ALSO BY STEVEN WATTS

The Republic Reborn: War and the Making of Liberal America, 1790–1820

*The Romance of Real Life: Charles Brockden Brown
and the Origins of American Culture*

The Magic Kingdom: Walt Disney and the American Way of Life

The People's Tycoon

The People's Tycoon

HENRY FORD

and the American Century

STEVEN WATTS

Alfred A. Knopf

New York

2005

THIS IS A BORZOI BOOK PUBLISHED BY ALFRED A. KNOPF

Copyright © 2005 Steven Watts

All rights reserved under International and Pan-American Copyright Conventions.
Published in the United States by Alfred A. Knopf, a division of Random House, Inc.,
New York, and simultaneously in Canada by Random House of Canada Limited, Toronto.
Distributed by Random House, Inc., New York.

Knopf, Borzoi Books, and the colophon are registered trademarks of Random House, Inc.
www.aaknopf.com

All photographs are courtesy of the collections of The Henry Ford.

Library of Congress Cataloging-in-Publication Data
Watts, Steven, [date]
The people's tycoon : Henry Ford and the American century / [Steven Watts].
p. cm.
ISBN 0-375-40735-9
1. Ford, Henry, 1863–1947.   2. Industrialists—United States—Biography.
3. Automobile industry and trade—United States—History.   4. Mass production—
United States—History.   I. Title.

HD9710.U52F6684 2005
338.7'6292'092—dc22   2004048594

Manufactured in the United States of America

Published August 15, 2005

Second Printing, October 2005

For my parents, Kenneth and Mary Watts,
and my siblings, Tim, Lisa, Daniel, and Julie,
with my love and thanks for a lifetime
of support and encouragement.

Contents

Prologue

The Legend of Henry Ford

In the early summer of 1919, the familiar, slender figure with the sun-browned face, sharp features, gray hair, and homespun manner took the witness stand at the courthouse in Mount Clemens, Michigan, a small town twenty miles northeast of Detroit. Henry Ford, industrialist and American legend, was pursuing his libel suit against the Chicago *Tribune*. A few years earlier, the newspaper had published an editorial describing him as "an ignorant idealist . . . [and] an anarchistic enemy of the nation" when he opposed President Wilson's use of the National Guard to patrol the border against raids from Pancho Villa's Mexican guerrillas. An outraged Ford had sued, and now the *Tribune*'s lawyer bent to the task of disproving libel by trying to demonstrate the truth of the famous carmaker's ignorance. The task proved easier than anyone had ever imagined.

For several days, under relentless questioning from the chief defense attorney, Ford disclosed an astonishing lack of knowledge. He asserted that the American Revolution had occurred in 1812; he defined chili con carne as "a large mobile army"; he described Benedict Arnold as "a writer, I think"; he could not identify the basic principles of American government. As listeners cringed, Ford, like a negligent schoolboy, fumbled question after question, finally responding to one, "I admit I am ignorant about most things." Even the defense attorney grew embarrassed and asked, mercifully, if Ford would consent to read aloud a brief book passage or whether he wished to leave the impression that he, in fact, might be illiterate. "Yes, you can leave it that way," the witness replied calmly. "I am not a fast reader and I have the hayfever and would make a botch of it."

The jury, facing abundant evidence of ignorance but none proving anarchism, found that Ford had been libeled. But it awarded him only six cents in damages. Newspapers and magazines around the nation, however, largely ignored the verdict and the legal issues and had a heyday with his incredible testimony, chortling about the crudeness and shallowness of this American hero. Yet, as the episode played out, two unexpected things became apparent.

First, Henry Ford seemed perfectly content to appear the provincial rube whose productive endeavors left little time for book learning. When pressed on his lack of knowledge about public affairs, he confessed that, regarding newspapers, "I rarely read anything else except the headlines." He was even more frank in a private interview with a reporter, commenting, "I don't like to read books; they muss up my mind."[1] Second, common people, rather than being scandalized by Ford's predicament, seemed to appreciate it. They indulged his lack of learning and were amused by his response when he was asked what the United States had been originally ("Land, I guess"). They applauded him for a refreshing lack of pretension and sympathized with his frank admission that he was too focused on work to get much formal education. Ministers around the country offered prayers for Henry Ford's deliverance from his snobby oppressors. Small-town newspapers urged busy farmers, laborers, and merchants to send sympathetic letters of support to the carmaker, and tens of thousands did so. Thus, to the shock and consternation of highbrows everywhere, Ford emerged from a seemingly embarrassing debacle an even greater American folk hero than he had been before.[2]

This episode put on display one of the great stories, and mysteries, of modern American history. The trial revealed a love affair between a pioneering automaker from Detroit and common Americans that transcended all reason. The same Henry Ford who disgusted so many intellectuals, cosmopolitans, and opinion shapers, enjoyed for some four decades a special bond of affection with workaday citizens who drove his automobiles and hung on his utterances. But what explained his enormous popularity, prestige, and influence? Obviously, it was not based on intellectual achievement. Nor was it a product of mere wealth, since legions of rich industrialists in the United States failed to attain his public stature; in fact, many were denounced by the public as robber barons. Ford's exalted status did not result from technological achievement. Contemporaries realized that he did not invent the automobile, as many naïve observers later assumed, and they certainly knew that his celebrated Model T was not the best car on the market.

The mystery of the man and his influence only deepens when one searches more widely. Socialists such as Vladimir Lenin admired Ford as one of the major contributors to twentieth-century revolution, and it was not unusual to see portraits of Ford and Lenin hanging side by side in Soviet factories. Yet Adolf Hitler also revered Ford. He proclaimed, "I shall do my best to put his theories into practice in Germany," and modeled the Volkswagen, the people's car, on the Model T. In the United States, powerful capitalists such as John D. Rockefeller acclaimed Ford and described his production facilities as "the industrial marvel of the age," while at the same time Woodrow Wilson convinced the automaker to run for the Senate in Michigan as a progressive Democrat. Many artists on the left denounced Ford's impact on modern society. Charlie Chaplin hilariously satirized his system of mechanized labor in the film *Modern Times*; Aldous Huxley, in *Brave New World*, sarcastically dated the beginning of modern degeneration from "the year of our Ford." Yet a 1940 Roper survey of American workers found that they ranked Henry Ford above Franklin Roosevelt and Walter Reuther as the modern American leader who was "most helpful to labor."

Interpreters of Henry Ford's career, both during his lifetime and since, have done little to solve the enigma of his promiscuous appeal. For decades, journalists and historians have examined him in many guises. They have left a trail of contradictory assessments and unanswered questions in their wake. Was Ford an admirable titan who created an industrial empire, or a repressive tyrant who crushed everyone in his path? Was he a business innovator who pioneered pathbreaking productive processes, or a greedy capitalist who degraded work for millions? Was he a social revolutionary seeking to uplift American workers, or a cynical paternalist using subtle new methods of social control? Was he a public figure with the common touch, or an embodiment of the people's bad taste? Wildly divergent answers to these questions have never been reconciled, and Ford has been alternately denounced and deified since his emergence on the public stage in the early twentieth century. The genuine man remains elusive. The secret of his appeal and his significance continues to be largely unexplained.

This biography tries to capture Henry Ford in his complexity and uncover the sources of his public stature. It proceeds from the conviction that his unique relationship with America was shaped by the historical transformation of his age and a subsequent shift in cultural values. The period from 1890 to 1920, of course, framed the formation of the modern American order. These years witnessed the emergence of consumer capitalism, mass culture, bureaucracy, and the corporate state, all of which converged to create the century's most powerful nation. Ford, who leavened his enthusiasm for the future with a loyalty to the past, helped guide his fellow citizens through this wrenching period of historical change.

The scope of Ford's life was itself astonishing. Born just after the battle of Gettysburg, he lived to witness the dropping of atomic bombs at the end of World War II. But his significance went far beyond living through the vast changes separating the world of Abraham Lincoln from that of Harry Truman. Ford's life and career resonated most powerfully in three areas.

First, he moved front and center stage as a prophet of America's new consumer culture in the early twentieth century. He has gained a reputation, of course, as the American pioneer of industrial mass production, but a less appreciated role was, perhaps, even more critical. Coming to prominence amid the collapse of Victorian tradition with its values of self-discipline, thrift, and producerism, Ford popularized a new creed of consumer self-fulfillment. He was perhaps the first American businessman to realize that large-scale production depended on large-scale consumption.

Second, he played a key role in shaping the mass culture that began to emerge in early-twentieth-century America. In a new atmosphere of consumer abundance, Ford became a principal architect of a cultural order stressing standardized experiences, collective self-consciousness, and widely dispersed leisure among a popular audience. He first found fame in automobile racing, popularized camping, proselytized for positive thinking, and skillfully used the new media mechanisms of print and radio to enhance his personality in the public perception. As the Model T became the prototype of America's mass prosperity, Ford became the prototype of the mass-culture celebrity.

Third, he rooted his innovations in the rich soil of populism. He glorified the common man and made the judgment, dignity, and values of ordinary citizens his benchmark of achievement and worth. Powerfully shaped by Midwestern rural life and the strictures of the Protestant ethic, Ford's veneration of "just plain folks" nurtured a suspicion of sophisticated, urban elites and urged reliance upon an American folk defined by industrious self-reliance, rugged egalitarianism, and plainspoken piety. He parlayed this into a reputation as a social reformer who delivered high wages to working people and denounced wealthy financiers. At the same time, this creed carried a suspicious streak of anti-intellectualism and a wary hostility toward Jews and Catholics.

In other words, Henry Ford achieved a towering stature by drawing upon consumerism, mass culture, and populism to articulate an American way of life just beginning to take shape at the dawn of the modern era. But he became beloved, as well as influential, for another reason. Ford's striking innovations, rather than unsettling a mass audience, managed to assuage fears of the unknown. At the very moment he was transforming the world, he made new ideas and practices palatable by maintaining a conspicuous reverence toward the past. Whether mass-producing Model T's while reassuring the public that hard work, frugality, and community still mattered, or constructing his gigantic, centralized River Rouge plant while taking camping trips in the woods and promoting folk dances, he managed to combine modern permutation with respect for tradition.

Thus, Henry Ford became an American folk hero because he appreciated *both* the aspirations and the apprehensions of the American people as they struggled to enter the modern age. He understood their hopes and fears and mediated them through his larger creed of populist, consumerist progress. With one foot firmly planted in the past and the other confidently stepping into the future, Ford successfully crossed a great divide in American history. This maker of modern America comforted millions of his fellow citizens as he eased them through the dislocations created by breathtaking historical change.

Ford's complex personality fed this process. A Midwesterner born and bred, he displayed many characteristics shaped by rural life in the American heartland. Sparsely schooled yet possessing great native wit, he proceeded according to instinctive hunches rather than systematic analysis. Skeptical of received wisdom, he had a restless curiosity about the workings of the social and natural worlds. Committed to the virtues of the village folk, he viewed most outsiders with suspicion. Distrustful of fancy theories, he valued common sense and dispensed wisdom as a kind of cracker-barrel philosopher. In the manner of Mark Twain, Abraham Lincoln, and Will Rogers, he liked to play the part of the naïve provincial whose rustic image and sly humor barely covered the shrewdness lying beneath. Deeply ambitious, Ford combined a generous and idealistic view of humanity in the abstract with, all too often, a mean-spirited, self-aggrandizing attitude toward those around him. Like many uneducated people who become fabulously successful, he was utterly confident in his view of the world and never appreciated what he did not know. This amalgam of self-confidence and ignorance, insight and narrow-mindedness was at once his greatest strength and greatest weakness.

Ford's long, fascinating life and rocky climb to pre-eminence make for a story full of natural drama. His back-and-forth struggle to produce an automobile succeeded, albeit spectacularly, only when he was well into middle age. A series of highly publicized legal and political clashes over patents, company dividends, war, corporate power, anti-Semitism, and unionization punctuated his career. An intriguing array of activities—automobile racing, social progressivism, development of the assembly line, peace crusades, diet reform, political office-seeking, agricultural experimentation, historical preservation, and many others—kept him constantly in the limelight. Along the way, a number of people played key roles in Ford's life: his wife and son, a production manager and a preacher, an advertiser and an engineer, a race-car driver and a business partner, a mistress and a publicist, and a trusted, streetwise tough who nearly ruined his company. Sketches of these dramatis personae enrich an understanding of his accomplishments and ascendancy.

But this story also focuses on what was made of Henry Ford, not just what he made; what was said about him, as well as what he said. By describing and analyzing the substantial body of commentary on him in American newspapers, magazines, political speeches, and radio shows for some four decades, I have tried to dig into the Ford legend. The debate over his achievements and shortcomings tells us much about an America changing shape in the early decades of the twentieth century. Exploring the cultural mythology surrounding Ford also helps us to see him as his contemporaries must have—a protean figure who defined, energized, and comforted Americans as they rose to great power and wealth in an age of transformation.

Fortunately, the sources for reconstructing Ford's life are abundant. A pack rat, he saved nearly everything that crossed his path, from the trivial to the indispensable. After his death, hundreds of boxes of this material were gathered into a large archive now housed in the Benson Ford Research Center, which is appended to the Henry Ford Museum and Greenfield Village in Dearborn. The archives hold thousands of files full of printed material, objects, photographs, and records. Moreover, Ford was one of the most discussed and written-about of modern American figures in his time, so the volume of published interviews and articles is daunting. Nonetheless, this record can be misleading, because there is surprisingly little from Ford's own hand. There are no diaries and virtually no letters, and few uncensored recollections. The books and numerous articles appearing under his name, though reflecting his views, were ghostwritten. This lacuna is filled, in part, by perhaps the most revealing items in the Ford archives: dozens of transcribed oral interviews with company employees, family members, and associates, many of which contain a wealth of firsthand observations of, and quotations from, Ford.

As the twentieth century drew to a close, various magazines, academic groups, and television networks tried to identify the most influential American of the previous hundred years. Not surprisingly, Henry Ford emerged consistently at or near the top of these lists. *Fortune* magazine, for instance, chose him as the "Businessman of the Century" over Alfred Sloan, Jr., of General Motors, Thomas Watson, Jr., of IBM, and Bill Gates of Microsoft. Similarly, a recent poll of academic experts rated Ford, by a significant margin, ahead of Gates, John D. Rockefeller, and Andrew Carnegie as the greatest entrepreneur in American history.[3] The impact of Ford's career supports the wisdom of this choice. By presenting the automobile to the people as the symbol of a new consumer society, he changed modern life irrevocably. By defining American values in the mold of abundance and self-fulfillment, he strongly affected how we think about ourselves. By developing Fordism in the early twentieth century, with its formula of mass production and high wages, he offered a socioeconomic blueprint for the United States' climb to global prominence over the next half-century. Perhaps more than any other person, Henry Ford created the American Century.

But his story began many years earlier, and on a much quieter note, in a small town in the upper Midwest during the Civil War.

Part One

The Road to Fame

One

Farm Boy

By the early 1920s, Henry Ford may have been the most famous man in the world. His inexpensive, durable, and perky Model T had taken America by storm, and the pioneering industrialist had garnered enormous fame and wealth. The Ford visage seemed to appear everywhere, constantly. A torrent of interviews, newspaper stories, publicity handouts, advertisements, and popular biographies flooded into the public realm, carrying details of his life story and his comments on every imaginable topic. Often based on interviews with him, or legendary tales, these pieces told the story of Ford's life as he wanted it to be told.

They poured the events of Henry Ford's life into the mold of the American success story. This hoary genre dated back to Benjamin Franklin and his autobiography of the penniless, bright, and determined youth who had walked into colonial Philadelphia munching on bread rolls as the first step in his meteoric rise to distinction. Horatio Alger had updated it for the nineteenth century with popular novels such as *Struggling Upward* and *Mark the Match Boy*.

Now Ford sought to place himself squarely within this American mythology. His version of his life story could have been lifted from any one of Alger's cookie-cutter plots: the young man pursues his dream while others scoff, he undertakes a lonely journey from the country to the city in search of fulfillment, overcomes obstacles with a combination of pluck, determination, and talent, and finally rises to heights of achievement and prosperity. The Ford success story contained an additional element—the youthful hero had a stern father who was skeptical of the son's newfangled ambitions and sought to stymie his creativity.

The struggle against paternal authority, with its Oedipal overtones, became a key to Henry Ford's rendering of his own early life. His ghostwritten book, *My Life and Work* (1922), a runaway best-seller, particularly high-lighted this theme. Designed by Ford to popularize his ideas and enhance his legend, the book related how his father, William, sought to discourage his interest in machines. "My father was not entirely in sympathy with my bent toward mechanics. He thought that I ought to be a farmer," Ford told readers. When he finally decided to leave the farm, "I was all but given up for lost." Ford added that his later experiments with the gasoline engine while he was an electrical engineer "were no more popular with the president of the company than my first mechanical leanings were with my father."[1]

There was one problem, however, with this tale of triumph over over-weening paternal domination: it was as much the product of Henry Ford's imagination as a picture of reality. The facts suggest a different story. Though tension between father and son certainly existed, its causes were more complex and its results much less melodramatic than the younger Ford related. In part, it resulted from clashing personalities and private needs. Henry Ford's oft-told tale of rebellion and triumph over his father reflected a fundamental trait in his personality: a deeply felt need to present himself as a self-reliant individual who fought to prevail against lesser opponents and skeptics.

But this embroidery also went beyond personal issues. It was rooted in far-reaching currents of historical change that were broadly social as well as narrowly personal. By the late nineteenth century, America's industrial revolution was expanding explosively and beginning to overwhelm the traditional rural republic. Ford's story of rebellion, flight, and triumph was told thousands of times over as hordes of young men fled the countryside and streamed into urban manufacturing centers. This tidal wave of change, of which young Ford was a part, produced the machine age. Its alien values and unfamiliar landscape exhilarated many younger men, but it unsettled, even frightened many older citizens.

The younger and elder Fords were caught up in this larger social dynamic of America in the late 1800s. As William Ford occasionally remarked, "Oh, Henry ain't much of a farmer. He is more of a tinkerer." The son's tale of struggle with his father was destined to take shape in the stark, melodramatic terms of authority challenged, defied, and finally over-turned. Even if it was as much imagined as real, Henry Ford's story not only revealed the young innovator's state of mind but resonated with the kinetic energy generated by the larger remaking of the United States in this era.[2]

In late July 1863, much of the United States still was abuzz with reports of unimaginable fighting and bloodshed seeping out from the small Pennsylvania town of Gettysburg, where, a few weeks before, Robert E. Lee's invasion of the North had been thwarted by the Union Army of the Potomac. Far away, in the hinterland of the fractured American republic, in the early-morning hours of July 30, a healthy son was born to William and Mary Ford in Greenfield township, near Dearborn, Michigan. They had married two years earlier, and their first child had died at birth in 1862. So this pregnancy had caused much anxiety, and the safe arrival of the infant was the source of much relief. The parents decided to name the boy Henry.[3]

The child was born into a society barely emerged from the wilderness. Though Michigan had become a state in 1837, it remained predominantly a frontier area, sparsely settled with farmers who were beginning to hack their way through primeval forests of oak, elm, maple, ash, beech, basswood, and pine trees. By the 1840s and 1850s, the first signs of commercial endeavor had started to appear in the countryside. The Erie Canal had provided connections between the Great Lakes region and the Eastern port of New York City; later, the first primitive steamboats, turnpikes, and railroads moved into the interior of Michigan, carrying people and commercial goods. Detroit grew steadily, along with other trading towns such as Port Huron, Kalamazoo, Grand Rapids, Benton Harbor, and Ypsilanti. Agriculture remained the backbone of the state's economy, but by the 1850s timber harvesting, the fishing industry, and the mining of copper and iron ore were contributing significant wealth.

By the onset of the Civil War, Michigan stood as the embodiment of the nineteenth-century rural republic. With a population of roughly 750,000—immigration of large numbers of Irish and Germans had added to the stream of New Yorkers and New Englanders bringing settlers over its borders—the state presented a proud rural culture populated by self-reliant landowners and fiercely independent citizens. In the 1850s, like most of the Old Northwest, Michigan was swept up in antislavery politics and became a bastion of the new Republican Party, with its ideology of "free soil, free labor, free men." Staunchly Unionist during the Civil War, Michigan contributed ninety thousand troops to the federal armies; some fifteen thousand of them died from battlefield wounds or disease.[4]

Henry Ford's childhood, which began in the heart of this great civil conflagration, typified rural Midwestern life in the mid-nineteenth century. In the hundreds of towns, villages, and rural communities scattered throughout the area bounded by the Great Lakes in the north and the Ohio River to the south, and the Appalachians and Great Plains to the east and west, life was shaped by local influences. Several threads—extended family connections, seasonal farm labor, community gatherings, church—came together in a tightly woven web of social experience. Young Henry, like any toddler on a busy farm, stayed close to his mother, but he could not avoid being immersed in nature, the seasonal rhythms of agricultural production, and the workaday calendar of providing shelter and sustenance. His first childhood memory invoked this rural quality of life:

> The first thing that I remember in my life is my father taking my brother John and myself to see a bird's nest under a large oak log twenty rods east of our home and my birthplace. John was so young that he could not walk. Father carried him, [while] I being two years older could run along with them. This must have been about the year 1866 in June. I remember the nest with 4 eggs and also the bird and hearing it sing. I have always remembered the song and in later years found that it was a song sparrow.[5]

As a boy, young Henry increasingly came into contact with the adult male world of farm work. William pursued the typical, varied activities of a self-sufficient farmer: growing wheat, corn, and hay; raising livestock and smoking meat; tending a fruit orchard; hunting and fishing; preserving vegetables in cellars over the winter; cutting firewood for domestic use and to sell in nearby Detroit for extra cash. Labor was long and hard, and, in the words of a Ford neighbor, farmers set off for their fields and "went to work from daylight to dark, and then went home and did their chores." Tagging along with his father, Henry lent a hand with planting and harvesting, caring for livestock, and doing various chores. Inevitably, contact with hard-bitten farmhands produced a comical initiation rite. At about age six, the youngster was resting with some of the laborers when one of them innocently offered him a plug of chewing tobacco. Ignorant of the proper procedure for leisurely mastication and spitting, he chewed up the potent concoction and then swallowed it. As the men laughed, the boy grew light-headed and dizzy as he began walking woozily back toward the house. Sitting down by the creek near his home, he recalled much later, "I had the feeling that the water was flowing uphill." When he staggered in the door with his story, his mother burst into laughter but quickly reassured her son that he would be all right.[6]

In January 1871, at age seven, Ford trooped off to the one-room Scotch Settlement School, about two miles from his house. He had been well prepared by his mother, who already had conveyed the rudiments of reading by teaching him the alphabet and patiently leading him through simple texts. Among his early school instructors were Frank R. Ward, a sharp-witted neighbor; Emily Nardin, a young woman who roomed with the Ford family for a short time; and John Brainard Chapman, a large, stout man whose intimidating physical presence made up for his intellectual shortcomings. According to John Haggerty, one of Ford's schoolmates, Chapman "could have told Henry and me everything he knew in 10 minutes. But he weighed 275 pounds and it was the weight that really counted."

Young Ford settled into the typical routine of provincial public schools. The children of all ages met regularly during the winter and rainy seasons, but adjourned for weeks during planting and harvesting periods. School days began, after the woodstove had been stoked, with the reading of a Bible verse and recitation of the Lord's Prayer. Teachers closely followed a basic curriculum of reading, writing, and arithmetic and drilled into the heads of their young charges standards of honor, hard work, and fair play. Sitting at a desk on a raised platform at the front of the room, the teacher called students forward to recite lessons orally or write them on blackboards. Teachers sought to enforce discipline and instill self-control as well as impart information. As Ford recalled, students who misbehaved were brought to the front of the room and "placed directly under the teacher's eye."

Henry was an expert prankster. With typical ingenuity, he once bored two small holes in the bottom of another student's seat. In one hole he hid a needle with the point up, and then ran a connecting string down through the other hole and under the bench to his seat. During a dead space in the school day, he yanked on the string, and the resulting howls brought peals of laughter from his classmates. He also proved to be a bright, if unexceptional, student who particularly excelled at "oral" arithmetic, or working out number problems in his head. His greatest achievements, however, came from mechanical tinkering. Sitting at his desk while classmates recited at the front of the room, he would prop up his geography book as a cover; behind it, he took apart classmates' watches and put them back together. Once Henry and his schoolboy pals built a dam of stones and mud on a small creek near the school and installed a primitive water wheel that turned as water flowed over the dam. At the end of the school day, however, they forgot their construction project, left it in place overnight, and flooded the neighboring farmer's potato field. Another time, Henry led the group in building a crude turbine steam engine. Using an old ten-gallon can for a boiler, they attached to it a short length of pipe for carrying steam to revolving tin blades. A roaring fire built enough steam pressure to turn the turbine very fast, but eventually the contraption exploded. The spewing steam and flying tin slightly injured the boys, including Henry, who was left with a life-long scar on his cheek. As Ford recalled ruefully, the explosion "set the [school] fence on fire and raised ned in general."

Henry Ford commenced his lifelong friendship with Edsel Ruddiman, a neighbor boy, at the Scotch Settlement School. The two became nearly inseparable, and they spent much of their boyhood together. They played, walked, and talked nearly every day and carved their initials next to each other in the desk they shared. The two companions even went to church together on Sunday evenings—it was about a four-mile walk—even though neither was very religious. "It was more to be together," Ruddiman admitted. In later years, Ruddiman became a prominent pharmacist and chemist at the Ford Motor Company. When Henry's only child was born in 1893, he named him Edsel.[7]

Away from the school, Henry Ford spent his boyhood in the comfortable atmosphere of a bourgeois home set in a typical Midwestern village. Henry, the eldest child, had been followed by a succession of five siblings who arrived like clockwork every other year: John in 1865, Margaret in 1867, Jane in 1869, William Jr. in 1871, and Robert in 1873. Domestic life for the Fords revolved around simple pleasures. After the workday was complete, parents and children read, played card games, sang traditional songs and simple hymns around the pump organ in the parlor, attended the Christ Episcopal Church in Dearborn on Sundays, and joined in neighborhood picnics and church socials. The Ford brothers jostled and engaged in harmless antics. When their father decreed that the easiest chores would go to the boy who first got out of the house in the morning, William Jr. once filled Henry's boots with applesauce to slow him down. As an adult, Henry jotted down impressions that still remained with him from boyhood: "Remember sleigh, wood hauling, cold winters, setting sun, sleighbell, long walks, cold weather, boys and girls."[8]

Mary Ford, with her gentle but firm role in the household, provided the dominant influence in Henry's childhood. "Mother presided over it and ruled it but she made it a good place to be," he told many people in later years. He elevated her to near-sainthood in later life. Henry seemed especially struck by her moral influence. "I have tried to live my life as my mother would have wished," he told journalist Edgar Guest in 1923. "She taught me as a boy that service is the highest duty in the world. . . . I have tried to follow her teaching."[9]

Mary Ford's lessons clearly reflected the cultural values pervasive among mainstream, middle-class Americans during most of the nineteenth century. Victorian culture (as historians have termed it) forged a creed combining Protestant moralism, market individualism, the work ethic, and genteel restraint. It found expression in a variety of venues: advice manuals for young men and women, educational tracts, magazine articles, and religious pronouncements. The Victorian ethos demanded a standard of emotional self-control in personal life. It shaped a model of "domesticity" in family life, where women were expected to nurture in their husbands and children gentility, sentimentalism, and virtue. It promoted frugality and a nose-to-the-grindstone ethic, whereby citizens were expected to labor hard to turn out useful goods as the basis for market buying and selling.[10]

Mary Ford stoutly upheld this traditional moral code. She instructed Henry as to his duty to confront and complete hard work with a cheerful attitude. She did not offer sympathy when he grumbled about chores. " 'Life will give you many unpleasant tasks to do; your duty will be hard and disagreeable and painful to you at times, but you must do it,' " he recalled her saying sternly. "My mother taught me to work." Mary also urged her children to practice self-control. She sent them off to school with lunch boxes containing simple, hearty food, since indulging in sweets was morally dangerous. In her words, "Let your health, not your diet, be your guide. Never eat merely for the pleasure of eating."[11]

In her child-rearing practices, Mary displayed a similar sensibility. She favored the Victorian device of shaming children, rather than physically punishing them, to shape upright character. Henry was once caught telling a lie, and his mother simply expressed her utter disgust. "I was humiliated. Shame cuts much more deeply than a whip," he recalled. "For a day I was treated with contempt and I knew that I had done a despicable thing." Mary also provided sustained moral instruction. Many evenings, she would read aloud from the Bible, *Pilgrim's Progress*, and *Gems of Life*, a collection of inspirational essays and speeches which presented "a stirring call to service and duty."[12]

But two impulses in Mary Ford's nurturing struck her eldest son with special force.

First, she strove mightily to create harmony within her family, which Henry later described as "the art of being happy with each other." "More than once I have heard her say that if we couldn't be happy here in this house, we'd never be happy anywhere else." She gently insisted that work and play should occur in their proper proportions and that recreation was a reward for labor completed. "Fun we had and plenty of it," Henry related of his childhood, "but she was forever reminding us that life cannot be all fun. 'You must earn the right to play,' she used to say to me."[13]

Second, Mary made a lasting impression upon her oldest son as a paragon of efficiency. Hard work was fine and good, his mother would note, but results rather than motion were what really counted. According to

Henry's sister Margaret, everyone admired "the systematic and orderly way in which her work was done." Almost fifty years after her death, Henry recalled that "Mother believed in doing things and getting things done, not in talking about things and wishing they might be done. She was systematic and orderly and thorough, and she demanded that from us."[14]

But the matron of the Ford family provided her children with more than moral instruction and exemplary work habits. She gave large doses of love. Mary Ford seems to have successfully balanced affection with a long-range view of her children's well-being, and she earned their respect in the process. Margaret noted fondly how her mother allowed her daughters to "play ladies" and dress up in her clothes and imitate "the pictures in *Godey's Lady's Book.*" Henry often told the story of how one day he was feeding hay into the "chopping box" when his finger got caught in the sharp blades. Frightened and bleeding badly from the mangled finger—apparently, the tip was hanging by only a thread of tissue—the boy ran into the house. His mother quickly took control, calmed him, stopped the bleeding, and bandaged the wound tightly. Determined that he would not lose the finger, she checked and cleaned the wound daily and nursed it along for some three weeks, finally sharing his joy when the healing proved successful.[15]

Still, Mary Ford's maternal labors received major moral reinforcement from another direction. As Henry frequently acknowledged in later years, his character was also powerfully influenced by a series of books he read as a boy. Like countless other children in nineteenth-century America, he fell under the sway of one schoolmaster and children's author from the neighboring state of Ohio. The lessons absorbed from this source would stay with him throughout his life.

An observer of Henry Ford's career, with considerable truth, once asserted that the industrialist "found the McGuffey readers to be the greatest intellectual influence in his life." Ford referred, of course, to Professor William Holmes McGuffey and his legendary nineteenth-century textbooks. Formally titled *The McGuffey Eclectic Readers*, these didactic little texts, full of pithy verses and striking pictures, had taught reading fundamentals and moral principles to several generations of American children since the 1830s. (By the early twentieth century, they had sold some 122 million copies.) The McGuffey lessons, which were memorized so thoroughly that most people could recall and recite them decades later in adulthood, made a special impact on Ford.[16]

Henry first encountered McGuffey at home, when Mary Ford taught him to read by patiently leading him through the first number of these manuals. Some sixty years later, he recalled how "sitting by her side during the long fall and winter evenings he was fascinated by the pictures in the McGuffey First Reader." The images remained vibrantly clear in Ford's mind: an ax leaning against a log taught the letter "a," a cat lapping milk from a pan stood for "c," a running dog for "d," a zebra with an arched neck and vivid stripes for "z," and so on. When he went off to the local school, the lessons continued. As his sister Margaret explained, "The lessons in our *McGuffey's Readers* taught us honor, integrity, and fair play."[17]

What was the nature of the books internalized by so many American children during much of the nineteenth century? McGuffey volumes aimed at the youngest students provided basic reading skills—learning the alphabet, sentence construction, and proper word usage. For older children, they offered pictures and exercises on enunciation, punctuation, and elocution. Final texts in the McGuffey series contained selections of literature, poetry, and philosophy for more advanced students. But all of the readers were lively, occasionally even dramatic, as they used anecdotes, stories, and vignettes to illustrate the points at hand. They also provided children, most of them far removed from centers of learning, a veneer of civilization by serving up literary dollops in the Anglo-American tradition—poetry excerpts from Scott, Byron, Gray, Shelley, Wordsworth, Longfellow, Tennyson; prose from Dickens, Irving, Cooper, and Hugo. Most important, however, the *McGuffey Readers* presented a clear moral sensibility. Their lessons dramatized the need for piety, humility, hard work, integrity, patience, kindness, and temperance. McGuffey demonstrated to children both the moral and the material bounty that would flow from proper behavior, and the disastrous consequences of thoughtless or sinful actions. As one scholar of the *Readers* has put it, they "emphasized the hard moral discipline of self-improvement."[18]

The impact of McGuffey on Henry Ford's character and principles was profound. In the 1920s, he embarked upon an avid hobby of buying old *Readers*. While sitting at home one afternoon, he and his wife, Clara, heard a group of schoolchildren as they romped past dancing and talking. " 'Hear the children gaily shout, Half past four and school is out!' quoted Mrs. Ford, and then wondered what the rest of the piece was. We both recalled it as a McGuffey exercise," Ford noted. A search for the exact source of this common remembrance led him to dig around for old copies of McGuffey, and as schoolboy memories came flooding back his search became almost feverish. Within a few years, Ford had amassed probably the largest private collection of McGuffeys in the entire United States.[19]

Collecting old editions of this textbook, however, became much more than an antiquarian hobby for Henry Ford. His high regard for the content, lessons, and values of the McGuffey texts inspired him to a kind of revival. Aggressively seeking to rejuvenate their influence, beginning in 1926 Ford paid for the reprinting and distribution all over the United States of many thousands of sets of the *McGuffey Readers* from 1857. He also served as an associate editor for the volume *Old Favorites from the McGuffey Readers* and helped choose the 150 selections in it. He wrote an article in *Colophon: A Quarterly for Bookmen*, in which he argued for the relevance of the *McGuffey Readers* for the modern world. At a 1938 meeting of the Federation of McGuffey Societies, which he had sponsored and bankrolled, Ford made one of his typically brief and simple speeches: "I am glad to join with you today in giving honor to Dr. McGuffey. He was a great American. The McGuffey Readers taught industry and morality to the youth of America." He even established a McGuffey School near the Henry Ford Museum in Dearborn and used the schoolbooks as the basis of the curriculum. Harvey C. Minnich, author of a biography entitled *William Holmes McGuffey and His Readers*, dedicated it to "Henry Ford, lifelong devotee and patron of his boyhood Alma Mater, the McGuffey Readers."[20]

Ford helped bring McGuffey to perhaps his largest audience, however, in a radio broadcast of March 17, 1935, on the *Ford Sunday Evening Hour.* William J. Cameron, a close colleague and spokesman for Ford, gave "talks" during the intermission of musical performances on this CBS radio show, which had developed a large audience of some ten million listeners. Cameron consulted closely with Ford, and on this evening he declaimed upon "The McGuffey Readers." William Holmes McGuffey and his humble school readers had created a standard of character for over fifty years in the United States, he explained. In Cameron's lofty words, "The American people were made articulate, their moral ideals were elevated, their thought deepened and broadened through the influence of these tens of millions of unpretending little schoolbooks." As for Ford, Cameron concluded, he "is probably prouder of his knowledge of the six McGuffey readers than of any other volumes in his extensive library."[21]

Ford acclaimed the old-fashioned virtues of McGuffey at every opportunity. In an article in *Good Housekeeping*, he insisted, "The generations that grew up on McGuffey did better in common sense and common honesty. There is no escape from the need for moral precepts. The truths of life should be stated simply, clearly, and often to children." In another publication, he declared flatly, "Truth, honesty, fair-dealing, initiative, invention, self-reliance—these were the fundamentals of the McGuffey Readers and they are as timeless and dateless now as they were when he assembled his texts."[22]

But Ford's McGuffey mania was more than just an item for public consumption. Hamlin Garland, the best-selling Midwestern regionalist writer, became a friend of the industrialist in the 1920s, and they discovered a shared reverence for these old books from their youth. During one of Garland's visits, Ford

> brought out four volumes of McGuffey's Readers which he had rescued from the dust and reprinted, using the old type and retaining all of the illustrations. As I ran over these pages, I found myself back in the small bare schoolhouse on the Iowa prairie. The love I once had for the stories and poems which these readers contained came back to me. That they possessed a similar magic for Ford was unmistakable.

Ford and Garland engaged in a game challenging each other's knowledge and memory of McGuffey. Sitting on opposite sides of a desk, one would recite an opening stanza from a section of one of the textbooks, and the other would reply with the second stanza. They would trade lines in this fashion until one of them was stumped.[23]

So young Henry Ford, with the lessons of Mary Ford ringing in one ear and those of William Holmes McGuffey in the other, made his way through childhood. In a fashion that he would not fully realize until adulthood, their insistence on labor, service, temperance, and duty formed the bedrock of his character and sensibility. Victorian moral instruction made its mark. At least in most ways.

Two

Machinist

Mary Ford and William Holmes McGuffey nudged Henry Ford down a straight and narrow path, but they could not make him work. There the boy slouched to the beat of his own drummer. It became something of a standing joke among Ford family and friends that Henry could be counted on to slide away from hard physical labor. Margaret remembered her brother skipping farm chores "to go watch a threshing machine work." A neighbor, who occasionally worked as a hired hand on the Ford farm, laughingly noted that "that little devil was the laziest bugger on the face of the earth! . . . Henry would work along all right until about ten o'clock in the morning, and then he would want to go to the house for a drink of water. He would go and get the drink of water, but he would never come back!"[1]

But the youth's behavior was less a case of laziness or rebelliousness than a principled objection to wasting physical energy. As Margaret explained, Henry believed "that there was too much hard work connected with farming" and thus sought "easier methods" and "tried shortcuts to lighten the many chores." Henry admitted, "I have followed many a weary mile behind a plough and I know all the drudgery of it," and "When very young I suspected that much might somehow be done in a better way." Thus his mother's preaching about cheerful work appears in a new light— an admonishment aimed at the evasions of her eldest child. So, too, does Henry's admiration for Mary's example of the efficient handling of tasks. As Ford confessed to a reporter many years later, "My uncle once said that I am just like her in that respect." Ironically, the man who claimed work as the cornerstone of his philosophy had little fondness for physical labor.[2]

But this perception of the grind of farm labor dovetailed with a prominent part of young Henry Ford's personality: his growing mechanical bent. The inefficiency of farm methods, he once stated bluntly, "is what took me into mechanics." But this attraction to machinery also stemmed in part from a predisposition. "My mother always said that I was born a mechanic," Ford wrote later. Fascinated with the crude wind-up toys of his siblings, he habitually disassembled them to see how they worked and then successfully put them back together. Margaret noted that at Christmas the Ford children would surround their toys and cry out in unison, "Don't let Henry have them. He just takes them apart."[3]

The boy's fascination with mechanics produced a hobby that became almost an obsession: repairing watches. Adolph Culling, a German farmhand employed by his father, first took the back off his silver watch and showed Henry how the various parts worked. At the Scotch Settlement School, the boy often whiled away the time by tinkering with classmates' watches. He made himself a set of tools by grinding a tiny screwdriver out of a shingle nail, fashioning a pair of tweezers from one of his mother's old corset stays, and gained himself a reputation as a skilled repairman. Neighbors brought him malfunctioning watches and clocks, and he set up a small workbench at home, where he delightedly spent hours adjusting and correcting their tiny mechanisms. Henry haunted local watch shops, such as that of Englebert Grimm in Dearborn, to buy and trade parts and eventually went farther, into Detroit. There he visited watch shops in search of treasures, but also ventured out to the railroad yards to observe locomotives and to "engine works" shops to examine steam engines.[4]

Ultimately, these threads of work-related influences—his admiration for production but disregard for hard manual labor, his mother's example of focused accomplishment, his growing appreciation of mechanical power—were interwoven to create a notable personality trait. Early on, as many observers noted, young Ford became obsessed with work efficiency. In the late nineteenth century, this determination to get maximum production out of effort expended would be codified by industrial experts such as Frederick Winslow Taylor. Their doctrine of "scientific management," however, was second nature to this Michigan farm boy. His sister Margaret once described it clearly:

> Henry wanted things done with the least loss of time and energy. If a job could be done more simply that was the way it should be done. The farm gates were heavy to open and close, so Henry made hinges for these gates and a device for opening them and closing them without getting off the wagon.

Ford also displayed at an early age another managerial trait: he always took the lead in devising projects, but then stepped aside as others implemented them. "He had the ability of getting his brothers and his companions to work for him," Margaret noted. These basic traits would powerfully influence his career in later years.[5]

Many decades later, his close friend Thomas Edison would be amused at Ford's exuberant, youthful spirit. When they went on one of their camping vacations, the sixty-something automaker would cavort joyfully through the woods, running and jumping, climbing trees, and chopping logs. "At heart Ford is just a boy yet. He will never cease to be a boy," Edison noted. But this behavior may have been a kind of emotional compensation for a painful trauma that marked the end of his childhood. His idyllic, sheltered boyhood existence was about to end abruptly. As he approached adolescence, the stable and warm atmosphere of this respectable farm family would be blown apart by a sudden emotional storm.[6]

In the spring of 1876, the Ford family prepared to welcome another member into its midst. Mary had become pregnant midway through the previous year, and the birth of her seventh child promised to be a happy event. She was in good health, and her previous births had been uneventful. But something went terribly wrong, and both mother and newborn child died on March 29. Young Henry Ford's world was turned upside down, and the upheaval was especially terrible because of its unexpectedness. He was emotionally devastated. The passing of his beloved mother proved to be, perhaps, the most traumatic event of his life, and he carried the emotional scars for decades. Reacting with a combination of deep grief and adolescent self-absorption, he confessed much later that "I thought a great wrong had been done to me when my mother was taken." The boy expressed his bewilderment and pain in a revealing metaphor: "The house was like a watch without a mainspring."[7]

One profound development set in motion in Henry's young life by Mary's death was the beginning of a tense relationship with his father. At some deep personal level, Henry appears to have blamed him for the death. He had always been closer to Mary than to William. As a confidant wrote years later, "While Henry respected his father, it was to his mother that he turned for love and understanding."[8]

Following Mary's untimely death, a quiet but lengthy family travail began to unfold. The oldest Ford child—bright, curious, mechanically minded, and standing on the cusp of adolescence with all its emotional and hormonal disruptions—entered young adulthood riding a wave of deep pain. He careened into his father, a dignified, stubborn, but kindly authority figure. The growing tension between Henry and William also presented a broader, historical dimension. The son's restlessness at the constraints of rural life clashed with the father's values and experiences, and this lent additional force to their arguments about career prospects and the future.

William Ford presented his own version of an American success story. Born on December 26, 1826, in rural Ireland, he had fled the poverty and desolation of famine at age twenty along with other members of his family. They joined another branch of the Ford clan, already settled in the frontier village of Dearborn. By the early 1850s, dozens of Fords lay scattered throughout the Dearborn area and stood as prominent fixtures in the community. A mid-century photograph of the male Fords—dressed in their best black suits with vests and gold pocket watches, and facing the world as solid citizens with expressions of gravity and self-assurance—suggested the family's local prominence.

Upon arrival, William found employment as a carpenter for the Michigan Central Railroad, and during the next few years saved enough money to purchase his own tract of land. Working hard as a farmer, and acquiring additional acreage whenever the opportunity arose, William climbed steadily over the next decade and a half. By 1864, the year he finally went through the formality of becoming a U.S. citizen, he owned 120 acres, and over the next decade would add an additional hundred to his holdings. He also served in a number of civic capacities: member of the local school board, road commissioner, and, by the 1870s, justice of the peace.

In the meantime, William had married Mary Litogot, the adopted daughter of a local farmer, on April 25, 1861. He was thirty-four years old, and she was twenty-one. The couple settled into a seven-room white clapboard frame house built by the industrious groom to shelter his new bride and his father- and mother-in-law.[9]

By the time of Henry's birth, William had prospered and become a man of substance. He had bought the first buggy to be seen in the Dearborn area. Of medium height and slender build, with a ruddy complexion, neatly trimmed mustache and beard, and large, expressive blue eyes, he presented a dignified and stern appearance. A "merry twinkle in his eye" revealed a mischievous sense of humor lying just under the surface. A strong Episcopalian, the elder Ford nurtured "a very strong moral fiber and high ideals," qualities that flowered in his interactions with neighbors. Respected by local husbandmen and craftsmen, William had gained a reputation as a "good farmer" and someone who would help others in time of need. "Kindness and consideration of others was one of his characteristics," one of his children later noted, and he "was well-liked among the neighbors."[10]

Although reserved in temperament, William had a warm relationship with his children. He would take his sons to Detroit to deliver firewood or pick up farm supplies, and after the day's business was completed he showed them various sights around the city. When the circus came to town, he would pile his children into the wagon and head off to see the show. His delight was so obvious that observers wondered "who enjoyed it the most, father or children." According to Margaret, her father was a kindly, fair parent who "believed that children should obey." At home, he combined stern expectation of work and respect with easygoing tolerance of youthful high jinks. Unlike many stricter Protestant parents of his generation, he allowed the children to play cards around the table in the evening, stopping the games only when they became too rowdy or argumentative.[11]

William put much stock in being a well-informed citizen, and subscribed to several newspapers. He took great pride in his ownership of property and his involvement in the civic affairs of Dearborn, viewing local offices on the school board or the road commission as a responsibility to be shouldered willingly by responsible citizens. According to his daughter, William would often acclaim "the great miracle of America . . . [as] a place where a man could own the land upon which he lived and worked. Here there was personal independence." This proud tradition of the individual yeoman farmer deploying his labor and talents, of course, had deep roots in eighteenth- and nineteenth-century notions of republicanism and liberalism.[12]

Henry, however, increasingly appeared cut from a different pattern. He seemed to care little for the dignity of land ownership or the virtues of republican citizenship, and the routine of farm life inspired little beyond a growing disregard. Henry's rebellion, curiously, found focus in an aversion to horses. In the 1920s, he recalled for Edgar A. Guest how his father had assigned him the special chore of caring for the farm's horses. "I didn't like that job then and I wouldn't like it now," he declared, because "I was never fond of horses in the way that many are. I never really made friends with them." His grumbling had caused his mother to preach to him the necessity of self-discipline and persistence, so the boy reluctantly bent to the task. But, perhaps as a reflection of his distaste, Henry proved prone to horse-related accidents. Around age fourteen, while out riding on the road, he was thrown by a colt, caught his foot in the stirrup, and was dragged home over a considerable distance. After suffering many bruises and walking around sore for a week, Henry noted that the incident confirmed that he didn't "care much for horses." A few years later, the Detroit *Free Press* reported, "Henry Ford driving a manure wagon was seriously injured about 4 p.m. on Sunday, November 18 by the animal running away and collapsing the wagon. The horse was stopped by a fence." Ford's later involvement with the horseless carriage, it seems clear, may have resulted as much from equine aversion as from mechanical attraction. As he wrote triumphantly in one of his notebooks many decades later, "The horse is DONE."[13]

Henry's mechanical interests were intensifying almost daily as he spent many hours in the farm workshop, handling the tools and familiarizing himself with the mechanical operation of a number of agricultural implements. Then, in midsummer 1876, a few months after Mary Ford's death, an incident occurred that revealed the tensions of the present and portended the activities of the future. William and Henry were traveling by wagon between Dearborn and Detroit when they happened upon a crude steam engine trudging along the road under its own power. The younger Ford was amazed at the sight of this steam-belching, mechanical behemoth. As he reported many years later:

> I remember that engine as though I had seen it only yesterday, for it was the first vehicle other than the horse-drawn that I had ever seen. It was intended primarily for driving threshing machines and sawmills and was simply a portable engine and boiler mounted on wheels with a water tank and coal cart trailing behind. . . . [It] had a chain that made a connection between the engine and the rear wheels of the wagon-like frame. . . . I was off [our] wagon and talking to the engineer before my father, who was driving, knew what I was up to. The engineer was very glad to explain the whole affair.

This encounter became a turning point in Henry Ford's life, fostering a profound interest which would lead in new and fruitful directions. As he stated flatly many years later, "It was that engine which took me into automotive transportation."[14]

This incident suggested the knot of tension that tightened between William and Henry as the years went on. Increasingly, the son chafed at the constraints of rural life and yearned to immerse himself in the mechanical innovations inundating late-nineteenth-century America. The father upheld a more traditional standard of working the land. The farmer, as William liked to point out, "was his own boss" and could be sure of several things: "a reasonably good living for his family, security, sunshine not offered to factory workers, and good clean, fresh, air." This generational dispute, resonant with both personal and historical issues, gradually erected a barrier of misunderstanding between these two strong-willed individuals.[15]

Henry's version of this situation would become standard fare. In later interviews for articles and biographies, he habitually described his adolescence as a protracted struggle to overcome the backward-looking, even hostile opposition of his father. In the early 1920s, for instance, he spoke at length with writer Allan Benson, who wrote *The New Henry Ford* (1923). The boy's heart, Benson reported, "was always in his mechanical pursuits, which his father detested." Henry's labors in the farm workshop were not appreciated, for the youngster "worked with his tools always against the wishes of his father." In Henry's version, William's stubborn opposition to his mechanical endeavors had poisoned their relationship. The son reported that the father, displeased by his failure to charge for the work, had forbidden him to fix neighbors' watches. Thus Henry, unconcerned with money, was forced to "wait until I thought my father had gone to sleep" and then creep out of the house secretly to pick up malfunctioning timepieces from surrounding farms. "I did not get home until 3 o'clock in the morning," Ford noted. After his mother's death, Henry continued, the Fords' new housekeeper followed William's lead by banishing the boy's work from the downstairs parlor. He fled to his bedroom, where he set up a small workbench and worked late at night in the cold, huddled up to a small lamp for light and warmth. As Henry told Benson, his favorite book as a boy was a story of paternal rejection. *Herbert Mattison: A Bound Boy* told the tale of a youthful protagonist who was "bound out" by his father to work for a neighbor until he was twenty-one years old.[16]

According to Henry, William's intransigence later led him to a sour disapproval of the son's venture into automaking. He reported he had proudly returned to the Dearborn farm in the mid-1890s, wife and young son in tow, riding in his first "horseless carriage." But when he showed off the automobile prototype to the Ford family, William "got mad about it. He didn't like it at all. He thought it was something that would scare all the horses off the road." When Henry later quit a well-paying job to manufacture these machines, William dismissed his son as "an awful fool." Then his father declared that "I should hurry and build my automobiles or everyone who wanted one would be supplied before I got started." Ford could not resist a rather snide postscript: "We were building 100 cars a day in 1907 when father died."[17]

Henry's portrayal of his father's opposition, however, was more than a bit self-serving. Though it nicely framed a picture of his own heroic climb to success, it seriously distorted the facts. As other observers make clear, William Ford was not the man his son made him out to be. Far from being a dour, hidebound old fogy who blindly opposed his son's mechanical activities, he was a progressive farmer with a sincere interest in the dawning machine age. William, to be sure, tried to steer his eldest son toward becoming a farmer and citizen in the Dearborn community, and expressed some skepticism about his career adventures. As he once commented to a neighbor about his sons, "John and William [Jr.] are all right but Henry worries me. He doesn't seem to settle down and I don't know what's going to become of him." At the same time, however, the elder Ford clearly nurtured Henry's aptitude with tools and mechanisms and expressed pride in his skills.[18]

Margaret Ford Ruddiman provided a far different and more accurate rendering of the relationship between William Ford and his son. Henry's sister and the older daughter, she assumed an ever-larger role in running the household in the aftermath of her mother's death. She had abundant opportunity to observe sibling and father at close range, and her recollection of their relationship veered sharply from Henry's often repeated themes. Much of what the son related about the father at a later date, Margaret insisted, was simply a product of his imagination.

William Ford, according to his daughter, spent a great deal of time with his eldest child. From the time he could walk, the boy followed his father about, watching him work and "wanting to help as all little boys do." William himself was quite handy with tools, and he was proud that his son seemed to have inherited his knack for fixing things. "Father was quick to recognize Henry's ability in making new things," Margaret recalled. "He was very understanding of Henry's demands for new tools for the shop, and ours was one of the best equipped in the neighborhood." Moreover, William "never told Henry he should charge for the work he did on the neighbors' watches and clocks." As for Henry's tales about sneaking behind his father's back in the middle of the night to do repair work, Margaret described these as "fantastic stories" and recalled that throughout their childhood Henry's "workbench was at the east window in the dining-room just inside the door. This was his and we did not disturb the tools on it."[19]

William's own mechanical interests were evident. He was known for being handy with tools, and his reputation as a carpenter, craftsman, and repairer of farm equipment had spread throughout the community. According to Margaret, "our workshop was better equipped than most," and during the busy planting and harvesting seasons "many of the neighbors came to Father when an emergency repair job was needed." As a farmer, William "was willing to learn new methods and to purchase new farm equipment if it was practical and did an efficient job." In fact, over the years he purchased a McCormick reaper, a mowing machine, and a mechanical hay-loader to ease the burden of farm labor. As a member of the township committee set up to consider transportation linking Dearborn with Detroit, he played a key role in replacing horse-drawn cars with a system of electric cars based on a scheme already established in Cleveland.[20]

Perhaps most revealingly, the same summer when he and Henry stumbled across the self-powered steam engine on the trip to Detroit, William
Ford journeyed by railroad to attend the Centennial Exposition. Held in
1876 in Philadelphia to celebrate the centenary of the Declaration of Independence, this large exhibition displayed every kind of American engine and
mechanical innovation imaginable. Along with a nephew and two neighbors, William planned the trip to observe "scheduled tests of the steam
plows and road engines." Like most progressive farmers, he was interested
in the possibilities of steam power for agricultural work, a trend widely discussed in newspapers and magazines in the 1870s. The elder Ford had a
wonderful time on the trip—he marveled at the beautiful scenery of the
western-Pennsylvania mountains and visited historical sights in Philadelphia, such as Independence Hall—and returned with a perception that
because of machines "changes were being made in [farmers'] way of life."
For years, Margaret recalled, William and his friends talked about "the
mechanical exhibits and the wonderful things that could be accomplished
by steam power" they had witnessed in Philadelphia. Henry listened avidly
to these speculations.[21]

Later on, William's attitude toward Henry's automobile ventures was
more complex than the son ever acknowledged. William did refuse to ride
in Henry's horseless carriage the first time he brought it to the farm, and
Margaret admitted that the father may have resented his son's success in
pushing his beloved horses from the road. But it was in equal part fright, she
insisted: William "saw no reason why he should risk his life at that time for
a brief thrill of being propelled over the road." On subsequent visits, after
Henry explained the machine and offered assurances, his father consented
to climb aboard and rode many times. Once the ice was broken, "Father was
very proud of Henry's achievement. He talked about it to us at home and he
told his neighbors about it." In fact, some years later, William even offered
financial assistance to his son in developing the manufacture of his automobile. According to Margaret, Henry refused.[22]

In other words, this generational clash was much less melodramatic and
oppressive than Henry Ford ever admitted. To be sure, William was disappointed in his son's desire to leave the farm and evinced more caution about
the mechanical innovations of the age that so excited the young man. But he
did not crush the boy's spirit, curtail his interests, or tyrannize him. Father
and son had serious discussions about the future and harbored different perspectives about the wisest course for the future, but their disagreements
never exploded in acrimony. Such low-key differences of opinion, such
offering and rejection of advice, characterize relations between most fathers

and sons in most times and places. As Margaret explained, William and Henry "understood and respected each other." Edsel Ruddiman, Henry's best friend, confirmed that dissimilar ideas "didn't cause any hard feelings between father and son."[23]

In 1879, Henry Ford made a key decision in his young life that he later defined as a revolt against paternal abuse. At age sixteen, he left the farm to find his future in Detroit. Without informing anyone of his plans, as he told Allan Benson, he walked the nine miles to Detroit, rented a sleeping room, and began to look for employment in a machine shop, a move that ended "the struggle . . . between the father's will and the son's determination." Ford told other interviewers that he had fled to the city "against his father's commands." According to *My Life and Work* (1922), through this brash act "I was all but given up for lost" by his father and family. Henry Ford's version of the flight to Detroit, as did earlier stories, stressed his lonely heroism and determination in the face of his father's punitive resistance.[24]

But, once again, he mythologized this important event in his early life. As evidence from other observers makes clear, Henry's move to Detroit came with the cooperation, not opposition, of his father. According to Margaret, everyone in the Ford family knew that at some point he would leave for the city to learn more about machinery and steam engines: "It was just a question of when." Henry and William had discussed the matter, she claimed, and she pointed out that her brother did not walk Detroit streets looking for a room but stayed with "Aunt Rebecca Flaherty, father's sister." And after working for only six days at the Michigan Car Company Works, which built streetcars, he quickly found employment at the Flower Brothers Machine Shop. This job, Margaret believed, was the result of "some kind of previous arrangement" with William Ford, since he and James Flower were old friends. Frederick Strauss, a young apprentice with Flower Brothers, corroborated Margaret's story. Upon arriving at work one morning and glancing into the shop office, Strauss recalled, "I saw Henry Ford's father and Henry was with him. I didn't know who they were but the next day Henry came to work."[25]

Ford began work at Flower Brothers in December 1879 for $2.50 a week. Located at the corner of Woodbridge and Brush Streets, this shop made brass and iron castings on one floor and finished them on another. As an apprentice, Ford worked on a small milling machine shaping brass valves. The activities of this busy shop must have intoxicated the mechanics-mad youth. Frederick Strauss offered a description of Flower Brothers that captured the noisy, bustling atmosphere of this small-scale industrial enterprise:

> It was a great old shop. There were three brothers in the Com-
> pany, all in their sixties or more. . . . They were Scotch and believe
> me they could yell. They manufactured everything in the line of
> brass and iron—globe and gate valves, gongs, steam-whistles, fire
> hydrants, and valves for water pipes. There was a great variety of
> work. Some of the castings of the iron bodies of the large gate
> valves weighed a ton or more. They made so many different articles
> that they had to have all kinds of machines, large and small lathes
> and drill presses.

Strauss also related that when the heat became too oppressive in the low-
ceilinged shop, he and Henry often slipped away to a cooler building across
the street for half-hour breaks.[26]

After some nine months, however, Ford left Flower Brothers to
broaden his mechanical experience. As he explained later, apprentices in
Detroit had to serve four-year terms, and the masters "showed us how to do
a few things very well. That's why I changed; so that I could learn more
about different things." Thus, in August 1880, he moved to the Detroit Dry
Dock Company, the largest shipbuilding factory in the city, although he had
to take a pay cut to $2.00 a week. Sitting at the foot of Orleans Street on the
Detroit River, this enterprise sprawled along the riverfront for seven hundred feet and encompassed two large docks, a machine shop, an engine
works, a brass-and-iron foundry, and a boiler shop. The company manufactured a variety of iron ships—steamers, barks, barges, schooners, tug-
boats—and built engines ranging from 600 to 3,500 horsepower to power
them along. Ford was assigned to the engine works and came into contact
with a wide variety of power plants.[27]

He always looked back fondly upon his days at the Detroit Dry Dock
Company, viewing it as the place where he received his basic mechanical
training. "I passed my apprenticeship without trouble—that is, I was qualified to be a machinist long before my three-year term had expired," he
related in *My Life and Work*. While at this factory, he also had a memorable
encounter with its chief engineer, Frank E. Kirby. One day, as Ford related
the story, he was struggling to push a heavy wheelbarrow up a gangplank
into a ship when Kirby walked by, spotted him, and called out encourag-
ingly, "Stick in your toenails, boy, and you'll make it!" Ford added impishly,
"I've been sticking in my toenails ever since." He greatly admired Kirby,
and in 1918 he hired the engineer to help construct Eagle Boats during
World War I. When Ford built a huge engineering laboratory in Dearborn,
he ordered that the names of over a dozen celebrated scientists and inventors be carved above the large entry portal. Alongside Galileo, Copernicus,

Edison, Newton, and several others stands a name in letters equally tall: KIRBY.[28]

On weekends, after the long days spent laboring at the Detroit Dry Dock Company, Ford soaked up the sights and sounds of this booming industrial city. He would often accompany Frederick Strauss, who now was working at the Grand Trunk Railroad roundhouse, to his home for Sunday dinner, after which the two would stroll down to the river to watch the watercraft, especially the steamboats. They skipped rocks and engaged in boyish horseplay. According to Strauss, his companion was overflowing with plans for making things, although they were rarely fulfilled. Ford bought castings for a little steam engine that was never assembled; he secured a small galvanized boiler that was never put into operation; he got his hands on some lumber for building a boat, but the craft never made it into the water. "Henry always had another idea," Strauss recalled many years later.[29]

Ford's industrious nature proved more fruitful in another area. During evenings, he worked a second job, with jeweler Robert Magill, who had a shop on Baker Street, cleaning clocks and watches. One evening when the owner was absent, the youth audaciously exceeded his authority.

> I went to work on the watches waiting for repairs. Mr. Magill was alarmed when he first learned about it, but after he examined the watches he was pleased. So pleased that he gave me a steady job. But he was afraid his customers would not approve of a boy repairing their valuable watches, so I continued to work at the bench in the back room, out of sight.

After putting in a ten-hour day at the shipbuilding company, Ford spent six evenings a week laboring over watches for a wage of fifty cents per night. This was probably a necessity, since his lodging and food cost of $3.50 a week—by now he was staying at a boardinghouse—outstripped his modest salary of $2.00. Around this same time, according to Ford, he began to dream that "I could build a serviceable watch for around thirty cents and nearly started in the business." He figured that a production of two thousand watches a day would allow him to meet this low cost, and he started planning and designing machinery. The prospect of selling over a half-million watches a year eventually scuttled the plan, but, as Ford observed, "Even then I wanted to build something in quantity."[30]

Within a couple of years, Henry had settled into the life of a young Detroit machinist. When Magill sold his clock shop, the youth's Dry Dock Company salary had risen sufficiently for him to quit evening work altogether. He visited the Ford farm occasionally on weekends, and increasingly spent after-work hours pondering mechanical issues. He read back copies of publications such as *Scientific American* and studied closely Michael Faraday's book, *Treatise on the Steam Engine*. In an English magazine, *World of Science*, he encountered a story about a new "silent gas engine" that had recently appeared. Called the Otto engine, it featured a single large cylinder and ran on illuminating gas. Ford followed the development of this innovation, particularly "the hints of the possible replacement of the illuminating gas fuel by a gas formed by the vaporization of gasoline." He began tinkering with mechanical gadgets. He built a small turbine, powered it with water pressure by attaching it to a faucet in the shed behind his boardinghouse, and hooked up a small lathe to the turbine. He ran the lathe in his room most evenings, but politely refrained from doing so on Sunday to avoid offending the family who owned the boardinghouse, who were "Sabbatarians of the old-school, rigid type."[31]

Happily ensconced in an urban world of manufacturing and machines, Ford seemed to have made a complete transition from farm boy to city mechanic. So why, given the relatively smooth course of this youthful vocational journey and its happy conclusion, did he continue to embellish the story of his father as obstructionist, even a tyrant? Several factors came into play. First, resentment of William over Mary's untimely death continued to fester. Second, Ford betrayed a fundamental personality trait that would reappear throughout his life: an unwillingness, or inability, to grant others any measure of credit for his achievements. This impulse forced him to demonize his father to emphasize his own heroic, mythical quest to discover the mechanical future. Finally, by mid-adolescence his mechanical bent had become so single-minded that any kind of opposition, no matter how measured or mild, seemed like a gigantic barrier. Thus William's caution and mild skepticism cast him as a villain in his son's dream of abandoning farm life altogether and making the pilgrimage toward the mechanical glow of the nearby city.

But Henry Ford's melodrama with his father, all the more potent for being largely imagined, still had one more act to play out. After some three years in Detroit, his life took another important turn.

In late summer or early fall 1882, Henry halfheartedly returned to the family farm. As he had done nearly every year since his move to the city, he took some time off from the Detroit Dry Dock Company to help his family with the harvest for several weeks. But this time he ended up staying much longer. Abandoning his job as a machinist, he began nearly a decade of ambivalence, in which he tried to straddle the worlds of Detroit and Dearborn, the city and the country, the future and the past.

A new mechanical opportunity, complete with an independent role, caused him to abandon his life as an urban mechanic. John Gleason, a neighboring farmer, had purchased a portable steam engine from Westinghouse with plans to use it on his place and then hire it out for threshing grain and sawing timber later. But his skills proved inadequate to operating this high-speed engine, and the local engineer he hired turned out to be inept. So Gleason called upon Ford for assistance. "I have an idea he was afraid of his machine," Henry related much later. "To tell the truth I was frightened myself." William Ford believed that the high-speed, quick-steaming engine might be too much for his son's limited experience, but he reluctantly approved. So Henry took up the task. In his own words, "It was not long before my doubts entirely disappeared, and getting a grip on the engine, so to speak, I got a grip on myself." He seems to have discovered part of his life's calling by working and maintaining Westinghouse No. 345, with its steam boiler mounted on the rear of a small, sturdy, four-wheeled chassis:

> At the end of that first day I was as weary as I had been nervous at its beginning, but I had run the engine steadily, inducing it to stand up nicely to its work, and I forgot my griminess and weariness in the consciousness I had actually accomplished what I had started out to do. There are few more comforting feelings.
>
> I was paid three dollars a day and had eighty-three days of steady work. I traveled from farm to farm, and I threshed our own and the neighbor's clover, hauled loads, cut corn-stalks, ground feed, sawed wood. It was hard work. . . . I became immensely fond of that machine . . . and [its] complete and expert master. I have never been better satisfied with myself than I was when I guided it over the rough country roads of the time.[32]

Ford's mechanical work for Gleason opened other avenues. He started experimenting with building his own "farm locomotive," or prototype tractor. Rescuing an old, discarded mowing machine from his father's farm, he mounted a homemade steam engine upon its large frame and connected a crude belt to its cast-iron wheels. When fired up, the contraption crawled along for forty feet but then broke down. It was a victim of what would be a long-standing problem: power insufficient for the weight of the vehicle. He thought about alternative sources of power, such as electricity or gasoline, and continued to experiment.

In addition, while working area farms with Gleason's portable steam engine, Ford met John Cheeney, a regional manager for Westinghouse. Impressed by the young man's knowledge and enthusiasm, Cheeney hired him as a demonstrator and repairman for the company's machines. Ford traveled from farm to farm throughout southern Michigan from 1883 to 1885 working as a company troubleshooter, setting up and fixing Westinghouse steam engines. He began to encounter other types of engines, made by the Mills and Daimler companies, and broadened his knowledge by familiarizing himself with their design and characteristics. He also expanded his training in another way. During the winter season, when outdoor work with farm machines was impossible, he entered a Detroit business school called Goldsmith, Bryant & Stratton Business University—it was part of a national chain of institutions founded in the mid-nineteenth century—to study the rudiments of mechanical drawing, bookkeeping, and business practices.[33]

In 1886, in light of his son's successful work with farm machines, William Ford made a final effort to anchor him to the land permanently. He offered Henry eighty acres he had purchased in the 1860s, the Moir place, named after the previous owner, which included a small house and abundant forest growth. As Ford noted, William's offer was good only if "I gave up being a machinist." But he decided to accept, not out of a newfound desire to be a farmer, but because it offered an opportunity to use his mechanical expertise. He set himself up in the lumber business. He purchased a large circular saw, rented a portable steam engine to run it, and started to harvest the timber on the tract. Within a short time, he had built up a flourishing business and was supplying lumber to neighbors and to shipyards, factories, and shops in Detroit.[34]

But Ford had another compelling reason for taking his father's offer. At a dance on New Year's Night, 1885, at the Martindale House in nearby Greenfield, he had been introduced to a pretty local girl named Clara Jane Bryant by one of his cousins. He was enthralled. They courted, and were engaged on April 19, 1886. Since Ford had so little money, a quick marriage was not possible. So, when William offered the Moir place, Henry saw an opportunity to amass a respectable sum of money. After two years of hard work and saving, he married Clara on April 11, 1888. Though they set up housekeeping in the small house he had been occupying as a bachelor, they began to design a new abode; over the next year, Ford constructed what became known as the Square House. This story-and-a-half cottage was built with lumber from his farm and featured a wraparound porch, dormer windows, and gingerbread columns and balustrades. The couple moved into their new home in June 1889.[35]

For the next few years, Henry Ford led a kind of mixed existence, with one foot planted in the agricultural past and the other stepping toward the industrial future. He operated his sawmill in the winter months, and in the summer labored for the Buckeye Harvester Company, where he had been hired to set up and service its Eclipse portable farm engines. But much of his interest and energy focused on a new project.

Increasingly, Ford was bringing up a topic in conversation with his family: building a "horseless carriage" that could transport people about with its own power. One evening, while talking with Clara, he excitedly drew a sketch of his idea for such a contraption on the back of an old piece of sheet music. The big problem, of course, was developing an engine that was lightweight yet powerful. In 1885, Ford had been called to repair one of the new Otto engines from England, about which he had read during his apprentice days in Detroit. "No one in town knew anything about them," he related. "There was a rumor that I did and, although I had never been in contact with one, I undertook and carried through the job." Drawn to the unique potential of gasoline engines as an alternative to heavy, unwieldy steam engines, he became obsessed. He spent spare time in the shop behind his house building his own version of the Otto model: a one-cylinder, four-cycle internal-combustion engine that ran on gasoline. "The little model worked well enough," Ford observed; "it had a one-inch bore and three-inch stroke, operated with gasoline, and while it did not develop much power, it was slightly lighter in proportion than the engines being offered commercially." This engine required a heavy flywheel, however, which made it impractical for any kind of transportation device. So Ford started a process of building, and discarding, a series of "experimental engines."

Finally, he hit upon a new approach. "It was in 1890 that I began on a double-cylinder engine," he recalled. "The plan of the two opposed cylinders was that, while one would be delivering power the other would be exhausting. This naturally would not require so heavy a fly-wheel to even the application of power." Ford pondered the idea of mounting the engine on a bicycle with a direct connection to the crankshaft. Tinkering for hours in his farm workshop, he slowly built his engine and modified it by a process of trial and error. "A gas engine is a mysterious sort of thing—it will not always go the way it should," he noted many years later. "You can imagine how those first engines acted!"[36]

After several years of such modest experimentation on his Dearborn farm, Henry Ford made a momentous decision. Restless with rural life and eager to develop his horseless carriage, he looked about among his connections in Detroit for a position. Having concluded that development of the vehicle demanded a greater knowledge of electricity, he was delighted when the Edison Illuminating Company offered him a job as engineer and machinist for the handsome salary of $45 a month. After consulting with Clara, who was happy on the farm but supportive of her husband's endeavors, he decided to accept. "I took it because that was more money than the farm was bringing me and I had decided to get away from farm life anyway," Ford explained later. "The timber had all been cut." So, in September 1891, he and his wife packed up their belongings and departed for Detroit. Ford had finally severed all ties with the farming world of his father.[37]

Or had he? Many years later, in the 1930s, after spending several days with Henry Ford, a reporter for *Fortune* came to a curious conclusion about his seventy-year-old subject. "When you first meet him, you think he is a mechanic with a bent for farming," he wrote; "later you decide that he is a farmer with a bent for mechanics." This observer had shrewdly perceived that Ford's heart did not beat to the rhythm of his huge plant at River Rouge, where, amid the billowing smokestacks, bustle of unloading ships, and metallic clanging of an enormous assembly line, the aging industrialist oversaw, at its highest point, the labor of nearly one hundred thousand workers at a two-square-mile facility producing four thousand automobiles a day. In a wistful, revealing comment, Ford had admitted that the Rouge, the largest plant in the world, was "so big that it's not fun any more."[38]

So where did Henry Ford's heart lie? As *Fortune* reported, he spent most of his time away from the industrial empire he had created, at folk dances, harvest re-enactments, experimental farms, and tractor development projects. When not immersed in these activities, he whiled away the days at Fair Lane, the rural estate he had built in Dearborn on some two thousand acres only two miles from the place of his birth, or at his seventy-five-thousand-acre plantation in Georgia, Richmond Hill. In other words, the architect of mass production in America, having amassed incredible wealth from building and distributing millions of automobiles to a grateful public, seemed happiest when he escaped the industrial city crowded with cars. He thrived in the countryside, immersed in the rhythms, smells, labor, and traditions of rural life.

This impulse flowered fully in Henry Ford's most cherished adult hobby. After achieving worldwide fame by the 1920s, he poured money and effort into rebuilding the world of his youth. In 1929, after years of preparation, Ford opened to the public a large tourist park and museum built on 252 acres in Dearborn. Visitors could inspect a display of Americana—antiques of every imaginable variety—painstakingly collected by Ford's agents. In the enclosed buildings of the Henry Ford Museum, visitors saw an array of everyday goods from eighteenth- and nineteenth-century America: farm implements, railroad engines, furniture, cookware, wagons, woodstoves, and much, much more. Outside, in Greenfield Village, stood many architectural artifacts—a courthouse where Abraham Lincoln practiced law, Thomas Edison's laboratories, the homes of Stephen Foster and Noah Webster, a Southern plantation house, the Wright Brothers' bicycle shop, a gristmill, and a stagecoach tavern, to choose just a few examples—that had been purchased, carefully disassembled, and then rebuilt by Ford's carpenters and craftsmen.

William Holmes McGuffey's log-cabin birthplace occupied a conspicuous place in the village. Carefully moved from Washington County, Pennsylvania, the McGuffey cabin stood next to a log schoolhouse (now heated, lighted, and ventilated by modern methods) where children in the primary grades from the Greenfield Village school read and studied the old textbooks. Walking about the village with a New York *Times* reporter in 1936, Ford reaffirmed his reverence for this boyhood mentor. "This school house is an inspiration to us, for we are trying to produce a generation similar to that which learned its first principles under McGuffey and his type of school."[39]

But there was another architectural icon at Greenfield Village, one that stood even closer to his heart than the McGuffey cabin—Henry Ford's own boyhood home, lovingly rebuilt to the blueprint of his memories, and accurate to the tiniest detail. In part, the house stood as a living monument to his mother, replicating exactly her wallpaper, room decorations, china patterns, books, woodstoves, and kitchen utensils. It also offered a rendering of Ford's youthful struggle to succeed, as in the conspicuous placement of his workbench upstairs in order to stress his lonely endeavors as a watch repairman. The house conveyed a portrait of Ford as Horatio Alger, the boy who emerged from the countryside nurtured by his mother before she was snatched away, leaving him to pursue a lonely destiny.

Greenfield Village, with its evocation of a vanished age and its displays of personal meaning, demonstrated clearly that Henry Ford maintained a deep emotional attachment to the old-fashioned, prefactory world of his youth. For all of the mechanical zealotry and frustration with farming life that had marked his life as a young man, his rural roots ran much deeper than he realized at the time.

But this place devoted to the world of Ford's youth carefully concealed an old, unhealed wound. As is often the case, that which is missing reveals as much as that which is present. William Ford could scarcely be found at Greenfield Village. There appeared just a trace of his father's existence—a mention of his name at the homestead—and nothing about his activities and influence. The son, it seems, never forgave William for holding tight to the traditional world that he himself would come to love in later years. Well into advanced age, in fact, Henry continued to inveigh against his father. He fed stories to reporters and biographers that disparaged the older man. Privately, when he showed the old Litogot house to relatives, he angrily described it as "my mother's house—my father just walked into that place!"

But, typically for this American legend, the story was more complicated than it seemed. Henry never rejected his father as completely as he wished others to believe. All of his agriculture-tinged projects—his devoted production of tractors, his endless experiments with soybeans, his attempts to manufacture synthetic milk—emerged from the world of William Ford. Moreover, although few people knew this, William lived with or near the family of his eldest son for many years after retiring from the Dearborn farm in the 1890s. Most significantly, Henry revealed a debt to his father in a hobby he passionately pursued throughout his adult life. Perhaps reflecting the ancient childhood memory of William taking him by the hand to see the bird's nest he had carefully left alone in the field, Henry created at Fair Lane an elaborate sanctuary filled with hundreds of birdhouses, dozens of birdbaths, and abundant species of birds. Watching these feathered creatures through binoculars from his veranda, or strolling about among them on long afternoon walks through the woods and pastures of his estate, provided perhaps his keenest private pleasure. Henry Ford certainly found fortune and fame in the crowded, smoky factories of Detroit. But emotionally, in many ways, he never left his father's farm.

Three

Inventor

Thomas Edison, the great American inventor and close friend of Henry Ford, once described the carmaker as not only a "natural mechanic" and a "natural businessman," but that rarest of types, "a combination of the two."[1] By the 1920s, when Edison offered this assessment, most observers of Ford would have agreed. But in his early career, Ford's mechanical abilities and business talents fluctuated wildly and often divergently, and they were not harnessed in tandem. His skills as a machinist, of course, were evident when he arrived in Detroit in 1891. They provided a livelihood while he worked his way up in the electrical industry and inspired an obsessive, after-hours hobby as he tried for years to develop a horseless carriage. But Ford's adeptness as a businessman grew much more slowly and sporadically. In fact, on this front he failed consistently for many years; his first entrepreneurial ventures fell flat.

Ford's halting progress in the business world was partly the result of his personality. Inexperienced in the ways of commerce and stubborn to boot, he compounded mistakes in business judgment with an unswerving determination to follow his own instincts. But his long struggle for success also became caught up in historical developments beyond his control. Swimming against the current of business evolution, which was producing ever-larger corporate bureaucracies by the turn of the century, he pursued an older, more traditional goal of individual entrepreneurship. He was determined to maintain control of an organization, to shape personally the making of his product, and to direct the course of his enterprise according to his own vision. As he labored throughout the 1890s to be both mechanic and businessman, he mirrored an anxious question on the minds of many ambitious individuals of his age: was it still possible to be a creative, independent, self-made man in the dizzying new corporate world of bureaucracy, specialized production, mass markets, and managerial expertise? Eventually, Ford realized a hard-won answer in the affirmative. But that achievement may have been the exception that proved the rule.

Henry Ford left Dearborn with his wife, Clara, in September 1891 and journeyed up Michigan Avenue to Detroit with their household goods piled high in a haywagon. The couple took up residence in the right half of a rickety two-story double house at 618 John R Street, in a modest neighborhood inhabited by respectable working families. The Fords paid $10 a month for their half-house and settled in with their furniture and domestic goods. The John R Street house would be the first of a dozen residences they occupied over the next few years.[2]

To secure his position as an engineer with the Edison Illuminating Company, Ford had approached Charles Phelps Gilbert, then general manager of the company, and inquired about work. Gilbert hired him to replace a man recently killed at a substation located at the corner of Woodward and Willis Streets, and Ford started at midnight on the very day he and Clara moved to Detroit. Edison Illuminating, founded in 1886, focused on the residential market and was furnishing electricity to three-fourths of electricity-using Detroit houses by the 1890s. Ford would be employed by Edison for much of the next decade.

He worked the night shift, from 6:00 p.m. to 6:00 a.m., for $40 a month. The Willis and Woodward substation contained three large engines that generated electricity for houses in the vicinity: a 100-horsepower Beck steam engine, a 300-horsepower Rice dynamo, and an Arlington and Sims 150-horsepower generator. Ford's job was to supervise the operation of these generators and maintain them in smooth working order. Within a month, he took advantage of a disaster to enjoy his first professional triumph. The Beck engine failed, and inspection revealed major damage with a broken piston rod, a hole in the cylinder block, and a broken valve. Repairs promised to be costly and time-consuming, but Ford, confident of his abilities with steam engines, volunteered to undertake the task himself. To the amazement of his superiors, within a week he had made his own pattern, patched the block, and also fixed the piston rod and valve. Gilbert immediately gave him a $5.00-a-month raise, and did the same thing the following month. Ford's reputation and salary rose steadily, he moved to the day shift, and was promoted to the company's main station, at Washington Boulevard and State Street, within a few months. By 1893, the thirty-year-old engineer had become one of the company's most valuable employees.[3]

Years later, journalists interviewed Alexander Dow, who had succeeded

Gilbert as manager of Edison, and John R. Wilde, who had been Ford's first supervisor at the substation. Ford, they recalled, had been quiet, good-natured, deeply interested in his work, and unusually dedicated to learning about engine technology. In Dow's words, Ford had been a "very resource-ful" figure at the company:

> We found that out in the course of some repairs we were mak-ing. I recall that in putting in some new boilers we ran into a great pocket of quicksand. The foundations of our engines began to give way. Henry kept those engines running on wedges for six weeks. As the foundations of the engines sank into the quicksand, he would drive the wedges in a little more, day by day. He was very inge-nious.[4]

Many of Detroit's machinists were similarly impressed by Ford and his evident skill. Charles T. Bush, a fellow mechanic who first met Ford in the early 1890s, was struck by his drive to improve the steam engines at Edison. "He always figured that there was some little improvement that he could make," noted Bush. "He thought he could make them run better, make them use less steam, and get more out of a ton of coal." Ford also made an indelible impression on Frederick F. Ingram, a Detroit manufacturer who had a machine malfunction in his factory that no one could repair. He appealed to his friend Alexander Dow to send over the engineer about whom Dow always was bragging. Ingram related the following tale:

> In a little while, a slim, wiry man came out to my place. He said his name was Ford. I shall never forget the occasion as long as I live. Ford stood around a minute or two while we told him of our trou-bles. He walked around the balky engine once or twice and maybe fussed with it a little bit. Then he walked up to the throttle, turned on the steam, and away it went.[5]

Though Ford's engineering expertise and dedication became well known in Detroit machinist circles, it was not matched by intense ambition. On the contrary, he became notorious at Edison for his relaxed work habits and prankster personality. While at the main station, Ford once got even with an employee who had left his tools and work clothes scattered about by nailing his shoes to the floor with long spikes. Another time, workers repair-ing an engine in the basement of an old building felt faint and began gasp-ing for air. They ran outside to discover Ford, along with his friend John Wilde, dropping sulfur onto a large shovel filled with hot coals and squeez-

ing a bellows to blow the acrid fumes into the building through a knothole
in the wall. Jim Bishop, one of Ford's cronies, was heading home from work
one day when he saw a man riding away on his shiny new bicycle. Yelling
"Stop thief!," he ran off in pursuit. To his surprise, the thief began laughing
so hard he fell off the bicycle, and Bishop caught him. It was Ford.[6]

In fact, Ford evinced a rather casual attitude toward his job. By 1893,
his skills had made him something of a troubleshooter, so his work schedule
consisted of many hours of slack time punctuated by maintenance duties
and an occasional emergency repair on one of the company's generating
machines. As Ford himself once admitted of his Edison days, "There wasn't
much to do around the plant." Frederick Strauss—Ford's old apprentice
friend, who now worked at a neighboring shop—painted a similar portrait
of the engineer's slack work routine. "Henry never used his hands, to tell the
truth. He never came to work until after nine o'clock either," Strauss
recounted. "Henry was a free lance at Edison. He had to stand no watch. He
would be over at my shop every day three or four hours, just monkeying
around there."[7]

But Ford's real interest and energy were flowing elsewhere. Though he
performed his job at Edison with great dedication and skill, he was less
interested in meeting the electrical needs of Detroit than in pursuing a
hobby that had become a passion. Working in his spare time at home and at
Edison during slack time, Ford had become consumed with building a
crude internal-combustion engine. Such a motor, he had become convinced, eventually could be connected to a moving vehicle and fulfill the
dream of a horseless carriage. Back in Dearborn, of course, he had tinkered
with developing a farm tractor that would move under its own power, but
then his focus had been on steam engines. Now he began to veer in a new
direction with his experimentation.

In particular, Ford was caught up in a national craze for bicycles in the
early 1890s. He bought one and began to pedal about Detroit. These jaunts
on a two-wheeled machine seemed to trigger new thinking about the
mechanical possibilities of transportation. Ford had begun to read articles
about new, gasoline-powered engines that were starting to appear. He also
visited the 1893 Columbian Exposition in Chicago and witnessed a two-
cylinder Daimler engine from Germany that had been mounted on a fire-
hose cart. But Ford thought it might be possible to mount the engine on a
bicycle. Even though this idea proved impractical because of the engine's
weight, the seed had been planted.[8]

Thus, in 1893, he embarked upon what would be his life's work. In
December, Henry and Clara had moved to 58 Bagley Avenue, where they
occupied the left half of a two-story brick house. Ford built a workshop in a

small shed behind his home, and at the Edison Company he squirreled away some tools in a basement room across the alley behind the main building. During weekends, evenings, and odd moments in the workday, he constructed a small gasoline engine from scrap-metal parts that he had salvaged. It was a crude contraption of old steam pipes, pieces of brass, steel tubing, and a handwheel from an old lathe. The four-cycle engine featured a homemade piston and rings fitted into a cylinder bored from a one-inch pipe. It was mounted at one end of an old board a foot and a half long; a flywheel was placed at the other end; a rod connected the piston to the crankshaft; and a small, two-to-one gear arrangement operated a cam, which opened the intake and exhaust valves and timed the spark, which came from the building's regular electrical current.

After several weeks of tinkering, Ford finally got the engine to run on Christmas Eve, 1893. According to the legendary story, he brought it into Clara's kitchen while she was preparing food for the next day's holiday meal. He clamped the small engine to the kitchen sink, and secured his wife's help to trickle gasoline into the intake while he turned the flywheel. After a couple of false starts that required Ford to make adjustments, the engine finally roared to life and ran for about thirty seconds. The sink vibrated intensely from the shaking, and small flames shot out of the exhaust. Ford was ecstatic. Having proved to himself that a gasoline engine could be built to run, he immediately aimed higher. "I didn't stop to play with it," he said of his engine much later. "I wanted to build a two-cylinder engine . . . and started work on it right away." Within a few days, Ford was working on this bigger engine, one that would be powerful enough to run a vehicle.[9]

Around this time, an important family matter also pressed upon Ford's life. A few weeks before the successful trial in the kitchen, Edsel Bryant Ford had been born to Clara and Henry, on November 6. He would be their only child. The birth inspired a burst of professional zeal on Ford's part as he launched a campaign to secure promotion and a salary increase to meet his new responsibilities. The push was successful. He had been appointed chief engineer at Edison late in 1893, and his salary almost doubled, to $90 a month. But, even more important, this new position gave him flexibility in his work schedule. Though Ford was on twenty-four-hour-a-day call, his supervisory duties varied with the demands of any given day. This allowed him considerable free time to tinker at home, to visit machine shops, to trade tips and shoptalk with mechanics, and to experiment with improving his little gasoline engine. An evening job teaching a metalworking class at the local YMCA gave him access to the school shop to work metal parts for his hobby.[10]

Over the next two years, Ford spent nearly every free minute refining his engine and building a carriage that he hoped it would power. He recalled later, "Every night and all of every Saturday night I worked on the new motor. I cannot say that it was hard work. No work with interest is ever hard." Some of Ford's experimentation took place in the shed behind his home at 58 Bagley. Felix Julien, a retired coal-seller who occupied the other half of the house, had become fascinated with his neighbor's mechanical work, and surrendered his half of the shed to Ford in return for being allowed to observe. So, in the evenings, the old man would pull up a chair in the shop, or sit on the windowsill, and watch Ford tinker with his engine.[11]

But much of the work occurred in the informal shop he had established behind the Edison Company, in a basement room across the alley. A number of cronies gathered around Ford as they built and discarded engine parts, experimented with mechanical techniques, and shared no small amount of horseplay and male camaraderie. Jim Bishop and George Cato, both skilled mechanics for Edison, were regular participants. Bishop helped Ford build the carriage body, while Cato worked on the ignition for the new engine and developed a pair of "ignitors" for the cylinders. Ed "Spider" Huff, another mechanic friend, helped with electrical work. Charles B. King, a college-trained engineer who also was working on his own motor-powered carriage, lent assistance. Oliver Barthel—King's young assistant, whom Ford had instructed in the YMCA metalworking class—joined the group and contributed his considerable skills as machinist and designer.[12]

Ford lured Frederick Strauss, who was now working at the Wain Machine Shop, into the mechanics circle. Strauss left a picture of the group and the setting behind the Edison Company:

> The shop was across the alley; only one-quarter was above the sidewalk. It was a storage place. Henry used it as a hangout.
>
> There were other fellows who would come and sit in there. He had this little lathe. . . . We didn't work every night. We would just joke away. Sometimes we would work and sometimes not. On Saturday nights we had quite a crowd. Henry had some kind of a "magnet." He could draw people to him; that was a funny thing about him.
>
> When we ran that little engine in the basement, of course, there would be quite a few people outside listening to the noise, wondering what was going on.[13]

As the months went on, Ford made slow but steady progress toward bringing his prototype to completion. A crucial advance came in 1896.

Barthel, an avid reader of technological literature, called Ford's attention to a pair of articles from *American Machinist* dated November 7, 1895, and January 9, 1896. The first described the successful Kane-Pennington gasoline engine, and analyzed the strengths and weaknesses of this light, powerful motor. The second explained how a machinist might build a similar model from common scraps of material in any shop, and offered detailed drawings of such a project. Ford pored over the articles, as did many other machinists, and used them as the basis for his engine design.[14]

The labor of Ford and his associates reached a fever pitch during the winter and spring of 1896. Ford scrambled to procure materials from all over Detroit:

> Most of the iron work was got from a firm by the name of Barr & Dates; they were located at that time on the corner of Park Place and State Street, Detroit. The wheels I made; the seat I got from the Wilson Carriage Company, and from the C. A. Strelinger & Co. bolts and screws and nuts; I made the handle myself; I don't know where I got the balance wheel from; I made the pattern and got it cast; I made the sparking device; the springs from the Detroit Steel and Spring Co.

Clara Ford became concerned about the constant purchasing of materials. As Henry's sister Margaret recalled, Clara "wondered many times if she would live to see the bank account restored."[15]

The Quadricycle, as Ford and his assistants were now calling it, gradually took shape. The engine, which moved toward completion at the Edison shop, was a four-cycle motor with two cylinders of two-and-a-half-inch bore and six-inch stroke. It generated between 3 and 4 horsepower and relied upon an ignition system with a spark breaker fitted into a hole in the cylinder. The carriage, which Ford and Bishop had mounted on sawhorses at the Bagley Avenue shed, had the look of a small, boxy buggy. A carriage seat sat above and in front of the engine, flywheel, and transmission belt; the vehicle's squared front housed its "steering bar," connected to the front wheels. The whole was mounted on four twenty-eight-inch wire bicycle wheels with rubber tires. The vehicle's transmission system featured two speeds—a "low" of ten miles an hour and a "high" of twenty miles an hour—and a neutral gear. A clutch lever tightened and released a belt that dictated among these three choices, and power was transferred by this belt from the motor to a countershaft, and then from the countershaft to the rear wheels, by a chain. A flywheel was spun to start the engine; a crude brake could stop the vehicle when it was placed in neutral. The Quadricycle had a total weight of around five hundred pounds, a gasoline tank with a capacity of three gallons, and no reverse gear.[16]

For all of his labor, Henry Ford was not the first to drive a gasoline motor vehicle on the streets of Detroit. On March 6, 1896, Charles B. King debuted his own horseless carriage. With the assistance of Oliver Barthel, King rolled out his vehicle for a public demonstration and ran it a short distance. Detroit newspapers noted, "The first horseless carriage seen in this city was out on the street last night," and described how "when in motion the connecting rods fly like lightning." Though this contraption impressed casual observers, however, it disappointed the more knowledgeable. King's vehicle weighed over thirteen hundred pounds, could reach a speed of only five miles an hour, and was little more than a gasoline engine clamped to a horse wagon. Ford, eager to analyze the competition, observed King's maiden voyage as he followed on a bicycle.[17]

Finally, the stage had been set for one of the seminal moments in American history: Ford was ready for a test run of his Quadricycle. In the early morning of June 4, 1896, after hours of last-minute adjustments at the Bagley Avenue shed, Ford prepared to wheel the vehicle out for its maiden voyage. He and Jim Bishop looked out into the night and saw a slight drizzle dampening the streets. But as they turned the Quadricycle to leave the building, Ford, to his horror, realized a terrible oversight. In his determination to build the vehicle, he had failed to notice that it was too large to fit through the shed door. He grabbed an ax and doubled the opening by knocking out some bricks. The pair then wheeled the Quadricycle out onto the cobblestoned alley.

While Clara Ford watched from the back door under an umbrella, her husband adjusted the gasoline flow, turned on the electrical current from the car's battery, choked the engine by covering the valve's air opening with his finger, and gave the flywheel a turn. After a couple of tries, the engine sputtered to life, and Ford slipped the clutch lever into low. He headed off, turning quickly from the alley onto the street, and proceeded down Grand River Avenue toward Washington Boulevard. Bishop pedaled ahead on his bicycle, ready to alert any passersby and clear the path. Suddenly, however, the car stopped; Ford heard the engine die. An inspection revealed only a minor problem—a spring supporting one of the electrical "ignitors" had failed—and a quick repair got the vehicle up and running once again. After a brief jaunt, the two returned triumphantly to Bagley Avenue for a nap and a sturdy breakfast, then headed off to work at Edison.

After the Quadricycle's successful trial run, Ford's immediate concern was repairing the Bagley Avenue shed. He hired two bricklayers to fix the damage and had come home to supervise their work when William Wreford, owner of the residence, showed up to collect the rent. Viewing the damage to his shed, Wreford grew angry until Ford explained the story of the previous night's adventure with the horseless carriage. The landlord asked to see the machine, and immediately his fascination overcame his temper. According to Ford's report, Wreford exclaimed, "If those fellows put that wall back up, how are you going to get your car out again? I've got an idea. Tell those bricklayers to leave that opening and then you can put on swinging doors. That will let you in and out." Thus was born the first automobile garage in American history.[18]

The early-morning run of the Quadricycle through the rainy streets of Detroit dramatically marked a new stage in Henry Ford's career: his years-long dream of building a self-powered vehicle had finally become a reality. But this episode, by itself, took him only to the threshold of success. Like the spark needed to explode the gasoline in the chamber of the Quadricycle's engine, another element was required to ignite a burst of energy and carry Ford forward. In the form of a dose of encouragement, it came from an unexpected quarter.

Two months after the maiden voyage of his Quadricycle, Henry Ford had an epiphany. In August 1896, he accompanied Alexander Dow, manager of the Edison Illuminating Company, and Hoyt Post, the company attorney, to a professional convention in New York City. Held at the Oriental Hotel at Manhattan Beach—this late-Victorian pleasure palace welcomed visitors with a forest of turrets, vast expanses of spacious verandas, and a constellation of elaborate light fixtures—the meeting gathered representatives of Edison electrical companies from all over the United States. Ford heard lectures, talked with electrical technicians and executives, walked on the beach, and attended receptions.

But the decisive moment at this conclave occurred on August 12, the third evening of the convention. Somehow, Ford wrangled an invitation to an exclusive dinner held in the hotel's private banquet room. In attendance were some of the leading lights in the American electrical industry. The small group included Samuel Insull of Chicago, John W. Lieb of New York, Charles Edgar of Boston, John I. Beggs of Cincinnati, and Dow from Detroit. But most important was the guest of honor, seated at the head of the table: the great inventor himself, Thomas Alva Edison. Far down the table sat the young engineer from Detroit, who so idolized Edison that he had already taken several candid snapshots of the great man on the previous day, as he loitered about the Oriental Hotel and napped on one of its huge verandas.

During a lull in the dinner conversation, which had been addressed to the problem of charging storage batteries for electric cars, Dow offered an interesting observation. "This young fellow here has made a gas car," he informed the group, and nodded at Ford. Someone asked the young engineer how he got his vehicle to go, and he started to explain his gasoline engine. Edison, who was hard-of-hearing, strained to listen, so his neighbor traded places and allowed Ford to move up and sit near the head of the table. Edison peppered him with questions about the workings of the engine—he was especially interested in how an electric spark was used to explode the gas in the cylinder—and Ford took a pencil and began to draw on the back of a menu card. In Ford's account:

> He asked me no end of details and I sketched everything for him, for I have always found I could convey an idea quicker by sketching than by just describing it. When I had finished he brought his fist down on the table with a bang and said:
>
> "Young man, that's the thing; you have it. Keep at it! Electric cars must keep near to power stations. The storage battery is too heavy. Steam cars won't do it either, for they have to carry a boiler and fire. Your car is self-contained—it carries it own power-plant— no fire, no boiler, no smoke, no steam. You have the thing. Keep at it."

Henry Ford never forgot the encounter. Up to this point, many of his professional acquaintances had scoffed at his project. They dismissed the gasoline-driven Quadricycle, insisting that he was wasting his time since the future of power lay clearly with electricity. But now the demigod of American technological progress had offered words of encouragement. "That bang on the table was worth worlds to me. No man up to then had given me any encouragement," Ford related later. "I had hoped I was right, sometimes I knew I was, sometimes I only wondered if I was, but here . . . out of a clear sky the greatest inventive genius in the world had given me a complete approval."[19]

Ford's conversation with Edison initiated a famous friendship. Over the following three decades, the two men would see each other frequently. The Michigan mechanic admired the New Jersey inventor and considered him to be the greatest man not just in the United States but in the world. Ford would acclaim Edison's accomplishments in public print at every opportunity, memorialize his work at Greenfield Village, and glory in the many conversations they enjoyed on rustic vacations they took together. But in the 1890s, at the outset of their relationship, Edison personified something that the younger man yearned to be: a practical-minded inventor whose technological creations transformed daily life. As the last decade of the nineteenth century drew to a close, this desire had become a crucial element in the makeup of Henry Ford.

By 1896, of course, Thomas Edison already had achieved legendary status as a technological revolutionary. The Wizard of Menlo Park—so named after the New Jersey town that housed his research laboratory—had migrated from rural Ohio to New York City in 1868 and burst on the scene with his invention of the stock-quotation printer, which was quickly adopted by Western Union. In subsequent years, a long parade of Edison's creations came out of Menlo Park to transform the American landscape: the "talking machine," or phonograph, in 1877; the incandescent light in 1879; the multiplex telegraph; improved versions of the telephone and the typewriter; the basic elements of a central power-generating system for bringing electricity to homes, businesses, and factories; a new, efficient dynamo suitable for industrial use; and many other patented devices. These achievements popularized Edison as a kind of self-made genius of the Gilded Age. He captured the American imagination as both a heroic individual and a modern organizer who could put together a research organization, manufacture millions of lightbulbs, and gain the financial backing of J. P. Morgan to establish the nation's first power-generating plant in New York City. Part rural self-made man and part urban industrial engineer, Edison appealed to Americans in their struggle to accommodate the old and the new.[20]

To Ford, he was a god. As he once confessed, "The Edison who came into my life in this remarkable way [at Manhattan Beach] had been my ideal since boyhood. I first heard of him in a way that impressed me during 1879 or '80 when the invention and quick adoption of the incandescent light made him a world figure and filled the newspapers with articles about him." Edison's electrical technology alone had cut a wide swath in the daily lives of modern Americans, providing the wherewithal for a great leap forward in industrial production while also illuminating the homes of common citizens. Edison's inventions had ushered the United States into the modern age, and Ford noted, "He takes the strictly practical view—which he has carried through all his work—that results and results alone count."[21]

Even more important to Ford, however, were two other qualities. First, Edison brought to his work a combination of mental habits that Ford found inspiring. Edison's clarity and logic in addressing scientific issues were matched by his imagination and creativity in coming up with technological innovations. His practicality led him to use science not for abstract or esoteric purposes, but to solve daily problems in life. "He was a scientist but also he was a man of extraordinary common sense. It was a new combination," Ford observed. "[He] ended the distinction between the theoretical man of science and the practical man of science." Edison matched this utilitarian bent with a finely honed sense of efficiency in concentrating his mental resources. As Ford said, "His whole life is arranged on a program of economy of effort—he dislikes doing anything which is not necessary for him to do."[22]

But Edison's powerful work ethic most impressed his disciple. As Ford confessed:

> What hit my mind hardest was his gift for hard, continuous work. . . . Mr. Edison has a wonderfully imaginative mind and also a most remarkable memory. Yet all of his talents would never have brought anything big into the world had he not had within him that driving force which pushes him on continuously and regardless of everything until he has finished that which he started out to do. . . . He believes that unflinching, unremitting work will accomplish anything. It was this genius for hard work that fired me as a lad and made Mr. Edison my hero.[23]

Edison's concern for bettering the lot of common people also prompted Ford's veneration. Rather than seeking to build a huge fortune, the inventor found greatness as "a servant of humanity." Money in itself had little meaning for Edison, but provided merely the means to a greater reward: conducting more experiments and providing service to the public. In "the age of Edison," Ford insisted,

> . . . each and every person among us has gained a larger measure of economic liberty. . . . Already our general prosperity leads the world and this is due to the fact that we have had Edison. . . . His work has not only created many millions of new jobs but also—and without qualification—it has made every job more remunerative. Edison has done more toward abolishing poverty than have all the reformers and statesmen since the beginning of the world.[24]

Edison served as a role model for Ford. From the moment of their first acquaintance, Ford sought to emphasize their kinship as inventors. He liked to tell others, for example, how Edison, the day after their dinner meeting at Manhattan Beach, invited him to go on the train back to New York City. "We talked mostly of the difficulties of obtaining the right kind of materials and supplies in the working out of new inventions," Ford described. "For instance, I told him that for my first car I could find no suitable tires and had to use bicycle tires, and he told me something of the trouble which he had met in finding suitable bulbs for the incandescent light and how he had to have them blown himself." Ford's conclusion spoke volumes about his identification with the great man: "The pioneers in every art may plan perfectly, but always their first products must be compromises, for they can never obtain the right materials."[25]

This strong sense of kinship appeared even more clearly in Ford's description of their next encounter. Two or three years later, Ford visited Edison's New Jersey laboratory to discuss the problem of developing an electrical storage battery for the automobile. Once again, his telling of this tale emphasized their common impulses. "As I began to explain to him what I wanted, I reached for a sheet of paper and so did he," Ford related. "In an instant we found ourselves talking with drawings instead of words. We both noticed it at the same moment and began to laugh. Edison said: 'We both work the same way.' " Ford's form of hero-worship, it seems, revealed more about the worshipper than about the hero.[26]

Ultimately, Ford's veneration of Edison had deep roots in his own character and beliefs. He saw the inventor as the embodiment of American achievement: "The American spirit of endeavor as represented in its fullness by Thomas Alva Edison is the real wealth of the nation." But the Edisonian influence involved more than abstract representations. In a very practical way, that first conversation sparked Ford's enthusiasm for plunging ahead with an improved version of his horseless vehicle. After getting encouragement from his idol, "I was in a hurry to get home and go ahead with the work on my second automobile," he said. "The first thing I did when I reached Detroit was to tell my wife what Mr. Edison had said, and I wound up by saying, 'You are not going to see very much of me until I am through with this car.' " Thomas Edison's fist-banging seal of approval at Manhattan Beach provided an emotional springboard for a new leap forward in Henry Ford's career. But it soon would land him in new, unfamiliar, even threatening terrain.[27]

By the fall of 1896, Ford had become a familiar, if somewhat eccentric figure on the streets of Detroit. With his Quadricycle performing reliably, he could be seen puttering about the city on short trips that often proved adventurous. Ford once described the reactions of his fellow townsmen and -women as he sat perched behind the tiller of his vehicle:

It was considered to be something of a nuisance, for it made a racket and scared horses. Also it blocked traffic. For if I stopped my machine anywhere in town a crowd was around it before I could start up again. If I left it alone even for a minute some inquisitive person always tried to run it. Finally, I had to carry a chain and chain it to a lamp post whenever I left it anywhere. And then there was trouble with the police. I do not know quite why, for my impression is that there were no speed-limit laws in those days. Anyway, I had to get a special permit from the mayor and thus for a time enjoyed the distinction of being the only licensed chauffeur in America.[28]

Though Ford's motorized adventures were certainly unusual, they were not unique. In the early 1890s, European engineers such as Carl Benz in Germany and Émile Constant Levassor in France had developed reliable vehicles with ever-larger, more powerful engines. In the United States, mechanically minded individuals were also tinkering with horseless-carriage models all over the country. In 1893, Charles and Frank Duryea had built the first successful American vehicle powered by an internal-combustion engine in Springfield, Massachusetts. Other innovative mechanics, such as Elwood P. Haynes, Hiram Maxim, Ransom E. Olds, and Alexander Winton followed suit. In 1895 alone, two periodicals devoted to the automobile, *Motorcycle* and *Horseless Age*, appeared; over five hundred applications for patents related to motor vehicles were filed in the U.S. Patent Office; and the Chicago *Times-Herald* sponsored the first American automobile race on Thanksgiving Day, which was won by the Duryea brothers.[29]

Thus, by 1896, when Henry Ford first began piloting his Quadricycle through Detroit, a highly energized and competitive atmosphere was taking shape in the fledgling American automobile market. His vehicle, though skillfully built and charming, was too small and unfinished for large-scale production. No one realized this more than Ford, who sold his first car to Charles Ainsley, an acquaintance in Detroit, for $200, in order to raise funds for continued research and development. As he described later, "I had built the first car not to sell but only to experiment with. I wanted to start another car. Ainsley wanted to buy. I could use the money and we had no trouble agreeing upon a price."[30]

Ford began work on a second automobile with an eye toward manufacture for a mass audience. "I was looking ahead to production," he noted with his usual practical bent. Once again, he turned to the circle of mechanics who had helped him with the Quadricycle. In 1897–98, Jim Bishop and George W. Cato continued to perform a variety of mechanical tasks. Ed Huff, who had proved to be something of an electrical genius and possessed a creative temperament to match, had left Edison and begun bouncing from job to job as his interest waned. He remained loyal to Ford, however, and threw himself into refining the electrical system for the second automobile. Huff designed a key electrical part—the magneto—that made it superior to many of its competitors.

David Bell was a new addition to the team. Ford had hired him as a blacksmith at Edison, and he became invaluable by helping his supervisor forge new, sturdier metal parts—wheel spokes, steering rod and mechanism, iron pipe in the undercarriage for the vehicle, handrails on the seat—for the new horseless carriage. As for Ford himself, he supplied more brainpower than brawn. In Bell's words, "I never saw Mr. Ford make anything. He was always doing the directing."[31]

Ford purchased a stream of materials from Detroit suppliers as the second car slowly took shape. He purchased a lathe from the Detroit Motor Company, wrenches from the Strelinger Company, and a whole list of items from Whitehead and Lewis and S. Harvey's Sons Manufacturing Company: locknuts, brass bushings, flanges, plugs, nipples, gears, electrical parts, and collars. Charles T. Bush, a young mechanic who worked at the Strelinger Company, recalled that Ford

> would be in our place two or three times a week buying something that had to do with something he was making. As a rule he paid cash. Later . . . he opened a charge account. . . . Mr. Ford loved anything in the way of tools, any kind whatsoever. Anything new that came out in a tool, he wanted to see it. . . . We often wondered when Henry Ford slept, because he was putting in long hours working, and when he went home at night he was always experimenting.[32]

This flurry of designing, construction, and purchasing soon brought results. By late 1897, Ford's second car was complete, although he still continued to refine it and tinker with details. In most respects, it represented a striking departure from the Quadricycle. The original boxlike carriage, with its four bicycle tires and tiny carriage that barely accommodated two passengers, had given way to a larger, elongated, flowing design with elevated rear tires and smaller front ones. A large, stuffed seat, big enough for two, sat above a more powerful, sophisticated engine, a glass-jar battery system, and a gearbox. Although this model still retained a tiller for steering the vehicle, a throttle and "sparking" control had been installed near the driver's right hand, just below the seat.[33]

With his second vehicle running dependably, Ford began to venture out for weekend excursions to the family farm in Dearborn with his wife and son in tow. Margaret Ford Ruddiman had a clear memory of her brother's first appearance at the family homestead in his car:

> It was Sunday, and he brought Clara and Edsel out to the farm to show us the horseless carriage of which we had heard so much. . . . My first sight of the little car was as it came west along what is now Ford Road. The wheels on one side were deep in the rut made by the farm wagons while the wheels on the other side were high in the center of the road. . . . Clara and Edsel were with him, and all of them were sitting on the slanted seat. . . . Henry and Clara were proud of their little horseless carriage that day. Henry took all of us for rides during the day, and I well remember the peculiar sensation of what seemed to be a great speed and the sense of bewilderment I felt when I first rode in this carriage which moved without a horse. Henry particularly enjoyed explaining the mechanical details to his younger brothers, and I am sure that he enjoyed scaring the life out of his sisters.[34]

By 1898, Ford's schedule of alterations on his second car had been finished, and he made it available for public inspection. One engineer and horseless-carriage enthusiast, R. W. Hanington of Denver, stopped in Detroit after a trip to the East Coast. He had examined several motorized vehicles under development, and he had been told of the Michigan machine. After visiting with Ford and inspecting his prototype, he returned home and wrote a highly favorable analysis of the vehicle. Hanington offered much praise for the engine design, cooling tanks, carburetor, and transmission mechanism, but judged the gear system only adequate. Though there was nothing particularly novel about Ford's automobile, the engineer noted, its virtue lay in the way that it refined and compactly arranged existing elements. "The whole design strikes me as being very complete, and worked out in every detail," Hanington concluded. "Simplicity, strength, and common sense seem to be embodied in Mr. Ford's carriage, and I believe that these ideals are the essential ones for a successful vehicle." When manufactured and sold to the public, "this carriage should equal any that has been built in this country."[35]

Using his own skills and drawing inspiration from the encouragement of his hero, Thomas Edison, Ford had taken a major step forward. His new automobile prototype came near to a version salable to the public. But one move remained to be made. In modern, industrial America, even minor-scale manufacturing required both an organization and an extensive commitment of capital, and Ford lacked these resources. As the 1890s drew to a close, he began to search for financial support among those who did. Henry Ford the mechanical inventor stepped aside as Henry Ford the businessman strode forward.

Four

Businessman

On a Saturday afternoon in July 1899, Henry Ford pulled his motor vehicle up in front of the house of William H. Murphy, at the corner of Putnam and Woodward Streets, in a fashionable area of Detroit. Some months earlier, this prominent businessman had expressed an interest in Ford's horseless carriage, and told him to come see him when the car could travel from Detroit to Orchard Lake and back by way of Pontiac—a total distance of some eighty miles. Now Ford announced, "I am ready to take you on that ride." The two climbed aboard and set out, with Ford driving and Murphy keeping a log of the trip, in which he recorded the fuel consumed, the behavior of the car, and the condition of the roads it navigated. The businessman was satisfied. Upon returning to his house several hours later, he said simply, "Well, now we will organize a company."[1]

Securing Murphy's support was no small achievement. With his position in Detroit, his agreement to back Ford sent a clear financial signal that the horseless carriage carried significant economic potential. But actually manufacturing and selling these motorized vehicles, like any industrial enterprise in modern America, was a daunting task. It demanded considerable capital, the construction of a complex business organization, and the deployment of marketing skills to get the product to buyers. Murphy would be a key figure in this process as it unfolded over the next few years. The relationship between the two major actors in the drama—the innovative mechanic and the wealthy investor—yielded a progress report on Henry Ford's evolving business sense.

Ford's relationship with Murphy was the culmination of a search for financial backing that had begun with a series of quiet inquiries. By 1898, with the successful development of a second vehicle, Ford looked to identify and woo investors. One of his earliest contacts was George Peck, president of the Edison Illuminating Company and the Michigan National Savings

Bank. Peck had developed an interest in horseless carriages through his son, Barton, a young dilettante who was tinkering unsuccessfully with his own motorcar in a shop. Ford's friendship with this family led to his use of part of Barton's shop space for his own work, and the elder Peck ended up a shareholder in Ford's enterprise. William C. Maybury, an old friend of the Ford family and newly elected mayor of Detroit in 1897, proved to be a much more important figure. This energetic, charismatic businessman and Democratic politician took an early interest in Ford's project, helping him to secure credit for purchasing materials, loaning money to pay for outsourced labor, and issuing him an official "license" when some citizens complained about the car's noise.[2]

A number of factors—Ford's expertise and growing reputation, excitement about the profit potential of motor carriages—inspired broader entrepreneurial interest. In the fall of 1898, Mayor Maybury and a trio of businessmen became the first investors in Ford's automobile enterprise. Ellery I. Garfield of the Fort Wayne Electrical Corporation, Everett A. Leonard of the Standard Life and Accident Insurance Co., and Dr. Benjamin Rush Hoyt, a physician, joined Maybury to advance money for Ford to meet development expenses. They each put up $500, worked out provisions with Ford to share any patents, and anticipated the formation of a corporation to manufacture the automobile when it was ready. When such a corporation was formed, the contract provided that it would employ Ford "on fair compensation."[3]

This financial lifeline had allowed Ford to complete the second version of his automobile by midsummer 1899. This prototype looked promising for production. An article entitled "Ford's Automobile Has New Features and Is a Novel Machine," in the Detroit *Journal*, described the car in detail. Complete with one illustration of the whole car, and another of its chassis and gear mechanism, the article offered information on Henry Ford and his financial backers. It devoted most attention, however, to an extensive description of the "self-propelling carriage's" mechanical features and engine, and concluded with a reporter's account of a brief trip in the vehicle.[4]

With the appearance of this prototype, other Detroit investors began to crowd in around Ford and his original backers. They included William C. McMillen, scion of a wealthy family of capitalists who, among their vast holdings, owned the Detroit Dry Dock Company, where young Ford had worked years earlier; Dexter Mason Ferry, owner of a large seed firm; Alfred E. F. White, director of several McMillen and Ferry corporations and banks; Thomas W. Palmer, lumber magnate and U.S. senator from Michigan; Frank R. Alderman, a prosperous life-insurance salesman; Safford S.

DeLano, heir to the fortune his father earned as president of the Detroit Steel Works; and the aforementioned George Peck. In other words, the elite among Detroit's financial community stepped forward to put their capital behind the manufacture of Henry Ford's horseless carriage.[5]

But Murphy was the linchpin. Though Ford's other backers were certainly impressive, Murphy's towering reputation in Detroit commercial circles granted Ford instant credibility, and reassured other potential investors. Moreover, unlike the other investors, he took an active role in the Ford enterprise over the next few years.

Murphy had been born in 1855 in Bangor, Maine, in a long line of lumbermen. The son of a prosperous sawmill owner who migrated to Michigan, he had attended the University of Michigan before going to Boston to study business and music. Upon returning to the Midwest, Murphy took a position in his father's company at a mill in Bay City. This became his schoolroom for learning the lumber business, and after a few years he returned to Detroit to become involved in his father's endeavors. The family lumbering operation spread from Michigan to Wisconsin, and then to northern California with the organization of the Pacific Lumber Company. Growing profits gradually took the Murphys into real-estate investments—by the 1890s, along with the McMillen family, they owned large sections of downtown Detroit—and other commercial ventures included the formation of the Murphy Power Company, the Murphy Oil Company, and the Simon J. Murphy Company. The elder and younger Murphy, in a visible sign of their wealth and power by the 1890s, began construction on Detroit's first skyscraper, the Penobscot Building, which would reach thirteen stories by 1905 and forty-seven by the 1920s.

Of calm and dignified demeanor, well dressed, with thinning hair and spectacles, William H. Murphy projected a quietly powerful presence to the world. In his business affairs, as Ford would learn, he combined hard-nosed commercial judgment with attention to detail. Ironically, since Murphy had suffered from near-total deafness since boyhood, the great love of his life was music. As a youngster, he had tried to play the violin; as an adult, he organized and supported orchestras. Murphy became the leading force in the Detroit Symphony Society, pouring his money and time into creating the Detroit Symphony and building Symphony Hall. In 1925, four years before his death, the development of radio allowed him to have powerful speakers and headphones installed in his private box. To his joy, the sounds of the orchestral music that he loved, but had strained to hear only faintly for decades, now came through fairly clearly.

Murphy had a long-standing interest in horseless carriages. In 1883, he traveled to Philadelphia to inspect a steam-engine fire wagon and was so impressed that he purchased a model for the Detroit Fire Department. Apparently, Ford had met Murphy many years earlier, when he was running his small sawmill on his father's property in Dearborn. In 1898, they became reacquainted through Mayor Maybury, who was boosting Ford's horseless carriage to anyone who would listen. This had set the stage for Ford and Murphy's pivotal automobile journey to Orchard Lake in July 1899.[6]

With Murphy's stamp of approval wiping away any doubts, Ford and his investors officially formed the Detroit Automobile Company on August 5, 1899. Papers for the corporation, filed with the county clerk on that date, indicated that the company was capitalized at $150,000, with $15,000 actual cash put into it in the form of fifteen hundred shares. Though a stockholder, Ford contributed no money: he was assigned shares on the basis of his mechanical expertise as architect of the company's automobile.

One final step remained. Ten days after the birth of Detroit Automobile, Henry Ford resigned from the Edison Illuminating Company to bet his future on the new world of the motorized vehicle. But in doing so, he indulged in an old habit. Just as he had once described his departure from William Ford's farm, he now cast his leaving the company as an escape from a disapproving authority figure. "My gas-engine experiments were no more popular with the president of the company than my first mechanical leanings were with my father," he wrote. "The Edison Company offered me the general superintendency of the company but only on the condition that I would give up my gas engine and devote myself to something really useful." As he observed dramatically, "I had to choose between my job and my automobile."[7]

Again, however, Ford's need for mythmaking twisted the facts. According to all evidence, there was no angry split with Edison Illuminating, his employer for almost the last eight years. According to Alexander Dow, Edison's manager, he and Ford had an amiable discussion of the future in the spring of 1899. In Dow's words:

I knew that he was giving a great deal of thought to the gasoline car he was trying to make. He made the parts for his first car right here in our shop on company time, and I never objected to it. But I knew the extensions we were about to make would so increase his duties as to take all of his time. I simply wanted Henry to know what we were planning so that he could make his plans accordingly, but there was no threat to discharge him nor any time limit set before he must decide. The talk was entirely friendly.

Once more, Ford's proclivity for portraying himself as the lonely, heroic individual triumphing over the odds had surfaced. Now it was relatively harmless. Later it would become a much more troublesome trait.[8]

The Detroit Automobile Company, after signing a three-year lease, set up operation in a three-story brick building at 1343 Cass Avenue. Clarence A. Black, Detroit city controller, was installed as president, and Frank R. Alderman became the company secretary. But the real powers behind the scenes were Murphy, McMillen, and Maybury, the trio who dominated the board of directors, and Ford, who directed production endeavors as mechanical superintendent. Within a couple of weeks, the organization had purchased a number of small machines and tools, and Ford assembled a manufacturing team of thirteen workers who began the task of preparing the plant for production.

The future looked rosy. Alderman, who served as the organization's spokesman, issued a confident statement to the Detroit *Free Press* on August 19, 1899, on the young company's prospects. Ford's vehicle, he announced, promised great things as it moved toward production:

> We have several new devices in connection with the construction of our automobiles, on which patents are now pending, which will make them as near perfect as they can be made. We have solved the problem of overcoming the bad [gasoline] odor by securing perfect combustion, and with our improved method of applying the power to the axle and of keeping all the machinery hidden from sight, we will have a fine motor carriage. We expect to have 100 to 150 men employed before the year is past.[9]

But problems emerged. For reasons that are not entirely clear—his investors may have demanded a larger, more expensive model that would sell for a higher price—Ford had set aside his second car and was developing a third model. High-sided, enclosed with an overhanging roof, and much heavier than his earlier vehicles, it struck many who saw it as a horse-drawn delivery wagon without the horse. But newspaper stories waxed enthusiastic. On January 12, 1900, the Detroit *Journal* provided a long description of the automobile. Then, on February 4, a laudatory story appeared in the Detroit *News-Tribune* carrying the headline "Swifter Than a Race-Horse It Flew Over the Icy Streets." This colorful narrative came from a reporter who took a ride in the new car with Ford. As they traversed the streets of the city in the heart of winter, this "thrilling trip on the first Detroit-made automobile" included acceleration to the heart-stopping speed of twenty-five miles an hour, a demonstration of the car's braking capacity, and the deft evasion of pedestrians and horse-drawn vehicles. In the reporter's memorable phrase, as they arrived back and turned into the Cass Avenue plant, the auto "slipped like a sunbeam around the corner." Thus, as the new century began, Henry Ford seemed poised to take the final step onto the summit of success. His new automobile appeared ready for presentation, and sale, to an enthusiastic public.[10]

But the spirit of optimism and anticipation at the Detroit Automobile Company proved to be an illusion. Behind the scenes, the real story was unfolding much less happily. For all the promise of Ford's automobile work, for all the wealth and prestige of his backers, and for all the public fascination with horseless carriages, the enterprise was floundering. It would become the first of several frustrating failures for Henry Ford, automobile manufacturer. Several problems plagued the new company, and most of them were his doing.

First of all, Ford's new prototype was simply not a very good vehicle. Despite the glowing newspaper accounts, the car had few virtues. In violation of his stated preference for a lightweight, sturdy, efficient automobile, this new "delivery wagon" model appeared big, heavy, even clunky. In addition, most of the time it didn't run very well, if at all. Many of its body and mechanical parts were being machined elsewhere, and they were slightly deficient and required reworking. An inexperienced workforce faced difficulties in correctly assembling these parts, because a number of minor problems had plagued the manufacturing process. Frederick Strauss, who had gone to work for Ford, described how the manufacturing team struggled continually with the vehicle's balky ignition and carburetion system. "We did get one of the engines to run on this car," he stated, "but we had an awful time doing it." Apparently, one of the few times Ford's automobile actually worked correctly was for the "sunbeam around a corner" newspaper story. More often, the appropriate metaphor would have been that of a candle feebly flickering in a dark room.[11]

Even more fatally, Ford was dallying and equivocating in finalizing the prototype for production. The nature of the problem was murky. According to some observers, Ford worked hard. William Pring, who joined the Detroit Automobile Company soon after it started up, insisted that his boss was deeply involved in the development of a prototype: "Mr. Ford worked right in the plant with us. He was more or less an instructor." But others offered a different judgment. "Henry never put much time in the shop," recalled Ford's old friend Strauss. "He might come in every day for an hour or two." In fact, Strauss continued, when company president Alderman pushed Ford to get a car into production, the latter engaged in some trickery:

Henry wasn't ready. He didn't have an automobile design ready. To get it going, Henry gave me some sketches to turn up some axle shaftings. I started machining these axle shafts to show them we were doing something . . . but they didn't belong to anything. We never used them for the automobile. It was just a stall until Henry got a little longer onto it.

Oliver Barthel—Ford's old accomplice, who now worked for him—may have come closest to identifying the real problem. Ford, he asserted, never stopped changing various features as he strove to improve his automobile prototype. He refused to "freeze" the design. "Too many changes were made," Barthel insisted. "They'd design something and build it, and then they'd discard it and build something else to take its place."[12]

As this drama of delay and deception unfolded, Murphy began to play a larger role. According to observers, he stood as the bulwark of the company's financial structure, and Ford was especially concerned not to alienate him. But as Murphy paid closer attention to the troubling delays at the Cass Avenue plant, Ford concocted a ruse to fool him as well. A peculiar situation took shape—the most powerful business figure in the company was being systematically misled by its supervisor of manufacturing. Strauss explained how Ford temporarily misled Murphy by a show, rather than the substance, of progress. "We had parts for about a half-dozen automobiles. We had a long bench, and all the parts we had finished were on it," Strauss explained. "Mr. Murphy and some of his friends would come along and see all these parts on the bench, and they were all machined perfectly, and it looked wonderful. They were very well pleased with them."[13]

By the fall of 1900, however, such stratagems were failing to hide Ford's evident lack of progress in bringing a car to production. The situation deteriorated to the point of breakdown. As months went by with no automobiles appearing, some of the stockholders grew disgusted, jettisoned their holdings, and walked away, while others tried to shore up the enterprise. Maybury bought most of the malcontents' shares, and Murphy pumped additional cash into the enterprise to keep it afloat. Eventually, Henry Ford would spend about $86,000 trying to develop a car with which he was satisfied. The patience of the company's remaining investors finally ran out completely. The board of directors convened a special meeting in November 1900 and demanded that Ford present an accounting of the situation. But he got wind of the meeting in advance and told Strauss, "If they ask for me, you tell them that I had to go out of town." With Ford's absence providing final evidence of the company's problems, the board decided to lay off most of the workforce and give up much of their shop space at Cass Avenue.

A few weeks later, in January 1901, after not quite a year and a half of operation, the board dissolved the Detroit Automobile Company outright.[14]

Thus Henry Ford's first adventure in car manufacturing crashed to earth after a high-flying start. All was not lost, however. Some of Ford's financial backers remained hopeful, including Murphy. This small group immediately purchased the Detroit Automobile Company's assets and continued to support Ford in developing an automobile for manufacture. So Ford experimented and tinkered for several months in a much-reduced shop at the same Cass Avenue facility. He abandoned the "delivery wagon" model and turned once again to a smaller, lightweight automobile.

He made progress, because on November 30, 1901, articles of incorporation were filed for the Henry Ford Company. Capitalization stood at $60,000, while Ford was given a thousand shares, a $10,000 interest, as compensation for his mechanical expertise to the company. Hope burned brightly once more. The Detroit *Journal* reported, "Mr. Ford has, in fact, with the backing of Mr. Murphy, succeeded in inventing an entirely new machine, departing in every respect from the lines of the old one and showing a vast improvement, as he believes, upon any automobile now on the market." Ford, unlike most participants in the burgeoning, volatile new world of car manufacture, where failures were commonplace, had secured a second chance.[15]

But once again, his conduct scuttled a promising enterprise, and this time it happened much more quickly. A familiar problem set in: Ford failed to get a commercial model ready for manufacture. The dynamic this time was a little different—he had become interested in automobile racing, and began pouring most of his energy into developing a race car rather than a vehicle for market—but the result was identical. The company never finalized a design for a commercial car, let alone actually manufactured a car. Moreover, Ford harbored a growing resentment over his financial share in the company, which he considered to be paltry. As tensions and tempers flared, the situation increasingly focused on two people: the company's namesake, and his wealthy, influential backer, William H. Murphy.

Frederick Strauss, having followed his old friend into this new venture, provided an insider's view of the gathering crisis. According to him, in the months after the dissolution of the Detroit Automobile Company a team consisting of Ford; Ed Huff, his old assistant from the Bagley Avenue garage; C. Harold Wills, a young toolmaker and draftsman; and Strauss designed and constructed a new, small, commercial car. Murphy and the other investors were quite pleased with this prototype and assumed that Ford would push it into production. Though they were aware that Ford was also developing a racing automobile, they believed he was spending most of his energy on the commercial vehicle. "Murphy had the idea that they were going on with the little car, and he didn't get onto us until we got that second car [the racer] about half machined up," Strauss explained. "After he found out that we were making a different car altogether, he was very disappointed. . . . When Murphy found out what Henry was doing, he got disgusted."[16]

Oliver Barthel provided additional information on the widening rift between Murphy and Ford. He confirmed that, as Murphy uncovered the truth about the situation, he grew angry. He confronted Barthel, and "he told me not to do it [work on the racer], and that he would fire me, and if I valued my job I'd better not do any work on it." But Barthel, at Ford's insistence, continued to labor on the race car, a move that led to a series of acrimonious arguments over the course of several weeks between Murphy and Ford. The situation settled into an uncomfortable stalemate. According to Strauss, Murphy quit speaking to Ford entirely. "Murphy came in every morning before he went to his office, but he had nothing to do with Henry," he reported.[17]

Eventually, Murphy acted decisively to resolve this contest of wills. Concluding that Ford had acted negligently in failing to develop a commercial automobile to the point of manufacture, he took the drastic step of bringing in an outsider to review the situation and restore order. Henry M. Leland, the director of Leland & Faulconer, a Detroit machine shop well known for its high-quality work, had been trained at Colt's factory, the Springfield Armory, and several other machine establishments in New England. By the 1890s, he had gained a reputation for the precision, elegance, and strength of his machined parts. Along with his son, Wilfred C. Leland, Henry Leland was producing motors for Ransom E. Olds and his car. Murphy knew Leland as a social acquaintance and convinced him to come to the Cass Avenue plant, inspect Ford's work, and offer advice and recommendations. Leland seems to have frankly criticized Ford's methods, vehicle, and lack of progress. According to William W. Pring, Leland miscalculated. "He figured he could tell Ford what to do," Pring related, "but Mr. Ford wasn't the type of man to take it." Not only did Ford bridle at Leland's critique, but he resented the board for undermining his authority. According to Charles T. Bush, his boss wanted to develop a car according to his own standards but now saw the board as a hostile, elitist group who wanted to constrain him.[18]

The situation proved untenable. Unwilling to have another mechanical expert looking over his shoulder, Ford grew even more sullen and uncooperative. The crisis came to a head within a few weeks, and Ford left the Henry Ford Company on March 10, 1902, only three months after the enterprise had been launched. Accounts differed, with some insisting that Ford resigned and others claiming that Murphy fired him. Whatever the case, the terms of Ford's departure were clear: he received a cash settlement of $900, the drawings and plans for his racing car, and assurances that Murphy and the board would discontinue using his name for their company. The agreement was kept. Following Ford's departure, the investors reorganized as the Cadillac Automobile Company—Murphy became its treasurer and largest stockholder—and they installed Henry Leland as its manufacturing supervisor. Cadillac began manufacturing reliable motorcars of high quality, and in 1909 it was purchased by the young General Motors Corporation.[19]

In this unseemly fashion, Henry Ford, the mechanical inventor, and William H. Murphy, the prominent businessman, parted ways only two and a half years after the beginning of their promising alliance. At the time, there appeared to be considerable hard feeling on both sides, although as years went by animosities mellowed. Much later, for example, Murphy attended a social function at the Ford home where the host was overheard remarking that "he had always regretted Mr. Murphy had not gone along with him and the Ford Motor Company." However, a curious twist of fate brought their relationship full-circle. In 1917, Henry and Wilfred Leland launched the Lincoln Motor Company, another enterprise devoted to making high-quality automobiles, with Murphy's support as a major stockholder. But the company went into receivership after a few years and was purchased by the Ford Motor Company. Within five months, Ford dismissed Leland and his son with two weeks' severance pay. Though Ford always claimed it was a business decision, it also seems clear that in a not-so-subtle way he got his revenge on the man brought in to discipline him two decades before.[20]

But in the spring of 1902, Henry Ford was in no position to visit revenge on anyone. To most observers, he appeared little more than another casualty of the viciously competitive motor-vehicle market. A carefully researched table compiled for *Motor* magazine by Charles E. Duryea, himself a pioneer carmaker, revealed that from 1900 to 1908, 501 companies were formed in the United States for the purpose of manufacturing automobiles. Sixty percent of them folded outright within a couple of years; another 6 percent moved into other areas of production.[21] Despite Ford's impressive financial backing and his own mechanical expertise, he seemed but another statistic in the vagaries of enterprise. His only distinction lay in squandering not one but two golden opportunities.

But, curiously, Ford's resounding failures in this time period did not disturb him unduly. He apparently drew only positive lessons from these disasters. He adopted an unconcerned, even lackadaisical attitude that showed twenty years later in comments during an interview:

> Now why should anybody be in such a hurry to accomplish what he sets out to do? He should work diligently, of course, but why should he be discouraged if success be somewhat delayed? . . . These were very useful years to me and very well employed. What better use could I have made of my time? So far as I was concerned, I was never happier in my life. I was learning something every day and what I was learning was of use to myself and everybody else.[22]

These philosophical words offer little satisfaction to one seeking an explanation for Ford's early lack of success at automobile manufacture. For his prominent investors, the reason was apparent—he had wasted their money on excessive tinkering and refinement, and never brought a manufacturable prototype to market. He had engineered his own demise by a failure to perform.

Ford, however, offered a different assessment, one that reflected his developing sensibility as a businessman and an industrialist. He insisted that he was a victim of greed. The backers of the Detroit Automobile Company and the Henry Ford Company, in his view, harbored misplaced priorities. A couple of weeks after his final departure from the second of those ventures, Ford encountered Charles T. Bush, who had worked under him at Cass Avenue. Naturally, they fell into a discussion of the recent tumult, and Bush reported how Ford lashed out at his former backers:

> I think I'm going to open a shop. I think I'm going to carry on the work that I've been doing. I just can't go along with the way those people run it. . . . They were to stay by me to have the experimental work done. Now when they pull in somebody else from the outside [Henry Leland] and back away from me, I'm all through. . . . From here in, my shop is always going to be my shop and that's the way it's going to be. *I'm not going to have a lot of rich people tell me what to do.*[23]

Two decades later, Ford's analysis remained harsh. In *My Life and Work*, he argued that his early investors had no interest in making a quality product for the public but only wanted "to get the largest price possible for each car. The main idea seemed to be to get the money." Ford rebelled and, in his own words, "resigned, *determined never again to put myself under orders.*"[24]

Ford's reading of his early business reverses provides a revealing glimpse into his psyche. As he took his first tentative steps into the manufacturing arena at the onset of the twentieth century, he clearly carried two deep commitments. First, he resented and resisted any attempt by wealthy business elites to direct his course of action. Second, he was stubbornly determined to follow his own instincts and values, to maintain his independence, and to keep control over his own destiny as a manufacturer. Both of these commitments would remain critical parts of Ford's mature personality in coming years, and they would shape, in many ways, his fabulous climb to success. But this dogged self-reliance and hostility to elites bespoke more than personal character. They also reflected larger historical pressures which bore down upon Ford.

His early adventures in car manufacture, it is important to remember, unfolded in the heart of a great transformation of socioeconomic life in the United States. Beginning in the late nineteenth century and extending into the twentieth, the country experienced what one historian has described as "the incorporation of America." This broad process involved much more than the technical matter of corporate forms of ownership in business endeavors, which were spreading rapidly throughout the economy. It also gave rise to the rapid expansion of industrial capitalism across the United States, the development of accompanying transportation, communication, and bureaucratic systems, intensified urbanization, and the emergence of a managerial class of white-collar workers. Incorporation also generated a tremendous cultural impact. The vast "organizational revolution of the late nineteenth and early twentieth century," according to scholars, created not only a different socioeconomic environment but "an altogether new outlook on life." In the new corporatized America, old-fashioned, self-reliant individualism was increasingly subsumed by the concerns, ambitions, and opportunities generated by bureaucratic organizations.[25]

This profound reshaping of American social and economic life unquestionably brought great benefits—economic growth, with its explosion of industrial productivity, more available consumer goods, and a rising standard of living for American society as a whole. But it also created great strains and uncertainties. Many citizens worried about deeper inequality and class divisions in the United States, dubious business methods, and the threat that corporate institutions would reign unchallenged over national life. Incorporation also created intense cultural anguish. Even among the business groups propelling it forward, there appeared widespread anxieties about abandoning the values of the past. They worried about advancing luxury and materialism, urban anonymity and confidence games, overrefinement and isolation from real life, and declining opportunities for the self-made man.[26]

It seems clear that Henry Ford, as he struggled unsuccessfully to manufacture his automobile around the turn of the century, shared in large measure both aspirations and anxieties about the incorporation of America. In fact, his position was fascinating in its ambiguity. On the one hand, he was clearly attuned to the new business world of mass manufacturing and mass marketing, especially in its technological dimension. As events would soon prove, more than any other American business figure he grasped the vast economic potential of a mass-consumer economy. On the other hand, he remained in many ways a Dearborn farm boy rooted in the soil of William Ford's agricultural republic. He defined himself, in the best traditional terms, as a self-reliant individualist who owned his property, earned his way, and was beholden to no one.

In other words, Ford strode into the new century carrying a load of ideological baggage. Affiliated with no particular political party or individual, he might best be described as an instinctive populist. Ford's ideology, shaped in the cauldron of the provincial Midwest, was not so much a product of the agrarian Populist revolt of the 1890s, which attacked the bastions of urban industrial life and the "money power," as a reflection of the rural, village culture that nourished it. This broader populist persuasion drew upon several sources—the residue of republicanism, with its tradition of civic obligation; the Protestant work ethic, with its insistence on the moral value of labor; and the values of market "producerism," which claimed that the ownership of property and the production of useful goods bestowed social dignity and economic independence upon the citizen. Deeply suspicious of the machinery of high finance, this populist culture, in the elegant words of historian Richard Hofstadter, attempted "to hold on to some of the values of agrarian life, to save personal entrepreneurship and individual opportunity and the character type they engendered. . . . [It promoted] the ideal of a life lived close to nature and the soil, the esteem for the primary contacts of country and village life, the cherished image of the independent and self-reliant man."27

Part progressive in its advocacy of economic reform, part traditional in its defense of old-fashioned individualism, this populist culture constituted the seedbed in which Henry Ford's attitudes sprouted. Floundering in his first attempts at manufacturing, he drew upon these notions to denounce the greed of his investors and uphold a standard of quality production. This populist orientation also was mirrored in Ford's insistence on maintaining self-reliance as he struggled to create a bureaucratic business organization.

Yet his position was complicated. Ford was no solitary entrepreneur from the early nineteenth century, heroically carving his own path through the thickets of enterprise. He appreciated the need for large group structures in modern business and technology. Part of his admiration for Thomas Edison stemmed from an appreciation of the inventor's organizational talents. Edison, according to Ford's reading, discovered early on that "he needed assistance, for no matter how long he worked he could not by himself complete all of the needed experiments. . . . [So he decided] to start forward with something of an organization. Thereafter he was always the director of a laboratory and conserved his time by devoting it to the things where his brain and not his hands alone were needed."[28] Clearly, Henry Ford was no hidebound reactionary worshipping at the shrine of individualism while condemning all complex forms of business organization.

At the same time, many of Ford's instincts ran across the grain of the culture of incorporation. Though respecting the need for intricate business structures, he adamantly refused to be swallowed by any variety of bureaucracy, especially one dominated by financiers. Ford's goal appeared in an elusive middle ground: to develop the right *kind* of organization, where his self-reliant, populist instincts would not be completely subsumed in a larger entity. The difficult period of the late 1890s, with its slow prototype development, manufacturing delays, financial misfires, and limited progress, was but the first stage in his career-long quest to maintain personal control over a large-scale industrial enterprise.

Thus the Henry Ford of the late 1890s—the failed businessman who chastised his financial backers for their greed and their infringements on his independence—was a product of this rural, Midwestern culture of populism. Even while embracing technological advances, he rejected the notion that wealth carried special prerogatives in a republic of merit, and he insisted, to the point of leaving before surrendering the principle, on keeping personal control of his enterprise in an age of growing corporate bureaucracy. Though still unsure about exactly how to do it, Ford made clear that somehow he intended to hold on to a populist ethic of old-fashioned individualism as he strained to create a modern corporate bureaucracy.

After several years of effort, the mechanic and businessman seemed to have failed at reaching these goals, succeeding only in entangling himself in frustrations and false starts. But within a short time, he found a way to break the logjam. Unexpectedly, with his typical mix of shrewdness and audacity, he turned to an exciting feature of the new leisure-and-entertainment culture sweeping through early-twentieth-century America: Henry Ford became a racing-car celebrity.

Five

Celebrity

In 1901, Henry Ford presented an image that marked a dramatic departure from his earlier life. The large crowds pouring into the Grosse Pointe racetrack in Detroit did not encounter the farm boy, steam-engine mechanic, backyard tinkerer, or failed manufacturer of horseless carriages. Instead, spectators saw a glamorous public celebrity: the automobile racer. Covered with oil and grime, with the wind sweeping through his hair and thousands of excited viewers screaming their approval, Ford shot down the dirt track in his powerful race car, its enormous engine roaring and its tires sending clouds of dust flying into the air as it skidded through the turns and sped down the straightaways. Winning races and setting speed records, the exhilarated driver received a hero's acclaim and basked in the glow of newfound fame. Henry Ford demonstrated, for the first time, the instinctive feel for publicity and its benefits that would become a hallmark of his career.

In fact, this often forgotten chapter in Ford's life encompassed one of the most important maneuvers he ever made as an automaker. Temporarily abandoning straightforward attempts at car production, he plotted an indirect strategy. Because he saw the need for public attention that would revive interest in his motor vehicle, he embraced an exciting activity that seemed to attract the notice of growing numbers of Americans. The best way to bring the Ford car and name before great masses of people was to join the fad for racing.

But there was a larger dimension to this maneuver. This foray into automobile racing also typified a larger pattern in his career: a natural feel for the public pulse. Although certainly no sophisticated student of American values and culture, he had an instinctive appreciation of the leisure-and-entertainment culture emerging in turn-of-the-century American society. Like Theodore Roosevelt in politics or D. W. Griffith in filmmaking, Ford grasped the essence of a new mass culture beginning to emerge by the early

1900s and sensed its enormous power in terms of advertising and celebrity. Roosevelt, with his colorful personality and bombastic rhetoric, made himself into a political figure trailed by newspapermen and photographers wherever he went. Griffith, emblazoning his initials on every frame of his movies, adopted the persona of the artistic *auteur* whose own personality became as celebrated as his creations. Ford, in similar fashion, manipulated this popular culture to boost his technological enterprise. He devoted his considerable energies to constructing a powerful, winning race car and secured the services of a daredevil driver who soon became a household name. Within a short time, as he anticipated, this winning formula had generated substantial publicity for the Ford name and associated with it an image of racing victories and speed records.

When the dust had settled on the racetrack, Ford's fame had secured his larger, practical objective. The publicity of automobile racing provided the leverage that he needed to return to his real quest—the production of an inexpensive, sturdy, lightweight motorcar for the average American. Trading upon his racing fame, Ford secured new financial support in the form of a partnership and created the Ford Motor Company in 1903. Within a short time, however, he would take sole control of this enterprise. By 1908, Ford finally had created a corporate structure that he could live with—one where only he could direct its destiny.

Henry Ford began the new century on an inauspicious note. His earliest car-production ventures had folded because of his failure to bring an acceptable prototype to the point of manufacture. But another difficulty had also undermined his initial attempts at forming a viable company. Automobile racing had seduced him, much to the detriment of his commercial endeavors.

Ford first became interested in racing while still involved with the Detroit Automobile Company, when he had begun working secretly on a racing car. As with his Quadricycle, he was assisted by associates who were attracted to this enticing vision of barrier-breaking speed embodied in a high-horsepower racing vehicle. The group included his old friends "Spider" Huff and Oliver Barthel. Newcomers included draftsman, toolmaker, and commercial artist C. Harold Wills; lathe operator Ed Verlinden; and blacksmith Charlie Mitchell. By the summer and fall of 1901, this team had built the first version of the Ford racer. The vehicle's enclosed, water-cooled engine featured a pair of large, opposed cylinders, seven by seven inches each, that could generate up to 26 horsepower. The chassis had thirty-six-inch wire wheels, a steering wheel set on the right side, and a "patented reach and trussed front and rear axles." Built low to the ground, the race car weighed twenty-two hundred pounds.[1]

Ford's racer first drew attention for its appearance rather than its substance. Before the car ever competed, *Scientific American* praised it for revising the dominant look of early motorized vehicles, most of which still remained "horseless carriages of a horsey style." In an article entitled "Style in Automobiles," author Hrolf Wisby argued:

> Only a single class of automobiles is progressing toward a definite style, namely the racing machines. . . . The latest American racing automobile, the Ford, possesses features entitling it to credit as being the most unconventional, if not the most beautiful, design so far produced by American ingenuity. It is a model that commends itself strongly to the automobile experts because of the chaste completeness and compactness of its structure . . . [and its] neat tapering stern; the chauffeur seat has been shaved down to a mere toadstool perch and the forward condensers, instead of being enclosed in a pyramidal casing, have been placed in an inverted shield. . . . The carriage element, so detrimental to a clear, unsophisticated style, has been avoided.[2]

But more than style points were needed for success in the exciting new world of competitive racing. In July 1899, the Tour de France had created a sensation as cars from several countries successfully traversed a 1,428-mile course, with the winner averaging thirty-two miles per hour. By 1901, the Frenchman Henri Fournier stood unchallenged as the leading European racer; in the United States, Alexander Winton of Cleveland (also a manufacturer) had emerged as the most successful driver. Winton set the world record for the mile in 1897 and then drove his vehicle from Cleveland to New York. In 1901, he again set the world record for the mile, at one minute and fourteen seconds.[3]

Automobile racing required speed, endurance, and a strong dose of courage. It was a dangerous proposition that involved two people—one to steer and one to provide balance. In his racing team, Henry Ford drove the car, with shoulders down and head hunched over to peer down the track (there were no windshields on these early prototypes), while "Spider" Huff, with much bravery but little evident sense, crouched precariously on the running board. Holding on to metal grips with both hands, he provided ballast by leaning out from the vehicle to help the car negotiate through turns on an oval racetrack. In the fall of 1901, Ford and Huff made several trial runs on broad streets on the outskirts of Detroit, and once hauled the car out to Dearborn to test its speed on the old Scotch Settlement Road. Ford had his mind set on breaking the speed record held by Winton. His opportunity would appear within a few weeks.

In the summer of 1901, a trio of entrepreneurs—Daniel J. Campeau, head of the Detroit Driving Club; William B. Shanks, Alexander Winton's business manager; and William Metzger, a Detroit bicycle-shop owner and businessman—organized the first automobile race to be run in Michigan. It was to be held at the mile-long Grosse Pointe racetrack on October 10. The organizers set up a program of five preliminary events for electric, steam, and gasoline vehicles of various sizes and weights, to be followed by a ten-mile main event. Winton agreed to compete, as did five other drivers from around the United States, including Ford, who paid his entry fee the day before the race. As the prize for the winner of the championship event, the promoters offered an elaborate, expensive cut-glass punch bowl and serving set.

As plans were finalized, there was intense interest in the race, and Ford immediately reaped the benefits. "The event is all the talk of Detroit's smart set," reported the *Free Press*. "One of the most promising contestors is the Detroit chauffeur, Henry Ford. His machine was tried out on the boulevard recently and without great effort covered a half mile in 38 seconds." The streetcar company in Detroit announced that, on the day of the race, cars would be leaving for the Grosse Pointe track every thirty seconds. A number of public offices even closed up shop for the event. A judge in the Detroit Recorder's Court printed this notice in the local newspapers: "Gentlemen: This court has received several requests from attorneys and others to adjourn court tomorrow afternoon on account of the automobile races and as there is nothing of importance on, court will be adjourned for the day at one o'clock."[4]

Although rain had threatened, October 10 dawned clear and dry. In the morning, large crowds gathered to observe a long parade of some one hundred assorted motorized vehicles—steam, electrical, gasoline—winding its way through Detroit. An equine-preferring journalist sourly described their arrival at the track as an "invasion of the temple." "The horse was forgotten," he wrote. "Outside along the fence, where usually are found tally-ho's and coaches with gay parties, were long rows of those things instead." What one newspaper described as a "Blue Ribbon Crowd" of about eight thousand packed the grandstand and congregated along the rails, waiting expectantly for the festivities to start. Finally, in early afternoon, the first events began, and the excitement deflated almost immediately. The early races were slow, with the winner in the "steamer" class of vehicle going about thirty miles per hour, and the victor in the "electrical" class scoring with an excruciating fifteen miles per hour. The pace of this last group was so slow that the Detroit *Journal* described, with some amusement, how the two lead drivers actually conducted a conversation as they puttered around the track side by side. The crowd grew so restless that one of the promoters, Metzger, convinced Winton to placate them by attempting to break the world's speed record for the mile in a special exhibition. The obliging driver took to the track and roared off for a three-mile test ride. When his time was announced—the second mile had been completed in 1:12, for a new world record—Detroiters roared their approval.[5]

For the day's biggest race, disappointment once again threatened as mechanical difficulties kept most of the entries from even starting the contest. It was announced that only two drivers would compete in the championship race, Winton and Henry Ford. Though initially the crowd groaned, in a curious way the reduced field worked to heighten the drama of the event. Spectators saw unfolding before them a one-on-one match race between two automobile manufacturers, one the clear favorite as national champion and world-record holder, the other an upstart local figure. The ensuing battle between this mechanized David and Goliath more than lived up to expectations.

One could feel the atmosphere at the track grow charged as Winton and Ford sat behind the wheels of their "big express-train racers" as they rolled onto the track, each with a mechanic clinging to a perch on the running board. According to the Detroit *Tribune*:

> . . . after refusing to take the events seriously for a time, the mob of onlookers grew almost hysterical with excitement and cheered the huge monsters in the big race. . . . There was unquestionably reason for excitement. The huge machines of Winton and Ford as they sped about the track looked and sounded more like runaway locomotives than mere road vehicles. They ate up the miles one after the other at such a terrific pace that it all seemed unreal and like a chapter from the Arabian nights or some tale of Munchausen.[6]

The race began with Winton taking the early lead and using his superior driving skills to keep his vehicle hugging the inside fence. Ford seemed to go faster on the straightaways, but then struggled to control his racer on the curves as it veered toward the outer fence, and he steadily lost ground. As one journalist described, "E. S. Huff, Ford's mechanic, hung far out in his efforts to ballast the car, but she swung wide at every turn." To enhance his control, Ford even tried shutting off his power entirely on the curves, so that, as he later told reporters, "two-fifths of the time . . . his machine was simply coasting." At the end of three miles, Winton held a fifth-of-a-mile lead, but then Ford's handling of his car improved and he began to make up lost ground steadily. On the sixth lap, the Detroiter "shot up perceptibly, and the crowd cheered frantically." With Ford closing the gap, the race reached its decisive point during the seventh lap, when a bearing box in Winton's car began to overheat under the strain of the competition. A thin line of blue smoke rose from the rear of the machine, and it grew into a cloud as Winton's mechanic, still clinging to the running board, frantically freed one of his hands to pour oil on the box in an attempt to cool it. But this maneuver was ineffective, and the car lost speed. In the words of the Detroit *Free Press*, "Mr. Ford shot by them as though they were standing still. Down the stretch he came like a demon, and the crowd yelled itself hoarse." He lengthened his lead over the last three laps and won by a full three-quarters of a mile as spectators exploded in a frenzy of celebration.[7]

Clara Ford, who witnessed the race from the grandstand, wrote her brother a description of the race as her husband won his shocking victory. "I wish you could have seen him. Also have heard the cheering when he passed Winton. The people went wild. One man threw his hat up and when it came down he stamped on it, he was so excited. Another man hit his wife on the head to keep her from going off the handle." Detroit newspapers proudly affirmed Clara's judgment that her husband had succeeded in "covering himself with glory and dust." Ford "ran a marvelous race and defeated his Cleveland rival by a good margin," wrote one. According to another, "Henry Ford broke into the front ranks of American chauffe[u]rs by the wonderful performance of his machine yesterday." With his unlikely victory, the automobile maker with the checkered past had emerged as a local hero.[8]

Yet, amid the cheers and adulation accompanying this glorious episode in Henry Ford's life, a question lingers uncomfortably. Why did he seemingly abandon his life's work of creating a serviceable commercial automobile and divert his creative energy into this relatively frivolous, albeit exciting, endeavor? According to some observers, he had contracted an infectious disease. Oliver Barthel claimed that Ford had come down with "what was termed by many of his friends, racing fever." Galvanized by the promise of public acclaim and the thrill of competition, "He talked mostly about wanting to build a larger and faster racing car."[9]

Indeed, Ford provided evidence of feverish enthusiasm in a letter of this period. On January 6, 1902, several weeks after his great victory over

Alexander Winton, he wrote to his brother-in-law, Milton D. Bryant. Clara's brother had expressed an interest in becoming involved in Ford's new career in a managerial capacity by setting up races. In a short missive, the new champion revealed his eagerness to meet the record-holding Frenchman Henri Fournier in a contest. "If I can bring Mr. Fournier in line, there is a barrel of money in this business," Ford burst out to Bryant. "I will challenge him until I am black in the face."[10]

But excitement and the promise of quick cash had its limits. Ford was a serious and calculating man, and never one to be caught up completely in frivolity. While racing must have provided a kind of visceral thrill that he seldom, if ever, experienced in his lifetime, sensation-seeking was never a deep-seated impulse in his personality. A deeper motivation—the sense that the new entertainment form could generate enormous publicity—clearly lay at the bottom of this career move. In some instinctive way, Ford sensed that racing would get his name before a mass audience in a dramatic way, and that this, in turn, would promote his larger plans. Years later, he explained rather matter-of-factly his strategy in 1901: "I never thought anything of racing, but the public refused to consider the automobile in any light other than as a fast toy. Therefore . . . we had to race."[11]

In fact, Ford's judgment on this matter was probably shrewder than he fully realized at the time. Instinctively, he had tapped into a powerful trend in American life. In the years around the turn of the new century, the United States was witnessing the first flowering of a cultural revolution in its morals and manners. Victorian standards from the nineteenth century had mandated behavior characterized by emotional self-control, genteel propriety, and hardworking producerism. For those in respectable society, entertainment and leisure, whether formal dances or lectures or concerts, were cast in the mold of moral uplift. Taverns, roughneck sports, and bawdy melodrama were the purview of the uneducated working class. But with the evolution of an economy increasingly oriented toward consumerism by 1900, managers of mass culture perceived new forces at work. The explosive growth of an urban society with its corporate bureaucracies, white-collar workers, and organized industrial workforce had created a new audience, eager, in the words of one historian, to purchase "instant pleasure and momentary release." Under such pressures, Victorian tradition began to crack and buckle. The 1890s saw the first stirrings of a new culture of entertainment that bowled over old-fashioned notions of self-restraint. Vigorous, rowdy, competitive sports such as prizefighting, baseball, and football began attracting large followings, while, musically, exuberant forms such as the cakewalk and ragtime emerged from African American communities to be commercialized for a larger, mass audience. Amusement parks, of which New York's Coney Island was the largest and most spectacular, sprang up all over the country and drew enthusiastic crowds. Even more spectacularly, movies outgrew their early accommodations in penny arcades and nickelodeons to become a national pastime.[12]

This commercialized mass culture of cabarets and sports parks, picture palaces and dance halls provided the material setting for a new leisure ethic in America. These venues offered amusements where exuberance, sensuality, physical release, pleasure, and personal self-fulfillment could flourish. White-collar and blue-collar workers alike, faced with increasingly regimented and tedious work, were eager for recreation. "Recreation and play were not luxuries but necessities in the modern city," one scholar has stated in summarizing the new leisure ethic. "The fear of idle time as the devil's workshop gave way to a reverence for play, promoted alike by middle-class reformers and working-class organizers." Showmen, entertainers, and sportsmen quickly grasped this new logic and began shaping public entertainment for the masses where excitement and low prices combined to attract the largest possible audiences.[13]

Thus automobile racing arrived on the American scene as an exciting facet of this new culture of leisure. Like baseball or Coney Island, speed contests between motor vehicles were mass events that brought big, paying crowds, excitement, recreation, and reams of newspaper publicity that created popular celebrities. Henry Ford, demonstrating an instinctive feel for the popular pulse, sensed that racing offered a rich opportunity to connect with the new zeitgeist. As he noted later, his great victory over Winton "was my first race, and it brought advertising of the only kind that people cared to read."[14]

Ford clearly understood that the publicity accompanying his racing endeavors would enhance his name and give a boost to his efforts to develop a commercial automobile. Investors at the Henry Ford Company may have groused about his racing efforts, he noted in early 1902, but "they will get the Advertising and I expect to make $ where I can't make cents at Manufacturing." Around the same time, Clara conveyed her husband's view of his racing victory over Winton. In her words, "That race has advertised him far and wide. And the next thing will be to make some money out of it."[15]

At first, Ford struggled to connect his racing success directly to the engineering of a commercial automobile. With the formation of the ill-fated Henry Ford Company after the victory over Winton, he announced, "We have the fastest machine in the world. We shall . . . begin making commercial machines, with the best prospect of success." But behind the scenes, the two endeavors did not mesh smoothly. Ford's racing success and his enthusiasm for it only highlighted his painful slowness in bringing a car to production. The marked contrast between Ford the racer and Ford the manufacturer only increased tensions with his financial backers. "He seemed to be so taken up with the racing car that that is the thing which made the others dissatisfied," Oliver Barthel observed of Ford's festering relations with his stockholders. "They merely said that he had the racing fever and they were through with him." This situation contributed to Ford's dismissal from the Henry Ford Company in March 1902.[16]

Set adrift from the world of commercial manufacturing in the spring of 1902, Ford was forced to focus even more intensely on developing his race car. He set up a temporary workshop in a small brick building at 81 Park Place owned by a friend, Barton Peck, and worked on developing a larger, faster racing vehicle. More important, he gained a new supporter who shared his enthusiasm for the sport. Tom Cooper, a young, athletic bicycle-racer, had amassed a small fortune by winning road races all over the United States and Europe. He had witnessed Ford's victory over Winton at Grosse Pointe and was awed by the exciting spectacle of speedy motorcars flying around dirt tracks to the cheers of thousands. Eager to get into the game, he contacted Ford early in 1902 and decided to put up money to help him develop an even more powerful race car. As Clara Ford noted in a letter from this period, "Tom Cooper . . . has got the racing fever bad, he is very anxious to get a good racing car." Within a few weeks, Cooper and her husband became partners.[17]

With this lifesaving injection of funds, Ford agreed to build two new race cars, one for himself and one for Cooper. Work began late in the spring of 1902. He was assisted by Cooper and his old friend Spider Huff. The talented young designer and machinist C. Harold Wills, whom Ford had first hired at the Detroit Automobile Company, also provided invaluable help in the early mornings and evenings. As the twin racers took shape, Ford painted his own vehicle red and named it "999," after the New York Central train that had made a record run between New York and Chicago before being exhibited at the 1893 World's Columbian Exposition. Cooper's vehicle was painted yellow and christened the "Arrow." In late September, an article in *The Automobile and Motor Review* described the racers at length and praised their combination of a powerful engine and a stripped-down chassis. "Built to speed, and speed alone, the new racing machines made by Henry Ford and Tom Cooper, of Detroit, are first-class examples of how an automobile may be simplified by the leaving off process," the magazine observed.[18]

As for Ford, he seemed more unsettled than inspired by the tremendous power of the vehicles. As he and Cooper began test runs in the fall of 1902, he provided a rather terrified description of the racing monsters he had created:

> I put in four great big cylinders giving 80 H.P.—which up to that time had been unheard of. The roar of those cylinders alone was enough to half kill a man. There was only one seat. One life to a car was enough. . . . We let them out at full speed. I cannot quite describe the sensation. Going over Niag[a]ra Falls would have been but a pastime after a ride in one of them.

In fact, the roar of the 999 was so window-rattlingly loud and fearsome that Ford and his helpers dared not drive it through Detroit streets to the racetrack. Ironically, it had to be towed there by horses.[19]

A local newspaper reporter observed one of Cooper and Ford's test drives:

> The oily appearance of the fence is nothing to the look of chauffeur Henry Ford after he had made a few dashes around the track yesterday in his new speed machine which he and Tom Cooper have built. Mr. Ford was a daub of oil from head to foot. His collar was yellow, his tie looked as though it had been cooked in lard, his shirt and clothes were spattered and smirched, while his face looked like a machinist's after 24 hours at his bench.[20]

Thus Ford's new race car stood poised for achievement, the product of the combined efforts of a talented team of associates. But his collaboration with Tom Cooper and Harold Wills loomed relatively unimportant in comparison with another new friendship. In 1902, Ford made the acquaintance of a man who would become one of the celebrities of the new century. Emblazoned in newspapers across the country and acclaimed by thousands, his name would become synonymous with speed and daring. And his career was launched in concert with Henry Ford.

In the early 1930s, Henry Ford and Barney Oldfield met for the first time in many years. Both were attending the Indianapolis 500 race, and as they warmly shook hands and reminisced about earlier days, a number of reporters took notes. Ford grew sentimental. "We started together at the bottom and we owe each other a lot," he declared. "After all, it could be said that you made me and I made you." Oldfield, his trademark cigar clenched tightly in his teeth, grinned devilishly as he pulled out his wallet and opened it. It was empty. "Yeah," he replied to Ford, "but I did a damn sight better job of it than you did!"[21]

This reply summed up his personality. Pugnacious, fearless, and always at the ready with a colorful quip, Barney Oldfield had become one of the great popular heroes in early-twentieth-century America. Constantly chewing on a cigar, his handkerchief knotted around his neck, and using his famous "underhand" grip on the steering wheel—his hands lay at the bottom of the wheel, palms facing his body, as his fingers curled around from behind and his thumbs from the front—he guided smoke-belching behemoths around dirt tracks throughout the country to the cheers of thousands. Oldfield won races and set speed records in great batches from 1902 to 1918, and in so doing he became the public symbol of this thrilling new sport. His name became synonymous with speed. Meanwhile, this outlandish Ohioan, with his colorful quotes and flamboyant style, cut quite a figure. Equal parts showman and athlete, Oldfield demonstrated an instinct for the publicity limelight. His barnstorming antics and reputation as a fearless speed demon were carefully constructed images, and the fact that they drew widespread notice came as no surprise to the man who built them.

Born on January 29, 1878, to a farm family in Fulton County, Ohio, he had been named Berna Eli Oldfield. Around age ten, the boy had accompanied his family to Toledo when his father sought steadier, more lucrative employment. As a teenager in the early 1890s, young Barney became enamored of bicycling at the time of its national craze. He was particularly attracted to racing, a sport that had begun generating much attention from newspaper accounts. Oldfield entered his first race at age sixteen and started winning prizes. After a brief and undistinguished career detour in the boxing ring—he fought as "The Toledo Terror"—Oldfield signed on with the Stearns Bicycle Company and became a professional racer. He spent much of the late 1890s traveling the circuit in the Midwest, and gradually drifted into motorized-bicycle racing. From there it was but a short step into automobile racing, which he took up in 1902.

Within a short time, Oldfield emerged as a nationally known driver, his quick reflexes, physical strength, and daredevil temperament making him a natural. In 1903, he was the first person to break the mile-a-minute barrier in an automobile, an achievement that earned him the newspaper title of "America's Premier Driver." His purple-prose description of the feat demonstrated Oldfield's gift for self-promotion:

You have every sensation of being hurled through space. The machine is throbbing under you with its cylinders beating a drummer's tattoo, and the air tears past you in a gale. In its maddening dash through the swirling dust the machine takes on the attributes of a sentient thing. I tell you, gentlemen: no man can drive faster and live![22]

In succeeding years, Oldfield's reputation soared. He first joined up with Alexander Winton to drive his "Bullet" racer, and then contracted with the Peerless Company to operate its "Green Dragon." He won numerous races in both cars, and then purchased his own machine in 1907, the German-built "Blitzen Benz," in which he set an astonishing world record by going 131.7 miles per hour at the Daytona, Florida, track. By the 1910s, his racing career had exploded into national prominence. He drove a "Christie" early in the decade—other drivers had walked away from this front-drive 300-horsepower monster machine, deeming it uncontrollable—and won numerous races and set speed records all over the United States. Suspended for a time by the American Automobile Association for participating in unauthorized events, he advertised himself as "Speed King of the World" and took to driving exhibition races at county and state fairs. He supplemented this lucrative endeavor by striking a commercial deal with Harvey Firestone. As Oldfield tore around racetracks throughout the American hinterland, tens of thousands of fans saw the slogan painted on the side of his race car: "Firestone Tires Are My Only Life Insurance."

Oldfield demonstrated the showman's instincts, for example, in deciding on the matter of racing apparel when he began driving the Peerless Company's Green Dragon racer. "Resolving to set myself apart, I decided to do all my driving in a suit of green leather to match the color of my car," he wrote. "I got a good many laughs and comments from spectators, who said I was trying to bring the customs of the running-horse track to the automobile business. They were doing just what I wanted them to do—notice me."[23]

He also manipulated newspaper reporters shamelessly, as when he allowed them to spread exaggerated estimates of his income. "As it was good publicity, I let the newspapers tell me how much money I made, without raising a dissenting voice," he explained. "I knew that all the world loves a successful man, and I was willing to have them make me highly successful if they cared to." He also attracted headlines and drew crowds all over the country with outrageous stunts. In 1914, for example, Oldfield set up a series of match races with the aviator Lincoln Beachey. Advertisements blared out "The Demon of the Sky vs. the Daredevil of the Earth for the

Championship of the Universe!" Unbelievably, these two would tear around large dirt racetracks, Oldfield hunched over the steering wheel of his car while Beachey's low-flying biplane skimmed along no more than ten feet above his head. A series of spectacular car crashes—Oldfield always seemed to walk away, albeit with a series of bone fractures and lacerations—only added to the mystique.[24]

Oldfield's private life enhanced his reputation. His extravagant habits—ordering Havana cigars in two-thousand-lot boxes, wagering large sums at the horse track, staying at the fanciest hotels and dispensing $5 tips, drinking and brawling in saloons all over the country—kept his larger-than-life image before the public. He even ventured into acting, making a brief appearance in a Broadway musical before taking a starring role in a Mack Sennett film entitled *Barney Oldfield's Race for Life*. He fraternized with roughneck sports figures such as the baseball hero Ty Cobb, and set up a grudge race with the controversial African American boxer Jack Johnson. Shortly after his retirement from the racing game in 1918, Oldfield demonstrated his public appeal at the opening of the new Beverly Hills Speedway. As the festivities unfolded, he shared a front-row grandstand, casually mixing with movie stars Douglas Fairbanks, Charlie Chaplin, Wallace Beery, and Tom Mix.

Thus, in the new leisure culture of early-twentieth-century America, where baseball jostled with boxing, movies with music halls, and automobile racing with amusement parks, Barney Oldfield became a "star." But as the years unfolded, many forgot that his career had been launched in the early years of the century when he joined forces with a little-known carmaker named Henry Ford. This alliance revealed much about both men. Their joint undertaking not only started Oldfield on the path to fame and fortune, but demonstrated Ford's own knack for finding the limelight.

In 1902, Oldfield, who was racing motorized bicycles, came to Detroit at the request of Tom Cooper to inspect Ford's racing cars. It would be the turning point in his life. Up to this point, Ford had driven his own race cars, but the new models were so powerful that, like Dr. Frankenstein, he grew leery of his own creation. Bluntly put, Ford was scared to drive his own car. After several test runs around Detroit tracks, he had sensibly concluded that he had neither the nerve nor the skill to operate them at optimal level. In Ford's words, "I did not want to take the responsibility of racing the '999,' [and] neither did Cooper." So he turned elsewhere, and Cooper's friend entered the picture.[25]

Oldfield was attracted immediately by the situation. Not only did it present the allure of steady work and "a chance to make a chunk of money," as he recalled later, but it offered "a chance to fool with America's coming game—racing automobiles." He instinctively sensed the possibility of fame, and he leaped at it without hesitation. In Oldfield's words, "When Opportunity knocked in that letter from Cooper, I jerked the door open so quickly that she almost fell on her nose in the middle of the room."[26]

When Oldfield arrived in Detroit, he quickly sensed that Ford's interest in racing was serious but ephemeral. As the new arrival noted matter-of-factly, Ford had been trying to build a commercial car and was pursuing racing because he knew the value of advertising. These vehicles were in the last stages of completion, and Oldfield pitched in to help finish them along with Ford, Cooper, Wills, and Huff. Quickly sizing up the situation, he grasped that he had been summoned because of his "reputation for having plenty of nerve," not because of his skill. But Oldfield's risk-taking temperament, strength, quick reflexes, and addiction to speed made him a natural race driver. Ford showed him the ropes during a few practice sessions, and Oldfield's reckless courage did the rest. As Ford said of his new accomplice, "He had never driven a motorcar, but he liked the idea of trying it. He said he would try anything once. It took us only a week to teach him how to drive. The man did not know what fear was. All that he had to learn was how to control the monster."[27]

The racers were completed by the early fall of 1902, and the team began the test runs noted earlier. Newspaper reporters were curious about the car, and Ford would explain its special features. He unintentionally highlighted the extreme danger involved in navigating this powerful vehicle at high speed without benefit of a windshield while an open crankcase continuously spewed a mist of oil onto the driver. According to Ford, the car's "tiller"—instead of a steering wheel, it had a straight two-foot length of steel with two handles on each end sitting atop a shaft connected to the car's front-wheel system—provided special benefit to the driver.

> You see, when the machine is making high speed, and for any reason the operator cannot tell at the instant because of the dust or other reasons, whether he is going perfectly straight, he can look at his steering handle. If it is set straight across the machine he is all right and running straight.

This provided but scant comfort, one imagines, to the frequently blinded race driver struggling to keep this roaring machine, with flames spurting out of its four exhausts, from careening off the track.[28]

Nonetheless, the Ford-Oldfield team looked ahead to the Manufacturer's Challenge Cup race to be held at the Grosse Point track on October 25. Alexander Winton remained the foremost American racing champion, and he promised to be there. For Ford, this offered another golden opportunity to publicize his expertise as a maker of automobiles. According to Oldfield, he "wasn't satisfied to have Winton the champion driver of America" and saw the Challenge Cup as the perfect opportunity to wrest the top position away from his rival.[29]

Ford, Cooper, Huff, and Oldfield took turns test-driving the racer in the weeks before the big contest. The 999 was even shipped to Ohio for a race in mid-October. It was agreed that Oldfield got more speed out of the 999 than any of the others, so he was chosen to drive in the Challenge Cup. Then, the two leaders of the racing team had a falling out, and Ford ended his business relationship with Cooper by selling his financial interest in the race cars. According to a letter from Clara Ford to her brother in late October, Ford sold to his associate when he uncovered some "dirty tricks" in which his partner "was looking out for Cooper and Cooper only." "I am glad we are rid of him," Clara confessed with obvious relief. "He thinks too much of low down women to suit me." Ford agreed to remain on board, however, to assist with the big race.[30]

On October 25, after four preliminary races for smaller vehicles, the prestige event of the day began as four drivers entered the Challenge Cup, a five-mile race. The field consisted of Winton, driving the Winton Bullet; his business manager, William B. Shanks, in a modified model called the Winton Pup; a racer named Buckman in the Geneva Steamer; and the unknown youth Barney Oldfield at the tiller of the Ford 999.

Under this pressure, fears for Oldfield's safety suddenly surfaced. "One of my friends came up to me just before the race and said, 'You better be careful, Barney; you're liable to get killed,' " Oldfield recalled. " 'I might as well be dead as dead broke,' I answered." Even Ford caught a case of the jitters. Believing that Oldfield was risking his life because of his lack of experience, he urged him to stand aside and let someone else drive. But Oldfield laughed off such concerns. Ford reported, "As he took his seat [for the big race], while I was cranking the car for the start, he remarked cheerily: 'Well, this chariot may kill me, but they will say afterward that I was going like hell when she took me over the bank.' " Lee Cuson, a mechanic who was helping with the racer, discovered a potential disaster in a prerace inspection of the car: a six-inch bolt had worked itself completely loose from the gear housing in the rear end, a problem that would have wrecked the vehicle in a short time. "Mr. Ford was leaning on the rail of the fence," Cuson reported. "He hopped over the fence and we replaced the bolt together. He was grease up to his elbows with me."[31]

The race began on an auspicious note for the Ford team as Oldfield accidentally turned a stumble into an advantage. He lagged behind the other drivers as they moved their cars toward the starting tape, and thus was forced to accelerate in order to pull even. In Oldfield's words, "I had to put on so much speed to catch up with the field that when we all crossed the tape together I was moving much faster than anyone else. That gave me a better start." Oldfield shot into the lead quickly, and his full-throttle style kept him there. Later, he offered a gripping description of his first race as seen from the driver's seat of the 999:

> I didn't know anything about automobile racing. I managed to get into the middle of the track, and I stayed there throughout the race. I slid all the way around the first turn, the 999 trying to jerk away from me and go straight ahead through the outside fence. The rear wheels insisted on getting ahead of the front ones. I used to stop skids on the bicycle by turning the front wheel in the direction of the skid, so I jerked the tiller bar of my racer so as to point the front wheels toward the outer fence. The idea worked! I showed that bunch of wood and iron where to head in! I got out of the curve and into the backstretch.
>
> When I reached the second turn I went right on into it, using the same tactics I had on the first one. I certainly got a few thrills jerking that car around and putting her nose where I wanted it. . . . I kept this up for five miles. I really had got so interested in getting around the corners that I didn't pay much attention to anyone else on the track. Some of my friends told me afterward that I scared the other participants and the spectators half to death by my crazy driving.[32]

Oldfield held a substantial lead at the end of the first mile. Winton used his driving experience to narrow the gap gradually between them. By the third mile, however, the Winton Bullet fell back with mechanical difficulties as its engine began to misfire, and it quit the race entirely on the fourth mile. Oldfield lapped one of his remaining opponents, and nearly lapped the other as he sped to a convincing victory. Moreover, his time of 5:28 for five miles set an American speed record. Hundreds of spectators rushed onto the field, hoisted the beaming, grimy young driver onto their shoulders, and carried him around to cheers, whistles, applause, and the exploding flash powder of photographers. Even Ford was swept up in the moment. "Mr. Ford rushed out on the track at the conclusion of the race," Oldfield related. "Coming over to me, he shouted, 'I'll build another car for you, Barney, and we'll challenge the world with it.' "[33]

After Oldfield's retirement from active racing, he described the summons from Cooper bringing him to the Manufacturer's Challenge Cup race as "the letter that changed my whole life." "The afternoon of October 25, 1902 will be my red-letter day forever," Oldfield confessed. "Later on I was to win bigger races, to get more publicity, perhaps, but not the same thrill that came to me then." He always cherished his early association with Henry Ford and believed that it had launched both their careers. "A few years later I had managed to keep pace with him in fame, though not in dollars," Oldfield later wrote of the race. "Mr. Ford, by virtue of his building a car for the masses, had become leader of the automobile industry; I held the title of master driver of the world."[34]

As for Ford, he also understood the significance of the Challenge Cup victory and took immediate advantage. After a disgruntled Winton promised to build a faster car and recapture the speed record, Ford summoned reporters. "If Mr. Winton does lower this time, I'll build another machine that will go him one better if I have to design a cylinder as big as a hogshead," he declared. "I am bound to keep the record in Detroit." But despite such determined rhetoric, this master of publicity realized that racing had already fulfilled its larger purpose. The Ford-Oldfield victory, having splashed his name before the public as a skilled automaker, served as a springboard to launch him back into his real field of interest—building a commercial car. In a frank assessment of the Challenge Cup race, Ford asserted, "The '999' did what it was intended to do: it advertised the fact that I could build a fast motor car. A week after the race I formed the Ford Motor Company."[35]

Ford's racing career, however, was not quite over. A little more than a year later, in January 1904, he once again took advantage of the sport's capacity to attract publicity. Having resumed work on commercial motor vehicles, Ford decided that his new company's four-cylinder model, which he had dubbed the Model B, needed a boost. "Winning a race or making a record was then the best kind of advertising," Ford recalled years later. So he reacquired the old Arrow racer from Tom Cooper—it had been wrecked in a 1903 race—and rebuilt it. Ford announced that the vehicle would be outfitted with a Model B engine, and that it would break the world's record for the mile. Moreover, he picked a theatrical venue that would have done Barney Oldfield proud. He chose to accomplish this feat just northeast of Detroit, on the ice-covered surface of Lake St. Clair. Detroit newspapers featured stories on the upcoming event, and the Hotel Chesterfield, located close to the race site on the lake, provided additional advertisement by distributing handbills. What unfolded was a prototypical publicity stunt.[36]

Assisted by Harold Wills and Spider Huff, Ford made some modifications on the Arrow—they installed a V-shaped fuel tank and a bullet-shaped water tank on the front of the racer, above the engine, and replaced the old tiller with a steering wheel located on the left side behind a new "blast breaker" windshield—and shipped the vehicle to the New Baltimore powerhouse at Lake St. Clair. He hired a team of local farmers to remove the snow from a path four miles long and fifteen feet wide on the icy surface of the lake. He then had them haul cinders from the powerhouse and spread them on the ice, hoping that the tiny, hot nuggets would melt into the surface just enough to provide traction for the racer's tires. On January 9, around noon, Ford, Wills, and Huff wheeled the vehicle onto the lake surface. The weather was so bitterly cold that the car's intake manifold had been wrapped in burlap to keep it from freezing. Hot water was poured into the engine's cooling system while Huff used a plumber's blowtorch to warm the engine parts. After a brief preliminary ride, Ford reported that he was having trouble keeping his foot on the accelerator because the car bounced when it hit fissures in the ice. They decided that during the time trial Huff would crouch on the floorboards next to Ford and hold the gas pedal down with his hand so the driver could concentrate on steering.

A crowd gathered along the makeshift racetrack. Locals eager to witness this unusual display were there, along with many of Ford's associates and his family from Detroit, including Clara and Edsel. Finally, the Arrow made its run. With Ford steering grimly and Huff holding on for dear life as he pressed the accelerator to the floor, they went flying down the track. According to the accepted plan of procedure, the first two miles were for acceleration, the third mile would be timed for the record, and the last mile would allow for slowing down. As Ford and Huff went hurtling down the ice, they twice grazed the snow embankments while gathering speed. Ford steadied the racer, however, and they hit the third mile at top speed. After slowing the vehicle to a stop over the fourth mile, the driving team was given the incredible news: the racer had completed the third mile in thirty-six seconds, which meant that it had been going an astonishing hundred miles an hour. This shattered the existing record of seventy-seven miles per hour.[37]

Years later, Ford recalled his misgivings as he began this unusual, and dangerous, undertaking on Lake St. Clair:

> I shall never forget that race. The ice seemed smooth enough, so smooth that if I had called off the trial we should have secured an immense amount of the wrong kind of advertising, but instead of being smooth, that ice was seamed with fissures which I knew were going to mean trouble the moment I got up speed. But there was nothing to do but go through with the trial, and I let the old

"Arrow" out. At every fissure the car leaped into the air. I never
knew how it was coming down. When I wasn't in the air, I was skidding, but somehow I stayed top side up and on the course, making a
record that went all over the world.[38]

The Detroit newspapers amply repaid Ford for his risk with much
favorable commentary. Describing the world record run as "the wildest ride
in the history of automobiling," the *Tribune* breathlessly depicted the scene:
"Humped over his steering wheel, the tremendous speed throwing the
machine in zigzag fashion across the fifteen-foot roadway, Ford was taking
chances that no man, not even that specialist in averted suicide, Barney Oldfield, had dared to tempt." Ford's feat was so dumbfounding, according to
the Detroit *News,* that "even the most enthusiastic supporters of American
speed machines admitted that they would like to see further proof before
accepting the figures."[39]

Ford milked the incident for all it was worth. His new company immediately launched an advertising campaign that trumpeted "World's Mile
Straightaway Record Broken by a FORD MACHINE." Once again, he had
proved the power of publicity in America's new mass culture. It was a power
that he would use frequently in the future.[40]

Six

Entrepreneur

Henry Ford put his newfound celebrity to use. Drawing upon the favorable publicity surrounding his racing successes, he worked to clothe himself once again in the more familiar guise of an automobile manufacturer. He returned to the old problem that had haunted his failed efforts of the late 1890s—finding investors—only this time he had additional leverage. Newspapers noted, "Mr. Ford is one of the best known auto men in the middle west," and magazines proclaimed, "Ford Is King." For thousands of citizens in Detroit, and, indeed, throughout the nation, who read about such racing exploits, the Ford name was now associated with a winner.[1]

Ford was determined to overcome his earlier failures and bring a viable vehicle into the commercial market. The problem, as his earliest disappointments had demonstrated, lay in finding the right kind of investors: capitalists who would be sympathetic to his vision, patient enough to put up with his perfectionist streak, and willing to allow him to control and direct the company with little outside interference. With a typical combination of big ideas and stubborn independence, Henry Ford set out to be a successful entrepreneur. It was probably his last chance.

Ford actually began casting about for new sources of capital for manufacturing early in 1902, a few months after his first victory over Alexander Winton. Though to outsiders he seemed consumed by racing fever, such was not the case. After the collapse of the Detroit Automobile Company and the Henry Ford Company, he had continued to develop ideas for a passenger car. Initially, his hopes were frustrated, as many Detroit businessmen, aware of his two earlier failures, shied away from financial involvement with the maverick automaker.

Then Ford hooked a new financial partner from an unlikely source. Official histories of the Ford Motor Company, and, indeed, Henry Ford himself, have tended to slight the crucial role played by Alexander Y. Malcolmson in the founding of the company. In hindsight, it seems clear that the enterprise could not have been launched without his help. This aggressive, energetic Detroit businessman had accumulated considerable assets over the previous decade, and, although completely unversed in the automobile game, he now entered Ford's orbit.

Born June 15, 1865, in Scotland, Malcolmson had come to Detroit in 1880 and steadily worked his way up from grocery clerk to grocery-store owner. By early in the next decade, he had entered the coal business, establishing his first yard in 1893. He focused on delivery, using many small, three-horse wagons to make faster deliveries in greater volume and satisfying customers in thousands of homes around Detroit. Advertisements declared that Malcolmson's coal was "Hotter Than Sunshine," a slogan that was also posted on the sides of his delivery wagons. By 1903, he had bought out two competitors, set up ten coal yards around Detroit, purchased the city's only coal trestle, constructed a steam coal-plant, gained an interest in a West Virginia mine, and branched out southward to establish the Crescent Fuel Company in Toledo. "We now have 120 horses and 110 wagons constantly at work, which gives an average delivering capacity of 1,800 tons daily," he told a newspaper in that year. Malcolmson also secured several large industrial accounts to supplement his fleet of wagons, supplying coal to steamships, railroads, factories, and state institutions in and around Detroit.[2]

Small, lean, and muscular, full of nervous energy and ambition, the Scotsman with the dark hair and full walrus-style mustache threw himself into his business endeavors. According to his son, Malcolmson was "the plunger type, a man who did not hesitate to take chances." He "had a fiery temper and would blow up fiercely when anyone did something he considered wrong or stupid." After the death of his first wife, in 1901, Malcolmson had married a woman from his church to help care for his six children.[3]

He had first met Henry Ford in the 1890s, when the latter was the chief engineer of the Edison Illuminating Company and in charge of coal purchases for its furnaces. Ford would go to Malcolmson's yard every couple of weeks or so to check the quality of the fuel. In subsequent years, Malcolmson supplied coal to Ford's residence. The two became reacquainted in 1902. Ford may have simply approached Malcolmson as a likely investor, or vice versa, since the coal dealer had witnessed Ford's racing victory over Winton. The contact may have come through William Livingstone, Jr., a prominent businessman who knew Ford and had extended much credit to Malcolmson for his business activities. Whatever the case, by late summer the two men were talking seriously about a joint venture.[4]

Malcolmson agreed to put up money to finance Ford's development of a commercial automobile. John W. Anderson, Malcolmson's attorney, met with the two prospective partners on August 16, 1902, to discuss the organization of an automobile company. In Anderson's words, Malcolmson "was interested in automobiles, had become interested in Mr. Ford's idea and thought it was a good one, and was willing to back his faith by advancing money to supply materials and pay the labor necessary to create a car." On August 20, the two signed a preliminary accord drawn up by the attorney. According to this contract, Ford would contribute to the enterprise all of his drawings, machines, models, and patents, while Malcolmson would provide cash to finance the building of a prototype. The partners also agreed that within a short time, once the car's design was completed and a working vehicle actually constructed, they would create a corporation, fold the partnership's assets into it, and seek additional investment capital. Finally, the pair decided to maintain majority control of the corporation, with Malcolmson handling its financial affairs and Ford its mechanical and manufacturing endeavors.[5]

So, throughout the fall of 1902, at the very same time they were scrambling to complete the 999 and Arrow racers, Ford, Spider Huff, and Harold Wills used any spare moments to develop plans for a commercial automobile. Riding the wave of enthusiasm following Oldfield's victory in the Manufacturer's Challenge Cup, in the last few months of 1902 Ford began hiring workers to finalize the commercial prototype and put the manufacturing process in place. These included old friends such as the design engineer Oliver Barthel, and Frederick Strauss, who became manager of the machine shop. New employees were a draftsman, Gus Derenger; a patternmaker, Dick Kettlewell; and mechanics John Wandersee and Fred Seeman. By Thanksgiving, the two-cylinder motor for a pilot automobile was in running order; by Christmas, the chassis had been made.[6]

Malcolmson offered encouragement as his partner's development work progressed. "Hope you will get everything running in good shape at the shop, so that the work can be pushed ahead with all possible speed," he wrote Ford on October 30, 1902. "Our salvation for next season will be in getting the machine out quickly and placing it in the market early. It is pleasing that you have been so successful thus far in getting the right kind of help." Malcolmson and Ford maintained an amiable personal relationship during this period. When the coal dealer's car, a Winton, broke down near Pontiac,

Ford, along with a pair of his mechanics, rushed to the rescue. They discovered that a piston had come loose, harming the gasoline pump and causing it to leak fuel everywhere. Ford and his colleagues repaired the problem.[7]

By the late spring of 1903, the Ford team had made two significant advancements in their project.

First, an "assembling plant" was established on Mack Avenue near the Belt Line Rail line. One of Malcolmson's acquisitions in the coal business had brought him the lease on an old wagon shop at this site, and it was enlarged according to Ford's specifications. After some twelve weeks of remodeling, a small workforce moved in on April 1.[8]

Second, the prototype of Ford's new car—he and his team had decided to call it the Model A—was completed in late spring and contracts were arranged with parts-makers throughout the city. Ford and Malcolmson signed an important agreement with the Dodge Brothers Machine Shop to provide 650 engines, transmissions, and axles for the new automobile. John and Horace Dodge, owners of the largest and best-equipped machine shop in Detroit, rejected offers from the Oldsmobile Company and the Great Northern Automobile Company to throw in their lot with Ford. The new enterprise also contracted with the C. R. Wilson Carriage Company to construct wooden bodies and cushions, the Prudden Company to build wheels, and the Hartford Rubber Company to provide tires.[9]

In the meantime, of course, a hunt for investors sought capital to incorporate the enterprise officially. Malcolmson and Ford approached everyone they knew. Progress was slow. Ford, for example, spoke with his old boss at the Edison Illuminating Company, Alexander Dow. Dow refused politely; he ruefully recalled, many years later, "I didn't know then, of course, that he was going to make millions of the blamed things." Malcolmson contacted his myriad associates in the Detroit business community. As investors slowly came on board, they also pitched in to help raise additional funds. John W. Anderson, who had drawn up the original partnership agreement, recruited his law partner, Horace H. Rackham. Lacking funds himself, he also wrote a long letter to his father seeking a loan of $5,000 for investment purposes. "I earnestly believe it is a wonderful opportunity, and a chance not likely to occur again," Anderson wrote earnestly. "Mr. M. is successful in everything he does, and such a good businessman and hustler, and his ability in this direction, coupled with Mr. Ford's inventive and mechanical genius . . . makes it one of the very most promising and surest industrial investments that could be made."[10]

After much struggle and persuasion, enough investors were corralled to allow the crucial step. On June 16, 1903, Ford and Malcolmson filed incorporation papers for the Ford Motor Company and transferred all of their assets and holdings to this new corporation. The two partners listed twelve individuals (including themselves), who invested a total of $28,000 in cash and promised $21,000 more in notes, receiving $49,000 worth of stock in return. Malcolmson, it is clear, had been the driving force on the financial front, for nearly all the investors were his friends, relatives, or business associates. The Malcolmson group was impressive: John S. Gray, a banker and his uncle; John W. Anderson and Horace H. Rackham, his lawyers; Vernon E. Fry, a businessman and his cousin; Charles J. Woodall, his bookkeeper; James Couzens, his business manager; and Albert Strelow, the contractor who had built his coal yards. One outsider investor, Charles H. Bennett, president of the Daisy Air Rifle Company, also joined the group. The final two contributors were highly interested parties. Brothers John and Horace Dodge invested in the company, but did so as part of a larger business arrangement. Each contributed a $5,000 promissory note, but they covered their investments by demanding up front $10,000 in cash to cover the cost of manufacturing the 650 engines, transmissions, and running gears for the company. By June 20, Detroit newspapers had announced the formation of the new company, complete with praise for "a commercial venture that promises strong competition for the auto manufacturers already in the field."[11]

In the summer, Henry Ford's work teams began assembling the first Model A's at the Mack Avenue facility. The plant, sitting on a corner right next to a railroad spur line, measured some 50 by 250 feet, about a third of an acre, and had a wooden clapboard exterior with numerous tall windows that gave the interior a light, airy feel. A second story was added within a few months at a cost of about $5,000. A large Olds gasoline engine provided power for a milling machine, a planer, and several lathes. As engines and body parts manufactured at the Dodge Brothers plant and the Wilson Carriage Company arrived in quantity, about a dozen workmen hired by Ford at $1.50 a day assembled them into complete vehicles. Methods were crude. As one employee recalled:

> The cars were assembled on the spot. They would bring the chassis and the motor and the body to one place. I would say there was [sic] ten or fifteen spots for assembling, and there would be just one or two men for each assembly. . . . After they were assembled, they were driven out. Some testing was done right on the blocks. You'd have to get the motor started and run it. . . . Sometimes the valves needed grinding, and we'd do it right there.

Production also was minimal. "I remember that we used to try and get out fifteen [cars] a day," another early employee remembered. "We would work our hearts out to get fifteen a day."[12]

The Model A was a solid, reliable vehicle, and it embodied Henry Ford's principles of lightness, simplicity, and durability. "Excess weight kills any self-propelled vehicle. . . . The car that I designed was lighter than any car that had yet been made," he described many years later. "The cars gained a reputation for standing up. They were tough, they were simple, and they were well made." But sales failed to materialize, and for several weeks the company led a hand-to-mouth existence. Funds dwindled rapidly as a steady stream of payments for parts and labor flowed out with no cash returning. The company's balance fell to a total of $223.65. Finally, on July 15, the company made its first sale: a check in the amount of $850 from Dr. E. Pfennig, a Chicago dentist, was recorded for the purchase of a Model A. This punched a hole in the dam, and over the next few weeks additional orders and payments came trickling, and then pouring, into the Ford factory. By the end of August, the balance stood at some $23,000. The new enterprise had taken its first breaths of life.[13]

As the company scrambled to its feet, Henry Ford assumed a dominant role. In the beehive of activity that surrounded both the assembly of Model A's and the design work for new models at Mack Avenue, he seemed to be everywhere at once. Workers at the plant encountered their quiet, amiable, yet energetic boss daily and in varied situations. Ford, usually dressed in casual work clothes, mingled with the men and provided injections of energy and inspiration. Walking among the assembly groups, he offered friendly encouragement, asked questions, and helped supervise the labor process. Occasionally he pitched in to help. "If there was a dirty job and he had a good pair of trousers on," one employee noted, "he wouldn't hesitate a minute in those days to tackle any job." The original employees of the Ford Motor Company idolized their boss as a man who treated them even-handedly and expressed genuine appreciation for the work of a mechanic. According to Fred Rockelman, one of the earliest workers, "At that time we looked upon Mr. Ford as our great godfather or benefactor. We were always able to go into his office because he would have an open door and we felt that he had a great sense of understanding of mechanics."[14]

Ford also provided a calming, soothing influence on the frantic, occasionally contentious work atmosphere of an early industrial plant like this one. With an even, cheerful disposition and quiet reputation as a "square shooter," he mediated explosive situations that arose. Charles Bennett, one of the original stockholders, became involved in an argument with James Couzens over a financial matter. Others were drawn in, and soon a bitter shouting match erupted. At this point, Ford "stepped right forward and took hold of my arm and said, 'Aw, come on, let's calm down. Let's all calm down,' " Bennett recalled. "He meant *all* of them too. . . . We started talking about something else, and it all melted away." This calming influence was enhanced by a reputation for full-blown, authoritative involvement in shaping the company's product. The design engineers, as well as the assemblers on the plant floor, knew who was in charge. "Mr. Ford kept in touch with everything in the experimental room, with every piece of paper on the board and everything in the shop, looking at the parts as they progressed," noted John Wandersee, one of the key early development engineers. "Mr. Ford always gave the designers a lineup of what he wanted designed. The ideas, I believe, were original with him."[15]

Ford's image as a strong yet approachable figure was enhanced by his love for horseplay and practical jokes. His tomfoolery at the Mack Avenue plant became legendary. Ford liked to wrestle, for example, and he would leap into a grappling contest with one of his men at the slightest show of interest. "He had just a little neck on him, but he could throw a very big man," reported Frederick Strauss. "Henry had some kind of way that he could get you around the back and trip you." His compulsive practical-joking came from the same sensibility, and many of his antics were aimed at Dick Kettlewell, a particularly somber and gullible pattern-maker, who never seemed to catch on to the drift of these tricks. Once, Ford arranged for a loaded cigar to be given to Kettlewell, which, when lit, exploded and singed his eyebrows. Another time, with the assistance of Spider Huff, Ford fixed a lever on one of the Model A's so that when moved it triggered a small explosion in the car's muffler. It was arranged for poor Kettlewell to sit in the car and adjust the lever, and the resulting boom frightened him so badly he nearly fell out of the vehicle. Ford, with his accomplices, was lurking behind a partition and "laughing his head off to think that he scared Dick so." Perhaps Ford's most memorable trick occurred when, along with Harold Wills, he hot-wired the urinal in the men's toilet and waited patiently until Kettlewell went in during the day to relieve himself. The switch was thrown, and when the stream of urine made contact, the resulting shock produced an outburst of hilarity. "Dick just gave one yell and came running out of the toilet before buttoning up his pants," reported a witness; Ford and his workers collapsed in laughter.[16]

As the company expanded and prospered, its leader's public image also began to grow. Calls and inquiries after Henry Ford mounted as his new secretary, Myrtle Clarkson, scrambled to locate her energetic boss roaming the factory. "He came and went at his own sweet will, observing no office hours," she noted. The area around his office often became congested, with car dealers seeking contracts and visitors clambering to see the successful manufacturer. Letters also poured in. One of them, according to Clarkson, was Ford's first fan letter. From a young woman who lived in the Western part of the United States, it described her recent encounter with a picture of Ford as he sat behind the wheel of one of his cars. Smitten, she offered to marry him sight unseen.[17]

As the Model A began to sell steadily, production and profits both mounted. But success brought new and unforeseen problems. It became evident that the Mack Avenue facility was being swamped by the volume of sales. On April 1, 1904, responding to the need for increased output, the company secured a larger factory site on Piquette Avenue, conveniently located near several railroad lines. The new facility consisted of a three-story brick building measuring some 402 by 56 feet. The plant featured special fire walls and sprinkler systems and relied upon a one-story powerhouse to provide electrical power. By the fall of 1904, this structure, almost ten times the size of the Mack Avenue plant, neared completion. The company shifted its manufacturing operations there in late 1904 and early 1905, and within a short time it was employing some three hundred.[18]

During this early spurt of growth from 1903 to 1905, Henry Ford assembled a group of associates who would play prominent roles in developing the company's earliest automobiles. Harold Wills, assisted by J. C. Smith and Harry Love, specialized in experiment and design; Gus Derenger and P. E. Martin supervised the assembly process. Fred Seeman, with the help of Charles E. Sorensen, directed the pattern-making efforts; and a trio of engineers—Joseph Galamb, Oscar C. Bornholdt, Carl Emde—came to play important roles in tool design and model development. Frank Bennett and Fred Rockelman were in charge of the motor-testing room—at that time a rather perilous operation, because of ineffective ventilation for carbon-monoxide gas. But Henry Ford oversaw the entire production process. No important decisions were made without his approval. "His was the final say," one employee emphasized. "The other people did the work, but when it came to 'shall we put this here or there?' Mr. Ford would say, 'we'll put it here,' and that was the end of that."[19]

On the business front, however, Ford's contributions faded. In fact, in matters of finances, billings, payments, and sales they disappeared almost completely. During the company's first, occasionally precarious few years of existence, another figure proved to be particularly valuable and influential. Alex Malcolmson, up to his elbows in various business ventures, had overextended his credit by 1903 and wished to hide his adventures in the automobile industry from his bankers. So he transferred his chief clerk from the

Malcolmson Coal Company to a position of authority in the automobile company. This able young man was put in charge of the partnership's business operations. No one could have predicted the influential role that this brilliant, methodical young clerk would come to play in the fortunes of Henry Ford and his company.

James Couzens knew nothing about automobiles. Occasionally he would go for a ride with Malcolmson, who would adjust a control on the dashboard of his Winton and explain that he was changing the mixture. "I thought he meant that he was mixing water with the gasoline, and continued to think so for a long time," Couzens confessed, not understanding about gasoline and air. But he did know about business. In the late summer of 1903, the Ford Motor Company had sold a few cars and had others ready for shipment, but Henry Ford was delaying, offering the familiar excuse from his earlier days as a manufacturer: his automobile was not yet as good as he could make it. This time, however, someone intervened. "I urged H.F. to get the cars out and get the money for them, regardless of whether he could improve them," Couzens noted. "We had but a small working capital and it was getting low." To make sure that the automobiles went out to buyers as planned, he personally helped transport them to the railway, crate them up, and nail shut the doors of the railcars.[20]

Here was Couzens in a nutshell—smart, tough, blunt, willful, and self-confident. A man with an incredible capacity for work, a volcanic temper, and an attention to detail, he overflowed the official confines of his position to emerge as a powerful force in the early Ford Motor Company. Joining forces with Henry Ford, who quickly and favorably sized up this talented new associate, he dominated the business operations of the growing enterprise. Couzens' prodigious talents and powerful personality made him a man to reckon with, and his contribution to building the company ranked second only to that of Ford himself.

Couzens had been born in 1872 in Chatham, Ontario, some fifty miles from Detroit, to a pair of hardworking English immigrants. He worked for his father, who had risen from workman to small-business owner, and often accompanied him on business trips in the community. The ambitious youth harbored big dreams, once chiding his mother for dampening his prospects by allowing him to be born in Canada: "I can never be King of England, but if I had been born in the United States, I could be President." After high school, he trained as a bookkeeper at the Canada Business College in

Chatham, paying expenses by working as a news butcher on the Erie and Huron Railroad. In 1889, at age seventeen, he left Chatham to take a job as a car-checker with the Michigan Central Railroad in nearby Detroit.

For $40 a month—twelve-hour days, seven days a week—Couzens checked freight cars and affixed labels to them confirming their contents. His obsession with efficiency soon became storied, as did his steely, no-nonsense temperament and prickly personality. Couzens avoided beer-drinking and carousing at his boardinghouse, and seemed to face everything, and everyone, with the same stern gaze. He dressed impeccably, carefully clipped his hair, and wore steel-rimmed glasses, thus creating an image of self-discipline and determination. He was also known for an unpleasant but effective forcefulness as he bluntly denounced those with whom he disagreed, and often displayed a powerful temper. Seldom smiling and deadly serious, he seemed someone to cross only at one's peril.

By 1893, at age twenty-one, Couzens became supervisor of the freight office in the railroad yard and established a reputation for strictness and dis-cipline. Unconcerned with popularity, he earned little affection but much respect from workers and railroad managers alike. He treated customers honestly yet candidly. For example, he minced no words in insisting that customers pay "demurrage" charges, a much-resented new tariff established by Michigan Central. "The way Jim Couzens talked with these patrons on the telephone, giving them holy hell, was just astounding," said one of his associates. Couzens clashed with Alex Malcolmson, who resisted the new tariff, and the two engaged in several shouting matches. Malcolmson admired the young man's spirited defense of his employer's interest, and offered him a job.

So, in 1895, James Couzens went to work for Alex Malcolmson as a clerk and car-checker, but soon rose to the position of manager of opera-tions in the coal company. His habits of stern attention to duty, efficiency, and dogged pursuit of profit held firm. "He had a direct, blunt way of speak-ing to fellow employees and to customers," a stenographer at the company testified. "He expected to be obeyed without any question." Couzens' strong personality was appreciated by his boss, but it also produced frequent clashes of will between the two. Once, an argument over a business matter created a heated exchange during which Malcolmson called his manager a liar. Red-faced, Couzens flung his office keys at the tycoon, shouted his res-ignation, and stalked out. He returned only when Malcolmson sent a con-trite note asking him to resume his duties. "How Malcolmson and Couzens managed to remain affiliated is one of the mysteries of destiny," reported Ross Schram, Couzens' secretary.[21]

In the late 1890s, Couzens first encountered a Detroit mechanic who worked in the electrical industry and tinkered with horseless carriages. "The first time I ever saw Henry Ford was when I asked Malcolmson who was that man with the big mustache, who was looking at some coal in our office. Malcolmson said it was Henry Ford, the Edison Company's engineer," Couzens recalled later. "We supplied the Edison Company with coal, and Ford used to come over, every little while, to see that he got the kind of coal he wanted." Couzens became much more familiar with Ford when Malcolmson entered into the automobile partnership.[22]

The connection, however, followed a curiously indirect route. Malcolmson was afraid, as Couzens explained to a writer many years later, that "his credit with the banks would be injured if it were publicly known that he was backing anything so risky as an automobile venture." So a ruse was created: Malcolmson shifted Couzens to the automobile company, created a special account in Couzens' name with Malcolmson secretly providing funds for deposit, and Couzens was directed to pay Ford's bills in his own name. Thus the coal dealer was able to mask his involvement by deploying a surrogate. Couzens' task was simple—protect Malcolmson's interests and keep a tight financial rein on his boss's new partner. This he certainly did, warning Malcolmson many times as Ford's bills began to pile up.[23]

But Couzens' ambitious, forceful nature soon propelled him into other areas. He became intimately involved with nearly every business aspect of this manufacturing enterprise, and Malcolmson soon relied upon him for advice and counsel on larger questions. During negotiations with the Dodge Brothers over a contract to build the chassis for Ford cars, John Dodge demanded provisions that Couzens believed were unfair. "I won't stand for that," he told Dodge at a meeting. The quick-tempered, bar-fighting Dodge bristled, and demanded, "Who in the hell are you?" Malcolmson quickly interjected, "That's all right. Couzens is my adviser in this." A bit later, Couzens joined in the quest to gather investors as the new company attempted to incorporate. Telling friends that he intended to "beg, borrow, or steal" as much money as he could, Couzens scraped together $2,500 in cash, salary advances, and promissory notes to stand as one of Ford Motor Company's original investors. He also helped beat the bushes for other contributors, although the process was a discouraging one. In later years, Couzens recalled that at one point, having suffered rebuff after rebuff, he slumped down the stairs following another unsuccessful appeal and sat down on the curb, almost in tears.[24]

With the incorporation of the company in June 1903, Couzens was appointed as its general business manager and secretary. Malcolmson had wanted that position for himself, with his lieutenant placed in command of the coal business, but other investors, relying upon Malcolmson's experi-

ence in the energy operation, persuaded him to stay with his original enterprise. Besides, his chief clerk had made a strong impression upon the new
stockholders. As John W. Anderson noted in a letter to his father, "Mr.
Couzens . . . is going to leave the coal business, for the present at least, and
devote his entire time to the office and management of the automobile business. And he is a crackerjack."[25]

As the company geared up for production, Couzens set up an office on
the first floor of the Mack Avenue plant and began to grapple with key issues
facing this fledgling firm on the business front: payment of bills for parts,
purchasing, meeting the payroll, and particularly sales. His support staff was
small—a stenographer, a secretary, and a one-armed bookkeeper named
Talmadge. Couzens took care of everything that smacked of business and
worked heroic hours in doing so. "In those days," reported *Ford Times*, the
company magazine, a few years later, "J.C. was the entire office management—he hired and fired—he kept the books, collected, spent, and saved
the cash, established agencies, and dictated policies." Everyone at the Ford
plant perceived the clear division of responsibility at the top: Ford handled
engineering and production, Couzens handled business matters.[26]

He made one crucial move in setting up a sales structure for the new
Ford vehicles. He began attending automobile shows held in big cities
throughout the United States and scoured their displays and meetings looking for sales agents. Within a short time, Couzens had secured agents in
nearly all major urban areas, such as the Duerr-Ward company in New
York, the William L. Hughson Company in San Francisco, and McCord
and Company in Chicago. By the fall of 1905, he had signed up more than
450 agencies to sell Ford automobiles. He handpicked dealers and salesmen,
looking for men who shared his devotion to the work ethic. Couzens also
played the innovator in shaping his sales force, placing salaried employees,
rather than independent agents, at key points, and setting up a system of
incentives and bonuses to reward the diligent. One day, an individual from
the West Coast visited the Piquette Avenue plant to order a single car as a
first step in becoming a Ford dealer. "Mr. Couzens asked him for the population of his town and when he learned the answer, said, 'For a town that
size you ought to order 100 cars!' He talked the man into doing just that,
and what's more, collected in advance for the ordered cars."[27]

Ruling his business fiefdom from the hub of the Ford operation,
Couzens established a larger-than-life image. Attired in a dark business suit
and bow tie, with his habitually severe expression highlighted by steel spectacles, he imposed his will on nearly everyone with whom he dealt. Subordinates entered Couzens' domain gingerly, aware of his tough temperament
and his ability to "squeeze a penny and watch it as carefully as any living

human being could." Workers suffered similar fates. Fred Rockelman, a Ford mechanic, described the business manager as "a terrific man-handler" when confronted with personnel problems and complaints. "In the old days, we always called him the fire hydrant. We went in enthusiastically and he opened up the hydrant on us and cooled us off." To many, Couzens appeared tough but fair, brooking no nonsense from employees but also encouraging those who worked hard and believed in the future of the company. For others, however, his domineering ways caused resentment. "I called Couzens 'Sunny Jim' because he was so God-damn mean," Frank Bennett once noted. "There were a great many people who didn't like 'Sunny Jim.' "[28]

But Couzens' hard-driving intensity was not of the bullying sort. He did not just torment those lower on the food chain at the factory, but applied the same standards to everyone, regardless of rank. He established a rigid sales policy and grew angry when he discovered Malcolmson had violated it by giving a business friend a discount on the sale of a car. At the next stockholders' meeting, Couzens denounced this practice so vigorously that a chagrined Malcolmson agreed to pay the difference out of his own pocket. Years later, Couzens explained his attitude. "I am one of those who hold that it is not worthwhile to attempt to be popular," he wrote in *System: The Magazine of Business*. "I should prefer to be a hard taskmaster—but a fair one. Popularity is more often a liability than an asset."[29]

As the Ford Motor Company accelerated its production and sales and broke into the car market after 1903, one factor in James Couzens' evolving role proved essential—his relationship with Henry Ford. Originally, he made little impact on the company's namesake. But Ford soon sensed that this manager could be an invaluable ally. After an early organizational meeting of the board of directors, Ford offered Couzens a ride home in his own automobile. As the two drove along, they discussed plans for the new company, and the issue of salaries arose. Then Ford posed a question. "What do you think we ought to ask from *those fellows*?" he asked. Couzens immediately grasped the implications of Ford's wording: "*those fellows*," or the stockholders not really involved in the actual work of the company, stood on one side; he and Couzens, the workhorses of the enterprise, on the other. They agreed that a figure of $3,000 for Ford and $2,400 for Couzens would be reasonable. Couzens immediately sensed that his future no longer lay with Malcolmson but with the clear-sighted man sitting next to him. Instinctively, they entered into an unofficial partnership that blended distinct talents into a larger, fruitful whole.[30]

First at the Mack Avenue plant, and then at the facility on Piquette Avenue, the Ford-Couzens alliance emerged in force. Though outwardly formal—they commonly addressed each other as "Mr. Ford" and "Mr. Couzens"—the two acted in friendly concert regarding company affairs. Couzens took Ford's side in all differences of opinion regarding manufacturing and development, and Ford nodded silently when Couzens spoke on business issues. A Chicago dealer who observed the two in action at the Ford factory noted that "they were like brothers."[31]

Ford's organization of the manufacturing process, and Couzens' skillful erection of a supporting financial structure, prompted an explosive rate of growth. During Ford Motor Company's first three months of operation, it earned a profit of $37,000, and on November 21, 1903, it paid out a 10 percent dividend to stockholders. Over the next nine months, the company realized nearly $100,000, and by the autumn of 1904, sales were averaging $60,000 per month. Gross sales for the year October 1, 1904, to September 30, 1905, were nearly $2 million. During this start-up period, the company was selling roughly seventeen hundred motorcars per year. As Couzens told the Detroit *Journal* in the spring of 1905, "We are now turning out twenty-five machines a day on average and giving employment to three hundred men."[32]

But prosperity brought problems. Malcolmson, observing the company's success and the tight relationship between his partner and his business manager, grew nervous and moved to reassert himself. He asked Couzens to return to the coal company so he himself could take over the directorship of the car company's business affairs. When Couzens balked, Malcolmson asked the board of directors to discharge him. But Ford convinced the board to oppose this move. "I told Malcolmson that I did not want him but that I wanted his man Couzens," he explained later with typical candor. Couzens made his own sentiments clear. "I did not want to change, and H.F. and the Dodge Brothers stood by me. So I stayed."[33]

Yet this brewing controversy involved more than personalities and power. A deeper issue lying dormant during the first few years of the Ford Motor Company gradually came to life and fueled dissension as the company expanded rapidly. It involved a vision of the Ford automobile—what kind of car would the company develop, manufacture, and market?—and questions about how to capitalize on that vision. At the heart of things stood a growing difference of opinion between the two majority stockholders, Malcolmson and Ford. That difference swelled and festered, forcing stockholders to one side or the other, until it finally reached an explosion point. James Couzens' role in resolving this larger policy dispute would prove critical for the fortunes of the company.

Malcolmson, though standing on the sidelines during the company's early years of growth, knew exactly the kind of car he wanted to make—an expensive, luxury automobile aimed at prosperous buyers and promising a larger profit margin. Henry Ford sized up the situation quite differently. In mid-1903, describing to John W. Anderson his vision of an inexpensive, simple, lightweight car for a mass audience of buyers, he said he believed the best way to make such cars was to simplify and standardize the manufacturing process.

> When you get to making the cars in quantity, you can make them cheaper, and when you make them cheaper you can get more people with enough money to buy them. The market will take care of itself. . . . The way to make automobiles is to make one automobile like another automobile, to make them all alike, to make them come through the factory just alike; just as one pin is like another pin when it comes from a pin factory, or one match is like another match when it comes from the match factory.[34]

For the first two years of the company's existence, Ford and Malcolmson papered over their differences. In the 1904–5 season, the company offered to the public two different styles of automobile. The Model A and its successors, the Model C and Model F, represented Henry Ford's vision of a light, inexpensive, two-cylinder car. At Malcolmson's insistence, however, the company also built and marketed the Model B, a much heavier, faster, and more expensive four-cylinder touring car. Henry Ford's models were bought up by consumers as quickly as they could be made; the Model B sold only moderately well.[35]

Bolstered by the popularity of the lightweight runabouts, Ford and his engineers focused attention during the 1905–6 season on a new model that became the workhorse of the company: the light, durable, inexpensive four-cylinder Model N. Out of deference to Malcolmson, they also developed the six-cylinder Model K, a more powerful and expensive model. Whereas the Model N weighed 1,050 pounds and sold for $600, the Model K weighed some eighteen hundred pounds and cost $2,800. Ford and Malcolmson continued to stand by their respective positions. Ford pointed to sales figures and volume of demand for his smaller, affordable motorcar. But Malcolmson believed that another fact pointed up the company's path to future prosperity—in 1906, two-thirds of cars sold in the United States were larger, more expensive models, and these brought a greater profit margin. The two increasingly found themselves at loggerheads over this issue. Board-of-directors meetings throughout 1905 and 1906 turned acrimonious as the stockholders, following the lead of the two partners, quarreled over the company's future direction. Malcolmson gained support from several board members, but Ford's argument proved persuasive to a sizable majority.[36]

As tensions accompanying this disagreement increased, Henry Ford began to sour on his partner. Memories of the Detroit Automobile Company resurfaced, with the images of wealthy investors trying to force him in certain directions against his better judgment. He was determined to avoid a replay of this situation. His private comments turned harsh as he told associates that "anyone who did not have a part in the manufacturing of the company was actually not contributing and was a parasite." On the board of directors, Couzens was a key ally, of course, as were John Dodge, who did not like Malcolmson, and John Gray, who agreed with the long-term logic of Ford's position.[37]

As the situation grew more contentious, it became clear that a resolution needed to be found. Late in 1905, Ford and Couzens decided upon a clever maneuver that would serve two purposes at the same time. Thinking strategically, they had become convinced that the company should manufacture its own parts as another source of profit. As parties to a struggle for power within the company, they also were faced with what they saw as the wrongheaded thinking of an intransigent partner. So Ford and Couzens proposed to create a new entity, the Ford Manufacturing Company, that would solve both problems. It would produce Ford engines and parts, thus capturing the profit from selling them to the parent company that theretofore had gone to the Dodge Brothers. Equally important, it would be organized without the participation of Malcolmson. The ploy was ingenious. This new company and its stockholders would receive profits on the manufacture of engines and gears for the new Ford Model N, and henceforth Malcolmson would realize profits only on the *sale* of the completed vehicle. Thus Ford Manufacturing Company was incorporated on November 22, 1905, and the operation was set up in a rented facility on Bellevue Avenue. A stockholder election made Henry Ford its president, John F. Dodge vice president, and James Couzens treasurer. The intent was transparently clear. As John Gray noted to a skeptical stockholder, "I have Mr. Ford's promise that when things get straightened out with Mr. Malcolmson, the Ford Manufacturing Company is to be taken into the Ford Motor Company, just as if it had never existed."[38]

Malcolmson immediately understood the thrust of this move, and he fought back. He dashed off a long, angry letter to the board of directors, denouncing its actions as calculated

... to sacrifice the interest of the general body of stockholders to those of some individuals. The most striking instance of this tendency . . . is the organization of the Ford Manufacturing Company, comprised and controlled by the holders of the majority both of stock and directorships of the Motor Company, and designed, as I am reliably informed, to sell its products to the Motor Company—presumably not without profit. In this new company the minority stockholders were not invited to join. . . . [It offers] the prospect of participating in the profits and of confining the injury to those stockholders of the Motor Company that are left on the outside.[39]

Unwisely, Malcolmson went further. Letting his anger get the better of his judgment, he impulsively founded his own company to manufacture automobiles. In early December 1905, the Detroit *Journal* and the Detroit *Free Press* announced "Detroit's Newest Auto Company" and carried stories on the establishment of the Aerocar Company. Complete with a picture of its majority stockholder, Alex Y. Malcolmson, the accounts described the new company's capitalization of $400,000, the building of a three-story factory on Mack Avenue, and its plans to produce five hundred large touring cars for sale in 1906. Aerocar presented its advertising slogan: "The Car of Today, Tomorrow, and for Years to Come."[40]

This ill-conceived move gave Ford and his allies the opening they were looking for. With Aerocar standing as a direct competitor to the Ford Motor Company, Malcolmson could no longer act to promote the well-being of the company he had largely financed in 1903. Thus the Ford board of directors asked for his resignation on the grounds that his creation of the Aerocar enterprise was "inimical to the best interests of the [Ford] company." Malcolmson angrily refused and threatened a lawsuit.[41]

The internally divided young company now faced an outright civil war. In this battle of wills, Ford and Couzens insisted on Malcolmson's resignation and rallied support among the factory management. According to Fred Rockelman, Couzens told him "that Mr. Malcolmson was getting out of there and he was awful glad because there would be a much more cooperative group between Mr. Wills and Mr. Ford and himself." Couzens confessed to suffering "very severe headaches" from the stress of the situation. Ford moved to bolster morale among the troops, urging stockholders, "Don't sell out. You'll be taken care of. I'll see to that."[42]

After several months of unsuccessful negotiations with Malcolmson, Ford and Couzens mustered a majority to make another decisive move. In May 1906, the board of directors voted to remove Malcolmson as treasurer of the company. Finally, hemmed in and outmaneuvered, the bitter and resentful partner agreed to sell his 255 shares in the company for the price of $175,000. Couzens' uncle, businessman A. A. Parker, helped arrange for a loan to Henry Ford at the Dime Savings Bank, which was headed by William Livingstone, Jr. Couzens endorsed the notes. Within a short time, Malcolmson's few supporters among the directors also sold their shares—Charles H. Bennett said he was no longer comfortable with "a crowd of fellows that had frozen out somebody"—and Ford and Couzens bought them as well. With the unexpected death of John Gray in the summer of 1906, the presidency of the company opened up, and the board elected Henry Ford to fill the position. Thus, by 1907, the upheaval in the company had brought about a revolution. "Managerial control had been fused with stock control," in the words of one observer. Henry Ford owned 585 shares and directed production of the company's automobiles; James Couzens owned 110 shares and managed its business affairs; the other stockholders together held 305 shares and were content to leave the company in Ford's and Couzens' capable hands.[43]

Alex Malcolmson would go on to a checkered career. By September 1907, his Aerocar Company had filed for bankruptcy, and within a short time he was sued, first by a firm that had made auto engines for Aerocar, and then by representatives of the company's creditors. He recovered from this debacle to find financial success in several Detroit ventures: his old coal business, building supplies, and real estate. But by the late 1910s, Malcolmson had once again fallen on hard times. In 1919, he actually approached the Ford Motor Company, arguing that he had received insufficient compensation for his early Ford stock and asking for financial assistance. The company refused. Malcolmson suffered a nervous collapse and died in 1923. Henry Ford, in spite of the bitterness of their split many years before, served as an honorary pallbearer at Malcolmson's funeral. According to a newspaper account, as the minister eulogized Malcolmson, "Mr. Ford seemed lost in thought as if remembering the days when he was but a struggling mechanic with a vision and Malcolmson the financial colossus ready to bear his burdens."[44]

Indeed, Malcolmson's ill-fated clash with Ford constituted one of the great blunders in American business history. His shares, which he sold for $175,000, would have been worth hundreds of millions of dollars only ten years later. Yet the resolution of this crisis, though drawn out and painful, had clarified the future for the Ford Motor Company. It was now evident that the self-contained, visionary mechanic from Dearborn had gained control of the enterprise that displayed his name. And he knew it. One day near the end of the Malcolmson affair, Ford asked Fred Rockelman to drive him home. As they motored along, he confided that he had just bought out his partner. An exultant Ford, Rockelman recalled, waxed enthusiastic about the future of his motorcar and its vast social implications:

> Fred, this is a great day. We're going to expand this company and you will see that this company will grow by leaps and bounds because this transportation system as I have it in my mind is to get it to the multitude. If you get people together and get acquainted with one another and get a neighborly idea, it will be a universal thing.

Rockelman's reaction to the idealistic outburst mirrored that of most other Ford employees. "He wanted to help people and we as the young men in the shop looked up to that," he noted approvingly. "We could see that Mr. Ford's mind went to the farmer and the mechanic and to the people who lived in the hinterland."[45]

Ford now stood in a position to realize his vision. The man who wanted farmers and mechanics driving his car had emerged as the unchallenged director of company fortunes. His friend and ally James Couzens stood second-in-command as the manager of the business operation. With Couzens' help, Ford had drawn up the blueprint for the future, and the company would rise or fall accordingly.

With a new, vigorous leadership clearly in command, the Ford Motor Company blossomed. The clearest sign of progress came with the Model N, which truly represented Henry Ford's ideas, at least in nascent form, about the efficient, rationalized production of an inexpensive, universal vehicle. The conceptualization, manufacture, and marketing of this motorcar laid the groundwork for a business explosion that would rocket the Ford name into the industrial stratosphere within a few short years.

In 1906, Henry Ford proudly informed the Detroit *Journal* that this lightweight motorcar, which carried a price tag of only $500, would change the face of American transportation. He did not mince words:

> I believe that I have solved the problem of cheap as well as simple automobile construction. Advancement in auto building has passed the experimental stage, and the general public is interested only in the knowledge that a serviceable machine can be constructed at a price within the reach of many. I am convinced that the $500 model

is destined to revolutionize automobile construction, and I consider my new model the crowning achievement of my life.[46]

The Model N had resulted from many months of development work by Ford and his engineers. The experimental room stood next to Ford's office on the second floor of the Piquette Avenue plant, and throughout 1905 and 1906 he had directed the effort toward designing a four-cylinder car that would sell for $500. Harold Wills did yeoman work in developing this model, as did Joseph Galamb, a talented draftsman and engineer. Galamb had caught Ford's attention with his neat design drawings of the rear axle, differential, and housing for the new Model N. Impressed, Ford would frequently drop by his drafting table to offer encouragement and exchange ideas. By the fall of 1906, the manufacturing operation at the Bellevue Avenue plant was turning out a hundred engines per day, and the assembly teams at Piquette were frantically putting together the final product. Henry Ford aimed at producing more that ten thousand Model N's a year.[47]

As the Model N entered the market, trade magazines and newspapers carried glowing reports. The *Cycle and Automobile Trade Journal* published a nine-page article detailing every element (complete with photos and drawings) of the Model N's chassis, engine, steering, brakes, axles, and transmission. The reporter also described the forty-nine-mile test drive he took in the company of Henry Ford himself. The car performed admirably, steering smoothly and running steadily as it traversed miles of rough roads and accelerated nicely in climbing an extremely long hill with a turn halfway up. Ford commented, according to the author, that "he had never made that rise before so easily, in any car whatever." The article concluded that the Model N was "distinctly the most important mechanical event of 1906 . . . [and] supplies the very first instance of a low cost motor car . . . which is well built and offered in large numbers."[48]

However proud he was of the Model N's technical features, Henry Ford based his fondness for the car on a different source. With almost religious fervor, he preached the social virtues of this dependable, inexpensive vehicle. He told colleagues, "There are a lot more poor people than wealthy people. We'll just build one car for the poor people." This message became a mainstay of Ford Motor Company advertising for the Model N. "Henry Ford's idea is to build a high-grade, practical automobile" at a reasonable price, declared a 1906 publicity campaign, "thus raising the automobile out of the list of luxuries, and bringing it to the point where the average American citizen may own and enjoy his automobile." Buyers responded; sales of the Model N soared to some 8,423 cars in 1906–7, over five times better than the company's previous record for a twelve-month period.[49]

Production of the Model N reflected the growth of the company and its increasingly large and sophisticated operation. Advertisements explained that its low cost came from mind-boggling volume in production: "We are making 40,000 cylinders, 10,000 engines, 40,000 wheels, 20,000 axles, 10,000 bodies, 10,000 of every part that goes into the car—think of it! Such quantities were never heard of before." Much of this mass production took place at the Piquette Avenue factory. According to manager John Wandersee, "They were manufacturing everything there: blocks, connecting rods, everything but axles." The Ford Manufacturing Company, although absorbed into the parent company in 1907, after Malcolmson's departure, also produced engines for the Ford Model N.[50]

In this atmosphere of growth and expanding production, Ford moved to solidify his operation. In August 1906, he took an important step by hiring Walter E. Flanders, an expert in machine tools who made Ford's acquaintance when overseeing the installation of large lathes and grinders at Piquette Avenue. Very knowledgeable about the design and management of factories, Flanders took over as production manager. He immediately began reorganizing the process of making Model N's. A large, rough-hewn, heavyset man with a great head of woolly hair, he quickly assessed the situation and began issuing orders. Flanders informed Ford and Couzens that he intended "to manage the different manufacturing departments of your companies, [and] reorganize same, on what, in my judgement, is the most economical basis of manufacture for producing commercial products at the minimum cost."[51]

Flanders realigned machine placement for smoother flow and trained workers in more efficient production methods. He instituted a system whereby the workmen were given specific tasks to perform in assembling the Model N while "runners" were assigned to keep materials on hand and to supply small tools at the exact moment they were needed. He also established a schedule for monthly production, and integrated the parts-purchasing department into the larger scheme of manufacture. Along with his assistant, Thomas S. Walborn, he made Ford's factory the most efficient in Detroit. "Walter Flanders was a man of great ability," noted a colleague at Ford. "The men believed in and worshipped him. He was a very clever individual."[52]

Although Flanders stayed with Ford only a short time—he resigned in April 1908 to go into business for himself—his innovations provided a foundation for rationalized production methods. Near the end of his tenure, a move toward even greater production efficiency came when the Model N chassis was placed on a wooden truck and pushed along from one assembly station to another. A Ford employee described the process:

They'd roll them from spot to spot. . . . So they had the beginning
of an assembly line with the [car] frame on a truck. The supplies
would come in and each spot would order the parts they would use.
They had what they called stock chasers. They'd go downstairs to
the stock room and get most of the stock on a truck and bring it
upstairs and deliver it to these different cars according to the stage
of their assembly. . . . The men would help each other along the
line. They became specialists in certain operations on the assembly
of the car.[53]

While Ford, Flanders, and managers and engineers revamped production at the Piquette Avenue facility, important adjustments appeared on the
business side. Couzens, of course, remained, in the words of a subordinate,
"what you'd call 'the man who pulled the trigger.' He was *everything*. Whatever was to go, had to pass him." But, stretched beyond capacity, he reached
out for assistance. In November 1907, Couzens hired Norval A. Hawkins as
"commercial manager," a position that encompassed the entire sales organization. This appointment proved to be as important for Ford's marketing
operation as Walter Flanders was for its production. Over the next several
years, Hawkins would expand and revamp the Ford sales operation
throughout the country.[54]

As his company expanded rapidly in terms of production and structure,
Henry Ford influenced its evolution with his relaxed management style. He
roamed amid the growing workforce dispensing encouragement and advice
and cultivating a spirit of relaxed camaraderie. Everyone called him Hank or
Henry. The fact that he now tended to wear business suits during the workday did not stop him from lending a hand in the dirty work. According to
one workman at Piquette Avenue:

He'd leave the office and ramble through there. He'd make it his
business to show a new man how to handle a machine. If he got his
hands oily and greasy, that didn't make any difference to him. . . .
He'd stand there and do half a dozen articles for him and show him
how to do them. Finally the man got the swing of it and how to
handle it. Mr. Ford would say, "That's the way, John! Just take it
easy. You'll learn!"

Telling funny stories and bantering with the men, he would often pose rid-
dles or ask peculiar questions and then, according to one worker, "laugh his
fool head off to think that he had something on you that you couldn't
answer right. He was pretty witty." Ford's horseplay continued. Two of his

favorite activities were footracing with Fred Rockelman, a vehicle tester with the company—the pair would sprint, usually neck and neck, the length of the factory—and wrestling with George Holley, a young mechanic who was developing a carburetor for the Model N. According to one astonished observer, Ford and Holley would be talking and "the first thing you knew, they'd both be on the floor wrestling."[55]

Henry Ford spent much time, however, in the development room at the Piquette Avenue factory, where he and a cadre of company engineers put in long hours working on the newest model innovations. It was a rather unimpressive space, with a blackboard, several drafting desks, a kitchen table, and a couple of chairs. It also featured a small couch that lay low to the ground, and Ford would occasionally be glimpsed stretched out on it, hands behind his head, eyes closed, quietly pondering the issues at hand. Among the development team, he promoted his agenda for making light, inexpensive cars and demonstrated an instinctive skill for coordinating efforts toward this larger goal. Disagreements arose, of course, over ideas involving mechanical and design issues. Ford would grease the creative wheels to keep them turning:

> When tension had built up and Mr. Ford would come into the room . . . he would notice that the feeling wasn't there of full cooperation, of everybody working together. Then he would go around and talk to this fellow and that fellow, and pretty soon he'd play a trick on somebody . . . and after that happened, it seemed that the boys all got together in a more cheerful mood. He was very observant, and if everything wasn't going smoothly, he would notice it immediately. . . . He'd try to smooth it out.[56]

Ford's managerial skills, however, did not carry over into finances. In fact, his ineptness in that area became notorious. One day, shortly after the move to the Piquette Avenue plant, a young bookkeeper named Frank Klingensmith spent a long time unsuccessfully searching for an invoice. Frustrated, he finally looked into the shop, saw Ford, and inquired whether the company's chief had seen it. Ford thought for a moment, shrugged his shoulders, and suggested that the bookkeeper might check in an upstairs room by his office. Klingensmith was stunned to find the invoice there, lying in the middle of a huge pile of unopened mail. The bookkeeper filled two wastebaskets with this correspondence, carried it to his office, and spent the next two hours sorting through several weeks' worth of invoices, bills, and checks that Ford had absentmindedly set aside without opening. When Klingensmith informed Couzens of this situation, the latter blanched and immediately issued a directive: "From now on it will be part of your job to open Mr. Ford's mail."[57]

Financial acumen aside, Henry Ford established a broader reputation as production figures rose and the Model N emerged as one of the most popular motorized vehicles in the United States. Coming out as an industrial debutante on the national stage, he publicized himself and his company with an article in *Harper's Weekly* on March 16, 1907, proudly explaining his company's development of new kinds of steel for Ford cars and asserting the growing primacy of the automobile industry in the United States. "American methods of manufacture and American workmanship, both of the hand and the machine, are superior to those of older countries—many hoary superstitions and beliefs to the contrary notwithstanding," Ford declared. "European makers are studying American methods and importing American automatic machinery as fast as they can get it." Unquestionably, the booming production and escalating sales figures from Piquette Avenue fueled this optimistic statement.[58]

The *Harper's Weekly* piece marked a stage in Henry Ford's life. The first five years of his company, he said years later, constituted "an experimenting period," defined by steady movement toward producing an automobile for the American people and financial restraint. "We sold for cash, we did not borrow money, and we sold directly to the purchaser. We had no bad debts and we kept within ourselves on every move," he observed. Ford's own energy and vision, however, clearly provided the driving force during this formative era. Charles Sorensen, who joined the company in 1905 and quickly rose into the ranks of management, related the story of a chat with Ford after a meeting regarding the start-up for Model N production. Couzens had just warned that escalating production costs were outpacing profits and severe financial difficulties lay ahead. Obviously upset, Ford confessed despair about his ability to build an inexpensive car that working-men could afford to buy. A sympathetic Sorensen offered to help in any way he could, and this reaction seemed to galvanize his boss.

> He replied immediately, "Charlie, I'm going to do that job" . . . and he slapped me on the back. He left me with a little casual remark that, "You go on, Charlie, with what you were going to do. I'm going to see that this job is finally accomplished. *I'm* determined to do it and nobody, Couzens or anybody else, is going to stop me on it."

Sorensen, who became a major figure in the company, noted decades later, "To this day, this conversation has always remained very firmly in my mind.

I always consider it as the real turning point in the Ford Motor Company's future."[59]

This episode, as Sorensen sensed, symbolized a new stage in the journey of Henry Ford and his company. By 1908, he had clarified his vision of the automobile he wanted to make and consolidated a structure for realizing it. Sooner than anyone could imagine, his dream of a low-cost car for the people would burst through all existing market restraints and expand his operation on a heroic scale. In so doing, Ford would create a new world.

Part Two

The Miracle Maker

Seven

Consumer

They were as common as horseflies and as American as apple pie. First announced in the autumn of 1908, these modest automobiles appeared for sale early the following year. Pouring out of the Ford Motor Company's Detroit factory, they reached millions of consumers among the nation's middle and working classes. Eventually, some fifteen million of these vehicles would be manufactured, and by 1920 they constituted almost half of the cars on the country roads and city streets of the United States. They were given nicknames—"tin lizzies," "flivvers," "rattlers," "Little Henrys," "mechanical cockroaches"—and for millions of Americans they became like members of the family, by turns annoying with their unruly temperaments and endearing with their loyal service. They made Henry Ford a household name and granted his company iconic status. For most Americans in the early twentieth century, the Model T was the vehicle that transported them, literally, into the modern age.

The Model T was the culmination of Henry Ford's long-standing determination to produce a light, sturdy, inexpensive car for the American people. During the first five years of the Ford Motor Company's existence, he had turned out several models, especially the Model N, that aimed at this goal. But none fully met the standard. Beginning in 1909, however, Ford presented the new, affordable, durable Model T as a truly "universal car," and citizens of modest means purchased it in unprecedented numbers. More than any other single development, it put America on wheels in the early twentieth century.

The car culture created by the Model T would change forever how ordinary Americans led their daily lives. "Automobility," as one observer has defined the multifaceted impact of the car, became the backbone of a new society and economy in the early twentieth century. Within fifteen years of the Model T's appearance, car manufacturing had emerged as the leading

American industry in terms of value. In turn, this enterprise became the lifeblood of the petroleum industry and a leading customer for a variety of enterprises: steel, rubber, glass, lacquers. The automobile inspired street and road construction all over the country, stimulated suburban real-estate development, and nourished the growth of new service businesses such as gas stations, tourism, and roadside lodging. This vehicle moved Americans from home to job, from work to play, and tightened connections among regions, between urban areas and the countryside. By the 1920s, as Robert and Helen Lynd noted in *Middletown*, their sociological study of Muncie, Indiana, the purchase of automobiles on the installment plan had made consumer credit a key part of everyday life. According to the Lynds, "Ownership of an automobile has now reached the point of being an accepted essential of normal living." Only a few years later, the President's Research Committee on Social Trends offered a simple conclusion about the American love affair with the car: "The automobile has become a dominant influence in the life of the individual and he, in a very real sense, has become dependent on it."[1]

Yet Ford's Model T, for all of its practical impact, represented something even larger and more far-reaching: a new vision of the good life in America. As Henry Ford made clear both in his statements and in his company's advertising, this "universal car" was intended to spearhead a new era of consumer prosperity. By the early 1900s, many Americans believed that the enjoyment of material goods brought unprecedented social harmony and personal fulfillment. And as the ability to consume became the essence of Americanism, ownership of an automobile became the quintessence of consumption. In the hands of Ford and his associates, the Model T appeared as the most common symbol of a new age of material comfort.

Thus Henry Ford, the farmer's son from Michigan, emerged as the major architect of a new value system in modern America. Though we are accustomed to think of this automaker as a pioneer of production, it was, in fact, his vision of a consumer utopia that underlaid the quest for a universal automobile. With his new car for the people, Ford certainly changed how his fellow citizens lived. But, even more significantly, he changed how they thought about what was important.

Henry Ford liked to tell a story about how he stumbled across the lightweight material that became the basis for the Model T. While attending an automobile race at Palm Beach in 1905, he witnessed a crash wherein a

French race car was wrecked. After the race ended, he walked out to the site of the pileup. As he recalled, "I picked up a little valve strip stem. It was very light and very strong. I asked what it was made of. Nobody knew. I gave the stem to my assistant. 'Find out all about this,' I told him. 'That is the kind of material we ought to have in our cars.' " When it was discovered to be a special kind of steel containing vanadium, Ford located an Englishman who could make this material commercially and found a small steel company in Canton, Ohio, that could run extra-hot furnaces, at three thousand degrees Fahrenheit (the temperature required for normal steel production was twenty-seven hundred), to manufacture it. Ford then authorized a series of tests that led to the use of vanadium steel in half the car's components.[2]

This tale, like many others Ford liked to tell, was probably exaggerated in its dramatic details. The centrality of vanadium steel to his manufacturing project, however, was not magnified in the least. This material provided the final, crucial piece of the production puzzle of how to construct a "universal car" that would combine light weight, durability, and a low price tag to appeal to a mass audience of consumers. "The vanadium steel disposed of much of the weight," Ford explained years later. "The other requisites of a universal car I had already worked out and many of them were in practice." This list was imposing in its demanding simplicity—quality materials, low price tag, uncomplicated mechanical operation, sufficient power, reliability, adequate control, inexpensive operating costs—and it found a focus in a new car model.[3]

The first sign of Ford's new project came in late 1906. One morning he asked Charles Sorensen, supervisor of the pattern department and assistant production manager at the Piquette Avenue factory, to come along as they walked up to the north end of the third floor, which had a small space unoccupied by machinery or workmen. "Charlie, I'd like to have a room built in right here," Ford said. "You put up a wall around this and put a door in big enough to run a car in and out and get a good lock on this door. . . . We're going to start a completely new job." A short time later, Ford corralled Joseph Galamb, the company's chief design engineer, and told him to install a design board and a blackboard in this special room. He issued a final directive: the room was to be off-limits to everyone except Sorensen, Galamb, and their key assistants.[4]

In 1907, the small group took its first steps toward bringing to life Henry Ford's dream of a universal car. Design work on various components—the engine, transmission, chassis, suspension, body—moved along briskly as Galamb, along with his assistant, Eugene Farkas, put in long hours in the experimental room. Ford, however, stood at the center of the process. According to Galamb's description, he and Farkas would draw designs on the blackboard while their boss observed intently from a special seat:

> Mr. Ford wanted to get a look at everything where he could see from his big rocking chair. He had a rocking chair in there of his mother's. He brought it up for good luck. The chair was a good, comfortable rocking chair and he would sit in it for hours studying the blackboard to see what we were doing and talking to us. He would give instructions when we were drawing on the black-board. . . . He was right in there changing things that he didn't like. He followed everybody closely.[5]

Once designs had been refined and approved by Ford, Sorensen stepped in. Because blueprints were never Ford's strong suit (he preferred the finite to the abstract), he demanded a physical model of the part or component at hand so he could see it, touch it, evaluate it. "Everything they were designing, I would make a model of it and then Mr. Ford would look it over," Sorensen recalled. The group would spend hours whittling away at the model, calculating its strength, efficiency, and efficacy before finally approving a final design. According to Sorensen, amid this painstaking process of piecing together the right parts for the universal car, Ford's enthusiasm grew steadily. "Almost daily I would hear the same comments from him," the production supervisor related. " 'Charlie, we are on the right track here. We're going to get a car now that we can make in great volume and get the price way down.' "[6]

For months, Ford, Galamb, and Farkas worked late into the evening, altering and improving their designs. Then development moved into another stage when the small experimental room gained a milling machine, drill press, and lathe. Parts for the new car's chassis were machined, engine components cast outside were assembled, and everything was examined, tested, and modified. Once again, Ford dominated the proceedings. "Mr. Ford spent a lot of time in that department. He was in there every day," reported the mechanic Charles J. Smith. "Our job was to get the advance designs, the ideas that Mr. Ford and others would bring in to us, and actually put them together and test them. We would machine them all up, even get the castings and everything, and take them and build them in a car, and take the car out and test it."[7]

As this process of brainstorming, experimentation, and testing unfolded, the centrality of vanadium steel for Ford's universal car became evident. "Mr. Ford was always for a light car because it could cut rings around the big cars," John Wandersee explained, so he demanded that the new Model T be strong and durable in construction, yet lightweight. Vanadium steel proved ideal for this task. The material became essential for the new prototype, although its adoption came about rather differently from the fanciful, dramatic tale of the Palm Beach race often told by Ford.[8]

The actual story was more mundane. Information, some of it published, had been circulating among engineers for several years about a new kind of heat-treated steel incorporating vanadium; this malleable alloy added tensile strength. When J. Kent Smith, a noted English metallurgist and pioneer in making this material, came to Detroit in 1906, he met with Ford and Harold Wills, and demonstrated the alloy's unique qualities. "Immediately Mr. Ford sensed the great value of this for use in the motor car," Charles Sorensen noted. "After the first time he saw Mr. Smith, he said to me, 'Charlie, this means an entirely new design requirement. We can get a better and lighter and cheaper car as a result of it.' "[9]

Wills, the company's chief engineer, was particularly enthusiastic about the possibilities of vanadium steel alloy. He began to oversee its testing, first at various steel mills outside Detroit and then at a new laboratory set up in the Piquette Avenue plant. He planned on hiring a college-trained metallurgist to head the project, but Ford insisted on appointing Wandersee, who had first come to the company as a floor sweeper and then rose through the ranks to become a mechanic and then an engineer. Ford had little use for university graduates, preferring men who proved their value on the basis of talent and achievement. So Wandersee spent several months in training at the United Alloy Steel Laboratory, learned how to manage a lab, and became the company's expert on metallurgy and vanadium steel.[10]

Ford sang the praises of the new steel alloy in his 1907 *Harper's Weekly* article. He claimed that vanadium "imparts qualities to steel which are little less than magical," creating "a metal of such toughness and tenacity as would successfully resist the ravages of vibration and fatigue." He claimed that with vanadium steel "the strength of an automobile axle or a crankshaft may be doubled without increasing the dimensions or weight, and the working capacity and shock-resisting qualities of that member in actual usage multiplied many times." These characteristics were vital to Ford's goal of increased strength and light weight.[11]

With the finalization of the vanadium-steel components, the time arrived for the last step in the development process: road tests. When new parts were added to the Model T, it was taken out for examination under road conditions. Then the handmade model was returned to the development room at the Piquette Avenue factory, torn down, inspected for wear in engine and body parts, and reassembled for more tests. Ford closely monitored the proceedings. His office stood next to the experimental room, and he spent hours every day checking on test results and inquiring about specific achievements and problems. On numerous occasions, he tested the Model T prototype himself. "He went out with us many a time," related one of the mechanics on the team. "Mr. Ford wouldn't let anything go out of the shop unless he was satisfied that it was nearly perfect as you could make it. He wanted it right."[12]

After nearly two years of development and testing, the car that emerged from the brain of Henry Ford and the hands of his engineers met the stringent requirements of his "universal car." The Model T was a utilitarian, inexpensive, lightweight, and durable automobile that offered many attractive features to the buyer. Boxy in its basic design, this open-top vehicle came in one color—Brewster green in the early years, and then black after 1914—and offered a tonneau at extra cost. Weighing in at only twelve hundred pounds, it was propelled by a four-cylinder, 20-horsepower engine that was crank-started. The car could achieve a maximum speed of forty-five miles per hour on a smooth, straight road. Its steering wheel and controls were located on the left side instead of the right, a logical place for them in a country where vehicles drove on the right side of the road (this innovation was adopted by all carmakers within a few years). The engine, transmission, flywheel, and universal joint were all enclosed within one case, which was lubricated by a splash-and-gravity oil system. Unlike earlier automobiles, the Model T featured an engine whose four cylinders were not cast separately but drilled into a solid block covered by a single, detachable cylinder head. A three-point suspension system gave the car great flexibility, and a high clearance offered much forgiveness in navigating rough, rutted American roads.

The Model T presented three pedals to the driver—one for forward motion, one for reverse motion, and a brake. A multiuse hand lever served many functions—releasing the clutch in one position, putting the car into high speed in another, and serving as an emergency brake when pulled completely back. The unique planetary transmission was a vast improvement over earlier systems for gear shifting; an ingenious magneto was incorporated into the flywheel to supply current for the ignition and the lights. The car was simplicity itself in terms of its basic systems, and any driver handy with a screwdriver, pair of pliers, wrench set, and some wire could repair most problems and get the car up and running in the event of breakdown. Perhaps best of all, the modest price for the Model T—the earliest model sold for $850, and the price fell steadily in succeeding years—made it affordable for many consumers.

Aside from its technical features and attractive price, one habit of the Model T caused it to appear almost lifelike to many of its owners. When the car was crank-started, its planetary transmission created a subtle forward movement that warmed many a heart. In the sentimental words of one owner:

> . . . there was always, in the Model T, a certain dull rapport between engine and wheels, and even when the car was in a state known as neutral, it trembled with a deep imperative and tended to inch forward. There was never a moment when the bands were not faintly egging the machine on. . . . Often, if the emergency brake hadn't been pulled all the way back, the car advanced on you the instant the first explosion occurred and you would hold it back by leaning your weight against it. I can still feel my old Ford nuzzling me at the curb, as though looking for an apple in my pocket.[13]

Once the prototype was approved by Ford, the Model T went into production, late in 1908. P. E. Martin and his assistant, Charles Sorensen, masterminded a reorganization of the Piquette Avenue plant and its production process as "operation sheets" were prepared, machine requirements were calculated, new equipment was purchased, new tools were designed, and floor layout was improved. Perhaps most important, a stock-control department was established to regulate the flow of parts and maintain steady production. The company hired new workers, till by mid-1909 it employed some twenty-two hundred individuals, a fourfold increase over the previous year. In other words, the "universal car" forced a swift systemization of the Ford Motor Company. As Sorensen later noted, "The Model T just drove us into this planning so that by 1909 we realized what it meant to have an organization."[14]

As production of the new automobile began, in late 1908, Ford took to the factory floor to prod and inspire his workers. Kidding with the men, he would shake his head in mock discouragement and declare, "I wonder if we'll get up to number ten." Company accountant George Brown, many years later, recalled witnessing Ford's performances:

> He'd be out there in the factory, watching them and kidding them and telling stories. God! He could get anything out of the men because he just talked and would tell them stories. He'd never say, "I want this done!" He'd say, "I wonder if we can do it. I wonder." Well, the men would just break their necks to see if they could do

it. . . . Every time he'd meet somebody, he'd give him a kick in the
pants or a punch between the shoulders. He was just like a kid with
a new toy.

Ford's efforts were rewarded handsomely. From October 1908 to September 1909, the company manufactured 10,660 cars, the great majority of them Model T's, a total that eclipsed the sixty-four hundred of the year before.[15]

When advertisements for the Model T first appeared, in the fall of 1908, and brochures on the new car went out to Ford dealers, a bonanza of sales began. Within a few months, the Piquette Avenue factory had been overwhelmed, and on May 1, 1909, the company was forced to declare, "We will not be able to take any further orders for any type of delivery until after August 1st." This explosion of consumer approval indicated that a connection between Ford and his audience had been established, but its nature was not immediately apparent. What was Henry Ford really aiming for with his "universal car"? And why did ordinary citizens respond with such enthusiasm? The answers to such questions could be found in the social underpinnings of the Model T, which were constructed not of vanadium steel but of the values and aspirations of many Americans in the early twentieth century.[16]

In 1928, on the twentieth anniversary of the launching of the car that made him famous, Henry Ford created controversy over his comments during an interview with the Associated Press. When asked for his advice about how to become successful in modern America, he said that traditional injunctions to work hard and save your money—such advice had been a staple of American success writers from Benjamin Franklin to Horatio Alger—were wrong. He insisted that, though hard labor was still a good idea, thrift was fruitless. "No successful boy ever saved any money," Ford declared. "They spent it as fast as they could for things to improve themselves." Almost immediately, an uproar ensued over Henry Ford's "gospel of spending," as one publication termed it.

Denunciations of his position appeared immediately. The Detroit *Free Press* sniffed, "We are old-fashioned enough to believe that . . . the philosophy of Poor Richard is more salutary than that attributed to Mr. Ford." Chicago's *Journal of Commerce* insisted that, even if exceptional individuals might prosper from Ford's advice, saving was "the only hope for people of mediocre ability." It added pointedly, "For all men, exercise in self-denial is a wholesome experience."

Significantly, however, the dissenters were overwhelmed by publications that lined up in support of Ford's injunction to spend. The New York *Herald Tribune* praised his intelligent position and opined that youth needed to enjoy life because fun was worth "a treasure far greater than any fortune which could be built by counting pennies and dimes." Another publication lauded Ford for raising the question of "how money may be spent wisely, and that is quite as much a test of success as earning it." The Asheville, North Carolina, *Citizen* supported him for downplaying the miserly aspects of business and stressing its "adventurous" qualities. "He who nurses the nickels misses the knockouts," declared this paper. "He probably will have enough to live on, but no sculptor will get a fee for making a statue of him when he is dead. The world belongs to the audacious."[17]

Ford's "gospel of spending," in fact, had captured a new sensibility in turn-of-the-century America. Since the 1890s, many citizens had been endorsing an ethos of consumption, pleasure, and self-fulfillment. The Model T, a universal car for the people, became an influential vehicle for spreading the consumer gospel throughout modern America.

As this new, lightweight car burst into the American market, Ford consistently defined its appeal in consumer terms. To be sure, he delighted in praising the Model T's utilitarian features, but the pleasure and contentment to be derived from this vehicle also played prominently in his assessments. His enticing descriptions of the universal car prompted newspaper headlines informing readers that "Henry Ford Says Comfort His Aim." His public announcement of the Model T was awash in the rhetoric of leisure and enjoyment, emphasizing his vision of the vehicle not as a luxury item for the elite but as a pleasurable necessity for the masses.

> I will build a motor car for the great multitude. It will be large enough for the family but small enough for the individual to run and care for. It will be constructed of the best material, by the best men to be hired, after the simplest designs that modern engineering can devise. But it will be so low in price that no man making a good salary will be unable to own one—and enjoy with his family the blessing of hours of pleasure in God's great open spaces.[18]

Defining the motorcar as a necessity "that would meet the wants of the multitude," Ford linked his vehicle to a larger vision of contentment through consumption. In *My Life and Work*, he dismissed some business-

men's fears of overproduction and market saturation with a utopian vision of
consumer abundance:

> We believe it is possible some day to reach the point where all
> goods are produced so cheaply and in such quantities that overpro-
> duction can be a reality. But as far as we are concerned, we do not
> look forward to that condition with fear—we look forward to it
> with great satisfaction. . . . Our fear is that this condition will be too
> long postponed.

A few years later, in 1926, Ford used a second autobiographical volume,
Today and Tomorrow, to point out that America's consumer values had created among its citizens a happy problem of how to spend leisure time. The
eight-hour day and five-day workweek was creating all of the manpower
production required by the nation's industry. "What is really bothering
most people is how to put in their spare time," Ford observed. "That used to
bother only what was called the 'leisure class.' "[19]

Ford's notions of consumer prosperity caught the crest of a wave of historical change sweeping over early-twentieth-century America. Whereas
citizens in the Victorian nineteenth century had lived by a creed of hard
work, self-control, and delayed gratification, shifting socioeconomic reali-
ties were pushing forward leisure, material abundance, and emotional self-
fulfillment. As one historian has described, from the 1890s on American
society became "preoccupied with consumption, with comfort and bodily
well-being, with luxury, spending, and acquisition. . . . Different kinds of
people and groups—cultural and non-economic, religious and political—
. . . worked together to create what merchant John Wanamaker called the
'land of desire.' . . . Merchants cooperated with educators, social reformers,
politicians, artists, and religious leaders to bring into existence the new
economy and culture."[20]

Henry Ford, perhaps more than any other American industrialist and
businessman of the early twentieth century, grasped the essence of this cultural shift. He instinctively appreciated the allure of consumer abundance;
in fact, he shared the dream. Though far too busy building Ford Motor
Company to articulate a coherent philosophy before 1920, he eventually
formulated his thoughts into a basic creed stressing consumer demand, people's desires, and the critical importance of leisure. He dropped nuggets of
advice at every opportunity. In an *American Magazine* interview with Bruce
Barton, a journalist who would become one of the great boosters of American consumerism as a popular success writer and advertising man, Ford
insisted that satisfying the American desires for material goods lay at the

heart of modern commercial life. "Well, say, we're creating new wants in folks right along, aren't we? And we no sooner get those wants satisfied in one class of society than another class bobs up to present its needs and demands," Ford declared. "The wants keep right on increasing, and the more wants the more business, isn't that so?"[21]

Ford infused his published writings and interviews with aphorisms about how the importance of business began with the consumer:

> Ordinarily, business is conceived as starting with a manufacturing process and ending with a consumer. . . .
>
> But what business ever started with the manufacturer and ended with the consumer? Where does the money to make the wheels go around come from? From the consumer, of course. And success in manufacture is based solely on an ability to serve that consumer to his liking. . . .
>
> We start with the consumer, work back through the design, and finally arrive at manufacturing. The manufacturing becomes a means to the end of service.
>
> The question behind manufacturing is not: "How can I best serve the salesman?" It is: "How can I best serve the consumer?" If you find the answer to the second question, then it is quite inevitable that you will also find the answer to the first question.[22]

In a 1926 article in the magazine *The World's Work*, he summarized his thinking about the new culture of consumption. The old-fashioned denigration of leisure as either wasted time or a privilege of wealth, Ford said, must be abandoned once and for all. Leisure was neither idleness or shiftlessness, but an activity with "positive industrial value . . . because it increases consumption." The smart businessman supported higher wages and shorter work hours, because "people who have more leisure must have more clothes. They must have a greater variety of food. They must have more transportation facilities. They naturally must have more service of various kinds." Demand created jobs and profits because "the people who consume the bulk of goods are the people who make them. That is a fact we must never forget—that is the secret of our prosperity." Ford viewed leisure as the lifeblood of modern consumer capitalism, coursing through the commercial arteries of the United States carrying the nourishment of desired goods and services and prompting people to buy.

Ford's Model T was the final piece of the puzzle. The automobile, he recognized, provided the linchpin in this new system of leisure, consumption, and prosperity. It served as a commodity itself, of course, but it did much more.

> ... the automobile, by enabling people to get about quickly and easily, gives them a chance to find out what is going on in the world—which leads them to a larger life that requires more food, more and better goods, more books, more music, more of everything.[23]

Even if not portrayed fully and colorfully until some years later, an early version of Ford's consumer vision had been in place since the turn of the century and provided the conceptual foundation upon which the Model T was built. Americans grew used to thinking of Henry Ford as a pioneer of mass production because of the massive building and distribution of his universal car, but it was his endorsement of consumer abundance for the ordinary citizen that provided the impetus for the process. The Model T, he understood at some basic level, was a revolutionary event in the evolution of a modern consumer consciousness. "Nothing could be more splendid than a world in which everybody has all that he wants," Ford once declared. This consumer ethos, the industrialist realized more clearly than anyone, was in the air of early-twentieth-century America. But, practically speaking, it usually came riding into the cities, villages, and farms of the United States in the front seat of Ford's flivver.[24]

As modern consumer society gradually took shape in the early twentieth century, one activity emerged above all others to bind together notions of business profit, leisure activity, prosperity, and personal happiness. Advertising—a long-standing endeavor in American business, dating back to the early republic—was transformed into a kind of commercial religion in the booming new consumer economy. It offered social redemption through the partaking of material goods. Like other business enterprises, the Ford Motor Company embraced this gospel and won converts by means of an inspiring advertising vision of prosperity, abundance, and self-fulfillment. These qualities were built into the Model T as surely as its vanadium-steel axles, planetary transmission, and recalcitrant cranking mechanism.

Modern advertising, as historians have pointed out in recent years, shifted significantly around the beginning of the twentieth century. Traditional advertisements in newspapers, magazines, and flyers had employed a practical palette of durability, quality, and usefulness to paint attractive portraits of commercial goods. By the early 1900s, however, advertisers had begun using brighter cultural colors to portray commercial goods as conveyors of emotional happiness, personal desire, and private satisfactions. Advertising increasingly appeared as a kind of commercial therapy that promised varieties of self-fulfillment: fantasies of play and fun, possibilities of romance, excursions into progress and modernity, pathways to increased social status. The Ford Motor Company's efforts on behalf of the Model T reflected this transition in advertising from meeting practical needs to fulfilling desires.[25]

The Ford advertising operation had accelerated in 1907, as the Model N was going out to the public, when the company hired LeRoy Pelletier as its first advertising manager. *Motor World* described this colorful figure as "a brilliant, plausible, rapid-fire conversationalist" and "a clever writer" who, "in the art of 'putting them over,' has few peers. Even the great Barnum himself would have found him a valuable assistant." Before coming to Ford, Pelletier had served as an advance man for a circus, a correspondent for the New York *Times* in the Klondike, the owner of a real-estate firm, and the developer of an air-cooled automobile. He affected a theatrical appearance, with a great bushy head of hair and long, flowing black ties, and impressed all who encountered him with his enormous energy and winsome style. Specializing in light, glowing, imaginative copy, he put together the major ad campaign for the unveiling of the Model N in New York City. This dynamic adman formulated the first great advertising slogan for the company— "Watch the Fords Go By"—and emblazoned it in unforgettable style on a giant, first-of-its-kind sign set atop the Detroit Opera House. Made in the shape of the Model N, it featured turning wheels, burning headlights, and the new slogan in blinking lights below the giant automobile. By early 1908, however, Pelletier had left the company to pursue other business opportunities.[26]

As the Model T prepared to go on the market, Ford advertising efforts escalated. With Pelletier's departure, ad policy was shaped by several individuals, including H. B. Harper, Robert Walsh, and sales manager Norval Hawkins. The company started a monthly in-house publication in April 1908, the *Ford Times*, and used it to inspire promotional efforts among the growing network of Ford dealers and salesmen. Articles entitled "Does Advertising Pay?," "Living Advertising," and "Suggestions for Advertising" spurred dealers to greater publicity campaigns and promised to supply them with "good-selling advertising copy and electrotypes or cut-outs of the cars." Ford also launched its own national publicity campaign in 1909 with a flurry of ads in trade journals, newspapers, magazines, and special pamphlets.[27]

Ford advertising employed current tricks of the trade by deploying slogans, logos, and images. "Watch the Fords Go By" appeared constantly, of course, as did the phrase "The Universal Car." The company created its famous trademark of "the winged pyramid"—a pyramid shape with wings sprouting from each side, with "Ford" emblazoned across the middle and "The Universal Car" in smaller letters beneath it—to adorn its ads as well as the show windows of most Ford dealers. Company boilerplate explained this imagery from ancient Egypt: "The pyramid suggests strength, permanency, stability—the conventionalized Sacred Ibis wings typify lightness, grace, speed. And on the winged pyramid is our advertising endeavor centered." Then there was the flowing script of *Ford* that appeared not only in advertisements but on the radiator fronts of the Model T itself. Thus, in the years after 1909, an array of symbols clearly established Ford's new car in the mind of the average consumer. As a 1912 ad declared, "You can't get beyond the domain of 'The Winged Pyramid.' "[28]

The company and its dealers, embracing the philosophy that the best kind of advertising is free, did not shy away from headline-grabbing stunts and promotions. Ford distributors utilized hot-air balloons with the name of their business and "Ford Model T Cars" splashed in large letters across the side, which sailed around their towns attracting enormous amounts of attention. Many dealers offered demonstrations of stair-climbing. Max Gottberg of Columbus, Nebraska, for example, took one of his Model T's to the town's YMCA building, gathered a crowd, and proceeded to drive up the stone steps to show its ability to maneuver up steep, rough grades. The *Ford Times*, in a pictorial write-up, urged all its dealers to duplicate this feat for its publicity value.[29]

Perhaps the best example of Model T publicity came in the summer of 1909 with the great Transcontinental Race from New York to Seattle. Set up as part of a publicity campaign for the Alaska-Yukon-Pacific Exposition held in Seattle that year, this endurance race appeared a heaven-sent advertising opportunity for the company and its new car. The race was scheduled to begin in New York City, proceed through St. Louis, and conclude in Seattle. Henry Ford immediately issued a challenge to all other automakers, offering to match the Model T against any of their models for "any sum of money that acceptants may suggest as a suitable purse."

The race began on June 1, with two Model T's among the field of six. The Fords pulled into a quick lead in an uneventful first stage that brought them to St. Louis on June 5. In the Western portion of the race, however, problems mounted. Torrential rains and hailstorms bogged the drivers down in mud and washed-out roads; mountainous areas in the Rockies, with roads that were little more than goat paths, caused broken wheels and bent

axles. Bad maps and lack of dependable gas and oil sources did not help matters. After a series of adventures that included skidding down a fourteen-
foot embankment into a stream, suffering a fire started by a careless
bystander who struck a match on the side of the gas tank, getting lost so
completely that the car had to travel eight miles on railroad ties and dash
through a mountain tunnel to get back on track, and sinking through the
crust of a four-foot snowdrift in a mountain pass and being dug out by a railroad crew with shovels, Ford No. 2 dashed into Seattle the winner on June
22. A crowd of two hundred thousand, including Henry Ford, who had traveled west for the occasion, were there to cheer the Model T home. It had
completed the run in twenty-two days and fifty-five minutes. Another car,
the Shawmut, arrived seventeen hours later, closely followed by Ford No. 1.
The other entries failed to complete the race.[30]

The Transcontinental Race generated tremendous publicity. The Ford
Motor Company, boasting two out of the top three finishers, benefited from
headlines and dramatic photos of the grime-covered victors that appeared in
newspapers all over the country. Company advertising took full advantage
of the race. During the contest, it urged dealers to publicize their Model T's
by painting a large map of the United States on the salesroom window,
marking out the route and all checkpoints, and then moving small car icons
along as telegrams announced progress of the Ford entries. This "has never
failed to keep an interested crowd before the window," the company told its
dealers. After the victory in Seattle, Ford launched an advertising blitz in
newspapers that announced in giant letters, "FORD—WINNER OF THE
O. to O. CONTEST." The text noted, "The important consideration for
automobile buyers is that the winning car was a standard stock car, an exact
duplicate of the regular Model T. . . . Nothing special, nothing better than
regular, nothing different from what any buyer gets." Employing David-
and-Goliath imagery, ads argued that the great race demonstrated the superiority of the lightweight Model T over its much heavier opponents. "The
little fellows led the way . . . [and] practically ran away from their powerful
adversaries," they noted.[31]

Beyond such special events and attention-grabbing stunts, however, the
company's steady flow of advertisements offered an intriguing mix of messages. On the one hand, these early ads featured traditional themes that
trumpeted the Model T's utilitarian virtues. Typically, buyers were told that
"the mechanical perfection, strength, light weight, and simplicity of the
Ford car make it the people's utility. And they average only about two cents
a mile to operate and maintain." The Model T's low price and dependabil-
ity also generated much ad copy. A 1909 advertising catalogue displayed
vanadium steel in key components providing strength and lightness; the

best materials for tires and castings; dependable planetary transmission and rugged three-point suspension; sophisticated lubrication and cooling systems; and overall, as the pamphlet stated at the bottom of every other page, "High Priced Quality in a Low Priced Car."[32]

Many early Ford advertisements for the Model T, however, stressed a subtle, seductive new consumer vision. Visual and verbal images invoked not durability or performance but the pleasure, self-fulfillment, happiness, leisure, and romance likely to be gained. In 1908, a Model T ad described the vehicle as "a roomy, commodious, comfortable family car that looks good, and is as good as it looks." Others underscored its role in democratizing leisure. "If there were no Fords, automobiling would be like yachting—the sport of rich men," declared one ad, but this vehicle "brought the price down within reason—and the easy reach of the many." As another ad noted succinctly, "It's a universal servant because it serves everybody. It's a universal luxury because it gives pleasure to everybody."[33]

Explicit messages of pleasure and comfort pushed to the fore in many Model T ads. How much better to step into this vehicle and "drive, warm and dry," than "to get wet and cold, walking to and waiting for the trolley car, and then stand up in the crowded car on the wet floor while the cold breezes chase the dangerous chills up and down your back every time the door opens." Such promises of physical comfort were a prologue for assurances of emotional enjoyment. "The family car of pleasure," one ad described the Model T; another assured that the vehicle met "the requirements of pleasure" for men of business, who would "find this car a dignified appearing and entirely satisfactory assistance in the fulfillment of their engagements, both business and social." Ford ads followed the pleasure trail into the realm of romance. A 1911 promotional pamphlet for the Model T featured a gentleman assisting a fashionably dressed young woman out of the car above these enticing words: "A very pretty girl and a charming scene from California." A 1910 effort depicted an eager, grinning young man, straw hat tilted back, sitting in the back seat of a Model T with *two* attractive females. The irreverent caption made the possibilities clear: "He loves me—he loves me not—he loves me—he loves me not—Oh pshaw, we haven't got the time to finish this. Look at the picture and decide for yourself."[34]

Many of the most vibrant Ford ads, however, argued that the Model T offered to ordinary citizens the prospect of new and exciting experiences through greater mobility. "No Ford owner ever doubts the ability of his car to go wherever he desires to travel," the text of one ad informed consumers rather breathlessly. "He tours in it, travels in it, hunts in it, climbs mountains and crosses deserts." The automobile, according to a strategy urged upon all Ford dealers in *Ford Times*, provided a unique way to travel and enjoy American historic sites. A 1913 ad underscored the enriching possibilities of tourism. "Every day is 'Independence Day' to him who owns a Ford," it declared. "Liberty from confinement to a narrowing environment—and that at small cost—is one of the many boons which the sturdy, powerful Ford has brought to untold thousands. Why not to you?"[35]

The liberation theme found a special focus with regard to American women. In a pamphlet entitled *The Woman and the Ford* (1912), the company contended that the Model T's easy mode of operation, lack of expense ("Trust women to find the bargains"), uncomplicated mechanical structure, and cleanliness ("no grease or dirt to soil dainty gowns") made it "a woman's car." Moreover, its lightweight durability offered special opportunities to roam the countryside and visit interesting sites, an important desire among vigorous, modern women who "crave exercise and excitement, who long for relief from the monotony of social and household duties." In fact, escape from Victorian restraints was the pamphlet's centerpiece. The opening passage of *The Woman and the Ford* punched the message home:

> It's woman's day.... She shares the responsibilities—and demands the opportunities and pleasures of the new order. No longer a "shut in," she reaches for an ever wider sphere of action— that she may be more the woman.
>
> And in this happy change the automobile is playing no small part. It has broadened her horizon—increased her pleasures— given new vigor to her body—made neighbors of far away friends— and multiplied tremendously her range of activity. It is a real weapon in the changing order.[36]

The advertising appeal to the new consumer ethos of leisure, status, and emotional self-fulfillment was summarized in the 1910 *Ford Times*. Aimed at dealers all over the country, an article entitled "Why Doesn't More Auto Copy Talk My Language?" noted many car ads concentrated on a vehicle's features, such as toughness, speed on a straightaway, climbing ability on hills, mechanical innovations, and maintenance costs. This emphasis missed the special ability of the automobile to bestow status, emotional satisfaction, and invigorating new experiences. The shrewd Ford dealer learned this lesson: "The time is now come for automobiles to be advertised as a necessity for one's health and comfort, and the pleasure which they give."[37]

As the company deployed advertising to present an image of the Model T as a quintessential consumer item, no one played a more crucial role than a charismatic, silver-tongued salesman who emerged as an influential figure in 1908. Ford's universal car was in the last stages of development, standing poised to enter the market, and this young man positioned himself at the center of things. His energetic activities in promotion, sales, and advertising proved essential to the vehicle's popularity. In his skillful promotion of the Model T, he was a pioneer in the creation of a new consumer America.

In 1908, *Ford Times* carried a pithy article entitled "The Man Who Does Things." Aimed at employees in the company, it defined the type of person whom every business sought to hire: someone who took the initiative, spent as many hours as necessary to complete a task, sought to advance the interests of the organization, was absorbed in his work, and valued results. He also radiated confidence. "There is usually a settled, well-defined air of assured success in his manner and movements," the essay noted. The message of this tract was predictable to anyone who knew the author, a dynamic figure who had burst into the Ford company only a few months earlier and transformed its marketing efforts. Perhaps more than anyone else, Norval A. Hawkins presented the Model T to the American consumer as the harbinger of a new age.[38]

Born in Ypsilanti, Michigan in 1867, Hawkins had grown up with a youthful interest in business which led to a position with a small kerosene company when he moved to Detroit in 1888. Within a few years, he joined the Detroit office of Standard Oil as an assistant cashier, and his exceptional talent for business soon led to a position as an accountant. Then a foolish action brought disaster. In 1894, he was convicted and sentenced to a jail term for embezzling $3,000 from Standard Oil. Convinced that the crime was an impulsive, youthful mistake—Hawkins candidly admitted the felony and apologized for it—friends in the business community assisted in getting him pardoned by the governor of Michigan in 1896, after he had served part of his prison sentence. They helped him get re-established in business, and in the late 1890s he founded the accounting firm of Hawkins, Gies, and Company. This endeavor grew steadily, and by 1904 he had an account with the new Ford Motor Company, where he impressed James Couzens with his work. Overwhelmed by the business demands of the rapidly growing company, Couzens convinced the accountant to take over its sales-and-marketing operation in November 1907. Hawkins made an immediate impact.[39]

With great energy and talent, he began revamping and rationalizing the entire marketing operation. Hawkins' new colleagues were overwhelmed. "God, that man had a wonderful set of brains! When he went there, he revolutionized the old sales division," declared one. "He just turned things topsy-turvy and everything seemed to thrive. He had something new in salesmanship." Hawkins moved quickly on a number of fronts.[40]

First, he began formulating accurate estimates of future sales, a procedure that helped Ford production managers to establish an effective schedule for turning out Model T's. He also systematized the entire business operation in terms of departmentalization, cost accounting, auditing of branch accounts, purchasing, stockpiling, and bookkeeping. The new sales manager formulated a plan to set up assembly plants outside of Detroit, a move that brought significant savings, because it was much cheaper to ship parts to a region for final assembly than several completed automobiles in a freight car. "A circle was drawn on the map around Detroit with the circumference on the points where freight rates began to affect the profits on sales, and in cities on the edge of this circle we established our assembly plants," Hawkins explained. "By 1913 we had six to ten times as many branch houses and assembly plants as other companies had."[41]

Most important, however, Hawkins revitalized Ford's sales operation throughout the United States. One observer proclaimed him to be "perhaps the greatest salesman that the world ever knew . . . original in ideas, forcible in presenting them, a perfect dynamo for work, and a man who gets the quickest execution of any man I ever knew." When starting out, Hawkins was asked where he would sell the first Model T: "I pointed to a grocery store on the opposite corner and said we could start there." He soon unveiled a dynamic agenda of expansion by authorizing Ford field representatives to draw up exhaustive "territory reports" on every town in the United States with a population of over two thousand. These reports assessed road conditions, banking facilities, local economic conditions, and the financial state and personal habits of potential Ford dealers. Hawkins used this raw information to divide the country into a patchwork of sales zones, which he steadily filled with a network of seven thousand dealers by 1913. He regularly visited dealers throughout the country and urged them to ring doorbells and contact prospective buyers. He would ask a dealer to choose five likely purchasers. "Then I would say, 'Let us, you and I, get in a car and see if we can't sell these five cars today or tomorrow and bring in some money for the fall season or the winter season.' "[42]

Hawkins' enthusiasm was matched by insights into the psychology of selling. He once explained how he would closely examine a dealer's salesroom for anything that might leave an unfavorable impression with a prospective buyer. Posters advertising tire chains were removed because they suggested the possibility of accidents; clear glass separating the salesroom from the repair garage was replaced with opaque, grilled glass so buyers would not see dilapidated cars being fixed; the stockroom was separated from the sales area, so buyers would not overhear someone buy a new carburetor with the complaint, "Yours is the worst carburetor in the world." "We didn't want anything around that might deter the buyer," Hawkins reported. "Such a thing was called a negative selling point."[43]

To help weld together the geographically scattered Ford sales force, Hawkins inaugurated *Ford Times,* as noted earlier, and filled it with items about automobile models, dealer activities, effective sales techniques, and buyer testimonials. It went out to dealers, branch managers, and prospective buyers. He personally guaranteed its focus on inspiration as well as information and instruction. A typical copy of *Ford Times* contained one of his essays exploring some aspect of salesmanship. Carrying titles such as "Can a Man Learn to Be a Salesman?," "Hard Work First," and "The Man Who Merely Fills the Position," these pieces implored the Ford employee to demonstrate "the energy, ability, and determination to stretch his job into something bigger."[44]

Hawkins' great success with the company made him a renowned figure, both in the Detroit community and in the automobile industry. His prowess as a salesman carried over into his private life, where he had a growing reputation as a fund-raiser for civic causes. In a long, laudatory article subtitled "A Modern Midas," the Detroit *Times* praised his achievements in raising money for hospitals, the Board of Commerce, and numerous charities. "Norval Hawkins can lure money from sources whence it was never lured before," the reporter noted, "and can make it do large and useful work after he has it." Henry Ford and his company's board of directors also appreciated this smooth talker with the golden touch. On October 19, 1909, they voted unanimously to award him, after not quite two years on the job, a princely bonus of $13,000 in appreciation for his efforts over the past year.[45]

Hawkins relied upon the singular appeal of the company's new automobile in igniting a sales revolution at Ford. The Model T, he believed, offered unprecedented advantages. For the salesman in the field, the Model T was easy to sell because "there was no conflict in the buyer's mind as to what to buy. There was only one thing to buy from a Ford dealer." For the consumer, not only did the car offer many attractive qualities, such as vanadium-steel components, but there was no fear that it would become obsolete or out of style. The Model T, Hawkins said repeatedly, was the special creation of Henry Ford, a courageous man with a "wonderful vision in the automotive industry," whose determination and skill had brought this special car to life.[46]

But Hawkins' spectacular success in marketing the Model T also reflected his sensitivity to a larger, transforming cultural atmosphere. He displayed an instinctive sense of the new consumer world coming to life in the early twentieth century. He understood that advertising played an important role in its operations. He demanded that Ford dealers put up signs in their communities showing the way to their establishments and encouraged them to display prominently the company's "winged pyramid" logo. He funneled publicity about Ford and the Model T to newspapers around the country. In *Ford Times*, Hawkins employed call-to-arms imagery in telling Ford dealers that advertising "is a most serious sort of business; it is arming the trade to do business in the largest possible measure; it is literally baptizing civilization with the name FORD, and the merits of Ford cars."[47]

Hawkins' understanding of the ethos of modern consumption penetrated more deeply, however. Advertising brought consumers and goods together, but what really mattered, he concluded, was the nature of that connection. He explained the psychological substance of buying and selling in *The Selling Process: A Handbook of Salesmanship Principles* (1920), a book that he wrote after a decade of spectacular success with the Model T. The first two-thirds of the text drew upon Hawkins' long experience in sales to describe basic techniques for getting the attention and holding the interest of the potential buyer. These "preparatory" and "presentation" steps, as the author termed them, involved such things as the salesman's offering a friendly, confident, sincere persona; driving home the merits of his products through sensory appeals and mental images; and shaping positive, affirmative impressions of the product in the mind of the buyer.[48]

In the last third of *The Selling Process*, however, Hawkins turned to the heart of the matter: the "convincing steps" that clinched the purchase. Here lay the matter of "Persuading and Creating Desire," as he termed it, and the shrewd salesman must realize that, ultimately, "the appeal must be made primarily to the heart instead of to the mind. A man's emotions, not his thoughts, control his Desires." "You do not sell goods, but ideas about goods," Hawkins insisted. Rational or utilitarian considerations carried but little weight in the act of buying, he explained, because people seldom reasoned their way into purchase. Instead, they usually sought to fill some kind of void in their emotional lives:

> Desire means want; and a man *wants* things, *longs* for things with his heart. He realizes a lack, and has a *heart hunger* for something to fill this lack. His mind may oppose his heart, and may hinder his heart from getting what it Desires. His mind has no *feelings*; so it cannot experience hunger. . . . The ache is in his *heart*, the place where he hungered. . . .
>
> The process of persuading and creating Desire . . . [demands

that] the salesman should work to get old *feelings* (not ideas) to move out of the prospect's heart with longing for the salesman's goods or proposition.[49]

But how does the salesman create or enhance this emotional longing? Hawkins proposed various methods. He should use "suggestion" as a subtle psychological technique to prod the buyer's imagination of future fulfillment. He should "never sell disappointment" but make sure that his product can meet the desire that is aroused. He should cultivate faith in the buyer by making him believe that the salesman is really interested in his welfare. But all such efforts, Hawkins concluded, should converge on a primary goal: "to arouse vivid images of the satisfaction the prospect would derive from using the goods that will fill a lack he feels. That is, the salesman must start imagination to working toward Desire's fulfillment."[50]

Clearly, Hawkins understood that, in America's emerging consumer culture, inspiring imagination, expressing emotion, and fulfilling desire drove the hunger for material goods. And he helped make the Model T one of the first great expressions of this new sensibility. Perhaps the best gauge of his achievement came from Charles Sorensen. This hard-nosed production manager was already on the path that would make him Henry Ford's right-hand man within a few years, and he did not bestow compliments lightly. Sorensen always believed, however, that Hawkins' efforts were at the center of the Model T's exploding popularity. In his words, Hawkins was "the greatest sales manager the company ever had and my hat is off to his natural-born genius in this line." Sorensen sensed, perhaps more than anyone but Henry Ford himself, that Norval Hawkins had pushed the Model T to the cutting edge of a consumer revolution.[51]

With the introduction of the Model T in the autumn of 1908, the Ford Motor Company leaped to the top of the automobile industry. In so doing, it also assumed a leading role in shaping America's new consumer economy and culture. As the company expanded dramatically, its guiding force, Henry Ford, demonstrated a keen awareness of his new car's cultural and social impact and the larger promises of happiness that it embodied. His devotion to the Model T and its consumer destiny was absolute and unwavering. In fact, Ford's faith in this automobile and its role quickly became the stuff of legend.

In 1912, for example, a few years after the release of the Model T, Ford returned to Detroit after an extended trip to Europe. While he was gone for

several months, the company's leading managers and engineers had con-
spired to present him with a pleasant surprise. During his absence, they
designed a successor to the Model T, which featured a longer chassis, four-
door body, windshield and top, and sleek, stylish lines. It was painted a rich
red, and plans were drawn up for its production. The hand-built prototype
was placed in an area between the business offices and the factory floor, and
it became the subject of much admiring commentary for several days. Then
Ford returned a day earlier than anticipated.

He strolled into the office area, glanced at some paperwork, and then
noticed the gleaming red car sitting outside. His reaction, according to an
eyewitness account from a company manager, was like a slow-gathering
storm. After some small talk, he inquired about the unfamiliar vehicle and
was told that it was the new Ford car. He was also informed that plans for
production were well under way.

> He kept looking at it. He'd tip his head this way and that
> and look at it. . . . I said, "Is there anything more I can . . . ?" "No,"
> he said. "I'm going over and look at the new car." He kind of
> smiled. . . .
> He had his hands in his pockets and he walked around that car
> three or four times, looking at it very closely. It was a four-door job
> and the top was down. Finally, he got to the left-hand side of the car
> that was facing me, and he takes his hands out, gets hold of the
> door, and bang! One jerk, and he had it right off the hinges! He
> ripped the door right off! God, how the man done it, I don't know!
> He jumped in there, and, bang, goes the other door. Bang, goes
> the windshield. He jumps over the back seat and starts pounding on
> the top. He rips the top with the heel of his shoe. He wrecked the
> car as much as he could. . . . Mr. Ford was in there, and his hands
> were going, and his feet were going, and you talk about cussing! It
> was the first time I had ever heard Mr. Ford cuss, and oh, the other
> fellows were just taking it in. He was going to it.

After a furious Ford finished demolishing the new model, he ordered all
production plans halted and all contracts canceled. With this angry outburst, he had made his position clear. The Model T alone would define the
destiny of the Ford Motor Company, and anyone who questioned its status
did so at his own risk.[52]

A few years after this remarkable display, another incident dramatically
demonstrated that Ford not only revered the Model T but understood its
social and cultural impact. His advertising staff approached him with a new

slogan they had crafted over the previous weeks. Taking their cue from Ford's many public pronouncements about bringing a sturdy vehicle to the ordinary person at a modest price, they hit upon an ideal phrase: "Buy a Ford and Save the Difference!" When they showed it to Henry Ford, however, he took a pencil and crossed out one word, replacing it with another. His revised slogan read "Buy a Ford and *Spend* the Difference!" Saving money was good, Ford explained, but if carried too far it would strangle American industry. Spending, rather than saving, now held the key to happiness, and it "is the wiser thing to do," Ford insisted. "Society lives by circulation, and not by congestion."[53]

This incident, in concert with his destruction of the prototype a few years earlier, revealed worlds about Henry Ford's keen grasp of the age in which he lived. Perhaps better than anyone, he understood that, whereas thrift and self-control had been the hallmarks of success in an earlier age, spending and self-fulfillment were becoming the cultural lubricant that kept the mass society of the new century moving ahead smoothly. With his fierce loyalty to the Model T and his successful association of it with a new ethos of buying and enjoyment, Ford made his name and his car synonymous with the deepest instincts of an emerging consumer America.

Eight

Producer

Those who saw the sight never forgot it. Tens of thousands of Model T's began appearing as if by magic from Henry Ford's marvelous new factory at Highland Park. Lined up wheel to wheel in the huge clearing lots outside the assembly buildings, they stretched nearly as far as the eye could see, a sea of automobiles waiting to be loaded onto railcars to meet their purchasers. Highland Park had lurched to life like a giant mechanized octopus with its grasping tentacles extending in every direction, drawing in great chunks of raw material and exuding finished Fords. But, far from presenting a gruesome or unsavory spectacle, this sparkling new factory made industrial manufacturing into a modern art form. It offered unprecedented economies of scale and employed thousands of workers. It brought acres of production area under one roof. An example of the most innovative industrial design, this monument to American productivity with its massive windows and glass-encased roof was dubbed the "Crystal Palace."

Then, in 1913, Highland Park upped the ante even more. Adopting a novel manufacturing technique called the "assembly line," Ford and his managers installed a system that sent production soaring to unimaginable heights. In the assembly line's first year of operation, output of Model T's shot up from 82,000 to 189,000. By 1916, it stood at 585,000. In 1921, Ford produced one million automobiles; by 1923, two million. Highland Park had become the site of a miracle. Like the New Testament story of the loaves and fishes, Ford seemed to be creating material sustenance for thousands of people by a superhuman process. His fellow citizens responded with a kind of worship, and his assembly line, much like the Model T it produced, became a symbol of modern America and its prosperity.[1]

In fact, Henry Ford employed religious imagery to describe his company's stunning technological and organizational achievements. Mass production, he declared, had so improved the lot of human beings that it could only be described as a gift from God. In an article entitled "Machinery, the New Messiah," Ford explained how the intelligent use of technology had made goods available and affordable for popular consumption while also lifting the physical drudgery of hard labor from the shoulders of factory workers, farmers, and housewives. Organized machine production had provided the means by which a consumer utopia of prosperity was being realized. In Ford's words:

> Human demands are increasing every day and the needs for their gratification are increasing also. This is as it should be. Gradually, under the benign influence of American industry, wives are released from work, little children are no longer exploited; and given more time, they both become free to go out and find new products, new merchants, and manufacturers who are supplying them.... Machinery is accomplishing in the world what man has failed to do by preaching, propaganda, or the written word.[2]

Yet Highland Park also performed an important cultural function by alleviating anxiety. The new consumer world so skillfully shaped by Ford and others inspired, even thrilled, millions of Americans in the early twentieth century. But it also unsettled them. To a population raised on Victorian proprieties, the new consumer values of self-fulfillment, material comfort, and leisure raised unnerving moral quandaries, unfamiliar dilemmas, and challenging questions. Ford's highly publicized productivity, in subtle yet profound ways, salved people's fears. It reassured Americans that productive effort brought rewards, and that labor was a form of virtue. In so doing, he tapped the wellsprings of the Protestant ethic, an American tradition insisting that work was morally meaningful, even while twisting the work ethic into new shapes that would eventually become nearly unrecognizable. Appearing the defender of producerism as well as the disciple of consumerism, Henry Ford demonstrated that work still mattered.

By 1906, Ford was suffering a happy problem. As he told a reporter for *Motor Age*, his company was five months behind on orders and struggling to keep up with the growing demand for the Ford Model N. A few months later, the Detroit *Journal* carried a front-page story confirming progress on this front. The Ford Motor Company, it announced, had decided to purchase the grounds and racetrack of the old Highland Park Hotel, on the northwest edge of Detroit, as the site of its new automobile factory. The fifty-seven-acre tract stood at the intersection of two thoroughfares, Woodward and Manchester Avenues, and offered convenient access to the Michigan Central, Grand Trunk, and Detroit Terminal Railroads snaking in from the north. Design work and planning began in 1908, and construction of the new facility continued through the next year. The company moved from Piquette Avenue to Highland Park at New Year's 1910, even though the factory would not be completed until 1914.[3]

Noted architect Albert Kahn had designed the Highland Park plant. Ford had summoned him in 1907 after rejecting the original design for the factory. "I don't like it, and they think that the kind of building I want is impossible," Ford complained to Kahn. "I want the whole thing under one roof. If you can design it the way I want it, say so and do it." He gave a rough verbal sketch of his plan. Kahn agreed to try, and drew up designs, which Ford modified. This process went on for months until the automaker was satisfied. "All I ever did was to take his instinctive hunch and reduce it to a working formula," the architect described later. Kahn, a German immigrant, was a pioneering figure in factory design. Most of his fellow architects believed that the creation of museums, libraries, monuments, and mansions stood on a more dignified, elevated plane than meeting the utilitarian demands of industrial enterprise. Kahn disagreed, and his innovative design for the Packard Motor Car Company factory brought him to Henry Ford's attention. His creation at Highland Park was so astounding that it launched his career, making him the most famous and accomplished industrial architect in the world.[4]

The factory born from Henry Ford's imagination and Albert Kahn's blueprints was unlike anything yet seen in industry. Instead of the traditional design, in which separate functions were performed in separate buildings, an entire industrial complex was placed under one roof. The proportions were enormous. The main, four-story structure fronted Woodward Avenue and stretched to a length of 865 feet and a width of 75 feet. Another, one-story edifice, with a sawtooth roof, 140 feet wide and 840 feet long, paralleled the main building and was connected to it along the entire length by a huge glass-roofed craneway for the transfer of materials. Over the next few years, more parallel structures were added, along with a host of support buildings—power plant, foundry, engine house, underground tunnel system, and administration building—until the sixty acres were filled. All of the structures were built of steel and reinforced concrete, with minimal use of bricks except on ornamental bastions at the corners. The most notable feature of the Highland Park factory, however, was its fifty thousand square feet of glass windows (nearly 75 percent of the wall area), an expanse of transparency that was supplemented by skylights and glass roofs in the craneways. This created the impressively light and airy atmosphere of the Crystal Palace.[5]

Highland Park's rationalization of automobile manufacturing dwarfed all previous efforts in the field. The first floor of the main building was divided into compartments, each of which focused on machining various parts of the Model T chassis, such as camshafts, crankshafts, axles, transmissions, and connecting rods. Across the craneway in the one-story machine shop, several departments worked on the power elements—machining cylinders and cylinder heads, piston rings, differential gears and gear cases, and assembling the motor. The fourth floor of the main building witnessed the construction of large metal components of the Model T body, such as fenders, radiators, hoods, and fuel tanks. It also housed the upholstery operation. On the third floor, Ford workers in one large area busily fashioned the car's wheels, tires, lamps, and floorboards, while those in another painted and trimmed the car's finished body. The second floor housed a great variety of activities, including body assembly, stock areas for repair parts, and the shipping department. The experimental department, drafting room, and pattern department sat in the front areas of the second floor and had direct access to the administration building sitting at the front of the complex.[6]

This careful organization according to function aimed at maximum efficiency in production, and it was enhanced by several operational principles mandated by Henry Ford and his managers. These entailed the skillful use of machinery. First, Highland Park deployed an enormous power source—a 3,000-horsepower gas engine turning huge generators—to distribute electrical power throughout the facility. Within a few years of the factory's opening, an additional, 5,000-horsepower gas engine increased the power potential. Second, from its inception, when P. E. Martin and Charles Sorensen used layout boards to create an overall plan, the new Ford factory deployed its machines in a logical progression that matched the sequence of production for the Model T. This encouraged a smooth flow from beginning to concluding processes. Third, the factory became noted for its close grouping of machines, something allowed by the abundant sunlight and ventilation. With tightly placed machines discouraging the accumulation of work in aisles, a continuous flow of production from site to site became the norm. Fourth, because of Henry Ford's decision to produce only one chassis model for all his company's automobiles, Highland Park relied heavily upon single-purpose machines. Machines, such as the large apparatus in the engine department that drilled forty-five holes in the side of the engine block at one time, greatly increased efficiency of production.[7]

But Highland Park encompassed more than machines and flowcharts.

Within two years of its opening, the factory employed some fifteen thousand workers. Yet here, too, the Ford devotion to organization and efficiency shaped significantly the configuration of human labor. "System, system, system!" was the accurate conclusion of a reporter for the Detroit *Journal* who visited Highland Park soon after it opened in 1910. That ethos pushed Ford managers to create labor systems that encouraged maximum productivity. In the subassembly of various components, for instance, such as the engine or the rear axle, workers labored at stations where they were provided easily accessible bins filled with appropriate parts for the task at hand. Then, in the general assembly of the Model T, a line-production system held sway: a skeletal chassis was placed upon a stand, or "horse," as teams of workers, each specializing in a specific task, added sections of the car. Supplied with the necessary components, these teams followed one another sequentially, moving from horse to horse, until the automobiles began to emerge. When the wheels had gone on the car, it would be rolled along from station to station until its completion. The smooth operation of this system demanded the timely delivery of parts and the careful orchestration of assembly teams.[8]

Ford's success with his new factory system was evident not only in the swelling production numbers—20,700 Model T's in 1910, 53,500 in 1911, 82,400 in 1912—but in the admiring commentary of experts who witnessed the operation. Fred H. Colvin, a respected industrial journalist, wrote a series of articles on the new factory for *American Machinist*, and could barely contain his enthusiasm for its efficiency and productivity. He noted several characteristics that permeated the plant's operation: simplicity in its productive processes, the constant testing of parts to ensure their standard size and interchangeability, an emphasis on speed and accuracy in machine design, use of "motion study" to determine the minimal movements required of a laborer to perform certain tasks, a standard of cleanliness throughout the factory, and constant examination and modification of machines and processes to increase production. "What more could the greatest high priest of efficiency expect?" he noted of Highland Park.[9]

The tremendous productivity of Ford's new factory—by 1913, this single plant was responsible for half of the entire automobile output of the United States—soon generated publicity throughout the country. Stories about Highland Park appeared in newspapers all over the country. Headlines announced, "Ford Factory Is a Wonderful Place," "Figures on Ford Production Amaze," "New Idea in the Big Ford Factory," "Ford's Gigantic Output Marvel in Auto Industry." Texts praised every aspect of the plant's operation, from the giant cranes that distributed material throughout the factory to the abolition of stockrooms in favor of delivering material directly to the production spot where it would be used, from the elimination of wasted motion to the creation of machines especially designed for the requirements of the Model T.[10]

Popular accounts of the Highland Park facility focused on the links between its efficient methods. "Everything is highly systematized in our factory and every possible waste motion is eliminated," Ford noted in one piece. "How important it is that the utmost care be used to guard against the loss of a minute of a workman's time, can be realized when it is considered that if each of the 16,000 men employed wasted one minute a day the company would be losing about 266 hours a day of productive labor." The notion of a consistent, efficient flow of material fascinated journalists and readers alike. According to a reporter for the *Christian Science Monitor*, at Highland Park

> . . . the Ford engineers devised a plan whereby there is a steady progression of materials as they enter the factory on the one side in a crude state and, without one backward movement, go straight ahead until the completed car leaves the factory on the other side. The general movement is from north to south.

The process so impressed a movie studio that it convinced the company to set up a special demonstration whereby several teams of workmen assembled an entire Model T in two and a half minutes. "This Remarkable Record Caught in Moving Pictures," ran the headline. In early 1913, Norval Hawkins sang the praises of Highland Park in a Detroit speech that was reported by many newspapers. "Our factory, which now practically covers sixty-five acres, is about as complete and up to the minute as modern architecture and the latest machinery and labor-saving appliances can make it," he enthused. The resulting productivity was so astonishing, Hawkins concluded, that it could only be compared to a fairy tale such as "Aladdin and his wonderful lamp."[11]

The Ford Motor Company added its own voice to the chorus of acclaim for Highland Park. Two years after the factory opened, in 1912, it published *Ford Factory Facts*, a publicity pamphlet for mass distribution. The text led the reader step by step through the entire factory, proudly detailing various architectural features and manufacturing techniques, while accompanying photographs provided striking images. Beginning in the administration building, the tour continued through the power plant and engine room, the foundry, and the craneway. Upon entering the machine shop, a visitor would be "looking into a hopeless tangle of machinery, shafting, and belts," the pamphlet declared. "It seems incredible that a thousand men are working calmly and effectively among this maze of whirring, groaning, grinding wheels and gears, but as you walk along the main aisle and study each section carefully, the impression of confusion is dispelled and is replaced by amazement at the perfect system that prevails." The text concluded with a survey of the experimental laboratory, assembling department, and testing area, where the Model T's were started, inspected, and driven out for shipping. The pamphlet offered a stirring summary: "Today the home of the Ford Model T stands pre-eminent as the most complete manufacturing establishment in the world, devoted to the production of one motor car—a profoundly impressive monument to the creative and constructive genius of Henry Ford and his associates."[12]

As events unfolded, however, it became clear that the opening of Highland Park was only the first stage of something much bigger in the evolution of the Ford Motor Company. The gleaming glass of the Crystal Palace constituted but the shell of a truly revolutionary idea that, like a pearl, slowly took shape within before appearing in 1914. American industry, and American history, would never be quite the same.

Even though Highland Park surpassed the expectations of most observers with its production during the first years of operation, company leadership was not satisfied. In the spring of 1913, certain managers and engineers began to experiment with a technique that took production methods into a new realm of efficiency. Henry Ford described it simply: "The first step forward in assembly came when we began taking the work to the men instead of the men to the work."[13]

What he referred to, of course, was the "assembly line," which became perhaps the most revolutionary development in industrial history. Rather than having teams of laborers doing many different jobs as they built a car from the ground up, this new process placed workers, each performing a minuscule task, at stationary positions along a conveyor belt that moved the developing vehicle along. The relentless, steady culmination of these tiny jobs, performed incrementally, produced a finished automobile in record time.

Although the assembly line changed forever the nature of industrial production, its roots have remained rather tangled and obscured. Conflicting stories about the origins of the assembly line circulated widely as Ford operatives, given the great success of this technique, later scrambled to take credit for it. Henry Ford's own version of things changed. At one point, he declared that the inspiration came from observing the overhead trolley that

Chicago packers used in dressing beef at the slaughterhouses. Another time, he claimed that he got the idea from observing a watch factory where parts sat on a moving belt and assemblers took them off as required. Others offered different stories. William C. Klann, foreman of motor assembly at the Highland Park facility, asserted that the conveyors used to transport sand in the factory foundry inspired the idea of using a similar method in the assembly process. Charles Sorensen, in a memoir written many years later, averred that as early as 1908 he and several subordinates had arranged stock parts sequentially on the floor of the old Piquette Avenue factory, put a tow rope onto a car chassis with wheels, and pulled it from pile to pile, attaching appropriate components one after another. "Over several weeks we developed it as well as we could," Sorensen wrote. "Then we laid it away and put it on the shelf until we were ready to use it."[14]

But whatever the exact inspiration or point of origin, it seems clear that the Ford assembly line did not appear suddenly or wholly formed. Like most innovations in the industrial world, it was the product of various influences, numerous people, and extensive experimentation. Once initiated, however, it spread rapidly throughout most production sectors in the Highland Park plant. Evidence suggests that the first actual use of the assembly line came on April 1, 1913, when workers in the flywheel-magneto department stood alongside a waist-high table with a smooth metal surface and were instructed by foremen to install one part and then slide the component along to the next worker, who would add something else. This soon led to the idea of pulling the evolving component along at a set rate with a chain, a move that steadied the process by speeding up the slow workers and slowing down the speedy ones. By tweaking this system in various small ways over the next few months, Ford supervisors were able to cut the man-minutes required for assembling the flywheel magneto from twenty to five. This quadrupling of productivity caught the attention of nearly all Ford production engineers, and they began to develop the technique in various areas.[15]

Klann, for example, brought the assembly line to the building of the Model T engine. He established in 1913 a conveyor system that took a cylinder block past a number of men who installed various parts, including the crankshaft, bearings, and bearing-cap bolts. The primary parts were very heavy, of course, and at one point the process demanded that the cylinder be clamped down while the crankshaft was turned over with a three-foot metal bar. The system worked well for a day, but on the second day disaster struck. In Klann's words, a workman

  . . . forgot to tighten his clamp and when he turned over the crankshaft with the three-foot long bar, he threw the cylinder block off the bench and the cylinder block hit his leg and he was sent to the doctor. They found his leg was broken above the knee. . . .

We continued working, but at four PM that afternoon Mr. James Couzens came out to see the "Goldberg job," as he called it. He said to me, "If you are just going to break legs, let's shut this thing off."

Klann consulted with P. E. Martin and Charles Sorensen, however, and they instructed him to install safety precautions and try again. The foreman did so, the line continued, and within several weeks it was working smoothly. As in other sectors of the plant, production increased dramatically.[16]

The assembly-line technique was adopted quickly for transmission assembly. Using a chain conveyor rather than a belt conveyor, construction of this major system for the Model T added gears, clutch, and drums to the back side of the flywheel, and each of these components demanded a number of pins, disks, screws, and springs. This complicated process culminated with the attachment of sixteen magnets to the front of the flywheel, which involved the installation of sixteen sets of spacers, screws, and clamps. By November 1913, Ford production engineers had put the entire engine assembly on an integrated assembly line. As in other areas, production time plummeted, with requirements dropping from 594 man-minutes to 226 man-minutes for engine assembly. Within months, the assembly line had been adapted to making the body, pistons, and upholstery for the Model T.[17]

Then came the most dramatic step of all. By the fall of 1913, Ford was facing a happy problem created by the boost in productivity from the first assembly lines. As Klann explained, "We found that we were making parts a hell of a lot faster than they could put them together on cars." In an effort to catch up, production managers decided to use the new method in Model T chassis construction. This was a spectacular success, and in the public mind, it became *the* Ford assembly line, with its image of a conveyor belt some hundred yards long, relentlessly moving the chassis along as nearly two hundred workers performed a series of tasks, each adding parts and components to the whole, until, at the end, the radiator was filled, the engine started, and the completed car driven off to the holding lots.[18]

The mature form of the assembly line was influenced particularly by Clarence W. Avery, a Ford production engineer. Avery had studied at the Ferris Institute and the University of Michigan before taking a position as director of manual training at the Detroit University School. There he encountered Henry Ford's son, Edsel, as a student. In 1912, Edsel helped bring Avery into the company, where he became Charles Sorensen's assistant. This thoughtful and articulate young man (he was only thirty-one in

1913) took a special interest in problems of mass production, and he soon gravitated toward the emerging technique of the assembly line. Working closely with Klann in putting together the transmission and engine sub-assembly lines, he became an advocate for putting the entire chassis assembly onto a conveyor system. He was, according to one associate, the "guiding light" of this concept. Avery organized a series of experiments. The chassis was pulled along by various means at various speeds while assembly operations were timed, the workers' physical movements were analyzed, and methods of work division were assessed.[19]

The process was refined in a series of steps, which Avery described many years later:

> The first continuous assembly line had no mechanical means of movement. The wheels of the car were assembled at a very early stage and channel iron tracks provided for them. At intervals, giving sufficient time for the operations to be performed, the foreman blew a whistle and all hands pushed the cars forward to the next position, and then returned to their original locations to perform their next operations.
>
> In the next stage we provided rigid spacers between the cars, and introduced a pusher chain about three cars long at the beginning of the line. This worked well for a few weeks. The cumulative resistance, however, was too close to the safety factor. One day the complete line buckled and pushed a section from the side wall of the building. It was then that the continuous chain was introduced.[20]

Avery and his team designed, modified, and finalized the new chassis assembly line over a three-month period during the fall of 1913. By April 1914, three complete lines were in operation, fed by a tributary system of subassembly lines. Avery always modestly insisted that Henry Ford deserved the credit, because he had insisted that "the cars should move, rather than the men and the stock. It was my privilege . . . to put into operation many of the ideas he so carefully outlined." But whatever the origin of the technique, the production result proved astonishing. Under the old, stationary system, the best time for assembling a chassis had been twelve hours and twenty-eight minutes. By the summer of 1914, the new assembly line was accomplishing this task in one hour and thirty-three minutes.[21]

The first professional critique of Ford's new assembly system came from two mechanical experts who visited Highland Park in early 1914. Horace L. Arnold and Fay Leone Faurote, both trained engineers and technical writers, spent several weeks examining assembly-line production for a series of articles printed in *Engineering Magazine*. The following year, the pair gathered the pieces into a book and published *Ford Methods and the Ford Shops*. This text provided an exhaustive look at the entire Highland Park operation and offered many valuable insights into Ford's revolutionary methods.[22]

The preface, written by the editor of *Engineering Magazine*, Charles B. Goings, dramatically framed the book's theme. "Ford's success has startled the country, almost the world, financially, industrially, mechanically," he wrote, by achieving "an absolutely incredible enlargement of output reaching something like one hundred fold in less than ten years." Arnold and Faurote then examined every detail of the plant's operation, consulted with company managers and engineers, observed every facet of the factory's labor, and interviewed Henry Ford at length. "The urgent demand for maximum production is the dominant condition which governs every activity of the Highland Park shops," they discovered. This impulse dictated both the organization of the factory and its development of highly specialized machinery. Once, a representative of an Eastern manufacturing concern came to Highland Park to consult with Ford engineers about building a certain machine, Arnold and Faurote reported. After looking at the blueprints, the visitor pointed out a mistake: it specified an output of two hundred parts per hour, whereas obviously the goal was two hundred parts per day. The Ford experts affirmed that the original specification was correct. The outsider pointed out that, since forty units per day was considered a good production, the Ford expectation was impossible. A heated debate ensued, and the machine's designer was summoned and told by the visitor that this output was impossible. "Well," he replied, "if you will go down into the machine shop on the main floor, you will find a machine doing it—we built one to try it out, and it is doing what we thought it would." Needless to say, the discussion ended there.[23]

After a painstaking analysis, Arnold and Faurote concluded that the key to Ford's rising output was its new method of "moving assembly." Fascinated by the assembly line, they examined it in every detail and concluded that it represented a complete overhaul of traditional, stationary methods. It brought "remarkable labor-saving gains," "great reductions in floor space required for assembly operations," and "almost unbelievable reductions in assembling time." Moreover, the authors concluded that Ford's assembly line had much broader implications for American industry because the principles of "moving assemblies in progress, and of minutely dividing assembling operations," could be applied to nearly every kind of manufacturing.[24]

The most spectacular expression of the assembly line, of course, came with chassis construction of the Model T. Arnold and Faurote were awestruck by the sight:

> The Ford chassis assembling in moving lines affords a highly impressive spectacle to beholders of every class, technical or non-technical. Long lines of slowly moving assemblies in progress, busy groups of successive operators, the rapid growth of the chassis as component after component is added from the overhead sources of supply, and, finally, the instant start into self-moving power—these excite the liveliest interest and admiration in all who witness for the first time this operation of bringing together the varied elements of the new and seemingly vivified creation.[25]

By 1914, publicity about Ford's new technique had begun to engulf the public as journalistic accounts of this production miracle appeared all over the United States. The magazine *Interstate Motorist*, published in Sioux City, Iowa, proclaimed that the "Ford Factory Is an Ideal"; an essayist for the Boise, Idaho, *News* wrote, "What I saw at the Ford factory impressed me as being even more wonderful than the world-renowned falls at Niagara." Writers scrambled for metaphors in trying to convey the significance of the assembly line. According to a reporter for the Houston *Chronicle*, a visitor watching this process "thinks of chickens hatching by wholesale in an incubator."[26]

Most journalists were stunned by the volume of cars pouring off the assembly lines and into American households. A September 1913 article in the Washington *Times* described the "Ford Production Industrial Marvel" that had produced 185,000 automobiles during the previous twelve months. Newspapers published stories of Ford speed records for assembly, as when a Ford team put together a complete Model T from a pile of preassembled components in two and a half minutes. A nationally reprinted story in the spring of 1914 explained that a Model T "is born every twenty-four seconds during the month of April." For customers, of course, the great payoff of the speed and volume of the assembly line was the declining price of Ford automobiles. The extraordinary production at Highland Park had allowed Ford to reduce the price of the Model T to $500, as another widely reprinted article announced in August 1913.[27]

On August 8, 1913, one of the most celebrated photographs in American industrial history appeared in papers all over the country under a compelling headline: "The Most Expensive Picture That Was Ever Taken." Ford amassed twelve thousand of his sixteen-thousand-strong workforce in a large open area outside the Highland Park factory—the factory had to be closed for two hours to do this, hence the expense—and the photographer snapped an unforgettable image of a great sea of laborers. Another story explained how the vast scale of the Ford workforce required that wages be paid out daily to some portion of it. The most striking measure of Ford productivity, of course, could be seen around the country. The Model T was appearing everywhere on American roadways. As one headline noted succinctly, "Half Million Fords in Use—Every Third Car a Ford."[28]

Henry Ford was delighted to feed the popular hunger for news about his new production methods. In the midsummer of 1915, the company presented an exhibit at the Panama-Pacific International Exposition in San Francisco. In a brilliant publicity move, a truncated version of the assembly line was constructed, complete with conveyor chain to pull along a Model T chassis while stationary workmen attached various components until the vehicle rolled away under its own power, completely equipped. Trucks replenished the stock supply with new batches of parts every morning, between 1 and 6 a.m. "The crowds seem never to tire of watching a rear axle grow into a complete motor car," reported a local newspaper. They flocked to see the spectacle, breaking the restraining railing on the first day and forcing a temporary shutdown while Ford workmen sank the support pipes even deeper into the floor.[29]

Thus a series of successful experiments at Highland Park in 1913–14 brought to life the vision of "moving assembly." A bird's-eye view of Ford's factory would have revealed a systematic but complex picture. Rather than one great assembly line snaking through the factory, taking the vehicle from lumpen metal to finished automobile, a kind of industrial river system appeared. A number of subassembly tributaries, each of them producing components, ran through various areas of the plant before feeding the main assembly line, where all the already assembled systems, along with a host of specialized parts, were placed on the chassis to produce a completed Model T. Every few seconds, one of these sturdy automobiles rolled off the line to be started, inspected, and driven onto the storage lots to await shipment.

As Henry Ford and his staff developed the Model T and produced it in large numbers, many managers and engineers contributed to the company's explosive growth. But none loomed larger than a man who had stood beside the company owner for more than a decade. He had spent many long, cold evenings lending mechanical expertise to Ford in the development of his early race cars. He had been around during the dark days when the Detroit Automobile Company and the Henry Ford Company first sprang to life, then withered and died. Now he moved into the spotlight, an industrial magician who helped shape the factory churning out tens of thousands of Ford's modest little car.

In November 1915, *Ford Times* featured an arresting photograph. Seated on one side was the company's owner and namesake, while facing him sat its chief designer and engineer. The caption read, "Mr. Henry Ford and Mr. C. H. Wills, the two men who have developed the Ford car." This photo publicly acknowledged what company insiders had known for a long time: though James Couzens served as Henry Ford's mainstay on the business side of things, Wills stood as his right-hand man on the mechanical, production side. As the company developed and mass-produced the Model T, no one played a more critical role than this talented, headstrong engineer.

Childe Harold Wills was born on June 1, 1878, in Fort Wayne, Indiana, and was named after Lord Byron's epic poem "Childe Harold's Pilgrimage." The Wills family moved to Detroit in 1885, and by his teenage years, young Harold (he hated the name Childe and refused to use it) had shown an aptitude for commercial drawing and mechanics. He served an apprenticeship at the Detroit Lubricator Company from 1896 to 1899, and within a few years had risen to the status of journeyman toolmaker and started supplementing his practical training with night courses in metallurgy, chemistry, and engineering. Then he took a job with the Boyer Machine Company, and within a few months became its chief engineer.

Meanwhile, in 1899, he had made the acquaintance of Henry Ford, and began working for him in the evenings, drawing a small salary and assisting him with drafting and design. In 1900, Wills labored part-time as a draftsman for Ford's Detroit Automobile Company, and when it failed, continued to do so with its successor, the Henry Ford Company. He also assisted his employer with the development of the 999 and Arrow race cars. By 1902, Wills was working for Ford full-time, and the following year, when Alexander Malcolmson provided the necessary capital for a new venture, he became chief engineer, designer, and metallurgist for the Ford Motor Company.[30]

Perhaps the most striking aspect of Wills' early career at Ford was his close personal and professional relationship with the founder. During their earliest collaboration, when Henry Ford was developing his racing car, Wills worked with him every evening in the small machine shop at 81 Park Place. There was no heat in this facility, and after long hours spent drafting plans and machining parts in the frigid climate, the pair would often become too cold to work. As Wills liked to tell acquaintances in later years, they "would put on boxing gloves and flail each other until they felt warm." The pair also shared misadventures. While they were repairing a large gas tank for the racer in the alley outside the shop, an explosion from trapped fumes blew Wills and Ford backward and flat onto their backs, also putting a hole in the wall. A few years later, Ford and Wills, continuing to work closely, in the experimental room of the Ford Motor Company, created its earliest automobile models. The highly trained Wills complemented Ford's instinctive but less articulate mechanical talents. Ford had difficulty understanding designs that were not put into a three-dimensional model, so Wills read and translated blueprints for him.[31]

In addition, they seem to have been genuine friends who shared a number of traits. Like Ford, Wills had a deep love of outdoor life and pursued hobbies of fishing, hunting, and boating. Both men displayed a gift for quickly grasping and solving mechanical problems. Perfectionists, Ford and Wills worked obsessively on refining a product until it was exactly the way they envisioned it. Perhaps most important, Ford and Wills shared a hard-nosed approach to the world. Oliver Barthel, an associate in Ford's earliest automobile projects who had much contact with Wills, described the engineer's difficult temperament. "He had the right kind of disposition to get along with Mr. Ford," Barthel added. "In order to get along with Mr. Ford, you had to have a little mean streak in your system."[32]

As the Ford Motor Company began to push its way into the national automobile market, many noted the close relationship between Ford and Wills. At the time of the crisis resulting in Malcolmson's ouster, Ford's steadiest ally did not come from among the board of directors. "A man who had no stock at all was the closest to Mr. Ford. That was Mr. C. H. Wills," noted Charles H. Bennett, one of the original stockholders. "He and Mr. Ford were great friends and got along very well together." Fred W. Seeman, a pattern-maker who worked closely with both men during the early years of the company, affirmed their close relationship. "I think Mr. Wills and Mr. Ford got along about as well as any engineering pair I've run across in my life," Seeman stated, "and I've run across a lot of them."[33]

Wills' importance to the early Ford Motor Company, however, far exceeded his friendship with its founder. On any number of fronts, he played a key role in developing the automotive product. As chief engineer, he made design contributions to Ford automobiles that were basic to their creation. In the simple words of pattern-maker Fred Seeman, "Most of the ideas for the cars came from Mr. Wills and Mr. Ford." In fact, Wills worked so closely with Ford that their contributions were indistinguishable in developing the first wave of automobiles (Models A, C, F, and B) as well as the more sophisticated prototypes that emerged a bit later (Models N, R,

and S). His influence was not limited strictly to engineering. Acutely interested in production, he strongly supported Walter Flanders' reorganization
efforts. His longest-lasting influence, however, came when the company
began searching for a trademark. He remembered that as a teenager he had
earned spending money by printing calling cards using a crude, home-
printing set. He recalled that its graceful script had featured a particularly
striking "F" similar to that in Henry Ford's own signature. So he dug the old
set out of his attic and used it to letter the familiar, flowing *Ford* logo that
would be affixed to millions of automobiles and advertisements in the
decades to come.[34]

Wills' professional profile was enhanced by a striking appearance and
forceful personality. When he was a young man, his handsome demeanor—
tall, with dark hair, strong facial features, including large brown eyes, and
outfitted in impeccably tailored suits—had turned many heads. In later life,
he would move toward baldness and add weight to his frame, but the powerful presence remained. Wills struck all who worked with him as headstrong, confident, persuasive, and rather high-strung. Some perceived a
kind of selfish arrogance. One colleague observed that the engineer "was all
for Mr. Wills, not so much for the Ford Motor Company or somebody
else." But most found his tough-mindedness to be tempered by kindness.
Fred Rockelman described Wills as a "great educator" who constantly
taught the young mechanics; Charles Sorensen, whose temper and ambition
were already producing clashes with his peers, conceded that Wills was "a
very pleasant man to work with."[35]

In fact, many co-workers described a man whose professional kindness
leaned toward extravagance. Sorensen reported that Wills had negotiated a
special agreement with Henry Ford wherein his regular salary would be
supplemented by a percentage of company profits and special dividends. As
the company grew, so did Wills' bonuses and his generosity. "I always knew
when Wills got one of these dividends. He would look me up and also [P. E.]
Martin and present us with a nice little check," Sorensen wrote later. "The
first one I remember he gave me was for $100. After that, as his income
increased, he did the same with Ed and I. The last one I remember was for
about $1000." Irving Bacon told a similar tale. As official photographer for
the company and "court painter" for Henry Ford by the 1910s, he made a
decent, if undependable, living. Wills admired Bacon's work and once used
one of his bonus checks to grant the artist a stipend of $2,500 a year so he
could paint unencumbered by other responsibilities. "Now, you paint anything you care to," Wills told him. "When you get through, I will pick out
what I want [from among your paintings], and you can keep the rest." Sitting on top of the world financially, Wills once quietly bought a farm for an

old shoemaker he had known as a boy when the old man failed to save enough money to realize his lifelong dream.[36]

Wills' lavish style spilled over into his private life, where he embraced the new consumer ethic of leisure and consumption. He converted his first $1,000 bonus into dollar bills, brought them home in a suitcase, and tossed them in the air like confetti before his delighted wife and children. A few years later, after divorcing his first wife and marrying a much younger woman, he purchased a waterfront house on Jefferson Avenue. He acquired a fine yacht, as well as several smaller craft, and was noted for hosting friends on weekend boating trips and duck-hunting excursions. He also had a weakness for gems, showering them on his new wife and even carrying them in his pockets to display to admiring friends. At one point, to the surprise of the pugnacious recipient, he presented a diamond finger ring to Sorensen.[37]

Despite his extravagance, Wills was no frivolous playboy. A highly intelligent and competent engineer, he demonstrated an independence of mind that occasionally created tension at the company, particularly with its chief. He kept his own schedule, often coming to the factory at 11 a.m., rather than 8 a.m. with the rest of the managers. Because of his long familiarity with Henry Ford, he refused to bend automatically to the founder's ideas. Wills would engage in lengthy arguments with his boss over the best procedures and designs, and occasionally would alter agreed-upon designs to suit his own ideas. As Sorensen once noted:

> I found that Wills was very critical at times of Mr. Ford and his demands for certain products. The design problems were ones that rolled around a good deal between the two of them, with never any apparent, real satisfaction on the part of Mr. Ford. I must say that Wills was a very clever and able designer. But one thing he lacked terribly, and that was to try to give Mr. Ford just exactly what he was trying to make.

In Sorensen's view, "Wills would not accept full control by anyone. He was a very independent, haughty person."[38]

The culmination of Wills' early career at Ford came with his work on the Model T. He contributed to the design of the car in its development stage, working with Joseph Galamb and Henry Ford as they spent months drawing and modifying plans on the large blackboard in the experimental room. Wills was instrumental in designing the Model T's pathbreaking planetary transmission. But his biggest contribution came in terms of materials. For all of Henry Ford's later claims, it was Harold Wills who led the way in the use of lightweight, powerful vanadium steel in the construction of the revolutionary automobile. He had trained extensively as a metallurgist, and around 1905 he attended an engineers' convention in Atlantic City where he studied an exhibition of this alloy. He then spent much time with J. Kent Smith, the English metallurgist who had developed vanadium, at his laboratory in Canton, Ohio, and supervised experiments that led to vanadium steel's use in the light yet strong gears, axles, and linkages in Ford's new automobile.[39]

Wills' efforts, in concert with those of many other talented figures, helped make the Model T a booming success. Knowledgeable observers recognized his role. The Dodge brothers, embroiled many years later in a bitter lawsuit with Henry Ford over the payment of stock dividends, made a point of exempting Wills from their criticism. "As a stockholder, I have no objection to the salary paid Wills," testified John Dodge. "Mr. Wills is a very valuable man. I have always considered him the brains of the company." Sorensen, usually a harsh critic of his fellow managers, also made an exception for Wills, whom he described as "an important factor in building the Ford Motor Company. . . . In my books he remains one of the greats." In producing the automobile at the center of the consumer revolution, Wills helped bring about a subtler but equally far-reaching change.[40]

The assembly line churning out Model T's at the Highland Park factory impressed all who witnessed it: hundreds of workers lined up almost shoulder to shoulder, each busily tightening a bolt or adding a metal sleeve or sliding a bearing into place while a conveyor moved the growing automobile from station to station, and completed cars relentlessly emerged at the end. With its division of labor, grand scale, massive efficiency, and continuous forward movement, the assembly line reconfigured the production process. Just as important, it revolutionized the very idea of industrial labor and changed forever the traditional world of the artisan mechanic.

As none knew better than Henry Ford, the assembly line fundamentally redefined work according to several new principles. Besides "taking the work to the men instead of the men to the work," it broke down work into the smallest possible components and eliminated all waste motion on the worker's part. As Ford explained, the assembly line brought "a reduction of the necessity for thought on the part of the worker and the reduction of his movements to a minimum. He does as nearly as possible only one thing with only one movement." It also reduced the need for skilled labor and emphasized the rote completion of simple, repetitive tasks. The innovations of the assembly line brought clear results, according to Henry Ford: "By the aid of scientific study one man is now able to do somewhat more than four did only a comparatively few years ago."[41]

But Ford's assembly line, for all of its radical redefinition of industrial work, was not so much a completely new idea as the culmination of a decades-long process. Since the mid-nineteenth century, the rise of the factory system in the United States had inspired industrial engineers to slowly reshape and rationalize the work process. Factory managers struggled to break the hold of artisan craftsmen, with their traditions of stubborn independence, and fought to eradicate a larger "premodern" work culture, with its agricultural aversion to disciplined, time-oriented labor. They sought to construct a new model of labor, more attuned to the demands of efficiency and mass production. This movement reached a climax with the pioneering work of Frederick Winslow Taylor, the father of "scientific management." Wielding his stopwatch as a weapon against waste and inefficiency, this engineer had conducted time-and-motion studies throughout the 1880s and 1890s that sought to reformulate and systematize industrial work tasks. Taylor hoped to eliminate all wasteful motion, redesign all tools for maximum impact, and place all decision-making in the hands of foremen rather than workmen. By the time he published his collected work in *The Principles of Scientific Management* (1911), "Taylorism" was already sweeping through American industry with its gospel of standardization and rationalization of work.[42]

Ford's development of the assembly line emerged from similar principles. With his visceral dislike of anything smacking of bookish ideas, he denied that his new system owed anything to systematic theories of organization, including scientific management. Though this is technically true—Ford certainly never read Taylor, and there is little to suggest that his managers did, either—much evidence indicates that the spirit of scientific management was in the air at Highland Park. The broad impulse to rationalize the labor system, to break down and reorganize its component parts, to eliminate waste motion through time-and-motion studies, and to select workers for tasks scientifically, animated Ford managers in the years when the assembly line was developed. As one scholar has commented astutely, the Ford Motor Company was "Taylorized without Taylor."[43]

By 1913, before the assembly line was installed, a time-study department had been established at Highland Park, and Ford efficiency experts, stopwatches in hand, closely studied every aspect of all work tasks in the cause of increasing productivity. Once they had decided how to eliminate waste motion, foremen on the plant floor were expected to enforce their reforms. Ford management, according to engineer Harold Wibel, grew

obsessed with saving time. "They weren't interested in anything except efficiency of production," he noted. "They wouldn't talk dollars and cents at
all. They talked in terms of the minutes that the thing cost." This drive, in
the words of one observer, pushed the men "into the condition of performing automatically with machine-like regularity and speed." Charles Madison, an assembly worker, labored at Highland Park in 1910, left for several
years, and then returned in 1914. He reported that he, like all the workers,

> . . . was frequently timed by efficiency experts, a way of driving a
> worker to function at maximum speed, and a cause of constant ten-
> sion. . . . [Upon returning in 1914] the harried foreman told me
> that my operation had been timed by an efficiency expert to pro-
> duce a certain number of finished parts per day. I timed myself to
> see what I could actually do, and realized that I might achieve the
> quota only if all went well and I worked without letup the entire
> eight hours. No allowance was made for lunch, toilet time, or tool
> sharpening.[44]

The spirit of Taylorism also could be seen in the general atmosphere of
the Highland Park factory. Journalists O. J. Abell and Fred Colvin, who
studied the pre–assembly-line facility for articles in *Iron Age* and *American
Machinist*, described how "the pressure of rush" was omnipresent. Ford
foremen drove workers to new heights of productivity. In Abell's words, a
foreman must "see to it that the men under him turn out so many pieces per
day and personally work to correct whatever may prevent it." His quota
came from a daily schedule setting out work to be completed by his department. William Klann gave a glimpse of this atmosphere. Highland Park
employed many recent immigrants, he related, and "one word [*sic*] every
foreman had to learn in English, German, Polish, and Italian was 'hurry
up.' "[45]

With the advent of the assembly line, Ford managers created the quintessential system for regulating and rationalizing the labor process. The
basic procedure made management the absolute arbiters of when, at what
speed, and in what fashion work was performed. It also provided the means
for Ford engineers to reorganize labor completely, according to standards
of efficiency. The assembly line's smooth, continuous flow, in the words of
Horace Arnold, worked by "hurrying the slow men, holding the fast men
back from pushing work to those in advance, and acting as an all-around
adjuster and equalizer." It was the apotheosis of scientific management.[46]

But this revolution in the conduct of labor also transformed its soul. For
generations, American attitudes about work had been rooted in the Protes-

tant work ethic. From the Puritans through the periodic evangelical up-
surges of the eighteenth and nineteenth centuries, this tradition insisted
that work must be morally meaningful and spiritually fulfilling as well as
economically sustaining. Laboring hard to fulfill one's "calling" was a way to
praise God, build character, and turn a profit simultaneously. Work exercised the moral as well as the physical faculties.[47]

The assembly line, by making labor monotonous and unfulfilling,
eroded the foundations of the ethic. It raised troubling questions about the
meaning of work in modern society, and Henry Ford, as well as anyone,
confronted them. Although he later gained a reputation as a soulless
exploiter of labor, he anguished over the work issue in his early career. He
was a diehard defender of the traditional work ethic, but he viewed it as ill-
suited to a new industrial age. He sought to redefine the modern meaning of
labor by softening its physical demands and linking it to consumer abundance. Ford's struggle to construct a new moral foundation for labor
reflected the uncertainty of his times.

Long after the advent of the assembly line, Henry Ford defended the
old-fashioned view that work was morally, as well as financially, rewarding.
The compulsion to labor, he believed, was rooted in human nature. "The
natural thing to do is to work," Ford proclaimed, "to recognize that prosperity and happiness can be obtained only through honest effort." He
agreed with a long line of Western political economists such as John Locke,
Adam Smith, and Karl Marx, who held that labor is what added value to raw
materials, and thus people were entitled to "the right of property" created
by that labor. In the best tradition of the Protestant work ethic, he insisted
on the moral discipline of labor. Work and play should not be mixed.
"When we are at work we ought to be at work. When we are at play we
ought to be at play," he wrote. "When the work is done, then the play can
come, but not before."[48]

As Ford wrote in *My Life and Work*, "Work is our sanity, our self-
respect, our salvation. . . . The man who does not get a certain satisfaction
out of his day's work is losing the best part of his pay. For the day's work is a
great thing—a very great thing! It is at the very foundation of the world; it is
the basis of our self-respect." In interviews, Ford stressed the same theme.
"Work for the joy of working. Work regardless of profits," he told a journalist. "[Most people] work hard, in order to be able to quit working. They
need to work for the sake of the work; and it's hard to make them understand that."[49]

At the same time, however, he recognized that modern mass production
had changed the nature and meaning of labor. Ford supported Taylorized
work not just for its efficiency. He pointed out that the assembly line had

lifted the burden of physical drudgery from the backs of workmen, a humane agenda that critics often overlooked. Employees did little lifting or trucking of materials at Highland Park, and, as Ford noted proudly, "We have succeeded to a very great extent in relieving men of the heavier and more onerous jobs that used to sap their strength." Moreover, he argued that this reduction of physical demand actually supported the Protestant work ethic by eliminating waste. "A cardinal principle of mass production is that hard work, in the old physical sense of laborious burden-bearing, is wasteful," he observed. "Save ten steps a day for each of twelve thousand employees and you will have saved fifty miles of wasted motion and misspent energy."[50]

He also contended that the assembly line, far from violating people's desire for meaningful work, was a welcome reform for most workers, who did not wish to think when they worked. "The average worker, I am sorry to say, wants a job in which he does not have to put forth much physical exertion—above all, he wants a job in which he does not have to think," he wrote. And for those not satisfied with repetitive work, the assembly line actually *increased* the opportunity for creative endeavor. "The need for skilled artisans and creative genius is greater under mass production than without it," Ford declared. Highland Park demanded a host of machinists, pattern-makers, and tool-builders whose jobs required great skill. "Today we have skilled mechanics in plenty, [but] they do not produce automobiles—they make it easy for others to produce them," Ford explained. The assembly line simply recognized the differences in human makeup by separating those who treasured job skills from those who sought easier tasks. "We have to recognize the unevenness in human mental equipments," Ford insisted. "If every job in our place required skill the place would never have existed."[51]

If Ford was unblinking in his appraisal of human frailty, he was equally so in his promotion of the discipline required by a Taylorized workplace. In a factory like Highland Park, where an extreme division of labor had created a web of interconnectedness, workers had to perform tasks as they were defined. "We expect the men to do what they are told," Ford said bluntly. "The organization is so highly specialized and one part is so dependent upon another that we could not for a moment consider allowing men to have their own way." For Ford, once again, this impulse was partly rooted in tradition. The discipline required by the assembly line, he believed, was little different from that required by the old-fashioned demands of the work ethic.[52]

Ford's advocacy of Taylorized work, however, did not render him insensitive to its dangers. On occasion, he lashed out at the "theorists and bookish reformers" who romanticized the fulfillments of "medieval toil." And he insisted that company investigations revealed that assembly-line workers did not wish to switch tasks. "They do not like changes," Ford concluded. "If [a worker] stays in production it is because he likes it."[53]

In calmer moments, however, Ford confessed to being troubled, even anguished by the implications of routine, thoughtless assembly-line labor. "Repetitive labor—the doing of one thing over and over and always in the same way—is a terrifying prospect to a certain kind of mind. It is terrifying to me," he admitted. "I could not possibly do the same thing day in and day out." In a philosophical moment, he went even further. Though scientific management had removed much of the physical burden from modern industrial labor, he noted, it was now time to take reform forward:

> The time has come when drudgery must be taken out of labor. It is not work that men object to, but the element of drudgery. We must drive out drudgery wherever we find it. We shall never be wholly civilized until we remove the treadmill from the daily job. . . . We have succeeded to a very great extent in relieving men of the heavier and more onerous jobs that used to sap their strength, but even when lightening the heavier labor we have not yet succeeded in removing monotony. That is another field that beckons us—the abolition of monotony, and in trying to accomplish that we shall doubtless discover other changes that will have to be made in our system.[54]

Ultimately, however, Ford dismissed his doubts about Taylorized work by turning to a familiar source of comfort: consumer abundance. The best rationale for the new forms of mass-production labor, he concluded, lay in the rewards of consumption. Assembly-line work meant more productivity, which brought higher wages, which provided more money for workers to enjoy material goods. For Ford, this opportunity, more than anything else, compensated for the monotonous aspects of modern industrial labor. Taylorized methods, he believed fervently, had opened new doors for "the increasing supply of human needs and the development of new standards of living . . . the enlargement of leisure, the increase of human contacts, the extension of individual range." Ford condensed this belief into a maxim: "The methods of mass production enable the worker to earn more and thus to have more."[55]

In a larger sense, Ford grasped that mass consumption provided the very raison d'être for mass production. The powerful surge of consumer demand in the early twentieth century provided the impetus for new production techniques like the assembly line. To anyone who would listen, Ford preached this message: "The necessary, precedent condition of mass production is a capacity, latent or developed, of mass consumption, the ability to absorb large production. The two go together, and in the latter may be traced the reasons for the former." The desires of consumers underlaid the outpouring of modern industrial production. Workers' ability to participate in this consumption is what reconciled them to the monotony of the assembly line. In his view, it was a wise and fulfilling trade-off.[56]

In another way, however, Ford's understanding of the problems of Taylorized labor was self-interested to the point of brutality. He believed that workers could simply be molded to fit the requirements of mass-production labor. Charles Sorensen told a story of how, on a Monday after Easter, when many of the men were missing from the factory after too much celebrating over the holiday, several managers were upset that production schedules would fall behind. Ford walked up when they were complaining, listened, and said, "Well, that is an easy thing to fix." Flabbergasted, Sorensen asked for his magical solution. Ford replied, "Well, go ahead and make some more men for these jobs." This formula was vintage Ford—simple, effective, and slightly unsettling. If men would not, or could not, embrace the new system of labor, you "made" new ones who would do so. Henry Ford believed that workers could be mass-produced in the same way that he mass-produced cars.[57]

Ultimately, it was an ironic situation. With his simpleminded belief that men could be made like so many interchangeable parts, Ford exhibited an inhumane streak that undermined the work ethic to which he was devoted. Mass-produced workers, by definition, could never appreciate the old-fashioned moral dimension of labor that he valued so highly. So, at the very time he proclaimed the importance of work, he unintentionally degraded it in ways he never really understood. In trying to straddle the divide between two worlds of work in such an awkward fashion, Ford lost his balance, and thus did the only thing he could do. Having robbed labor of any joy, sense of accomplishment, and moral meaning, he made the *fruits* of labor, or consumption, the real standard of happiness and achievement in one's work life in modern America. The circle was completed. Producing the Model T, as well as purchasing it, helped realize Henry Ford's vision of a consumer paradise.

Nine

Folk Hero

In the summer of 1914, *Collier's Magazine* published a long article entitled "Detroit the Dynamic," which examined the explosive growth of this Great Lakes city. It described booming industrial activity, with new factories shooting up almost weekly, a bustling commercial scene with merchant ships cruising down the Detroit River into Lake Erie, an expanding transportation hub that sent large railroad lines snaking out to every section of the United States, a growing population that kept street construction lagging behind multiplying neighborhoods, and an ambitious civic leadership that oversaw the construction of banks, office buildings, museums, and libraries. Julian Street's article culminated with a description of his trip to Detroit's westernmost boundary, where he came face to face with the city's most celebrated feature. He spoke with Henry Ford.

The industrialist's rapidly rising reputation intrigued Street. Along with the Model T, Ford's name had spread throughout the United States—indeed, throughout the world. Yet, Street noted, "little had surfaced that gave me a clear idea of Mr. Ford's personality. I wanted to see him. . . . I wanted to know what kind of man he was to look at and to listen to." After jousting with a battalion of protective secretaries in Ford's office, and delaying for a day while he toured the factory, Street finally ran his mysterious prey to ground. He walked away mightily impressed with Ford's physical and mental qualities.

Ford, wrote Street, was a lean, wiry man of good height with gray hair, rather sharp features, and a casual yet determined way about him. The eyes were impressive—keen, set wide apart with a net of wrinkles at the edges, and expressive in their reflection of shrewdness, kindliness, humor, and a distinct wistfulness. The mouth, determined, collaborated with the eyes to form a dry grin that punctuated many of his statements. Overall, Street observed, Ford radiated a presence of understated power. Exuding quiet confidence, he leaned back in his chair, his legs crossed and resting atop a wooden wastebasket.

But for Street, the shape of Ford's character was even more striking. A man of common tastes and ordinary habits, Ford conveyed a powerful sense of honesty and trustworthiness. He confessed to having little use for money and noted that he avoided high society while still socializing with friends he had known for twenty years. Plain culinary tastes completed the picture. Ford related that over the previous few months he had hired a series of cooks but remained dissatisfied because "they try to give me fancy food, but I won't stand for it. They can't cook as well as Mrs. Ford either—none of them can."

One of Ford's comments particularly revealed his utter lack of pretense. When asked his opinion about art, "he replied, 'I wouldn't give five cents for all the art in the world.'" This unwillingness to posture struck Street as refreshingly honest, even admirable. True, with such an admission "Ford declares himself a barbarian of sorts. But a good, honest, open-hearted barbarian is a fine creature." In Street's assessment:

> There never was a man more genuine than Mr. Ford. He hasn't the faintest sign of that veneer so common to distinguished men, which is most eloquently described by the slang term front. Nor is he, on the other hand, one of those men who (like so many politicians) try to simulate a simple manner. He is just exactly Henry Ford, no more, no less; take it or leave it.[1]

Such images of Henry Ford had begun to permeate American public life. As his Model T spread throughout the United States, a similarly simple, utilitarian, and dependable image of the Detroit automaker followed in its wake. He appeared as an unassuming man of the people, a "just folks" producer, guileless and honest, a heroic defender of the little guy, and a provincial whose native wit and shrewdness elevated him above more sophisticated classes. Ford molded a public image of himself as a self-educated, native genius with a homespun manner and unsounded depths of wisdom. In the process, he demolished an older, ruthless image of the American big businessman and remolded it for a new century. Unlike robber barons such as John D. Rockefeller, J. P. Morgan, and Cornelius Vanderbilt, Ford emerged as a folk hero in the eyes of ordinary citizens. He became a symbol not only of responsible business, but of the most cherished American values. Henry Ford, it is fair to say, emerged as a beloved figure in the popular imagination.

How did this happen? Ford's status as folk hero was partly accidental, partly purposeful; it was partly the product of events beyond his control and partly the product of his self-conscious manipulation of them. As Model T's began to blanket the country, Ford's "just folks" image seemed a genuine reflection of his personality. But Ford publicized this persona at every opportunity to gain fame for himself and sales for his automobile. He took full advantage of the commercial drawing power of his rough-hewn, man-of-the-people image.

One of the most important factors launching Ford's persona into its elevated public orbit was a bitter lawsuit that entangled him for years in legal maneuvers and courtroom litigation. From 1903 through its final settlement in 1911, this lawsuit threatened the very existence of the Ford Motor Company. Battling for his life as an automaker, Ford assumed a stance that earned much admiration from his fellow citizens.

On October 22, 1903, George B. Selden and the Electric Vehicle Company filed suit against the Ford Motor Company in the United States Circuit Court in New York. Henry Ford's production of automobiles, the lawsuit argued, was infringing upon the patent granted to Selden for his invention of a motor carriage with an engine running on gasoline or kerosene. The ensuing legal battle would rage for seven and a half years, gathering attention not only within the automobile industry but among a national audience increasingly addicted to buying cars. The stakes were high. If Ford lost, he could be forced out of business. But he fought back in a fashion that appealed to the deepest, most revered American values. He gained much of his folk-hero status during the contentious proceedings of the Selden suit.

An attorney from Rochester, New York, Selden had first filed a patent application in 1879 for a road vehicle of his own design. Over the next decade and a half, he amended his application with minor improvements that delayed the granting of the actual patent until the infant automobile industry had struggled to its feet and began to walk. In November 1895, Selden finally secured his patent for "a road-locomotive featuring a liquid hydro-carbon engine of the compression type." The patent extended backward to cover all such vehicles designed since 1879, and forward to cover those manufactured or sold until 1912. In 1899, Selden assigned the patent to the Electric Vehicle Company for cash and a percentage of whatever royalties it could collect. This company proceeded systematically to file suit against the largest automakers in the United States, such as the Winton Motor Carriage Company of Cleveland and the Buffalo Gasoline Motor Company.

Car manufacturers and automobile experts uniformly saw Selden's patent claim as preposterous, because it described a motor carriage in only the most general terms. Avoiding any exact mechanical descriptions, Selden noted vaguely that his vehicle was to have a compression engine, a steering mechanism, a tank for liquid fuel, a power shaft, some kind of clutch mechanism, and a carriage body for carrying passengers. In addition, rather than pretending that any of these elements were new, he claimed that combining them constituted an invention. Most galling of all, Selden never actually built his vehicle. Thus critics scoffed at the patent, observing that mechanics and engineers all over the United States had been developing motorized carriages in many forms throughout the 1890s. Selden's claims, they believed, were so broad as to be meaningless.

By 1903, however, twenty-six automobile companies had caved in to legal pressure and decided that settlement would be cheaper than litigation. After negotiation with the Electric Vehicle Company, these companies recognized the validity of the Selden patent and formed the Association of Licensed Automobile Manufacturers (ALAM). ALAM members agreed to pay a royalty of 1.25 percent of each car's price to the Electric Vehicle Company, which then sent a portion of the money to George B. Selden, kept part for itself, and gave the rest to ALAM. In turn, ALAM granted licenses to manufacturers who recognized the Selden patent, and sued those who refused to cooperate. In other words, the Selden patent became the basis for a monopoly that controlled the manufacture of automobiles through the issuing (or nonissuing) of licenses to companies.

Henry Ford responded initially in the summer of 1903 by approaching ALAM and inquiring about a license. The organization refused, noting its skepticism about Ford's ability to meet its manufacturing standards and to become a respected part of the industry. A short time later, ALAM began running advertisements in Detroit newspapers proclaiming its leadership of American car manufacturing and warning that all unlicensed manufacturers would be prosecuted for patent infringement. At this point, Ford, distrustful of ALAM from the outset, reacted defiantly. His company ran a series of ads blasting the validity of the Selden patent, denouncing the claims of ALAM, and refusing to purchase a license. The company promised protection to all consumers and dealers who might handle or purchase Ford cars.[2]

As the Ford resistance took shape, two themes came to the fore. First, the campaign portrayed ALAM as a monopolistic, greedy "trust" seeking to dominate the market and drive out legitimate competitors. Second, it made Henry Ford the centerpiece of its effort, portraying him as a heroic individualist who was not afraid to stand up to the forces of corrupt power. This strategy depended on cultural values as much as technical legalisms, and sought to try the case in the forum of public opinion as much as in the courtroom.

The issue of monopoly emerged quickly in Ford's assault on ALAM. In a public letter to the editor of the *Cycle and Automobile Trade Journal* that was essentially a declaration of war, James Couzens sarcastically noted that ALAM was "not a philanthropic institution. . . . Its members have joined together because of some expected pecuniary benefit in monopolizing the market under cover of the Selden patent, and not because they believe the patent to be impregnable." A barrage of Ford advertisements over the next year repeated this characterization over and over. In response to ALAM's attempts to scare consumers away from purchasing unlicensed cars, a 1904 Ford ad claimed, "The Ford Motor Car cannot be beaten by the Trust in competition; so they have erected a scarecrow, to frighten the buying public." Subsequent ads proclaimed "The Ford, Boosted into Popular Favor by the Trust," and insisted that "The Ford has sounded the death knell of the Trust with its attempt to make a monopoly of the motor car industry and to charge exorbitant prices for inferior cars."[3]

The antitrust flavor of the Ford campaign against ALAM shrewdly capitalized on one of the most heated issues in American public life in the early 1900s. By the turn of the century, concern about the unchecked power of large American corporations was influencing debate and policy-making throughout the country. The emergence of the Progressive movement in politics had helped secure Theodore Roosevelt in the White House with his famous reputation as a trustbuster. Muckraking journalists such as Ida Tarbell, whose series in *McClure's* on "The History of Standard Oil" had brought to light the ruthless tactics and monopolistic bent of John D. Rockefeller, had helped raise a cry for government regulation of unfair corporate practices. The spirit of political reform was in the air, and Ford's denunciation of ALAM as the automobile trust found a responsive audience.[4]

Another motif emerged alongside Ford's trustbusting theme during the Selden controversy. Henry Ford himself, appearing as an individual entrepreneur and straightforward competitor, took center stage as a compelling symbol. In an image shaped by advertisements and interviews, he appeared before the public as an industrial David standing alone against a powerful, monopolistic Goliath.

Company advertisements shaped this image of lonely heroism by presenting its leader as a man of ability and principle. Henry Ford, they noted, had put his "extraordinary mechanical ability into building the best motor cars yet produced for popular use. . . . [This car] costs only $900. The Trust car that compares with it costs $1500." References to "the mechanical genius of Mr. Henry Ford" and to the fact that "Henry Ford alone has done more to develop the automobile industry than the combined members of the Licensed Association" became mainstays of Ford advertising during the Selden suit. Ads insisted that his real quarrel with the automobile trust concerned its attempt to restrain his individual initiative. ALAM must allow him "to pursue his own course and work out his own inventions unhampered and without interference."[5]

Ford's own words reinforced his growing image as a heroic individualist. He entered the fray directly, with articles and newspaper statements, lashing out at his legal foes in forceful, indignant language. George Selden's patent, he claimed, "has never been considered seriously except as a foundation to keep the field of motor car manufacture in the hands of a limited few." Ford exuded optimism, insisting that his company's crusade was inspiring resistance among other independent manufacturers. "The ingeniously built structure that proposed to have a monopoly of motor car manufacture and [to] boost prices accordingly," he wrote confidently, "is nearing its end. . . . Trust methods have failed to produce results."[6]

Ford defined his opposition to the Selden patent in terms of deep-rooted American traditions. In his words:

> We possess just enough of that instinct of American freedom to cause us to rebel against oppression or unfair competition.
>
> It goes against the grain of Americanism to be coerced, or bluffed, or sandbagged; and men who will not fight in such circumstances do not, in my estimation, possess the highest degree of self-respect or even honesty—for I protest it is dishonest to bow to expediency in such a case, and thereby not only become contributors of graft money, but subject the entire automobile industry and buying constituency to a tax that is unjust and uncalled for.

He contended that his ALAM opponents were not actually automobile makers who had contributed to the industry's development, but manipulators "whose talents take the peculiar slant of smart practice and bluff." Here was the old contest for control in American commerce between honest producers and confidence men, hardworking entrepreneurs and unscrupulous schemers.[7]

After years of litigation and evidence gathering, the Selden suit finally reached its conclusion dramatically. In the initial stage, on September 15, 1909, Judge Charles Hough of the Circuit Court of the Southern District of

New York rendered a favorable decision to ALAM by affirming the validity of the Selden patent. Though elation swept through the ALAM ranks, more experienced observers counseled patience. They knew that Judge Hough had little expertise in patent law, and that an appeal would likely bring a different judgment. Such prudence proved well founded. In stage two, ALAM and Ford attorneys presented their cases to a three-judge panel in the New York Court of Appeals on November 22–25, 1910, and then turned over their briefs, exhibits, and transcribed testimony. The trio of judges rendered their unanimous opinion on January 9, 1911, ruling in Ford's favor and overturning the lower court's decision. The Selden patent, they wrote, did not cover the great variety of engine types, transmissions, body carriages, and ignition systems that had been developed independently by many engineers and mechanics since 1879. The idea of the automobile, they noted, was not the property of any one person.[8]

Ford's victory inspired an avalanche of public acclaim. Over one thousand telegrams from ordinary citizens as well as figures such as Charles E. Duryea, the automobile pioneer, and Harvey S. Firestone, the tire manufacturer, congratulated Ford on his great victory against "trust methods." At a victory dinner held in New York City's Hotel Rector on January 13, testimonials to Ford's fortitude flowed as abundantly as the fine food and libation. Friends, associates, and employees of the Ford Motor Company vied with one another in congratulating the victor and applauding his strength of character. Unexpected recognition of Ford's newly won stature came from a special guest, Alfred L. Reeves, director of ALAM, whose generous words took his former opponents by surprise. "Henry Ford is the greatest man in the automobile world; the Ford plant is the greatest automobile plant in the world; and the Ford organization is the greatest automobile organization in the world," he declared.[9]

The press, however, played the largest role in proclaiming Henry Ford's virtues. Trade publications such as *Horseless Age* and *Motor World* praised him as a great individualist, a heroic opponent of monopoly, and a dominant force in the automobile industry. The Detroit *Free Press* ran an editorial entitled "Ford the Fighter." The struggle against ALAM, the newspaper opined, had revealed Henry Ford to be "a man of backbone" who single-handedly took on a powerful opponent in defense of his convictions. It was "a spectacle to win the applause of all men with red blood." The Detroit *Journal* declared the victor to be a genuine American hero. "It would have been considerably to Mr. Ford's personal advantage, in dollars and cents, had he compromised with or capitulated to the Selden patent holders years ago," it wrote. "But for more than seven years now he has fought on, almost alone, against huge odds—for a principle. He believed that his own rights were imperiled and the rights of every American citizen who is entitled to the rewards of his enterprise, industry, and brains." Many other newspapers followed suit in praising Ford's struggle against the forces of economic privilege.[10]

The positive effects of the Selden suit victory reverberated for years. About a decade later, in *My Life and Work*, Ford speculated, "Perhaps nothing so well advertised the Ford car and Ford Motor Company as did this suit. It appeared that we were the underdog and we had the public's sympathy." Many years later, he was still trading on the popularity that he accumulated during the Selden struggle. On the *Ford Sunday Evening Hour* of January 6, 1935, W. J. Cameron, Ford's spokesman in this period, told a national radio audience that a single automaker's struggle against the forces of monopoly a quarter-century earlier had guaranteed competition in the auto industry. Through this action, Cameron argued, Henry Ford "liberated the entire industry," and the American people were the beneficiaries.[11]

Ford's impressive victory in the Selden suit greatly elevated his stature in the public eye. It was, however, only the beginning. With the runaway success of the Model T becoming evident around the same time, Ford's national image assumed larger and larger proportions. More than just an inspiring curiosity—the businessman as antimonopolist—he began to appear as a homegrown folk hero.

In the early 1910s, flattering portraits of Henry Ford appeared in journalistic venues all over the country. They created an image that was curiously mixed: a common man of the people who was, at the same time, larger than life. It rapidly became the stuff of legend, for the mythic Ford taking shape in the public mind was America personified.

Journalists were delighted to discover a traditional American success tale. Ford, they wrote, provided a modern update of an old ideal of the self-made man. Of modest background, he had relied upon diligence, hard work, and unwavering commitment to a new idea to climb to an eminent position. Headlines proclaimed this up-by-your-bootstraps success: "Henry Ford in Fifteen Years Rises to Be, in Point of Income, One of the Richest Men in the World." Stories detailed his rags-to-riches story and concluded that his achievements made him "at once one of the world's marked men, entirely aside from his enormous wealth." They attributed his success, in the best American tradition, to a relentless, self-directed individualism.

According to one magazine article, Ford had achieved so much because "he was determined to make the kind of automobile he wanted in the way he wanted it, and for the price he wanted. He was determined to do the thing he liked best without interference."[12]

A sign of Ford's new prominence came in the summer of 1914, when President Woodrow Wilson summoned him to the White House for discussions about the sluggish national economy. Ford assured the President that everything would be fine and encouraged patience. Stories on this conference carried a picture of Ford and described him as "A New Adviser to the President." He was described as "a self-made man . . . unassuming, of the utmost simplicity of character."[13]

In fact, some of these favorable stories adopted a highly romanticized tone. In 1913, an interviewer asked him about the future of the auto, and then offered readers a description that could have been lifted from a popular novel of the day:

> Mr. Ford looked out of the window toward the sunset. His face, bronzed by country life, was tinged by a ruddy glow. He passed a hand over his iron gray hair and his eyes took on a contemplative look. Again that suspicion of a tolerant smile hovered at the corners of his mouth. It seemed to say that the man who had made a $10,000,000 dividend possible, recreating Sinbad's diamond valley out of a mechanic's brain, was thinking of the painful early path. It suggested that eagle flights of 200 or 300 years do not belong to the inventor but [instead] toilsome days and wakeful nights with infinitesimal progress.

With such puffery, it was little wonder that Americans began looking at him as a national treasure.[14]

The glowing Ford image particularly stressed one theme: instead of being spoiled by his success, he cherished his roots and retained a down-to-earth sensibility. By the early 1910s, nearly all stories on Ford stressed his rural background, simple style, and modest material desires. His unwillingness to upgrade the Model T with fancy accessories, his wife's hobby of darning, his preference for home cooking, and his penchant for wearing overalls on his farm were characteristics of a man who had risen to great heights but never forgot where he came from. As *Harper's Weekly* noted, Ford's advocacy of ordinary people flowed from his own status as one. It informed readers, "Faith in the everyday man, exalted faith, is an integral part of the Ford character. I have been a workingman myself, he says." In

Ford's words, "When a man's hands are callused and women's hands are worn, you may be sure honesty is there. That's more than you can say about many soft white hands."[15]

Ford's fondness for the commonplace became apparent in his attitude about money. The rapidly escalating sales of the Model T had made him a rich man. But as scores of newspaper and magazine articles made clear, Ford seemed supremely unconcerned with money. "What do I want with more money? I shall never use what I have, most likely," he typically told journalists. As *Harper's Weekly* informed readers, Ford's conversation seldom touched on matters of profit, but focused almost entirely on the usefulness of his car and the productivity of his factory. "Money-making is only incidental to Henry Ford's work," it concluded.[16]

Thus the Henry Ford viewed by Americans was a man unswayed by his growing affluence who loved his work and enjoyed nature and rural life. He did not smoke or drink and had unsophisticated tastes in music, the theater, or art. Avoiding the nouveau-riche role, he shunned gambling, horseracing, yachting, and other forms of fancy entertainment. Ford was deeply antielitist. He disparaged intellectuals, particularly those who criticized his factory: "I would like to get all the college professors in the world, bar none, and put them out in that factory, and then see what they would do with it." He came before the American public as a Thoreau-like figure, whose deep love of nature was reflected in his hobby of bird-watching. His simple tastes in life, concluded one magazine writer, "bear incontrovertible testimony to the sincerity of his philanthropy and the glory of his self-reliance."[17]

Ford's public spirit gave another boost to his status as a folk hero. In 1913, he stepped in when the city of Detroit failed to sell enough bonds to pay for several civic-improvement projects and purchased $1 million worth of the bonds. Around the same time, he launched a project to help poor, wayward youth in Detroit. He ensconced several dozen of them at Valley Farm, on his Dearborn property, where they were fed and clothed, taught in the local school, and put to work at agricultural labor under adult supervision. Here was a new kind of businessman who saw "no good reason why business cannot be conducted that will add to the world's stock of good will," opined one magazine article.[18]

Ford stressed his dedication to benevolence, stewardship, and goodwill in the conduct of his company. In 1915, he spoke of his belief in helping his fellow man. "You have seen two fellows on a street corner," he told a magazine. "Both of them are down and out; but one has ten cents. With that he can buy a bun and a bed for himself. Or he can buy a bun for himself and a bun for his chum, and take chances on getting a bed. If he does that he is my kind of folks."[19]

As his public image became more radiant in the early 1910s, some journalists began to dig deeper into its essential nature. Different explanations
emerged. Harry Nimmo, after spending a good deal of time with Ford and
evaluating his popularity, concluded that the automaker uniquely reflected
the reformist spirit of the times. Ford's benevolence toward his fellow man,
Nimmo argued, was the product of the popular spirit of progressive amelio-
ration that "breathed into his soul the brotherhood of man."[20]

Gerald Stanley Lee, in a 1914 *Harper's Weekly* essay entitled "Is Ford an
Inspired Millionaire?," offered a more trenchant analysis. Henry Ford, he
argued, had stumbled across a key dynamic in the modern world of mass
production and consumption: to advertise oneself was to advertise one's
product. While producing a car for ordinary citizens, Ford had discovered
that this feat created "personal news to every man on this planet." Moreover, he understood that if you wanted to get favorable publicity you needed
to be interesting. According to Lee, Ford learned a fundamental lesson in
the early 1910s:

> To make a sensation, be one. Then other people will attend to it—
> people in general, people going by in the streets—anybody and
> everybody will do your advertising for you and do it for nothing.
> The real reason that the Ford car is a sensation is that Ford is. A man
> like Ford in business today—the way he is made inside and the way
> his mind works, is personal and necessary news to everybody. Every-
> body has to advertise Henry Ford whether they want to or not.[21]

Lee unearthed something fundamental. In the glare of growing media
attention after the Selden suit and the Model T, Ford certainly loomed large
and virtuous in the public eye. Yet this involved more than good fortune.
Perceptively sizing up the situation, Ford grasped the possibilities latent in
his popular image. While newspaper and magazine stories were telling his
story, he simultaneously maneuvered to take advantage of this newfound
personal status. Company advertising and publicity used the picture of its
founder as a homespun hero. Quite self-consciously, Henry Ford set about
making himself a sensation.

As early as 1908, Ford Motor Company's advertisements displayed a unique
strategy. While praising the sturdy features and low price of the Model T,
they claimed that its quality was guaranteed by the individual at the head of
the company:

Henry Ford promised three years ago to build a high grade touring car, and sell it at a heretofore unheard of price, and now just as surely as every claim made for the small car was made good, just so surely has Ford made good this promise. . . . You know that Henry Ford can build a better car for less money than any other manufacturer on the face of the earth. You know it because he has always done it, and that is your guarantee of his ability, and your security in dealing with him.

Such assertions became a key feature of Ford ads over the next several years. Merging with a swelling stream of news stories, company efforts steadily raised Henry Ford's stature in the early 1910s.[22]

The company's promotional literature to its dealers and sellers also encouraged this cult of personality. A 1909 pamphlet prominently featured a photo of Henry Ford and described him as "the pioneer automobile manufacturer of this country." Another pamphlet claimed that Ford made a quality car at half the price of other manufacturers. "That's a statement that would appear to be out of reason if Henry Ford did not have five years of continuous success," it added. "Henry Ford has built more automobiles than any other manufacturer and he has never designed or built a failure."[23]

Similar portrayals became a staple of company newspaper and magazine advertisements in this era. Sometimes they featured his personal success story, as in the 1910 ad claiming, "Henry Ford has been the greatest factor in the development of the automobile industry, greater than any other man in the world." Other ads stressed Ford's character. "The mechanical genius of Mr. Henry Ford enabled the Ford Motor Co. to produce a car so perfect in construction and so low in price that it has sounded the death knell of the Trust," read an ad released during the Selden suit. Some advertisements played upon the founder's growing prestige, noting that Henry Ford "stands out independent and alone, clear and strong, as the most dominant factor in the automobile industry of today." Finally, of course, Ford's loyalty to the common people featured prominently in its advertisements. A 1912 advertising pamphlet entitled *The Woman and the Ford* acclaimed "Mr. Henry Ford's determination to build an automobile for the people. . . . He has stricken the motor car from the list of luxuries, and made it a commodity, within the reach of all."[24]

A particularly interesting use of Henry's image played off the growing impersonality of modern big business. Company publicity liked to stress that its founder, unlike many tycoons in this age of incorporation, personally directed his company's affairs. A pamphlet entitled *Ford Motor Cars*

(1912) reassured readers that Ford was an old-fashioned, hands-on businessman rather than a paper-pushing bureaucrat:

> Mr. Ford is continually moving through the large Ford plant, here,
> there, everywhere; alert, observing, thinking, doing. No part of this
> great manufacturing establishment is strange to Mr. Ford. He
> knows every nook and corner of it. He knows every bit of machin-
> ery and what is expected of each machine. He knows of the heat
> treatment of metals. He is everywhere—in the designing room, in
> the engineers quarters, in the superintendent of production's office,
> in the foundry . . . and his active, inventive mind is continually
> thinking out improvement of product, reduction of costs, increase
> of output.[25]

The convergence of advertising and journalism to shape Ford's folk-
hero status could be seen in the efforts of Elbert Hubbard. He had been a
leading American promoter of the Arts and Crafts movement in the 1890s,
which sought to revive traditions of craftsmanship to counteract modern
dissipation caused by technology, urban luxury, and bureaucratic work.
Hubbard became the editor of *The Philistine*, an iconoclastic magazine that
playfully mixed literary assaults on the genteel tradition, quasi-socialist
political rants, and Arts and Crafts encomiums. A few years later, in 1908, he
founded *The Fra: Exponent of the American Philosophy*, a more intellectual
journal that promoted his new message of human brotherhood through
enlightened capitalism and business prosperity. Hubbard saw Henry Ford
as a paragon of the new American businessman who would lead the country
to prosperity, and he did his best to publicize the automaker in the early
1910s.[26]

In 1912, Hubbard's enthusiasm for Ford earned him access to a company publication. His article, entitled "A Little Journey to the Workshop of
Henry Ford," which appeared in *Ford Times*, presented its subject as an heir
to the democratic creed of Thomas Jefferson and Abraham Lincoln. Ford,
Hubbard insisted, was a manufacturer with many other talents and virtues:
hard worker, teacher, manager, leader, farmer, nature lover. This businessman had proved his merit by writing "a Declaration of Independence for
the automobile business" with his triumph during the Selden suit. In the
author's simple conclusion, "Henry Ford is a Public Servant."[27]

Ford's greatest display of virtue, according to Hubbard, came in his
business practices. "Henry Ford is not the typical American businessman,"
Hubbard asserted. "He is more than that." Rather than merely pursuing

profit, he sought to make a quality, affordable product while maintaining a respectful relationship with his employees. He shouldered personal responsibility for the performance of his automobiles. Moreover, he saw business as a means to "human betterment" and became the "man who made it possible for all humanity to ride in motor cars." In fact, the Model T mirrored the qualities of its creator. "A Ford automobile looks like Henry Ford," Hubbard wrote. "It is light in physical weight, strong in every part, well-balanced, safe, effective, and thoroughly efficient."[28]

The following year, Hubbard offered another Ford-as-folk-hero piece. In November 1913, *The Fra* published an article that polished the industrialist's image to a bright sheen. In modern America, Hubbard asserted, "the theme is Henry Ford. You hear it in barber shops, barrooms, smoking-rooms, ad-clubs, Sunday Schools, sewing-circles." There were several reasons for his popularity. Ford produced a sturdy, economical car; he was a brilliant businessman who directed a massive yet highly efficient organization; he had pioneered techniques of standardization that transformed industrial manufacturing. But even more, Hubbard argued, Ford displayed a variety of attractive personal qualities that connected him to ordinary Americans:

> He is a man of few words—simple, plain, unaffected, democratic, direct. . . . He uses no tobacco, no strong drink and no strong language. Moderation is his watchword. He is temperate in all things, except in the manufacture of automobiles. . . .
>
> Into his car Ford has put the truth, integrity, simplicity, sanity, and commonsense which he himself possesses. . . . Henry Ford is not a highbrow, not a theorist, not a professional reformer—he is a worker and an executive. Also, he is a teacher and a learner. . . . He has the work habit, the health habit, the play habit, and the study habit.

As the author summarized, "Here is a new kind of millionaire."[29]

Hubbard's promotion of Ford reached its apex with the publication of what was probably the first biography of the car manufacturer. In a brief hagiography of twenty-nine pages, Hubbard analyzed his achievements as a master of standardized production, unfolded his life story as a tale of success, and compared his public influence to that of Thomas Jefferson. "As an inventor, creator, manufacturer, humanitarian, and public servant, the name of Henry Ford will endure," Hubbard concluded. "He will live in history . . . as one of the Makers of America."[30]

Thus, by the mid-1910s, writers, journalists, advertisers, and everyday citizens had joined forces to make Henry Ford one of the most famous and publicized figures in the United States. But what of the man himself? Were the virtues enumerated in dozens of articles genuine, or just a public-relations ploy? Was he really devoted to stewardship, common taste, and his fellow man, or was this simply a strategy to sell more Model T's? Like the questions, the answers were complex.

In 1914, a startling story broke on news wires around the United States. Former President Theodore Roosevelt, in a public statement, complained that Henry Ford was getting too much attention. The Detroit automaker, he noted sourly, was receiving more publicity than even President Wilson. Nor did Roosevelt let up. Years later, he was still complaining that Ford had employed "an army of press agents" to keep himself in the public eye. "Henry, like Barnum, has been a great advertiser," groused the old Rough Rider. How could Teddy Roosevelt, whose notorious love of the limelight had earned the quip that "he wants to be the bride at every wedding and the corpse at every funeral," complain that someone was gaining excessive public attention? This was like hearing Ty Cobb denounce fierce competition in baseball, or Lillian Gish criticize the popularity of the movies. A newspaper captured the irony. "The Terrible Teddy has so long maintained the mastery of the spotlight that he brooks with impatience any rivals," it observed sardonically. But, as the editorial concluded, Americans were fascinated by Ford because he was "doing something for the country in general all the time and he is unusually modest about his work."[31]

The Roosevelt episode revealed not only that Ford was becoming a celebrity by the mid-1910s, but that his folk-hero status was now a subject of public fascination. Newspapers and magazines commented on both the man and the growing cloud of publicity that surrounded him. Clearly, Ford's popularity had become news.

The Associated Advertising Clubs of the World, at their annual convention in Atlantic City, voted Ford "the best advertised individual in America, though at least 99 percent of his publicity comes to him without his lifting a finger to seek it." A Detroit publication suggested that an epidemic of "Ford-osis" had swept through the United States:

It's on the brain and in the blood of the American people. They gobble the Ford stuff, and never stop to reason whether they like it, or whether it has any real merit in it. . . . Some of his words and acts, if spoken and done by any other man, would strike you as being more or less silly. Yet, under the spell of Ford-osis, you would hail them as matters of boundless consequence, and you would be the first to snatch from the fingers of a screaming newsboy the edition that breaks this news to the world.[32]

The growing hoopla surrounding Ford made it difficult to judge his genuine qualities. In certain ways, his image seemed to capture his essence. At the same time, however, the motivations of a complicated man pulled in a different direction. Moreover, a process of evolution was at work. Under the pressure of escalating fame that came with the launching of the Model T and the successful conclusion of the Selden suit, Ford changed. He may have entered this era as a provincial who eschewed sophistication, clung to several deeply felt ideas, manufactured his unique car for the people, and avoided the public limelight. But, inevitably, he did not stay that way.

To be sure, in certain aspects and at certain times, Henry Ford lived the principles he espoused. Much of the time, he was indeed a man of the people, defender of the work ethic, and responsible steward of wealth who shied away from the glare of direct publicity. A genuinely shy man, Ford loathed most public appearances. The larger the crowd, the more uncomfortable he became. According to one longtime associate, "He was a very good speaker with two or three people, just sitting around a table, but with half a dozen or more he became very retiring and could not express himself as freely." By the early 1910s, stories of Ford's woeful public appearances were becoming legendary. At a Detroit banquet in 1913, where fellow industrialist Charles M. Schwab spoke glowingly of him, *Motor Age* reported, "Ford became so embarrassed that he slid down in his chair, and before Schwab had finished, had completed a vanishing act . . . almost under the table." At a 1915 dinner celebrating the production of the one-millionth Model T, Ford displayed his notorious terror of public speaking. When asked to say a few words, he reluctantly stood up, said, "Gentlemen, a million of anything is a great many," and sat down as the audience looked around in bewilderment and then slowly began to applaud.[33]

In his public writings, Ford displayed his homespun virtue by consistently defending the interests of ordinary citizens. In a 1916 essay, he argued that the humane, wise manager remembered that workers were much like himself. "He must not make the mistake of thinking of them as units of wage earners or as being in any way different from himself," Ford wrote. "If he is going to get their best work and effort, their interest, and consequently the best results in his business, he has got to realize that he has human beings working for him who have the same ambitions and desires that he has." He also insisted that businessmen should focus on service rather than profits. "If people would go into business with the idea that they are going to serve the public and their employees as well as themselves, they would be assured of success at the very start," he asserted.[34]

Ford did more than just talk. In 1914, he backed up his rhetoric by launching the construction of a new hospital in Detroit with his own money. In a statement to the press, he linked this medical institution to a larger vision of enhancing the public good. Good health and the prevention of disease, he said, should be promoted by factory owners and businessmen as well as by the family. New hospitals and safe, sunny factories, he suggested, would nourish "healthy, happy living—the common sense of living, it might be called."[35]

But although Ford sincerely supported an ethic of public virtue, there were self-serving elements also at work. He not only sensed that publicity had the power to spread his fame and to promote his company, but he began to enjoy the attention. This convergence of influences pushed him to manipulation of his public image. He encouraged company advertising to focus on his biography while he eagerly seized every opportunity to talk about his regard for common people. In a philanthropic venture such as building the hospital, he made sure that Detroiters knew about it by announcing a contest to choose a suitable name for the institution. Increasingly, Ford kept one eye trained on public opinion in nearly everything he did.

Insiders at the company knew that their boss was more than a simple mechanic who only wanted to make cars and avoid crowds. Charles Sorensen wrote with characteristic candor. "No, Henry Ford was not modest. . . . He pretended to be humble when with people who did not know him. But I knew this was an act. . . . He sought publicity. . . . He wanted to be observed." E. G. Pipp, managing editor of the Detroit *News* and Ford's informal public-relations counselor by the mid-1910s, claimed that Ford's great skill as a "publicity getter" had one goal: "self-glory." Fred L. Black, a longtime advertising and public-relations man at the company, probably came closest to the truth. His boss, he argued, was basically a bashful man who acquired a taste for, and a skill at generating, publicity. According to Black, "Nobody made Henry Ford from a publicity standpoint except himself. . . . The rest of us just merely helped. . . . It was a very strange combination; he was a very shy man with this amazing sense of publicity values."[36]

Perhaps the most penetrating analysis of Ford came from Samuel S. Marquis, the family minister, who joined the company in 1915 as director of its social programs. Marquis became a friend and adviser to the industrialist and had occasion to observe him closely and speak with him intimately. His reading of Ford's nature, published in a book in 1923, carries a special weight. Marquis believed Ford's folk-hero image was partly genuine and partly contrived, accurate in its essence yet self-consciously magnified.

To Marquis, it was clear that Ford truly identified with the life of the common man. Wealth and fame had but small impact on his tastes, values, and style of life. He lived relatively simply, enjoyed the seclusion of family life, and pursued quiet pleasures, such as bird-watching, that he had learned as a boy in rural Michigan. "Since becoming rich Henry Ford has acquired no expensive tastes, formed no costly habits," Marquis noted. "His personal habits and pleasures remain very much as they were in the days of his obscurity. Wealth has simply lifted the lid, and that which is coming out . . . was always there." The reverend liked to tell a story about Ford's modest taste. The automaker once explained his aversion to servants: "I still like boiled potatoes with the skins on, and I do not want a man standing back of my chair at table laughing up his sleeve at me while I am taking the potatoes' jackets off."[37]

But then, Marquis asserted, in the mid-1910s a different side of Ford began to emerge, one that did not shun the public gaze or avoid reporters. Increasingly, he seemed to fall in love with creating publicity about himself. As Marquis put it, Ford "suddenly faced about, hired a publicity agent, jumped into the front page of every newspaper in the country, [and] bought and paid for space in which he advertised what were supposed to be his own ideas." In a chapter of his book entitled "The Art of Self-Advertising," Marquis argued that Ford became addicted to creating publicity after learning the important lesson that "from the self-advertising point of view, a sensational attempt is almost always as valuable for immediate purposes as a sensational achievement." Ford's theory became "It is a good thing to keep people talking about him, no matter what they say." Thus, by the mid-1910s, a new person had emerged who "would rather be the maker of public opinion than the manufacturer of a million automobiles a year."[38]

It seems clear that in many ways Henry Ford was exactly what he seemed: an extraordinary man with ordinary tastes. At the same time, however, he clearly came to savor the role of celebrity in the modern world. He had sought attention years earlier with automobile racing, but Ford made a quantum leap in this regard in the Model T era. He understood the lesson that publicity translated into sales. But he also seemed to grasp a more profound point: his folk-hero image provided a kind of comfort for ordinary Americans come face to face with a rapidly urbanizing, bureaucratizing, and modernizing society. They found it reassuring to know that a simple, honest, rural-raised entrepreneur was making their automobiles and leading them into a strange new future. Workaday citizens *wanted* to believe in Henry Ford, folk hero, and he helped them do it.

Thus Ford became one of the most famous men in the United States. He was not only wealthy, but an admirable figure who seemed to represent all that was best in the American character. A proponent of hard work and honesty, a down-home genius who outdistanced the sophisticates, an up-by-the-bootstraps success who remained loyal to his roots, an innovative inventor and engineer who respected fellow citizens of even the most modest means, Ford appeared as a new kind of industrialist who sought to serve the public. But his adventures with the Selden suit, the Model T, and the public print proved to be just a prelude to bigger things. Early in 1914, he made an announcement that sent him into the highest orbit of public approval.

Ten

Reformer

In early 1914, the Ford Motor Company announced that it was immediately doubling the standard wage of automobile workers. This startling news generated tremendous publicity and fervent debate. For months Americans seemed to talk of little else, as labor leaders praised it, business magnates denounced it, politicians cautiously tested the wind, and newspapers endlessly debated its merits and dangers. The Five-Dollar Day, as it soon became known, would forever be linked with the name of Henry Ford.

With this policy, Ford overturned the older robber-baron image of the American big businessman, whose instincts for profit and power rode roughshod over the public good. He came forward as a new kind of business leader, who sought to share the wealth and prosperity generated by his company. He represented an unfamiliar yet inspiring social type: the businessman as reformer. It was an image that made him, perhaps, the most admired man in the United States.

On January 5, 1914, Henry Ford and James Couzens summoned representatives from the Detroit press to Highland Park. They handed out a two-page typed statement announcing several new policies. Couzens read the news release aloud in his office as Ford stood by quietly, looking out the window. First, the company was reducing the workday from nine hours to eight; second, it was establishing three daily work shifts instead of two, so that the factory would be operating continuously. The third new policy, however, left reporters startled. Ford Motor Company vowed that within one week it would establish a basic pay rate of $5.00 per day for its workers, an amount that roughly doubled their existing paychecks.

The announcement's tone reflected its astonishing content. "The Ford Motor Co., the greatest and most successful automobile manufacturing company in the world, will, on Jan. 12, inaugurate the greatest revolution in the matter of rewards for its workers ever known to the industrial world," it began. The statement then explained that 90 percent of Ford workers would receive the bonus rate immediately and the other 10 percent would be able to qualify shortly. After listing details of the plan, it ended with another stunning pronouncement: "It is estimated that over $10,000,000 will be thus distributed over and above the regular wages of the men."[1]

After a brief discussion with Ford and Couzens, reporters sped from Highland Park to file stories for the late edition of city newspapers. Headlines announced the Ford action. "HENRY FORD GIVES $10,000,000 IN 1914 PROFITS TO HIS EMPLOYEES" was on the front page of the Detroit *Journal;* "NEW INDUSTRIAL ERA IS MARKED BY FORD'S SHARES TO LABORERS," said the Detroit *Free Press.* Within hours, news of the Ford action was spreading around the country—indeed, the world. "FORD AGAIN STAGGERS THE WORLD" appeared in *Motor World;* "FORD FACTORY HAS A HEART," in the Keokuk, Iowa, *Gate City;* "HENRY FORD, WHO MADE 26,000 EMPLOYEES HAPPY," in the New York *Sun;* "CRAZY FORD, THEY CALLED HIM, NOW HE'S TO GIVE AWAY MILLIONS," in the St. Louis *Post-Dispatch.* New York papers devoted fifty-two front-page columns to the story over the next two weeks. Dozens of editorial endorsements appeared, while a raft of cartoons illustrated the popular impact of Ford's new policy. One pictured a frustrated farm boy exclaiming to his father, "I want $5 a day for eight hours work or I'll quit right now an' go to Detroit, I will!"[2]

Moreover, the company was swamped by a deluge of mail from job seekers. Within one week of the announcement, nearly fourteen thousand such letters had arrived at the company's employment office; two months later, it was still receiving some five hundred letters a day. Even more astonishingly, within twenty-four hours of the announcement a crowd of men began gathering at the Highland Park gates hoping for employment. The shortening of the workday and the expansion of work shifts had opened up about four thousand jobs. These were filled quickly, but eventually ten to twelve thousand workmen descended on the factory—"anxious men, some ragged and unkempt, others seemingly prosperous," according to one newspaper—and stood in line in the bitter cold. At first, the situation was jovial, as the men built fires from scrap lumber and tree limbs and cheered Henry Ford at every opportunity. Soon, however, the situation became tense: tempers fraying, the men destroyed a wooden barrier, began pushing against metal fencing that had been erected to protect the Highland Park entrance, and refused to let company employees enter the facility. Detroit police tried to contain the crowd peacefully, and when that failed they resorted to drenching them with fire hoses. At this point a riot erupted, demonstrators hurling bricks, swinging crude clubs, and bombarding the factory with any debris at hand. Several agitators were arrested when the police finally gained control of the situation.[3]

Although the public reaction inspired by the Five-Dollar Day was easily understood, another question lingered. What prompted the company's decision to create this groundbreaking new policy? Friendly observers credited Henry Ford's genius or beneficence, but skeptics claimed that it was a shrewd maneuver designed to get free publicity. In fact, a number of practical labor problems at the Highland Park plant had provided the impetus for this new wage standard.

By mid-1913, Ford and his managers were wrestling with a mysterious difficulty. The assembly line had raised expectations dramatically for production, but the actual increase, though significant, was less than planned. In 1909, the first full year of Model T production, 1,548 Ford workers, using old-fashioned methods, produced 1,059 automobiles per month. In 1913, after the installation of the assembly line, 13,667 workers turned out 15,284 automobiles per month. In other words, the productivity of Ford workers only increased from an average of .70 to 1.12 cars per worker per month, and part of this could be attributed to larger economies of scale. Ford managers had anticipated a much greater rise in productivity.[4]

Baffled by the discrepancy, the company turned to John R. Lee, its leading labor expert. Lee had come to the company in 1911, when it purchased the Kiem Mills in Buffalo, New York, and he quickly displayed his talent for handling personnel and labor problems. Now, called upon to explore the productivity gap at Highland Park, he conducted intensive investigations of the work process at the factory throughout 1913. Lee's studies suggested that the problem lay not with the machinery, or the plant layout, or the organizational schemes of managers. The culprit was something initially left out of the calculations: human beings. Ford assembly-line efficiency had institutionalized technological and organizational factors, but had failed to control the human element.[5]

Lee identified several problems among the workers who manned the assembly line: absenteeism, shoddy performance, and, most important, rapid turnover of personnel. He also discovered several causes of worker dissatisfaction—excessively long hours, low wages, poor housing and home conditions, undesirable shop conditions, and arbitrary handling of workers by foremen. What Lee did not fully understand at the time, however, was the underlying source of this discontent. The assembly line had created pressing demands for work discipline. Men spent long, monotonous hours performing the same tasks over and over—tightening the bolt on a wheel housing, or lowering the car body onto the chassis, or attaching the gasoline tank. They were physically repetitive, emotionally deadening, and nearly devoid of satisfaction. Workers slyly resisted with several tactics. Through loafing ("soldiering") or sometimes outright subversion, they created what Ford managers called "output restriction." They absented themselves from work as often as they could without losing their jobs. Ultimately, droves of workers simply left the factory when they were fed up. For example, daily absences at Highland Park in 1913 amounted to 10 percent; the rate of labor turnover during that same year reached a stunning 370 percent.[6]

A significant social development exacerbated the work-discipline problem at Ford. In the early days of the company, it had employed American-born workers of Anglo and German descent, most of whom had trained as mechanics. By 1913, however, Highland Park and its assembly lines were relying increasingly on new immigrants. Detroit, like urban areas throughout the United States, had seen a massive influx of people predominantly from eastern and southern Europe in the early twentieth century. In particular, it absorbed large numbers of Poles, Russians, Hungarians, Romanians, Italians, Greeks, Lithuanians, Ukrainians, and Finns. By November 1914, such foreign-born workers constituted 71 percent of the sixteen thousand employees at Highland Park. The problem, of course, was that the demands of the assembly line required conformity, clear communication, and synchronization of effort. The fact that many Ford workers now spoke little or no English hindered this process. So, too, did the preindustrial, rural, and village background of many southern and eastern European workers, which ill suited them for the discipline of the assembly line. Facing such barriers, Ford managers found it difficult to enforce standards of efficient production.[7]

In short, the company's labor problem stemmed from its inability to make human efficiency as great as technological and organizational efficiency in the production of the Model T. Ford managers tried to ameliorate the situation. Since nearly its founding, the company had established a tradition of humane treatment of workers, with a regular bonus system and a medical department. By the 1910s, it had implemented additional programs, such as the Ford Motor Band for musicians among the workers, *Ford Times* to foster a sense of cooperation and common purpose, and a twenty-acre park with athletic fields, playgrounds, and a bandstand for workers and their families. In 1913, under Lee's prodding, the company went further by increasing wages by 15 percent and tying them to a new "skill-wages-classification system," creating an Employees' Savings and Loan Association, and establishing a new employment department that mediated disputes between workers and foremen.[8]

Thus Ford's electrifying announcement of the Five-Dollar Day did not appear out of the blue. Rather, it was the culmination of a process of study and problem-solving. Based on the general approach indicated by the Lee investigations, this reform offered a dramatic incentive for workers to cement their loyalty to the company and increase their effort. Enhanced productivity would be the payoff.

Yet there was more to it. As Henry Ford made clear at the time—in fact, he much preferred talking about this aspect of the move—the Five-Dollar Day concept also flowed from his genuine desire to share the company's prosperity with its workers. Here was an impulse rooted not so much in bottom-line calculations of business profit, but in Ford's instinctive worldview. His sympathy for working people, and his sincere desire to spread the benefits of consumerism to them, helped fuel the revolutionary wage increase.

In his brief comments to reporters at the press conference announcing the Five-Dollar Day, Ford provided a glimpse into his own thinking about the new policy. "Mr. Ford said simply that he had determined upon a plan to share his prosperity with his employees," reported the Detroit *Free Press.* He also clearly expressed his appreciation for the workingmen who made the company a success. "The commonest laborer who sweeps the floor shall receive his $5 per day," Ford noted with quiet earnestness. He promised that under the new guidelines no factory foreman would be able to fire a worker arbitrarily, and that the company would strive to find suitable jobs for all who wished to put in an honest day's work. Then Ford made the striking statement that was picked up by newspapers around the country: "We believe in making 20,000 men prosperous and contented rather than follow the plan of making a few slave drivers in our establishment millionaires."[9]

Ford had privately expressed the same sentiments in meetings leading up to the announcement. In early January, he had called together Couzens, P. E. Martin, John R. Lee, Harold Wills, Norval Hawkins, and Charles Sorensen. This conclave considered budgetary and production matters for the upcoming year, but discussion turned quickly to deeper issues. Ford was concerned with the morale and performance of workers at Highland Park. A recent walk through the factory had made him a witness to a fistfight between two men, an incident that left him depressed. Now, at this meeting of top managers, Ford began to write wage figures on a blackboard and compared them with anticipated company profits. The obvious discrepancy prompted discussion, and Ford scribbled higher and higher wage figures. He first put down a raise in wages to $3.00 a day, then raised it to $3.50, then to $4.00 and $4.50, and then, finally, to $5.00. Although some at the meeting remained skeptical, there was general consensus in favor of this dramatic hike.[10]

Fundamentally, Ford believed that high wages helped business in the long run by enhancing workers' ability to consume. In later years, he insisted that "the real progress of our company dates from 1914," because with the wage increase "we increased the buying power of our own people, and they increased the buying power of other people, and so on and on. It is this thought of enlarging buying power by paying high wages and selling at low prices which is behind the prosperity of this country." At another point, Ford said that with the Five-Dollar Day "we really started our business, for on that day we first created a lot of customers."[11]

But the Five-Dollar Day also stemmed from a populist strain that colored his thinking throughout adulthood. His career as an automaker had been marked by a loyalty to working people and suspicion of financial power. Several episodes in Ford's life had illustrated this: the clash with early investors who sought to restrict his initiative and build a vehicle for the wealthy, the concept of the Model T as a car for the average citizen, the cultivation of a folk-hero image as a man of the people, and the struggle against the forces of monopoly capital in the Selden suit. Ford drew upon an American tradition of populism supporting the interests of ordinary citizens against the malefactors of great wealth, a tradition that had flourished with the assault by rural radicals in the Populist Party on the "money power" of urban industrialists in the nineteenth century, and lingered in the Progressive movement's attempts to regulate the power of capital and big business in the nation's affairs. The Five-Dollar Day sat atop this political foundation.[12]

However, a cultural version of populism proved especially crucial to shaping Ford's worldview. This tradition bestowed social dignity and economic independence upon the average citizen and defended a kind of old-fashioned, property-owning individualism. As Richard Hofstadter, a perceptive student of this movement, has noted, cultural populists upheld "a life lived close to nature and the soil, the esteem for the primary contacts of country and village life, [and] the cherished image of the independent, self-reliant man." In his many public statements during this period, Ford revealed his kinship with this spirit of cultural populism. The Five-Dollar

Day, he sincerely believed, would enhance the prosperity of workers in his company and help protect them from powerful financial interests in industrial society. Ford also hoped that such reforms would help rural as well as urban workers in modern America. "What I want to do is to make the farmer as independent as I am; independent of the trusts, independent of the banks, the railroads," he explained in phrases borrowed from the populist rhetoric of the late nineteenth century. "I think the normal life for a man is to get back on the land. The land is the healthiest way to be."[13]

In newspaper interviews throughout 1914, Ford contended that his new wage policy flowed from several populist principles.

First, it expressed the notion that "good will" toward working people was the key to harmonious relations in industrial society. "I have been accused of being a philanthropist. I am not. I am an ardent believer in the gospel of good will," he told journalists. "Because I happen to be the head of a factory that employs an army of men who are working to make profits for me is no reason why I should look upon them as chattels." Yet this notion did not reflect an impulse of self-sacrifice. As Ford made clear in his statements, the attitude of goodwill kept his army of workers "contented, prosperous, and faithful . . . [thereby] increasing the greatest assets a factory can have—that of the ability to produce better goods for less cost." The drastic pay raise was, in Ford's words, "a piece of efficiency engineering, too. We expect to get better work, more efficient work, as one result." Goodwill, in Ford's realistic formulation, was a reflection of enlightened self-interest.[14]

Second, Ford drew upon a benevolent philosophy of wealth that became a mainstay of his social philosophy. To the dismay of businessmen and financiers throughout the country, he insisted that profits were not the property solely of capitalists. Instead, he offered a theory of stewardship. "The money I have gathered together is not mine to do with altogether as I please. I do not own it. It is mine to control simply as the steward of it. The men who have worked with me have helped to create it," he asserted. Programs such as the Five-Dollar Day would pass back to them their fair share. Ford offered another declaration: "No one made himself wholly what he is: in a sense all humanity cooperated in the success that some men think they won alone." Here was a challenge to individualist profit-seeking of which any populist would be proud.[15]

Third, Ford insisted that manufacturers and capitalists must recognize the simple humanity of industrial laborers in modern society. His new policy, he asserted repeatedly, pursued this objective by giving workers "wages that will support them without constant worry as to making both ends meet." Five dollars per day "made in many homes the difference between pinching penury and a wage that permits pleasure and a little savings besides." Anyone who worked, Ford argued, deserved "sufficient wages to keep him out of debt, to keep him in comfort, to give him a good home, and to educate his children." At bottom, this position rested on a roughly drawn, but deeply felt, social egalitarianism. When factory owners "realize that their laborers are human like themselves and should be treated humanely, the dawn of the ideal will approach," Ford believed.[16]

Fourth, and finally, Ford's perspective was more beholden to old Populist Party attacks on financial power than he ever admitted, or even recognized. The automaker indignantly denied that his policy had any ideological components. Annoyed that some had defined his wage policy as socialism, he told reporters, "As for this plan of mine, it has nothing to do with any 'ism' whatever. Our company is making money enough to do some good in the world, and I'm glad to do it." But Ford's debt to the Populist Party became evident in his explicit attack on one of its favorite bugaboos: wealthy financiers and banks. In New York a few days after the Five-Dollar Day announcement, Ford lashed out at Wall Street bankers, many of whom had criticized his $5.00 day. "Wall Street can't control the automobile industry," he exclaimed angrily. "Most of the automobile manufacturers 'under' Wall Street are closed down in Detroit, because the money they needed to use in their business went elsewhere. Then they had to wait for the money market to get in a proper condition for them to borrow." Ford's conclusion was defiant: "I'm not 'under' Wall Street." Such rhetoric—contrasting the sweaty virtue of common workers with the greedy manipulations of big financiers—could have been lifted from any populist speech of the late nineteenth century.[17]

Many of Ford's most striking pronouncements appeared in national magazines. Popular journals such as *Everybody's Magazine* and *Harper's Weekly* were full of expressions of his high regard for, and identification with, workers. "You can trust your employees every time if you give them half a chance. . . . I have been a workman myself, and I know," he declared in one piece. "Whatever I leave behind [in terms of wealth] I would rather leave to those boys out in the factory who have helped me make it than hand it out to a lot of relatives who never helped to earn a dollar of it." At one point, Ford let slip that his sympathy for the lower classes even extended to hired ex-convicts at his factory. In the reporter's words, "Nobody knew it but himself and the judges and the police. He personally vouched for them in the beginning and went good for their board to get them started. They were turning out very well. 'People are all right,' he announced."[18]

When asked about potential problems at Highland Park between an intelligent, educated managerial class and an ignorant workforce, he rejected such an assumption outright. Though a gap might exist between these groups, he replied, "there is less difference than we might imagine. What one can do another may." Ford "refused to think it [his workforce] unintelligent at all. He could take a man off the street, out there, quite raw, and make a good molder of him in a few weeks. He knew because he had done it."[19]

Correspondingly, Ford freely criticized American elites in these magazine forums. He took a swing at Wall Street financiers: "We never let a contract to a company owned by absent capitalists and managed by a hired hand. We do business only with a man who owns and conducts his own business." In typical populist fashion, he also disparaged intellectuals who criticized his new wage plan. Professors and writers who had never earned a living by the sweat of their brow, in his view, had no business opposing his attempt to help working people.[20]

To the journalists who interpreted his words, Ford looked like a genuine man of the people. As one of them put it, "By a very fortunate miracle Ford had got rich without being spoiled—without the time to forget that he, too, had been very poor, and had never been paid what he earned when he worked for others." Others observed, "Faith in the everyday man, exalted faith, is an integral part of the Ford character," or commented ironically that many did not know how to react to "Mr. Ford's monstrous way of treating everybody alike." Perhaps the most striking confirmation of Ford's populism, however, came in *Everybody's Magazine*. It disclosed that Detroit newspapers and the Ford Motor Company had been inundated with verses written by people who were grateful to Ford for the Five-Dollar Day. "Most of it was very bad as poetry, but touching for what it meant, written by men and women, some of whom could hardly spell, let alone set words into feet."[21]

Ultimately, Ford's populist rendering of the Five-Dollar Day drew nourishment from his personal image. To many American citizens and consumers, this wage policy dovetailed neatly with his folk-hero image as a man of the people. Some two weeks after the public announcement, the San Francisco *Bulletin* carried a prominent article entitled "Millionaire Ford's Tastes Are Worker's." It featured a photograph of Ford with a caption reading, "Prefers Giving to Spending: Henry Ford, the rich man with a poor man's tastes." The article described him as the same unassuming person that he had been two decades earlier, who wore modest clothes, tinkered with mechanical problems, and enjoyed quiet evenings at home with his family after a hard day's work. "Personally there is not much outward difference between Henry Ford, maker and dispenser of millions, and many of his workmen," the article concluded. "Money has not made the slightest difference in his habits, his manner of life, or his friendships."[22]

But Henry Ford and his populist notions did not stand alone in shaping the Five-Dollar Day. In fact, they received powerful support from another quarter. Unexpectedly, the hard-driving business manager of the company proved to be Ford's strongest ally in formulating this revolutionary labor policy. For those who had encountered his tightfisted protection of company funds over the previous decade, his support for handing over $10 million must have seemed surprising.

James Couzens stood at center stage in the dramatic press conference announcing the Five-Dollar Day. After reading aloud the statement doubling workers' salaries at the company, he commented at length on the significance of this move. "It is our belief that social justice begins at home," he declared. "We want those who have helped us to produce this great institution, and are helping to maintain it, to share our prosperity. We want them to have present profits and future prospects." Over the next few months, Couzens emerged as a strong advocate of the Five-Dollar Day and a man of powerful progressive principles and reformist sympathies. Observers of the Ford Motor Company, and particularly of its relentless business chief, must have been startled.[23]

As manager of company financial affairs since the founding in 1903, he had kept a close eye on its costs, wages, and profit margins. But much evidence suggests that Couzens, rather than Henry Ford, should be credited as the architect of this new wage policy. In several meetings of top managers in December 1913 and January 1914, Couzens spoke strongly on behalf of raising workers' pay. "When you get down to the wage scheme which we started at the Ford Motor Company," he wrote a correspondent in 1915, "I will say that I, personally, am responsible for it." But he also acknowledged that Ford's stamp of approval had been essential to the plan's success. "It was quite natural that Mr. Ford should be credited with this project, because he was the head of the company [and] a majority stockholder," Couzens wrote. Ford gave it "a personal touch which was greatly beneficial in an advertising way." But, whatever the origin of the idea, Henry Ford and James Couzens agreed on the Five-Dollar Day and worked together to promote it.[24]

In the months after the announcement, Couzens made a series of public statements that rivaled Ford's in their enthusiasm for the new wage policy. Full of reformist rhetoric, they framed the Five-Dollar Day as the kind of measure that would save modern industrial society. In making this argument, Couzens pursued three primary themes.

First, he confronted head-on the problem of class conflict in modern industrial society, confessing that capitalist businessmen had not given workers their fair share of profits. He declared that "a division of earnings between capital and labor is unequal" and that industry must "arrive at the point where we will divide more equitably between capital and labor." Couzens also took a swipe at Wall Street financiers. In good populist fashion, he insisted that the reason many large businesses failed was that "they are managed from Wall Street and other financial centers. The heads of the concerns are absent landlords, and absent ownership never pays."[25]

Second, Couzens argued that high wages and humane treatment of workers were, in fact, good business. It was a fallacy for factory owners to believe that they were saving money by paying low wages. On the contrary, men worked harder and more efficiently when well paid, and the result more than made up for the higher cost of wages. "I am talking sound business as I understand it. It is my experience that it pays to pay good wages. It pays because a workman is a human being and will work harder to make a high wage than a low wage," he observed. In fact, high wages were necessary to the very survival of business. Couzens believed that low wages and mistreatment made for "an industrial system that fails to protect the men engaged in it against want, temporary or permanent, against unemployment, against sickness or against old age. That is the kind of an industrial system that breeds discontent and unhappiness and strikes all manner of wasteful wars between capital and labor."[26]

Third, Couzens became most passionate in contending that respect for the dignity and humanity of common people demanded measures like the Five-Dollar Day. He told the press that the standard industry practice of laying off workmen in slack periods grated against his conscience. It ignored the "human element" in industrial production. Manufacturers considered machines, markets, materials, transportation, management, efficiency, and many other factors before "the needs, feelings, health, and happiness of their men." He offered a maxim: "If you are going to get the best possible service from a wage worker you must remember he is a man and treat him as a man."[27]

Couzens believed that the Five-Dollar Day embraced the humanity of Ford workers.

> [W]e are going on the principle that our business never could have been built up without the skilled, intelligent, careful work performed by our employees. If they have been responsible to a considerable degree for success of the company it is only right that they should share in its prosperity, and if such prosperity is of unusual extent, that they should share to unusual extent.[28]

What inspired James Couzens' late-blooming progressivism? It was not a logical outgrowth of his earlier business career, which had seen its share of cutthroat self-interest (joining Henry Ford to drive his own mentor, Alex Malcolmson, out of the company) and the determined pursuit of profit (his notorious tightfistedness regarding production costs and raises for employees). Indeed, the source of Couzens' reformism lay elsewhere. Much evidence suggests that it had flowed from discontent in his private life, which had been caused, ironically, by his great success as a businessman. By 1914, Couzens had become a millionaire, but he had not found happiness.

This self-made man, awash in money after the stunning success of the Model T, was suffering pangs of guilt over his wealth. By 1913, signs of his prosperity were evident. Couzens hired Albert Kahn to design a large brick house for his family in one of Detroit's most exclusive neighborhoods. He bought a farm near Pontiac, Michigan, and built a sturdy clapboard house for a summer residence. He joined the board of directors of several Detroit banks as well as companies selling tobacco, salt, and real estate. He became one of the most active business figures in Detroit, a status that led to his being chosen president of the Board of Commerce. Yet he grew increasingly uneasy about the impact of his growing affluence.[29]

To family and friends, Couzens confessed his deep suspicion of wealth's impact on character. In the best tradition of the Protestant work ethic, stretching back to the Puritans, he agonized that luxury would undermine self-discipline and cause dissipation. He lectured his children on the importance of self-control and character development and urged them to "buck up" under the weight of duress. Couzens allowed his children only modest allowances and forbade them to flaunt the family's wealth, saying, "I am always annoyed at any sort of display and have fought against that for years." One day, when his daughter, Madeleine, commented on a newspaper article outlining the growing fortune of the Ford Motor Company and its top managers, he turned grave. This money "doesn't belong to us," he replied. "It's a trust. It's a responsibility, and a tough one." In fact, the more money Couzens made, the more he seemed to retreat into an obsessive work ethic. "I am never happier than when I am working at top notch," he wrote to a friend, "and the only reason I let down at all is to be able to work at top notch the majority of the year."[30]

This growing guilt over wealth, in turn, was part of a larger midlife crisis. Couzens had turned forty in 1912, made his fortune by 1914, and, like many intelligent people, came face to face with larger questions of meaning. "You know, there comes a time when the fun of making money is all gone," he confessed. "The battle is won; the goal is achieved; it is time for something else." When interviewed by *Forbes* magazine, he admitted, "I got tired of making so much money. It became a burden. It was almost obnoxious, distasteful." Couzens grew listless, complained of mysterious physical ailments, began having trouble sleeping, and fled at every opportunity to his farm, where, as he groused to one newspaper, "my cows don't talk to me, don't ask questions, nor criticize my way of doing things." In the summer of 1913, he even contemplated resigning from the company. "I seemed to have no interest in life for a while," he recalled later. "I had achieved what I started out to do."[31]

Weary of wealth and searching for direction, Couzens was ripe for a burst of reformism. He was desperate to see the Ford Motor Company as something more than a mere profit-generating institution. When the company laid off several hundred men that winter, he became distraught. "All winter, I sat in my office on the second floor of the Ford Building and every time I looked out the window I saw a sea of faces looking up," he told one journalist. "There were men shivering in the cold with their coat collars turned up." Couzens contemplated the idea of instituting a pension plan for all workers and then issued an order forbidding foremen to fire any workers until they had been tried at other jobs in the factory. On the question of wages, he arrived at a simple remedy. "Why shouldn't the Ford Motor Company take a decided lead in paying the highest wages to its workers, thus enabling them to enjoy better living conditions?" he asked. "The company was making money hand over fist and could, therefore, afford to do something worthwhile." He brought the proposal to a sympathetic Henry Ford's attention, and Couzens argued for $5.00 while Ford pushed for a lower number. Couzens finally carried the day when he noted that a "five-dollar wage will be the greatest advertisement any automobile concern ever had." No one had to say that twice to Ford.[32]

In Couzens' eyes, the Five-Dollar Day emerged as a benchmark for judging the modern, humane, and progressive corporation. "The corporation that treats every employee as if he were an individual and an entity instead of a number will soon find that it has a soul, and can do things which its less intelligent competitor cannot do," he declared throughout 1914. The progressive business concerned itself with larger issues, such as the health of a worker's family, and paid a generous wage to its employees. In Couzens' formulation, when companies "are inspired by dollars and cents alone, the human spirit is missing. . . . System alone is not enough in any kind of dealing with human beings." And with reforms like the Five-Dollar Day, "the follies of socialism and the terrors of anarchy will fade away in an industrial system that guarantees to every man, rich or poor, a fair field and a square deal."[33]

In light of such public statements, Couzens' reputation as a progressive began to grow rapidly. Detroit newspapers described him as the "Wizard of Finance Who Combines Humanitarianism with Efficiency," while he chastised Detroit's business elite. A few months after the announcement of the Five-Dollar Day, he spoke to the Detroit Board of Commerce and excoriated its members for greedy business behavior. "You fellows sit back, smug and complacent, and don't give a damn what becomes of your workmen," he said. "They are just as human as you and I, but they are not as well taken care of." Citizens responded; in time he was elected mayor of Detroit and then to the United States Senate. "I think I know how the average man feels on most questions," he noted soon after his election. "I am going to try to be his spokesman on the floor of the Senate."[34]

James Couzens played a central role in formulating and promoting the new wage policy. But his efforts on behalf of the Five-Dollar Day were only a preview of what the Ford Motor Company launched in the weeks and months that followed. Never one to overlook a publicity opportunity, Henry Ford masterminded one of the great promotional blitzes in the history of his company.

As news of the Five-Dollar Day reverberated throughout the United States, newspapers and magazines were filled with commentary, feature stories, editorials, pictorial spreads, and publicity releases on the phenomenon. This provided a kind of free advertising, just as Henry Ford had hoped.

Following distribution of the original printed statement on January 5, Henry Ford carefully encouraged an outpouring of national publicity when he arrived in New York City on January 8 for its annual auto show. Staying at the Belmont Hotel, he attracted so many reporters, photographers, and admirers that the management deployed a squad of security people to protect him. Ford clearly welcomed the limelight. He submitted to interviews, answered questions patiently, and projected an image of modest, simple honesty. He also showed a talent for creating memorable quotes. "I believe it is a disgrace for a man to die rich," he declared. "Goodwill is about the only fact there is in life. With it a man can do and win almost anything. Without it he is practically powerless." Throughout the spring of 1914, a string of interviews, carefully crafted statements, and public appearances by Ford maintained this promotional momentum.[35]

The offensive produced hundreds of favorable newspaper stories throughout the United States. Their headlines provided a glimpse of the outlandish praise within. One proclaimed, "World's Economic History Has Nothing Equal to Ford Plan." According to another, "Social Justice Animates Ford, He Is Not for Multi-Millionaires." Other headlines followed similar themes: "Puts Capital and Labor on Equal Basis," "Ford Factory Has a Heart," "Henry Ford's Act Is That of a Far-Sighted Businessman." The stories that followed typically framed the Five-Dollar Day as a reform healing the rift between capital and labor while praising its creator as a "man of the people." A story entitled "Aid Man Who Sweats, Says Ford," for instance, quoted him as declaring that the man "who literally lives by the sweat of his brow, is the man entitled most to direct rewards for his labor wherever those rewards are possible."[36]

Most newspaper editorials were effusive about the Five-Dollar Day. Some praised it for diffusing wealth more widely in the new consumer-oriented United States, where an increased ability to buy goods and enjoy leisure meant higher status and enhanced happiness. Ford's wage plan brought "Prosperity Sharing," said the Cleveland *Plain Dealer*, and "opens the way to further wealth diffusion," said the New York *Globe*. The Omaha *News* stressed that "26,000 men and women are to have their leisure increased and their buying capacity multiplied." Ford, these papers believed, had transformed thousands of ordinary workers into consumers and customers.[37]

Other editorialists stressed that Ford's wage policy attacked the most vexing social problem in the United States over the previous forty-five years: the clash between capital and labor. Since the 1870s, rapid industrialization had pitted factory workers against their employers in disputes over wages, hours, and working conditions. Unionization, labor strikes, and violence had punctuated this lengthy encounter. Now the leading automobile manufacturer in the country, in the words of the New York *Times*, had intervened with an act of "originality and daring." "What marvels might not Mr. Ford's example work if only other capitalists would do the same," the editorial asked. "And what miracles might not the world see if capital and labor should cooperate on the same lines." Other newspapers agreed that the Five-Dollar Day would bridge the chasm between workers and owners with a new spirit of cooperation. In the words of the Peoria, Illinois, *Transcript*, Ford's plan was "a shining example for other employers of labor and if his experiment proves a success, it may blaze paths in the realm of profit-sharing which have received so much attention in theory and so little in practice."[38]

Not surprisingly, American labor leaders praised the Ford initiative. Samuel Gompers, the president of the American Federation of Labor, released a public letter noting that "the attitude of Henry Ford toward organized labor and toward his employees has always been fairer than usually obtains in the automobile establishments of the United States." The Five-Dollar Day, he continued, would "demonstrate its justice" and prod further reforms in American industry in terms of wages, working conditions, and hours. The Illinois Federation of Labor endorsed Ford's plan, stating that such "cooperation will be the solution of the labor wars in the country. It shows the right spirit in the employer and indicates that he understands his duty as a capitalist towards the masses of his employees." E. P. Usher, president of the Toledo Central Labor Union, described Ford's new policy as "an advance in the method of dealing with labor by the manufacturers." Thomas E. Burke, an official with the United Association of Plumbers, Gasfitters, and Steamfitters, contended that the Five-Dollar Day was "the last thing in unselfishness and so altruistic that it rises far above any previous innovation in the commercial world."[39]

But not everyone was convinced of the Five-Dollar Day's virtues. Many in the business community were skeptical of Ford's new wage policy. "Revolutionary" change and doubled wages did not sit well with Wall Street bankers, small businessmen, or competitors in the automobile industry. *The Wall Street Journal* led the counterattack. "To inject ten millions into a company's factory, and to double the minimum wage, without regard to length of service, is to apply Biblical or spiritual principles into a field where they do not belong," it asserted. "[Ford] in his social endeavor has committed economic blunders, if not crimes. They may return to plague him and the industry he represents as well as organized society." A corporate manager in New York dismissed the Five-Dollar Day as "the most foolish thing ever attempted in the industrial world" and promised that it would "only result in unrest among the laboring classes." Samuel Tilton, manager of auditing at Security Trust Company in Detroit, praised Ford for his altruistic spirit but insisted that most companies had thin profit margins and would be bankrupted by raising wages so dramatically. The average businessman, he said, "sees the lamp of Aladdin, but cannot touch it."[40]

The automobile industry was in shock following Ford's wage hike. The evening after the announcement, Alvin Macauley, president of the Packard Motor Car Company, phoned Charles Sorensen and complained, "What are you fellows trying to do? We got the news about your $5 day while we were having a board meeting. It was so astonishing that we broke up the meeting." Many automakers denounced the move, often with considerable bitterness. Contacted at the New York auto show a few days after the announcement, leading manufacturers such as Hugh Chalmers, Windsor T. White, Otis O. Friend, and C. W. Meers told reporters that Ford's precipitate action promised to throw the labor market into utter turmoil and harm the entire industry. Moreover, they insisted, Henry Ford might be wealthy enough to dabble in utopian experiments, but no one else had such means available. As J. J. Cole said bluntly, "If Ford wants to amuse himself, all right. He can afford it. Others can't." Growing companies such as the General Motors Corporation raised wages slightly to compete with Ford, but were not able to meet the $5.00 standard until years later.[41]

The forces opposing Ford's new policy were joined by a few newspapers. The Pontiac, Michigan, *Press*, complained that this dramatic pay raise, if adopted by companies nationwide, would launch a great wave of price increases as those companies struggled to fund higher wages. Higher prices would mean no real gain in purchasing power. Other papers wondered whether employees were willing to share in the market risks faced by their employers. Though taking a cut of company profits was attractive, "it is when loss-sharing is included that the pinch will come," one noted. Another sharpened the argument: even though workers "are quite willing to share in the prosperity few are ready or can afford to share in their employer's adversity."[42]

These pockets of dissent, however, remained small and scattered. A great chorus of affirmation for Ford's Five-Dollar Day came from nearly every segment of opinion in the United States. One approving group drew special attention. For perhaps the first time, an American business tycoon became the darling of the political left.

Two years after the announcement of the Five-Dollar Day, John Reed, the noted leftist gadfly and soon-to-be friend of the Russian Revolution, visited Detroit to interview Henry Ford. He toured the Highland Park factory and spoke with Ford workers, and was also welcomed at Ford's home, where he talked at length with the automaker and probed his thoughts about social and political issues. He interviewed Ford's neighbors and associates for insights into his character and business philosophy. When he returned to New York, Reed wrote a pair of articles that conveyed his favorable impressions.

"Why They Hate Henry Ford," published in *The Masses*, examined Ford's profit-sharing scheme in light of the hostility it aroused among many American big businessmen. The $5.00 wage, Reed asserted flatly, had made Ford a traitor to his class. "That is why the capitalists hate Henry Ford. That is why the Steel Trust would like to cut off his steel—and Wall Street curb his power." This wage reform, in Reed's assessment, had demonstrated Ford's concern for social and economic justice over merely making more

money. In Reed's ringing phrase, "This new Ford plan is turning into something dangerously like a real experiment in democracy, and from it may
spring a real menace to capitalism." A second article, "Industry's Miracle
Maker," which appeared in *Metropolitan Magazine*, reached the same conclusion. "He is that most dangerous of revolutionists—a man who translates
platitudes into action," Reed wrote of Ford. "Here is a powerful industrial
baron who is interested in human beings instead of stocks and bonds."[43]

John Reed's approbation was symptomatic of a much larger trend in the
aftermath of the Five-Dollar Day announcement. Over the next several
years, leftists of every stripe—socialists, radical progressives, liberal reformers, labor activists—competed with one another in praising Henry Ford.
They argued that his wage scheme promised to heal the wounds of class
conflict by signaling the long-awaited recognition by capital of the debt
owed to labor. It announced a new day, when industrialists and laborers,
management and workers would cooperate rather than clash, and achieve
justice and prosperity for all. The irony was profound. For several years
after 1914, the political left raised to heroic status a man who was rapidly
becoming the wealthiest businessman in the United States.

The panoply of progressives supporting Ford ranged widely. At the
local level, Detroit leftists such as the "gentle anarchist" Jo Labadie and
socialist organizer Robert A. Westfall endorsed the Five-Dollar Day as a
marked advancement toward improving economic conditions and increasing justice in the modern industrial system. The Michigan Socialist Party
published a pamphlet full of praise entitled *The Bombshell That Henry Ford
Fired*. William A. Moore, a Detroit pastor influenced by the Social Gospel
movement of the early twentieth century, defended Ford against attacks by
other businessmen. He preached a much-publicized sermon that described
big business as "conservative and afraid." "Dollars will not lead into heaven,
for the road to heaven leads up hill," he told listeners. "Some one must vol-
untarily give up something for a weaker brother." Ford's wage innovation,
Moore concluded, established "the beginning point for a new era in the
relations between capital and labor."[44]

At the national level, leftists vied with one another in their praise.
Noted progressive lawyer Samuel Untermyer, who had established his
reformist credentials in 1912 with a relentless interrogation of J. Pierpont
Morgan as chief counsel for a congressional committee investigating
the "money trust," painted Ford in glowing colors. "Henry Ford has a
prophetic eye. He is the first to see the inevitable readjustment of the relations between capital and labor looming on the horizon," Untermyer told
reporters. "He has established a glorious precedent." Clarence Darrow, the
attorney becoming known for his work on behalf of progressive causes, con-

curred. "He has established a magnificent precedent," he said of Ford's wage plan. "I honestly believe that what he has done is what all American employers of labor must eventually come to. Labor will demand its own. Ford has recognized the right of labor to make this demand."[45]

Many prominent socialists also praised the Ford plan. Eugene V. Debs declared that, though socialists had been insisting for years that workers would respond to generous wages, a humane working environment, and social justice, it took Ford's Five-Dollar Day "to prove these theories on a large scale." Kate Richards O'Hare, the socialist agitator from Kansas, journeyed to Detroit to interview Ford. Writing for the socialist journal the *National Rip-Saw*, she described Ford as "so absolutely 'just folks' that I felt quite as much at home with him as I would sitting on a cotton pile discussing the boll-weevil with a Texas farmer." After several hours of discussion, O'Hare became convinced of his genuine idealism and belief in democracy and cooperation. Moreover, she castigated her fellow socialists for not providing *more* support for "having our theories worked out and demonstrated, as Ford has done." Too many socialists, she accused, "in order to be perfectly orthodox, ignore Ford and read another chapter in Marx."[46]

For at least a half-decade after the inauguration of the Five-Dollar Day, American socialists continued backing Henry Ford. Upton Sinclair, who in a later period would attack Ford as a heartless capitalist in his book *The Flivver King: A Story of Ford-America* (1937), held a much more favorable view of him in the late 1910s. After speaking with Ford at length in 1919, when he came to southern California, Sinclair published the interview in *Reconstruction: A Herald of the New Time*, a journal edited by another socialist admirer of Ford, Allan L. Benson. At the outset, Sinclair described Ford as "a human and lovable person, with no reserves and no poses of any sort." The writer maintained a kind of ironic distance throughout, continually probing Ford as to whether his money made him genuinely happy. At the same time, however, Sinclair asked questions allowing Ford to define himself as a transportation innovator, a friend of the workingman, the enemy of idle stockholders, a hater of corrupt politics, and a reformer who was determined "to put these steel-trust fellows out of business." The Ford who emerged from the Sinclair interview was a reformer's dream. He valued his profits because these allowed him to make "better and cheaper cars" for ordinary people, and defined his happiness in terms of performing "public service."[47]

John R. Commons, the progressive economist from the University of Wisconsin, certified Ford's reformist credentials in an article entitled "Henry Ford, Miracle Maker." Part of a series in the magazine *The Indepen-*

dent on businesses that were finding solutions to labor problems, this piece praised Ford as a "plunger in social psychology" who "believes in ordinary, plain people as they come along." With his Five-Dollar Day, reluctance to fire workers, and attempts to find suitable jobs for his employees, the automaker demonstrated a "faith in human nature" and concern for his workers that were quite uncommon among industrial manufacturers. Through such policies, Commons concluded, Ford had created at Highland Park a harmonious system between capital and labor where "real team work is possible."[48]

Ida Tarbell, the legendary muckraking journalist, spent ten days in Detroit in the spring of 1915 investigating Henry Ford's manufacturing operation. Charmed by Ford's good-heartedness and lack of pretense, and swayed by her observations at the factory, Tarbell became convinced that Ford had opened a door to happiness for laborers. His philosophy of inexpensive cars and high wages, she believed, was providing to industrial workers "a chance for what we are pleased to call these days a good life. And if they are going to have a good life they must not only have money but have low prices."[49]

Some leftists, however, recognized that Ford's new wage policy would undermine the long-term radical agenda. The Five-Dollar Day, if successful, would strengthen, rather than weaken, the capitalist system. Jo Labadie warned of this danger. "Henry Ford's scheme is all right, but of course it doesn't dispose of the fundamental problem," he told journalists. "I haven't a doubt that Ford will find his profit-sharing plan good business. His men will work the harder." Journalist Gerald Stanley Lee, writing in *Harper's Weekly*, also pinpointed the danger of such wage reforms for leftist prospects. If powerful businessmen like Ford started thinking strategically, rather than instinctively defending their profits to the last penny, and then tried to improve the lives of their workers, he argued, radicalism would likely disappear. In his words, such actions would create "a new world, a world in which we will see Socialists and Syndicalists losing their jobs."[50]

Most radicals reacted like John Reed, however. After visiting Highland Park in 1916 and discussing an array of issues with Ford, he remained skeptical about certain aspects of the new wage system. In many ways, he noted, "Ford profit-sharing is still in the form of a gift." Handed out in generosity by a wealthy businessman, this policy was, in Reed's words, a species of "benevolent despotism" and "paternalism" rather than an attack on the structural inequalities of industrial capitalism. Ultimately, however, he decided that the strengths of Ford's wage reform outweighed its weaknesses. The automaker "knew the misery and waste of working-class lives," Reed observed, and the $5.00 wage was a sincere attempt to ameliorate such living conditions. As a test, Reed compared the results of two surveys of Ford workers, one done in late 1913 and one done five months after the inauguration of the Five-Dollar Day. The contrast was dramatic. "The increase in life insurance was 86 per cent. The value of homes owned increased 87 per cent. The value of homes bought on contract increased 95 per cent," Reed observed. "Employees with 'bad' home conditions decreased from 23 per cent to 1½ per cent while men living in bad neighborhoods decreased from 19 per cent to 2½ per cent." For Reed, the conclusion was obvious. He had to support a man who "felt that adequate incomes, freedom from anxiety about unemployment, and leisure, automatically made better workmen and better citizens."[51]

But even as the praise of leftists converged with that of other groups around the country, the situation turned cloudy. In the months after the dramatic announcement, a disquieting fact slowly began to emerge. Rather than being granted automatically, as many observers assumed, the Five-Dollar Day was extended by management in concert with a system of regulations that sought to shape how the company's employees lived as well as worked. Moreover, it soon became clear that this wage policy was only part of Henry Ford's larger social vision, one that saw people being molded into certain shapes so they could flourish in modern American life. A specter of paternalism hovered in the background of Ford's scheme for improving the lots of workers, and it cast a shadow over the reform. For many observers, misgivings replaced unstinting praise.

Eleven

Victorian

In their press conference announcing the Five-Dollar Day, Henry Ford and James Couzens adopted the rhetoric of social justice and industrial cooperation. Accordingly, reporters stressed those same themes when they left Highland Park to file their stories. As the Detroit *Free Press* explained in its front-page story, "Because Henry Ford believes that the distribution of wealth between capital and labor is too uneven, the world's greatest profit sharing plan . . . was announced Monday morning by the company."

Careful readers, however, may have noted an additional item mentioned casually in the coverage of the Five-Dollar Day. "Ford employees are to be further benefited by the establishment of a sociological department in the plant," the *Free Press* article noted deep in the story. "Its work will be to guard against an employee's prosperity injuring his efficiency. Employees who cannot remain sober and industrious will be dismissed, but not until an indisposition to become a valuable employee is shown."[1]

As more details came to light in 1914 and 1915, it gradually became evident that Ford's "sociological department" was more crucial to his wage reform than it first appeared. His new wage did not come to workers free and clear but was loaded with institutional and ideological baggage. In fact, it lay entangled in a web of requirements. Ford laborers who desired this new pay rate had to do more than work hard, effectively, and faithfully. They also had to meet certain moral standards and fulfill certain social obligations in the realm of family life and personal behavior. Nor were workers merely instructed to act in certain ways. Henry Ford created the sociological department to make sure they did so.

Moreover, as time unfolded it became clear that the Five-Dollar Day represented something much larger. This wage reform was but one dimension, albeit a highly publicized one, of a grand social project drawn up by Henry Ford and implemented by his company. The broader crusade was partly nationalistic in its determination to make good Americans out of the polyglot immigrants who worked in his automobile factory. Yet, ultimately, it transcended national boundaries. Ford's broader social agenda sought to shape human beings who could function efficiently in the new society of mass production and mass consumption that the Model T had helped create. As he frequently noted, to both associates and reporters, he wanted to make men as well as automobiles.

As with so many things touched by Henry Ford, however, a profound irony came to color this grand project of industrial reformism. The Five-Dollar Day and its sociological apparatus was at once a modern attempt to give working people their due and a blueprint for moral discipline rooted in old-fashioned Victorian values from the world of Ford's youth. Like the Model T, Ford's reform aimed to enhance the lives of ordinary citizens in an advanced industrial society. At the same time, however, it promoted a backward-looking moral mandate that demanded allegiance to nineteenth-century values of self-control and domesticity. This prescription for creating new people to inhabit a new world by dint of an old-fashioned Victorian creed was replete with tension. Eventually, the contradictions would prove fatal.

The Five-Dollar Day went into effect on January 12, and its eligibility rules addressed matters of age, gender, and support of dependents. All married men were eligible for the new wage, as were males under age twenty-two who were supporting widowed mothers or brothers and sisters. All women who were supporting families would receive the pay boost. But unmarried females and those men not supporting dependents were excluded from Ford profit-sharing. Perhaps the most striking qualification, however, concerned matters of a personal nature: character, morals, habits and behavior, and family arrangements.[2]

From the outset, the new Ford plan made clear that higher wages were linked to a proper private life. In the January 5 press conference, James Couzens noted, "Thrift and good service and sobriety all will be encouraged and recognized." In an interview with *Motor World* a few days later, he noted that employees "who cannot remain sober and industrious will be dismissed, but no one will be let out without being given every possible chance to make good." Over the next several months, such virtues and several others were elevated to the status of qualifications as an elaborate set of moral standards was put in place. To be eligible for the $5.00 rate, the employee needed to demonstrate that he did not drink alcohol or physically mistreat his family or have boarders in his home, and that he regularly deposited money in a savings account, maintained a clean home, and had a good moral character.[3]

John R. Lee, the first head of the sociological department, took the lead in defining its moral mission. He impressed all who knew him as a talented, honest, benevolent man well suited to the company's new social initiative. An associate described Lee as "the soul of the organization, the champion of the underdog. . . . He has a keen sense of justice and a sympathy with men in trouble that leads to an understanding of their problems."[4]

Lee often told people that the Ford Company's social work had begun in 1912, when a dependable employee operating a drop hammer began to fall off on the job. A brief talk with the man revealed that the problem lay in his domestic life. "Sickness, indebtedness, and fear and worry over things that related entirely to the home, had crept in and put a satisfactory human unit entirely out of harmony with the things that were necessary for production," Lee related. Such incidents prompted the company to turn its attention to reforming the private life as well as raising the wages of its employees. In particular, according to Lee, the sociological dimension of the Five-Dollar Day plan stemmed from two sources. First, preliminary investigations indicated that men who came from settled, thrifty, harmonious homes were happier and performed better as workers. Second, the greatly increased wages of early 1914 raised among Ford management a fear that the princely sum of $5.00 per day might trigger irresponsible behavior among its recipients. In Lee's words, such sudden prosperity "would work a tremendous handicap along the paths of rectitude and right living and would make of them a menace to society." In other words, for their own good workers needed to be instructed on how to manage their abundance responsibly. Thus the sociological department, Lee argued, tried to provide "something that is of great benefit both to the men and to the company."[5]

The moral injunctions of Lee and the sociological department were codified for employees within a few months. In 1915, the company published *Helpful Hints and Advice to Employees,* a manual that carried a lengthy subtitle: *To Help Them Grasp the Opportunities Which Are Presented to Them by the Ford Profit-Sharing Plan.* This forty-one-page illustrated booklet explained the standards and procedures of the sociological department in great detail. It began with a clear statement of purpose:

> The sole and simple aim of the entire scheme is to better the financial and moral standing of each employee and those of his household; to instill men with courage and a desire for health, happiness and prosperity. To give to father and mother sufficient for present

and future; to provide for families in sickness, in health and in old age and to take away fear and worry. To make a well rounded life and not a mere struggle for existence to men and their families, and to implant in the heart of every individual the wholesome desire to Help the Other Fellow, whenever he comes across your path, to the extent of your ability.[6]

This exhortation was followed by a long list of "hints and advice" for employees. The pamphlet devoted much attention to the issue of home sanitation and living arrangements, for example, instructing workers that they "should live in clean, well conducted homes and in rooms that are well lighted and ventilated." Dark, dirty, foul-smelling tenements should be avoided, and employees, wherever their lodging, should take special care to deal appropriately with sewage and garbage to avoid disease. The pamphlet also urged an ethic of personal cleanliness by praising the healthy effects of frequent bathing and abundant soap and water. It insisted that employees not take in roomers or boarders, arguing that such moneymaking expedients endangered wholesome family life by bringing people of unknown morals and habits into the household.[7]

Helpful Hints and Advice paid special attention to children. It urged workers to ensure their children's health and to provide them with clean, wholesome physical surroundings. Children required instruction in hygienic matters such as bathing daily and brushing teeth, and they needed to be taken to a doctor when illness or disease struck. Proper parents did not let their offspring run in the street but found safe spaces for play, directed youthful energies into useful channels, and sought to give them the best education possible. When their charges reached adolescence, parents should screen companions to make sure they were "decent and clean minded" and help children avoid vices damaging to their health or morals. Perhaps most important, the conscientious parent provided a moral model for the child: "THE EXAMPLE PARENTS SET THEIR CHILDREN GOES A LONG WAY IN FORMING THEIR HABITS. A GOOD EXAMPLE IS THE BEST SERMON."[8]

The pamphlet dispensed abundant counsel on the wise use of money. Now that the pockets of Ford workers were filling with the bounty of the Five-Dollar Day, "thrift" became the order of the day: "Every employee participating in profit-sharing is expected to save some part of the profits allowed him. No hard and fast rules can be laid down or adopted in this particular, as responsibilities differ with different persons and families." But the sociological department offered guidance about saving for retirement, banking with a reputable savings institution, securing a safe real-estate mortgage to procure a house and property, and buying fire and life insurance. Interestingly, however, in light of Ford's central role in the consumer revolution of the early 1900s, the sociological department made this admonition: "Avoid, as much as possible, making purchases upon installment plan." Nice furniture, musical instruments, and other household luxuries should wait for a cash purchase. Houses and automobiles, of course, were exempted from this restriction.[9]

To heighten the impact of the message, the pamphlet contained striking photographs. On the one hand, images of dirty, crowded bedrooms ("a breeder of tuberculosis"), children playing in cramped alleys filled with garbage, infected hands that resulted from medical neglect, toothless men who failed to practice oral hygiene, unsanitary kitchens and filthy bathrooms, and smoking shells of uninsured houses drove home warnings about cleanliness and prudent financial planning. The images were juxtaposed with cheerful photographs of neat, tidy homes, clean and airy bedrooms, school yards filled with joyful children, sanitary kitchens and bathrooms, and cozy dining rooms where families could gather for evening meals.[10]

The sociological department moved to put these principles and procedures into practice among its workers. Its key strike force lay in a battalion of investigators who carried the department's message to the homes and hearths of Ford workers. This group was chosen from various white-collar and supervisory sections of the company—medical department physicians, auditors, foremen, assistant superintendents—all of whom had established a reputation for reliability and solid character. By the end of January 1914, nearly a hundred investigators had been organized and deployed; by December, they numbered two hundred. However, within another six months, after preliminary investigations had been completed, the number leveled off to about fifty permanent investigators with supporting secretaries and staff.[11]

Fanning out into working-class neighborhoods of Detroit, Ford's sociological investigators performed a number of tasks. First, they identified flaws in a worker's home life. Investigators visited an employee's home in cases of persistent absenteeism, for example, to ascertain whether domestic difficulties such as illness, debt, or a strained marriage lay behind the problem. But mostly they arrived, forms and questionnaires in hand, to survey an employee's personal habits—whether he dependably brought home his salary, consumed alcohol and gambled, or physically mistreated his wife and children—and to inquire about household living arrangements, the care of children, and family spending and savings habits. One magazine recorded an encounter between an investigator and a worker's wife:

"Does Joe Polianski live here," he asks.

"Yes, he lives here all right."

"What sort of a man is Joe—pretty good fellow?"

"Sure, he's a fine man."

"What does he do evenings?"

"Always home evenings. Goes to bed early."

"Does he drink?"

"No! No! He does not drink."

"What does he do with his money—does he save any?"

"Sure, he save. Some of it he send to old country to help old folks, some of it in bank."

"Well now, if Joe should get more wages what do you think he would do with it?"

"Save it and buy a house, I guess."

"All right," says the investigator, snapping his book together. "Tell Joe to bring his bank book with him when he comes to work next week."[12]

The investigators also observed firsthand the tidiness and hygiene of the home. If problems were apparent, they offered advice and guidance on cleanliness, money management, child care, alcohol abuse, and related matters. As a company manual explained, representatives of the sociological department were to advise employees on their living conditions and handling of money. The manual carefully added, however, "The work of the advisor is not to pry into family affairs from a meddlesome standpoint, but rather to . . . help those who are the kind that desire to seize opportunities, but, for various reasons are unskilled in being able to seize the best opportunities when they present themselves."[13]

Ford investigators were also to make workers aware of the social services available through the company. For example, the company maintained a bank for employee use. First established in the fall of 1913, the Employees' Savings and Loan Association, administered by Lee and Frank L. Klingensmith, became a key repository for workers' funds, as well as a lending institution after the Five-Dollar Day announcement in January 1914. As Lee told the newspapers in April of that year, "The company encourages thrift by maintaining a savings bank for deposits and loans of a certain character. Thrift is one of the qualifications of the employee for profit-sharing, so the total deposits in the bank have more than trebled."[14]

The sociological department informed employees of the important services provided by the Ford Legal Department. Its lawyers offered to employees, free of charge, advice on a variety of matters: the process of purchasing a home, the relief of debt, the procurement of naturalization papers, the acquisition of life insurance. By 1917, the legal department maintained four attorneys and one real-estate specialist on its permanent staff. The medical department worked to treat employees' health problems, both as a humanitarian effort and to guarantee that employees "are in proper physical condition for their work." Company physicians were on duty twenty-four hours a day, seven days a week, to handle injuries, illnesses, or emergencies concerning workers' families. Investigators from the sociological department urged workers to take advantage of this service. By 1920, the medical department had evolved into a twenty-room institution with a staff of ten doctors, two dentists, two pharmacists, an anesthetist, and nearly one hundred first-aid attendants.[15]

Thus, by late 1915, the sociological department was implementing the moral strictures that framed the Five-Dollar Day and seeking to shape the character, domestic life, and financial habits of Ford workers. Clearly, much of the impetus for the company's massive social project emanated from Henry Ford himself. With the Five-Dollar Day, his inclination to manufacture men as well as cars became an imperative.

Though Henry Ford had been at best an intermittent moralist in his early life, the reform impulse was in his blood. Determined not to succumb to the evils of big finance, this populist-leaning manufacturer had avoided banks and gone his own way in the forming of his company. He was disdainful of the prevailing notion that the automobile was a plaything for the rich, and staked his career on manufacturing a car for the people. By the mid-1910s, flush with the astounding success of the Model T and making more money than he knew what to do with, he determined to reform the state of the industrial worker. Ford turned, in equal measure, to the issues of wages and morality and simultaneously established the Five-Dollar Day and the sociological department. He had concluded that he could mass-produce virtue as well as vehicles.

Henry Ford worked closely with John R. Lee in setting the moral agenda of the sociological department. According to one observer, "I know that Mr. Ford and John Lee spent a good deal of time in handling this question [of qualifications] and setting ideas and rules that were to be followed." Teaching the men responsible values so that their new abundance would go to their families rather than to saloonkeepers, prostitutes, or bookies, Ford believed, would ensure the benefits of the company's wage experiment. During their planning sessions, Lee once asked Ford how far he was willing to go in terms of establishing rules for conduct among his workers. Ford's reply revealed his moral passion: "Well, John, if you ever get track of the devil, you run and catch up to him and you try to reform him."[16]

In an appearance before the Congressional Commission on Industrial Relations on January 22, 1915, a little over a year after the launching of the sociological department, Henry Ford provided an overview of this new agency. His description revealed its linkage of private and public virtue. He described investigators' efforts to counsel employees about healthy living and immoral, self-destructive practices. "The whole effort of this corps is to point men to life and make them discontented with a mere living," he concluded. "The object was simply to better the financial and moral status of the men."[17]

What prompted Ford to launch this unprecedented industrial experiment in moral as well as financial uplift? In many ways, his concept of the sociological department was a grab bag of early-twentieth-century reform impulses. Inspiration arrived from different directions. Not surprisingly, Ford's populist principles led him to see his company's social program as supporting the aspirations and opportunities of common workers. "We are planning to help the man who is weak and needs our help," he once confided to an associate. "What [ordinary workers] need is the opportunity to do better, and some one to take a little personal interest in them—someone who will show that he has faith in them."[18]

Also evident was an influence from the Social Gospel, an influential movement in turn-of-the-century Protestantism that sought to mold a secular version of salvation. In 1916, Ford put a clergyman in charge of the sociological department, and the industrialist's comments were littered with allusions to "tracking the devil" through sociological investigations and "bringing Jesus Christ into my factory." Though no orthodox Christian, Ford once told an associate that "the Bible is the most valuable book in the world" and inquired about paying to have it rewritten in updated language, published, and distributed in a million copies to those who had never read it. Charles A. Brownell, an advertising specialist deeply involved with the company's social program, had many conversations with Ford about its intent. When asked by a reporter about Ford's motivation, he explained it as an exercise in "dispensing practical Christianity, interpreted through dollars and cents in the sharing of profits with employees."[19]

Ford's sociological program further drew upon the heritage of nineteenth-century Victorianism, the moral tradition in which he had been raised. Since the 1830s, bourgeois life in the United States had been dominated by genteel values of self-restraint, middle-class domesticity, and a strong ethic of character formation. Ford's embrace of these values colored the agenda of the sociological department. The company's social programs, he told interviewers, would have "a striking effect in the development of personal character" and help the typical worker become morally self-reliant, family-oriented, and socially responsible. The worker who was living in a salacious or improvident manner, Ford explained, would be assisted

> . . . in a friendly way until he is able to walk alone. . . . There are thousands of men out there in the shop who are not living as they should. Their homes are crowded and unsanitary. Wives are going to work because their husbands are unable to earn enough to support the family. They fill up their homes with roomers and boarders in order to help swell their income. It's all wrong—all wrong. It's especially bad for the children.[20]

But Ford also saw the sociological department as an important instrument for inculcating new values of consumer abundance. In his view, investigators needed to teach workers how to consume responsibly. Immigrant workers, he believed, especially required instruction in living more abundantly without falling into profligacy. "We have seventy-five supervisors who are under orders to go out to teach our people to live better and to want more," he declared. Teaching the wise use of wages was especially important. "We know there are some out there who can't stand prosperity," Ford told *Everybody's Magazine*. "It is our business to see that they spend their money right."[21]

Ultimately, Ford's vision of the sociological department reflected the social-engineering ethos of progressive reformers in the early twentieth century. Seeking to avoid both working-class revolt and business autocracy, progressives favored the rational, efficient management of human affairs to overcome problems of poverty, waste, and social inequality and create responsible citizens. In his interviews and writing, Ford stressed that his company's social programs followed precisely this route. Also, in typical progressive fashion, he argued that environmental factors lay at the root of social problems. Company investigators could identify and rectify them, and thus create fuller and happier lives among workers and their families. The sociological department could help workers become good citizens. As Ford noted of his social-engineering sensibility:

> We want to make men in this factory as well as automobiles. This company has outlived its usefulness as a money-making concern, unless we can do some good with the money. I do not believe in charity, but I do believe in the regenerating power of work in men's

lives. . . . I believe that the only charity worthwhile is the kind that helps a man to help himself. . . . I want the whole organization dominated by a just, generous, and humane policy.[22]

As the sociological department gathered these reform impulses and began its work of molding the private lives of company workers, Henry Ford turned to a friend to direct its operation. A leading minister in the Detroit area, he enthusiastically embraced the challenge posed by the company's social work. In 1915, he became the architect of the Ford Motor Company's moral mission.

The Reverend Samuel S. Marquis was exhausted. Over the previous few years, as dean of the newly constructed St. Paul's Episcopal Cathedral in Detroit, he had worked relentlessly, raising funds, energizing the congregation, and preaching. By early 1915, he had drained his body of energy, and his health had begun to decline. His physician grew worried and suggested a year's vacation, but Marquis rejected the idea. "A change in work would be more beneficial to me than being idle," he replied. A parishioner with whom he had become friendly, Henry Ford, came forward with a proposal. Ford encouraged Marquis to contact his company's new sociological department and offer his services. The minister found the idea attractive and arranged to become a volunteer. Ford was elated; using his nickname for Marquis, he provided a directive: "I want you, Mark, to put Jesus Christ into my factory."[23]

Henry Ford respected the kind of social reformism that the Reverend Marquis represented. For several years, this prominent preacher had spoken vigorously throughout Detroit on behalf of reconciliation between capital and labor. He had proselytized for a rigorous personal code, stressing moral improvement. He had articulated a view of human nature based on a mechanical model. To Ford, all of these qualities made Marquis the perfect choice for the job he would assume at the company within a matter of months—head of the sociological department and spokesman for its program of social reform.

Samuel Simpson Marquis had been born in Sharon, Ohio, in 1866, the offspring of several generations of Episcopalian ministers. He pursued his own ecclesiastical studies, first at Allegheny College in Pennsylvania, and then at Cambridge Theological School in Massachusetts, where he earned a bachelor-of-divinity degree in 1893. Marquis served as rector at two Massachusetts churches for several years before assuming that same position at

Detroit's St. Joseph Church in 1901. On May 15, 1906, he became dean of
St. Paul's Cathedral, where he gained public notice for advocating the principles of the Social Gospel movement.[24]

In the decade after his arrival in Detroit, Marquis steadily emerged as
an energetic, outspoken, and progressive public figure who spoke out not
only on spiritual matters but on social issues of the day. In 1904, he
appeared on the front page of the Detroit *Free Press* advocating the establishment of a local civic federation where leaders of capital and labor could
gather to work for "industrial peace." "The welfare of both depends upon
their getting together upon a basis of intelligence, good will, equal rights,
and equal power," he insisted. He also advocated equal rights for men and
women. Addressing the matter of divorce, he denounced a double standard
in matters of morality. "I do not see why woman should not exact the same
standard of morality of man as he would exact from her. Morals will not
improve until man and woman are on equal standard," he stated.[25]

Marquis enhanced his reformist credentials with a personal image as a
charismatic, masculine figure. He rejected the model of the pale, pious do-
gooder and embraced that of Theodore Roosevelt—the energetic, happy
warrior battling against sin. "His activities are perpetual, save as he sleeps.
He is in deadly earnest," wrote one newspaper. "He hits from the shoulder."
Marquis had an infectious laugh—"no clerical contagion of gloom for
him"—and told a rollicking story. No pasty-faced bookworm or ascetic, the
minister cultivated "the healthy primitive instincts." He often retreated
from the city to a small cabin, built by his own hands, in a remote area
where he rejuvenated himself through hard work and direct contact with
nature. "He comes back as the trained and militant sky pilot should be,
equal to and eager for the work to which his life is dedicated," concluded the
Detroit *Journal*. "There is not the mark of a weakling about him."[26]

So, by 1915, when Marquis made his first sojourn to the Ford Motor
Company, he had an established reputation as a vigorous proponent of
social as well as spiritual reform. Near the end of the year, when John R. Lee
resigned to pursue other business opportunities, Henry Ford asked Marquis
to become head of the sociological department. Within a short time, the
minister mustered his considerable energy and eloquence and went forth to
explain to the world the company's experiment in social reform.[27]

On February 23, 1916, Marquis appeared before the National Education Association to give a major address on Ford's sociological department.
He began in striking fashion. "The impression has somehow got abroad
that Henry Ford is in the automobile business," he declared. "It isn't
true.... [Cars] are but the by-products of his real business, which is the
making of men." The Ford factory at Highland Park, he argued, was as

much a school as a production center, and it fully aimed to improve the lives of its workers as well as to manufacture sturdy, reliable cars for the American people. With this goal in mind, Henry Ford had inaugurated the Five-Dollar Day along with "a plan for the education of the working-men in thrift, honesty, sobriety, better housing, and better living generally." Marquis listed its concrete objectives:

1. To improve a man's tastes and at the same time increase his earning power.
2. To teach a man to use his income in a constructive manner.
3. To put a man into a right relation with his family.
4. To put a man into right relations with his community.
5. To put a man right with his work and his employer.
6. To fit the foreigner to become a citizen and to encourage him to do so.
7. To give the man who is down and out a chance to come back.

This reform effort, Marquis explained, aimed to create better citizens and happier human beings. "The Ford idea," he explained, "is to increase a man's capacity for happiness and at the same time to increase his efficiency, his earning capacity, his worth to society, so that he may have access to the things he has been taught to enjoy."[28]

Over the next several years, Marquis stalwartly defended the principles of the sociological department. Its system, he stated, taught workers the value of hard work and self-reliance. Rather than handing out charity, the company sought to pay its men high wages and then assist them in learning how to spend their money wisely. Rather than making workers wards of the company and encouraging dependence upon outside support, it insisted that each individual "be put ultimately upon a self-supporting basis."[29]

For critics who accused the Ford Motor Company of interfering in the private affairs of its employees, Marquis had a rejoinder. Some employees did object to investigators' asking questions, but nearly always they were individuals who wanted to protect "such liberties as getting drunk and beating up one's wife, abusing one's family, and wasting one's money." To those who questioned the efficacy of the sociological department's program, he offered a long list of endorsements from Detroit judges and law-enforcement officials who praised the company for enhancing the well-being of both its workers and the broader community.[30]

Marquis also stressed that the Ford program helped industrial workers cope with the new consumer culture springing up around them. He said that newly affluent employees "do not know how to take care of their money or employ their leisure," and explained that Ford sociologists "not only teach a man how to earn more money, but . . . how to spend it." The company, in Marquis' words, sought to provide a wage "that provides for some of the luxuries of life, as well as for its necessities." The sociological department, in other words, provided instruction in responsible consumption.[31]

In addition to defending the Ford social mission to the outside world, Marquis served as its cheerleader within the company. A couple of years after assuming his position, he had changed the title of his department's representatives from "investigators" to "advisors," and in January 1917 he assembled the group to give them one of his famous pep talks. Marquis assured the groups that they were "the center of all sociological work in the world; there is no work being done anywhere that is attracting so much attention as this work in this department of the Ford Motor Company." He reiterated the humanitarian, economic, and social-justice dimensions of the Ford program and trotted out his favorite line: "It is not paternalistic . . . it is fraternalistic; we are not trying to be the fathers, but the brothers." Henry Ford, Marquis explained, had made the company's social advisers his agents in a special kind of work. "Five dollars a day won't do anything for a man," he declared. "You have to get the men in the way of right living, of looking toward the future." To accomplish this task, a Ford adviser must himself be a person of integrity, upright character, thrift, and sincerity, while holding fast to a faith in basic human goodness.

The stakes were high, Marquis pointed out. The failure of the Ford profit-sharing plan would represent a larger failure of enlightened labor policies, and could plunge industrial society into class warfare. The sociological department could stave off such a calamity, and Marquis stirred his advisers to this task:

> If you can do the work you are doing without getting a lump in your throat once in a while, you have not got the idea. You have one of the greatest chances a fellow ever had for the building up of his character. When we have got along to the end of the day, the richest thing you and I as men can have will be the memories of the hundreds of men we were able to take and help to a wider, finer, higher, and more constructive way of living.[32]

Samuel Marquis' reform work at the Ford Motor Company won him admirers among progressives around the United States. Labor leader Samuel Gompers was so impressed with Marquis that he appointed him to membership on the Section on Industrial Training, a division of the United States government's Committee on Labor during World War I. Marquis also struck up a strong friendship with Ida Tarbell when she visited the Ford plant in the spring of 1915. Over the next few years, she and Marquis exchanged letters, compliments, and ideas on reform work among industrial workers.[33]

More radical reformers were not so admiring. John Reed, who interviewed Marquis in 1916, claimed that he was little more than a lackey of the wealthy, "a man who for many years preached the gospel of Jesus Christ to the predatory rich so inoffensively that they built him the most sumptuous church in Detroit." Upon joining Ford, this writer continued, Marquis had become a moralizing busybody who subverted Ford's revolutionary wage policy by burdening it with insidious rules of conduct. The minister's smooth voice and assertive, confident manner underscored his powerful position, and his practical bent drove his interviewer to conclude that his "gospel, as far as I could make out, is Efficiency."[34]

But this was a minority report. Most reformers believed that Marquis' infusion of progressive political and social principles into the Ford sociological department—encouraging a fuller, richer life among industrial workers, creating habits of responsibility that encouraged private virtue and community cohesion, helping to heal the rift between capital and labor—portended to a brighter future for American society.

An even deeper impulse inspiring Marquis, however, involved spiritual yearning. He believed he was part of a great moral crusade at the Ford Motor Company. Shortly after taking over the sociological department, he told the New York *Tribune* that this work demanded the attention of every "public-spirited Christian." "I believe that I could have preached and lived a more vital, practical Christianity had I done something of this kind earlier in my ministry," he confessed. Marquis recalled years later that he had felt "part of a great experiment in applied Christianity in industry. The spirit of service, helpfulness and cooperation permeated practically the whole organization. . . . Here was a corporation with a soul." To this reform-minded minister, the company's melding of industrial regeneration with spiritual salvation created an intoxicating sense of mission.[35]

Marquis' vision of the sociological department gained power from one final source—a mechanistic view of human nature that mirrored the sensibility of the surging automobile industry. Combining a positivistic mind-set derived from nineteenth-century science with a modern managerial commitment to efficiency, Marquis viewed human beings as, literally, machines that required constant tune-ups to run smoothly and productively. He had unfolded this model in a 1912 essay in *Ford Times*, which the company later reprinted and distributed as a pamphlet. Marquis' title—*The Man: On the*

Scientific Self-Management of a One Man-Power Three Cylinder Engine—revealed much about its content.[36]

Marquis' mechanistic metaphor unfolded relentlessly. He noted the existence of an engine that was capable of producing enormous power if managed scientifically. "It has three cylinders; is cast in one piece; has a self-starting device, and is automatically controlled," he described. "It was first installed in the Garden of Eden and was called 'The Man.' " Each of the cylinders developed a different kind of power—physical, mental, and moral—but each needed to be in perfect condition for the human engine to obtain the best results.[37]

Although scientists and mechanics had been studying machines for centuries, Marquis argued, only recently had people found it worthwhile to examine the human mechanism. The results were remarkable. It had been discovered that "the human engine—like the steam plant in its early days—is wasting a great deal of power, and that this waste can be stopped by scientific management." Moreover, it was clear that the intelligent direction of one's own energies and talents—what Marquis termed "scientific self-management"—held the key to financial success, emotional contentment, and personal happiness. It was simply a matter of the individual's striving "to find out how he can get the most out of this three-cylinder engine of which he is the owner and engineer."[38]

Marquis told readers exactly how to go about it. The scientific self-manager must study each of the three cylinders in the human engine. First, he should observe the "physical cylinder" of the body and avoid abusing it with bad diet, excessive passion, or alcohol. Second, the scientific self-manager must examine the "mental cylinder" and practice "mental control" to acquire knowledge and avoid fear and worry. Finally, he must focus attention on the most powerful element in his engine, the "moral cylinder," and cultivate useful, respectful relations with others, a task that demanded firm moral principles. Proper self-management, Marquis concluded, kept "every cylinder running" to propel the individual on his journey to the top.[39]

Marquis ended his service with Ford in January 1921 when enthusiasm for the moral mission of its sociological department began to wane. This became evident when company production managers, after several years, objected to the constant scrutiny of workers' lives and behavior. Sociological investigators were calling men away from work during the day to discuss domestic or moral matters. Managers such as Charles Sorensen grew furious at such interventions and refused to let workers leave their jobs. A contest of wills ensued as the two parties took their quarrel to the top. Marquis complained to Henry Ford about Sorensen's countermanding his directives, and Sorensen denounced Marquis' meddling. After months of mutual recrimination, the two were summoned one day to Ford's office, where a shouting match erupted. Marquis proved a match for the volcanic Sorensen. "I had always treated clergymen with deference," Sorensen noted much later. "Many times in my life I have been called an s.o.b., but never before or after was I called one by a supposed man of God—in fact, that day I heard from Dean Marquis some words I had never heard before." But Ford refused to back Marquis, and he resigned his post a few days later. In a post-script penned several years later, Marquis noted that powerful men who "never ceased to ridicule, criticize, and misrepresent the efforts put forth to improve the human relations within the industry" had gained Henry Ford's ear and subverted the noble crusade of "the corporation with a soul." The days when an enlightened corporation "set justice and humanity above profits and production, were gone."[40]

But during the mid-1910s, everything had seemed possible in an industrial enterprise where moral conduct mattered as much as production. Samuel Marquis' efforts with the sociological department had demonstrated the Ford Motor Company's commitment to a curious kind of reform blending twentieth-century managerial efficiency with nineteenth-century Victorian moralism. This impulse also appeared in another company endeavor: an educational project designed to Americanize the tens of thousands of immigrants who had come into the Highland Park factory to help make the Model T. Here, too, the Victorian moral reformer joined hands with the modern industrial manager.

In Detroit, as throughout urban areas in the United States, immigrants constituted a large percentage of industrial workers. Almost half of the twenty thousand employees manning Ford assembly lines and machine shops were recent arrivals in the United States. Many of them were mired in poverty and spoke only their native tongue. Walking through Highland Park in the early 1910s, an observer hearing the babble of voices in languages from around the world would have faced an unavoidable conclusion. The Model T, much like America's industrial society in the early twentieth century, was produced by men from many nations.

In Henry Ford's eyes, however, this mass of immigrants created significant difficulties. As he told a journalist in 1914, "Foreign laborers cannot become American citizens, learn to spend more money for living and efficiently enjoy freedom and citizenship unless they can speak, read, and write

English." Two problems loomed particularly large. First, workers' lack of English-language skills presented an impediment to effective management at Highland Park. According to one Ford manager, it was "utterly impossible to reach these men with an explanation of our work through the medium of interpreters." Second, the failure of immigrant workers to assimilate into the American mainstream often translated into a reluctance to embrace the tenets of modern industrial society: disciplined labor in a factory setting, the pursuit of consumer abundance, the shaping of a clean, cozy domestic setting for the family. Too often, upon arriving in Detroit, recent immigrants had been set upon by corrupt ethnic bosses who steered them toward stores or tenement buildings owned by those same men. As a company official observed, "It is to the interest of such men that these foreigners shall know nothing of the English language, of American ways and customs . . . which would liberate them from the bondage."[41]

Henry Ford believed that these problems demanded solution. In his words, "These men of many nations must be taught American ways, the English language, and the right way to live." Acting partly out of self-interest, the company sought to Americanize workers as a way to instill work discipline and assert the company's control over the process of industrial production. Acting partly out of benevolence, Ford and his managers saw Americanization as a way to build a social and cultural framework that would support a raised standard of living for workers in the new atmosphere of consumer abundance. The sociological department had provided one prod toward Americanization, but the educational project launched about the same time proved even more far-reaching in assimilating immigrant workers.[42]

In April 1914, the company secured the services of Peter Roberts, a YMCA teacher, to develop a program in English-language instruction. He had a background working with immigrant miners in the Pennsylvania coalfields, where he had published an instructional booklet entitled *English for Coming Americans*. This text outlined a practical approach to teaching the language that offered three series of lessons—one focusing on domestic life, another on commercial transactions, and a third on industrial situations. With titles such as "Table Utensils," "The Man Washing," "Going to the Bank," and "Beginning the Day's Work," these lessons combined the learning of basic grammar and vocabulary with lessons in proper behavior and values.[43]

The Roberts Plan became the foundation for the Ford English School, which was established in May 1914. Henry Ford instigated the program and believed strongly in its mission. A journalist who interviewed him concluded that the school "is the child of his brain and is near his heart." The school faced a daunting task. The company estimated that workmen in the Ford shops represented some fifty-three nationalities and spoke more than one hundred languages and dialects. Classes began on a small scale, with a single instructor and about a dozen students. Within a few months, however, the operation expanded dramatically.[44]

By late 1916, the Ford English School was enrolling twenty-seven hundred students per session and had engaged 163 teachers. The school offered lessons taught in a thirty-six-week session, two lessons a week, for an hour and a half each. Three meeting times were created to meet the huge numbers: one at 8:30 a.m. for men leaving the night shift, one at 1:30 p.m. for men slated to begin an afternoon shift, and one at 3:30 p.m. for those leaving the day shift. Attendance was compulsory for non-English-speaking workers. According to Marquis, "A man who declines to take it is laid off for a couple of weeks in order that he may have time to think it over. If after further persuasion he refuses to attend the classes he is given an opportunity to find employment elsewhere." For teachers, the program drew upon company volunteers who had a solid grasp of English and a desire to help. They spent three months in a teacher-training course, then served as substitute instructors, and finally were eased into teaching regular classes. The instructors also enjoyed a fellowship of their own, forming a Teachers' Literary Club that met twice a month to discuss and debate books.[45]

The Ford English School taught by means of dramatization and mass recitation. Part of the Roberts method included "dramatization of all the sentences; that is acting out all of the ideas to be conveyed," as a way of teaching vocabulary, grammar, and practical phrases. The instructor would go through the motions of bathing, for example, while saying, "I wash myself," as the class recited the sentence in concert. This method encouraged a participatory, even carnivalesque atmosphere. According to one observer, "Twenty-five men shouting the lesson together arouse a great deal of good feeling, and in a few minutes, the day's work is forgotten." A few weeks after the birth of the school, Henry Ford, accompanied by two visitors, dropped by to observe a lesson. With twenty laborers who spoke eleven languages, the class presented this scene:

> "Kettle," says the teacher, with 20 pairs of eager eyes upon him.
> He holds up the common tea kettle of the kitchen.
> "I put water in the kettle," he continues. "I put the kettle on the stove."
> Each sentence is repeated in chorus, over and over again. Then the teacher takes them through the various uses of the personal

pronouns: "he puts the kettle," "you put the kettle," "we put the kettle." This brings up the mystery of singular and plural words. He can't get it into their heads. He grabs a man who is known to be unmarried. "Single," the teacher says, shaking the man. "Not married." They understand.

"Now," says the teacher, "one kettle," holding up one finger, "is what?" The answer comes at once. "Single."

"Now, what is two kettles," holding up two fingers and the kettle.

"Married!" shouts a bright laborer, beaming at his own show of knowledge. All he gets is a laugh. The class has learned enough to see the joke and the teacher laughs too.[46]

The school curriculum followed the Roberts blueprint by including practical lessons based on daily actions, social encounters, and work tasks. But it also sought to inculcate middle-class values of hard work, sobriety, punctuality, and cleanliness—"such matters as the proper care of the body, bathing, and clean teeth," according to a report in *Ford Times*. Some lessons focused on etiquette, such as the correct way to be introduced and shake hands, and the proper way to conduct oneself at the meal table in terms of being seated, using napkins and utensils, and adding condiments to food and drink. As Samuel S. Marquis once explained to an audience, "We have our professor of table manners who teaches the art of eating a meal in a manner that will not interfere with the appetite of the other fellow."[47]

The Ford English School made a special point of teaching the fundamentals of American government to its immigrant students. As Marquis put it, the curriculum sought to "make the men more efficient in our work in the shop, but also to prepare them for citizenship. The first thing we teach them to say is, 'I am a good American,' and then we try to get them to live up to the statement." After observing one of the lessons that instructed pupils in the democratic voting process and the basic principles of the Constitution, Henry Ford declared to an accompanying reporter, "Great, useful, and patriotic citizens are to come out of this school."[48]

One of the most fascinating aspects of the curriculum, however, concerned its subtle inculcation of consumer values. Many of the lessons underlined the skills necessary to purchasing goods and services in a modern society of abundance. With titles such as "Pay Day," "Going to the Bank," "Buying a Lot," and "Building a House," they taught immigrant laborers how to navigate among a host of bewildering choices regarding the spending of their enhanced paychecks. As Marquis explained, "We not only teach a man how to earn more money, but we begin at once to teach him how to spend it. Lessons on how to use money are just as important as lessons on how to earn it." Company pamphlets aimed at immigrant employees argued that learning to speak English would help them transact their own business and make their own choices about buying articles. The English School sought to convert immigrants to the American idea of abundant living. "Thrift is construed by the average foreigner as meaning to live cheaply as possible, while the American-born often construes it as meaning the opposite," one of its pamphlets stated. "[After proper schooling] the foreigner now knows the meaning of the phrase 'American standard of living.' "[49]

The Ford school's program of Americanization was illustrated dramatically in its graduation ceremonies. On July 5, 1915, all foreign-born employees of the company gathered for a patriotic march through the heart of Detroit. Some five thousand strong, and led by sixteen hundred students from the English School and a detail of Boy Scouts, the group walked in orderly fashion the two miles from Highland Park to City Hall. After a mass singing of "America," the crowd cheered a welcoming speech from Detroit Mayor Oscar B. Marx.[50]

A short time later, the school held its first graduation ceremony. The graduates and their guests listened to inspirational addresses, drank refreshments, and enjoyed several musical offerings. The graduates then lined up to receive official diplomas signed by Clinton D. DeWitt, superintendent of the school, as well as by Lee, Couzens, and Henry Ford himself. Then came the dramatic highlight of the proceedings—the pageant of the "Ford Melting Pot." Behind an elevated stage sat a large, painted backdrop of an ocean steamship, from which a gangway led down into an immense cauldron labeled "Ford English School Melting Pot." The graduates filed across the stage and down the gangway into the cauldron, from which they emerged waving small American flags to the cheers and applause of the audience. According to *Ford Times*, this exercise was "symbolic of the fusing process which makes raw immigrants into loyal Americans."[51]

To admirers of Henry Ford and his company, the sociological department and the English School complemented the Five-Dollar Day as important elements of an industrial reform agenda. For critics, however, these social programs represented unwarranted intrusions of corporate power into the private lives and values of workers. Though not an exercise of naked authority in the older style of the robber barons, they offered a subtler but equally sinister form of social control by a wealthy, powerful industrialist. A debate opened over the merits of Ford's social "reforms," one that began slowly but soon gathered momentum and passion over the years.

In mid-1916, John Reed sat in Samuel S. Marquis' office in Highland Park, on assignment to examine Henry Ford's experiment in industrial reform. Though an admirer of Ford's Five-Dollar Day and his enlightened senti- ments, Reed loathed the sociological department and its agenda. This pro- gram, he wrote, "interfered in the most sacred matters of a man's private life." It "set up a conventional settlement-worker's code of morals" and then "constructed an elaborate system of spying all over Detroit to report lapses of morality and bad habits." In his view, the investigators of the sociological department exercised "an intolerable tyranny" over Ford workers. Reed was determined to call Marquis to account for these sins.[52]

After Reed recited his litany of complaints, Marquis made his standard defense of the program. He argued that it helped workers take care of their money and improve their home lives while, simultaneously, helping the company because men worked better when their private affairs were in order. "It is not a paternal system," Marquis declared in his favorite turn of phrase; "it's fraternal." Unswayed, Reed peppered the minister with ques- tions suggesting that any self-respecting worker would resent the company's attempt to impose its standards of conduct. Marquis' anger flared. "We find that the only resentment comes from those that are doing wrong and want to conceal something," he shot back. "Besides, if they don't like it they needn't come here. A man has the choice of taking a job with the Ford Company or somewhere else."[53]

This confrontation between Reed and Marquis reflected a larger debate. As the acclaim over the Five-Dollar Day subsided and news spread of its accompanying sociological requirements, disagreements emerged, some of them acrimonious, among newspaper editorialists, social critics, and representatives of business and labor. The crux of the issue, of course, was the intrusion of the company into the private lives of its employees. Was Ford's attempt to mold personal values and private behavior a legitimate expression of social reform, or was it an unwarranted attempt to extend cor- porate social control into the very homes of industrial workers?

About a year after the announcement of the Five-Dollar Day, the Con- gressional Commission on Industrial Relations took up the issue. Henry Ford appeared before this body to answer questions on his industrial reforms and the mission of the sociological department. He was asked why the Ford Motor Company sought to assume "so large a measure of respon- sibility, not only for the labor conditions in its plants, but also for the social and moral surroundings of its employees?" Ford explained his goal of improving his workers' home lives, their moral character, and thus their prospects for leading a fuller and more abundant life. A follow-up question: "Is it desirable for a corporation to assume so large a measure of control of employees as the Ford Co. has done?" Ford replied that his social program reflected a "heartfelt, personal interest in the welfare of his employees" and that this concern not only helped the worker and his family but, by improving morale and contentment among employees, boosted the productivity of his company. This exchange—skeptical questions about the dangers of overweening paternalism on the one side, reassurances about the moral and economic virtues of the Ford social program on the other—occurred over and over in the larger public debate.[54]

Critics of the sociological department's agenda denounced Ford's intrusion in private lives as a thinly veiled exercise of power. The New Haven, Connecticut, *Journal-Courier* confessed that it did "not quite see Mr. Ford's right to regulate [his workers'] home life because he has made liberal allowances in their wage. . . . They want to live their own lives in their own way, advancing to a higher social status, if that is what it is, by processes of evolution, certainly not by processes of proscription." Other newspapers denounced the Ford program as subverting American principles of liberty. "It is the American theory that when his day's work is over a free man is free . . . that so long as a man observes his obligations to society he is his own master in his own house," declared an editorial entitled "Ford's Feudal System." "The payment of good wages does not give an employer the authority to seek to regulate the internal family affairs of any man."[55]

Most critics, however, focused on Ford's paternalistic impulse. The sociological department's requirements about personal values and private behavior, they argued, simply treated workers like children. This misguided agenda created dependence, not self-reliance. An editorial entitled "Paternalism at the Ford Works" put the matter eloquently. Though the Ford program had done good things in teaching English and encouraging proper living habits, the question remained "whether good citizens can be turned out mechanically, as are automobiles. Personal liberty is essential to good citizenship, and when the living of men and families is governed by outsiders as completely as if they were horses, it is to be feared that they may lose some of the stamina and independence which are inseparable from the best citizenship."[56]

As for Ford workers, their reaction to the sociological department was mixed. Some approved of the scheme or did not publicly object to it. After interviewing laborers at Highland Park, *The Survey* reported that Henry Ford's workmen were "all going around grinning. Contrary to all precedent they welcome the official [sociological-department] investigator with open arms. . . . And there is talk everywhere of savings banks accounts and of the purchase of homes." In fact, this state of affairs utterly frustrated radicals who sought to organize the Ford plant. An outraged John Reed denounced the American Federation of Labor in Detroit for endorsing the idea that "Ford paternalism was beneficial to the men." This action, he said, "makes one seriously doubt whether, after all, men should not be treated like slaves or children."[57]

Workers' approval of Ford's social programs was not unanimous, however. In various ways, dissenters and grumblers at the company made their views known, although they did so carefully, to protect their jobs. William Pioch, a loyal Ford employee for many years, grew disgruntled when company investigators "went to my home. My wife told them everything. There was nothing to keep from them. . . . It was kind of a funny idea, in a free state." John R. Lee confessed that the initial round of reports by investigators in the summer of 1914 "engendered a lot of apathy and ill-feeling" among workers. They complained, some in writing, that investigators were prying into their private lives. Lee warned his associates to be careful and steer clear of "things that are strictly private, that do not concern our work in the least." An internal report written a year later by a supervising investigator, William M. Purves, admitted that "private affairs were needlessly pried into, confidences violated, and ungentlemanly acts perpetrated in the employees' houses" by many of his associates. Other signs of resistance also cropped up. As late as 1919, thirty-eight workers were dismissed at Highland Park for refusing to attend the Ford English School.[58]

But Ford's supporters also spoke out. *Leslie's*, a popular magazine, lauded him as "an evangelist of the doctrine of industrial reform for the benefit of the laboring classes," and concluded that his social efforts at "encouraging the laborers to use their new-found wealth wisely" had benefited both the workers and the company. A trade journal, *The Automobile*, praised the Ford sociological department for pursuing a "kind of welfare work that is a man-to-man, character-building proposition," and asserted that other companies "can well learn from what has been accomplished by this wonderfully large organization." Newspaper editorials argued that Ford's program was based on the well-established connection among sociology, economics, and social uplift. "He does not wish to narrow their freedom or dictate to them where dictation is unwarranted," one stated. "He simply asks them to conform to the American standard of decent living." According to the New York *Sun*, the sociological department simply sought "to look after [workers'] health, to aid in their recreational opportunities, the education of their children, and in every legitimate way to further their general well being."[59]

Henry Ford's most enthusiastic support came from the ranks of progressive reformers, who saw their own principles of efficiency, expertise, and good citizenship mirrored in his program. Beginning around the turn of the century, centrist progressives in both major political parties had sought to tame, regulate, and rationalize corporate capitalism through strategies of social engineering. They believed that humans were fundamentally rational, so American citizens, if properly informed and empowered, would pursue the public good. They assumed that social-science experts were discovering the causes of the nation's social problems in various environmental causes and were working to shape solutions. Mustering a powerful moral energy, often Christian in character, they directed it toward obliterating social ills and reconstructing a purer, more ethical, and equitable life for all citizens. Prodded by thinkers such as Herbert Croly, John Dewey, and Walter Lippmann, progressives embraced bureaucratic planning and the expertise of disinterested professionals, planners, and technocrats. They strove to ensure abundance and security for American citizens through rational planning, management, and cooperation between capital, labor, and government in the public sphere. To many such progressives, Ford's sociological department appeared as an inspiring example of intelligent, efficacious reform.[60]

Within the company, of course, Samuel S. Marquis advocated a progressive vision of capital-labor cooperation, intelligent planning, and good citizenship. He presented the sociological department as a kind of welfare agency devoted to uplift of workers, with the investigator taking the role of caseworker. "The environment of a man must be right if you expect him to come clean and strong out of it," he explained. "If conditions are not right in the home, we set ourselves the very first thing to the task of making them right."[61]

Perhaps the most famous progressive supporter of the Ford social plan was Ida Tarbell. She admired the emphasis on mass production and endorsed the Five-Dollar Day as a boon to workers, of course, but she praised with equal enthusiasm the sociological department. Terming it "a thoroughly worth-while and deeply human method," Tarbell lauded the company and its investigators for their determination to add to what they were doing for the making of men inside of the factory a thorough overhauling of the men's lives outside. "There were certain things that were laid down as essential. You had to be clean—cleanliness had played no part in the lives of hundreds of these men. . . . Ford's men must be clean. Already it had made an astonishing difference in the general look of the factory. And this cleanliness was carried by the sociological department into the home. The men must be kept clean, and the women must do their part. Many of the women, as well as the men, were discovering for the first time the satisfaction of cleanliness."[62] Here was a species of reform that pleased many progressives—clean, cooperative, efficient, character-building.

Tarbell especially admired the sociological department's efforts to combat alcohol abuse, which she viewed as a scourge of working-class families in industrial America. Company investigators, she explained, went to extraordinary lengths to help employees overcome drunkenness—medical treatment, moral pressure, wage incentives, family counseling. She spoke with one young man who had been put on the path to sobriety by a determined Ford investigator, and his words reaffirmed her approval of the company social program. "Lady," he said, "if, when I was a boy somebody had talked to me as these people have, if there had been anybody to be interested in me like they are, I'd have money enough laid up to live without working. I'm a good worker, always was when I was sober, but generally I was in the gutter." Such testimonials convinced Tarbell that Ford was on the right path to rational, humane reform. In her words, "The truth is the Sociological Department at Ford's seems to hate to give up a man as much as the Sales Department hates to give up an order."[63]

John R. Commons, the labor historian and economist at the University of Wisconsin, had been at the forefront of progressive reform in that state since the early 1900s, where he advised Governor Robert La Follette and served on a commission on factory-working conditions. In a long article entitled "Henry Ford, Miracle Maker," he detailed the automaker's profit-sharing scheme and its sociological apparatus. Because the plan focused on the way a worker lived his life as a whole, Commons concluded, "It ought to be called a citizenship fund, a community-developing fund, a homemaker's fund. . . . It is based upon the value of the individual in citizenship and in society." He approved of the sociological department's basic principle: "The idea is that every man wants to be a sober, capable, industrious citizen, and that such a man is the best investment the company can make."[64]

Commons believed that Ford's social programs—not only the investigators but the company's medical department, legal department, English School, and bank—demonstrated a genuine concern for workers' well-being and a desire to show them the way to responsible citizenship. "It is just old-fashioned industrial autocracy tempered by faith in human nature," he concluded. Though the autocratic element may have troubled some, Commons decided that Ford's insistence on counseling workers rather than firing them, his trimming of foremen's power in the factory, and his establishment of an advisory committee to handle difficult employees removed any prospects of abuse. In his words, "It all goes back to faith in people and ends in a trouble department to make repairs where something goes wrong in the exercise of faith."[65]

Within a few years, the experiment in social reform ended. By 1920, Henry Ford saw that the sociological department, with its list of moral requirements, had outlived its usefulness, and he instigated a bonus and investment plan for workers to replace the older system. Within a short time, there were only about a dozen operatives left in the department, and by mid-1921 they had been incorporated into the medical department. There were several reasons for the demise of the program: resistance from production managers finally wore down its adherents, it became increasingly expensive to support, and the company's growth made it impractical. Perhaps the most important factor, however, was Henry Ford's change of heart. He grew weary of answering the sociological department's critics. "There were objections to the bonus-on-conduct method of paying wages. It tended toward paternalism," he admitted in *My Life and Work*. "Paternalism has no place in industry. Welfare work that consists in prying into employees' private concerns is out of date."[66]

Henry Ford's social program reflected his loyalty to old-fashioned Victorian values of self-control, sobriety, and bourgeois respectability. Yet it also embodied his more modern, managerial determination to pursue "the making of men" with the hope that, like axles and camshafts, they could be perfectly reproduced by the thousands. The resulting tension between the archaic and the visionary, the cultural and the economic, the paternal and the modern, doomed Ford's sociological experiment. But the impact on his career was minimal. By the late 1910s, his interests were turning elsewhere. Ever restless and increasingly unconstrained, he began looking at issues that stretched far beyond the horizon of industrial production. The results would make him a much more visible—and even more controversial—public figure.

Twelve

Politician

In the spring of 1917, business journalist B. C. Forbes examined Henry Ford as part of his series on "Men Who Are Making America." Writing in *Leslie's* magazine, he reported that, although Ford had earned the admiration of the world for his achievements in reshaping American industrial life, he had recently demonstrated a troubling penchant for overreaching his talents. In Forbes' words, Ford's "intoxicating success went to his head, and he became obsessed with the notion there was nothing, human or superhuman, he and his money could not accomplish." Some of Ford's colleagues agreed. Samuel S. Marquis, for example, wrote that the industrialist had succumbed to a temptation facing many wealthy men by "assuming that because they have made a great success and shown exceptional ability in one field of action, therefore their opinions are of equal weight in all others." In Marquis' view, Ford had begun commenting and acting upon issues "for which he has not the special fitness that distinguished him in his own particular field."[1]

This portrait of a man stretching beyond his intellectual means had been inspired by Ford's controversial entry into public affairs. With the tremendous acclaim for the Model T, the Five-Dollar Day, and the company social programs, Ford saw himself moving about on a larger stage. With the whole country taking him seriously, he felt compelled to do likewise. In the mid-1910s, Ford moved out into the public arena. Around 1915, he began to speak out on controversial issues, lend his support to political movements, and even run for public office.

Ford undertook this new endeavor as a populist reformer. He drew upon several ideological influences from his youth and early manhood that were shaped by his rural Midwestern background. Pulling together various elements of his rough populist creed—hatred of Wall Street finance, belief in hardworking individualism, faith in ordinary citizens, suspicion of social elites and corporate privilege, pacifism—he embarked upon a political crusade. Typical of Ford, it was equal parts vision, sincerity, and naïveté. But this crusade was both energized and undermined by an additional element: hubris.

Once again, Henry Ford received an enormous amount of attention throughout the country. In his new life as a political player, just as in his earlier endeavors as a pioneering industrialist, everything he did seemed to create another headline. But palpable excitement produced only negligible results.

James Couzens was furious. On a fall day in early October 1915, Charles A. Brownell, the advertising manager at the company, had entered his office. Brownell oversaw publication of the *Ford Times*, and he had brought page proofs of its next edition for Couzens' approval. Couzens had thumbed through the proof, nodding his assent, until he saw an article credited to Henry Ford himself. Then his face began to redden and his muscles clenched. "You cannot publish this," he exclaimed. When Brownell assured him that Ford had given his personal approval, Couzens grew even more emphatic. "This is the company paper. He cannot use the *Ford Times* for his personal views," he burst out. "I will talk to Mr. Ford tomorrow."

The next morning, Ford dropped by Couzens' office and the two associates chatted amiably for a few minutes about Ford's upcoming trip to California with Thomas Edison. Then Couzens noted that he had held up publication of the *Ford Times* because of the offending article. Ford's good humor vanished and, according to Couzens, he "just flew off the handle. . . . I was shocked, aghast." An angry exchange ensued and Ford declared, "You cannot stop anything here!" Couzens replied, "Well, then, I will quit." The atmosphere grew frighteningly calm, and Ford told him to think it over. "No, I have decided," Couzens said. "All right, if you have decided," Ford said quietly. He left the office, and a short time later Couzens, having placed on his desk a resignation letter written in longhand, walked out of the Highland Park plant. Upon departing, he told a shocked subordinate, "I decided that I had enough of this God damn persecution." Thus ended the partnership that had brought great prominence and profits to the Ford Motor Company.[2]

Couzens' anger was inspired by what had become a preoccupation with Ford by late 1915—a passionate condemnation of the war raging on the European continent and a fervent opposition to American involvement in it.

Over the previous year, he had started speaking out against World War I, and his pacifism had emerged as a matter of public debate. His statements to the press made headlines, of course, and kept his views before the public. As controversy mounted, Couzens protested to Ford, fearing that a patriotic backlash might harm the company. Ford ignored him, and the use of the *Ford Times* to convey pacifist views proved to be the final straw. In one sense, however, Couzens was attempting to stem a sea change in the career of Henry Ford. At some level, Ford had decided that his views on public issues needed to be heard. The antiwar crusade, an issue about which he felt strongly, proved to be the opening stage of a larger engagement with public affairs.

Ford's denunciation of World War I was part of a national debate about the wisdom of intervention in this massive conflict. The American government, inspired by President Woodrow Wilson's aversion to warfare, pursued an official policy of neutrality. But significant segments of the public worried that defense of American commercial interests and pressure from the combatants would not allow neutrality. Notable figures holding this view, such as Theodore Roosevelt, were calling for a program of "preparedness"—building up the armed forces, shifting industry toward armament production, psychologically acclimating the citizenry for war—to ready the United States for an inevitable entry into World War I. Opponents of the war demanded that the country remain at a distance from the corruption and destruction of this Old World fight.

Ford embraced the antiwar position. As early as February 1915, he reprinted George Washington's Farewell Address, with its warning about the dangers of foreign entanglements, in the *Ford Times*. By the summer, he had abandoned subtlety for polemics. On August 22, in a lengthy statement to the Detroit *Free Press*, he declared,

> I will do everything in my power to prevent murderous, wasteful war in America and in the whole world. I will devote my life to fight this spirit which is now felt in the free and peaceful air of the United States, the spirit of militarism, mother to the cry of "preparedness" . . . I would teach the child at its mother's knee what a horrible, wasteful, and unavailing thing war is. In the home and in the schools of the world I would see the child taught to feel the uselessness of war; that war is a thing unnecessary; that preparation for war can only end in war.

The common people of the world desired peace, Ford insisted, but their desires were thwarted by corrupt rulers who sought glory and political advantage. These misguided leaders were encouraged by commercial "parasites" who sought to profit from conflict.[3]

Over the next two years, Ford gained a national reputation as an antiwar activist. In a series of newspaper statements, he made many memorable declarations. "To my mind, the word 'murderer' should be embroidered in red letters across the breast of every soldier," he told a reporter in 1915. "The saddest thing about this war—about every war, in fact, is that the people acquiesce in it. . . . Two classes benefit by war—the militarists and the money lenders." The following year, in an interview with a socialist newspaper, Ford argued that war should be declared only after a referendum by the nation's citizens: "The people who do the fighting and pay the war debts should have a vote as to whether they wanted a war or not." In an article in the magazine *Farm Life*, Ford contended that the United States was "confronted by the greatest danger in its history. . . . We are confronted by the danger of militarism." He denounced cheap appeals to patriotism. In his view, "patriotism does not consist merely of dying for one's country. I believe that patriotism consists more in living for the benefit of the whole world, of giving others a chance to live for themselves, their country, and the world."[4]

Ford also launched an advertising campaign that nationally distributed antiwar articles appearing under his name. In an essay entitled "Concerning Preparedness," he noted, "I am having this statement printed in the advertising columns of newspapers and magazines throughout the United States. Others will follow. I have no other purpose than to save America from bloodshed and its young men from conscription." Another, entitled "Humanity—and Sanity," quoted Washington, Jefferson, and Franklin on the dangers of war and military establishments and proclaimed, "It is the duty of Congress to keep this country out of a war into which there is no reason for our entrance."[5]

Eventually, as a man of action rather than a thinker, Ford attempted to put his beliefs into practice. Well meaning but naïve, he embraced an initiative that would eventually absorb huge amounts of time and money before degenerating into an international fiasco. It became one of the most embarrassing episodes in Ford's life. The voyage of the "Peace Ship," as it came to be known, took shape in late 1915, as Ford made the acquaintance of several people who sought to use both his name and his money.

For many months, Rosika Schwimmer, a Hungarian journalist, political activist, and pacifist, had been agitating for an end to World War I by neutral mediation. Working with figures such as Jane Addams, she had helped persuade the International Congress of Women in The Hague to support this policy. She came to the United States in 1915 and toured the country speaking at antiwar gatherings. Schwimmer noted Ford's public opposition to the war, and wrote to him to secure an interview. Louis Lochner, a young American pacifist working with the International Federation of Students and International Peace Congress, had been similarly aroused by Ford's efforts. Schwimmer and Lochner visited Ford at his Dearborn home in early November. They presented their plan for convening a commission of representatives from neutral nations who would work to negotiate a peace acceptable to all warring parties. With little effort, the pair convinced Ford that the people of the belligerent nations desperately sought peace and would support mediation.

Ford agreed to finance a barrage of telegrams to President Wilson in behalf of this peace strategy. Moreover, to the surprise of Schwimmer and Lochner, he suggested that he accompany them to the East Coast to rouse support for "continuous mediation." Within a matter of days, the trio left for New York City and met with a group of prominent supporters—Jane Addams, Dean George W. Kirchwey of Columbia University, Paul Kellogg of *Survey* magazine—and hatched a plan. First, they would seek Wilson's support for sending an official commission to Europe to participate in a convention pursuing "continuous mediation." If this option failed, they would dispatch a private group across the Atlantic to participate. Ford procured an appointment at the White House, and he and Lochner traveled to Washington the next day for a meeting with the President. The conference was pleasant but unsuccessful. Though Wilson was sympathetic to the proposal and grateful for Ford's offer to finance a commission of mediators to Europe, he believed that such a move was unlikely to succeed and politically impossible. A disappointed Ford commented afterward, "He's a small man."

But Ford had another plan brewing. Back in New York City, he summoned reporters to a press conference on November 24. Flanked by prominent supporters such as Jane Addams, Oswald Garrison Villard, and Ida Tarbell, Ford made a dramatic announcement. Speaking in his usual halting fashion before a public audience, he said, "We're going to try to get the boys out of the trenches before Christmas. I've chartered a ship and some of us are going to Europe." He explained that he had leased a ship, the *Oscar II*, from the Scandinavian-American Line and planned to fill it, at his expense, with many of "the biggest and most influential peace advocates in the country." They would exert moral pressure and mobilize public opinion to convene a giant peace conference in a neutral European city. "I am for this thing because it is right and I am going to give my last cent to carry it through," Ford declared. "The world is with a movement to establish a lasting peace."[6]

Throughout late November, newspaper headlines proclaimed "Ford to Captain Peace Crusade in Chartered Liner," "Peace Ship Will Sail in

December," "Prominent People to Go with Ford." Ford encouraged the attention with a stream of news releases detailing his preparation. He distributed the texts of telegrams and letters of invitation he had sent to over one hundred progressives, peace advocates, and political leaders, including ex–Secretary of State William Jennings Bryan, Jane Addams, John Wanamaker, Thomas Edison, John Burroughs, William Howard Taft, Luther Burbank, Washington Gladden, and the governors of all the states. He also announced an idea for calling a general strike on Christmas Day among troops on both sides of the conflict. Through use of a powerful wireless telegraph, he planned to send a message in English, French, German, Russian, Italian, Serbian, and a number of dialects urging the troops on both sides to abandon the trenches. He appeared at a mass meeting of antiwar enthusiasts in New York and sat on the platform while Schwimmer and others made speeches. The audience began to chant, "We want Ford," however, and the terrified industrialist was finally coaxed to the lectern to say a few words. That is exactly what he did. "Out of the trenches by Christmas, never to return!" he cried out, and then fled the stage.[7]

As news of the Ford plan spread throughout the United States, he received plaudits from several quarters. He was praised as a "peacemaker," and a man of "pure mind and honest heart" who sought "the end of war and the reestablishment of decent regard for civilization in lands where humanity suffers and hell prevails." He was lauded for defying "the overlords of plutocracy" who sought to perpetuate the war as a profit-making enterprise, and refusing to play "according to the rules laid down by Vanderbilt, Gould, and Fisk, and perfected by Morgan and Rockefeller." Ford had revealed the secret that "our noble plundercrats are making billions in supplying the warring nations in Europe." As the New York *Herald* summed up, "We need more Fords, more peace talks, and less indifference to the greatest crime in the world's history."[8]

An undercurrent of difficulty and doubt, however, began to subvert the mission of the Peace Ship. First of all, Ford's high-profile invitees, one by one, offered support and good wishes but declined the offer to sail for Europe on the *Oscar II*. Matters became worse when Ford released a statement to the press indicating that Addams, Edison, and Wanamaker were joining him, whereas in fact they were not. As many newspapers noted, Ford "seemed to have some difficulty . . . in telling just who will and who will not sail on the peace ship Oscar II." The Louisville *Herald* observed that Ford's plight recalled this old verse:

> *A little girl right hale and hearty,*
> *Thought she would like to give a party.*

But, as her guests were wise and wary,
Nobody came but her own canary.[9]

Moreover, negative commentary about Ford's plan began to surface. By early December, newspaper editorials and public speeches were raising questions about the vagueness of the undertaking, the intrusion of a private citizen into the affairs of government, and Ford's hubris in thinking that a wealthy individual could somehow step in and stop a massive war involving millions of people. Some of the criticism was mild, acknowledging the good intentions while disparaging the tactics. "Mr. Ford is doubtless well-meaning and in earnest, but such busy 'Mr. Fix-its' must be a trial to the President," noted the Baltimore *Sun*. "All the amateur efforts of altruistic and notoriety-seeking millionaires only make matters worse." The New York *World* agreed: "Henry Ford says he would give all his fortune to end the war. So would many another man. But this is something that money will not do."[10]

Some critics of the Peace Ship offered severe chastisement. "Henry Ford's millions have gone to his head," the Philadelphia *Record* told its readers. "The fact that a man can make a cheap automobile is not necessarily a qualification for becoming a world leader and showing all the belligerents how much pleasanter and cheaper peace is than war." "It is worse than ineffable folly for pestiferous busybodies in this country like Henry Ford to nag the President to make an ass of himself," declared the Louisville *Courier*. Unlike Ford, the paper continued, "the President has already demonstrated that he carries brains instead of cold cream in his head."[11]

In a widely quoted remark about the Peace Ship, former Senator Chauncey M. Depew of New York stated, "In uselessness and absurdity it will stand without an equal." He questioned Ford's motives, suggesting that the industrialist well understood that "the greatest asset in advertising is widespread familiarity with a manufacturer's name." Depew compared Ford to Phineas T. Barnum, as did the evangelist Billy Sunday, who said, "As a winner of publicity, Ford takes the cake. I think that when Ford put over this advertising for the Ford car the late lamented P. T. Barnum turned over in his grave and said, 'You win, Henry, you've got me skinned.' " Alton B. Parker, the Democratic candidate for president in 1904, offered a more dignified but no less scathing dismissal of Ford's Peace Ship. "If we could only be sure that all other nations would estimate him as we do, as a clown, strutting on the stage for a little time, no harm could come of it," he stated. "But we have no such assurance. The chances are that his antics will be taken seriously and they will tend to bring us into contempt if not hatred."[12]

This torrent of satire, mockery, and sarcasm wounded Ford. For a man who sought to be taken seriously on the political stage, widespread public scoffing at his airy statements about peace must have been excruciating. The Philadelphia *Ledger* mocked Ford's claims that talking about peace would somehow force the belligerents to negotiate: "No one can tell what they may do under the flood of talk which Mr. Ford proposes to let loose upon them." Cartoons lampooned Ford and the peace expedition. One pictured Ford dressed as a clown, parting a curtain labeled "European War" as he prepared to step into the public arena waving a fun-maker entitled "Peace." Another showed a huge erupting volcano labeled "War," while Ford stood on a nearby peak shaking his fist and yelling, "Now You Stop!" Another depicted a giant bearded warrior with sword, shield, and plumed helmet glancing down as Ford, driving a tiny Model T, bumped into his foot. The scoffing became so prevalent that supporters of Ford pleaded for restraint. He did not deserve to become "a subject of flippant ridicule in the way that is now being done," wrote the Paterson, New Jersey, *Press-Guardian*. "The motive of this visit . . . is certainly worthy of respect, although it may be generally held as futile."[13]

Despite the criticism, Ford plunged ahead. The *Oscar II* prepared to set sail on December 5 from its Hoboken, New Jersey, pier as a crowd estimated at fifteen thousand gathered for the send-off. The guests aboard were a far cry from the celebrities Ford had hoped to entice. Instead of Bryan, Addams, Edison, and Wanamaker, the Peace Ship took on board Dr. Charles Griffin Pease, head of the Anti-Smoking League; editor S. S. McClure; Judge John B. Lindsey of Denver; Governor L. R. Hanna of North Dakota; and a motley collection of reformers advocating everything from temperance to sexual freedom, pacifism to vegetarianism.

The circumstances surrounding the *Oscar II*'s departure portended future developments with the peace mission. A circus atmosphere prevailed at dockside as reporters and participants milled about among the thousands of onlookers. A band played "I Didn't Raise My Boy to Be a Soldier" while pacifist, pro-German, and pro-Allies contingents shouted insults at one another. A prankster sent two squirrels up the gangplank in a cage to which was affixed a large sign reading "To the Good Ship Nutty." (Reporters aboard ship later would name the pair "William Jennings Bryan" and "Henry Ford.") The Reverend Jenkin Lloyd Jones, who looked remarkably like Santa Claus, amused the throng by presiding at the on-deck marriage of peace delegate Berton Braley, the "Hobo Poet." As the ship pushed off and Ford stood at the rail waving, a buzz went through the crowd: a fully dressed man dived into the harbor with a great splash and proceeded to swim after the *Oscar II*; when he grew tired and agreed to be pulled from the water, the dripping figure returned to shore, identified himself as "Mr. Zero," and informed bemused reporters that he was "swimming to reach public opinion. War must cease." Cartoons conveyed the carnival atmosphere. They depicted squirrels driving miniature Model T's waving goodbye to their fellows aboard the ship, or bums stumbling aboard the *Oscar II* boozily inquiring, "Is my berth made up?" One of the most effective cartoons portrayed a wide-eyed Ford steering a ship in the shape of a flivver while a crowd of passengers was identified by placards reading "Professional Philanthropists," "Plain Cranks," "Rah-Rah Boys," and "College Professors." Rather than a picture of dignity and effectiveness, which Ford had hoped to convey, the departure of the *Oscar II* appeared to the public as the first act of a comic opera.[14]

Once on the Atlantic, the Peace Ship became a scene of controversy as delegates feuded over principles and tactics. Within days, the situation had degenerated into a fiasco. News of President Wilson's message to Congress—though reaffirming the neutrality of the United States, it also called for a program of military preparedness—caused a rift. Pacifists in the group circulated a resolution denouncing Wilson's policy, and most of the delegates signed it. A significant minority, however, believed the resolution to be unpatriotic and unnecessarily political, and threatened to leave the group upon reaching Europe if it was adopted as the official platform of the Peace Ship. The two factions denounced each other, and, according to one reporter, "the conversation veered from acrimonious debate to violent altercations, in which the language became not only personal, but occasionally profane." The tense political situation was not helped by the fact that nearly all of the voyagers, having never traveled on the ocean, spent many of the first days violently seasick.[15]

Meanwhile, a group of over fifty reporters, increasingly bored and liberally lubricated with drink, were delighted by the Peace Ship spat. They formed the satirical Viking Press Club—it met daily in the *Oscar II*'s bar, featured an insignia of a nut bound upon the brow, and adopted as its secret signal "a violent and horrified clasp of the hand upon the forehead"—and reveled in detailing the disputes among the peace missionaries. They composed such headlines as "Ford Ship Is Scene of War" and particularly savaged Mrs. Schwimmer, who refused to discuss or display important mediation documents she claimed to have from European leaders. Cartoonists depicted shipboard battles between squirrels and doves and showed the French and German armies fleeing in fear from the angry peace pilgrims. According to an American newspaper, only one tactic could restore harmony among the feuding delegates: "chartering a vessel for each member of the party and then keeping them a mile apart."[16]

Ford's own position aboard the Peace Ship grew increasingly awkward.

During the thirteen-day cruise across the Atlantic, he courted the press by holding conferences with reporters twice daily. He tried to mediate among the acrimonious delegates and assured dissenters that approval or disapproval of Wilson's message would disqualify no one from participating in the peace mission. But his patience wore thin. Trying to navigate between bickering delegates and openly contemptuous reporters was stressful. Ford's irritability became noticeable when he saw an employee drinking at the ship's bar and snapped, "You cut out the booze on this trip, or I'll have you fired." His resolve also was eroded by the persistent, subtle pressure of Samuel S. Marquis, who, at the insistence of Clara Ford, had accompanied her husband to look after him. Marquis maintained reservations about the expedition and lost few opportunities to question it in conversations with his boss.[17]

Interestingly, however, the same reporters who detailed every shipboard dispute and described most of the peace reformers as buffoons came to respect Ford. They found him to be open, honest, and free from the self-righteousness that afflicted most of the peace delegates. "I came to make fun of the whole thing," confessed one, but "I believe in Henry Ford and I'm going to say so even if I lose my job for it." Another, who had initially seen Ford as a manipulator, concluded that he was a man "of goodness, of genuineness, of sincerity." The Viking Club met as a group during the voyage and agreed that Ford deserved more respectful treatment than that accorded to the more flighty members of the group. As the correspondent for the New York *Times* summarized, the reporters "have learned in these few days an immense respect and liking for the character and abilities of Henry Ford."[18]

But Ford's personal standing could not salvage the mission of the Peace Ship. The nadir of the *Oscar II*'s unhappy voyage came with an outbreak of influenza that swept through the crew and passengers about halfway to their destination. The disease incapacitated many and produced one death when it turned into pneumonia. Ford himself became very ill as the *Oscar II* sailed into European waters. By the time the ship made its way through the North Sea, endured a none-too-friendly inspection by the British Royal Navy, and finally approached the shores of neutral Norway, Ford was sick and depressed. Thin and ashen-faced, he avoided reporters and public dignitaries when the Peace Ship docked in Oslo in the early-morning hours of December 18. He left the ship in a temperature of twelve degrees below zero and immediately went into seclusion in the Grand Hotel.[19]

Contrary to the assurances of Mrs. Schwimmer, the Peace Ship was not greeted by cheering throngs. Many Norwegians favored preparedness and maintained a skeptical posture toward the peace delegates. Given this decidedly muted reception and his own poor health, Ford remained out of sight for four days. He finally met the press on December 22 but talked little about the peace crusade. Instead, he expressed the peculiar hope that armament manufacturers could make more profit from a new product he was interested in, tractors, than from instruments of war. He also gave a public statement pledging $10,000 for the construction of a student clubhouse at the University of Christiania.[20]

Clearly, Ford had had enough. "Guess I had better go home to Mother," he told Louis Lochner. "I told her I'll be back soon. You've got this thing started now and can get along without me." On the evening of December 23, Ford slipped out of his hotel suite and, accompanied by Marquis and Ray Dahlinger, his chauffeur and bodyguard, booked passage to the United States and left on a ship departing from Bergen. After an uneventful voyage—an ill, exhausted Ford spent most of the time resting in his cabin—the steamer *Bergensfjord* arrived at a Brooklyn pier on the morning of January 2, 1916. Ford was greeted by his wife and son and then, avoiding reporters, was taken to the Waldorf Hotel. After a consultation with William Jennings Bryan, who had traveled from Washington to meet him, Ford held a brief press conference and departed for Detroit.[21]

Ford's state of mind was curious. Though he had obviously deserted his Peace Ship associates before their mission in Europe even began, he denied that the expedition had been a failure. He insisted that the accompanying publicity had made it a success because discussions of peace replaced war propaganda. "It's got people thinking, and when you get them thinking they will think right," he told reporters. He also claimed that he had modified his critique of the war. Bankers, militarists, and munitions manufacturers were still guilty of fostering the conflict, he believed, but the mass of common people must also shoulder part of the blame. "The trouble is that [Europe's] citizens don't take enough interest in the government," he said. "They should express their own minds." More disturbingly, Ford made private comments that called his sincerity into question. When presented with a bill for the Peace Ship, Ford commented cynically, "Well, we got a million dollars worth of advertising out of it, and a hell of a lot of experience."[22]

Nonetheless, Ford's loyalty to his antiwar position remained steadfast. "If necessary I will go back [to Europe]," he told reporters in New York City. "If it will help matters I will charter another ship." Ford also continued to foot the bill for the efforts of the Peace Ship delegates who organized themselves as the Neutral Conference for Continuous Mediation. They met at The Hague for over a year, until early 1917, by which time their efforts had come to naught, and Ford ceased covering the group's expenses. Throughout 1916, he paid for full-page antipreparedness statements that appeared in newspapers and periodicals all over the country. They denounced military bills coming before Congress and the economic and political interests that supported them. Thus evidence of Ford's sincerity in opposing war was overwhelming. But where did his antiwar fervor come from?[23]

Ford never explained clearly the intellectual or emotional source of his antiwar views. Usually he stood on pragmatic grounds. "My opposition to war is not based upon pacifist or non-resistant principles," he claimed. "But the fighting never settles the question. It only gets the participants around to a frame of mind where they will agree to discuss what they were fighting about." Numerous public and private statements, however, suggested that Ford's denunciation of warfare had deeper ideological roots.[24]

First of all, Ford's worldview as a modern industrialist led him to view warfare as a wasteful folly. Everything he valued in terms of economic and social endeavor—an ethic of work and productivity, keen standards of efficiency, consumption and abundance among the mass of people—was violated by the wartime destruction of human beings and material resources. In a long string of pronouncements, Ford made it clear that he viewed war as an economic disaster.

He grew indignant about war's economic wastefulness. It destroyed human and material resources and offered a stark contrast to the positive ethos of modern industrial production. On the eve of the Peace Ship's departure, Ford issued a statement noting that the vessel carried "a spirit that appreciates the useless waste of war. . . . The business world wants the thing stopped so that it may go on in its work of construction—that is, all except that part of the business world that is turning out guns, battleships and other useless but costly products." For Ford, the horrendous sounds and images of war stood in contrast to those of a smooth-running factory. "Isn't it better fun to hear an engine purr than it would be to hear a big gun roar?" he observed to one reporter. "The one will give good men their living; the other would give good men death."[25]

Ford also believed that war hindered long-term economic growth. "The manufacture of munitions is a thing of the minute, and after the war the whole business will crumble," he declared in 1915. The losing side in the European conflict would likely suffer destruction of its economic infrastructure, and even the winners "will be suffering under heavy war debts and taxes." A greater stress on business efficiency would discourage rather than encourage warfare. "If every man who manufactures an article would make the very best he can in the very best way at the very lowest possible price the world would be kept out of war, for commercialists would not have to search for outside markets which the other fellow covets," he argued.[26]

Ford contended that war profited only a minority of businessmen. "Preparedness means war, and war, for some few business men, means big, immediate profits," he argued in one of his newspaper advertisements in 1916. But small businessmen faced a situation where wars "materially depleted the financial resources of the world, and the effects have been felt in all countries and localities, whether they were directly involved or not. It requires a good deal of time to recuperate from losses created by disturbances of this kind." Big business, particularly those involved in producing munitions and armaments, might favor wars. But the majority of business, Ford reported over and over in this period, sought to avoid armed conflicts in order to concentrate on making goods, providing jobs, and generating steady profits. In the business world, he insisted, productivity trumped destructive impulses.[27]

The debacle of destruction in Europe illustrated the economic folly of war, Ford believed, but another situation brought it even closer to home. By the mid-1910s, domestic unrest in Mexico had grown acute, and the threat of revolution raised talk about American military intervention. Ford was horrified. "We mustn't go down there with a rifle. We must go down there with the plow, the shovel, and the shop," he said to a reporter in April 1915. "Instead of sending soldiers down to Mexico we should send industrial experts down there—missionaries of the true and holy gospel of get down to work."[28]

Ford's economic misgivings about war appeared most clearly, perhaps, when he contrasted the European carnage of World War I with the efficient industrial operation of the factory in Highland Park. As he observed in an interview:

> Suppose Europe had been managed as we are endeavoring to manage the Ford factory. We are trying there to give every man a square deal, fair pay for his work, and enough time for play and educational development. Then there would have been no war [in Europe]. . . . We have peace in the Ford factory, and efficiency and happiness and success there, without anything in any sense approaching the use of force.

For Ford, industrial and mental progress went hand in hand, and war was the enemy of both. "Why not begin now to build a machinery of reason to do the work that the machinery of force has not accomplished?" he asked. "That is the great duty facing those who govern." The image of the busi-

I'm sure that New York is the place for giving it publicity." The phrase "out of the trenches by Christmas" was part of Ford's master publicity plan. "Expert advertiser that Mr. Ford is, he knew that he needed something startling to attract world-wide attention," Lochner explained of this slogan. After spending several months in close contact with his benefactor, Lochner concluded that, even though Theodore Roosevelt and Woodrow Wilson had reputations for understanding the value of publicity, "either of them might have learned a thing or two from Henry Ford."[36]

Critics may have branded Ford's antiwar rhetoric as self-indulgent and ineffective, but many Americans responded to his appeals for peace. After returning from Europe, Ford enjoyed substantial support, even from some who had denounced the mission itself. The New York *American*, which had ruthlessly lampooned the Peace Ship, now argued that Ford "deserves respect, not ridicule." If America's political leaders had "put forth one-tenth the individual effort that Henry Ford put forth," it wrote in an editorial, "the boys would have been out of the trenches by Christmas." The Saginaw, Michigan, *Herald* said that Ford had gained much sympathy from his efforts. "Mr. Ford stands before the people now very much like the farmer who stood on the railroad track and defied the train," it said; "they do not respect his judgement, but they admire his nerve and extend him sympathy."[37]

Perhaps the clearest indication of the admiration accorded Ford, however, came from an unexpected direction. Those in the press and the political establishment who viewed his entry into public affairs with contempt received a shock in the spring of 1916. Voters, acting of their own volition, pushed him front and center on the national political stage. In a development that few had foreseen, Henry Ford emerged as a genuine, if unorthodox, politician.

In 1916, Woodrow Wilson ran for re-election on the Democratic ticket while the Republican Party searched for a viable candidate. The leading contenders included former President Theodore Roosevelt, Charles Evans Hughes of New York, and a variety of favorite sons such as Senator William Alden Smith of Michigan and Senator Albert B. Cummins of Iowa. But as returns from the first presidential primaries came in, political strategists for the party were startled. Without mounting a campaign, or even announcing his candidacy—in fact, he said publicly, "I do not want anything to do with politics or political offices. The filing of my name . . . was a joke"—Henry Ford won the primary in Michigan and came very close in Nebraska. In both of those states, friends and supporters had placed his name on the ballot by popular petition. A few days later, Ford received about five thousand votes in the Ohio primary as a write-in candidate. When the St. Louis *Times* conducted a poll on potential Republican candidates in May 1916, he topped the list.[38]

Ford reacted coyly to these surprising developments. He described his electoral support as "an expression of the majority of voters that they believe, as I do, against military preparedness and the exploitation of the workingman by the moneyed munitions interests." But he shrank from a declaration of his candidacy. In New York City, he told reporters that political office should seek the man rather than the other way around. "I don't think any man should run for President," he declared. "In business, if we want a man to do certain things we look him up. . . . I think he [a presidential nominee] should be chosen without active participation on his part." Ford carefully noted, however, that he thought "a government should be run as a business organization." Reporters drew the obvious conclusion. "Ford Willing to Run If the People Call Him," ran the headline in the New York *Times*.[39]

Another sign of Ford's popularity was the letters pouring into Highland Park urging him to run. "I am just a humble farmer," wrote a North Carolinian, "but my three greatest desires are to vote for Ford, own a Ford, and see Ford elected president by the greatest majority given any man." A steelworker in Minnesota offered to use his knowledge of several foreign languages and go on the campaign trail stumping for Ford. A group of citizens in South Dakota printed handbills with the message "No names are greater in the whole universe than George Washington, Abraham Lincoln, and Henry Ford." Ford's popularity also prompted the American Party and the Prohibition Party to court him actively as a third-party candidate during the summer of 1916.[40]

Ultimately, however, this upsurge of political support for Ford was channeled in a different direction. Assistants in his office drafted a form letter informing supporters that Ford had no interest in public office. More important, Ford threw his support to another candidate. After Wilson was renominated by the Democratic Party at its June convention in St. Louis and adopted the slogan "He Kept Us Out of War," Ford moved steadily toward his corner. According to Ernest G. Liebold, his executive secretary, Ford met with members of the Democratic National Committee in New York City and agreed to help fund Wilson's campaign. At the recommendation of Liebold, who studied the election carefully, much of Ford's money went to California, where the election promised to be extremely tight. By mid-September, Ford had publicly endorsed Wilson's candidacy.[41]

Not surprisingly, he provided the public with a populist reading of the election, picturing it as a struggle of peace and democracy against war and economic privilege. In a long interview with the New York *World* in early October, he declared, "I hope every workingman who knows me and my attitude toward workingmen will vote for the President's return." Ford praised Wilson for his support of eight-hour-workday legislation and argued that the President was a protector of "the welfare of industrious people." He praised Wilson's peace sympathies, contending that the President would not "be pushed into carnage by the 'unseen hands' of Wall Street." As for the Republican candidate, Charles Evans Hughes, "Wall Street and all the big interests are all for him."[42]

Ford mounted an advertising blitz of full-page newspaper ads for Wilson. In "Humanity and Your Vote," which appeared under his name, he warned citizens to "guard against Wall Street influence again securing control of our government." "Although nominally a Republican all my life," he wrote, "I am for Wilson and urge my fellow citizens to stand for him." He praised Wilson's attempts to keep the United States out of war and chastised the "special interests" who complained that "he has not plunged the country into war for their profit." Given Wilson's principles and record, Ford posed an obvious question: "Why should we make a change?" This essay, as well as other political advertisements, appeared in some five hundred newspapers in October and early November.[43]

Ford remained a loyal Wilson supporter after the President's reelection. He even muted his antiwar, antipreparedness rhetoric and followed Wilson in accepting the inevitability of American participation in World War I. Though some accused Ford of betraying his pacifist principles, it was more a matter of patriotism. Wilson, Ford argued, had tried everything possible to keep the United States out of the conflict and mediate a resolution. In contrast, Germany had been aggressive and treacherous in its policies, using submarines to attack American ships and trying to gain a political toehold in the New World by plotting in Mexico. Thus, when the United States severed diplomatic relations with Germany on February 3, 1917, Ford declared, "I will stand with our President, and in the event of a declaration of war will place our factory at the disposal of the United States government and will operate without one cent of profit." A few weeks later, on April 6, when the United States declared war on Germany, the case was clinched. As Ford explained a few years later, his support of American neutrality "had no application, once the United States entered the war. From April 1917 until November 1918, our factory worked practically exclusively for the government." Ford was not alone in his conversion. "A declaration of war closes discussion," noted William Jennings Bryan. "There is no country in the world whose citizens would be so willing to die for their liberty as this one." Ford the peace activist moderated his views, musing that "perhaps militarism can be crushed only with militarism. In that case I am in on it to the finish."[44]

Once the United States entered the hostilities, the Ford Motor Company did indeed fully support the war effort. It used its mass-production methods to pursue two large projects: the making of thousands of ambulances, cars, and trucks for the armed forces, and the production of thousands of Liberty airplane engines. Two other projects—Eagle submarine-patrol boats and small, two-man "flivver tanks"—were aborted by the end of the war. In 1917–18, the company also participated enthusiastically in drives for Liberty Loans and the Red Cross, and pioneered in making films for military training and to publicize activities of various branches of the military.[45]

Ford's stalwart support for Wilson and his policies eventually produced a surprising result. The President called him to Washington in early June 1917—they met at Shadow Lawn, Wilson's summer place, and at the White House—and urged him to run for the United States Senate from Michigan in the 1918 election. Wilson saw Ford as someone who could win as a Democrat in a heavily Republican state, and who would support his policies, including the League of Nations. He told Ford that in difficult times men must give to their country and described him as "the only man in Michigan who can be elected and help to bring about the peace you so much desire." Although not eager to run, Ford saw the President's appeal as a patriotic duty.[46]

The Michigan Senate race began in peculiar fashion. Ford refused to run in the traditional way, eschewing both campaigning and the established political parties. He entered the contest as a citizen candidate from outside the political system and ran in *both* the Republican and Democratic state primaries. During these races, he made clear his distaste for actively seeking office. In a private letter, he noted, "If the people of Michigan chose to elect me to that office I would accept it, but I will not lift a finger to bring it about." Determined to avoid party affiliation and to exercise free and independent judgment, he dismissed politics as a dirty, unattractive business. As he put it, "I have already found from the Wall Street press that I have been guilty of breaking most of the ten commandments and the campaign has not yet fairly opened." Gathering support from workers and farmers, Ford came in second in the Republican contest, but won an overwhelming victory in the Democratic primary.[47]

In the fall campaign, Ford's Republican opponent was Truman H. Newberry, a Detroit businessman and secretary of the navy in the Roosevelt administration. With America's entry into World War I, Newberry became a lieutenant commander with a desk job in Washington, and then returned to Michigan in 1918. In the general election, he spent a great deal of money and followed a relentless schedule of speech-making. By contrast, Ford spent nothing and refused to campaign or give public speeches. Nonetheless, through interviews and press releases, the citizen candidate made clear his positions on several issues.

He pledged that, even though he would fully support the American war effort as senator, he would work for a resolution that "will give permanent peace to the world, and, I believe, infinite glory to the United States." He fully supported Wilson's plan for the League of Nations and declared that when the war was over he would take down the American flag from his factory and "hoist in its place the Flag of all Nations, which is being designed in my office right now." He promised not to accept a cent of profit from war production and polished his progressive credentials by endorsing women's suffrage.[48]

Ford provided perhaps the fullest explanation of his political sensibility in *World's Work* in September 1918. In a piece entitled "Why Henry Ford Wants to Be a Senator," which listed him as the author, he explained that he was running only at the request of President Wilson and had no interest in politics as a profession. "I shall not spend a cent nor make a single move to get into the Senate," he told voters. "I shall not have a campaign organization, nor pay any campaign bills." Having already served the people by "giving them the best car they can get for their money," now, if the voters so chose, he was willing "to do other things for the benefit of mankind."

Ford outlined his key political concerns. At the top of the list, of course, was peace. "I am willing to fight only to put an end to all war," he claimed, and promised to work toward finding ways of preventing armed clashes in the future and to work against "the kind of nationalism that tries to set one country up against another." He listed consumer comfort as the second of his political goals. Everyone in the world, he insisted, deserved "a chance to get what he wants at a price he can afford to pay." Human nature drove people to seek happiness and fulfillment, Ford believed, and they "cannot hope to be happy unless they are sure of a comfortable living with leisure in which to enjoy themselves." He promised to pursue policies that would promote this goal, pledging to work for social and labor reform, and noting that the modern industrial revolution "has not benefited the common man so much as it has benefited the profiteer." Finally, he promised to seek policies that would help farmers, decentralize industrial production, and develop new sources of power. Ford concluded, "Whatever will open up greater opportunities for comfortable, happy living for the ordinary man, and teach him and his family how to make the best use of those opportunities, is the proper function of government."[49]

A controversial personal issue arose during the course of the campaign. The fact that Edsel Ford, Henry's son, had secured a draft deferment to stay out of the armed forces and remain at work in the company aroused much criticism. Hostile newspapers pointed out, "Henry was more successful in keeping his boy out of the trenches than he was in getting other boys out by Christmas," and suggested, "The people of Michigan are not going to send the father of a slacker to the United States senate." The Newberry campaign picked up on this theme in a series of advertisements. "Truman H. Newberry is no new convert to preparedness," said one. "He backs up his belief in preparedness by being in the service himself. His sons are in the service. His whole family is serving." Another pictured Newberry and his two sons dressed out in military uniforms, along with the statement, "Truman H. Newberry believes in practical patriotism—So do his sons—They are all in the Service, just like lots of other fathers and sons."[50]

Despite these attacks and his supine style of electioneering, Ford's idiosyncratic noncampaign gathered significant public support. He received endorsements from many prominent national figures. William G. McAdoo, Wilson's secretary of the treasury and a leading national Democrat, wrote, "You have shown yourself to be a real patriot, and those are the kind of men who ought to be sent to the Congress of the United States these days." Bernard Baruch, chairman of the War Industries Board, said, "I am more than delighted that you are going into the race for the Senatorship, and I want to congratulate the State upon getting you to run." John R. Commons, on the other hand, urged Ford to reconsider his candidacy: "Please do not consent. The Senate would smother you. You have bigger work, namely to finish your job and be the next President."[51]

Ford's status as folk hero and reputation as a friend of the common man gained him much popular support. Many workers and farmers believed he would pursue their interests. Labor journals such as *The Union*, published in Indianapolis, editorialized that Ford's election to the Senate "would give labor a real representative in that body" and contrasted him with other big industrialists, who exploited their workers. Other reforming voices claimed, in the words of a newspaper headline, "Henry Ford Is Progressive, Therefore He Suffers Abuse." As the accompanying editorial contended, "Henry Ford has incurred the bitter and deadly hostility of the privileged classes, of the predatory interests, of those who look upon the plain people as their rightful prey."[52]

A particularly sympathetic and insightful assessment of Ford and his senatorial campaign appeared in *World's Work*. In a piece entitled "Henry

Ford, Amateur," Frank Parker Stockbridge suggested that Ford's candidacy was fueled by a personal sensibility rather than a specific political agenda. After talking with Ford, he perceived no limitations on his ability—or, indeed, the ability of mankind—to change the world. Combining the peculiarly American traits of egalitarianism, experimentation, and practical achievement, Ford was defined by his

> . . . unbounded confidence and belief in the ordinary man, his deep-rooted distrust of the professional expert in every line—in short, his ingrained, almost instinctive preference for the amateur rather than the professional in every phase of human activity. Mr. Ford believes that the ordinary man, given a task to perform and a free hand to perform it, will, nine times out of ten, work out a way of doing the job that is better than the way in which the professional in that line would do it. . . . He sees something he wishes to do and immediately proceeds to devise a way of doing it, confident in his own ability to work out a way that will be better than the existing methods, whatever they may be.

Here was a clear snapshot of Henry Ford the "amateur" citizen candidate— a man who refused to campaign, lacked respect for professional politicians, promised to bring fresh perspectives to public issues, believed that clear analysis and goodwill could solve problems, and exuded quiet confidence in his ability to reform the system. For many Michigan voters, the idea that Ford could remake government as he had remade the production of automobiles had great appeal.[53]

Yet Ford also aroused considerable opposition among segments of the population. Two issues particularly caused concern. Ford's highly publicized opposition to American preparedness did not sit well with a significant portion of the public. According to the South Haven, Michigan, *Daily Tribune*, Ford was "a leading figure among the pacifists who kept the country unprepared for the conflict that was inevitable, and who are responsible for the tremendous waste of blood and treasure that we must make to make up for those years of folly." The Flint *Journal* agreed, noting that when Ford "took his shipload of squirrel food to The Hague . . . he was the joke of the world." Now he had the nerve to run for the Senate, an act that prompted this conclusion: "As a come-back artist, Henry is the prize winner."[54]

A sharp attack on Ford's pacifism came from Theodore Roosevelt. A strident supporter of American entry into World War I, the aging but energetic Roosevelt had tried unsuccessfully to raise a regiment, as he had done in the Spanish-American War, before proudly seeing several of his sons go off to combat in the United States Army. Ford's pacifistic crusade had infuriated him, and his statements supporting President Wilson's plans for an international League of Nations now made Roosevelt nearly apoplectic. He burst into the Michigan election by lambasting Ford in a public letter that became the basis of an advertising campaign. In full-page ads in Michigan newspapers, the former President denounced Ford for the Peace Ship, his son's failure to enter the military, and his support for world government. In his unmistakable style, which mixed theatrics with sarcasm, Roosevelt declared:

> Michigan is facing the test, clear-cut and without shadow of a chance for misunderstanding, between patriotism and Americanism on one side, and on the other pacifism, and that foolish sham-cosmopolitanism which thinks it is clever to deride the American flag, and to proclaim that it would as soon be a Hindoo or China-man as an American. If there should be at any time in the future a Hindoo Senate, and it should choose, in a spirit of cosmopolitanism, to admit outsiders, there is no reason why Mr. Ford should not aspire to membership therein; but he would be signally out of place in the American Senate.[55]

In addition to suspecting Ford's views on war and peace, many voters also believed that his refusal to campaign for office smacked of high-handedness rather than virtue. It highlighted his central weakness as a candidate: a complete lack of political experience. Ford's success as an automobile manufacturer "is no proof that he is a master of public questions, that he has the qualifications of a statesman, that he can create, interpret, or guide and lead public opinion concerning those great problems of human conduct on which the destinies of nations turn," a magazine article argued. Even his friends and admirers, noted one newspaper, "still question the wisdom of his entrance into politics." Other commentaries were less delicate. Proclaiming that it was "A Hazardous Time to Take Chances," the Oswosso *Times* concluded, "The chances are ten to one that as an United States Senator he would be a fizzle." The Sanilac County *Times* agreed that "for the great state of Michigan to send a man with no more governmental experience than Henry Ford to Washington . . . would be a serious mistake." The Grand Rapids *News* offered a biting conclusion: "Mr. Ford would be about as useful in the United States senate as a pastry cook would be at the head of a receiving line."[56]

When Michigan voters went to the polls in early November, Ford lost the Senate seat to Newberry by the very thin margin of 212,487 to 220,054.

Ford demanded a recount—there was also an investigation by a federal grand jury into Newberry's excessively high spending—and it pulled him within five thousand votes of victory. But this was not enough. Though Ford had sought the office only reluctantly, he was unhappy about losing. Newberry's enormous campaign expenditures, Ford concluded, only proved that Wall Street "interests" lay behind his defeat. "If they would spend $176,000 to win a single Senate seat," he complained to an associate, "we may be certain that they would spend $176,000,000 to get control of the country."[57]

Ford had acquired a taste for the political limelight. A few years later, he would allow his name to be bandied about as a candidate for president, a political flirtation that had leading national politicians as well as commentators in an uproar for well over a year. Ford, it seems clear in hindsight, was a type that popped up periodically in American public life: the straight-talking nonpolitician who transcends party and promises to clean things up. Much like the protagonist in the 1930s Frank Capra film *Mr. Smith Goes to Washington*, Ford appealed to the public imagination as an honest reformer. "Mr. Ford Goes to Washington," if never actually projected onto the screen of national politics, offered an enticing political fantasy to many.

Henry Ford's entry into public affairs underlined his popularity among the common people. As a political figure he was viewed with suspicion by intellectuals, party managers, and social elites. But he generated considerable enthusiasm among voters, especially in the Midwest and West. His 1918 performance in Michigan revealed his extraordinary appeal.

Power brokers in the Eastern sections of the nation began to pay attention. An analysis in the New York *Tribune* examined Ford's appeal in the provinces. Although somewhat condescending, the editorial grasped something fundamental about this industrialist with the populist message. Ford, it concluded,

> ... has become the messianic hero of the impressionable West, and this exceedingly comic person is wearing a halo among his people.... This same Henry Ford, the butt of Eastern ridicule, returns from wretched peace-ship adventure the most admired man in the Mississippi Valley and the Great Lakes region.... The West remembers that the very best people almost succeeded in saving the country from the ignorant railsplitter, Lincoln.... So it turns to Henry Ford with renewed zeal after each blow which Henry rains

so indiscriminately upon the helm of Mars and the vault of Wall
Street. . . . This is a nation of industrial barons. But what industrial
baron ever became a popular hero? Certainly not Rockefeller, not
Carnegie, not Westinghouse, not Schwab, nor Armour. But Henry
Ford wears the nimbus of popular hero-worship. And he wears it
because he is in his heart the man of the people, the gentle fool who
lives and feels and believes with the common man.[58]

Ford's connection to ordinary citizens had been years in the making.
Since the advent of the Model T nearly a decade earlier, he had appeared
before the American people as a kind of miracle maker. His consumer vision
of the American future, innovations in mass production, humane model for
modern business, and status as a folk hero had made Henry Ford a household name and, for many, a truly beloved figure by the late 1910s. But in
many ways it was only a beginning. Over the next decade, he would build
upon this foundation to become one of the most prominent and powerful
figures in the United States.

Part Three

The Flivver King

Thirteen

Legend

The 1920s seemed to mark a new period in American life. In the aftermath of World War I, the flowering of the Jazz Age obliterated any remnants of stuffy, genteel Victorian values left over from the earlier century. In a new atmosphere of flappers and speakeasies, older traditions of self-control and propriety gave way as the mass of American citizens, especially youth, adopted relaxed sexual mores and embraced a leisure ethic of self-fulfillment. At the same time, this exciting new decade saw the enjoyment of unprecedented material abundance among the middle class. A series of Republican presidents—Warren G. Harding, Calvin Coolidge, Herbert Hoover—presided over a booming economy that presented a cornucopia of goods to the American people. Spreading prosperity seemed to mark the inauguration of a consumer bonanza in the nation's history.

In many ways, however, the twenties were the Age of Ford. He dominated the decade, commanding attention and respect, generating controversy, creating headlines, and launching ventures in economic, social, and cultural life. As Americans purchased automobiles in ever-expanding numbers, especially the Model T, his role in the economy was ever larger. In addition, his views on and his involvement in a series of compelling projects kept his name constantly in the public eye. Simply put, Ford became a colossus in the American consciousness. He seemed to represent everything that was modern, innovative, and vital in this triumphant new society.

Ford's reputation and influence in the United States were so enormous that commentators struggled to explain it. Assessing this situation midway through the decade, Reinhold Niebuhr concluded, "Henry Ford is America." In an essay published in *The Christian Century* some years before he emerged as perhaps the nation's leading theologian, Niebuhr argued that Ford had become "the hero of the average American" because he had made his fortune without ruthlessness, paid high wages to his workers, and made a cheap but reliable product. Ford had done well by doing good. Moreover, he had spanned successfully a key historical divide in American history. For Niebuhr, Ford was "the symbol of an America which has risen almost in a generation from an agrarian to an industrial economic order and now applies the social intelligence of a country village to the most complex industrial life the world has ever known." Like many common Americans, Neibuhr believed, Ford had kept one foot in the nation's rural past even as he was striding into its urban, industrial future.[1]

Other critics also tied Ford to deep social and economic impulses in American life. Arthur Pound, addressing "The Ford Myth" in *The Atlantic Monthly*, observed that in "a newspaper morgue the envelope filed under 'Henry Ford' bulks larger than that devoted to any other private citizen." Pound attributed this popularity to Ford's reputation as a humane manufacturer and his image as a man of the people. But he also suggested that the automaker benefited from something over which he had little control—the decades-long evolution of "the market," which made conditions ripe for the automobile by creating railroads, pipelines, and a prosperous country of consumers where wealth was widely distributed. In Pound's view, Ford had taken advantage of these conditions to become "a superman who has ploughed a straight, deep furrow through the crust of custom."[2]

Many national publications joined the parlor game. *The New Republic*, a progressive journal of opinion, concluded that Ford's political popularity came from "roots deep into the soil of the American character." The average citizen, it argued in 1923, "sees Ford as a sort of enlarged crayon portrait of himself; the man who is able to fulfill his own suppressed desires, who has achieved enormous riches, fame, and power without departing from the pioneer-and-homespun tradition." For all his wealth and power, Ford seemed to embody almost literally the common man and his humble origins and tastes.[3]

These varied critics captured aspects of Ford's appeal. Yet, for all its connection to cherished American values, the Ford legend also received a lustrous shine from a less lofty source. A series of incidents and controversies in the late 1910s generated much publicity as the new decade began. Like spotlights shining on a skyscraper in the evening hours, these events illuminated Ford's towering stature.

On September 23, 1916, a registered letter arrived at Henry Ford's office in Highland Park. Written by his longtime business associates John and Horace Dodge, it complained that they had been unable to get an appointment to discuss the company's policy regarding dividends to stockholders. The Ford Motor Company's most recent financial statement indicated a net profit of $16 million over the past year and a cash surplus in the bank exceeding $50 million. Yet all this money was going to expansion, none to stockholders. The Dodges demanded a meeting of the company's board of directors to rectify the situation with a new policy "to distribute a large part of the accumulated cash surplus as dividends to the stockholders to whom it belongs." Over the next several weeks, the company and the Dodge brothers exchanged several letters, with the latter demanding action and the former cagily promising to take up these issues at a future date.[4]

The Dodge brothers, of course, had been original investors in the company in 1903, putting $10,000 into the new venture. Over the next thirteen years, they remained vital to the Ford operation, building a variety of parts as the company moved into Highland Park. Throughout these years, the Dodges received around $5.5 million in dividends on their original investment, but with company profits running at almost $16 million a year by 1916 and capital assets far exceeding $100 million, this amount seemed meager. Frustrated by Henry Ford's lack of response to their queries on dividends, they sought redress by filing suit against the company in Wayne County, Michigan, on November 2, 1916. They asked the circuit court for an injunction to halt all expansion plans of the company and an order compelling Ford to distribute 75 percent of its cash surplus as dividends. The court immediately issued an order restraining Ford from using any of its cash resources for plant expansion.[5]

The lawsuit angered Ford on several counts. Initially, its timing seemed a calculated insult, the filing coming the morning after the wedding of Ford's son, Edsel, an event the Dodge brothers had attended. They had conversed congenially with the entire Ford family and said nothing about filing the suit, and "that's what made Mr. Ford so darned mad about it," according to Ernest G. Liebold. But the lawsuit also violated Ford's visceral need for control over his company and its destiny, an impulse that had driven him since his earliest days in the automobile business. Furthermore, the Dodges' assertion about their right to dividends also ran against the grain of his business philosophy, which stressed public service and expansion of products. Finally, the Dodge lawsuit threatened Ford's plans for expanding his factory further.[6]

As the legal proceedings began, it became clear that the lawsuit involved a clash of economic interests. The need to maintain a steady stream of capital—the Dodges had started their own automobile company in 1913—partly motivated the plaintiffs. E. G. Pipp, who had close connections to both parties in the suit, wrote that the Dodges sued "because they had grown too big 'to be carried around in Henry Ford's vest pocket,' as John Dodge expressed it," and they needed financial support to sustain their own enterprise. In his testimony, Henry Ford claimed that the Dodge brothers had filed suit when he refused to purchase their stock in the company at an inflated price to provide them with capital. "They asked me to buy them out," he testified. "They put a price of $35 million on their stock, and they told me unless I bought they would harass me in anything I tried to do." Clearly, Ford also had a great economic interest at stake in the suit: he did not want to distribute in dividends tens of millions of dollars that provided the wherewithal for future expansion of his company.[7]

As the case unfolded, however, such practical considerations gave way before a clash of philosophies. The Dodge brothers and Elliot G. Stevenson, their dynamic lawyer, insisted that the purpose of a business corporation was to earn profits for its stockholders. Just as vigorously, Ford and his chief attorney, Alfred Lucking, who was equally skilled if less flamboyant than his counterpart, defended a different conception of the modern business corporation and its duties. This model downplayed profits in favor of service, and valued consumers over stockholders. In particular, two principles became the centerpiece of Ford's defense.

First, in good populist fashion, Ford argued that stockholders were unproductive "parasites" and "idle drones." Though they contributed money to get an enterprise up and running, he believed this contribution was of limited value. "Mr. Ford didn't feel that the stockholders ever contributed anything to the company except in the early days when they contributed small amounts of capital," reported Ernest Liebold. This notion crept into his public statements. In his new manufacturing projects, he told a newspaper in 1916, "there will be no stockholders, no directors, no absentee owners, no parasites." Ford insisted that, even if stockholders deserved a fair return on their investment, they did not deserve millions of dollars of profit, year after year, when they did not contribute actively to the success of a company.[8]

Second, Ford maintained throughout the Dodge suit that the purpose of a modern industrial corporation was to make products as well and as cheaply as possible rather than just to make money. "I do not believe that we should make such an awful profit on our cars. A reasonable profit is right, but not too much," he said on the witness stand. "So it has been my policy to force the price of the car down as fast as production would permit, and give the benefits to users and laborers." Selling a large number of cars at a small profit was much better than selling fewer cars at a large profit, he asserted, because "it enables a larger number of people to buy and enjoy the use of a car and because it gives a larger number of men employment at good wages."[9]

Ford believed that profits generated by his company should be reinvested in the company to create even greater production, which would lower prices even more for consumers. As he explained to the court, his company was "an instrument of service rather than a machine for making money. If large profits are made—and working to serve forces them to be large—then they should be in part turned back into the business so that it may be still better fitted to serve, and in part passed on to the purchaser." He admitted that his philosophy did not agree with the usual business view. "I do not want stockholders in the ordinary sense of the term—they do not help forward the ability to serve." As he declared vehemently from the witness stand, "I'll fight it through to the highest court in the land, if my contract as president of the Ford Motor Company is to be interpreted as requiring me to squeeze every cent I can out of everybody."[10]

The decision in the Dodge lawsuit was not rendered for nearly a year. Ford lost. The judge of the circuit court came to a decision favorable to the Dodges and ordered the Ford Motor Company to stop its expansion project and pay a special dividend to its stockholders of a little over $19 million. This decision was announced on October 31, 1917, and Ford immediately appealed. After another year and a half of litigation, the state superior court modified the lower court's ruling. The higher court overturned the ban on Ford Motor Company expansion, noting that judges should not be posing as business experts. At the same time, it upheld the ruling that Ford had acted unreasonably in withholding dividends from his stockholders and ordered that the special dividend, with interest, be distributed in an amount exceeding $20 million. A disappointed Ford agreed to pay, but vowed in private never again to be tied to the desires of stockholders, a determination that bore fruit in a few years.[11]

Though the legal verdict went against him, Ford once again triumphed in terms of public reputation. His denunciation of idle stockholders, his insistence on the value of productive labor, and his definition of the modern corporation as an instrument of service struck a responsive chord with the public. The Dodge suit burnished his reputation as a businessman who had the common man's interest at heart. Newspapers asserted that this lawsuit revealed a contrast between Ford's philosophy of service to the public with that of businessmen such as the Dodges, who were "not so much concerned with lessening the cost of production in the future as they are in seizing the profits of the present."[12]

Some observers placed Ford in a favorable light by interpreting the

Dodge suit as a ploy by powerful economic interests to control him. The Detroit *Journal* reported that Ford's expansion plans included building a steel smelter for processing iron ore, and thus the "steel kings" were backing the Dodges in their legal action. According to an insider in Detroit banking and manufacturing circles, the implementation of Ford's plans would have undermined big steel manufacturing. "It would do much to shake loose the grip the trust has upon the throat of the industrial world," he noted. Thus portrayed as a victim of "the steel barons" and the "trust," Ford reaffirmed his populist credentials as a defender of the little man.[13]

Public sentiment seemed to embrace him as the symbol of a new, enlightened age of corporate behavior, in contrast to the Dodges, who represented an archaic model of big business. As an editorial in the New York *Evening Mail* argued, a great injustice would occur if the Dodges prevented Ford from "working out the great corrective ideas he has inaugurated in the realm of big business in America." He had become too valuable:

> Henry Ford is a great national asset. He is the master economist of the manufacturing world. His principles are the principles that must control if industry in this country is to be developed on sound, safe lines, profitable not only to producers but to consumers and to labor. . . . To standardize, to improve, to lessen costs, to widen his market until it has reached its utmost limit, and all this time to give to labor its just reward—these have been the aims of Henry Ford. His business philosophy is the only one upon which great and enduring success can be established.

Ford had played a huge part in creating an American economy of consumer abundance and demonstrated that both business and labor could flourish when productivity and wages were maximized. He was a national hero, this editorial concluded, because "he, more than any man of great wealth the world has ever seen, interprets the dream of democracy."[14]

So, though Henry Ford lost the Dodge lawsuit, he won a much larger prize—the hearts of ordinary American citizens. And the Ford legend, enhanced in a Detroit courtroom, gained even more brilliance from being showcased in another typical American setting—the great expanses of nature.

Henry Ford liked to tell an amusing story about an incident that occurred on one of his camping trips. While he was in the wild regions of northern

Michigan with some friends, the group parked their automobile and camped in the woods a short distance from a farmhouse. When they drove to the house to purchase some provisions, they found the farmer in his barn tinkering with a large automobile that was not a Ford. Without disclosing his identity, Ford inquired about the problem with the car and then helped the farmer get it running. He identified the problem, assisted with repairs, and even contributed some new spark plugs and tools to the project. When they were finished, the farmer turned to Ford and said, "What's the charge?"

Ford replied, "Nothing."

"But I can't let it stand that way," said the farmer. "You have not only given your time, but you have also given me spark plugs and tools. Here's a dollar and a half. I insist you take that much."

"No," said Ford. "I can't do it. I have all the money I want."

The farmer looked him up and down and drawled, "Hell, you can't have that much and drive a Ford."[15]

This incident reflected not only the omnipresence of Ford's modest Model T, but another topic that fascinated many Americans in the years after World War I. In the late 1910s, the public became entranced with news about Henry Ford and his regular camping forays with a group of high-profile companions: Thomas Edison, Harvey Firestone, and John Burroughs. The adventures of the "Four Vagabonds," as they called themselves, became a proven news generator with stories about their encounters with the wilderness. This "gathering of geniuses" around a campfire seemed to connect with something basic in the collective American psyche. Like Benjamin Franklin, the learned scientist who had cavorted through the salons of Paris dressed in Quakerish garb and fur hats, or Mark Twain, who masked his worldliness with a persona of provincial shrewdness, Ford and his fellow campers enhanced their technological achievements by seeking inspiration and amusement in the great natural spaces of the United States.

The Four Vagabond trips developed gradually. The Ford and Edison families, along with John Burroughs, had first vacationed together in 1914, on a trip to Florida. The following year, Harvey Firestone and his wife joined the group for a journey to the Panama-Pacific International Exposition in San Francisco, followed by a motoring trip southward, down the coast to Los Angeles and San Diego. By 1918, the four famous men had adopted a more rustic routine. Over the next few years, Ford, Edison, Burroughs, and Firestone traveled through sparsely inhabited areas of the Mid-Atlantic region, New England, upstate New York, Pennsylvania, and the upper Midwest to camp. Eagerly followed by reporters, the exploits of the Four Vagabonds became public rituals from 1916 to 1921.[16]

The camping trips followed a standard format. The men would drive off for an unknown destination at the head of a caravan composed of attendants, supply vehicles, and reporters. Edison served as navigator, always choosing the route, often deciding upon one itinerary in advance and then selecting another when the group actually departed. The group seldom knew their destination and usually improvised as they went along. As Firestone once joked about Edison, "We never know where we are going and I suspect that he does not either." Firestone functioned as commissary officer and general manager, securing foodstuffs and making general arrangements. Ford took on the duties of mechanical expert, repairing the automobiles on several occasions. Once on the road, the group would meander from day to day, setting up camp wherever and whenever they felt like it.[17]

Over the years, several traditions evolved among the Four Vagabonds. Edison forbade shaving while on the camping trips, but Firestone found it difficult to obey this edict. Being a rather fastidious man, he would occasionally sneak off to a local hotel for the night, where he could enjoy a bath and a shave. "You're a tenderfoot," Edison would laughingly say upon his return. "Soon you'll be dressing up like a dude." Edison enjoyed fleeing urban life and roughing it in the wild. "He is a good camper-out and turns vagabond very easily. He can go with his hair uncombed and his clothes unbrushed as long as the best of us," Burroughs once noted. "There can be no doubt about his love for the open air and wild nature."[18]

This was no small praise, since "Uncle John" Burroughs, the senior member of the group and a well-known naturalist, poet, philosopher, and writer, set the standard for communing with nature. He came from the same mold as Henry David Thoreau and John Muir. In his late seventies by the time the camping trips began, Burroughs had established a national reputation with his essays and books extolling the virtues of America's natural beauty. He had met Henry Ford in 1913, and they bonded on the basis of a shared love of nature and birds. Looking the part of the romantic rustic with his gaunt frame, weatherbeaten face, flowing white beard, and long hair often topped by a slouch hat, he would set his tent apart from the others, so that he could meander at will among the plants and woodland creatures that he loved. Burroughs' reputation even rescued the group from an occasional scrape. Once, when they set up camp on private land, an irate farmer was dissuaded from running them off at gunpoint because he recognized Burroughs as the author of some nature pieces he had read.[19]

While wandering through backwoods America, the Four Vagabonds typically filled their days and evenings with interesting diversions. When he wasn't taking naps or reading, Edison liked to gather rocks and break them open with a hammer to examine the mineral deposits within. Ford, Edison,

and Firestone often strolled along the banks of local creeks and rivers, calculating the drop, estimating the volume of water that was moving, and discussing how the building of dams could generate power for use in isolated
areas of rural America. As Firestone noted, "I doubt if, on our trips, we ever
passed an abandoned mill without Mr. Edison and Mr. Ford getting out to
measure the force of the stream, inspect the old wheel, and talk about ways
and means of putting the waste power to work." Led by Burroughs, the
group would take long hikes and then relax by bathing their feet in streams.
The vagabonds would pick berries, stop at farms to cradle oats and rake hay,
and ride on logging locomotives with Ford at the throttle.[20]

The four friends loved to engage in contests of physical prowess such as
sprinting and tree felling. Ford won the footraces, but Burroughs excelled at
cutting down trees. When the group stopped at small-town inns, at Ford's
prodding they would continue the competition by trying to kick away cigars
that were balanced on the edge of mantels. Or they would compete to see
who took the most steps in the fewest bounds, a contest usually won by
Ford. During the evening, the quartet would repose for hours around the
campfire, discussing current affairs and debating the merits of literary works
such as *Evangeline* and *Les Misérables* and authors such as Emerson, Thoreau,
and Shakespeare. They would also exchange jokes and stories, some of them
a bit risqué. As one of Ford's retinue testified, "I've never seen a bunch of
fellows—you know, big guys with big money—have more fun than they did.
They were just like a bunch of kids when they went on these trips."[21]

Ford cut the most energetic figure on the vagabond forays, leaping into
activities with boyish enthusiasm. He arose every morning around five-
thirty, hiked the longest and the fastest on daytime jaunts, and chopped
wood every night for the campfire. He also loved indulging in playing practical jokes. One of his most memorable came when he took several wooden
tent stakes and "had a fellow saw them up in little bits of square blocks and
put them in the soup for dinner, so Mr. Firestone would bite on them."
Another time, he came across a boy and girl living near a campsite, and discovered that the family's Edison phonograph had quit working and could
not be repaired. Ford fetched the phonograph, located the problem, and
repaired it. He got two laughs from his effort: one when he told the children's mother who he was, and another when he was able to report to Edison that he could fix the inventor's products better than his dealers could.[22]

Ford served as the main attraction for reporters and crowds that would
gather in small towns to greet the group. Burroughs reported, "The crowds
that flock around the car in which he is riding, as we pause in the towns
through which we pass, are not paying their homage merely to a successful
car-builder, or business man, but to a beneficent human force, a great prac-

tical idealist, whose good-will and spirit of universal helpfulness they have all felt." Such acclaim sometimes hurt Burroughs' feelings. On a stop at a local college, the nature writer expected appreciation and acclaim, only to be crushed when the president of the institution introduced Henry Ford to the crowd instead. Burroughs confessed, "My mental barometer fell from high to low on that occasion."[23]

Ford as vagabond galvanized the public imagination in several ways. The camping trips reinforced his stature as a genuine, rough-hewn American folk hero. He would arrange special events for local farmers, with picnics and exhibitions of farming implements. Once, he befriended a prominent country fiddler and organized an impromptu concert and dance for the vagabonds and some of the locals that featured "the old jigs, the square dances called as they should be called, and music which none of us had heard for twenty years."[24]

The camping trips also allowed Ford to display his work ethic. In Connellsville, Pennsylvania, one of the cars in the caravan broke down, and after local mechanics concluded it could not be fixed, Ford repaired the radiator and cooling fan. According to the local newspaper, "His hands were covered with grease and his new olive green suit was spotted here and there where he had placed his hands upon it." Its conclusion appeared in an admiring headline: "Mr. Ford Demonstrates He's Not Afraid of Work; Repairs His Damaged Car."[25]

Ford's demonstrations of physical vigor on the expeditions impressed his popular audience. When the group paused, Burroughs reported, Ford would "inspect the stream or busy himself in getting wood for the fire. Mr. Ford is a runner and a high kicker, and frequently challenges some member of the party to race with him. He is also a persistent walker, and from every camp, both morning and evening, he sallied forth for a brisk half-hour walk." Firestone expressed a similar admiration. "Mr. Ford, when he is out of doors, is just like a boy: he wants to have running races, climb trees, or do anything which a boy might do," he wrote. "He eats very little, is nearly always in first-class condition, and he likes to walk." Newspaper headlines declared, "Henry Ford Chops Wood."[26]

Publicity, of course, polished Ford's reputation as folk hero. Even as the camping trips provided an escape from the stresses and strains of the workaday world for these busy businessmen, they also became magnets for public attention. On their first trip to California, in 1915, when the group stopped so Edison could lay the cornerstone for a new building, they were unprepared for the brass band that appeared to escort them to the site. They were equally surprised by the hundreds of schoolchildren who lined the roads and threw flowers as they passed by. By 1918, people in towns and villages commonly turned out en masse to greet the Four Vagabonds, clamoring for speeches and pleading for money to support local causes.[27]

The vagabonds complained about the publicity. Firestone claimed that the attention stole the trips' charm: "We found ourselves in the midst of motion-picture operators, reporters, and curiosity seekers. We became a kind of traveling circus." Ford also complained, writing in his autobiography a few years later that "the trips were good fun except that they began to attract too much attention." But the facts indicate that Ford not only enjoyed the attention but encouraged it. In 1918, he instructed one of his staff to gather newspaper articles from all the areas through which the party traveled. He arranged for a photographer, George Ebling, to be a regular member of the group and helped stage scenes for the camera. He allowed newspapermen to follow the group on their rambles and talked with them frequently. Only occasionally did he demur, asking the press to stay a distance from the vagabonds' campsite.[28]

More often, Ford's desire for publicity frequently overwhelmed his fondness for privacy. "With squads of newswriters and platoons of cameramen to report and film the posed nature studies of the four eminent campers," wrote Charles Sorensen, "these well-equipped excursions . . . were as private and secluded as a Hollywood opening, and Ford appreciated the publicity." Newsmen and photographers reported every move and utterance of the campers, and newsreel cameramen made films that were shown in theaters. It seems clear that Ford and the vagabonds, for all their complaints, appreciated, even nurtured, the public attention that accompanied their backwoods excursions.[29]

An unmistakable sign of Ford's desire for publicity came on the 1921 trip. He helped arrange the participation of President Warren G. Harding, hardly a maneuver designed to avoid attention. Harding joined the group at their campsite in Maryland with an entourage that included his wife, his secretary, several Secret Service men, and a bishop of the Methodist church. Not surprisingly, journalists and cameramen flocked to the site. They were especially pleased to record Harding removing his coat to chop wood for the evening fire, and then, when he tired, Ford taking over and finishing the job.[30]

Perhaps the most significant aspect of Ford's camping hobby, however, involved its connection to recreation. In the early twentieth century, America's new consumer society was increasingly emphasizing the enjoyment of leisure time. Recreation gradually emerged as not only a new arena for indulging in consumer goods, but a space in which hardworking, productive, white-collar workers could escape the stresses and strains of modern corporate life. The camping trips of Ford and the vagabonds appeared as manifestations of the new recreation ethic of modern America.[31]

As newspaper stories and interviews revealed, much of the impetus for these backwoods trips came from the urgent wish of the three businessmen in the group—Firestone, Edison, and Ford—to escape the pressures of their work. During the 1918 expedition, Edison confided to reporters that Ford had been drained by overwork, and needed a rest because of "nerves, nerves, nerves." One of the automaker's retinue confirmed the therapeutic effect the camping trips had on his boss. "After these trips Mr. Ford would be a changed man—noticeably refreshed and rested," he noted. "He was just living another life. . . . [He was] a new man."[32]

The jaunts of the Four Vagabonds underlined the role of consumer comfort in modern recreation. Far from roughing it, Ford and his friends ventured into the wild supplied with a full array of modern conveniences. The 1918 trip saw the group traveling in six cars—two Packards, two Model T's, and two Ford trucks (which Ford had begun to manufacture in 1917)—accompanied by seven drivers and helpers. The following year, a veritable caravan took shape, as Ford introduced a pair of specialized vehicles that he had developed. Automobile A was a large kitchen car furnished with a pantry, a built-in icebox, and special gasoline stove mounted onto the running board. Automobile B had been constructed on a truck chassis and included an array of specialized compartments for tents, beds, and camping equipment. When Burroughs was asked by a reporter to describe his feeling about the latest camping expedition, he quipped, "I should say I am now seeking comfort in a luxurious way."[33]

The vagabonds ventured into the countryside armed with all the conveniences of home. Each man had a separate spacious tent with his name monogrammed above the entrance as well as a full sleeping outfit—a folding cot, mattress, blankets, pillows, and sheets. As one of Ford's attendants confessed, it was "just like living in a hotel." Ford developed a portable power plant with a generator and battery so the group could string up electric lights in the sleeping and dining tents. By 1921, an electric player piano was included. Perhaps most impressive, however, was the food. Ford brought Sato, a skilled Japanese cook, to prepare meals, and the group purchased fresh provisions as they meandered along. They ate well—steaks and chicken in the evenings, pies and cookies, huge breakfasts of bacon, ham, eggs, biscuits, and pancakes. They also ate in style. A large dining tent, with a round table supporting an enormous lazy Susan that rotated dishes around to the diners, made for very comfortable meals.[34]

Yet these trips, as newspapers were quick to note, were more than recreation. The vagabonds engaged in practical, useful activity. Their journeys into the countryside, in the words of one paper, also involved brainstorming about projects to improve American life. Ford and Edison, for example, pondered rural water-power projects. "Each has a great deal of vision along that line; Mr. Edison as to how flowing streams may be converted into adaptable power; Mr. Ford as to what uses that power may be turned to," noted a reporter. "Couple their talents and who knows what may be the result?"[35]

Around the same time as the camping trips, Henry Ford ignited an even larger explosion of publicity with his involvement in a legal confrontation that was part of the fallout from his antiwar adventures a few years earlier. Ford initiated a libel suit that went to trial in the courtroom of a small town in Michigan in the summer of 1919. It once again put him into national headlines for several months.

In May 1919, the sleepy village of Mount Clemens, Michigan, awoke with a start. Located some twenty miles northwest of Detroit, the town found its streets populated with over two dozen cowboys and ranchers from Texas who, according to one newspaper report, were "tall, tanned, and wear wide sombreros and cow punchers' high heels. They have suspicious bulges at the hip." Other characters—detectives, investigators, clerks, publicists, attorneys—also descended upon the town and took all the available hotel rooms. As the Detroit *Times* reported, there were "mysterious comings and goings, whispered consultations on hotel verandas, on street corners, long walks over country roads, messenger boys running hither and thither carrying notes and letters and an air of secrecy pervades everything." Meanwhile, a squad of carpenters remodeled the courtroom in the redbrick county courthouse, but left hanging a curious sign on the wall right outside the door: "If you spit on the floor in your own house, do it here. We want you to feel at home." Outside, trucks unloaded dozens of boxes of documents and books. The cause of all this activity—Henry Ford's million-dollar libel lawsuit against the Chicago *Tribune*—was the biggest event in Mount Clemens' history.[36]

Once the trial began, the circus atmosphere intensified. People poured into the small town, the interurban railway running special cars from Detroit and the local taxicab business enjoying a boom. Hundreds of residents neglected their jobs to jam the courthouse and absorb every detail of the case. A powerful sulfurous smell from local medicinal waters pervaded the air; the "rheumatic rich," as one newspaper termed them, hobbled from the Mount Clemens health resort to jostle for seats in the courtroom. Every day, the tall, slender, striking figure of Colonel Robert R. McCormick, publisher of the *Tribune*, could be seen strolling about town accompanied by a large retinue including his wife, "a strikingly beautiful woman . . . [who] is followed by admiring looks wherever she goes." Similarly, Henry Ford could be glimpsed every morning "taking a long hike over a country road or strolling along the grassy banks of the Clinton river, which runs close by his hotel."[37]

This extravagant episode of legal theater had been engendered by a *Tribune* editorial on June 25, 1916, denouncing Ford as an "ignorant idealist . . . [and] an anarchistic enemy of the nation." The newspaper had launched this attack because its reporter had concluded that the Ford Motor Company would not hold jobs for, or assist the families of, National Guardsmen who had been mobilized to protect the border with Mexico during an upheaval in that country. Ford denied this accusation and demanded a retraction, but the *Tribune* refused. Ford's attorney, Alfred Lucking, brought the editorial into Ernest G. Liebold's office and declared, "I don't think Mr. Ford should stand for it." A bit later, Ford came in, listened to Lucking, and said, "Well, you better start suit against them for libel." Within a few days, he filed suit against the *Tribune* for $1 million because the editorial had "sought to bring the plaintiff into public hatred, contempt, ridicule, and financial injury."[38]

After over two and half years of legal maneuvering and preliminary argument, the case finally came to trial in Mount Clemens on a change of venue. The Ford forces took over the second floor of a commercial building just opposite the courthouse and established the Mount Clemens News Bureau to send out information and stories to newspapers all over the country. Fifteen thousand weekly papers and twenty-five hundred dailies were given "copy" on the trial. On the office wall the Ford team hung a large map of the United States with colored pins: blue indicating newspapers that were favorable to Ford, yellow showing hostile papers. In the words of one visitor, there were "enough blue pins in the map to make everybody around the Mount Clemens News Bureau feel pleased." Ford also engaged some forty operatives, who prowled about the town checking on witnesses for the opposition and trying to get wind of any significant testimony.[39]

The trial opened on May 12, 1919, with the selection of a jury, a process that took four days. It was composed entirely of farmers. The primary attorney for the *Tribune* was Elliot G. Stevenson, who had represented the Dodge brothers in their suit against Ford; he was assisted by several other lawyers. The Ford team, led by Alfred Lucking, in their opening statement claimed that the *Tribune* had worked to embroil the United States in a conflict with Mexico in 1916 as a way to keep the country out of the war in Europe, and that Ford had been libeled because he opposed American military action against its southern neighbor. Defense attorneys for the *Tribune* stated they would prove that Ford was indeed an "ignorant idealist" and that his pacifistic campaign had so weakened the military preparedness of the American government that he deserved the label of "anarchist."

As the trial proceeded, expert witnesses called by each side pondered the meaning of anarchism and debated whether Ford's statements put him in that camp. His lawyers summoned figures such as Francis W. Coker, professor of political science at Ohio State University, who argued that the automaker's denunciations of war corresponded to those of such diverse thinkers as Victor Hugo, Martin Luther, James Russell Lowell, and Voltaire. Bishop Charles D. Williams of Detroit testified that Ford's antiwar views were more akin to Christian teachings than to anarchism. Professor William A. Dunning, chairman of the history-and-political-philosophy department at Columbia University, insisted that Ford's opinions were not anarchistic but common among thinkers ranging from the ancient Greeks to Dr. Samuel Johnson.[40]

The *Tribune* countered with witnesses such as Professor Andrew Reeves of the University of Michigan, who declared that Ford's ideas represented anarchistic hostility to government. But the newspaper's lawyers also employed a wider strategy. They called to the witness stand ordinary citizens from the Rio Grande region who recounted their victimization, frequently accompanied by tears, at the hands of Pancho Villa and his Mexican raiders. They summoned Texas Rangers, who told tales of gun battles along the border, all of which underlined the emergency situation to which the American government had responded. Such stories painted Ford's opposition to the deployment of American forces in rather dark colors. The defense also questioned his reputation as a reformer, suggesting that his inauguration of the Five-Dollar Day had been a clever ruse to hide his enormous profit-making. They depicted his proposal to fly an "international flag" at Highland Park during his antiwar campaign as a sign of anarchistic hostility to the American government.[41]

But the focal point of the *Tribune*'s strategy, and the central drama of the trial, came when its attorneys called Henry Ford to the stand for cross-examination on July 14. The defense, as part of its strategy to establish a broad definition of anarchism and the phrase "ignorant idealist," sought to prove that he was an untutored, unpatriotic extremist. Ford remained pinned on the stand for eight days of dissection. During this grueling ordeal, Elliot Stevenson's tactic was a simple one: to quiz Ford on basic matters of American history and government and thereby reveal the profound ignorance that lay behind his antiwar fervor. By making Ford appear the fool, the *Tribune* team hoped to lend credence to its editorial description of him. As one of its attorneys said to a reporter, "This lawsuit is like the tenth baby in a family. We didn't want it, but now that we have it we wouldn't take a million dollars for it. It is worth that to show Ford up."[42]

Ford proved to be more cooperative than anyone ever dreamed. Stevenson opened by asking him what the United States had been originally. Ford drew a laugh with his homespun parry: "Land, I guess." After that, his performance plunged. When Stevenson asked about the date of the American Revolution, he replied that it was 1812. As titters went around the courtroom, Stevenson reminded the witness about 1776, but even with prompting, Ford was unable to list any causes for the Revolution. When Stevenson inquired about the 1812 conflict, Ford could only lamely offer, "It was one of aggression." Piling error upon malapropism, Ford identified Benedict Arnold as a writer, described the Monroe Doctrine as "a big-brother act," and identified a mobile army as "a large army—mobilized." He could not recall the basic principles of American government. Confronted with words and phrases from his own antiwar statements, Ford proved equally inept. He defined ballyhoo as "a blackguard or something of that nature," anarchy as "overthrowing the government and throwing bombs," treason as "anything against the government," and an idealist as "anyone who helps another to make a profit."[43]

Ford's attorneys had foreseen this debacle and tried to avoid it. Operatives had gleaned information that *Tribune* attorneys were going to go after Ford on history questions, so they tried to coach him before his appearance on the stand. For several evenings, Lucking and his associates became tutors to a rather unwilling pupil. When the lessons began, Ford would wander to the window after a few minutes and observe "Say, that airplane is flying pretty low, isn't it?" Lucking would persuade him to return to his chair, but as the instruction proceeded Ford would again jump up, after a short time, and observe, "Look at that bird there, pretty little fellow, isn't it? Somebody around here must be feeding it, or it wouldn't come back so often." After many such episodes, Ford's attorneys had thrown up their hands in frustration.[44]

Now, as he fumbled Stevenson's questions one after another, Ford maintained a curious pose on the stand. He seemed content to play the provincial rube. When an attorney asked him whether he would rather read something aloud or leave the impression that he was illiterate, Ford replied, "Yes, you can leave it that way. I am not a fast reader and I have the hayfever and I would make a botch of it." But Ford occasionally grew testy and lashed out at his antagonist. At one point, as Stevenson badgered him about some detail of American history, for example, Ford snapped back, "I could find a man in five minutes who could tell me all about it." Overall, however, he presented a personal demeanor that was equal parts dignity, detachment, and long-suffering patience. A reporter described his strange serenity on the witness stand as his ignorance was laid open to public view:

> He is sitting in a chair that is tilted back against the wall. His thin knee is clasped in his long hands; good-natured patience dwells upon his face. Henry Ford looks his fifty-six years. Clean-skinned and tanned, grayish hair flowing back from his high retreating brow, prominently featured with the long arched nose and straight mouth, the blue of his deep-set eyes . . . When a question is asked him he rubs his hand across his long jaw, a rural gesture; he speculatively moistens his lips, lowering his eyes when he wants to think, bending forward when something interests him. Henry Ford, sitting in court with crossed legs, suggests the country store philosopher.[45]

But it was Ford's gaffe-filled testimony, not his philosophical demeanor, that created a sensation. Headlines described "Spectators Gasping at Ford's Story" and denounced his testimony as "A Shabby and Discreditable Hoax." Editorialists guffawed and public figures chortled at Ford's ignorance. The New York *Times* opined that "Mr. Ford has been submitted to a severe examination of his intellectual qualities. He has not received a pass." The Sioux City, Iowa, *Journal* contended that he had been "disclosed as a man with a vision distorted and limited by his lack of information. The public is disillusioned." The New York *Post* claimed, "The man is a joke. He may not be an anarchist, but his mind is anarchic." *The Nation*, with a more-in-sorrow-than-anger commentary, typified discussion in the national media: "The mystery is finally dispelled. Henry Ford is a Yankee mechanic, pure and simple, quite uneducated, with a mind unable to bite into any proposition outside of his automobile and tractor business. . . . He has achieved wealth but not greatness."[46]

Then a startling thing happened. Many common citizens, small-town editors, village leaders, workers, and farmers throughout the United States rushed to Ford's defense. Arthur Brisbane, a Hearst columnist syndicated in many small-town newspapers, urged readers to show their support by mailing this form letter to the Ford Motor Company in Detroit: "Dear Ford: I am glad to have you for a fellow citizen and I wish we had more of your brand of anarchism, if that is what it is. Yours truly, (sign here)." Thousands did so, mounting a counterattack on Ford's persecutors from the provinces and the working strata of American society in behalf of a man they viewed as their spokesman.[47]

Many of the letters pouring into the Highland Park offices went far beyond Brisbane's formula. Hundreds of working people, outraged by the attacks on Ford's character and intelligence during the trial, composed heartfelt missives of encouragement. Handwritten on stationery, ruled paper from a tablet, even postcards, these crude communications amounted to a huge outpouring of affection:

> You are the only rich man we know off [sic] who are willing to give the poor a living chance. . . . You are doing grand work, Mr. Ford and you have a heart, which few rich men seem to have. . . . Long may you live and prosper.

> You are my ideal of a self-made man whose opinions are sincere and justly righteous. Such a man was our noble Lincoln. Everyone who appreciates sincerity and worth looks up to you and admires your views. The others are not worth thinking about.

> You are loved by thousands of people all over the world, and you are prayed for and blessed whenever and wherever your name is mentioned. . . . You have done more good and accomplished more for the people than any man living. Do not let them discourage you.

Such loyalty and love occasionally spilled over into rant, as with the irate correspondent who characterized Ford's antagonists as "half-baked lawyers employed by those pollywog editors." He sarcastically suggested that the industrialist counter with his own questions: "Why does a brown cow that eats green grass give white milk? Who was the king of Ireland when the Chinese wall was built, and what are its dimensions? In what year and for what purpose was it built? Why do cats when making love make such a hell of a noise?"[48]

The case finally went to the jury on August 14, and the verdict offered an appropriate conclusion to this bizarre spectacle. After about ten hours of deliberation, the jury found that the *Tribune* was guilty of libel but awarded Ford only six cents in damages. Though both sides claimed victory in the courtroom, the real outcome had been decided in the court of public opinion. Ford's performance on the stand in Mount Clemens may have disgusted the American intelligentsia, but it only endeared him further to ordinary people. In the words of the Fairbury, Nebraska, *Journal*, "A few less smart-aleck attorneys and a few more Henry Fords, and the world would have less troubles and more to eat." Ford, added another small-town paper, "comes nearer being typical of the average, energetic, courageous, honest, uncultured American than any other one man in this country. . . . A great heart beats in Henry Ford, and in his clumsy earnest fashion he is manfully trying to make all men happier." The Chicago *Tribune* libel trial, like so many incidents in Ford's career, ended up as a triumph by enhancing his status as a man of the people.[49]

By the early 1920s, Henry Ford's views on modern society had become a staple of American public discussion. His legal wrangles with the Dodge brothers and the Chicago *Tribune,* and his high-profile camping trips, piled on top of the enormous publicity he had attracted earlier from the Peace Ship, the Senate race, the Five-Dollar Day, and the sociological department, made Ford a household name. His every utterance and activity was analyzed closely and reported to an interested public of millions. Newspapers and magazines scrambled to gain access to him, and his thoughts on everything from industrial relations to dietary issues, career paths to religious practices, international relations to modern marriage, went tumbling out into the public arena.

In part, this was Ford's own doing. Since his early days in the automobile-racing game, he had demonstrated a talent for generating publicity; by the 1910s, he had honed this skill to a sharp edge. As he once confided to an associate, "I don't care what anybody says, so long as they talk about Ford." But gradually he ventured further and carved out a new role as an oracle. He began issuing pronouncements on the state of the nation and the world and spent increasing amounts of time and energy seeking the public limelight. Moreover, by the late 1910s he had created a publicity machine to aid him in popularizing his views.[50]

In many ways, this new public persona represented a significant change in Ford's life. Earlier public attention had focused on his company and his automobile, while Ford the man stayed in the background. Throughout the 1910s, however, growing public attention began to change him. "For many years Mr. Ford shunned the public gaze, refused to see reporters, modestly begged to be kept out of print; and then suddenly faced about, hired a publicity agent, [and] jumped into the front page of every newspaper in the country," noted Samuel S. Marquis. Charles Sorensen, who worked closely with him for many years, offered a similar observation: "The world-wide attention accorded Mr. Ford changed him from a modest man content with remaining in the background to one who delighted to bask in the great white light of publicity." By the 1920s, some viewed this behavior rather cynically. Journalist E. G. Pipp, after leaving Ford's organization, claimed that the allure of fame had seduced his former boss. "All of his roads lead either to wealth, to power, or to self-glory, or to all three—for himself," Pipp wrote bitterly. As another observer of Ford's career concluded frankly, he was "one of the most skillful and avid self-advertisers of the century."[51]

Ford's yen for self-promotion led him to put together an organization to publicize his views. Throughout much of the 1910s, Ernest G. Liebold, Ford's executive secretary, had authorized his boss's interviews with the press. By about 1920, however, William J. Cameron, a former newspaperman with a talent for interpreting Ford's often enigmatic ideas, had become responsible for arranging interviews, editing his off-the-cuff comments, and vetting the resulting press stories. Assisted by a team of journalists and publicity agents—these included Fred L. Black, Ben Donaldson, and Walter Blanchard—Cameron oversaw the cascade of Ford publicity that began to blanket the country. A student of Ford's public image has concluded that in the last half of the 1910s only four Americans—Woodrow Wilson, Theodore Roosevelt, Charles Evans Hughes, and William Jennings Bryan—received more press attention than Ford. By the following decade, that group had dwindled to one: President Calvin Coolidge. "Mr. Ford felt a news story on the front page was of more value than a paid advertising campaign," Liebold explained.[52]

But Ford also aimed at loftier goals. Inspired by his experiences with the Five-Dollar Day, the Peace Ship, and his campaign for the Senate, he saw himself as a serious public figure with a historic role to play. Ford the oracle began to step forward onto the public stage.

Certain journalists and critics aided this process. Judson C. Welliver, writing in *The American Review of Reviews*, argued that Ford had emerged as a prophetic figure in a modern society characterized by technological advance, growing wealth, increased education, and spreading material abundance. Ford, according to Welliver, fully embraced this "new era." "A genius in mechanics, a revolutionist in industry, a Napoleon in business, he has visions of the future that are not distorted by any reflections from the background of a past about which he knows little and cares less. His eye and interest are all for the tomorrows," noted the journalist. Ford believed that the future had arrived and the new age would "see industry and enterprise operating for the greatest good of the community as a whole."[53]

The New York *World* also analyzed Ford's growing public presence. He had emerged as a social philosopher in the 1910s, and by the end of the decade he had become the most quoted citizen in the United States. "There is evolving around him a whole philosophy of ideas built up partly from casual roadside comments, partly from the books in which he has now begun to labor his ideas, partly from things which are said and thought of him by several thousand other people," the newspaper observed. For the first time in modern American history, it concluded, a wealthy entrepreneur had blossomed not as an art collector or a horse breeder but as "a fancier of ideas."[54]

Ford provided a notable boost to his own oracular status in 1919. In January of that year, the first issue of the Dearborn *Independent* appeared under his auspices. A few months earlier, Ford had purchased this small, financially troubled newspaper from his hometown and proceeded to make it a national mouthpiece for his views. Carrying the extravagant subtitle *The Chronicler of the Neglected Truth*, this tabloid-sized weekly covered a variety of topics, with pieces by diverse journalists and writers. In large part, however, the Dearborn *Independent* came before the public as Ford's own personal forum, a fact reinforced by "Mr. Ford's Own Page," an editorial appearing in every issue.[55]

Ford had come upon the idea for procuring a newspaper during his antiwar crusade, when he became convinced that a hostile press was controlled by banks and other powerful financial interests. "The capitalistic newspapers began a campaign against me. They misquoted me, distorted what I said, made up lies about me," he declared. He went on to note, "I have definite ideas and ideals that I believe are practical for the good of all, and intend giving them to the public without having them garbled, distorted, or misrepresented." In other words, Ford wanted to control the presentation of his ideas to the public.[56]

The Dearborn *Independent*'s first editor was E. G. Pipp, a muckraking journalist who had risen through the ranks to become editor-in-chief of the Detroit *News*. Pipp was "Henry Ford's favorite newspaperman," according to Fred L. Black, because the two men shared a strong measure of social idealism as well as friendship. Ford prohibited all advertising in the paper, instead picking up production costs himself. Leery of advertisers' control over the press, he also feared deception and "didn't want to advertise a product he didn't fairly believe in, or didn't know was absolutely what it claimed to be." Despite this, Ford's fame immediately brought tens of thousands of subscribers to the paper, augmented as the Ford Motor Company pressured its hundreds of car dealerships to buy multiple subscriptions to distribute to customers.[57]

Ford's newspaper carried a variety of articles on topics in public affairs, science, education, popular culture, religion, industry, and agriculture. It attracted between a quarter-million and a half-million subscribers between 1919 and 1928. Unquestionably, however, Henry Ford's personal editorials provided the most striking feature of the Dearborn *Independent*. Although appearing under Ford's name, they were ghostwritten by William J. Cameron, who talked regularly with Ford and extracted from him the epigrammatic nuggets that were refined into full-blown editorial statements. Indeed, Cameron displayed a unique talent for interpreting and expanding his boss's cryptic "intuitions," as Ford often described them. Whereas many journalists and members of Ford's staff would come out of an interview muttering, "What in the hell did the old man mean by this?" Cameron had the ability to discern Ford's meaning. He would go through several drafts of "Mr. Ford's Own Page" each week, eventually gaining the approval of both Ford and Ernest Liebold, who maintained a veto power over its content.[58]

The opening number of "Mr. Ford's Own Page," in the January 11, 1919, issue, established its avuncular tone. "This paper exists to spread ideas, the best that can be found," Ford stated. "It aims to furnish food for thought. It desires to stir ambition and encourage independent thinking." The editorial then alighted on some of the author's favorite themes: the great opportunities still existing for innovative and hardworking individuals, the need for industry to perform a useful public service as well as make money, the evils of "absentee ownership" and "speculative capitalists," and the scourge of war. Ford struck a characteristic note of folksy wisdom in explaining his own role: "I have never pretended to be a writer or an editor, but I can talk with plain Americans in a way that we can understand each other."[59]

Henry Ford's emergence as an author provided this final component of his publicity machine. With considerable fanfare, *My Life and Work* (1922) was published to an appreciative national and international audience. This book—part autobiography and part manifesto for industrial progress—had been ghostwritten by Samuel Crowther, a journalist who specialized in writing about politics and economics. He had won Ford's confidence by collaborating on projects with Thomas Edison and Harvey Firestone. The two established an unorthodox working relationship. Crowther would scour Ford's editorials, use his staff to help dig up materials, interview Ford himself to glean his thoughts directly, and then spend hours in discussion with Cameron. After composing drafts, Crowther and Cameron would consult with Ford to get his final approval.[60]

A compelling book emerged from this collaborative process. It offered Ford's version of his own life, which appeared in snippets throughout the text as a mythical tale in which hard work and perseverance triumphed. But much of the book focused on the principles upon which Ford believed modern industrial society should be based. *My Life and Work* offered his blueprint for progress, and it flowed from two basic principles: the pursuit of service over profit in business, and the necessity of serving the consumer above all else. As Ford insisted in his introduction to the book, the modern businessman must understand that "profit must and inevitably will come as a reward for good service." And the key to successful manufacturing, he continued, lay in "the process of buying materials fairly and, with the smallest possible addition of cost, transforming those materials into a consumable product and giving it to the consumer."[61]

My Life and Work not only sold vigorously, but received positive reviews, with critics describing it as a "unique autobiography" combining nuggets from "a practical idealist's philosophy" with a "human narrative" of the author's life experience. As the New York *Times* noted, the presentation of Ford's philosophy was enhanced by a casual style suggesting "a man sitting near you at his ease and talking earnestly and with a curious sort of impersonal, objective attitude about his life . . . [and his] principles of living and working." An adulatory review in *The Nation* praised *My Life and Work* as "one of the most significant books of this generation." Ford, it stated, clearly explained principles of mass production and showed the wisdom of "taking the desires and the purchasing power of the consumer as the starting-point of all business planning." He presented an enticing vision of a "Fordized America" characterized by a shorter workday, higher wages, and "a margin of leisure now unknown."[62]

Thus, by the early 1920s, the Ford publicity machine had conveyed his legend into the farthest recesses of American public life. The Dearborn *Independent*, *My Life and Work*, and a host of newspaper interviews, magazine stories, and press releases kept his name continually before the people. Looking at this barrage of publicity, some observers concluded that a squadron of public-relations people had "made" Henry Ford by molding and publicizing an image. Though not completely inaccurate, of course, this perception missed the essence of the situation. Ford publicist Fred L. Black revealed the truth: "Any Ford legend would start with the boss himself, and it was nursed along by the newspapermen, rather than engineered by any staff at Ford's. This idea that Henry Ford was an ignoramus, and had his smartness due to his public relations men who engineered all his stuff, is *absolutely untrue*."[63]

In other words, Henry Ford largely created his own legend by manipulating the mechanisms of modern publicity. The result—great stature as an oracle in the modern world—proved salutary as he prepared to embark upon a bold new project in automobile manufacturing. By the late 1910s, Ford was poised not only to consolidate his hold on the Ford Motor Company but to enlarge his already huge role in this key sector of the American economy. A new facility began to arise on the banks of the River Rouge, and with it a new prototype for modern industrial production.

Fourteen

Visionary

In the years following the inauguration of the assembly line and the Five-Dollar Day, Henry Ford completely dominated the American automobile industry. In 1916, his company produced over 523,000 Model T's, or some 32 percent of all cars made in the United States. This was four times the number manufactured by its nearest rival, the Willys-Overland Company, and more than any six of Ford's competitors combined. Manufacturing numbers continued soaring, and in 1919 the company built some 750,000 cars, or about 40 percent of the national total.[1]

Rising production brought declining prices. In 1912, the Model T Runabout sold for $525, but the cost had dropped to $345 by 1916. Ford's competitors lagged badly in bringing inexpensive automobiles to the mass of citizens. A few companies—Willys-Overland, Studebaker, Maxwell, and Buick—offered cars in the $600–1,000 price range; the likes of Hudson, Cadillac, Chalmers, and Oldsmobile presented models from $1,000 to $2,000. Chevrolet, soon to be the low-price division of the General Motors Corporation, launched its Model 490 in the summer of 1915 at $550 to offer some competition. But such moves did little to faze Ford, who continued to manufacture Model T's in unprecedented numbers to dominate the volume end of the market.[2]

Highland Park represented the perfection of the Ford system, with thousands of flivvers pouring off its assembly lines every day. By 1915, however, Henry Ford had become frustrated by the limitations of his Crystal Palace. He began to contemplate a scale of production that far outdistanced anything achieved at Highland Park—or, in fact, even imagined in modern industry. He envisioned a manufacturing complex of truly vast proportions, one that would encompass an unprecedented integration of the industrial process and make an automobile complete from raw material to finished product.

But just as he started to move on this front, Ford encountered a serious obstacle within his own organization. Two of the key stockholders in the company objected to his plans and moved to stop them. Thus, before he could create this manufacturing leviathan, Ford had to gain total control of his own company. Typically, he did so by one of the shrewdest maneuvers in American business history.

On March 5, 1919, the Los Angeles *Examiner* printed a headline reading "Henry Ford Organizing Huge New Company to Build Better, Cheaper Car." It reported that Ford was creating a new enterprise to make a quality automobile that would beat the price of the Model T. Ford also promised that his new company would build plants all over the world, because "I believe that every family should have a car and it can be done." What would happen to the Ford Motor Company? Ford was asked. "Why, I don't know exactly what will become of that," he replied.[3]

Here was astonishing news—Henry Ford was walking away from one of the greatest companies in the modern industrial world, one that had put America on wheels, made the Model T a household name, and earned him a fortune. Curiously, he did not appear overly concerned that his present company might go under as a result of his new plan. In words that must have chilled its stockholders, Ford's spokesman, Ernest G. Liebold, noted, "It is Mr. Ford's belief that when any corporation or organization dealing in commodities consumed by the public ceases to serve the public its usefulness is ended and it naturally ceases to exist." According to the Los Angeles *Times*, Ford was fully prepared to abandon his past and embrace his future. "Unlike that mythical student, Frankenstein, Henry Ford does not intend to be destroyed nor balked by that creature of his own making—the Ford Motor Company—in the realization of his newest dream child, the production of an automobile to be marketed for $250 or $300."[4]

An air of mystery surrounded the situation as Ford announced his grand plan while on vacation in California with his family, and the project seemed to come out of the blue. "Officials here of the Ford Motor Company declared today they had no knowledge of the scheme of Henry Ford to organize a new corporation and manufacture a lower priced automobile," reported the New York *Herald*. The magazine *Automobile Topics* wrote, "To General Manager F. L. Klingensmith, the news was in the nature of a complete surprise. He was disposed at a late point in the week to treat it as a rumor merely, preferring to await Ford's return to Detroit for details."[5]

To add to the confusion, there were rumors of high-level financial deals behind Ford's surprising move. Stories appeared about mysterious groups who were maneuvering to buy Henry Ford's stock in the Ford Motor Company. *Automotive Industries* claimed that General Motors was offering Ford $187 million for his shares; the New York *Herald* reported that General Motors, with the backing of Du Pont money, had already acquired the Ford Company and was poised to become "the biggest factor in the automobile business of the world." Another rumor involved Harvey Firestone. By the early summer of 1919, there were reports that an Eastern financial syndicate was trying to buy shares of minority stockholders in the company.[6]

Under headlines reading "What Shall We Call the Baby," newspapers speculated on an appropriate name for the proposed new car—"Fordlet," "Sub-Ford," "Ford Junior," the "Henry," and "Ford 2d" were early favorites. Wags joked, "Would a Ford be the same under any other name?" Meanwhile, letters of inquiry came into Ford's office at Highland Park. Citizens who could not afford an automobile were elated by the prospect of a $250 model, and they wanted to know when it would go on the market. Other writers expressed interest in securing an agency to sell the new car, or asked about buying stock in the new company.[7]

In this context of unsubstantiated rumor and public excitement, Ford Motor Company stockholders became frantic. If Henry Ford deserted his own company, would it remain a viable, profit-making entity at anything near its present scale? As Liebold wrote to a friend, "Mr. Ford's recent announcement has created quite a stir in this community; in fact I do not believe any of the stockholders are at all pleased over it." Some reacted angrily. The Dodge brothers issued a statement through their attorney, Elliot G. Stevenson. "There would be no attempt to keep either Mr. Ford or his son in the firm if they simply wished to retire, but Henry Ford is under contract to the Ford Motor Co. and he will not be allowed to leave the firm and start a competitive business," the statement said in part. "Both Mr. Ford's genius and his name are under contract to the present company, and certainly the organization will not allow him to withdraw these without legal protest."[8]

But more was going on than met the eye. Henry Ford was engaged in a sleight of hand. Far from abandoning his company, he was moving secretly and skillfully to gain complete control of it. The evidence suggests that he had floated the rumor about forming a rival manufacturer to create a situation of uncertainty, even foreboding, regarding the future prospects of his company. Ford's overall goal was clear—to frighten the minority stockholders about the future value of their holdings, thus making them amenable to a purchase offer. And the identity of the purchaser would soon become clear.

Two factors motivated Ford. He had been furious at the decision in the Dodge brothers' lawsuit, which forced him to pay millions of dollars in dividends rather than reinvest it in the company, and he vowed never again to be held hostage by stockholders who valued short-term profits over the long-term vitality of the company. He was also bent on expanding the company's productive capacity. Ford believed that the economies of scale he had achieved at Highland Park marked only the first step of what could be realized. He was determined to plot the future direction of his enterprise with a new, even more efficient factory.

From this determination had emerged a plan to force out minority shareholders. Other than Ford and his son, Edsel, the other key player in the plan was William B. Mayo, the chief power engineer and the designer of the new plant taking shape on the River Rouge. There is conflicting testimony as to who originally hatched the idea, Ford or Mayo, but, regardless of the source, Ford emphatically endorsed it and deputized Mayo, who contacted acquaintances at the Old Colony Trust Company and negotiated a loan to purchase the minority stock. F. M. Holmes, an Old Colony vice president, emerged as a key figure, along with Stuart W. Webb of the Bond & Goodwin investment house. This pair of experienced financiers worked behind the scenes, contacting the minority stockholders to purchase their stock without disclosing the identity of the real buyer. The stockholders believed Henry Ford's public denials of any interest in their holdings, and they speculated, according to attorney John W. Anderson, that "the potential principal [buyer] was J. P. Morgan [Company] or W. C. Durant [of General Motors]."[9]

While this situation was developing privately, publicly Ford played a game of deception. "He disclaims any desire to buy up that portion of its stock which he does not now own," *Automobile Topics* reported in March. At the same time, Edsel Ford was playing a careful game of stalling and reassurance with regard to company functionaries around the country. Though he did not deny the plans for a new company, he sought to reassure employees that massive changes were not coming immediately. Two weeks after Henry's announcement, Edsel sent a letter to Ford dealers stating: "A large majority of the rumors afloat are distorted. A new car may be manufactured, but as to when it will be manufactured we are not in a position to say, except that we know a new car could not possibly be designed, tested out, manufactured, and marketed in quantity [in] under two or three years."[10]

Meanwhile, the purchase of minority stock was proceeding steadily. Stuart Webb had contacted stockholders such as John W. Anderson and Horace H. Rackham, who knew only that Webb represented the Old Colony Trust. Negotiations proceeded throughout the summer, and it was only late in the process, according to Anderson, that "I had any inkling of who the purchaser of that stock was going to be." By late July, all minority stockholders had been bought out, including the Dodge brothers. Around eighty-three hundred shares were purchased for $12,500 a share, except that James Couzens was paid $13,000 because of his extraordinary contributions to the company. Henry Ford had stayed conspicuously on the sidelines throughout this process. "What interested me was the way I was left alone," Webb reported later. "I was amazed how Mr. Ford could keep his hands off details." When the deal was finally closed, however, the negotiators met with Ford to give him the news, at which time, according to one eyewitness, "he danced a jig all around the room."[11]

At last the truth emerged. On July 17, it was announced that Ford had bought out minority interests as part of a larger "reorganization plan" for the company. A news release detailed the purchase and noted, "Mr. Henry Ford, though owning the controlling interest, took no part in the negotiations, but consented to and approved the purchase." News stories reported that the Fords had received a $75 million loan to help cover the acquisition of the minority stock. The Chase Securities Corporation of New York, the Old Colony Trust Company, and Bond & Goodwin advanced this credit.[12]

Thus Ford gained total control of the company. As a headline in *Motor Age* put it, "Purchase Paves Way for New Ford Era." The success of the maneuver had freed Ford to conduct the affairs of his company according to his own lights, free of interference from the likes of John and Horace Dodge. Any talk of Ford's starting a new automobile enterprise vanished. As a public statement from the company noted, "Of course there will be no need of a new company now. We will develop our plans for a new car in the Highland Park plant." In fact, however, Henry Ford's vision had already begun to extend beyond the confines of that facility. He had set his sights some miles to the southwest, to a spot not far from his home, near Dearborn. There he planned to build a car factory like none ever before seen.[13]

In the spring and summer of 1915, Fred Gregory, a real-estate agent, and four associates quietly began to purchase tracts of land in a remote area southwest of Dearborn. Located near the Rouge River, this district contained dozens of small farms, patches of forest, and abundant pastureland on its flat landscape. By the time they were finished, the Gregory group had bought some two thousand acres, but their purpose remained secret. What only a few insiders knew was that Gregory was Henry Ford's representative.

The reason for the secrecy gradually came to light—Ford planned to build on this acreage the largest industrial complex in the world.[14]

By the end of June, the plan had gone public, at least in part. The ostensible rationale for the new facility, according to Ford's announcement, was the production of tractors, a project in which he had become much interested. According to stories appearing in the Detroit *Journal* and *Automobile Topics*, he wanted to build a large factory that would eventually produce a million tractors a year. Moreover, the facility would include a blast furnace that would allow "Henry Ford to bring iron ore in boats . . . and turn the ore into motor cylinder heads and other auto and tractor parts without having either ore or iron pass through the hands of the middleman."[15]

In fact, however, the blast furnaces and the tractor plant were but the first step in a much larger undertaking. Ford planned the creation of a massive manufacturing complex to replace Highland Park and produce automobiles on a scale that far surpassed anything in existence. Even more important, his blueprint called for a vast extension of the manufacturing process in order to construct an entire vehicle, from raw materials to finished product. The complex would include not only an assembly plant, but a port and a shipyard, a huge series of storage bins, a steelmaking operation, a foundry, a body-making plant, a sawmill, a rubber-processing facility, a cement plant, and a power plant. Thus the goal of River Rouge was not just a matter of sheer size but complete control of production, from the time iron ore came out of the ground until a Model T rolled off the assembly line.

The Rouge plant was Henry Ford's idea from the beginning, and two factors prompted his launching of the project. First, he became convinced that the company had maximized its productive capacities at Highland Park. Second, he believed that his company needed greater control over its supply of raw materials and parts. Having had several bad experiences with suppliers who withheld materials, Ford, according to one associate, did not wish to be "dependent to the point where he could be pinched . . . [and] having his whole set-up stymied." But at a deeper level, he sought to be placed beyond the reach of financiers who could interfere with, or even buy out, his company. "I would tear down the plant brick by brick and scrape off the mortar before I would let this business get into the hands of capitalists," he told a journalist who inquired about his new Rouge project and rumors that the Ford Company might be purchased. The best way to keep control of his company was to extend its reach to the very earliest stages of production.[16]

A site for the new complex had been the subject of a great debate at the highest levels of the organization. Most of Ford's top managers had favored a site on the Detroit River. But Ford was determined to build the plant at the River Rouge location, and his choice proved to be the wisest and most farsighted one. Though a manufacturing complex on the Detroit River would have made for easy water access, the Rouge site was convenient to a nearby web of railroads. Moreover, it contained hundreds of acres of flat-land, which would make an expansion of the facility feasible. As one of the managers explained later, a Detroit River location would have created a hub with only half a wheel. Constructing near the River Rouge placed the fac-tory "in the center of the wheel and you can go in all directions from that."[17]

When the decision about the location was finally made public, employ-ees were shocked that the factory was being built in the middle of nowhere. "Everybody was getting a map to find out where the Rouge was," recalled one Ford veteran many years later. "They weren't familiar with it, when they . . . found out where it was, they said, 'My God! They've got us out in the country in Highland Park, but look where we're going at the Rouge!' " Even though the location was remote, the company realized that announce-ment of the new factory would likely bring in real-estate speculators and drive up land prices. To forestall this impact, it downplayed the size of the factory, publicly stating that only five hundred workers would be hired.[18]

Development at the Rouge started during World War I, when, because they had to produce Eagle boats, the company constructed a large assembly building and did dredging work to widen and deepen the river. After the war ended, the assembly structure was reconfigured for auto-and-tractor pro-duction. By late 1918, some thirty-five hundred men were steadily building blast furnaces, coke ovens, and a foundry. Streets were laid, and railroad lines extended into the complex. In 1919, the foundation for a power plant was laid. The dredging of a "turning basin" and the creation of a slip a third of a mile in length allowed large ships to load and unload. In addition, con-crete storage bins for limestone, coal, and iron ore were erected near the factory docks.[19]

As construction of the Rouge progressed, one man proved crucial to the enterprise. William B. Mayo, who emerged as Ford's chief design engineer, played a key role in shaping nearly every dimension of this undertaking. Mayo had been vice president of Hooven-Owens-Rentschler, a company that made steam-gas power generators, when he met Henry Ford, to whom he sold several generators for the Highland Park plant. Ford was so impressed with Mayo that he hired him to serve as his company's chief power engineer. Mayo had helped Ford secure loans to buy out the minor-ity stockholders, and now he assumed responsibility for planning much of the Rouge complex. Ford and Mayo established a close working relationship and collaborated in supervising the wide variety of construction projects at the Rouge. Mayo had about 250 men working under him, who dealt with architectural engineering, mechanical engineering, powerhouse design, and general construction.[20]

By 1920, the multifaceted production envisioned by Ford was beginning to occur at the Rouge. The coke plant was operating; the sawmill was functioning; the foundry was turning out parts; some twenty-four miles of railroad track had been put in place; railroad cars and river barges were delivering iron ore and coal to storage bins; a plant was producing eight hundred sedan and touring-car bodies a day; and thousands of tractors were coming off the assembly line in the large B Building. In the spring, the first blast furnace at the Rouge was completed. As a large crowd of company managers and workers gathered, along with reporters and members of the family, Henry Ford approached the furnace carrying his grandson, Henry II. Leaning over a pile of kindling and coke, the older man helped the boy set fire to it. "The fun of playing with matches was almost too much for Henry II, who is only three years old, and he had some difficulty, but with his grandfather's aid the blaze was started and then he sat perched on his grandfather's shoulder while everyone cheered," reported the Detroit News.[21]

As the River Rouge complex came to life, Henry Ford's central role in its creation became apparent. He envisioned making ten thousand cars a day at the Rouge by controlling the production process from beginning to end. This notion, dubbed "vertical integration" by the experts, became a hallmark of American industrial development. Whereas horizontal integration meant taking over the competition in a given area of production and sales, vertical integration extended a company's reach both backward, toward the sources of production, and forward, toward the consumer. As Ford was overheard telling one of his managers when the Rouge was nearing completion, he "wanted the raw materials coming in on one end of the Rouge plant and the finished cars going out the other end."[22]

Ford's determination to sell an inexpensive car had forced the cost of production downward and inspired efficiency on all fronts. "The greatest development of all, however, is the River Rouge plant, which, when it is running to its full capacity, will cut deeply and in many directions into the price of everything we make," Ford contended. The various productive activities connected to this complex—the waterway for shipping, the mining and transporting of coal, the railway system, the coke ovens and blast furnaces for steelmaking, the sawmill and concrete plant, the use of waste products to fire the power plant, the body plant, the assembling plant—

promised huge cost savings, because "we save in so many directions—in transportation, in the generation of our power, in the generation of gas, in the expense in casting."[23]

Because of his commitment to vertical integration, Ford took a personal interest in the construction of the new factory that would embody it. In 1916, he sat for hours in Charles Sorensen's office and discussed the plats of the Rouge development that were hanging on the walls. He intervened to insist upon a uniformity of design that would encourage an efficient flow as the product moved through the successive stages of production. He became upset at the prospect of moving materials up and down through various structures. He asked, "Now why do all this building of three stories here, four stories here, two stories here, five over here, all these ups and downs? Why not build the building by putting the columns four rods apart, four rods square? We'll build an acre to a bay and make the columns four rods high." This became the standardized plan for the construction of the main buildings. Ford once strolled into the compression room of a new coke oven and examined a huge wall, just completed, that stood about thirty-five feet high and ran some two hundred feet long. After looking at it from several angles, he said, "That wall is off." The engineer first denied the accusation, then admitted that the wall was a half-inch out of line. "Take it down," Ford ordered, and walked away. Although it was expensive in the short run, news of this decision reverberated throughout the construction crews and made for a renewed emphasis on quality in building the factory.[24]

Ultimately, the Rouge embodied Ford's commitment to the growth of a modern consumer society. Increasing the scale of production not only provided more jobs for workers but became a vehicle for getting more consumer goods to the masses. In a 1916 *Ford Times*, Ford outlined his vision of the Rouge and how bigness could be used to spread material benefits more widely. "My ambition is to employ still more men; to spread the benefits of this industrial system to the greatest possible number, to help them build up their lives and their homes," he wrote.[25]

By 1920, Ford's vision of the Rouge was coming to life. A 1922 article in *Industrial Management* accurately captured the rhythm and flow of this gigantic factory complex:

> Ore from the Ford mines hauled on Ford's railroad is converted into pig iron at the Ford blast furnace and made into castings at the Ford foundry. Coke for foundry and blast furnace use is produced at the Ford coking ovens. Gas for steam-electric power production, ammonia, distillates, tar, and illuminating gas are produced at the Ford by-product house and gas house. All of these

units in the industrial chain are geared up as one huge and complete machine at River Rouge.[26]

Perhaps the most searching analysis of the Rouge and its significance for modern American life came in the New York *Times* in 1925. Evans Clark, in a long article entitled "The Super-Trust Arrives in America," examined several large industries and concluded that the Ford Motor Company "is probably the most completely integrated industry in the country if not the world. . . . Now almost the entire Ford car except the tires is produced—from the basic raw materials to the finished raw product—under a single management and control." Integration was completely realized in the Rouge, which stood as "one vast interlocking self-improvement organization" where increased efficiency in one area reverberated throughout the process. "Undreamed of standardization becomes possible" at this huge plant, the author contended.

Clark also reported that Rouge-style integration was promoting the good life in the United States through "lower prices, more prosperity all around, and the progressive elimination of the extremes of the business cycle." In other words, the Rouge was spreading ever wider the material abundance of consumer society. Such an achievement suggested a reworking of traditional beliefs, Clark concluded. After examining the Rouge, the reasonable person must consider that "big business may not be an unmitigated evil."[27]

As Ford's new factory began running nearly full-speed, one man rose to the forefront of the operation. A high-level manager since the early days of the Model T and utterly devoted to Henry Ford, this ruthless, ambitious, and highly intelligent executive saw in the building of the Rouge an opportunity for enhancing his own position and authority. His ascendancy signaled not only a personal triumph, but an important shift in the center of power within the Ford Motor Company.

In 1919, Charles Sorensen and his staff moved their operation to the new River Rouge plant. A longtime production manager at Highland Park, he had been directing the tractor division at the new facility and became involved in planning the larger parameters of the complex. Sorensen and his assistants needed offices, and the only suitable space was in the "Wash and Locker Building," which was already occupied by engineers and draftsmen. Sorensen surveyed the situation and made a quick decision to take over the building. According to an eyewitness, "They moved in and took the two floors over. They then threw the draftsmen out. I remember the trucks driving up outside, and they opened the windows and poured the drawings right out of the windows and into the trucks. The draftsmen moved somewhere else."[28]

The clear goal, brutal tactics, and force of will were vintage Sorensen. These qualities made him the prototype of the new Ford functionary. By the early 1920s, Sorensen had schemed and bullied his way to the top of the company as head of production and de facto plant manager at the Rouge facility. He left behind a wake of bruised egos and ruined careers. Utterly devoted to indulging every whim of Henry Ford, he saw himself as an agent for bringing his patron's vision to realization. And, as he understood better than anyone else in the company, this role provided the best tactic for advancing his own career. Sorensen's brilliant achievements and personal power at Ford's new factory were undeniable. Yet his strengths and weaknesses told a larger story. His success revealed much about the nature of the Ford Motor Company—both its productive potential and its fault lines—as it re-created itself as an industrial behemoth on the Rouge.

Sorensen had first joined the company in 1905 as a pattern-maker. Born in Copenhagen in 1881, he had emigrated with his parents and grown up in Buffalo, Milwaukee, and Detroit. After being employed in young manhood by several foundry companies, Sorensen was in 1902 introduced to Henry Ford by Tom Cooper, Ford's old bicycle-racing associate. Over the next couple of years, he did some work for the new Ford Motor Company, and its owner finally offered him a position at a salary of $3.00 per day. Over the next few years, Sorensen climbed upward through the ranks, becoming head of the pattern department and then assistant production manager under P. E. Martin. He played an important part in developing the Model T, especially in terms of the innovative casting of a one-piece engine block, and then worked with Clarence W. Avery on establishing the assembly line at Highland Park. By 1915, Sorensen wielded great power in the company. During World War I, he organized the production of tractors, first in England for the Allies and then back in Dearborn at Ford's new factory.[29]

Sorensen made a powerful physical impression. A tall, ruggedly handsome man with light hair and chiseled features, he strode about with a determined, even stern look on his face. He had a strong personality and exuded confidence. And as everyone knew among the Ford workforce, he was given to explosive outbursts of temper. Sorensen was fond of the outdoor life, especially boating. Perhaps reflecting a Scandinavian love of the sea, he spent many summer weekends sailing the Great Lakes; by the 1930s, growing prosperity allowed him to pass several weeks each winter cruising off the Florida coast, fishing for marlin. Closer to home, Sorensen purchased several hundred acres near Detroit and engaged in hobby farming by raising herds of cattle, sheep, and hogs. At the same time, he enjoyed a tranquil personal life, marrying Helen E. Mitchell, a bookkeeper for the Sun Stove Company in Detroit, in 1904, and becoming father to one son, Clifford.[30]

By the late 1910s, Sorensen's talents as a production manager had fully flowered. At Highland Park, he had overseen a host of important innovations: the revolutionary technique of the moving assembly line, the plant layout for its implementation, new machines for multiple drilling, and the purchase of a pressed-steel plant. Sorensen also became an expert at skillfully calculating production estimates and costs for the Model T. In terms of the actual functioning of the factory, he gained a reputation for demanding efficiency, workmanship, and effort. He was impatient with those who said "It can't be done," but encouraging to those who bent to solving problems and developing new techniques. "Charlie always put up with a lot of mistakes from a guy who really tried," noted one associate. To this spirit of innovation and dedication, Sorensen added a penchant for sheer hard work. In his memoirs, he described practically living at the plant: "My day would start there as early as seven o'clock; luncheon was at Dearborn. I would then be back in the plant until about three o'clock, when I would go into production planning or tool design. At 5:30 I would return to my office for another hour. Several nights in the week I would come back after dinner at home for more office work." As one associate recounted, of all the Ford managers he encountered over a long career with the company, Sorensen was "the man who made the deepest impression on me—the most brilliant man I have ever known with the ability to render the right decisions on the instant."[31]

But *how* Sorensen achieved results at the Ford Motor Company became as important as *what* he sought to do. He was, in the words of one of his associates, a "rough customer" who did not shrink from intimidation, physical confrontation, even violence in the interest of achieving his goals. According to Ernest G. Liebold, "Sorensen used to get things done, but he used to drive hell out of a man to get it done." In later years, Sorensen claimed that this reputation resulted from tall stories blown out of proportion. "The truth is that during my thirty-nine years with Ford Motor Company," he wrote, "I never laid hands upon a soul, no one ever laid a hand on me, and I never smashed a desk in my life." But many witnesses and a string of incidents testified otherwise.[32]

Charles Voorhess, a power engineer who worked on several projects with Sorensen over the years, saw him in action numerous times. Voorhess described Sorensen as speaking sharply to subordinates and being "a very poor listener." According to Voorhess, one afternoon when Sorensen became annoyed with certain office personnel in the tractor division, he and his lieutenants "went into their offices and pulled the drawers out and threw the materials on the floor." Mead Bricker, a production supervisor who worked closely with Sorensen for many years, provided an even clearer picture of his boss's tyrannical tactics:

> Sorensen would go out and upset a department, turn a bench or a desk over, and it was my job, or somebody else's job, to go out and straighten that all out again. When you'd go back the place was all demoralized and everybody wanted to quit.... I have seen Sorensen grab a hold of people, but he would never kick anybody. Several times I saved him from being beaten up by these same people. He was very disliked all through the plant.

Sorensen was feared by all and grudgingly respected by many. By the time the new Ford plant began to go up along the River Rouge, he had moved into a strong position for gathering even more power.[33]

In fact, Sorensen played a prominent role in planning and building Ford's new factory. In July 1915, he had attended a meeting on Miller Road, near the River Rouge, along with Henry Ford, Ed Martin, John Lee, and Fred Gregory. Sorensen agreed with Ford's assessment of the potential of this site. Over the next couple of years, Sorensen and Ford frequently discussed the need to build blast furnaces and a foundry at the Rouge because of the increasing difficulty of securing adequate materials. With typical prescience, Sorensen's analysis of production and supply problems helped lay the groundwork for Ford's decision to adopt vertical integration: "The bigger [Ford Motor Company's] production got the harder it became to find suppliers who could keep pace. And when a supplier couldn't keep up with our needs for parts or materials, the alternatives were either to cut production or shut down until supplies caught up, or make the things ourselves." Sorensen's conclusion cut to the heart of the matter: "If others would not provide enough steel for our needs, then we would. It was just as simple as that."[34]

As development proceeded at the Rouge, Sorensen dived into one of its most important projects: purchasing and reviving the decrepit Detroit, Toledo & Ironton Railroad. By the late 1910s, shipping delays caused by overtaxed, run-down railroads had become a vexing problem. With the Rouge project, Ford and Sorensen were determined to solve this difficulty. When the DT&I, which ran southward into Ohio, came to Ford and asked for financing to repair several old railroad bridges, Sorensen sensed an opportunity. "Here's a chance to pick up a railroad that will break our freight shipment bottleneck," he told Ford. "This road on its route south cuts across every main line going east and west north of the Ohio River. If we can buy it, we can run it into the Rouge plant and handle all our outgoing and incoming materials." Ford endorsed Sorensen's idea, bought the railroad, and modernized its operations. Bringing its line directly into the Rouge broke the shipping bottleneck, speeded up distribution, helped reduce the company's inventory en route by more than half, and allowed for coal, limestone, and iron ore to be transported directly from mines to the Rouge. Subsequent savings paid the railroad's purchase price several times over.[35]

Ultimately, however, for Sorensen the new Rouge plant provided an opportunity to realize personal ambition. He stood at the center of a striking aspect of the company's shift from Highland Park to the new complex: the exodus of prominent executives from about 1919 to 1921. "The business world is astonished by the procession of Ford executives moving out of the front door for the last time," noted *Detroit Saturday Night*. " 'Watch the Ford officials go by,' is the latest advertising joke." As Sorensen exclaimed with typical bluntness, "We are getting rid of all the Model T sons-of-a-bitches."[36]

The purge at the Rouge plant was partly Henry Ford's doing. By 1919, as he bought out minority stockholders to gain absolute ownership of the company, he also sought to consolidate his power within it. James Couzens had resigned in 1915, of course, and now a long line of old associates and lieutenants began to leave. C. H. Wills, John R. Lee, Norval Hawkins, Samuel S. Marquis, and production manager William Knudsen would depart by 1921, as would many less prominent but experienced and influential figures such as company treasurer Frank L. Klingensmith, chief auditor Louis H. Turrell, and head of advertising Charles A. Brownell; Hubert E. Hartman, general attorney; and Warren C. Anderson, the company's European representative. The old Highland Park group gave way to a new set of Rouge managers who were devoted completely to Ford. Sorensen, by helping purge top managers to satisfy his boss, methodically eliminated his own rivals in the company.

As operations geared up at the Rouge, Sorensen undermined company managers whose authority had been rooted at Highland Park. He engaged in a power struggle with Wills, Ford's longtime chief engineer, and helped drive him out. He rationalized this move as a defense of Henry Ford. "I found that one problem in getting things the way Ford wanted was Wills, who at times was extremely critical of his boss and his ideas," Sorensen wrote. "Instead of giving him what he asked for, [Wills] frequently tried to mold the Ford idea to his."[37]

Sorensen also clashed with Knudsen, a production manager at Highland Park who had directed the construction of fourteen Ford assembly
plants around the United States, helped oversee the making of Model T's at
Highland Park, and supervised the company's building of Eagle antisubma-
rine boats during World War I. In 1919, Sorensen and Knudsen disputed
division of responsibilities at the Rouge and nearly came to blows. Ford
backed Sorensen, and Knudsen left in 1921. Around the same time,
Sorensen countermanded the directives of Samuel S. Marquis and drove
him from the sociological department. Sorensen tried to ensure that trusted
Ford associates such as William B. Mayo did not solidify their power.
According to one of Mayo's assistants, Sorensen "planted his underlings . . . to needle Mr. Mayo," and as a result, Mayo gravitated toward
Edsel Ford, for whom he became chief consultant throughout the 1920s.[38]

The biggest potential for strife, however, lay with Sorensen and P. E.
Martin, the production chief at Highland Park. Martin had begun working
for Ford Motor Company in 1903 and rose to become head of the assembly
department at the Piquette Avenue plant by 1906. He helped launch production of the Model T at this factory, and then worked on implementing
the assembly line at the Highland Park facility. By 1913, Martin had been
appointed superintendent of production and Sorensen served as his assistant. When Sorensen left Highland Park to manage production in the new
tractor division, both men's authority rose in their separate spheres. The
two of them were hard-driving, demanding men—Martin was quietly stern,
however, compared with Sorensen's more volcanic style—so by the time the
Rouge opened there was great potential for conflict.[39]

Martin and Sorensen each believed he had earned the right to supervise
production at the new facility, and both attempted to do so. Confusion and
tension prevailed, for, in the words of one Ford manager, "nobody could
ever understand the dividing line of authority between Sorensen and Martin." But as time went on, Sorensen, the more ruthless of the two, gained
the upper hand. "Charlie was rather aggressive and he just butted in anywhere that he could and took whatever he could," noted Frank Hadas, a
production assistant at the Rouge. Eventually, the pair reached an accommodation. Martin, who shunned the limelight and was not power-hungry,
gradually deferred to his former assistant. Sorensen assumed responsibility
for the large-scale decisions and policy-making for the company as a whole,
while Martin focused on the day-to-day management of production.[40]

The purges at the Rouge, however, went beyond Sorensen's confrontations with a few highly placed managers. As entire departments were down-
sized or revamped in the shift to the new factory, an atmosphere of unease
pervaded the organization. "There was a great deal of apprehension because

virtually every day or every few days, purges were going on," stated L. E. Briggs, the new company treasurer. "Departments were being eliminated overnight." As old Ford hand W. C. Klann put it, "There was a very uncertain feeling about what was going on." Edwin G. Pipp noted sarcastically that, to escape this power struggle, "I have gone for relief to the wholesome atmosphere of the foundry, the blast furnace, the heat treatment, the machine rooms, the assembly room."[41]

Much of this fear could be traced to Sorensen's tactics in becoming master of the Rouge. He saw a desk he believed extraneous and ordered it thrown out; he saw file drawers locked and broke them open; he saw supervisors who were sitting and jerked the chairs from beneath them; he spotted men standing idle and issued an order: "Go fire those guys." As he explained to a subordinate, "I figure it this way; I probably don't get out into the yard more than once a month, or once every two months, and when I do come there, I don't want to find a bunch of men standing around doing nothing."[42]

He demanded order and efficiency at the Rouge. Once, when a workman could not find a certain screw from his cluttered workbox after searching for fifteen minutes, Sorensen and his assistant went through the whole area breaking open toolboxes and dumping their contents on the floor. On occasion, his tactics turned from intimidating to vicious. He created a special "service department" consisting of handpicked agents who enforced work discipline among the laborers and intimidated Sorensen's rivals. He approved their use of unsavory tactics—liquor, bribery, and women—to entrap and dismiss those who opposed his climb to prominence.[43]

Sorensen's tyrannical style also extended to his allies and underlings. Harry B. Hanson, a talented layout engineer who became chief of planning for the new Rouge plant, served Sorensen for many years as a loyal assistant. He praised his boss's energy and initiative and worked hard to implement Sorensen's plans. Nonetheless, Sorensen often abused him. Sorensen "was quite rough with me in conversations and he'd bawl me out in front of people whether I deserved it or not," Hanson recalled. The subordinate shrugged off the tirades as products of his boss's hot temper. "I knew that was the method of his training," he said. "I guess it was to show me how to be tough." Hanson endured the abuse because of respect for Sorensen's high standard of production and loathing of poor workmanship and poor effort.[44]

By the early 1920s, Sorensen had emerged triumphant at the Rouge. He appeared "like a king on a throne telling us what to do," in the words of one Ford operative. His power, however, was based on more than his prodigious talent or ferocious force of will. Ultimately, it lay in his relationship with Henry Ford. Perhaps more than any other individual in the company, Sorensen understood the proclivities and principles that governed Ford's direction of his enterprise. It was an understanding that he carefully culti-vated for many years.[45]

Sorensen's personal relationship with Henry Ford dated to his earliest days at the company. The two families lived fairly close to each other, and they began to get together, the wives socializing while the husbands took test drives in the new Model T. At this time Ford still resided in Detroit, but he had a modest country house in Dearborn. He would take Clara and Edsel there for weekends, and soon Sorensen, his wife, and young son began visit-ing on Sundays. "We brought our own lunches and sat on the lawn and 'vis-ited,' " Sorensen recounted many years later. "And when Henry Ford and I talked shop, Mrs. Ford would perk up and direct a little friendly sarcasm at us for our seriousness." When Ford built a new estate in Dearborn in 1913, he urged Sorensen to construct a home nearby. So Sorensen purchased a tract of land along the same river, about one mile north of his boss—the tract had once belonged to one of Ford's uncles—and built a white Colonial-style house. "After my wife and I got settled in our new home, Henry and Edsel Ford would ride over on horseback to call," Sorensen related.[46]

Confirmation of their friendship came when Ford played one of his practical jokes on Sorensen. In the mid-1910s, as the pair was conducting an inspection trip of Ford industrial properties, Sorensen received a telegram saying that the tractor plant in Dearborn, of which he was now the supervi-sor, was on fire and about to burn to the ground. "I was wild. I wanted the train stopped so that I might hire a car and drive to the disaster," Sorensen recalled later. After thrashing about and yelling for action, he was chagrined to hear from the laughing train official that Ford had paid him to send a fake telegram. Ford's regard also revealed itself in the bestowal of a nickname. Sorensen's dedication to using cast metal instead of forgings won from his boss the sobriquet that would last throughout his life, Cast-Iron Charlie. Sorensen described his association with Ford in his memoir: "We had a business relationship closer than even his family had with him, and in many ways I knew him better than did members of his family."[47]

Throughout their years of working together, Sorensen spent much time trying to grasp what made his boss tick. He realized that the task required not reasoned analysis but gut instinct and feeling. "It was useless to try to understand Henry Ford. One had to *sense* him," he explained. The ambi-tious Sorensen realized that Ford did not want a tight structure for his com-pany but preferred a more informal system, where competition and achievement meant more than job titles. Sorensen reduced this to a dictum: "Constant ferment—keeping things stirred up and other people guessing—

was Ford's working formula for progress." Other astute observers confirmed Sorensen's insight. As one of them put it, "It looked to me that Mr.
Ford was sitting back there and letting it be the survival of the fittest."[48]

Sorensen learned additional lessons that served him well on his drive to
power. He appreciated something that other Ford lieutenants, such as
Wills, Couzens, Marquis, and Hawkins, ignored. Henry Ford would not
abide any rivals in gaining public attention. He "didn't want his staff to be in
the public eye. No one else in the organization could stand out above him,"
Sorensen pointed out. Those who did so aroused Ford's jealousy, and one by
one they fell into disfavor and were eliminated. "My ability to keep out of
the public eye was one reason why I stayed as long as I did at Ford while
others left," Sorensen wrote.[49]

He also understood that working mightily to fulfill Ford's vision, rather
than modifying it with his own views or desires, marked the truest path to
advancement. From his first days at the old Piquette Avenue plant, Sorensen
was able to intuit what his inarticulate boss wanted. "I could sense Henry
Ford's ideas and develop them. I didn't try to change them," said Sorensen.
"Mr. Ford never caught me saying that an idea he had couldn't be done." By
the time the new factory was built, according to one observer, Sorensen had
distilled his job into "trying to build up the Rouge the way Mr. Ford wanted
it to be built up." Rivals felt that Sorensen's extreme solicitousness toward
Ford made him a mere toady for the owner. "That's why he got along with
Mr. Ford for so many years," Joseph Galamb once commented. "He did
everything Mr. Ford wanted. He wouldn't stand up for his own ideas." But
Sorensen shrugged off such criticism: "I pinned my flag on Henry Ford
and . . . am proud to have had the label 'Henry Ford's man.' "[50]

Sorensen made a study of his boss's quirks. After noticing early that
Ford did not read blueprints easily, he made tangible models when seeking
approval for future projects. His pattern-making experience proved useful
for constructing wooden models of automobile parts, such as the Model T's
planetary transmission, for Ford to examine. By the time of the Rouge construction, Sorensen had refined this technique to the point of making and
displaying a scale model of the entire factory near his office. "I set aside a
separate room with large tables on which the Rouge site was laid out to
scale . . . [that showed] what each building would look like," he related. "I
showed the ship canal, docks, and blast furnaces on a scale of one-eighth of
an inch with roads, railroads, highways, bus lines, and streetcars all fitted in
to the model." Ford loved it.[51]

He repaid Sorensen's solicitous attitude with much trust and respect.
Their friendship seemed genuine, and as the years went on, Ford increasingly depended upon Sorensen's management decisions. Ford liked to oper-

ate behind the scenes, but when forced into the open, he relied upon a stock phrase: "You heard what Mr. Sorensen said." In *My Life and Work,* Ford made no mention of men who had helped him build his company such as Wills or Couzens. Only one lieutenant was cited: Charles E. Sorensen.[52]

Ford appreciated Sorensen's vigorous nature and demanding style. In a 1921 telegram, he jokingly advised his subordinate, "Take it easy and do not throw too many things around." He once remarked to Joseph Galamb, "Joe, we have to have a man like Sorensen in a big organization like this, to raise the dickens once in a while." But even with this favored lieutenant, Ford played his usual game of competitive tension by deliberately setting P. E. Martin against him. Ford would occasionally warm up to Martin, and that "would irritate Sorensen and get him on the job," related Mead Bricker. "It was a balance that kept going up and down on either side." Fred Black detected the same strategy, describing how Ford "would give one of the men a job to do and at a later date he would give the other a job along the same lines. . . . This is the way Mr. Ford pitted Martin against Sorensen." The important point, however, was that Sorensen grasped the game, and, rather than grousing or resisting, he played it with consummate skill.[53]

One of the least appreciated aspects of Sorensen's relationship with Ford had little to do with issues of production. Sorensen understood his boss's central insight: the overwhelming importance of the new consumer economy in modern America. He knew that Ford had delivered the crucial message that "the wage earner is as important as a consumer as he is as a producer; and that enlarged buying power by paying high wages and selling at low prices is behind the prosperity of this country." Wholeheartedly endorsing Ford's effort to spread material goods among ordinary citizens, Sorensen argued that the Ford Motor Company "was destined . . . to demonstrate the superiority of an economy of abundance over one of scarcity, and to begin the elevation of a standard of living to a height never before dreamed of." In later years, Sorensen even went so far as to favor a guaranteed annual income for all American workers, arguing that it repre-sented "recognition of Henry Ford's principle that the producer is also the consumer."[54]

The strengths and weaknesses of Charles Sorensen mirrored those of the mature Ford Motor Company. As an extension of Henry Ford's domi-nance after the buyout of the minority stockholders, the managerial master of the Rouge embodied the commitment to large-scale production that brought abundance within the reach of millions of Americans. With great flair and determination, Sorensen helped bring to life Ford's dream of democratizing consumption. At the same time, however, his absolute sub-servience to the owner's desires reflected the uncomfortably dictatorial quality of Ford's management style. By the early 1920s, the Ford Motor Company was almost completely the expression of one man's views and values. Sorensen didn't care. "Sorensen would always tell me that Mr. Ford was the boss and he knows what he wants," Harry Hanson related.[55]

Most Americans probably would have agreed with Sorensen's attitude. As Henry Ford's vision of a massive, vertically integrated production facility came to life on the River Rouge, his fame and influence were unsurpassed in American life. He held absolute control over the largest manufacturing enterprise in the world. He was incredibly wealthy yet remained to ordinary citizens a hero whose every public utterance was a source of fascination. With an image that simply towered over that of his contemporaries, Ford truly became the people's tycoon.

Yet what of the private person behind the public persona? By the time the blast furnaces were bellowing and the smokestacks pouring at the Rouge, Americans were hankering, as never before, for glimpses of Ford's life and activities. But the man's private life was bound to disappoint. His quiet, unpretentious existence appeared determinedly, even eccentrically, old-fashioned.

Fifteen

Moralist

By the early 1920s, the first biographies of Henry Ford began to appear. They focused on his public life and industrial innovations, sketching out the notable achievements in automobile production that had made the Model T an icon of modern American life. Books such as *Henry Ford's Own Story* (1917) by Rose Wilder Lane, *The Truth About Henry Ford* (1922) by Sarah T. Bushnell, *Henry Ford: The Man and His Motives* (1923) by the Reverend William R. Stidger, and *Henry Ford: An Interpretation* (1922) by the Reverend Samuel S. Marquis told the compelling story of his career. They piqued the attention of tens of thousands of readers throughout the United States.

But these books also delved into another area that intrigued Americans—the personal life of the industrialist. Sarah Bushnell, for example, informed readers that Ford's "home surroundings were such a factor in keeping his hopes high and his determination unshaken." Other biographers followed a similar tack. They depicted the great innovator in modern American life, the architect of the assembly line, and the prophet of consumption as a decidedly old-fashioned gentleman at home.[1]

This picture was accurate: Ford's domestic life could have been glimpsed in any middle-class home several decades earlier. He and his family presented a picture of stability and harmony shaped by the Victorian ethic of nineteenth-century America. In the best tradition of the Christian gentleman, he affirmed a personal code of self-control and hard work. According to the venerable tradition of domesticity, he viewed his wife as a paragon of rectitude and depended upon her to manage their home life. A genteel social atmosphere prevailed in the Ford household, which influenced his marriage, his relations with his son, and the general atmosphere of his private life. Edwin G. Pipp and Samuel Marquis, otherwise critics of Ford as a public figure, agreed that his personal life was beyond reproach.

Marquis stressed that Ford cherished "the quiet and seclusion of his home and family" and described his "moral qualities" as "some of the highest and noblest I have ever known grouped in any one man." Pipp portrayed Ford as "one of the cleanest minded men I have ever known," adding, "I don't believe America or the world has a man whose personal habits and home life are better." Similarly, Charles Sorensen later described his boss as "puritanical in personal conduct" and a man who led an "exemplary personal life." Thus nearly everyone who knew Ford outside the public limelight reached the same conclusion—his personal values were those of an old-fashioned Victorian gentleman.[2]

Ford's own pronouncements on character, family, and self-control reinforced this image. "Marriage is a partnership in many things beside love. It is a partnership in life, and life is made up of love and other things which are just as important," he said in a 1923 interview. "A man's work is as important; character is as important." In the best Victorian tradition, he also insisted on the sanctity of separate spheres for home and work, women and men. Whereas men were obligated to work hard to earn a livelihood for their families, women's "natural" role lay in domestic affairs, and their "real job in life is get married, have a home, and raise a family." Labor belonged in the public sphere of production and competition, and should be left there. The man who brought work home "neglects his family and makes human exchange impossible in the home. He defeats the purpose of a home." A few years later, a writer for *Forbes* spent several days with Ford and noted that he "regulates himself better, I imagine, than almost any other famous man in the world. His private life is a thing apart from his industrial activities and he succeeds, pretty well, in living his own life in spite of the demands made upon him."[3]

The old-fashioned calm and decorum of Ford's personal life seemed to complement the dynamic achievements of his public activities. His private standard of propriety and gentility appeared most clearly, perhaps, in his marriage. This important facet of Ford's life moved into the public spotlight as his fame grew.

In 1923, many Americans were introduced to the most important figure in the life of the nation's greatest industrialist. Readers of the *Ladies' Home Journal* made the acquaintance of Clara Bryant Ford in an interview that detailed many aspects of their home life as well as the history of their relationship and their attitudes about marriage. As the magazine noted, "In all the millions of words that have been written about Henry Ford, there has been the barest mention of his wife and the part she played and continues to play in his enormous success."

That Clara had remained a mystery figure—even amid the explosion of publicity accompanying her husband's involvement with the Model T, the Five-Dollar Day, the Peace Ship, and the Chicago *Tribune* trial—revealed much about her character and her values. So, too, did the fact that her national debut came in the pages of a popular magazine devoted to the home life of American women. For she clearly shared the values of her husband regarding the appropriate female role. If Henry embodied the attributes of the Victorian "Christian Gentleman" and appeared as the hardworking breadwinner who deferred to the authority of his wife in the home, Clara represented those of the "True Woman," the morally pristine figure who loyally supported her husband's worldly endeavors while managing domestic and familial affairs. She was, to use the affectionate title that Henry had bestowed upon her many years before, "The Believer."[4]

Born on April 11, 1866, Clara Bryant grew up on a farm along Monnier Road, a few miles northeast of the Ford homestead. She was one of ten children. As a girl, Clara attended Greenfield Township District No. 3 School, a one-room schoolhouse with eight grades, where she absorbed the virtues taught in the *McGuffey Readers*. As the eldest daughter in the family, she bore much responsibility at home for cooking, cleaning, and caring for her younger siblings. Clara graduated from the eighth grade in 1883, at age seventeen. Like many young people in the Dearborn area, she liked to attend dances at inns and roadhouses that sat along the main highways. On one of these occasions, the 1885 New Year's dance held at the Martindale Four Mile House, she met Henry Ford, a young man some two years her senior. He made no particular impression, but when they met again a few weeks later at another dance, Clara was struck by his demonstration of his special watch, which showed both standard time and sun time. As she would tell friends later in life, this serious young man seemed "different."[5]

Clara and Henry began to keep company at the social events typifying rural life—husking bees, dances, picnics, church socials. She also was friends with Henry's sister Margaret, through their participation in the Bayview Reading Circle in Greenfield. A pretty, petite young woman, Clara charmed her suitor with a quiet, proficient, yet friendly manner and particularly impressed him when she visited a work site where he was pulling tree stumps with a steam engine and they sat side by side on the huge machine as he worked. Their mutual attraction grew steadily, and they became engaged on April 19, 1886. On Valentine's Day before this happy occasion, Henry wrote a love letter that adorned his own awkward prose and inventive spelling with a sprig of poetry:

Clara Dear, you can not imagine what pleasure it gives me to think that I have found one so loveing kind and true as you are and I hope we will always have good success. Well I shall have to Close wishing you all the Joys of the year and a kind Good Night.

> *May Floweretts of love around you bee twined.*
> *And the Sunshine*
> *of peace Shed its joys o'e your Minde.*
> *From one tht Dearly loves you.*

H.

The couple was married on April 11, 1888, Clara's twenty-second birthday, at her parents' home.[6]

They spent the first year of their marriage in an old farmhouse on property owned by William Ford, Henry's father. Meanwhile, Henry, who at this time was cutting and milling lumber from a piece of family land, began work on what became known as the Square House. Built with the help of a finishing carpenter, and from his own lumber, this charming one-and-a-half-story dwelling with a wraparound porch was designed by Clara. In 1889, the Fords moved in, and the young wife enjoyed not only her flower and herb gardens but the small pump organ Henry bought so she could play the simple music that they both loved.[7]

In the late summer of 1891, however, this idyllic rural scene changed dramatically. Henry informed Clara of his growing belief that a gasoline engine could be used to power a horseless carriage, and explained that he needed to learn more about electricity and mechanics to advance this project. He did not tell her he had already accepted a job working at a substation of the Edison Illuminating Company in Detroit. Clara patiently listened to Henry's plans and agreed to move to the city. She would tell a confidante years later that the decision to leave the farm and their lovely little house "almost broke my heart." She also confided that, though she did not understand Henry's horseless-carriage project, "if he said such things could be done this was sufficient for her. She had complete confidence that he could do them." It was at this time that a grateful husband dubbed her "The Believer."[8]

The move to Detroit launched a period in the Fords' lives that must have tested the resolve of even the most devoted believer. Over the next decade, the couple lived in a series of eight apartments and small houses in Detroit while Henry pursued his mechanical studies, built a prototype of the horseless carriage, tried unsuccessfully to start two automobile companies, and dabbled in automobile racing. Though they were never poor, the

strained finances and succession of residences must have been trying for
Clara, the conscientious young woman who was burdened with managing
the Ford household. She never complained, although she confessed in later
years that when she went to the bank to withdraw money to pay for Henry's
automobile parts, "she wondered many times if she would live to see the
bank balance restored." Clara's unquestioning support reflected her
strength of character, but it also expressed the Victorian female ideal she
had learned as a girl—a wife provided emotional support and domestic stability for her husband when he retreated to the domestic scene exhausted
and bloodied from the battles of the marketplace.[9]

Clara fulfilled another great injunction of Victorian femininity when
she became a mother on November 6, 1893, with the birth of her only
child, Edsel Bryant Ford. Dr. David H. O'Donnell, a young physician who
came to the Ford house on a bicycle because he could not yet afford a
horse and buggy, delivered the baby, and later described Clara as "a wonderful patient." "Mrs. Ford didn't give me any trouble at all. She never
complained," he wrote. He received payment of $10 for the service. The
first photograph of Clara and Edsel, taken several months later, in the
spring of 1894, showed a proud young mother dressed in a crisp, high-
collared dress of dark cloth, smiling gently as a pudgy, wide-eyed Edsel sat
on her lap.[10]

Clara proved as devoted to her son as to her husband, and she held the
young family together throughout the decade as Henry's career progressed
by fits and starts. She demonstrated a warm, sure touch with children.
Helen Gore, a neighbor child, recalled later that Clara did all of the cooking
for her family and would patiently supervise the activities of her son and his
playmates while Henry was gone during the day. "Edsel used to have a little
table in the kitchen and we used to have great fun when she would make
soup. She used to put the alphabet in it. That was how I learned the alphabet. We used to pick out the letters," Gore recalled. Mother and son were
close, sharing a host of activities, many of them involving the Bryant family.
Surviving pictures show the two-year-old boy posing in his father's vest and
hat in 1895 on the front stoop at the Bagley Avenue residence as his laughing mother steadies him; Edsel sitting on a rocking horse surrounded by
Clara, her mother, and two sisters at the Bryant farm in 1896; Edsel dressed
in a sailor suit at the Ford farm surrounded by family members; Edsel and
his cousins, along with the Bryant sisters and their mother, at a Belle Isle
picnic in the summer of 1902; Edsel mugging for the camera at the Bryant
farm as a straw-hatted Clara stands behind him preparing to fire a pistol
into the distance.[11]

With the founding of the Ford Motor Company in 1903, and its rising success over the next few years, Clara's domestic burden began to ease. Prosperity allowed the Fords to buy five adjoining lots at the corner of Edison and Second Avenues between 1905 and 1907. Construction of a dwelling began, and the Fords moved into the completed structure in 1908. An elegant, roomy house built in the Italian Renaissance Revival style, the redbrick structure with stone trim featured a large outdoor arbor and a garage with a second-story shop for Henry and Edsel. Clara supervised the furnishing of the house, which was far from ostentatious. Sorensen credited Clara's modest style: "It was far below what she could have had. She furnished it herself and it was not overdone."[12]

By the early 1910s, the incredible success of the Model T had brought great wealth and fame to the Ford family. It also created problems. A glut of gawkers, job seekers, inventors seeking capital, and reporters lined up daily at their Edison Avenue residence. Frustration finally prompted the Fords to seek a new home. For a time they considered moving to the fashionable Detroit suburb of Grosse Pointe, but neither felt comfortable at the prospect of mingling with the city's elite. Clara pushed to settle in the area where they had grown up. "If we could build the house we want, I'd like to build out in Dearborn," she told Henry. In 1914, construction started on a large limestone house in the middle of a two-thousand-acre tract the Fords had accumulated over the past several years on the banks of the River Rouge. They named their estate Fair Lane. The decision to remain close to family roots revealed much about Clara's, and Henry's, fundamental characters.[13]

Clara Bryant Ford projected a dignified, genteel air that was sweet-tempered yet reserved. According to a reporter who interviewed her in 1927, "Mrs. Ford is the most genuinely modest woman in the world." Clara was intensely proud of her husband's achievements and fiercely protective of his interests. "Henry has been covering himself with glory and dust," she wrote of his racing adventures in 1901. "Henry has worked very hard to get where he is." In the early days of his business career, she served as a sounding board as he confided his plans and problems, and offered advice and encouragement. Colleagues who visited the Ford family were struck by her knowledge of company affairs and the unwavering confidence she expressed in her husband.[14]

But Clara's temperament also contained a streak of iron. Though ambitious for her husband and supportive of his endeavors, she stood up to him on the rare occasions when she thought it necessary. Several times during their marriage she issued ultimatums to Henry. In 1924, for instance, when he was nurturing presidential ambitions, she discouraged the move on the practical grounds that he was temperamentally impatient with restraints, burdened with a meager education, and a wretched public speaker. Clara even made her sentiments public. At a Daughters of the American Revolution convention in Washington, delegates repeatedly described Ford as presidential timber, and one speech referred to Clara as an ideal First Lady. Obviously annoyed, she rose to her feet and addressed the assembly: "Mr. Ford has enough and more than enough to do to attend to his business in Detroit. The day he runs for President of the United States, I will be on the next boat to England." Upon returning to Detroit, she firmly instructed Henry's lieutenants to scuttle further efforts in this direction. Years later, when the Ford Motor Company had been racked by labor conflict and an intransigent Henry refused to negotiate with the United Auto Workers, Clara intervened once again. She told her husband that if he refused to sign a labor settlement to stop the bloodshed she would leave him. Such episodes revealed that Clara, usually content to remain in the domestic sphere, stepped into Henry's world when convinced she was morally right.[15]

Among those privy to the Fords' private life, Clara's frugality seemed her most noted personal trait. She had been raised to believe that nothing should be wasted, and never forgot the lessons of her youth. As a young wife and mother, she managed the small family's affairs with great thrift and efficiency. Even after Henry became a millionaire in the 1910s, Clara continued her careful ways. When she heard that her husband was paying more for a haircut than she thought acceptable, she asked chauffeur and bodyguard Ray Dahlinger to monitor the situation. Even more famously, she insisted upon darning her husband's worn socks. Though appreciating the gesture, Henry detested darned socks and mounted a discreet resistance. According to close friend Harry Bennett, "Many times when he was with me, Mr. Ford would have me stop the car in front of some store and ask me to go in and buy him a pair of new socks. Then he would change in the car, tossing the pair Mrs. Ford had so carefully darned out the window."[16]

Clara's careful way with a dollar was mirrored in her sense of fashion, which, like many other matters, she approached with restraint and dignity. Short of height—she stood about four feet eleven inches tall—and inclined toward plumpness by middle age, she disdained flashy clothes and jewelry, even when her husband's income would have allowed the most extravagant purchases. As a young woman in the 1880s and 1890s, Clara favored the typical garb of a modest Victorian lady: high-necked blouses or dresses of crisp linen with ankle-length skirts, and long puffy sleeves set off with a ribbon bow tie or brooch. She changed with the times, and adopted sleeker dresses with a shorter hemline, along with sweaters and jackets, by the 1920s, although she still chose dignified colors and wore minimal jewelry. Because of her diminutive appearance, Clara often wore tall hats that were

*The earliest surviving photograph of
Henry Ford, taken when he was
two and a half years old*

Mary Litogot Ford, Henry Ford's mother, and Henry Ford's father, William Ford

*Henry Ford and Clara Bryant
around the time of their wedding
in the spring of 1888*

ABOVE: *Henry Ford (left) and two co-workers at the Edison Illuminating Company*

BELOW: *Henry Ford with his first automobile, the Quadricycle,
on the streets of Detroit in 1896*

ABOVE: *Henry Ford and Barney Oldfield with the "999" race car in 1901*

BELOW: *Henry Ford and his son, Edsel, seated in the Model F*
outside their residence on Hendrie Avenue in 1905

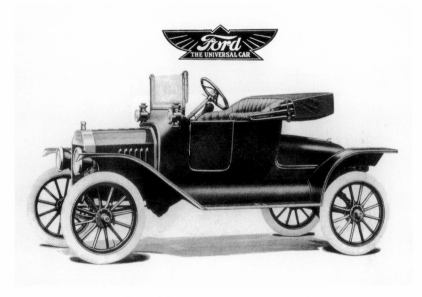

ABOVE: *1914 Model T runabout with Ford's famous "winged pyramid" advertising logo*

BELOW: *James Couzens and Henry Ford in the early 1910s*

ABOVE: *The assembly line at Highland Park in 1914*

BELOW: *Henry Ford and C. H. Wills in 1925*

ABOVE: *Workers lining up thousands of Model T's in storage lots at the Highland Park factory*

LEFT: *Advertisements in 1922 stressing Ford's consumer orientation with the founder's personal injunction to spend the money you saved in buying his inexpensive car*

LEFT: *Henry Ford departing on the Peace Ship in December 1915*

BELOW: *Henry Ford and the Reverend Samuel S. Marquis in 1915*

ABOVE: *The Four Vagabonds (left to right: Thomas Edison, John Burroughs, Henry Ford, and Harvey Firestone) on a 1918 camping expedition*

BELOW: *Henry and Clara's Fair Lane estate on the River Rouge*

ABOVE: *Ford's giant, vertically integrated River Rouge plant*

LEFT: *Charles Sorensen and Henry Ford*

ABOVE: *Evangeline Dahlinger in period costume at Greenfield Village in the 1930s*

BELOW: *Henry and Clara displaying their old-fashioned dancing skills*

ABOVE: *The Henry Ford Museum still under construction a few days before its celebratory opening at the Light's Golden Jubilee in October 1929*

BELOW: *A 1934 map showing the layout of Greenfield Village*

ABOVE: *Ernest G. Liebold*

BELOW: *Henry Ford and Edsel Ford with
the new Model A at a 1928 exposition*

ABOVE: *Henry Ford, typically surrounded by reporters,
demonstrating new Ford-Ferguson tractor in the 1930s*

BELOW: *William J. Cameron at the microphone of the*
Ford Sunday Evening Hour *in the late 1930s*

ABOVE: *Union organizer Richard Frankensteen being beaten by Ford thugs at "The Battle of the Overpass" in 1937*

BELOW: *Harry Bennett and Henry Ford in 1939*

ABOVE: *President Franklin D. Roosevelt, Henry Ford, and Charles Sorensen during FDR's visit to the Willow Run bomber plant in 1942*

BELOW: *A 1943 family photo taken a few weeks before Edsel's death. Seated left to right: Charlotte Ford, Clara Ford, and Henry Ford. Standing left to right: Henry Ford II, Eleanor Ford, Katrina Kanzler, Anne Ford, Josephine Ford, and Edsel Ford.*

exaggerated and occasionally outrageous—elaborate, elevated concoctions of feathers, ribbons, flowers, and various gewgaws. As she grew older, she became increasingly fond of furs because of their effectiveness in fighting the cold Michigan winters.[17]

Like many women from respectable families, Clara cultivated an interest in education and self-improvement. When the Fords moved into their new Edison Avenue home, she began accumulating a library of her favorite books, and continued the practice when they moved into Fair Lane in 1915. She particularly favored the traditional masterpieces of English literature, and publishers such as Scribner's and Houghton Mifflin regularly sent her purchase lists of appropriate titles. She read aloud to Henry, catering to his tastes by selecting books such as *Bambi* or, in later years, *The Yearling*. She subscribed to a number of women's magazines—*Good Housekeeping, Garden Magazine, Ladies' Home Journal, Vogue*—and by the 1920s and 1930s, she had become a regular moviegoer and a devoted fan of humorous radio shows such as *Jack Benny* and *Amos 'n' Andy*.[18]

Like Henry, Clara also loved music. In the 1890s, the Fords purchased a player piano, while they lived at Bagley Avenue, and upon moving into the Edison Avenue house bought a Steinway mahogany grand piano, a Themodist-Metrostyle player piano, and a Victrola record player. The Fords added a pipe organ when they occupied Fair Lane. They listened to music on many evenings on the player piano or the Victrola, and Clara enjoyed exercising her musical talents by singing and playing the organ. A journalist who interviewed Mrs. Ford in 1927 wrote, "She plays very well and sings in a soft, ingratiating voice; her slender hands bespeak the musician."[19]

But Clara Ford's unassuming personality found its truest expression in the hobby that became a passion during her adult life—gardening. She had loved flowers and plants since her youth. At Edison Avenue, she supervised a program of extensive landscaping and the building of a greenhouse. Henry's niece Catherine Ruddiman, who spent several months there in 1909–10, described her aunt's extensive garden with its phlox, roses, water lilies, ferns, geraniums, heliotrope, and a bright specimen known as the red-hot poker. At Fair Lane, Clara ordered three large greenhouses and began designing extensive landscaping schemes that culminated in her fabulous rose garden. Extending off to the north of the residence for some five hundred feet, it contained a pergola perched at one end and a series of small oval ponds, and held some ten thousand rosebushes. Clara spent several hours a day with her gardens, and this enthusiasm led to her election to the presidency of the Dearborn Garden Club in the 1920s.[20]

By the late 1920s, her horticultural interests had prompted involvement in a public project—roadside vegetable and fruit markets. Convinced that most farmers needlessly wasted excessive produce every year, and considering the increase in automobile travel, she saw roadside markets as a logical way to meet the needs of each group: they would provide better, cheaper vegetables and fruit to motoring consumers while bringing cash to the farmer. Clara designed an inexpensive roadside structure of whitewashed boards with neat shelves, a green roof, and a small porch. She displayed it at the North American Flower Show in Detroit and stocked it with produce from the Ford farms, along with homemade jelly and apple butter. She urged farmers nationwide to establish such structures along nearby roads and highways. "I am sure people will buy more quickly in the country provided they can do so from neat, well-kept markets where they receive courteous attention," she contended.[21]

Clara's interests quietly expanded along with her husband's growing fame and fortune. By the mid-1910s, she had gradually stepped outside the domestic realm to embrace a number of charitable, philanthropic, and reform projects. Like Henry, she held strong antiwar views, and in 1915 donated $10,000 to the Women's Peace Party to help finance a national campaign. A convert to the cause of women's suffrage, she was elected vice chairman of Dearborn's Equal Suffrage League and worked diligently in the successful 1918 campaign to gain the vote for women in Michigan. Clara had never been political, but an advocate for the female vote told her that just because she was fortunate enough not to need the vote there was no reason to deny it to women who did. Clara's response typified her unpretentious nature: "She was right. Her arguments for it were so convincing I became deeply interested in the cause."[22]

By the early 1920s, Clara was promoting several social-reform projects. She served as the primary backer of Williams House, a Detroit home for young female delinquents aimed at helping the "border-line girl—the girl who is in imminent moral danger." This clearinghouse assisted social-service agencies throughout the city by lodging and counseling girls who were in danger of running afoul of the law while plans were being made for their futures. She became an advocate for the mentally ill, writing letters to state legislators in 1921 urging them to pass legislation "making further provision for the feeble-minded in Michigan." A few years later, she attended a conference on social problems in Detroit sponsored by the Rockefeller Foundation as a representative of the Girl's Protective League.[23]

In fact, Clara's generosity with reform groups and charitable organizations became a source of frustration for her husband, who tended to believe that hard work provided the solution for most social ills. One day the ladies of the Detroit Community Fund visited Fair Lane and appealed for funds. Ford listened politely but remained noncommittal. "You can take a handful of coins and you can throw them at the ceiling. All that stick go to charity, and all that fall to the ground goes in someone else's pocket," he told an associate. Typically, however, his wife reacted differently and donated $50,000.[24]

Nonetheless, as Clara Ford made clear in her 1923 interview, such public projects stood second to family duties. When the *Ladies' Home Journal* asked if she had ever desired a career outside the home, she responded, "No, no. Motherhood is the best career." A woman's proper role, she insisted, should be played out on the family stage. "A woman puts her life into being a home maker," Clara explained. "I saw to it that Mr. Ford was never bothered by anything, that his energy wasn't wasted on things that could as well be done by others. . . . It's part of the woman's job." As another interviewer concluded, none of her various activities "compare with the vital job of being Henry Ford's wife."[25]

Clara's views on child-rearing honored a similar tradition. Like generations of Victorian parents dating back to the early nineteenth century, she stressed the necessity of moral instruction and character building among the young, assuring the *Ladies' Home Journal* that "sometimes even a spanking is necessary" for a recalcitrant child. At the same time, however, she proved receptive to newer notions of parenting, which stressed helping, understanding, and reasoning with children while encouraging "fun" in the home. "Times are different, and manners are different, and if children are more free it is because they must be so, because they know so much more than we did," she acknowledged in 1923. The modern world created a new atmosphere for young people, with "the automobile, the moving pictures, and country clubs," and parents needed to realize that it had become harder to keep kids at home. "If we helped our children more with their problems, didn't scold, and didn't antagonize them, we would have more success with them." Clara argued that being a good wife and mother now meant "being cheerful and generous and understanding of your husband and your children . . . having fun in the home, planning for things that will make your children want to stay home because home is so interesting."[26]

Clara's loyal support of her husband was repaid in kind. "Anyone who knows the Fords knows that Mrs. Ford discusses nearly everything with Mr. Ford, reads to him a great deal, talks business matters and publicity with him, entertains reporters and correspondents at the home when they are to write about him," reported E. G. Pipp. Charles Sorensen described them as "close-knit and devoted a married couple as I have ever seen." She was Henry's "balance wheel," in Sorensen's words. "When he would listen to no one else, he listened to her." At the same time, Clara's authority over the affairs of the Ford household stood unchallenged. She made all major domestic decisions, and her husband deferred. Henry's philosophy was "peace at any price." Edward Cutler, who became familiar with the Fords by the mid-1920s, reported that Henry once told him, " 'I never had a fight with my wife in my life. We never had a battle.' I kind of questioned that, but I found out afterwards *why* he never had a battle," Cutler noted. "He always ran away, got out of the room."[27]

But Henry Ford seldom failed to express his appreciation to the woman with whom he shared his life. In 1923, the *Ladies' Home Journal* asked him to explain the secret of his success. "Every great man has a great wife behind him," he replied immediately. Sixteen years later, at age seventy-six, Henry had not wavered in this belief. He told a reporter for *Liberty* magazine that the crucial factor in his life had been "a loyal wife who had helped him every minute—a woman who had never wavered in her faith in him, with whom he had had glorious comradeship through more than half a century."[28]

Clara and Henry Ford shared an old-fashioned marriage that radiated security, stability, and emotional comfort and lasted for fifty-nine years. The same old-fashioned ethos of genteel propriety that influenced Henry Ford's marriage also appeared in his personal values, which, like everything else connected to him, increasingly gained public notice. As Ford's stature grew in the 1920s, so did his determination to preach the gospel of self-regulation. He was delighted to take the public stage as a Victorian moralist, and he did so most famously as an opponent of two of Americans' favorite pastimes.

In 1914, Henry Ford published a passionate denunciation of cigarettes under the arresting title *The Case Against the Little White Slaver.* Vacationing with Thomas Edison that year in Florida, he had discovered that his idol shared a conviction about the evils of tobacco. He returned to Detroit determined to act, and secured the help of Len G. Shaw, a writer for the Detroit *Free Press,* to solicit testimonials from teachers, doctors, athletes, and social workers. Ford added a powerful personal statement of his own. The resulting pamphlet, reprinted several times over the next few years, was one of the first serious attacks on cigarette smoking by a public figure. It clearly indicated Ford's loyalty to a tradition of moral self-regulation.[29]

His opposition to tobacco had not developed suddenly. As early as 1908, Ford had insisted that salesmen at dealerships avoid smoking cigarettes and not "get yourself up like some young sport whose chief aim in life is to take his lady friends joy riding." A few years later, he issued an edict banning smoking in all Ford sales branches, even for customers and visitors.[30]

But *The Case Against the Little White Slaver* provided a full airing of Ford's beliefs about smoking. He prefaced his pamphlet with a letter from Edison, who denounced cigarettes because the burning paper wrapper formed a substance "producing degeneration of the cells of the brain . . . [that was] permanent and uncontrollable." Ford followed with his own essay, "To My Friend, the American Boy." Older smokers were addicted, and young women were not susceptible to the allure of cigarettes, he believed. But young males were a different matter. "Boys must be educated so they will know why cigarettes are bad for them," Ford wrote.[31]

Ford drew upon expert testimonials to illuminate the health problems caused by cigarettes. Under the heading "Some Scientific Facts," a long list of stories drawn from newspapers, magazines, health journals, and private letters illustrated the degeneration. Some pieces focused on cigarettes' contribution to "a decrease in mental efficiency," a slowing of brain activity, neurosis and other nervous diseases, and, in extreme cases, outright insanity. Ford's pamphlet quoted Dr. D. H. Cress, a Detroit physician whose analysis had appeared in *The Medical Times*: "The cigarette strikes a direct blow at the most vital organ of the body. It weakens the heart action. . . . The boy with a weakened heart is more apt to succumb to typhoid fever, tuberculosis, or other acute diseases which especially tax the heart. . . . It is generally recognized that any habit of life which places an extra tax upon the kidneys, heart, or other vital organs wears them out prematurely." As Ford summarized, "It is evident beyond question that the use of tobacco by the young man is injurious to his health."[32]

The Case Against the Little White Slaver underlined its health argument with a focus on athletics. A long list of doctors, coaches, sportswriters, and athletes explained smoking's physical costs. Dr. Frederick J. Pack, of the University of Utah, contended that smokers were only half as successful as nonsmokers in gaining a place on college football teams. Grantland Rice, the sportswriter, argued that tobacco use inhibited both physical and mental preparation in sporting competition. "A cigarette smoker would have but little chance in any red-blooded competition against one who stuck to training," he concluded of athletes. Connie Mack, the successful manager of baseball's Philadelphia Athletics, testified that "players who do smoke never amount to a great deal in the profession." Even Ty Cobb, the hard-driving bad boy of professional baseball, declaimed against "the evils of cigarette smoking. It stupefies the brain, saps vitality, [and] undermines one's health."[33]

But Ford reserved most of his passion for a moral denunciation of tobacco. The title of the pamphlet, connecting smoking to slavery, suggested this theme. In his introduction, Ford did likewise. "If you will study the history of almost any criminal you will find that he is an inveterate cigarette smoker," he claimed. "Boys, through cigarettes, train with bad company. They go with other smokers to the pool rooms and saloons. The cigarette drags them down."[34]

A battalion of experts in *The Case Against the Little White Slaver* supported Ford's claims of moral corrosion. Dr. Winfield S. Hall of Northwestern University argued that smoking encouraged the twin failings of "the dissipation of money for things unnecessary" and "sense gratification," both of which handicapped the young man seeking success. Other witnesses claimed that "the cigarette smoker is more likely to cheat, lie, and steal than the non-smoker." Judge Benjamin B. Lindsay of Denver asserted that smoking was pervasive among the young criminals who passed through his court because it "invited all the demons of habit to come in and add to the degradation that the cigarette began." Booker T. Washington described the smokers he had encountered during his many years at the Tuskegee Institute: "Their will power is broken down, their moral sense is blunted, and it is very difficult . . . to make anything of them."[35]

Ford underscored his moral critique of smoking with vignettes reminiscent of nineteenth-century Victorian reform tracts, illustrating how youth succumbed to the temptation of cigarettes and fell into moral ruin and social dissolution. A commander in the U.S. Navy, for example, related how a fellow officer's craving for cigarettes finally drove him from the service and to an early death. Another, longer tale described a star political reporter for a prominent newspaper whose insatiable appetite for cigarettes eventually undermined his journalistic writing. He lost his job and became an itinerant farm laborer, then fell even further to the status of panhandler, hobo, and part-time potato peeler in the county infirmary. Finally, he became a pathetic derelict, filthy and barely clothed, who could be seen drifting around the city while he "pulled away at a cigarette butt he had picked from the gutter." Inventor and scientist Hudson Maxim aptly summarized the pamphlet's moral assault on smoking: "If all boys could be made to know that with every breath of cigarette smoke they inhale imbecility and exhale manhood, it ought to deter them some. The yellow finger stain is an emblem of deeper degradation and enslavement than the ball and chain."[36]

For Ford, however, the moral nadir of smoking came with the sabotage of a young man's career prospects. He filled an entire section of his anti-tobacco pamphlet with tales of how smoking created barriers to success. A long list of prominent businessmen detailed their objections to cigarettes, and Ford put them under headlines such as "Cigarettes Spoils Boys for His

Business," "Non-Smokers Given Preference," "Cigarette Fiends Not Employed," and "Cigarettes Detrimental to Development." In Ford's assessment, employers had discovered that "the boy who is not addicted to the use of cigarettes will return larger dividends on the investment both to himself and his employer. . . . He will get to the front more rapidly." Ford's own policies reflected this belief: smoking was banned at all company plants, and this rule remained in place until after his death.[37]

Yet, however vehement Ford's opposition to smoking, it was perhaps surpassed by his disapproval of another American habit that had drawn the ire of reformers since the early nineteenth century: alcohol consumption. Ford was a temperance man. Throughout his adult life, he declared unequivocally, "Liquor never did anybody any good. I'm against it in every form. . . . Business and booze are enemies." His sociological department had made the eradication of drinking among company employees one of its central tasks. In his private life, Ford lived up to his public admonitions. As a 1923 magazine story announced, "It is a well known fact that Mr. Ford does not engage in intoxicating liquor in any form."[38]

As with most temperance reformers, Ford saw alcohol as the great enemy of self-control. The ability to regulate one's appetites was the key to virtuous character, controlling one's work and talent was the key to success, and liquor undermined all such capacities. Not surprisingly, Ford emerged as one of the most outspoken advocates for Prohibition in the 1920s. He gathered together his temperance declarations and published, at his own expense, a pamphlet entitled *Three Interviews on Prohibition* (1930).

Ford insisted that liquor, at the personal level, destroyed character. "Brains and initiative are dulled by even the occasional use of alcohol," he wrote. "They are made permanently dull by even the most moderate habitual use, and they vanish altogether in the steady, heavy drinker." Liquor channeled energy in wrong directions, subverted the capacity to work, and tempted the imbiber to improper behavior. The result was an individual who could not control his impulses or navigate his way in the world. In the author's words, drinkers "are not at home inside themselves. But a man cannot get away from himself; a man's or woman's drinking is just his or her confession of failure to be an interesting person, an alive person."[39]

Ford dismissed the argument that banning liquor subverted personal liberty. On the contrary, he asserted that the sloth and impropriety brought on by alcohol were a much greater danger to individual freedom. "I have never seen beverage alcohol do anything but destroy personal liberty," he insisted. "Not only does it destroy the personal liberty of the drinker, but it seriously curtails the personal liberty of his relatives, shopmates, and fellow citizens."[40]

Perhaps the greatest danger came from liquor's assault on women, children, and the family. The drunk's proclivities toward violence and unemployment threatened to undermine the stuff of domestic happiness— benevolence, material comfort, affection, respect. For centuries, liquor had caused a "mass of human misery," and "women and children were the chief sufferers." The sanctity of the family demanded that intelligent people confront the fact "that prohibition is a home problem, that it affects every man and woman and child in the country, their economic and spiritual welfare, their physical health and their happiness and work." As Ford concluded of Prohibition, "The whole world is benefiting from it—the family most."[41]

Three Interviews on Prohibition also argued that alcohol caused serious social problems. By impairing the skill and dexterity of workers, it hindered productivity in the modern factory. The worker "needs a keen brain. He needs a fine coordination between hand and brain," Ford explained. "But any use of alcohol at all seems to destroy that exact coordination, and the result is either slow work or spoiled work—or both." When drinking was widespread, factory owners could count on only three effective workdays a week. Echoing a lament about "St. Monday" made by employers since the early nineteenth century, Ford contended that they "used to fight beer and whiskey continually—and it was a hard fight—in order to have a fairly representative labor roster on Monday mornings."[42]

But perhaps the greatest social consequence of alcohol-addled behavior, in Ford's opinion, was poverty. As an idealist and industrial reformer, Ford lamented the manner in which drinkers seemed to fall behind in gaining good wages and a higher standard of living. Liquor threatened the ideal of widespread abundance. "The executive who drinks cannot so plan that high wages will result in low prices, while the workman who drinks cannot work intelligently enough to earn high wages," Ford argued. For him, Prohibition meant prosperity, and drink meant poverty.[43]

Ford's depth of feeling against liquor appeared in the historical comparison he drew upon. The Prohibition crusade, he said, could be compared only to the abolition of slavery. "If you will look back into our history, you will see that agitation against liquor began before the Civil War. This agitation was sidetracked, for a time, by the agitation against slavery," Ford wrote. "It happened that slavery got into politics first and brought on the Civil War which ended slavery. Otherwise, the abolition of alcohol would probably have come first." Liquor consumption, like slavery, obliterated self-control and gave rein to dangerous impulses. For Henry Ford, they were the twin evils that respectable Americans had been fighting for a century. Finally, with Prohibition, both had been vanquished.[44]

Ford's temperance views, though mustered in support of Prohibition in the aftermath of World War I, harked back to an earlier age of moral reform. In similar, if more ironic fashion, certain of his endeavors on the socioeconomic front also looked toward the past. The architect of modern industrial and consumer America sought to protect the rural life that he had done so much to destroy.

In 1918, Frank Parker Stockbridge, a journalist writing for *World's Work*, was surprised to hear a heartfelt outburst of sentiment from Henry Ford. Stockbridge had visited Highland Park, observed complex assembly lines and huge machines, seen thousands of laborers at work, and talked at length with the man who directed this extensive operation. Thus he was surprised when Ford stopped in front of the farmhouse he had lived in as a boy and declared emotionally, "I belong here. I am a farmer. I want to see every acre of the earth's surface covered with little farms, with happy, contented people living on them." Some years later, a reporter for *Forbes*, after spending considerable time with the master of River Rouge, felt a similar pang of cognitive dissonance. Ford's personality, he concluded, "is almost altogether rural. When you first meet him you think that he is a mechanic with a bent for farming; later you decide that he is a farmer with a bent for mechanics."[45]

These writers had discovered the great irony that the central designer of the modern American industrial order was in love with the virtues of rural life. This was no sudden development. Although Ford had physically fled the countryside as a youth to pursue mechanics, part of his heart remained behind. During his adulthood, this emotional attachment became steadily more evident. After spending time with Ford in 1912, Elbert Hubbard wrote, "Instinctively he is a farmer, a lover of the great out-of-doors, and is on good terms with the birds, bees, butterflies, flowers and trees."[46]

In 1916, John Reed was similarly struck by Ford's rural sympathies. When the sociological department discovered that Russian immigrants were saving money to return to the motherland and buy farms, Ford was delighted. "That's fine!" he replied. "I wish they'd all do that. I'd like to get two-thirds of the population of the earth back on the land." Moreover, Ford himself seemed a product of Midwestern rural stock and was fully imbued with such values: "puritanical narrowness, individualism run rampant, boundless energy, and a naïve political idealism." Reed noted that Ford avoided Detroit's sophisticated social circles and preferred "sitting on a neighbor's back porch of an evening and talking things over with the farmers."[47]

Around the same time, Ida Tarbell was astonished to hear Ford describe his dream for the eighteen thousand men working at his Highland Park plant. "I'd like to move them all out onto the land right now," he declared. "If they could have two weeks of out-of-doors planting this spring, two or three weeks more in haying time, help in harvesting next fall, they would be better workmen, better men, and there would be more food raised at cheaper prices." Tarbell toured Ford's thousands of acres of farmland in the Dearborn area and listened as he extolled the virtues of rural life. She concluded, "Whatever else Henry Ford might be, inventor, organizer, manufacturer, his real motive power was love of the soil."[48]

By the 1920s, Ford was consistently promoting rural life in interviews and public statements. "The farmer . . . lives amid conditions that make for sanity of mind," he told *Success* magazine in 1923. "He lives under the sky, he deals with the soil, he knows the flawless and beautiful order of nature's law." Many farm journalists made a pilgrimage to Dearborn during these years to visit Ford on his estate and discuss agricultural issues. Magazines such as *Farm and Fireside*, *Successful Farming*, and the *Farm Journal* sent writers to interview Ford, and they returned with stories describing his rural childhood, love of the land and its products, and determination to assist farmers in leading fuller and more prosperous lives. This image of the industrial magnate as "country boy" became an integral part of the Ford legend.[49]

Sentiment constituted part of Ford's veneration of farm life. In a tradition dating back to Thomas Jefferson and the earliest days of the United States as a nation, he proclaimed the farmer as the backbone of the American republic. For Ford, rural America was the real America. As he told the Chicago *Tribune*, cities like New York and Chicago did not really represent the United States: "America is out there among the old village sites, the small towns, and the farms." But an economic rationale also informed Ford's veneration for farming. He argued that, although agriculture, transportation, and manufacturing complemented one another in sustaining American prosperity, "the origin and sustenance of all is agriculture." Ford's 1922 message to company sales representatives reiterated this position: "Farming is and always will be the foundation on which the economic growth of our nation depends."[50]

In 1925, Andrew S. Wing, editor of *Farm and Fireside*, captured Ford's affection for American farm life. After a series of lengthy interviews with Ford, he informed readers that "at heart he is still a Michigan farm boy. I am convinced that he has a great affection for country life and all that goes with it." Wing toured the Ford farm, inspected its dairy herd, flock of sheep, and ponies, and talked to those who worked its thousands of acres under cultivation. He noted the presence of a lovely old barn and witnessed "five teams of horses plowing corn in one field." Ford concluded the interview in a manner that revealed his deep rural attachment. He asked Wing if any old numbers of his magazine were available. "I'd like to get hold of a bound volume of some of the old issues," he explained. "I used to read *Farm & Fireside* when I was a boy."[51]

In the early 1910s, Ford inaugurated old-fashioned "neighborhood threshing bees" that first convened at the farm of his cousin John Ford in Dearborn. Then they progressed to the adjoining farms of longtime friends and neighbors. Large work crews of Ford employees would labor all day at the harvest, and then join together at threshing tables for convivial meals. Henry himself often joined in this harvesting activity. Orla Ford, a male relative who also participated, described how the Ford farm crew would use its harvesting equipment and then pause for lunch. "Just before the meal, a limousine was sent to the various nearby farms to pick up the wives of the working crew, and they too were treated to the same hearty meal. Henry often would be there at that time to meet his friends." Ford seemed to have a natural affinity for farm folk.[52]

During the 1900s, Ford began accumulating thousands of acres of forest and farmland in the Dearborn area. Entitled the Henry Ford Farms, this operation was managed by Ray Dahlinger with much direction from Ford himself. Grain, especially wheat, provided the major crop, although there was also a sizable dairy operation. In 1917, the success of the Ford Farms prompted construction of a large grain elevator in Dearborn, and three years later the Ford Flour Mill was built nearby. It not only milled flour for commercial distribution but sold flour directly to employees of the Ford Motor Company.[53]

Ford's sentimental attraction to the land seemed odd in light of his championing the industrialized society of mass production and consumption that had undermined it. His populism explained part of his motivation. As numerous statements made clear, he idealized farm life as a counterweight to urban financial power. Drawing upon the traditional language of nineteenth-century populism, he told John Reed that he wanted to help farmers gain control over their land and liberate themselves from debt. "What I want to do is make the farmer as independent as I am; independent of the trusts, independent of the banks, the railroads," he declared. Throughout the 1920s, Ford continued to insist that agriculture and finance were diametrically opposed, "one productive and the other manipulative, pulling separate ways. One lives off increase, the other off interest." Ida Tarbell, who probed his ideas on such matters in 1927, reached a clear conclusion about his populist sensibility. "He began with the soil and he has never lost his conscious connection with it. . . . It was the farmer, not the banker in the cities, in whom he was interested."[54]

For all of his affection, however, Ford wanted to reform rural life. In the same spirit with which he built the assembly line at Highland Park, his desire was to revolutionize its work processes. As Andrew Wing observed, "He thinks of farming primarily in terms of efficiency, and his standards of efficiency are industrial standards." In short, Ford was an unabashed advocate of power-farming.[55]

Throughout the 1920s, Ford proselytized for agricultural mechanization. To Judson C. Welliver of *The American Review of Reviews*, he talked at length about the need for the farm to keep pace with technological advances. "My father bought a harvester in 1881," Ford said, "and I bought one last year. There was no difference except father's was rather better." He showed Welliver how farm implements such as plows and disk harrows were being tested at the Ford Farms. The Model T, in Ford's mind, had opened new horizons and "given the farmer a chance to get acquainted with the world, to see what is going on around him, to become a social being." If the Model T had liberated the farmer from the isolation of place, more sophisticated agricultural machinery would liberate him from the drudgery of toil.[56]

In *My Life and Work*, Ford stressed this theme. On the subject of the traditional American farm, he argued, "Power is utilized to the least possible degree. Not only is everything done by hand, but seldom is a thought given to logical arrangement." In contrast, the Ford Farms used machinery, pursued the efficient organization of labor, and saw productivity rise markedly. "We are not farmers—we are industrialists on the farm," Ford explained. Mechanization would dramatically improve the farmer's life by decreasing the amount of physical labor. "Power-farming is simply taking the burden from flesh and blood and putting it on steel," Ford wrote. Since hours of labor could be reduced dramatically, the rest of a farmer's time could be spent in other kinds of productive activity or in leisure. "Farming is too seasonal an occupation to engage all of a man's time," he believed.[57]

Ford's preoccupation with power-farming appeared in his strong support for the production of tractors. Two youthful prejudices—his hatred of horses and his enthusiasm for steam-powered machines—made the development of a motorized farm vehicle one of his first mechanical projects. "The first thing I ever set out to build was a tractor. I never could see any excuse for the way agriculture is carried on," Ford observed. "Nothing could be more inexcusable than the average farmer, his wife and their children, drudging from early morning until late at night." The tractor, he believed, would relieve this exhausting routine.[58]

As early as 1905, while still in the Piquette Avenue plant, Ford had begun experimenting with tractors. He secured an old house and carriage barn located a few blocks from the factory and set up a development team under Joseph Galamb. Eventually, they produced three tractors with a four-cylinder engine adapted from the Model B automobile, and then experimented with a machine based on the Model T—lightweight, mobile, inexpensive, and using the flivver engine. In the early 1910s, Ford tried to integrate tractor production into the new Highland Park plant, but the board of directors was cool to the idea. In 1915, he organized a separate company, Henry Ford & Son, and set up a production facility in Dearborn, overseen by Sorensen. By 1916, a prototype, the Fordson tractor, had emerged as a compact, simple machine with a relatively light frame of chrome-carbon steel and a 20-horsepower engine.[59]

Production of the Fordson tractor escalated steadily. During World War I, the British sought to mechanize farming as a way both to increase agricultural production and to free up manpower for the armed forces, and Sorensen negotiated a deal for the British government to purchase eight thousand Ford tractors. In April 1918, the first Fordson tractors for domestic use were produced. Ford presented the first two to his old friends Luther Burbank and Thomas Edison. By 1920, over ninety thousand Fordsons had been built; by 1924, the company was producing 750 per day. In 1927, production figures for the year reached 650,000.[60]

Throughout this period, Henry Ford used the bully pulpit to promote his tractor to American farmers. This machine "will eliminate drudgery and people will go back to the farm," he argued in good populist fashion. "I want to see the day when the country will assume the ascendancy over the city in the affairs of men." He also appealed to efficiency. "What a waste it is for a human being to spend hours and hours behind a slowly moving team of horses when in the same time a tractor could do six times as much work," he wrote in *My Life and Work*.[61]

Ford's belief in agricultural modernization went far beyond machinery, however. By the 1920s, he had become a disciple of scientific advances that would transform the nature of farm production and place the farmer side by side with the industrialist as a tribune of modernity. He became an enthusiastic advocate of "chemurgy," or the application of chemistry to develop new uses for agricultural products. "Everything that is produced from the soil can be used for some purpose," he announced. Describing cows as "the most inefficient creatures in the world," he charged Ford chemists with developing synthetic milk. He pioneered attempts to produce alcohol for motor fuel by distilling it from agricultural crops. He experimented with extracting rubber from nontropical domestic plants. He developed plastics from the cellulose in cotton, wood pulp, corn, wheat, hemp, and ramie. Perhaps his most useful experiments involved the soybean. Ford scientists devoted years of research to the uses of this versatile crop and discovered scores of applications, ranging from oil to food, fertilizers to plastics, cloth to synthetic milk.[62]

Ford also advocated the development of waterpower for rural electrification. Generating dams would allow the country to "develop its waterpower everywhere, keep them [farmers] from monopoly and exploitation, and lay bases for an industrial revolution through electrification." He insisted that the rivers crisscrossing the United States provided nearly limitless opportunity for producing cheap electricity in the countryside. Beginning in the late 1910s and extending well into the 1930s, Ford authorized the construction of small plants along various rivers in Michigan to supply automobile parts such as valves, headlights, carburetors, and ignition coils. "Why, we are putting nine dams in the little River Rouge here, and I don't know how many hundred horsepower it will finally produce," he said in a 1921 interview.[63]

Ford's support for rural life and his desire for the modernization of farming also inspired the most sweeping item on his agenda: decentralization. Ironically, the man who had masterminded the great River Rouge plant emerged in the 1920s singing the praises of small, integrated industrial sites that would dot the rural landscape of the United States and meld the tasks of the farmer and the worker. Ford envisioned modest village industries where small factories making a single item would employ part-time workers who also would spend a portion of the year doing farm labor. These institutions would offer fresh air, sunshine, and an opportunity to work the land to industrial workers, and steady work and income to farmers too often laid low by market forces. "I want to see mixed work," Ford said. "In the winter months a man should work in industry and in the summer months on a farm."[64]

In his 1918 race for the Senate, Ford proposed the decentralization of manufacturing to help rural residents. "What I am going to do is to establish plants for manufacturing parts of Ford cars and Fordson tractors in places where they will be within easy reach of farming districts, and provide employment for farmers and their families in winter," Ford explained during the campaign. Promoting decentralization in subsequent years, Ford the populist blamed cities and financiers for "robbing the worker and manufacturer of normal human conditions." He ritually denounced "the unnatural conditions of American cities, with their injurious effects on mental, moral, and physical life," and offered an alternate vision. "I want to see the day when the country will assume the ascendancy over the city in the affairs of men," he declared.[65]

Ford also used his autobiography to drum up enthusiasm for decentralization. *My Life and Work* offered a blueprint for a "combination of farm and factory." Each venue had slack times during the year, but with decentralization farmers could go to the factory and factory workers back to the farm as circumstances dictated. In Ford's words, this would "take the slack out of work and restore the balance between the artificial and the natural." He offered an idyllic vision of an America dominated by village industries: "You will find the smaller communities living along in unison with the seasons, having neither extreme poverty nor wealth—none of the violent plagues of upheaval and unrest which afflict our great populations."[66]

To the end of his life, Ford maintained a deep-seated affection for rural America. He hoped to save the farmer by wedding the organic connection of rural life with the efficiency of urban life, agricultural vitality with industrial productivity. In 1939, when he was an old man, Ford was asked by a reporter what he would do if he suddenly became director of the United States. He replied, "I'd put as many people on the soil as I could and manufacture farming tools at such low prices that everyone could find basic security on the land. I'd try to get as many city boys out into the country as I could and as many country boys into the city as possible. That would be a good exchange and both would profit."[67]

In this area, as in many others, Henry Ford proudly donned the mantle of an old-fashioned moralist. His defense of rural life, like his upholding of the traditional family and his crusade against alcohol and tobacco, sought to save traditional virtues both by defending them on their own terms and by bringing science to their support when necessary. By whatever means necessary, Ford hoped to nourish the virtues of self-control, hard work, and domestic "separate spheres" that he had absorbed as a youth. As with so many aspects of his career, however, the evident nature of his beliefs masked hidden complexities. Henry Ford's role as Victorian moralist, though played with enthusiasm and conviction, barely muffled a simultaneous attraction to several social and cultural projects that were ushering in a new era. These impulses gained much strength from the expansive energy of early-twentieth-century America. Paradoxically, they slowly eroded the very traditions that lay near to Ford's heart.

Sixteen

Positive Thinker

Henry Ford appeared the very epitome of Victorian gentility in his private life. His emotional self-control, dignified demeanor, domestic attachments, rural loyalties, and adherence to the work ethic bespoke the provincial, bourgeois culture of the nineteenth-century Midwest in which he had been reared. But, as is usually the case with most human beings, the truth was more complicated. For all of his traditional sensibility, Ford was not insulated from the impact of a changing cultural climate. In fact, throughout his adult life he became involved with certain ideas sweeping through the prosperous classes that were undermining the traditions he revered.

As a mature man, Ford became a public devotee of religious mysticism, mental revitalization, and physical vitality. In his private life, he engaged in a long-term intimate relationship with a much younger woman that reflected the new morality of a post-Victorian society. In one sense, as historians have discovered, the new movements that attracted Ford aimed to prop up a Victorian tradition that had grown brittle from excessively rigid expectations and weak from attacks by working-class immigrants and bohemian intellectuals. As early as the 1890s, nervous Victorian champions such as Theodore Roosevelt had campaigned for regeneration by urging prosperous citizens to adopt "the strenuous life." By the early decades of the new century, such calls for revitalization widened and intensified. In this atmosphere, vigorous new strains of religious thought, success ideology, physical well-being, and moral conduct blossomed.

At the same time, however, these cultural movements brought unintended consequences. Instead of just regenerating the culture of Victorian self-control, advocates of vigor and personal development nudged American values in a new direction. Ford, like countless others, encouraged a great cultural transformation that gradually replaced self-restraint with self-fulfillment, salvation with self-realization, and scarcity with abundance. Not surprisingly, this new ethic provided the emotional and intellectual fuel for the new consumer economy.

In Ford's case, the role of cultural revolutionary was largely unintended. He did more than he knew. Never a sophisticated thinker, Ford offered a mishmash of half-digested concepts and visceral intuitions rather than systematic analysis, so his social and cultural speculations did not probe very deeply. Ultimately, his ideas worked to push forward the notion of personal self-fulfillment in a consumer society. In religion and social values, as with so many other things, Henry Ford stood at the cutting edge of a great shift in the American experience that changed the accepted definitions of what was important in life. Ironically, the staunch advocate of Victorian tradition subverted it with his cultural enthusiasms almost as much as he did with his economic innovations.

On the day of President William McKinley's funeral in September 1901, Oliver Barthel lent Henry Ford a book entitled *A Short View of the Great Questions*, by Orlando J. Smith. Barthel, a skilled engineer who assisted Ford in his early automotive projects, had studied spiritual, philosophical, and metaphysical issues, and he hoped to stimulate the interest of his friend. Smith's brief volume examined various questions of human origins and destiny and summarized theories of materialism, religion, and reincarnation. In later years, Ford claimed that *A Short View of the Great Questions* changed his life. "I adopted the theory of reincarnation . . . from a book by Orlando Smith," he told a reporter in 1928. "When I discovered reincarnation it was as if I had found a universal plan." This belief that after death the human spirit goes on to inhabit another physical body seemed to connect with Ford's sense of destiny. It launched him on a long religious journey that took some strange twists and turns before it ended.[1]

Ford had been raised in a traditional Christian home. Baptized and confirmed in the Episcopal church, the boy had absorbed Protestant fare that was moderately demanding but not strict. He sang hymns and heard Bible recitation at home under the influence of his mother, a religious woman. In grammar school, as was the custom in the nineteenth century, he participated in daily "devotions" from the Bible and recited in unison the Lord's Prayer. The Ford family favored tolerance over orthodoxy, however, and Henry developed a sense of integrity, morality, and fair play but little spiritual passion.[2]

As a young adult, Ford paid scant attention to any church. "I was never especially religious," he admitted during this period. "Man has made many gods. How do I know and how can I find out which, if any, is the genuine one? I won't try. I'll just keep busy." After marrying, Ford and his family attended various churches in the Dearborn and Detroit area before settling in at Dr. Samuel S. Marquis' Episcopal cathedral. Then he became attracted to reincarnation, and by the 1910s, his views had become heavily tinged with mysticism. As Marquis observed, "He is not an orthodox believer according to the standards of any church I know."[3]

In fact, Ford became notorious for his rather outlandish religious ideas. He spoke often of reincarnation. Upstanding Protestant citizens with a belief in the infallibility of the Bible must have been startled to read his declaration that "the body, by its instincts, [and] the soul, by its intuitions, remember and utilize the experience of previous lives. . . . We all retain, however faintly, memories of past lives." To an interviewer, he claimed that the earth had nourished and lost many civilizations over millions of years that had developed modern items such as cars, airplanes, and radios. "What is 'new' about each individual is merely a new combination. The human mind is a channel through which things-to-be are coming into the realm of things-that-are," Ford said.[4]

He did not shy away from airing such beliefs. In fact, the thought of life's regenerating itself seemed to inspire him, and he wanted to share that feeling. "I expect to go on and gather more experience. I expect to have opportunities to use my experience," he once observed. "I expect to retain this central cell, or whatever it is, that is now the core of my personality. I expect to find conditions of life farther on, just as I found conditions of life here, and adapt myself to them." Ford frequently confessed his beliefs privately. Irving Bacon, an artist who painted many works for Ford on commission, recalled a conversation in which his patron announced, "We have lived several lives before. Memory never dies. We remember things from past lives in our present life." Similarly, Ford's cousin Artemus Litogot once heard him say, "You know, when a person dies I think their spirit goes into a newborn baby. I think that's why some people are so much further advanced in knowledge than others and are gifted."[5]

Ford's belief in reincarnation led him to a fundamental conviction about life's meaning. A person's time on earth, he told anyone who would listen, was meant to gain experience, and when you learned everything you could, you died and went on to another life. In such diverse venues as *Forbes* and the London *Express*, Ford claimed, "What you're here for, and what every living person is here for . . . is to get experience. That's all we can get out of life." The process of accumulating experience through several lives provided "an ideal, a purpose beyond it all, that keeps up the human procession."[6]

Ford's spiritual speculations led him away from Christian tradition and into the expansive atmosphere of religious mysticism. He came to view God not as the divine presence revealed in the Bible but as "a Master Mind which sends brain waves or messages to us—the Brain of Mankind, the Brain of the Earth. . . . There is a Great Spirit. Call it creative evolution or world mind. Call it collective intelligence or call it God. It is this Spirit which determines our actions and our thoughts." Ford became attracted to the essays of Ralph Waldo Emerson, which he kept scattered about his house and read regularly, and his theorizing mirrored the New Englander's notion of an "Over-Soul." Like Emerson, Ford believed that divine power permeated everything at all times and was "the essence and the substance of all there is. What we call spirit and what we call matter is one, and the All."[7]

Ford's conception of the human soul overflowed the model provided by Christianity. He did not deny the soul's existence. "The wind is invisible, electricity is invisible, the soul is invisible. They are, nevertheless, real," Ford contended. "Air can be weighed, electricity gauged, and I am sure that some day it will be possible to measure the soul." But he rejected the Christian duality of body and spirit by insisting that "a fundamental unity underlies all things. Matter and mind are one. They are different aspects of the same thing." He also moved away from Christianity in his stress on the self as the seat of universal consciousness. Ford was convinced that each person is "a universe in miniature, with the Self as the center and numberless millions of entities making up the thing we call I—that we function not only on the planes we see, but on others we do not see."[8]

Ford's spiritual proclivities produced some rather unconventional doctrines. He told reporters that, since "the earth is just a clearing station between past and future lives," surely life existed in the universe outside of the earth's confines. "We don't know anything about what's on those other planets, except life. I'm sure there's life there." He also became a believer in mental telepathy, arguing that thoughts could be passed from mind to mind without need for print or speech. "There is nothing to me that is more thoroughly established than thought transference," Ford told Ralph Waldo Trine. In his view, thought consisted of "a stream of little living organizations" that swirled about an individual at all times. "When thought goes out some of the energies of personality go out with it" and are conveyed to other people.[9]

But Ford's spiritualism, ironically, also nudged him in the direction of certain Christian traditions. His endorsement of reincarnation and a pervasive Master Mind, for example, produced a doctrine very much like that of Protestant predestination. "I feel that I have never done anything by my own volition. I was always pushed by invisible forces within and without me," Ford confessed. "In all likelihood every human range of experience is predestined. . . . Forces beyond our control determine the highway we take through life."[10]

Ford struggled to come to terms with the background from which he had emerged. Although rejecting the letter of Christian doctrine throughout much of his adult life, he sought to meld its spirit into his expansive new worldview. He took great pains to profess Christian loyalties. "I believe in God and in Jesus Christ. I was brought up in the church. I belong to the church. I attend church. I never go to hear a sermon, whether it is by a preacher in a small church or a large one, that I do not get help," he told the New York *Times*. He publicized the pledge he had taken during World War I, along with President Woodrow Wilson and evangelist Wilbur Chapman, to read a chapter in the Bible every day—a pledge he labored to keep. He even supported a move "to get the Bible back into the public schools," arguing that it provided a wealth of valuable moral and ethical directives.[11]

Most of the time, however, Ford tried to bend Christianity to fit the shape of his mystical convictions. His view of life as gaining experience produced some singular interpretations. Speaking of the scriptures, Ford said, "I look upon it as a record of experience. No matter what knocks we receive in life, we find, reading the Bible, that others have received similar knocks. It is a true book of experience." Jesus offered one example. In Ford's words, "My belief is that Jesus was an old person, old in experience; and it was this that gave him his superior knowledge of life."[12]

In the last few years of his life, Ford relented somewhat in his unorthodoxy and drifted closer to Protestant tradition. In a series of interviews and articles in the mid-1940s, he meditated upon his religious convictions in the New York *Times*, the *Christian Herald*, *Woman's Home Companion*, and the *American Magazine*. He professed his love for the old Protestant hymns he had heard since boyhood and claimed, "The associations of the church are beneficial to all." The Sermon on the Mount, Ford said, was the greatest pronouncement ever made in human affairs. Talking with a reporter, Ford pulled from his suit pocket a well-worn volume of biblical quotations, and suggested that he "read it every now and then. It is surprising how much help you will get from it." Even in old age, however, he quietly affirmed his long-standing belief in reincarnation and a vague "Power that is everywhere for good."[13]

Ford's eclectic blend of spiritual notions did not fit neatly into any religious category or denomination. Mainstream Protestants undoubtedly regarded his ideas as unsettling, even horrifying. His unorthodox spiritualism, however, found kindred spirits in a much broader cultural movement in early-twentieth-century America. Combining elements of religion, success ideology, and therapy, this cultural crusade cut a swath through great sections of the populace with its promise of mental and economic abundance.

In 1928, Ralph Waldo Trine traveled to Dearborn to meet with Henry Ford. Trine had written a number of popular inspirational books over the previous three decades, such as the best-selling *In Tune with the Infinite: Fullness of Peace, Power, Plenty* (1898). Having read certain of Ford's religious ruminations in the press, he was determined to interview the industrialist and claim him as a spiritual brother. Ford, Trine believed, was a prime example of what new-style religious thinking could produce in the modern world.[14]

Ford eventually found Trine to be something of a pest, with the interview stretching over several days, but initially he greeted him warmly. He told Trine he had read *In Tune with the Infinite* around 1914 and found it so insightful that "I used to keep a stock of your books in my office to give to friends or associates who, I thought, would be benefited by them the same as I." As their discussions unfolded over many hours, the two men touched upon a host of matters regarding religion, reincarnation, success, positive thinking, diet, metaphysics, and the general meaning of life. The result was Trine's *The Power That Wins: Henry Ford and Ralph Waldo Trine in an Intimate Talk on Life* (1928), which recorded their exchange of views. The book's subtitle, *Things of the Mind and Spirit, and the Inner Powers and Forces That Make for Achievement*, suggested how Ford's spiritual notions were entangled with the larger New Thought movement.[15]

New Thought had emerged in late-nineteenth-century America as a loose confederation of individuals and groups committed to the powers of positive thought and the possibilities of material and emotional abundance. Rooted partly in transcendentalism, with its emphasis on an "Over-Soul" and intuition as a window into reality, and partly in new therapeutic doctrines associated with study of the human psyche, this metaphysical movement stressed the restorative, generative, healing qualities of the human mind. In many ways, New Thought combined traditional religion with modern psychology. Founded by the self-educated healer Phineas P. Quimby, and inspired by the metaphysical philosophy of Ralph Waldo Emerson, the New Thought movement was led by figures such as Trine; Mary Baker Eddy, the originator of Christian Science; and Annie Payson Call, whose mind-cure program appeared in her popular book, *Power*

Through Repose (1891). Its disciples plumbed the human "subconscious" to retrieve mental powers that could be mobilized to increase emotional vigor and material success.[16]

New Thought advocates promoted several ideas. They postulated that the human mind was the primary causative force in the universe; that God was an immanent spirit ever-present in everyone and everything; that the remedy for all defects and disorders lay in the mental and spiritual realm; that evil was not a permanent reality in the world but merely the temporary absence of good; and that health and abundance were available to those who could effectively muster their spiritual and mental resources. The influence of New Thought spread widely at the turn of the century. Its adherents ranged from respected thinkers such as William James, the psychologist and philosopher, to popular magazines such as *Good Housekeeping*, which by 1908 ran a regular column for women on "How to Become Beautiful by Thought." Within a few decades, New Thought would enter the American cultural mainstream with the likes of Norman Vincent Peale, the influential minister whose message of positive thinking resonated powerfully with a large Protestant audience.[17]

Though never formally affiliated with any New Thought group, Henry Ford clearly displayed an affinity with their beliefs. His advice on achieving success endorsed not only the work ethic but newfangled techniques of positive thinking and mental mobilization. The new consumer age, he argued, had created a desire for goods, and there was great opportunity for achievement and advancement. In Ford's assessment, "We are entering the comfortable age, and the opportunity to make life more comfortable offers us the widest field mankind has ever known."[18]

In this atmosphere of abundance, Ford believed, positive thinking would work wonders for the success-seeker. "I refuse to recognize that there are impossibilities," he told a reporter in 1923, and he urged others to adopt the same attitude. One of his "Half Dozen Rules for Success," offered in *Leslie's Illustrated Weekly*, was "Be Optimistic." When interviewed by Allan Benson in the early 1920s, he waxed effusive about positive thinking. "I was never discouraged in my life," Ford insisted. "Most men are entirely too confident of their ability to fail—and they fail. If they were as confident of their ability to succeed, most of them would succeed." He reported his stock answer to inquiries about how his day was going: "The best day I ever had in my life." As Ford told friends such as Irving Bacon, "I never keep anything that reminds me of sorrow, trouble, disagreeableness, or bad things."[19]

It was imperative for the positive thinker, Ford believed, to abandon habits shaped by an older economy of scarcity—namely, the urge to save money constantly and hoard psychological resources. In the modern atmosphere of abundance, he was certain that it was far better to "invest in yourself." "Spend your money! Spend it for things that will put you ahead of where you were yesterday," he urged. "It is time enough to save when you can earn more than you can spend wisely." In addition, Ford urged the positive thinker to muster his mental resources and focus them in a constructive way. "After work, the next duty is to think. . . . Your thought makes great advances possible," he told the New Thought journal, *National Brain Power*, in 1923. Ford offered a dictum: "Let every man think for himself. Let him call a conference of his powers, his common sense in the chair, his desires and his knowledge of things as they are pleading the case before him." In his view, the positive thinker must cultivate a "belief in your ability to accomplish that which you set out to do."[20]

Ford probably revealed his New Thought agenda most fully in his interviews with Trine. Prompted by one of the leaders of the movement, he reflected at length upon the nature of modern society and the qualities required to thrive in it. Abundant opportunity beckoned to the individual. "There was never a better time to be young," Ford told Trine. "These times are richer in material for new combinations of knowledge, of grit and of power than any. . . . Here are over a hundred million people, inexhaustible resources and no limit to expansion." He denounced fear, praised positive thinking, and urged readers to focus their mental powers: "Intensify your thought and you set up attraction. Concentrate on a job, and you attract all the things necessary to accomplish it." He endorsed visualization as a technique for achievement. "To see a thing clearly in the mind makes it begin to take form," he explained. Every person harbored abundant psychic resources, Ford assured Trine: "A man is like a well. There is a vast amount in him, if he can only get it out."[21]

During the Trine interviews, Ford strove to connect positive thinking and mental focus with reincarnation. He argued that individuals who galvanized their mental powers also galvanized palpable spiritual forces—"little entities—invisible lives—that are building him up, and adding to and building up whatever he is doing. Whatever he has concentrated his thought and work upon is helped and shaped by these little lives that come to him. . . . These entities are the material of growth and achievement." These tiny forces, he insisted, "become a part of us; and then they work under our direction, and according to our character."[22]

Toward the end of his discussion with Trine, Ford neatly tied his spiritual and psychological beliefs to economic reality. He suggested that a New Thought orientation naturally reflected a new atmosphere of consumer abundance:

Our old ideas of thrift grew up in a country where the farms were rocky, where income was fixed beyond any possibility of increase, where poverty and need were always around the corner. In the economic sense, life was pinched and narrow for most of the people, and the pinching habit became almost a religious virtue. . . . [Now] the best form of thrift is to increase your income. The best way to increase your income is to increase your own productive powers. And the best way to increase your productive powers is to invest in your own development.[23]

Ford's belief in mental revitalization and the power of positive thinking reflected broader currents of change in early-twentieth-century America. It captured both the sense of unlimited opportunity that was spreading in a society of abundance, and the determination of New Thought advocates to take advantage of it. But his faith in the power of an energized mental state expanded to take in physical activity. He came to believe that the body, like the mind, could be used to generate vigor, energy, and creativity.

In the spring of 1926, H. William Klare, manager of a Detroit hotel, arranged a rather unusual banquet in honor of Henry Ford. The automaker had become noted for his dietary interests, and his latest enthusiasm—carrots—figured prominently in the evening's festivities. When the diners took their seats, the banquet hall grew dark and a spotlight shone on a figure dressed in black and orange who was standing next to Ford at the head of the table. The figure announced, "I am King Carrota! I am full of vitamins, full of iron, full of iodine, full of bottled sunshine. I have no enemy but a bad cook. I am a friend of flappers and the bald-headed, the spindly baby and three-chinned monsters, but who shall mix me with canned peas shall be consigned to outer darkness." Following this proclamation, the lights rose and the guests dug into a twelve-course meal consisting entirely of carrot dishes: carrots à l'orange, carrot soup Crécy mirliton, pickled carrots Greek style, carrots hors d'oeuvre, mousse of carrots, carrot loaf ravigote, carrots au gratin, carrot marmalade, carrot salad Henri Ford, carrot ice cream, and carrot tarte, the meal accompanied by large glasses of carrot juice. While the guests ate heartily, one of them, a dietitian, deflated the atmosphere of good cheer. Near the meal's end, he noted that a New York orphanage had overfed its children with carrots a few years earlier and was shocked to find that they had turned yellow. He hastily added, "The discoloration actually is not harmful, but I do know the children"—and here he paused and stressed the last three words—"*did turn yellow.*" As the diners left the banquet hall, each one, including Ford, glanced nervously into the large lobby mirror to check his pigmentation.[24]

This bizarre incident reflected an important dimension of Henry Ford's adult sensibility—a preoccupation with matters of diet, health, exercise, and physical development. Like his denunciations of liquor and alcohol, Ford's interest in food reform was rooted in Victorian tradition. Since the mid-nineteenth century, reformers such as Sylvester Graham had suggested that dietary purity, like sexual propriety and emotional restraint, fostered self-control. Ford followed in this tradition, but he also transcended it. Rather than just urging reform as a matter of moral character, he preached a "gospel of health" that promoted physical revitalization as a highway to worldly success. Here he converged with the movement for "physical culture" in early-twentieth-century America.[25]

Ford believed that diet was a crucial factor in human development, both physical and mental. By the early twentieth century, he had become convinced that food intake determined a variety of physical, emotional, and behavioral characteristics. "Most of the ailments of people come from eating too much, or eating the wrong things," he said in 1928. "Ailments are caused by, if not entirely due to, faulty eating." Ford denounced sugar, excessive starch, coffee and tea, too much wheat, and red meat as harmful to the human body. He was convinced that certain combinations of food caused particular kinds of sickness. To a friend who was hospitalized with gastric ulcers, Ford said, "Too much roast beef and milk, eh? It does it every time."[26]

He also linked diet to certain mental qualities. "Food specialists should try to find some food or combination of foods that will help to develop strong will-power. There are food regulations for almost every kind of physical disorder, why should there not also be a possibility of feeding a man so that he may be built up against mental or moral weakness?" he asked an interviewer. He liked to tell a story about how once he was able to assuage an angry company stockholder because he had an empty stomach. "I could prevent him from irritating me because I wasn't full of food," Ford explained. "My mind was clear. The blood was in my head instead of my stomach and I had self-control."[27]

Ford became convinced that diet produced patterns of behavior. Crime, depression, nervousness, lethargy—all were rooted in bad eating habits. "Most wrong acts committed by men are the result of wrong mixtures in the stomach," he told *Redbook* magazine. The individual seeking to live efficiently and effectively should seek to "discover the vital connection between food and attitudes of mind, between food and the energies of mind and of body." In fact, social harmony depended largely on diet. "Hospitals and jails and prisons would all have less to do if people learned right feeding habits," he said.[28]

People who sought mental vigor, physical vitality, and proper behavior should eat vegetables. Though not a strict vegetarian, Ford told the Detroit *News* in 1919, "the world would be better off without meat." He also became a fan of the Hay Diet, which warned against the ill effects of combining starches, proteins, and fruit acids at one meal. Beyond these two enthusiasms, Ford's dietary advice veered wildly from one fad to another. At various times he warned against fresh dough and said that bread should be eaten only after it has sat for a day; argued that "chicken is fit only for hawks"; depicted fried pork, boiled potatoes, and oranges as unhealthy; and defined cottage cheese as nothing more than spoiled milk. For a while, he advocated that people eat nothing until after 1:00 p.m. because of likely digestive problems at an earlier hour. He sang the praises of carrots, butter, celery, and sarsaparilla, although his enthusiasms fluctuated from year to year. By the 1930s, Ford had become convinced that soybeans were a magical food for good health. Visitors to the Ford exhibit at the 1934 World's Fair in Chicago were treated to a special menu: tomato juice with soy sauce, celery stuffed with soy cheese, soybean soup with crackers made from soy flour, apple pie with soy-flour crust, and soybean milk.[29]

Ford's dietary views often were downright eccentric. In the 1890s, he told Oliver Barthel of his conviction that sugar was harmful because its tiny crystals would lacerate the tissue in the digestive system after being swallowed. Throughout his life he denounced the pasteurization of milk, saying that it should be drunk fresh, "before it strikes the air." He insisted that colds came from overeating, or eating wrong combinations of foods, and recommended a forty-eight-hour fast as a remedy. To those suffering from ulcers, Ford suggested that a cure would result from "swallowing a ball of butter right down whole, once daily." A fan of salt, he contended that it should be used for brushing the teeth and rubbing into the hair to keep it healthy and vibrant. Such odd notions struck a sour note with some experts. Dr. E. V. McCollum of Johns Hopkins Hospital, a leading authority on diet and nutrition, stated, "Henry Ford knows about as much about food as he knew about history when they had him on the witness stand [in Mount Clemens]."[30]

By the 1910s, Ford's interest in the human body was moving beyond diet issues, as he began to embrace doctrines of physical development. In the same way that his New Thought convictions promised increased mental vigor, he believed that devotion to exercise promised to pay physical dividends. On this front, Ford's relationship with the early-twentieth-century "physical culture" movement proved especially revealing.

In the late nineteenth century, fears of weakness and dissipation among the genteel classes had prompted concerns about growing softness and "overcivilization" in American society. The image of the flabby, complacent, overstressed, convenience-addicted businessman began to haunt the bourgeois imagination. A number of factors—an epidemic of "neurasthenia," or nervous prostration, among prosperous men and women; the extreme emotional repression demanded by genteel standards of conduct; growing fears of lower-class revolt caused by labor agitation and social unrest—converged to create an atmosphere of crisis. As a result, there were calls for physical regeneration in American public life. Theodore Roosevelt's campaign for the "strenuous life," as well as popular movements extolling the invigorating virtues of camping, hunting, and athletics for both men and women, became part of the American cultural landscape. Building upon this foundation, Bernarr Macfadden appeared at the turn of the century as the messiah of health and bodily vigor.[31]

Emerging from a background of family impoverishment and illness, Macfadden became an advocate of physical fitness as a young man. Although slight of stature, he earned a livelihood as a weight lifter and professional wrestler. His enthusiasm for health and fitness, along with a love of publicity, led him to found a magazine. *Physical Culture*, first published in 1898, promoted an agenda of exercise, diet reform, and physical regeneration. With its slogan—"Weakness Is a Crime, Don't Be a Criminal"—the magazine promoted Macfadden's pet projects of vegetarianism, fasting, athletic exercise, and robust sexuality. It insisted that "sickness is a sin" and argued that such activities as calisthenics, bicycle riding, swimming, and hiking constituted obedience to God's natural laws of health. His "gospel of health," as one scholar has termed it, combined physical revitalization, religion, self-improvement literature, and marketing into a compelling whole that lasted well into the 1930s.[32]

As with New Thought, Ford never formally announced his endorsement of Macfadden and the "physical culture" agenda. His actions, however, made the affiliation clear. In June 1923, an interview entitled "Smooth-Running Henry Ford" appeared in *Physical Culture*. That same month, another of Macfadden's publications, *National Brain Power*, featured several pieces on Ford. All of them were written by P. L. Atkinson, a journalist and physical-culture enthusiast, who spent several days interviewing Ford and touring his plants at Highland Park and River Rouge. Years later, Macfadden himself interviewed Ford for a pair of articles in his magazines

Liberty and *Physical Culture*. An advertisement aptly suggested the theme of these stories. Entitled "The Story of Henry Ford—Physical Culturalist," the ad noted that Ford's "bodily fitness can be compared only to the efficiency of his business and manufacturing methods. His clean, athletic life stands as a model lesson in keeping fit and in the fine art of living."[33]

In the early 1920s, Macfadden publications portrayed Ford as a physical ideal. *Physical Culture* described him as having "an astoundingly well-knit, powerful, disease-resisting body and a physique that any physical culturalist must envy," attributing this to the fact that he had avoided sedentary occupations and, "whenever possible, done his thinking on his feet, among the men in his shops and his factories, at their side and not behind a desk." The author even made the ultimate comparison, picturing Ford as a man with "all the latent energy of mind and body that characterized Colonel Roosevelt." Articles praised his regimen of outdoor exercise, which consisted of walking cross-country and jumping fences in warm weather, and ice-skating in the winter. At one point, Ford pulled a pedometer from his pocket to show Atkinson that he had covered six miles that day while performing his duties.[34]

In 1923, *Physical Culture* specifically tied Ford's industrial achievements to his superb physical condition. "It is but natural that a man who has so revolutionized industry by methods that show astonishing common-sense should care for his physical well-being," the magazine noted. Years later, Bernarr Macfadden elaborated: "Mr. Ford is perhaps one of the most remarkable demonstrations we have in this country at this time of the advantage of the physical culture life in securing and maintaining the success that we all crave. . . . As a demonstration of the value a natural, healthful life in bringing out the talents and powers that reside in the soul of every human, Mr. Ford's career could hardly be improved upon."[35]

The Ford image of robust health and physical development, however, did not just grace the pages of Macfadden's magazines. It appeared in public statements throughout his adult life. In *Psychology* magazine, Ford promoted the virtues of exercise and vigor in an article entitled "Keep Interested and Stay Fit." "Personally, I believe in movement. I do not stay in one place very long," Ford said. "A man who sits at a desk all day becomes logy; he is using only part of his powers. Let him get up and move around. It will be good for both his mind and his body." He urged white-collar and blue-collar workers alike to exercise in off hours by walking, skating, doing sit-ups, any of "a multitude of things to take the kinks out of the spine." Ford followed his own advice, pitching hay during harvest on his farm, skating during the winter, and walking daily. Years earlier, he had joined his workmen for boxing contests over the noon hour. To the surprise of onlookers, when facing a burly opponent the slender factory-owner "was over him like a swarm of bees" and triumphed with his quickness and tenacity.[36]

Ford also preached the "gospel of health" to Ralph Waldo Trine and detailed his own physical regimen. He suggested that the study of diet and physical exercise was producing new knowledge that could enhance the quality and length of life. "We are already putting more mileage into the body by learning what is causing it to wear out," Ford observed. "Man will soon be able to use his body for a much longer time, because he will discover what is necessary to do so."[37]

In his day-to-day activities Ford indulged in a lifelong habit of footracing friends and acquaintances. According to Charles Sorensen, "He could run like a deer. Often when I was on a trip with him he would have the car stopped and say, 'Let's take a run.' He always won easily—even, when he was seventy, over active men half his age." This mania for physical fitness influenced Ford's hiring of managers at his company. "The first thing I would consider is health. I would never choose a man who looked sickly, weak, or run down," he told Allan L. Benson. "A man who does not care enough about his own body to take proper care of it and keep it in a high state of efficiency is not likely to care enough about somebody else's business to give it efficient management."[38]

Thus Henry Ford's health agenda, like that of the larger physical-culture movement, combined an ethos of physical and mental strength with ideas of personality, unlimited human potential, and self-development. It promised success to the vigorous, healthy individual operating in a new economic atmosphere of consumer abundance. Ultimately, however, Ford's physical energies overflowed the confines of exercise and diet, just as his New Thought principles transcended the goal of mere material success. Both the physical and the mental converged to shape a new morality that found an outlet in a different, more intimate area.

Henry Ford liked to visit an old farmhouse sitting on land near the Ford dairy in Dearborn. He would settle in a favorite rocking chair that cradled a small pillow given to him by the mistress of the house. He conversed with her for hours, reflecting upon his ideas and dispensing advice about various daily issues in her life. After a time, however, Ford invariably liked to take a brief nap, and he would fuss with the pillow, plumping it and arranging it to fit the small of his back. It became a standing joke that, despite this elaborate ritual, the pillow would be on the floor five minutes after he fell asleep. When he awakened, she would tease him by saying, "You see, you can handle an empire but you can't handle a pillow. Now, *I* can do both."[39]

The comment typified the woman who made it. Evangeline Dahlinger was a bright, vivacious, ambitious, and outspoken young woman who enjoyed an intimate relationship with Ford that lasted over three decades. A close companion who shared many of his interests as well as his high energy level, she lavished attention, affection, and respect upon a man thirty years her senior. In turn, she became the object of Ford's largesse, receiving not only his personal devotion but an outpouring of gifts that made her comfortably wealthy. Evidence also suggests that Eve Dahlinger enjoyed Ford's physical attentions, bearing him a son in 1923 whose existence became a source of obvious, if muted, pride for him. But, as with nearly everything about Henry Ford, this was no simple matter of a powerful man keeping a secret mistress. The tangled relationship involved company intrigue, marital compliance, and peculiar physical proximity in terms of their living arrangements. Overall, the romance bespoke Ford's embrace of a personal morality that undermined the Victorian traditions of nineteenth-century America.

Sixteen-year-old Evangeline Côté had joined the Ford Motor Company in 1909. Of French Canadian background, she was born in 1893 as the oldest of four children. When her father, a professor, became ill, she went to work to help support him and her three younger brothers. She entered the stenographic department at Ford, and within three years had become its head. Shortly thereafter, she caught the eye of Harold Wills, who asked her to become his personal secretary. In 1913 and 1914, as the company expanded, Wills worked closely with Henry Ford, and Côté made his acquaintance. She became increasingly friendly with the industrialist, first as a special assistant, and then as much more.[40]

Côté presented obvious attractions to Ford. Physically, she was a petite young woman just over five feet tall, with dark eyes, a curvaceous figure, and toothy grin. Her personality, however, made a bigger impact. Naturally vivacious, Côté was headstrong and independent-minded and tended toward outspokenness. She tempered these traits, however, with a charming and flirtatious personal style. Fun-loving and quick to laugh, she appealed to the opposite sex and, according to one observer, "easily twisted men around her little finger."[41]

Moreover, Evangeline Côté broke the mold of expected behavior for females. In many ways, she represented the youthful, liberated "new woman" on the American scene by the 1920s, who was determined to reject traditions of female propriety and self-restraint. Rather than engaging in sewing, cooking, reading, and domestic management, Côté embraced a vigorous lifestyle of physical activity. An excellent horsewoman who became the women's harness-racing champion in the state of Michigan, she so excelled at riding that she mastered the trick of cantering about while standing atop two horses at the same time. She also loved flying, becoming the first woman in Michigan to earn a pilot's license, and kept a Curtiss Flying Boat at a lake in the northern part of the state. She also adored speedboats and piloted a thirty-six-foot craft with a large Liberty engine. In more sedate moments, she enjoyed long walks through the countryside and ice-skating. In fact, she was so much the tomboy that Ford gave her the nickname Billy. Not surprisingly, Côté rejected the Victorian standard of thrift and, according to one witness, "threw money around riotously. Ford loved it." Thus, though fully feminine and something of a coquette, this energetic young woman was determined to break free from traditional female stereotypes.[42]

In particular, two things seemed to attract Henry Ford to Eve Côté.

First, unlike nearly everyone else in his life, she dealt with him honestly and stood her ground when she thought he was wrong. "She was not afraid of him, and I can still hear her giving Mr. Ford a piece of her mind," an observer noted. To a man often surrounded by sycophants, such conduct was a refreshing change. At the same time, Côté evinced a larger attitude of respect and admiration for Ford, verging on hero-worship. She followed his daily activities with intense interest, deferred to his judgments on many practical matters, and solicited his opinion, even on issues about which she had already made up her mind. This could shade into manipulation as she laughed and gazed at him tenderly with her large light-green eyes.[43]

Second, Eve's active, vigorous lifestyle proved alluring to a man enamored of health reform and physical culture. The pair loved to ice-skate together and spent many hours taking long walks in the woods and fields near his Fair Lane estate. "They loved to walk the railroad tracks; they would start from Dearborn and walk all the way to Detroit on the tracks—a distance of seven or eight miles," Eve's son reported. "However, at the end of the line, Ford's car and driver would be waiting to take them back." Ford drew the line at horseback riding. His well-known distrust of horses kept him on the sidelines as an admiring observer of Côté's riding and racing achievements.[44]

Ford found himself drawing closer to Evangeline Côté. When he returned from the Peace Ship mission in early 1916, for instance, he brought her an expensive silver brooch set with six large moonstones. Eve returned the devotion, spending as much time as possible with Ford and keeping track of his various endeavors in her diary. By the time of America's entry into World War I, however, their relationship had reached an impasse.[45]

Perhaps from a desire to extricate himself from an improper entanglement, or perhaps from a wish to create a façade of propriety behind which the romance could be conducted, Ford decided to find Evangeline a husband. By 1917, he had picked his chauffeur and assistant, Ray Dahlinger, and began maneuvering to position the young man near the attractive Côté. Dahlinger was totally devoted to Ford. He had secured a job at the company and worked his way up from assembly to testing to the experimental room at Highland Park, where he performed stress tests on Model T's. There Dahlinger met Ford, who would come by occasionally to be driven around the track and observe his car's performance firsthand. He became Ford's bodyguard and accompanied him on the Peace Ship. Upon returning, he assumed the duties of Ford's chauffeur and was responsible for upkeep of his automobiles. A hardworking, pleasant-looking young man, Dahlinger was nearly engaged to a good friend of his sister when the Ford plan materialized. Loyal to his boss and aware of Evangeline's charms, Dahlinger became her suitor.[46]

Côté responded. Strongly desiring children, and resigned to the fact that she could never marry Ford, she cooperated with the scheme. A relationship flowered, and Ray and Evangeline were married on February 20, 1917. They moved into an old farmhouse on Ford land in Dearborn, not far from his Fair Lane estate.[47]

From nearly the outset, the Dahlinger marriage was strained. After several years, Eve had failed to get pregnant, and the couple were sleeping in separate beds, and eventually separate bedrooms. As a flood of gifts from Henry Ford came pouring into the household, the relationship between Ray and Eve deteriorated. Ford provided a three-hundred-acre farm in nearby Romeo, and stocked it with three hundred head of cattle. He gave the Dahlingers a vacation house in upper Michigan, a number of expensive horses, and a large "flying boat" airplane. Though he was fond of both Dahlingers, the presents obviously reflected his affection for Eve and focused upon her outdoor interests.[48]

Ford's generosity culminated in a gift of 150 acres situated just downriver from his own home on the River Rouge. This became the site for the Dahlinger estate in the late 1920s, a palatial property whose worth obviously surpassed the financial resources of its occupants. The Tudor-style main house had nine fireplaces, eight bathrooms, servants' quarters, and a refrigerated fur-storage vault. It was surrounded by a gatehouse, several barns, a blacksmith shop, a lake and skating house, quarter-mile and half-mile racetracks, a gardener's house, a greenhouse, a boathouse, and a very large garage. The main house had a secret staircase. After entering a small, out-of-the-way room on the main floor, one could climb these stairs and emerge into Eve's bedroom suite upstairs without being observed.[49]

Ray Dahlinger cut a sad figure in this complex situation. On the one hand, he displayed occasional bitterness about his peculiar domestic life. Always a convivial consumer of alcohol, he began drinking more heavily. As the mansion went up on the River Rouge site, funded by Ford money, he bridled. "He said he was perfectly happy living in the old farmhouse and he didn't want to live in a 'goddamn castle,' " according to a friend who overheard him complain. Ray and Eve cooperated on various Ford projects, but any real intimacy seems to have evaporated. Though accepting the situation, Ray occasionally betrayed his emotional wounds. In a newspaper story in the Detroit *Times* about his management of the Ford Farms, Dahlinger declared, "Let me tell you one thing that I've always noticed. If a man is a success it is always because of a woman. And I believe it's up to every woman [to guarantee] whether her husband is a success or not." The irony of this comment turned pathetic within a few years. In a letter to Eve, he pleaded to be rid of their twin beds as something "made for only sick people, not people that love each other." "I wish our room would have *one* bed just for *you* and *me*. Is it alright for me to say that?" Yet Ray did not lead a monkish existence. He was observed at a Dahlinger party, for example, behind a tree, kissing a woman who had been flirting madly with him for several weeks.[50]

On the other hand, as compensation for his aggrieved status, Ray enjoyed a privileged position in the Ford organization. He was appointed supervisor of the Ford Farms, an important job that included not only agricultural sites but an airport and Greenfield Village, the historical attraction that Henry Ford had begun constructing in the late 1920s. Dahlinger also helped with special projects, such as a publicity film for the new Model A in the late 1920s. He jealously guarded his position, often in artless fashion, and made many enemies in the process. He sought to hamstring anyone who seemed a threat, causing many to describe him as "unscrupulous" and "a good fellow to stay away from." Others rolled their eyes at his penchant for telling tall tales designed to exaggerate his own importance, and denounced his habit of appropriating company equipment to use for his seasonal projects. Trying to throw his weight around, he alienated powerful figures in the Ford organization, such as Charles Sorensen.[51]

Yet Dahlinger remained devoted to Henry Ford as his "ambassador at large" or, more nastily, his "henchman." He followed the orders of "The Boss" doggedly and without question, even when those orders involved things about which Dahlinger knew nothing. According to many, that was the case most of the time. As Dahlinger once confessed to Eugene Farkas, a company engineer, "I never do anything unless Mr. Ford tells me to do it. There are a lot of things that I don't like to do, but I've got to do it." The picture of loyalty, he carried out Ford's wishes and cemented their special relationship. Because others could read the situation accurately and feared crossing his patron, Dahlinger was able to accumulate considerable power.[52]

But Dahlinger's relationship with his boss was more complex than it appeared. Ford was genuinely fond of him and appreciated his loyal friendship. At the same time, however, Ford accorded him little respect. Periodically he would administer "an awful licking" to Ray, chewing him out for poor performance, threatening his job security, and reducing his responsibilities. Such encounters would leave Dahlinger "scared to death," but he always rebounded and came back for more. "He seemed to be a hound for being kicked around" by Ford, noted one observer. Sometimes Ford intimidated Dahlinger in subtle ways, such as deliberately instructing that equipment be stored in spaces Ray was using for his work, or calling him at all hours of the day or night to run errands. Occasionally, Ford would even publicly embarrass Dahlinger. Knowing the underling's penchant for embellishing stories to exaggerate his own importance, Ford would stop Dahlinger in mid-sentence and tell him to start over and tell the truth. It seems clear that the two men were involved in a complicated dynamic of sex and power, in which the cuckold was utterly dependent, both psychologically and materially, upon the man who was cuckolding him.[53]

Eve Dahlinger faced no such ambiguity in her relationship with Ford. She was widely recognized, in the words of engineer Harold Hicks, as "quite a power in the Ford organization." Her assertive personality, in concert with her well-known closeness to Henry Ford, made her a fearsome figure. The fact that her father had a Ford agency in Ferndale, a Detroit suburb, and her brother had one in Highland Park, provided additional evidence of Eve's special pull. Her authority also stemmed partly from respect for her competence and intelligence. She was generally considered to be "the brains of the [Ford] farm," and most assumed that she was the reason Ray had been made superintendent. By the late 1920s, she was supervising many of the activities in Greenfield Village, including the several schools on the premises. She also helped train the servants who worked at Fair Lane. According to an admiring associate, "Mrs. Dahlinger was the go-getter type and got things done with dispatch, without red tape." In the blunt assessment of another, "She gave orders like a man."[54]

The crucial event in the Ford-Dahlinger relationship occurred on April 9, 1923, when Eve gave birth to a son, John, in Henry Ford Hospital. Ford appeared at the hospital immediately after the birth and showed a keen interest in the new baby. He hired the maternity-ward nurse to accompany the infant to the Dahlinger home and take care of him. A few days later, he gave Eve the baby crib in which he had slept as a child. When only a month old, young John received his first present from Ford, a Shetland pony. In such fashion the industrialist lavished attention upon the boy, a pattern that would hold throughout his childhood.[55]

Over the next several years, Ford sent a caravan of gifts for the child. These included a rocking horse, a miniature gardening wagon and tools, a small-scale motorized roadster, a small horse-drawn sleigh, a miniature electric car, a horse-drawn buckboard, a red bike, a trick horse from the Ringling Brothers Circus, and a small tractor. At age seven, young John Dahlinger received perhaps his most prized gift—a race car from the 1923 Indianapolis 500 that had its engine governed and its interior modified to allow him to reach the pedals. The delighted boy spent hours speeding about the half-mile horse track on the Dahlinger estate.[56]

Ford also communicated personally with John. On his sixth birthday, in 1929, when Ford was away on a business trip, he sent the following telegram: DEAR JOHN HAPPY BIRTHDAY MUCH LOVE HENRY FORD. Ford also talked regularly with him. "I learned even as a small child that wherever I was, Mr. Ford was sure to show up," Dahlinger recalled later. "He would find me, come upon me casually and sit down beside me, starting a casual conversation and imparting his philosophy or knowledge about life as he poked a stick at the ground. He seemed bent on telling me how to live, how to think, how to grow up to be part of his empire." These visits would often take place on Sunday afternoon, when Ford would take John for long rides up and down the River Rouge, trying to instill in the youth "his principles and prejudices."[57]

In fact, Ford regularly visited the Dahlinger estate throughout the 1920s and 1930s, coming by boat, bicycle, or, later in life, by chauffeur. He would see John, and then spend private time with Eve, or "Billy." Ray disappeared during most of these visits. According to John Dahlinger, Ray would typically come out of the house and Ford "would call out and say, 'Hello there, Ray. Is Billy home?' Then he'd go to see Mother, and they'd go cycling together. Dad would go driving off in his car. He accepted it. It was our way of life." In turn, young Dahlinger became a regular visitor at Fair Lane, where he played with Ford's grandchildren, Henry, Benson, Josephine, and William. The Ford-Dahlinger personal connection was unbreakable. "My parents and I always had access to the Fords," John stated. "We had a private telephone line to Fair Lane."[58]

The obvious question concerned John Dahlinger's patrimony. Was he Henry Ford's son? Circumstantial evidence—Ford's constant personal attention to Eve, the mansion and privileged position in the organization for Eve and Ray, the attention and gifts lavished on the boy—suggests strongly that he was. Eve Dahlinger, even several decades after Henry Ford's death, refused to divulge the nature of their private relationship, but she provided several hints. When John was old enough to understand and confront his mother about the rumors of his paternity, she replied, "I don't want to talk about it." Since that was her habitual response when she did not want to admit something, John noted, he immediately concluded that the rumor was truthful. Another time, he asked Eve if Mr. Ford loved him, since the older man seemed so concerned about his welfare. Eve responded, "Mr. Ford loves you very much, much more than I can express. And someday he wants you to help him run his whole company." John continued, "Does he love me like you do?" She replied, "Yes, that's the way he loves you." Thus, when Eve did deign to talk about it, even obliquely, her words suggested that Ford was the father.[59]

Irving Bacon, the Ford artist-in-residence, encountered Henry and Eve's relationship a number of times. When Ford sent Bacon to the Dahlinger household to do some decorative painting, the artist noticed the large number of expensive toys on the porch, which had to have come from Ford. When John was a bit older, the artist complimented the mother on her son's polite behavior and good nature. Eve gave Bacon a curious look and replied, "He has more sense than someone else I know." The artist reacted impishly: "I wonder who she meant?" Bacon's own conclusions about the boy's patrimony appeared clearly in the late 1920s. Asked by Ford to do a series of paintings based on his early life at the farm in Dearborn, the artist sought a boy model to help him accurately portray the youthful Ford. He did not look long before selecting John Dahlinger. Henry approved the choice and told Eve, in his typically dry way, "Well, John will do. It's close enough."[60]

In fact, the relationship between Henry and Eve became something of an open secret in the Ford organization. Rumors ran rampant about John Dahlinger's status as a love child. Many employees speculated privately about the situation, although none would comment publicly. Harold Hicks, for instance, told an interviewer many years later that Ford had him design a fancy barn for the Dahlingers that included a kitchen, toilet, and lounge. "The lady slept in the house, and he [Ray] slept in the barn," he explained. Hicks quickly added, "That was the story, anyway, but I'd better shut up." Not only were employees afraid to cross Ford, but they were reluctant to alienate Eve Dahlinger herself.[61]

Henry Ford's attitude toward women probably played a role in this tangled affair. Though holding to the traditional Victorian view that females were morally superior, he displayed a misogynistic streak. Privately, he declaimed against women's influence in the world and drew examples from the Bible to warn John Dahlinger that "women were behind all evil." He also had a roving eye, and had at least one awkward dalliance with a servant girl at Fair Lane. Thus he seems to have officially honored the tradition of female virtue while privately disparaging it. Harold Hicks once joked that a prominent engineer had ensured his demise at Ford Motor Company because of a fondness for women. Ford's reply revealed much about his underlying attitude: "Women! Why, Hicks, women don't do you any harm. You can screw any woman on earth, excepting for one thing; never let your wife find out."[62]

In less crass fashion, Ford publicly explained his views on adultery with words that may have illuminated his own situation. In a 1923 interview, he was asked to comment on men's proclivity to engage in affairs when they reached their forties. His response—that women needed to practice forbearance, and men needed to understand their own weakness—seemed to have a personal resonance. Men, he argued, are "simply trying to hold on to their youth. I say to the woman whose husband is in this situation: Treat it like the measles! It's a disease that strikes lots of people. That's all it is, at the most. Help your husband through it. Stand by. Don't let it hurt you. Don't let it break up your home."[63]

Henry's decades-long relationship with Eve Dahlinger raised equally intriguing questions about Clara's attitude. Given the widespread rumors about her husband and his young female assistant, and the fact that the Dahlingers were ensconced in grand style next to Fair Lane, it is impossible to believe that she was unaware of the situation. In fact, several incidents revealed her irritation. In the late 1920s, Irving Bacon did a painting of the grand banquet hosted by Ford to honor Thomas Edison and celebrate the opening of the Edison Institute. The canvas included Eve Dahlinger as one of the onlookers. A few days later, Ford appeared at his studio and exclaimed, "Take her out. Mrs. Ford wouldn't like her to be in it." As Harry Bennett put it plainly, "Mr. Ford admired Mrs. Dahlinger a great deal. Mrs. Ford did not."[64]

Yet some evidence suggests that Clara, for all of her resentment, may have tacitly agreed to look the other way. A genteel, dignified woman, she shared neither her husband's robust physical energy nor his habit of displaying affection. Whereas Henry would grab her hand or stride up and throw his arms around her, Clara viewed such demonstrations as unladylike and studiously avoided them. Rosa Buhler, the head maid at Fair Lane, reported that Mrs. Ford abhorred any kind of physical display with her husband. Moreover, it is likely that Clara had a hysterectomy in 1907, at age forty-one. Several physicians examined her in the fall of that year, before she underwent major surgery at Harper Hospital, probably the best medical facility in Detroit. This procedure incurred a payment of $2,700 to Dr. William F. Metcalf, who specialized in "Abdominal & Pelvic Surgery."[65]

When one considers that Clara turned fifty in 1916, it seems reasonable to suspect that she may have lost interest in the physical side of marriage while remaining fully confident of her husband's love and respect for her. Henry hinted at this scenario. Fred Black recalled that, though Ford was not partial to ribald stories, when he did tell one it "had a very definite point." At lunch one day, he told a story about a young man who ventured into a bordello only to be shocked when he spotted his elderly Uncle Charlie sitting in the parlor with a young, scantily clad woman on his lap. When the embarrassed youth expressed his surprise, Uncle Charlie replied, "Well, James, I find the active cooperation of these young ladies to be far more satisfying than the passive acquiescence of your Aunt Jane." If Ford's joke reflected the state of affairs at home, Clara may have found Henry's affair with Eve to be acceptable as long as discretion kept it officially private.[66]

The fact that Clara eventually developed an odd friendship with Eve Dahlinger lends credence to this view. By the 1930s, Eve was serving as a kind of secretary to Mrs. Ford, at least part-time, helping her with correspondence and to arrange social events. Clara began to depend on Eve, writing instructions about various tasks to be fulfilled, handing over shopping lists, and complaining about work that was falling behind at Fair Lane. A nurse at the Fords' summer home discovered the relationship between Eve and Clara. A local doctor was treating Mrs. Ford for arthritis, but when the nurse offered assistance, Eve refused the help. "Mrs. Dahlinger didn't even want me to know that she had it," the nurse reported. That Eve felt protective of Clara's privacy about a matter of personal health suggests the closeness of their friendship.[67]

The scene of Henry Ford's death may have clinched the case for Clara's acceptance of her husband's special relationship with Eve. When he became quite ill, late one evening in April 1947, the Ford maid and chauffeur located Henry's doctor and eldest grandson, both of whom rushed to Fair Lane. A phone call also went out to another residence. When Henry Ford II and the physician arrived, about an hour later, Ford had expired. But Eve Dahlinger was already present, summoned by Clara. She was standing at Ford's bedside to say her last goodbye.[68]

Henry Ford's long, intimate relationship with a woman thirty years his junior, like his attraction to New Thought and physical culture, reflected his instinct for cultural innovation. In many ways, Ford's new morality was that of modern America. Like the millions of Americans who were buying Model T's in the 1910s and 1920s while jettisoning traditions of self-restraint, Ford was reveling in a culture of mental and physical abundance.

Seventeen

Emperor

In the late 1920s, Henry Ford became one of Will Rogers' favorite topics. In addresses, articles, and radio commentaries, the popular humorist frequently joked about the industrialist's traits and influence in modern America. Ford "changed the habits of more people than Caesar, Mussolini, Charlie Chaplin, Clara Bow, Amos 'n' Andy, and Bernard Shaw," Rogers once claimed. He poked fun at the Model T, noting that in Ford's America "a man's castle is his sedan." Noting Ford's often expressed belief that a university education needed to be more oriented toward practical job skills, Rogers quipped, "If Henry Ford can educate a college boy to make a living right after he gets out of college, Ford is really the greatest living American."[1]

Rogers' humorous commentary on Ford reached its apex in "The Grand Champion," a 1929 essay appearing in the *American Magazine*. He satirized the vogue for success in the 1920s and the public's fascination with wealth, noting, "Why, the rich is getting so common now that it's almost a novelty to be poor." Rogers focused on champions, however, a category he defined as being the best at any one thing, whether it was Bobby Jones and golf, Houdini and magic, or Al Smith as a second Columbus because "he discovered 14 million Democrats in this country when it was thought the race was practically extinct." Rogers nominated as grand champion, however, a man who had influenced the world more than anyone: "our plain old friend, Mr. Henry Ford."

The choice set off a landslide of Rogers one-liners. Ford, "along with Brigham Young, is the originator of mass production." Ford was responsible for more building in the United States than any other man, since garages and filling stations now outnumbered schools and churches. Ford's cars "made more business for an undertaker than any other one thing, with the exception of Prohibition." Ford created the two biggest problems in modern America: first, "where am I going to park it," and second, "after it's parked (and you come back and get it), how am I going to get home in it through the traffic?" Ford "has taken the Police Force of the towns off watching criminals and got 'em standing in the middle of the streets waving their arms." Ford had driven all levels of government into debt, since "we owe more for roads than we do for persuading the Germans to 'please leave Belgium.' " Ford must be credited for the fact that there were "23,078 Ford radiators boiling over on the hills of this country every day" while there were "43,000 people just holding up the hoods of Fords looking at them, 42,598 with the same expression." Ford had allowed thousands of entrepreneurs to get rich "by just making things that go onto Fords after they are supposed to be finished." Ford had "caused more profanity than the Congress and Senate combined." Rogers concluded, "A marriage certificate and a Ford car are the two cheapest things known. Both lead to an ambition for something better." That Rogers was confident that his vast audience was familiar enough with Ford to get the jokes provided a clear sign of the industrialist's enormous popularity.[2]

By the late 1920s, Henry Ford had reached the pinnacle of his reputation and influence. The basis of his popularity, of course, remained the Model T, which the Ford factories continued to produce by the millions throughout the decade. In addition, Ford's activities as an industrial reformer and erstwhile political candidate, along with his image as a folk hero and success icon, made him perhaps the most esteemed private citizen in the United States. His thoughts on every conceivable topic provided grist for the journalists' mill on almost a daily basis, and his comments were a surefire attraction for readers throughout the country. Stories about him and by him appeared regularly in nearly every major magazine and newspaper in the United States.

In 1926, Charles Merz described this phenomenon as "The Canonization of Henry Ford." "We are approaching the point where anything is all right if Ford does it," he wrote in a magazine article. Merz pointed out that the steady stream of press releases from the Ford Motor Company was supplemented by journalists' determined solicitation of Ford's opinion, as well as his penchant for making off-the-cuff pronouncements when changing trains or attending public gatherings. Ford, Merz wrote with only slight exaggeration,

> . . . is besieged by an army of quite eager and quite earnest journalists who stand in line for his views on everything from foreign loans to modern marriage, including world peace, world war, mass production, the younger generation, the essentials of a good life on the

farm, the care of babies, and the business outlook in the Orient. . . .
He is [as] steadily pelted away at, with requests for an opinion, as
the oracle at Delphi.

Ford was no longer just the head of an industrial empire. He had become a
seer and a sage. As Merz observed, "Here he is, the man who made the Tin
Lizzie, now busily interpreting Twentieth Century industrialism to itself."[3]

At the very moment of Ford's triumph, however, several deep-seated
problems created an undercurrent of uneasiness. Amid the chorus of praise
for his unprecedented achievements, a few jeers and catcalls could be heard.
A small coterie of critics questioned Ford's treatment of labor, his managerial practices, and his reputation as a reformer. As this criticism gained
adherents, the suspicion arose that Ford's sterling reputation as an innovative industrialist may have rested on a shaky foundation.

Signs of a brewing storm also appeared on the practical front. After
reaching new levels in 1923, sales of Ford's beloved Model T began to
decline in the face of growing competition. The General Motors Corporation, under the dynamic leadership of Alfred P. Sloan, developed a modern
marketing-and-organizational scheme in the 1920s. It created automobiles
for consumers in every price range—Chevrolets, Pontiacs, Oldsmobiles,
Buicks, Cadillacs—offering, according to its slogan, "a car for every purse
and purpose." Its research staff, led by Charles F. Kettering, developed better tires, brakes, and gears; a "styling section," headed by Hollywood
designer Harley Earl, improved the appearance of its cars. By the mid-
1920s, these innovations had culminated in the yearly model change, which
was introduced with great fanfare by the company's advertising division.
The General Motors Acceptance Corporation offered loans that allowed
consumers to buy on credit. At the managerial level, Sloan developed a corporate structure of "centralized decentralization" that protected the entrepreneurial independence of its divisions while integrating them within an
efficient governing structure. General Motors' sales began to soar, as did
those of Chrysler, the final member of the "Big Three." Organized by Walter Chrysler in 1925, the company developed a popular medium-priced car
with a high-compression engine, purchased the Dodge Brothers Company
in 1928, and presented the low-priced Plymouth that same year. Firmly
grasping third place in the automobile market, Chrysler began to bite into
Ford's share of the market.[4]

Such pressure from competitors caused an internal division in the Ford
organization, wherein a determined group of managers, including his own
son, pressured Henry Ford to admit the obsolescence of the Model T and
develop a new model. In addition, an economic recession early in the decade

inspired a reorganization of the system by which the company distributed cars to its dealers, a move that caused bitter and lasting resentment. Meanwhile, an ambitious Ford proposal to harness the waterpower of the southeastern United States aroused growing opposition that eventually scuttled the project. This array of difficulties worked steadily, if imperceptibly, to undermine Ford's public standing.

Thus the Ford Motor Company showed serious signs of strain at the moment of its greatest ascendancy. External criticism of its emperor was mounting while internal problems in his organization were festering. The discrepancy between Ford's towering reputation and brilliant success of his company, on the one hand, and the malignant problems in his empire, on the other, were becoming harder to ignore. Before long, the resulting tensions reached a crisis point.

The influence of the Ford empire extended widely by the mid-1920s. The Model T provided its foundation, of course, and in 1923 the company reached its highest point of production by making and selling two million automobiles. The addition of trucks and tractors drove total sales figures well above that number. Looking at the numbers from another perspective, since about 1918, Ford had controlled at least 40 percent of the American automobile market, and that figure generally held steady throughout the first half of the 1920s.[5]

The booming market in the United States was augmented by the internationalization of the Ford product. Sales of Ford vehicles outside the United States climbed steadily after World War I, from fifty thousand in 1919 to ninety-one thousand in 1925. Even more important, the Ford model of mass production, high wages, low prices, and widespread consumption, or "Fordismus," had become all the rage in Europe by the mid-1920s. In Germany, an infatuation with Ford influenced the public discussion. The German translation of *My Life and Work* sold rapidly, and at least a dozen books on Ford and his industrial innovations appeared. German engineers and government officials visited the Highland Park and River Rouge plants and departed awestruck by their scale, efficiency, and order. A vigorous debate over the merits of Fordismus sprang up in the German industrial sector, with both supporters and opponents agreeing that this system, whatever its merits, stood at the cutting edge of modern economic life. Similar public discussions, although less intense in nature, also took place in France, Britain, and Italy.[6]

The most striking instance of Fordismus, however, appeared in Russia. The Bolshevik philosophy of Lenin and the capitalist philosophy of Ford may have seemed miles apart, but in fact their interests and ideologies intersected at several points. At the outset of the decade, the Soviet government ordered a shipment of Fordson tractors to help address the crop failure and famine that were devastating the economy. Over the next few years, it would purchase about twenty-five thousand tractors, and Russian peasants came to see the Fordson as a magical machine. In addition, the Soviet government viewed Ford as a revolutionary figure who had overturned tradition and transformed the industrial process. His "Fordizatsia" was a system that could bring inexpensive, durable goods to the masses. The Soviets sent dozens of engineers and technicians to be trained at Ford factories in Detroit, unsuccessfully tried to entice Ford to build a tractor factory in Russia, and eventually lured the company into a cooperative venture. Ford consultants spent several months in Russia in the late 1920s overseeing the construction of two large factories in the cities of Nizhni Novgorod and Moscow to build Ford cars and trucks. Ford managers also assisted with upgrading several Soviet tractor and automobile factories.[7]

The importation of thousands of Model T's further spread the Ford name, and translated versions of *My Life and Work* and *Today and Tomorrow* were devoured by the Russian public. By the mid-1920s, Henry Ford had become a household name and emerged as a kind of popular hero. When a writer for the magazine *Outlook* traveled to Russia in the summer of 1927, he was startled to see signs of Ford's popularity everywhere. "The most popular word among our forward-looking peasantry is Fordson," Leon Trotsky stated in a speech. "The peasant speaks of the Fordzonishko (dear little Fordson) gently, lovingly." At a village wedding along the Volga, the reporter observed the gaily costumed bride, groom, and wedding party sitting in a cart as they were pulled along to the celebration by a Fordson tractor. When the villagers discovered the journalist was an American, they bombarded him with questions: "Who was this man Ford, anyway? Where and how did he live? Was everyone in America as clever as he?" An Englishwoman touring Russia in 1926 observed Ford's name on large banners carried by workers in parades.[8]

In the United States, the powerful expansion of the company, along with the tremendous publicity surrounding Henry Ford, reached new highs in the 1920s. There were fawning articles in popular magazines such as *Good Housekeeping* and *McCall's*, and admiring treatments in technical journals such as *Industrial Management*. Business magazines like *Forbes* and *Nation's Business* surveyed his management practices; journals of opinion such as *The*

Atlantic Monthly, The New Republic, The Nation, Cosmopolitan, Current Opinion, and *The Literary Digest* debated the merits of his social and political views. Ford gained praise as an educator because of the Henry Ford Trade School in Dearborn; his purchase of an Atlantic freighter to convey vehicles to Europe—of course, he doubled the existing pay scale for the crew—attracted attention as a revolutionary move. Besides the large numbers of readers who bought Ford's *My Life and Work* and *Today and Tomorrow,* millions more encountered them excerpted in *The Saturday Evening Post.* His opinions, business philosophy, social commentary, and assessment of the future pervaded the public arena. As Charles Merz noted, "Henry Ford is our most quoted citizen."[9]

But signs of trouble had appeared. Sales of the Model T had begun to dip. After the two-million mark in 1923, company production slipped to 1.87 million vehicles in 1924 and 1.675 million in 1925. In 1926, despite two substantial cuts in price, the number fell to 1.465 million. And the competition was gaining. In the same year, despite a price *increase,* the General Motors Chevrolet model nearly doubled its sales. The Ford share of the American market shrank noticeably, to about 33 percent, and the falling sales trajectory predicted a drop to 25 percent the following year. This decline raised fears among managers that its famous car was losing its appeal among American consumers. Though the notion was nearly impossible to comprehend, the Model T seemed in danger of becoming a relic.[10]

In addition, an abiding bitterness among Ford dealers prevailed throughout the decade. The 1920 recession in the American economy had caused a serious decline in the automobile market, and Ford responded decisively. He lowered the price of the Model T and demanded further economies in the production process at the Highland Park and River Rouge plants. More important, however, he pressured Ford suppliers and dealers by sending them new shipments of automobiles whether they requested them or not and demanding that they pay the company for them. Dealers were forced to procure loans from local lenders to cover their consignments, thus shifting the financial burden from the company to its representatives in the field. As one observer commented, "Instead of borrowing money himself, Ford compelled his dealers to borrow." While allowing his company to survive economic hardship, Ford's move created much rancor among his dealers. Years later, they were still complaining, in the words of one, that the "Ford dealer is of but not in the Ford organization. Let him pledge his home, borrow the last penny he can at his bank, and then things continue. . . . Let him turn to the Ford organization and he will find that there is no balm in Gilead; no, not for him." The fact that many dealers felt saddled with an outdated car only increased their doubts about the future.[11]

Ford's ambitious proposal concerning waterpower in the Tennessee River Valley was another source of lingering controversy. In 1921, his interest in hydroelectric energy led him to propose to lease several inefficient installations near Muscle Shoals, Alabama—two nitrate-producing plants and an electricity-generating facility owned by the federal government—for ninety-nine years at a cost of $5 million. He proposed to modernize the plants and produce ammonium nitrate for fertilizer, and to install updated power machinery at the dam to develop hydroelectric power for distribution in this economically depressed region. The Chamber of Commerce, the American Federation of Labor, and the Farm Bureau Federation, among many other groups, immediately endorsed Ford's proposal. Rural organizations and farm magazines also threw in their support. Ford explained his vision of waterpower fueling economic development with factories, new cities, and modernized farms. His populist impulse surfaced when he stressed that the Muscle Shoals project would help liberate the power industry from the clutches of big financial interests. "Wall Street will have no part either in financing or operating Muscle Shoals if I can help it," he promised. "The great private financiers own the bulk of the country's coal mines. The financiers, centered in Wall Street, have a stranglehold on the industry and transportation of the country. . . . I am consecrated to the principle of freeing American industry."[12]

Conservative Republicans in the Harding administration were critical when electric-power companies and chemical corporations complained that Ford would be awarded an unfair advantage in the marketplace. Progressives such as Senator George W. Norris advocated public ownership of the water resources of the Tennessee Valley. They argued that turning over Muscle Shoals to Ford would grant to an individual rights to public resources that would last for several generations. Such a huge gift of the people's property would be unconscionable. Debate and indecision in Washington dragged on, and then another imbroglio muddied the waters. In late 1923, Calvin Coolidge—now president, after Harding's death—made public statements implying that he and Ford had made a deal: Coolidge agreed to back the Muscle Shoals project when Ford promised to stand down from the upcoming presidential race. The subsequent uproar caused Ford to withdraw his proposal in October 1924. Thus the Muscle Shoals project not only alienated portions of the American public, but suggested that Ford had overreached himself.[13]

This growing set of problems appeared even more threatening when critics, as never before, began to question the Ford Company and its future, its founder and his values. Such criticism came increasingly from some of the leading intellectuals and organs of opinion in the United States. Reinhold Niebuhr wondered about the man who had become "the hero of the average American." Ford's popularity, he argued, was based on the perception that he had accumulated his fortune and created his vast enterprise without being ruthless. Niebuhr argued that the facts—Ford's opposition to organized philanthropy, a stagnant rate of pay for his workers, the tendency of his company to dismiss older workers when they had outlived their usefulness—told a different story. At the Ford Motor Company, "human material is used with a ruthlessness and a disregard of ultimate effects which may be matched, but is not surpassed, by any industry." Though Ford's image as a benevolent reformer may have swayed public opinion, Niebuhr was determined to pursue "a thankless but an important task to set history against mythology."[14]

Rexford G. Tugwell, a prominent political economist who would assume a key role in the New Deal within a few years, wrote a searching review of *Today and Tomorrow* (1926). After examining Ford's business and social philosophy, he concluded, "Much of what he says is sound, and some of it illuminating . . . [but] some of it is nonsense." He compared Ford's social theorizing to the shallow ideas of college freshmen "of which they have to be disabused before they can begin, if they ever do, to think." Tugwell condemned Ford's simplistic views on banking and finance, his myopic denunciation of any kind of business regulation, his misunderstanding of the nature of the labor market, and his primitive attitudes toward the function of capital in a modern economy. Full of sensible views on matters involving mechanics and industrial production, Ford excelled when he could discuss facts, techniques, and concrete situations. But he stumbled badly, Tugwell concluded, when attempting to discuss matters involving ideas, values, and contingencies. Ford displayed "a mind alert and effective within its range, unusually suspicious and frightened outside it, a mind which conceives things simply or not at all."[15]

Many prominent publications brought attention to another difficulty in the Ford empire—its leader's absolute control over the organization. The New York *Times* ran a lengthy story entitled "The Mussolini of Highland Park" that described Ford as an "industrial Fascist." Written by Waldemar Kaempffert, it depicted "the world's outstanding example of complete autocratic control of a vast industry." It showed how Ford controlled everything in his giant enterprise—treatment and wages for workers, the design of every part in his automobile, the setting of prices and costs, the nature of sales and marketing strategy. "His despotic control over the greatest manufacturing organization that the world has ever seen is the expression of a fearless independence," the article noted. "Ford brooks neither opposition nor dictation from others. . . . Ford yields nothing. He is either all right or all wrong."[16]

Some of Ford's own managers also delicately questioned his decisive style of leadership, wondering "whether it is not a curious instinct rather than a logical reasoning that leads to his swift decisions." An essay in *The New Republic* explored this issue and reached a less diplomatic conclusion. It asserted that the "pioneer atmosphere" of the early Ford Motor Company, with its spirited self-made men, "has been replaced by something much more like the court of an oriental monarch in its combination of sycophancy and ruthlessness."[17]

Edmund Wilson, already establishing his reputation as a trenchant social critic, skillfully dissected the Ford psyche as well as the Ford Company. He offered the usual accolades, describing Ford as "a mechanical and industrial genius" who had created an inexpensive, indestructible car for ordinary Americans. But he also decried the fact that as the years went by Ford seemed to care less and less about his workers' welfare, had become increasingly addicted to self-advertising, and had surrounded himself with yes-men who feared to disagree with him. The discrepancy between declining wages and a speeded-up assembly line for employees on the one hand, and Ford's image as a benefactor of the workingman on the other, constituted a fraud at the heart of his reputation. In Wilson's view, the automaker's public pronouncements also revealed that "his mind is illogical and volatile; his genius seems purely intuitive. It is as if he had been born with a special sense of materials and mechanical processes. . . . He is, however, completely naïve in dealing with other things and of an extreme instability of opinion." Ford, Wilson concluded, had become "The Despot of Dearborn," whose great talent and force of will, originally focused on developing his vast enterprise, had now degenerated into a kind of tyranny.[18]

Mounting criticism of Ford also came from former supporters in the business community. B. C. Forbes of *Forbes* magazine wrote a scathing article in May 1927 that described Ford as "a democrat turned autocrat." For years, he confessed, "I swallowed unquestioningly all the encomiums I read about the Detroit manufacturer," before the growing volume of complaints from Ford workers and dealers around the United States became impossible to ignore. After investigating these charges of brutal treatment, Forbes issued an indictment: "I know of no employer in America who is so autocratic. I know of no employer who adopts a more dictatorial attitude toward associates. Time was when Ford was the most democratic of men. He is no longer." Power and wealth, Forbes charged, had corrupted this great industrial innovator. Since he was surrounded by lackeys and free to indulge his every whim, Ford's "sense of his own might has become grotesque," Forbes wrote. This had become manifest in his high-handed treatment of his executives, his relentless demands for productivity from his workers, and his determination "to compel the buying public to take exactly what he chooses to offer them" with the outdated Model T. For Forbes, however, Ford's narcissism may have appeared most clearly in the grandiose social theorizing in his books. There he appeared to be "posing as a writer when all the world knows that—well, that he is not a writer."[19]

The recurring words in these critiques—"despot," "monarch," "fascist," "autocrat," "dictator"—suggested the essence of the company's looming problems. The idea had taken root that Henry Ford, for all of his innovations and spectacular successes over the first two and a half decades of the twentieth century, had become too powerful. Insulated and unchecked, he worked according to his own lights and decided according to his own whims. This difficulty was compounded, many observers believed, by the fact that Ford's choices reflected outdated thinking. Ironically, he seemed to be falling out of touch with the society he had played such a large role in developing. Henry Ford's power appeared all the more grating because it served anachronistic ends.

This was nowhere more evident than in Ford's engagement with the American consumer. By the late 1920s, the pioneering figure in defining modern notions of the good life had become uneasy with the onrushing development of consumer culture. The forces of material abundance he had helped unleash twenty years earlier were now rushing headlong into the future, as Americans explored new areas of self-fulfillment and adopted new social, cultural, and economic strategies for buying goods and achieving happiness. Ford found this transformation to be confusing, deeply unsettling, and, ultimately, dangerous.

In many ways, Ford maintained a snug relationship with consumer society throughout the 1920s. Early in the decade, he reassured Allan L. Benson that although people should work diligently they "should also have time for home and recreation." A few years later, in *Today and Tomorrow*, he repeated his long-standing belief in the centrality of consumerism and leisure to the modern industrial economy. "What is really bothering most people is how to put in their spare time. That used to bother only what was called 'the leisure class,' " Ford argued. "Now, we find in our own industries that eight hours a day through five days a week gives all the production that is necessary. . . . Our workmen have leisure." This situation, he concluded, demanded that manufacturers continually ask themselves a simple question: "How can I best serve the consumer?" As Charles Sorensen observed, Ford had shaped his life's work "to demonstrate the superiority of an economy of abundance over one of scarcity, and to begin the elevation of a standard of living to a height never before dreamed of." The 1920s seemed to mark the zenith of this endeavor.[20]

In a 1928 series of articles in *Forum* magazine, Ford fully revealed his consumer orientation. Modern mass production, he pointed out, was not only providing an unprecedented volume of goods but liberating women and children from their former exploitation as laborers in the industrial system. Husbands, wives, and youngsters were now entering the marketplace seeking new products as manufacturers and merchants scrambled to supply them. "Human demands are increasing every day and the needs for their gratification are increasing also. This is as it should be," Ford wrote. A key factor in this new consumer economy, he continued, was the emphasis on endeavors outside the workplace. "There was a time when leisure was regarded as lost time," Ford wrote. "We, in America, have changed our thoughts in this regard very much during the last few years. We have come to see that leisure is not waste time. . . . It has been discovered that the workingman very soon finds a desirable and healthy way to use his leisure time to his own personal advancement and for the greater happiness of his family."[21]

At the same time, however, Ford had second thoughts about the excesses of modern consumer society. Older, cherished values of hard work and self-restraint were endangered by frivolous self-indulgence in materialism. Ford believed that the purchase of consumer items, if pursued imprudently, could be socially inebriating in the same way that the undue imbibing of alcohol produced drunkenness. Ford began to promote a version of the consumer ethic that appeared archaic compared with the one galloping forward in America.

He criticized buying on credit, an increasingly popular technique in the modern consumer economy. In an earlier day, Americans had known the value of a dollar and maintained a strong sense of utility. They spent money when they could afford it and made sound decisions about buying useful, long-lasting products. But now people had fallen under "the spell of salesmanship" as "the American people seem to listen and be sold; that is, they do not buy. . . . Things are pushed on them." Ford believed that the easy extension of credit facilitated this impulse and did harm by "taking up income before it is earned." Such a practice, by saddling the consumer with debt, enriched lenders "at the expense of public benefit."[22]

Similarly, he dismissed installment buying, another popular practice for the purchase of more expensive consumer items. Allan Benson, who interviewed him at length on this topic in 1927, reported that Ford foresaw a slippery slope where unsuspecting consumers would slide into a morass of indebtedness. "Ford believes that the whole system of deferred payments, not only on automobiles but on anything else, is bad for business and bad for the country," Benson wrote. He felt that, though installment buying brought goods to people who ordinarily could not afford them, this practice proved dangerous in the long run, because consumers "cannot buy as much as they used to when they paid cash. They cannot buy as much because they are in debt as far as they can go and part of their current income goes to pay the 'finance charges' upon what they bought last year."[23]

Ford also viewed advertising, an endeavor that American businessmen increasingly saw as the lifeblood of a consumer economy, with suspicion. He drew a distinction based on utility—ads that provided information about worthy goods were desirable, whereas those that merely promoted images about unworthy goods were undesirable. "Advertising?" he replied to a newsman's query in 1921. "Absolutely necessary to introduce good, useful things; bad when it's used to create an unnatural demand for useless things, as it too often is." "A good thing will sell itself," Ford declared. "We must make good things in this country, and not do too much talking about them. You've just got to let people know where to get them, and that's all." In 1926, he rejected his company's promotional campaign with an angry denunciation of advertising: "It's an economic waste and I never did believe in it!"[24]

Thus several fears—of debt, of unearned bounty, of the triumph of salesmanship over substance—kept Henry Ford from a full-blown endorsement of the modern consumer ethic. These concerns reflected his desire to hold on to older traditions of producerism, self-control, and hard work even while encouraging the new impulses of commodity purchase, self-fulfillment, and leisure activity. Ford Motor Company's capricious marketing policies in the 1920s reflected its leader's increasingly ambiguous attitude about American consumer values.

Its handling of advertising was consistently erratic. At Henry Ford's insistence, the company had discontinued all paid advertising in 1917, a policy it maintained for the next six years. This policy reflected the booming sales of the Model T and Ford's conviction that ads were unnecessary, but it also expressed his belief that he could generate free publicity whenever he wished and that this constituted the best kind of advertising for his car. The company, however, demanded that Ford dealers advertise at the local level as part of their contract. The majority did so throughout this period to the tune of about $3 million per year.[25]

Then, in 1923, the company suddenly reversed course and resumed advertising on a massive scale, becoming one of the biggest advertisers in the country over the next three years. With great fanfare, it announced the hiring of the Norton T. Brotherton agency to supervise an annual expenditure of up to $7 million. In fact, Ford would spend nearly $15 million on ads during this period. This was an attempt to bolster sagging sales of the Model T, which had failed to respond to other measures such as price cuts, nickel-plated accessories, and a palette of body colors in addition to the traditional black. Part of Ford's campaign focused on reaffirming the company's image as a national treasure. A series of double-paged advertisements in newspapers and magazines throughout the country carried the headline "A Nation's Institution Pledged to a Nation's Service." Beneath it appeared a promise "to insure, not only for the present but for years to come, that more and more people may benefit in greater prosperity, happiness, and leisure through low-cost transportation."[26]

But Ford also linked its automobile with the most modern impulse for self-fulfillment. A series of advertisements pictured the Model T as an instrument for satisfying all of the desires—for recreation, travel, adventure, social advancement, romance, style—that fueled the drive to purchase goods. The most prominent ad featured the slogan that had been personally approved by Henry Ford, urging buyers to use the money they saved on the Model T to buy other consumer products: "Buy a Ford and *Spend* the Difference."[27]

Other advertisements from 1923 to 1926 suggested the emotional yearnings and social aspirations that could be met by buying the Ford product. Some ads appealed to style, stressing that the Model T sedan had become a "better looking, roomier car" with "a stylish sweep to its body lines." Other ads conjured up visions of social mobility, such as those that pictured the Ford coupe amid sparkling images of consumer abundance in a luxurious ballroom and described it as specially suited to "the needs of the salesman and professional man." Here was a car, the text noted, "reflecting the good taste of its driver, and fitting profitably into a wide range of activities." Special ads appealed to a new audience for the automobile: women. Some of them invoked an older, reassuring idea of the woman as family manager by picturing the Model T as a safe, sturdy vehicle to meet the needs of mothers and children. But others were directed at emerging notions of female independence, such as the one promising "Freedom for the Woman Who Owns a Ford." It featured two women gathering colorful sprigs of autumn leaves at the edge of the woods as their car sat in the background. "To own a Ford is to be free to venture into new and untried places," the text said. Finally, a raft of ads appealed to the ethos of recreation, travel, and vacations that played such an important role in the new culture of consumption. As one of them promised, "You can, literally, get 'recreation'—be 'made over' again, when your physical self is rested, your energy and your strength conserved by the use of this Ford Runabout."

With such pledges to revive weary businessmen or enhance opportunities for women, Ford advertising drew connections between the Model T and a modern life of abundance, leisure, travel, health, and personal fulfillment. The company recognized that an ethos of immediate gratification inspired the process of consumption. To those who hesitated at participating in this cultural bonanza, Ford counseled abandoning restraint. "Delay invites disappointment. Why wait? Buy now!" urged one ad. "Now Is the Time!" said another. "You who have been promising yourself a Ford car, saying it was 'only a question of time'—should buy NOW!"[28]

Despite such full-blown appeals to consumer values, sales of the Model T continued to slide, and Henry Ford decided in 1926 to abandon advertising once again. In an attempt to save money and lower the price of his car, he abruptly killed the advertising budget even while competitors such as General Motors and Chrysler poured additional resources into theirs. Ford told his dealers to fund any advertising they wished to advance. "What Will Take the Place of Advertising in Ford's Marketing Scheme?" asked *Printers' Ink*, the advertising journal. Ford provided the answer—"a price concession to the public is the very best kind of advertisement." Thus Ford reverted to his old logic of fear, figuring that such promotional appeals wasted company funds and encouraged bad habits among consumers at the same time.[29]

As with advertising, the company's policies regarding credit and installment buying followed an uneven, foot-dragging course. It refused to offer a time-payment plan to Model T buyers for many years because, in the words of a company spokesman in 1921, "Ford products sell so readily." In 1923, however, the company responded to popular credit programs offered by competitors by establishing the "Ford Weekly Purchase Plan." Consumers could choose a Ford model from a dealer, pay a set amount of money every week, and have it deposited in a local bank to draw interest. When sufficient funds were accumulated, the sale would be consummated and the consumer would pick up the automobile. Although promotional material claimed that the Ford Weekly Purchase Plan "opens the way for millions of wage-earners and their families to enjoy the benefits and advantages of automobile ownership," such was not the case. Clearly, it was a savings plan rather than a time-payment plan, because it did not allow the buyer to possess the car until it was fully paid for. Not surprisingly, consumers responded unenthusiastically. Many Ford dealers, frustrated by the company's failure to establish a genuine installment program, set up their own credit policies by working through local banks. The Ford Motor Company lagged behind its competition in developing this key mechanism in a modern consumer economy.[30]

The company was obviously falling out of step with the march of modern American consumer culture, and Henry Ford's statements only underlined that fact. In 1928, he ventilated his ambivalent, cranky attitude toward modern consumer values in an article entitled "When Is a Business Worth While?" Writing in the *Magazine of Business*, Ford celebrated the opening of a new age of consumption. For millennia, people had struggled to provide the staples of existence—food, shelter, clothing—but in recent decades, that picture had fortunately changed. "Automobiles, bathtubs, and telephones are now simple necessities," he observed. "Buying begets buying, if the things are there to buy." In modern America, incomes were rising, purchasing power was growing, and new buyers were entering the market daily, while those already there were moving up into higher brackets. This trend obliterated the old notion of limited consumer dollars for which businessmen must compete. "There is no consumer's dollar," Ford pointed out. "Thinking of consumers as having definite incomes is only going back to the old days when the saturation point for goods was supposed to be fixed." Besides, traditional values that restrained buying habits and desires were disappearing in the mobile, fluid society of the modern United States. As Ford explained, "In former days a new kind of article was opposed just because it was new, but now it is likely to be welcomed just because it is new."

Yet he was deeply worried about consumer excess. Though recognizing that manufacturers must meet the expectations of the public, he resisted selling mere images or catering to the whims of buyers. Instead, he wanted attention to focus on producing basic products in quantity to keep prices low for consumers. Providing such "service" was more important than flashy marketing. Ford's words clearly reflected a stubborn, old-fashioned loyalty to substance over style. "Changes in the design of articles . . . are not lightly to be undertaken," he wrote. "The greater pressure for change comes always from the salesmen who are trying to resell old purchasers instead of going out for new purchasers. That pressure has to be resisted."[31]

This tension between forward-looking consumerism and concern about modern buyers' self-indulgence became a central issue in Ford's company by the late 1920s. More than abstract theorizing was at stake. Ford's ambivalence colored the anguished, increasingly angry debates in the Dearborn headquarters about the fate of the Model T. It also influenced—indeed, infected—one of the most important relationships in Henry Ford's life.

Eighteen

Father

"Henry Ford's greatest achievement was changing the face of America and putting the world on wheels," Charles Sorensen once declared. "His greatest failure was his treatment of his only son, Edsel." Many others who observed the relationship between father and son over the years agreed. Edsel, a sensitive and diligent boy, idolized his father as he rose through the ranks of the Ford Motor Company to assume its presidency in 1919. But Henry, jealous of his own prerogatives and suspicious of his son's "softness," sought to toughen up his offspring by undercutting his decisions and fomenting rivalries. Growing tension between Henry and Edsel became entangled with the question of replacing the Model T with a newer model as the two Fords lined up on opposite sides. The result was a personal as well as professional crisis.[1]

Edsel Bryant Ford was a quiet, obedient son who enjoyed the love and attention of doting parents and nearby family members. "Edsel is as happy as a bird toddling around in the snow. I have been taking some pictures of him," Clara wrote to an absent Henry in 1896. "He has been making some caves. Sam [a family friend] picks him up and throws him up and lets him down in a [snow] bank." The boy enjoyed typical childhood activities—ice-skating, making fudge with his mother, going on family excursions to visit relatives—and engaged in his share of horseplay, such as sliding down the banister of the Ford house with his childhood playmate Faye Beebe. He also suffered the inevitable juvenile mishaps, as when he fell and broke his arm after climbing a tree with Beebe. In a letter dated December 24, 1901, eight-year-old Edsel sought advantage: "Dear Santa Claus, I haven't had any Christmas tree in 4 years and I have broken all my trimmings and I want some more & I want a pair of roller skates and a book & can't think of any thing more I want you to think of something more. Good Bye, Edsel Ford."[2]

As an only child, Edsel spent much time with his parents and was particularly close to his mother. The boy shared his father's alertness and quickness of mind, "but in practical matters he was more like his mother . . . [and] their interests were more alike," noted Mrs. Stanley Ruddiman, who saw the Fords frequently. Even after he entered adulthood, acquaintances would note, "Mrs. Ford's mind and Edsel's mind were more the same . . . [and] on the whole his tastes and opinions more nearly coincided with his mother's than his father's."[3]

But Edsel matched affection for his mother with respect for his father and his achievements. As an adult, he recalled the proud day when the mayor of Detroit visited the Ford house to see Henry's horseless carriage. Edsel also had fond memories of hanging around his father's shop a few years later, where "he built the '999,' which Barney Oldfield drove." Henry lavished attention on his only child. In 1900, when Edsel was on a trip to Kentucky with his mother, his father wrote an affectionate, joking note to "My Dear Little Son." "I am well and hope you are all OK. Say, do they carry whiskey jugs and bandwagons in their blouse in KY? I hope you are having a good time and will be back soon for I am lonesome. From your loving, Pa Pa." Henry frequently took Edsel to the old plants on Mack Avenue and Park Place. Usually, Henry would not allow Edsel to enter the factory floor because of safety concerns, so the boy would remain outside and play with his wagon, kneeling on the seat and pushing himself along. "I used to look at him sometimes and notice how he had his father's alert, quick way and his mother's good common sense," noted a relative.[4]

Even as a boy, Edsel showed an artistic sensibility. Attracted to music, he also liked to draw detailed sketches of automobiles, making drawings of a Ford coupe and a Packard in colored crayon. By his teenage years, Edsel had graduated to more sophisticated forms—charcoal still-life drawings, landscape paintings, and watercolor portraits. The artist Irving Bacon first met Edsel with this introduction from Henry: "Edsel is the artist in our family. Art is something I know nothing about." As an adult, Edsel and his wife would collect valuable paintings, and donate many of them to the Detroit Institute of Arts.[5]

As the son of a wealthy and prominent family, Edsel enjoyed a comfortable adolescence. He attended public grade schools and then enrolled in the Detroit University School, a private prep school for boys. He ran on the track team as a sprinter, and pursued hunting, boats and water sports, golf, and automobile travel. Slightly shorter than his father, but possessing an

athletic frame and dark good looks, he began to cultivate his lifelong reputation as a snappy dresser, purchasing tailored suits in New York City. After
graduating in 1912, he decided to skip college and join his father's business
at the Highland Park plant. Edsel later regretted his decision: "I think it was
a mistake, for, whatever else college may or may not do, it helps one to meet
a great many different kinds of people and also it helps one to get more
enjoyment out of life."[6]

From an early age, with the encouragement of his father, Edsel had cultivated an intense interest in automobiles. In 1903, at age ten, he received a
new red Ford Model A Runabout from Henry. In this age before driver's
licenses, the youth drove the car about the Hendrie Avenue neighborhood
and transported his mother to do her shopping. He also amused his friends
by pulling their sleds along behind his vehicle. A few years later, he received
another car, a 1906 Model N, and started his lifelong hobby of automobile
collecting. The youth applied his artistic bent to the motorcar, and an interest in design began to blossom. In 1910, he designed a sportier version of
the Model T that lowered the seats and steering column, added doors to the
open body, and lengthened the hood. His father was intrigued by Edsel's
"Torpedo" but never authorized production of the car. In 1912, Edsel drew
up plans for a low-slung six-cylinder speedster that featured bucket seats,
wire wheels, and a V-shaped radiator. Company engineers built the car, and
he drove it for several years.[7]

Partly from paternal pride and partly from a desire to keep his family
company out of the hands of Wall Street, Henry began to groom his
teenaged son for future leadership. He put Edsel to work in various areas of
the company; the son later described "going from one department to
another, and trying to absorb as much as I could." Edsel also spent much
time with his father to observe company operations and the decision-
making process. George Brown, a company accountant, described how
Edsel, at age thirteen, would come by the factory after school and disappear
with his father into the experimental room. "We wouldn't see Mr. Ford or
Edsel. When we went home the both of them would still be in the experimental room, probably with Mr. Wills," Brown continued. "Mr. Ford and
Edsel were very close." As the father would say, "I've got one boy I can be
proud of. He's sure taking an interest in this work."[8]

Even as a youth, the modest, polite Edsel earned the respect and affection of his associates. He impressed Ford operatives with his considerate,
respectful, low-key manner. One day, while he was learning the ropes at the
motor-assembly section of Highland Park from Ed Harper, Edsel wanted to
go to a formal party at three o'clock. He had packed a suit in the back of his
roadster, so he changed clothes in the employment office and sneaked out of

the factory. His supervisor and fellow workers covered for him. When Henry checked on his son later that afternoon, he was informed that Edsel was working on a project in the foundry. The father discovered the white lie a few days later and chastised the conspirators, but they accepted the reprimand gladly. Engineer William C. Klann expressed the consensus about Edsel: "He was well-liked by everybody because he was what you would call a gentleman."[9]

In the mid-1910s, Edsel also took an important step in his personal life. Henry and Clara had tried to keep him at home (and attract his companions) by including several special features in their new Fair Lane estate—a swimming pool, a bowling alley, and a small golf course. Increasingly, however, Edsel left the domestic nest to spend time with friends and classmates. Active and energetic, he loved driving sophisticated automobiles, dancing, and golf. He also developed an interest in boating—particularly yachts and speedboats—that would provide a hobby throughout his adult life.[10]

Inevitably, he met a young woman who caught his fancy. As a student at the Detroit University School, Edsel took regular dancing lessons that were attended by students from the Liggett School, an academy for girls. At one of these dances, Edsel met Eleanor Lowthian Clay, the niece of Joseph L. Hudson, the prominent Detroit businessman. After a courtship of several years, they married on November 1, 1916, when Edsel was almost twenty-three. The couple took their vows at the Hudson home in Detroit. John Dodge reaffirmed Edsel's popularity, telling the groom's father at the reception, "Henry, I don't envy you a damn thing except that boy of yours." For their part, Edsel's parents were delighted with their son's choice of Eleanor. As Clara Ford wrote to a friend a few years later, she and Henry "could not love Edsel's wife more if we had picked her ourselves."[11]

It soon became clear, however, that Edsel had entered a different social orbit from the modest one traveled by his father and mother. After honeymooning in Hawaii for several weeks, the younger Fords took up residence at a spacious home on Iroquois Avenue, in an area popular with Detroit's elite families. Several years later, they moved to the Stephens mansion, on the Detroit River. Between 1917 and 1925, Edsel and Eleanor's four children—Henry II, Benson, Josephine, and William—would be born at these residences. In the mid-1920s, Edsel began building a new estate, Gaukler Pointe, located in Grosse Pointe. In subsequent years, he would acquire homes in Seal Harbor, Maine, and Hobe Sound, Florida, as well as a two-thousand-acre farm, Haven Hill, near Milford, Michigan. Edsel and his wife became benefactors of the arts, giving generous donations to the Detroit Institute of Arts, the Detroit Symphony Society, the New York Museum of Modern Art, and many local groups.[12]

Meanwhile, Edsel continued to climb toward the top of the company. He became a member of the board of directors in 1915, at age twenty-two, and was appointed secretary a year later. With the onset of World War I, however, Edsel was caught up in perhaps the nastiest public controversy of his life. When the United States entered the conflict in 1917, he applied for and eventually secured a draft exemption because of his work at the Ford Motor Company, which was busy producing a variety of war commodities. Critics attacked both father and son, accusing the younger of cowardice and the elder of using his money and influence to gain special privileges for his offspring. Edsel, ever the gentleman, was appalled by the public attention and stung by the accusations hurled at him. "My action in claiming exemption on industrial grounds is for the sole reason that I believe I will be of far greater service to the country right here in the plant," he wrote indignantly; "if the officials see fit to deny my exemption I am perfectly willing to be drafted with the rest of the young men of this community." He also refused to pull strings to get a desk assignment in the military. "There is one job in this war I do not want and will not take, and that is the job of a rich man's son," he asserted.[13]

The war's end finally brought an end to Edsel's troubles, and a few months later he reached the summit of his career. On January 1, 1919, he became president of Ford Motor Company, as part of his father's move to buy out the minority stockholders. In his new position, Edsel played a key role managing construction of the River Rouge industrial complex, making decisions about production and engineering, and supervising expansion of its marketing operation. Unlike his father, he did not roam widely throughout the company, but worked quietly in his office. Only a few months after assuming the presidency, Edsel testified at the Chicago *Tribune* trial, displaying a familiarity with all operations of the company. In marked contrast to the bumbling performance of his father, he appeared well informed, thoughtful, and articulate.[14]

But this image of authority and control was deceptive. As observers inside the organization gradually discovered, Edsel served as president in name only. His father, though officially in the background, continued to steer the course of the company and make all major decisions. Edsel, ever the obedient and loyal son, swallowed any resentment and acquiesced. In fact, this increasingly awkward situation played to the weaknesses of both father and son—domineering tendencies in the former and excessive deference in the latter. The presidency of the company soon became the greatest ordeal of Edsel Ford's life.

During the 1920s, the situation graduated from awkward to painful.

Within a few months of Edsel's ascendancy, it became clear that Henry had no intention of handing over power to his son. The elder man often said, according to one associate, "Well, you talk that over with Edsel, and do whatever he says. I'm going to turn more of these responsibilities over to him. He's got to run this company." Inevitably, however, Henry reversed his son's decisions and set policy. His unwillingness to act forthrightly—rather than clearly asserting his own pre-eminence, he insisted on Edsel's authority and then undermined it—poisoned the atmosphere. As a longtime Ford engineer summarized, "Every time Edsel starts to do something, the old man knocks it down."[15]

Not long after Edsel assumed the presidency, William Knudsen and Frank Klingensmith appealed to him for additional office space at the Highland Park plant. After studying the issue, he concurred and had plans drawn up for a new addition on the administration building. The bulldozers arrived and began digging a hole for the foundation. At this point, Henry entered the picture and demanded an explanation. Unconvinced by his son's rationale, Henry declared, "Edsel, we don't need that extra building." A tight-lipped Edsel surrendered and promised to fill in the construction hole. But Henry was not finished. "No, don't do that. Just leave it that way for a while," he replied. For the next several months, thousands of company employees passed a muddy mess as they entered and left work every day, a symbol of the father's authority and the son's humiliation.

A short time later, a similar incident occurred at River Rouge. William B. Mayo met with Edsel and outlined the need for additional coke ovens to make the steel required by the production schedule. Again, after evaluating the facts and consulting with other experts in the company, Edsel approved the project, and told Mayo to proceed with construction. Henry heard of the project and disapproved, but this time he waited until the ovens were completed before stepping in. He confided his plans to one of his henchmen, Harry Bennett: "Harry, as soon as Edsel gets those ovens built, I'm going to tear them down." Henry did exactly that. A despondent Edsel told a friend, "I don't know what kick Father gets out of humiliating me this way."[16]

This pattern of paternal domination soon moved from the cruel to the perverse. Henry employed a favorite tactic of divide and conquer by setting other Ford managers against Edsel. The bickering, of course, reinforced his own authority. Most often, Henry chose Charles Sorensen as the foil in this twisted process. The elder Ford would maneuver his son into making a decision on some issue, and then push his tough production manager to make the opposite decision. Ford managers instinctively followed

Sorensen's directions. As one of them said, "There was an understanding that Sorensen bypassed Edsel on decisions." The situation grew even more complex as it became obvious that Henry Ford was employing Sorensen as a role model for his own son. "Sorensen is being employed here to toughen up Edsel, and that's why Mr. Ford let Edsel go ahead and then had Sorensen stop him," Ray Dahlinger admitted. Fred L. Black confirmed this. Henry "felt that Edsel had to be harsher, act faster, and be turned into a personality something like Sorensen's. Mr. Ford didn't think that Edsel was tough enough."[17]

In fairness, Sorensen was caught in an awkward situation. On the one hand, his own position depended upon the approval of Henry and his domineering instincts pushed him to assert his authority. On the other hand, he was genuinely fond of Edsel and often defended him to his father. In his memoir, Sorensen wrote about his "fatherly feeling" toward the young heir and claimed that he dissuaded him from resigning on several occasions. "I was devoted to him, and he knew it. The only possible fault I ever found in him was that he was too kind," he noted. "Edsel Ford was a gentleman in the finest, fullest meaning of the word." With a rare display of sensitivity, Sorensen even grasped the essence of the older Ford's paternal failing: "What Henry Ford was unable to realize was that his son could not be a second edition of himself without being a mere copy of the original."[18]

So why did Henry Ford act with such calculated insensitivity, even cruelty, toward his son? In part, his actions stemmed from the same autocratic impulse that slanted all of his professional relationships. A desire for absolute control of the Ford Motor Company had motivated Ford to buy out all other stockholders, to purge the organization of almost all of his old associates, and to pit subordinates against one another from the earliest days of the company. This same impulse now resurfaced to shape his relations with Edsel.

In fact, Ford's autocratic instincts had become so strong that many of his subordinates and associates came to see him as a victim of his success. Howard Simpson, a design engineer who worked closely with Ford for two decades, analyzed his boss's megalomania. "I think he began to get the feeling that he was infallible and his decisions were always right. He depended upon himself instead of depending on teamwork and family spirit in the organization," he concluded. "Mr. Ford made this into such a personal corporation that he himself was the only source of authority in it." This need to dominate, so evident in his relationship with others in the company, extended to the treatment of his son.[19]

But Henry's harsh handling of Edsel also reflected his sense that the young man was too soft to survive in the rough-and-tumble world of auto manufacturing. He felt compelled to train his son "to be perhaps a little more shrewd, and a little more crafty, and perhaps a little more tricky than he was," reported Harold Hicks. The father increasingly looked askance at Edsel's sophisticated life—the philanthropy, the art collecting, the vacations in Europe, the enthusiasm for yachting, the golfing—and morally disapproved of Edsel's occasional use of tobacco and liquor. All of this pointed to a soft, weak character, the elder Ford concluded. Henry had come to value "a brutal-type fellow, . . . who would haul off and smack a guy and then talk to him after," one Ford manager explained. "He probably wished that Edsel was the same kind of fellow." Two men who worked closely with Ford in the 1920s and 1930s, William J. Cameron and Frank Campsall, sized up the situation in nearly identical terms: Henry was disappointed in Edsel because he "wasn't tough enough in some situations" and "didn't have enough boldness."[20]

Henry grew irate about Edsel's choice of friends. The same Detroit elites whom Henry had despised for decades constituted his son's social circle, the younger Ford moving about easily among the fashionable and wealthy in Grosse Pointe rather than the farm and village folk of Dearborn. Henry believed they encouraged the vices corroding his son's character. He complained about the cocktail parties of the Grosse Pointe set and once exploded in anger at the mention of Paul Strasburg, a wealthy young Detroiter who drove one of Edsel's racing speedboats: "Oh, that dirty rotten puke." "Mr. Ford was always a little leery of people who helped Edsel. He had the feeling that anyone who helped Edsel was trying to work in through [him]," noted an associate. Such concerns swelled when they involved representatives of Detroit's wealthy families. In other words, Henry Ford's class resentment found a target in his own son.[21]

Henry's attitude toward Edsel contained many elements of tragedy—salutary intentions, flawed perceptions, unintended consequences, misplaced jealousy. Everyone, it seemed, could see this situation except him. Yearning for Edsel to show an independent, even fiery spirit, he crushed any expressions of initiative and, in the words of one observer, "never could realize that Edsel had grown up." Suspicious of anyone who moved close to his son, he seemed unable to grasp that no father can ever be the sole mentor of a boy. Strangely, Henry seemed bent on replicating his own father's treatment of him in late adolescence, when William Ford had tried to force the mechanically inclined youth to remain a farmer. It was as if he, perhaps unconsciously, wanted his son to revolt as he had and throw off the paternal yoke. So Henry tightened his hold, and family intimates began to notice the growing strain between father and son. In this sad situation, Henry couldn't help himself—he seemed intent on driving his only son into total acquiescence or open rebellion.[22]

For his part, Edsel responded to his father's stifling maneuvers with bewilderment, repressed resentment, and long-suffering pain.

In public, he always displayed the greatest respect for Henry, and throughout his career made numerous public statements expressing admiration for his father's achievements, judgments, and values. Edsel clearly deferred to his father. In a 1929 interview, he noted his great regard for Henry in the language of submission and self-deprecation:

> Father seems to know in advance how things are going to turn out, but he just waits and does not say a word, hoping that a man will discover his own mistake. Then, if he does not discover it, Father steps in and sets things right before too much damage has been done. That is what he has done with me and I only hope that I can make all of my big mistakes while he is still here to show them to me. . . .
>
> But I am free to say that I do not seem able to originate on the spot the way that my father does. But then again no one else that I have ever met can do as he does.

Respectful to the point of being awestruck, Edsel refused to rebel.[23]

Yet he also grew despondent over his father's treatment of him. When Henry derailed one of his projects, according to one insider, "there would be sort of a woebegone expression come over Edsel's face as if to say, 'Well, what's the use!'" Others at the company noticed that he never seemed to be very happy and "always looked to me as if he was wishing he was someplace else. . . . He didn't seem to have his heart in the job at all." William C. Klann, who brought the bad news to Edsel that his father had ordered a halt to construction of the Highland Park office addition, reported that a stricken Edsel could only reply, "Well, Bill, you better do as you are told." That sentence served as a sad epitaph for the son's entire professional relationship with his father.[24]

Edsel's personal qualities exacerbated the tense relationship with his father. His sensitivity, kindness, and deference clashed with Henry's aggressive style. Unlike the father, who sought the limelight, the son wished to work behind the scenes. When asked to appear at a celebration or public function on behalf of the company, Edsel would demur. "See if you can't get Father to do that. He likes that sort of thing. I don't," he would say. He kept his emotions under control and presented a sober, reflective demeanor to the outside world. Clearly, he also sought to have a well-rounded life out-side of the company, once telling Fred Black, "I work for this institution, and when I put in my forty hours a week, I like to consider that I have the other time for things in which I am personally interested." To someone like Henry Ford—an assertive manager and publicity hound who lived and breathed his work—such attitudes must have been infuriating.[25]

The conflict between Henry and Edsel grew more complicated as it spilled over into broader questions of policy-making at the company. Not surprisingly, the personal differences between father and son translated into a clash of managerial philosophies. Henry continued the modus operandi in place since 1903: he alone made all major decisions in the administration of the company, utility defined the essence of the Ford automobile, and low prices attracted buyers. This philosophy had launched his company toward greatness, and he saw no reason to change it. Like many others, however, Edsel believed that modern industrial corporations, with their enormous size and complex operations, demanded modern management methods. By the 1920s, he was stressing teamwork in managerial decision-making, style in making the Ford car, and sensitivity to consumer desires as the keys to inducing purchases.

This philosophical difference divided company managers. Though reluctant to cross Henry publicly, in private many of them complained about his capricious managerial procedures. Henry, as one said typically, "didn't believe in big organization. He wanted to be the whole cheese and everything had to go through his hands first." Even Sorensen had to admit that Henry relied upon "hunches and intuition" rather than facts and logic in charting the course of the company. Henry "had this philosophy of con-flict where he believed the best way to run a plant was to set the different boys against each other so the best one would win out," Howard Simpson added. "He never got the idea of teamwork."[26]

To these men, the younger Ford's vision of cooperative, team-oriented management seemed much more appealing. "Edsel reasoned out his prob-lems after listening to and tolerating the opinions of others," Sorensen observed. Some chimed in to approve Edsel's methods of dividing responsi-bility, listening to ideas, and collaborating. Others even asserted that the promise of Edsel's eventual ascendancy kept many Ford managers from quitting the company. "You always figured that there was one person who was a perfect gentleman, and that some day he was going to run the place, and it would be a fine place to work when he was running it," Harold Hicks claimed. "You stuck around because of him." Joseph Galamb put the matter curtly: "You could reason with Edsel. . . . You couldn't reason with Edsel's father."[27]

But in management issues, as in all other things, Edsel invariably deferred to Henry. He told associates, "Well, after all, my father built this business. It's his business." Often sitting silent in important meetings as Henry dominated, he created an image of meekness among many managers. "The impression I got was that the father was completely dominant over the son," William Verner noted. "That stayed with me." Edsel "allowed himself to be submerged by his father," said Charles Voorhess.[28]

The increasingly tense relationship put a strain not only on their personal lives but on the management of the family enterprise. It became emblematic of a critical problem confronting the Ford empire by the mid-1920s. As Edsel Ford and most other company operatives realized, the Model T was meeting the needs of ever-fewer American consumers. It had become an albatross, and they yearned to remove it and develop a new model. Henry Ford, emotionally wedded to his beloved flivver, resisted mightily. For once, however, the son did not back down, but engaged in a protracted struggle with his father. The result was a battle for the heart and soul of the company that, when the smoke cleared, left casualties piled up in Dearborn.

On January 20, 1926, company vice president Ernest C. Kanzler presented Henry Ford with a six-page typed memorandum. Carefully prepared over several weeks, and marshaling its author's considerable intelligence and powers of persuasion, this document directly addressed a major problem facing the Ford Motor Company. Kanzler began on an elaborate note of deference that was almost obsequious: "Please, Mr. Ford, understand that I realize fully that you have built up this whole business, that it has been your battle and your creation." He also confessed to misgivings about writing the memorandum, because "I am afraid it may change your feeling for me, and that you may think me unsympathetic and lacking in confidence in your future plans."

Having paid homage to his liege, Kanzler plunged ahead. The problem that could no longer be avoided, he bravely told Henry Ford, was the primary product of the company. "I do not think the Model T will continue to be a satisfactory product to maintain our position in the automobile field," he wrote. A growing body of evidence, Kanzler argued, showed the old automotive warhorse to be outdated. In the last few years, the company had barely held its own in sales, while its competitors had "gained tremendously." Ford customers were migrating toward other models, and "our best dealers are low in morale and not making the money they used to." Kanzler assembled an array of facts and figures to demonstrate that Ford's share of the market was steadily shrinking. He then offered a brief solution to the problem: "new product necessary." Kanzler offered one final argument to clinch the case: "Practically every man in your organization to whom you have entrusted the greatest responsibility holds this same opinion."[29]

In the political atmosphere of the company, where Ford's devotion to the Model T was legendary, Kanzler's memo was courageous to the point of recklessness. But the situation was even more emotionally treacherous. Kanzler was Edsel Ford's brother-in-law (he had married one of Eleanor Clay's sisters, Josephine) and his staunch ally. Educated at the University of Michigan and Harvard, this young lawyer had launched a distinguished legal career with a Detroit firm in the 1910s. He made the acquaintance of Henry Ford through his friendship with Edsel and his legal work on the opposing side in both the Dodge brothers and Chicago *Tribune* suits. Impressed by his performance, and with Edsel's endorsement, Henry convinced Kanzler to abandon his law practice and come to work for him, as Charles Sorensen's assistant at the Rouge, in 1919. Kanzler performed brilliantly and became an expert in production and shipment. The situation started to sour rather quickly, however. According to Sorensen, Kanzler openly criticized Henry Ford's habit of undermining Edsel. "One Sunday afternoon in 1920, Mr. and Mrs. Kanzler called on my wife and me at our home," Sorensen recalled. "To this day my wife remembers how shocked we were at their unrestrained tirade against Mr. Ford and the way he held Edsel down." A few days later, Sorensen, ever protective of his patron, dismissed Kanzler, who immediately went to Highland Park, where Edsel hired him. He served as Edsel's right-hand man from 1921 to 1926, supervising production, overseeing the branch assembly plants, and helping develop sales strategy. In 1924, Edsel arranged for his lieutenant to be elected a vice president and director of the company.[30]

Though Henry Ford did develop professional suspicions about Kanzler, personal animosity carried even more weight. This sophisticated, well-educated young attorney was part of the Grosse Pointe establishment toward which Edsel had gravitated in early adulthood. For Henry and Clara, Kanzler came to symbolize the social elitism that had contaminated their son. When they examined the generational breach that had opened in their family, "their deepest suspicion and animosity was directed at Ernest Kanzler," Sorensen explained. "At the Ford mansion one day, Mrs. Ford opened up on Kanzler to me. Too many people, she said, were taking advantage of Edsel, and of these Kanzler had the most influence over him." Henry

Ford came to despise Kanzler and denounced his drinking, partying, and golfing as symptomatic of the evil influence playing upon his son.[31]

Given this background of tension and resentment, it was no surprise that Kanzler's memo infuriated Henry Ford. He took such umbrage at its contents that he immediately moved to freeze Kanzler out of his company. Ford made his displeasure evident to everyone by giving Kanzler the silent treatment, interrupting him and ridiculing his comments in the executive dining room, commenting loudly, "That young fellow is getting too big for his britches." Ray Dahlinger, widely seen as Ford's mouthpiece, began making the rounds with stories of how Kanzler was taking advantage of Edsel to gain power in the company. Sorensen also maneuvered against Kanzler and forced lower-level managers to take sides in a power struggle. The outcome was never really in doubt. On July 26, 1926, six months after submitting his assertive memorandum, Kanzler resigned from the company.[32]

The Kanzler imbroglio not only heightened the tension between Henry and Edsel, but added fire to the major crisis facing the company by the mid-1920s—what to do with the obsolete automobile that had made Ford but now threatened to take him under. This problem was no secret to the outside world. Kanzler's memorandum, for all of Henry Ford's enraged reaction, contained little that was not already being discussed outside the gates of Highland Park and the River Rouge.

James Dalton analyzed the situation for *Motor* magazine and made a gloomy prognostication. He argued that the rising standard of living in the 1920s, coupled with the falling prices of other cars such as the Chevrolet, spelled dark times for Ford. After analyzing the numbers, Dalton demonstrated that the pool of first-time car buyers (Ford's most dependable constituency) was shrinking steadily, while repeat buyers were willing to spend more money to purchase an up-to-date automobile with attractive options. To maintain his customer base, Dalton concluded, Ford would have to "produce something different, distinctive, and attractive, as well as to offer superior values."[33]

James C. Young, in the New York *Times*, corroborated. Henry Ford had been the giant of the early automobile industry, Young wrote, but now, because of growing problems, "rivals say that Ford is about to lose his grip." Declining sales and profits had forced cutbacks, and as Ford walked through his plant, many departments "are deserted now, and his footfall sounds loudly in the unaccustomed stillness." For the first time in the industry, Young reported, "Ford domination has been seriously challenged." Carmakers believed that failure to develop a new model would send sales plunging further. Noting the split between Henry and Edsel and the Ernest Kanzler controversy, Young concluded that internal divisions were exacerbating external problems. If changes were not forthcoming, an uncertain future faced the company.[34]

Other influential voices joined the chorus. *Liberty* magazine asked the question on the minds of many American consumers: "What will Henry Ford do?" It cited statistics of declining sales, dug into the rumored rift between Henry and Edsel, and added a new item to the litany of bad news. For the first time in some fifteen years, the magazine pointed out, Ford Motor Company "failed to show the largest estimated earnings of any organization in the automobile industry." General Motors had surpassed it in the profit margin column. In *Forbes*, B. C. Forbes declared that the Ford company had lost its position of leadership in the industry. Its production and sales were falling, its "dealer organization is rapidly being shot to pieces," and its "management is a hot-bed of jealousy and intrigue." And all because Ford refused to abandon the automobile he had been making for seventeen years.[35]

Despite this barrage of doomsday predictions, Henry Ford refused to be budged from his stubborn defense of the Model T. About 1923, he had authorized preliminary work on an experimental "X Car" that might someday replace the flivver, but he had urged so many outlandish ideas—eight-cylinder engines, four-wheel drive, four-wheel steering—that practical development of this model was impossible. Meanwhile, reporters who interviewed him returned with headlines declaring "Ford to Fight It Out With His Old Car." Radiating an attitude of calm confidence, he told associates, "The only trouble with the Ford car is that we can't make it fast enough." He reassured the public that his company would ride out the storm with a product that had been proved dependable over many years. "The Ford car is a tried and proved product that requires no tinkering. . . . It is not our intention to change our cars except as we always have done by constant improvement," he told the New York *Times*. During this period, Ford visited a gathering of his salesmen in Detroit, all of whom were complaining about various defects in the Model T and demanding a new model. When they asked his opinion, he replied, "I think that the only thing we need worry about is the best way to make more cars," and strode out of the room.[36]

Ford's reasons for this stance were personal, and obvious. Even Charles Sorensen, not noted for his sensitivity to human needs, understood that his boss "could not abandon the biggest single purpose of his life." "That achievement had brought him world-wide renown. . . . Henry Ford was in no mood to abandon it. None of us was sure that he would ever do so," Sorensen said. This deep emotional commitment to the product that had made him famous may have been accompanied by a damping of his competitive fires. After hearing another appeal to develop a new car to recapture the market, he confessed to Sorensen, "Charlie, I don't want all the business. Twenty-five per cent will satisfy me."[37]

As Henry dug in his heels, however, he came face to face with an unprecedented situation. Proponents of a new model, led by Edsel, refused to retreat. Instead of bowing to his father, even after the Kanzler fiasco, Edsel, with the implicit support of many other top-level managers, kept up a campaign of persistent pressure to convince him to change his mind. During "the years of the great debate," as one observer described this period, "everyone but Mr. Ford wanted to change the Model T. . . . Openly, Kanzler and Edsel were against [continuing] it. Rockelman was against it, not openly but quite frankly. Sorensen and Martin were against it in a very veiled way." The fight was long and bloody, and Edsel carried the flag. Week after week, he offered suggestions for a new car, and, just as dependably, his father ignored the ideas or dismissed them outright. One day, after another such exchange, a tight-lipped Henry walked away and left his son and other advisers standing at a drafting table. Sorensen was summoned to Henry's office. "The elder Ford told me to tell Edsel to take a trip to California. 'Make it a long stay,' he said, 'and tell him I will send him his paycheck out there. I'll send for him when I want to see him again,' " Sorensen reported. Wisely, Sorensen delayed in following these instructions, and the storm blew over in a few days. But the struggle soon resumed, as did the tension between the two Fords.[38]

Finally, late in the summer of 1926—it is difficult to pinpoint a precise date—Henry Ford succumbed. Though he never explained his rationale, it seems that the combination of pressure from associates and falling sales finally got to him. Ford approved the design of a new four-cylinder automobile to replace the Model T and appointed an engineering team to begin development: Lawrence Sheldrick served as project director, Joseph Galamb worked on the body and frame, Eugene Farkas on various mechanical systems, Frank Johnson on clutch and transmission, and Harold Hicks on engine and exhaust system. The old production bosses, Charles Sorensen and P. E. Martin, advised on the project, and Edsel took the lead in styling the model. Henry Ford was also deeply involved, often spending half of every day in Sheldrick's office, where he would monitor each detail of the new car as it emerged.[39]

Almost immediately, fresh debates erupted over the nature of the new car, and once again Henry and Edsel were at loggerheads. Predictably, Henry fought for the traditional features of the Model T; Edsel insisted on more modern innovations. Henry wanted to keep the planetary transmission and traditional brakes; Edsel successfully urged adoption of a sliding-gear transmission and brakes with balanced pressure on all four wheels. The Fords also clashed over the new car's suspension system, the son promoting the new coil-spring system against his father's opposition. But Edsel clearly carried the day on a number of stylistic issues, such as inclusion of a grille to cover the radiator at the front of the car, a larger frame with a lower ground clearance, a sharply designed instrument panel, a comfortable interior with cushions and trimmings, and a series of attractive color schemes.[40]

Henry accepted some of Edsel's judgment as the new Ford model took shape, even going so far as to comment, "We've got a pretty good man in my son. He knows style—how a car ought to look." But on many other matters, Henry stubbornly insisted on old-fashioned features, in defiance of Edsel's advice. Tensions waxed and waned as father and son argued over the central issue of meeting the public's taste. "It was the old man's belief that he knew best what was good for them [the public] and he was going to give them what was best," explained Lawrence Sheldrick, who witnessed these disputes. "Edsel, on the other hand, would try to give the public what they wanted." Eugene Farkas saw Edsel's frustration. "I know that he would have liked to make the Model A even more modern than we started out to do," he claimed.[41]

Despite fits of obstructionism, Henry threw himself into development of the new Ford car with his usual energy. Since he liked to see things full-sized, Sheldrick and Farkas set up a large drawing board covered with blackboard cloth on which they drew true-to-scale sketches of the car and its components. They even used crayons to depict various mechanical parts in different colors, so they could refer to the blue piston or the red cylinder block. Ford would examine the drawings, stand back to get an overall picture, discuss matters with the engineers, and issue directives. According to Sheldrick, "He was continually making comments and suggestions with reference to any element of design whether it was weight, or size, or strength." Ford observed tests run on the new prototype. After seeing the new car—it could reach speeds of sixty to sixty-five miles per hour, in contrast to the Model T's limit of forty-five—go careening into a ditch as the test driver banged his head and bruised his limbs, an agitated Ford burst out, "We can't put that car out on the public! We'll kill them all!" Once, Henry even conducted his own seat-of-the-pants test, commandeering the prototype from his startled engineers and driving off to traverse a field full of ruts, stones, and branches. Upon returning, he issued an order: "Rides too hard. Put on hydraulic shock absorbers." Thus was born one of the best features of the new car.[42]

Finally, after months of internal debate and continuous experimentation, wrinkles were ironed out and a design for the Model A emerged. On

May 26, 1927, a telegram went out under Edsel Ford's name announcing the imminent production of an "entirely new Ford car." Accompanying it was a statement from Henry Ford praising the Model T as a "pioneer" and promising that his new model would have "speed, style, flexibility, and control in traffic." Moreover, on that very day, the fifteen-millionth Model T rolled off the assembly line at Highland Park and was commemorated by a ceremony featuring Henry, Edsel, and various company dignitaries. The last Model T came off the line around the beginning of June, and a few weeks later another news release described the Model A as "an accomplished fact." Ford's new car, it seemed, would appear on the market at any moment.[43]

But such was not the case. The development of the Model A had created a massive new problem—the need to retool Ford factories that had been structured over the last fifteen years, down to the tiniest detail, for the single purpose of mass-producing the Model T. The protracted debate over the need for a new model, followed by a sudden decision to plunge ahead, had made planning for a production changeover nearly nonexistent. Henry Ford underestimated the problem. In a statement to the press, he reassured the public that retooling "will not necessitate a total shutdown. Only a comparatively few men will be out at a time while their departments are being tooled up for a new product. At one time it looked as if 70,000 men might be laid off temporarily, but we have now scaled that down to less than 25,000 at a time." This assessment proved wildly optimistic, and as the scope of the problem became evident, Ford managers blanched. Lawrence Sheldrick described these months as "the most terrific pressure period that anyone ever spent in their lives."[44]

In fact, all Ford production closed down for six months when the assembly lines for the Model T were terminated in June 1927. Tens of thousands of Ford workers were laid off as a massive retooling project started. The New York *Times* described it as "probably the biggest replacement of plant in the history of American industry." Henry Ford and his managers decided that the River Rouge facility would be the primary production factory for the Model A, and thirty-four assembly plants around the United States and twelve overseas would require retooling to produce the new car. In 1927, the company owned forty-three thousand machine tools, of which thirty-two thousand were used for production of the Model T. With the changeover, about half of these needed to be rebuilt or refurbished, a quarter scrapped, and a quarter used unchanged. Ford also purchased forty-five hundred entirely new machines to make the Model A. In addition, the company built over a million square feet of new factory space, installed new systems for using power, and formulated new machine layouts. After months of

frantic work, mass production of various components began in October, and
the first Model A was assembled on October 21. By early November, the
new assembly line at the Rouge was sending forth a steady stream of cars.
Ultimately, the cost of this retooling amounted to $250 million.[45]

Facing this immense project, Henry Ford turned to an activity in which
he had always excelled—publicity. As he had done so many times in the past,
he transformed a pressing situation into a public-relations bonanza. He
adopted a two-pronged strategy. First, Ford created a great sense of anticipation about his new car by initially withholding information from the public and then releasing tantalizing tidbits a little at a time. Second, even
though his associates in the company had dragged him kicking and screaming into replacing the Model T, he presented himself as a heroic, wise innovator who once again had decided to meet the needs of the American
consumer.

Ford masterfully manipulated the natural suspense that grew up regarding his new car. As the old assembly lines shut down, Ford factories closed,
and secret design work on the new car began, owners of those fifteen million Model T's were intrigued by its successor. Rumors ran rampant, and
the publicity buzz grew louder as newspapers, magazines, and people speculated endlessly. *Time*, for instance, analyzed some fuzzy photographs
snapped of the prototype on a test run in the Michigan countryside. Ford
played the game for all it was worth, denying false reports but offering nothing really illuminating. The New York *World* described how the story stayed
on the front pages:

> It is rumored that the car will be a six [cylinder]. A startled
> country rubs its eyes. The rumor is contradicted. It is rumored that
> the famous hood [of the Model T] will undergo a change and that
> the time-honored radiator is to have its face lifted. This rumor too
> is contradicted. But pictures purporting to represent the new-
> model car in action and at rest are smuggled to the press, debated
> by the nation, disavowed by the Ford Company, replaced by other
> pictures which in turn are half-confirmed, debated, disavowed—
> and the car that-is-to-be remains consistently on the front pages of
> the newspapers.

Jokes circulated. St. Peter, it was claimed, had begun stopping all deceased
Detroiters when they arrived at the gates of heaven and promising immediate admittance to anyone who could describe the new car. With typical
insight, Ford understood that by saying nothing he gained more publicity
than automobile companies who spent millions of dollars for that purpose.[46]

"Never was a publicity story so adroitly managed," noted *The Nation*. "A dozen times during the last few months alleged details about the new car slipped out and were duly featured on the front pages of the newspapers. Each time denials came from Edsel Ford, from the Ford plant in Detroit, or from the great man himself. Yet the stories persisted." Cartoons appeared, such as one that depicted two dejected circus barkers standing alone at their stalls as a huge crowd clamored around a Ford booth, with one inquiring, "How does he do it, Bill?" and the other replying, "Search me, I'm beat." The Ford publicity bubble, according to the Kansas City *Star*, was "the most remarkable exhibition of salesmanship in the history of the country." The Springfield, Massachusetts, *Union* described Henry Ford as "the master showman of all times." "To create a feeling of suspense, with its thrill of expectancy, is the aim of every dramatist who knows his art," the Chicago *Evening Post* pointed out. "Mr. Ford has achieved that aim." With his subtle gambits, Ford galvanized the American imagination for about six months, between June and December 1927.[47]

Henry Ford's image assumed a prominent position in the publicity surrounding his new car. In a sense, his performance was shameless, since everybody in the company knew that their leader had resisted eliminating the Model T. Nevertheless, articles appeared praising Ford as "The Driving Force and Guiding Spirit Behind the Ford Organization" as it labored at "designing a car which should meet the requirements of the market." He was described as "unique among men, a great thinker, a quick doer, a man of intense force but simple tastes; Lincolnian in character; a great American, the mechanical genius of the age." News stories explained how Ford spearheaded the development of the new car, telling his engineers, "I represent the public," as he "worked like a garage hand. He lay on his back under the cars, hitching and crawling from place to place, and when each design was completed, tried it out on the road." The New York *Times* described Ford as "still the restless, dynamic revolutionist that he always was," and claimed that he led the crusade to change the company's car. "No one fought to retain the old Lizzie. . . . Not a sentimental tear was shed over her," ran its fanciful rendering. "The fact remains that Ford himself specified exactly what he wanted [in the new model], that he passed on every gear and valve stem in the finished product, and that his was the spirit that dominated and animated the designing staff." Ford helped create this mirage, claiming that his engineers had been at work for several years on the new model but "it has been on my mind much longer than that." He explained the philosophy behind the new model. "Nothing is permanent but change. . . . If a manufacturer or a merchant has an ambition to avoid the junk pile, then his program has to be one of driving change," he declared.[48]

By early December 1927, the Ford campaign for the new car had reached its climax. The company had hired the advertising agency N. W. Ayer & Son of Philadelphia, and for five straight days after Thanksgiving, full-page ads appeared in every English-language newspaper in the United States, some two thousand in all. This created such a sensation that many papers reproduced the Ford ad copy on their front pages. On December 2, the Model A was introduced officially in New York City at the Waldorf-Astoria Hotel, as well as in showrooms and venues all over the country. The response was overwhelming. In Detroit, over a hundred thousand saw the car on display on its first day at the city's convention hall. Huge crowds descended on showings of the car in Denver, Kansas City, Dallas, New Orleans, and Cleveland, with mounted police summoned to control the situation. A scholar examining this outpouring of interest estimates that some ten million Americans saw the new Ford within thirty-six hours of its first display, and more than twenty-five million viewed it within a week.[49]

The Model A lived up to the hype surrounding it. This lightweight vehicle possessed a powerful four-cylinder, 40-horsepower engine that could reach a cruising speed of sixty-five miles per hour. So stylish that many described it as a "baby Lincoln," it featured low, sleek body lines and a variety of color combinations. The Model A, in contrast to its utilitarian predecessor, offered a variety of comfortable touches, such as safety glass, hydraulic shock absorbers, automatic starter, windshield wipers, nickel hardware, dashlight, and theft-proof locks. And, equally important, it continued the Ford tradition of inexpensive transportation. Ranging in price from $385 for the basic Roadster to $570 for the spacious Fordor Sedan, it cost no more than the last Model T's.[50]

The introduction of the Model A seemed to signal the triumphant revival, perhaps even rebirth, of the Ford Motor Company. It promised to solve profound problems in this enterprise. Even with its development costs, it promised redemption by offering the American public a stylish, comfortable, dependable vehicle suited to the social conditions and cultural values of the age. Just as the new car was coming before the American public, however, another controversy enveloped the company and its leader. More than any previous episode in his storied career, it illuminated Henry Ford's deepest personal weaknesses. By the time this controversy abated, his reputation had been sullied forever.

Nineteen

Bigot

On Sunday evening, March 27, 1927, Henry Ford was driving home alone from the engineering building in Dearborn. As he motored along Michigan Avenue not far from Fair Lane, another car suddenly sideswiped him and sent his coupe veering over an embankment, where it wedged between two trees. Ford managed to extricate himself from the wreck and stumble toward home. Scratched and stunned, he made it to the gatehouse of his estate, where the attendant immediately called Clara. She gathered her husband, put him into bed, and summoned his physician. Henry recuperated at home for two days, and then was moved to Henry Ford Hospital. Two boys were apprehended shortly thereafter. They claimed that Ford had been hogging the road and that the sideswipe had been an accident. Ford's attending physicians assured the public that his injuries were not serious, although he may have suffered a blackout, because "he did not seem to remember what happened."[1]

Such was the official story released to the press by the Ford Motor Company shortly after the accident. There may have been more to this incident, however, than met the eye. When Harry Bennett, Ford's security chief at the company, inspected the crash site, "there were some things that seemed phony to me," he later recalled. Then, when Bennett visited Ford later that day and vowed to find the culprits who had run him off the road, the victim insisted that he drop the whole matter. Bennett persisted, however, until Ford made a startling admission. "Well, Harry, I wasn't in that car when it went down into the river," he confessed. "I don't know how it got down there. But now we've got a good chance to settle this thing. We can say we want to settle it because my life is in danger."[2]

Why might Ford have concocted this episode, and what did he want to settle? In fact, he was under an enormous amount of stress on two fronts. First, having decided to jettison the Model T, he was about to authorize the closing of all company assembly plants for an extremely expensive retooling to produce a new model. Second, he was on the verge of being called to testify in what was perhaps the most embarrassing, controversial trial in which he had ever been embroiled. After years of anti-Semitic statements and articles published under his name in his Dearborn newspaper, Ford had been sued for libel by an outraged Jewish farm organizer. The trial was going badly, and his reputation was taking a beating.

Under pressure from these difficulties, Ford had grown fearful of being toppled from his lofty public standing. Desperate to recover his equilibrium and protect his image, he may have staged the car "accident" as a stratagem to position himself as a victim and arouse public sympathy. If nothing else, the accident allowed his lawyers to keep him off the stand. But the reprieve was temporary. Ford's anti-Semitism earned him a large portion of public disgrace that, coming near the end of the 1920s, accelerated his fall from public favor. Though the result of this process—a mortifying trial and humiliating public retraction—may have materialized fairly quickly, its gestation was lengthy. Ford's malignant strain of bigotry and ignorance was years in the making.

On January 11, 1919, Henry Ford presented a new publication to the American public. In 1918, as noted earlier, he had purchased the Dearborn *Independent*, a small community weekly, when financial difficulties were about to kill it. Now he launched the newspaper into the national arena. It became a forum for bringing his views directly to the American people unadulterated by a press, in his view, "owned body and soul by bankers. When they tell it to bark, it barks." True to his populist principles, he vowed, in the words of an associate, to use this publication for "giving the average citizen a truer and better analysis of matters which now reach him only from one point of view." Ford hired Edwin G. Pipp from the Detroit *News* as editor and built circulation by hiring people to sell subscriptions door-to-door and pressuring his automobile dealers throughout the nation to buy subscriptions and hand out copies.[3]

Ford also put his personal stamp on the Dearborn *Independent*. "Mr. Ford's Own Page," an editorial expressing his views, appeared in every issue. Although penned by William J. Cameron, the pieces resulted from daily conversations where Ford would talk, sometimes with his feet propped on Cameron's desk, expounding his philosophy while the ghostwriter took notes. Cameron would take Ford's epigrammatic, even cryptic declarations, and transform them into essays that would capture the speaker's meaning.

The *Independent* also carried an interesting mix of articles. Some addressed social and economic questions, such as "Speculation vs. Production: Which Creates Wealth?," while others urged Americans to be informed consumers. Many articles sounded a reformist note by promoting the League of Nations, supporting the 1919 Southern Race Congress, or advocating government ownership of telephone companies. General-interest stories examined foreign countries, offered cultural criticism of jazz and the movies, or reported on the evolution of the airplane. History articles sought to uncover the "real" John Wilkes Booth, and fiction appeared from writers such as Robert Frost, Hugh Walpole, and Booth Tarkington. Ford's newspaper proved popular. By 1924, circulation had climbed to 650,000; in 1926, it reached 900,000.[4]

A little more than a year after beginning publication, however, Pipp abruptly resigned as editor. In part, he was bothered by the growing intrusion of company politics, with its bureaucratic maneuvering and malicious competition, into the newsroom. Pipp described it as "the most depressing place I was ever in. There was so much intriguing and backbiting that one could feel only uncomfortable in the atmosphere." The editor also grew weary of Ford's obsession with using the newspaper to gain vengeance upon the victor in the 1918 election, Senator Truman H. Newberry, who Ford believed had stolen the count.

Most disturbing to Pipp, however, was Ford's plan for a new initiative in the *Independent*. He was preparing to mount a campaign against a group he considered to be the most dangerous in the world, and Pipp wanted no part of it. He spent much of March 1920 agonizing over his position. "I put in that month getting material ready for several editions ahead and on the first of April, resigned," he recalled later. "It was in May that Mr. Ford commenced printing his attacks on the Jews."[5]

On May 22, 1920, the Dearborn *Independent* began a controversial series that would forever be linked with the newspaper and its publisher. Appearing on the front page week after week for over two years, "The International Jew: The World's Problem" examined a purported conspiracy launched by Jewish groups to capture social, cultural, and economic power and achieve domination around the world. It began with a racial definition:

> Among the distinguishing mental and moral traits of the Jews may be mentioned: distaste for hard or violent physical labor; a strong family sense and philoprogenitiveness; a marked religious instinct;

the courage of the prophet and the martyr rather than of the pioneer and soldier; remarkable power to survive in adverse environ-
ments, combined with great ability to retain racial solidarity;
capacity for exploitation, both individual and social; shrewdness
and astuteness in speculation and money matters generally; an Oriental love of display and a full appreciation of the power and pleasure of social position; a very high average of intellectual ability.

Following this list of stereotypes and slurs, the essay argued that the growing influence of Jews in financial, political, and social life since the end of
World War I had raised concerns. "The Jew's" formation of a "money aris-
tocracy," a "corporation with agents everywhere," and a movement "linked
in a fellowship of blood" needed to be brought before the public gaze and
examined. After ninety-two such articles had appeared in the *Independent*,
they were collected and published in book form under Ford auspices.[6]

"The International Jew" castigated Jewish influences around the world
but focused on American manifestations of this supposed campaign for
power. The titles of individual essays suggested its basic thrust:

"The Jew in Character and Business"
"Does a Definite Jewish World Program Exist?"
"Does Jewish Power Control the World Press?"
"Jewish Testimony in Favor of Bolshevism"
"How Jews in the U.S. Conceal Their Strength"
"Jewish Supremacy in the Motion Picture"
"Jewish Rights Clash with American Rights"
"Jewish Degradation of American Baseball"
"Jewish Jazz Becomes Our National Music"
"Jewish Idea Molded Federal Reserve Plan"
"How Jewish International Finance Functions"
"Gigantic Jewish Liquor Trust and its Career"[7]

After exploring these corrosive manifestations of the "Jewish problem"
in nearly every aspect of American life, the series concluded with two broad
essays. Their contents were chilling.

The penultimate piece, entitled "Candid Address to Jews on the Jewish
Problem," urged Jews to mend their ways and "bring their misbehavior to
an end." It expressed the hope that criticism would "arouse a sense of social
responsibility among the Jews" so they would end their social isolation. In
other words, the essay suggested that Jews should control their own worst
instincts before others stepped forward to do so.[8]

The concluding essay contained another veiled threat. Entitled "An Address to Gentiles on the Jewish Problem," it offered an agenda to those who wished to curb Jewish influence. Though it explicitly disavowed violence, it urged vigilant citizens to open their eyes to Jewish subversion and stop it peacefully but firmly. It pressed responsible Americans to scrutinize commercial practices in their communities, identify shoddy goods and inflated prices, and reject these "Jewish" practices. "Let the business men of the country adopt the old way of the white man," it declared. The essay encouraged citizens to look carefully for degenerative themes in movies and books, to scrutinize those who stirred up social unrest, and to remain sensitive to "the subversive influence" in civil institutions such as schools and government. Eternal vigilance against such Jewish inroads was the price of American freedom. The essay concluded, "It is perfectly obvious that the cure for all this is to become awake, alert, to challenge the foreign influence, and to seek out again the principles which gave us our greatness. . . . The church must be un-Judaized and Christianized. The Government must be Americanized."[9]

The blatant anti-Semitism of "The International Jew" caused an uproar. The articles gained support from journalists and critics such as W. J. Abbot, John C. Chapman, and C. Mobray White, and the financier J. P. Morgan reportedly expressed approval. Evidence also suggests that the *Independent*'s subscriber list began to grow after publication of the anti-Jewish pieces. Anti-Semitism, as historian Leo P. Ribuffo has pointed out, appealed to powerful traditions in American life, such as nativism and several variants of Protestantism. Moreover, by the 1920s other ideological impulses had come into play. Conservative critics of the Russian Revolution frequently identified Bolshevism as a Jewish doctrine. Progressives insisted that a conspiracy of economic powers worked behind the scenes to oppress ordinary American citizens. Many of these reformers, such as the critic Burton J. Hendrick, the muckraker Jacob Riis, and the sociologist Edward A. Ross argued that Jews had played a significant role in such corruption. Thus the paranoia of left and right found a convenient convergence point in anti-Semitism.[10]

Yet many Americans were appalled by the crusade of the Dearborn *Independent*. In December 1920, the Federal Council of Churches adopted a resolution condemning the "International Jew" series. In early 1921, over one hundred prestigious Americans—the group included Woodrow Wilson, William Howard Taft, and Cardinal William O'Connell—signed a statement entitled "The Perils of Racial Prejudice" that repudiated "vicious propaganda" against Jews. Officials in several large cities considered removing the *Independent* from public libraries; certain automobile dealerships, such as the Barish Brother Company in Sioux City, Iowa, were so incensed by the "prejudice, hatred, and intrigue" of the articles that they canceled their contracts with the Ford Motor Company. Jewish leaders such as Louis Marshall and Herman Bernstein denounced the bigotry of "The International Jew" and supported rebuttals in books such as *The History of a Lie.* E. G. Pipp publicly broke ranks. "I regard Henry Ford's attack upon the Jews as absolutely without reason, unfair, cruel, bigoted, and contrary to the American spirit," he wrote. "Condemning 3,000,000 in this country for the acts of a few is not right, and I didn't want to be a party to it."[11]

As controversy swirled around "The International Jew," its genesis remained something of a mystery. William J. Cameron had succeeded Pipp as editor of the *Independent,* and he wrote most of the articles. He based them in part on a reading of books and essays such as Werner Sombart's *The Jews and Modern Capitalism,* and in part on a notorious manuscript entitled *The Protocols of the Elders of Zion,* which claimed to detail an international Jewish conspiracy to capture global political and economic power. Cameron also relied upon a team of agents whom the Ford organization paid to investigate every suspected strain of Jewish influence in American life. Headquartered in New York City under the direction of C. C. Daniels, a former lawyer for the Justice Department, this group forwarded rumors, newspaper clippings, and documents to the *Independent.*[12]

Clearly, however, Henry Ford's own ideas and proclivities fueled this project. He visited the offices of the *Independent* nearly every day and consulted with Cameron about the two projects at the newspaper that most interested him—"Mr. Ford's Own Page" and "The International Jew." Ford's ideas about Jews were certainly no secret. He spoke freely to associates, journalists, and other visitors about his hostile sentiments. "I never had a visit with him, at lunch or dinner, when he did not talk about the Jews and his campaign against them," noted writer James Martin Miller. Allan Benson, author of the *The New Henry Ford,* had a similar experience. "Ford often talked to me about the Jews," he reported. "He gave me two leather-bound books composed of articles printed in the *Independent* and asked me to read them." When Benson confessed that he did not share those views on the subject, Ford threatened to shun him.[13]

In his public statements on "the Jewish question," Ford was equally candid. "The Jews are the scavengers of the world," he declared in 1923. "Wherever there's anything wrong with a country, you'll find the Jews on the job there." Two years earlier, Ford had defended *The Protocols of the Elders of Zion,* contending that "they fit in with what is going on. They are sixteen years old, and they have fitted the world situation up to this time. They fit it now." In *My Life and Work,* he noted a "marked deterioration in our literature, amusements, and social conduct" that was attributable to "not the robust coarseness of the white man . . . but a nasty Orientalism which has insidiously affected every channel of expression—and to such an extent that it was time to challenge it."[14]

Although the nature of Ford's anti-Semitic views was clear, their inspiration was much less so. His intense dislike of Jews had various sources. There is no evidence of any telling personal episode involving him or his family with Jews. Nor is there any record of intellectual conversion, in which Ford read a tract or heard a speech that sent him down the path of bigotry. Instead, typically, his anti-Semitism lay entangled in a web of half-formed ideas, vague perceptions, and impulsive yet deeply felt readings of the world around him. This web, one suspects, was more than anything the product of his famous "hunches."

One of its strands emerged from Ford's populist political sensibility, with its distrust of financiers, bankers, and institutions of economic power. As did the Populist Party in the 1890s, his denunciations of Wall Street combined economic radicalism with a strong anti-Semitic element. "The Jew is a mere huckster, a trader, who doesn't want to produce, but to make something out of what somebody else produces," he told an interviewer in 1921. "Our money and banking system is the invention of the Jews, for their own purposes of control, and it's bad. Our gold standard was founded by the Jews; it's bad, and things will never get right until we are rid of the power they hold through it." For Ford, "Wall Street finance capitalists" and "New York Jews" were practically synonymous terms, and in 1922 he denounced the "greed and avarice of Wall Street Kikes" to the Detroit *Free Press*. Specifically, he viewed Jews as antithetical to the populist ideology of hard-working producerism. "He always stressed the fact that the Jews were the type of people who preferred nonproductive enterprises," an associate explained. He also blamed Jewish financiers for his defeat in the 1918 Senate election. Again like his populist predecessors, Ford endorsed a strategy of agitation and exposure to undermine this economic power. "Ford is a great believer in what he calls 'stirring people up.' He thinks the average man is too lazy and unprogressive," noted a reporter who talked with Ford about his criticisms of Jews.[15]

Ford's opposition to war provided a second strand in his mental web of anti-Semitism. He came away from his crusade against World War I with the clear conviction that international Jewish bankers lay behind the bloodbath. This conviction, of course, neatly dovetailed with his populist critique of Jewish financial power. He told Allan Benson that he had learned of Jewish culpability on the cruise of the Peace Ship. "It taught me who starts the wars—the International Jew, the International Jewish banker—and we're going to write some articles about him sometime," he confirmed to Fred Black. The war, Ford became convinced, had been fomented by wealthy Jewish lenders such as the Rothschilds and the Warburgs. In fact, while the Peace Ship was in mid-journey he had shocked fellow traveler Rosika Schwimmer by bursting out, "I know who caused the war—the German-Jewish bankers! [He slapped his breast pocket.] I have the evidence here. Facts! The German-Jewish bankers caused the war."[16]

In a 1925 interview with *Farm and Fireside*, Ford clearly delineated the connection he saw between Jews and international conflict. "What I oppose most is the international Jewish money power that is met in every war," he declared. "No matter what happens to the nations in a war the money power always wins. No war starts without it and every war stops when it says so. That is what I oppose—a power that has no country and that can order the young men of all countries out to death." For Ford, ironically, opposition to Jewish financial power was part of the noble reform crusade to bring peace to the world.[17]

A third strand of Ford's anti-Jewish sentiment came from his growing cultural conservatism. In the postwar years, he became increasingly drawn to the American past as he began to collect antique furniture, support old-time American music, re-create historical buildings from the eighteenth and nineteenth centuries, revive *McGuffey Readers*, and refurbish old machines and implements from traditional farms. From such a cultural palette, he painted an attractive portrait of traditional Anglo-Saxon Protestant village life that had little room for Jews. In fact, Jewish influences were blamed for lascivious new styles in music and dress, loose standards of sexual propriety, and scandalous productions in theater and movies. Associates heard him launch tirades against Jews in the entertainment industry who were subverting sturdy American traditions with jazz and movies. In *My Life and Work*, he defined America as a Christian nation and demanded that Jews "labour to make Jews American, instead of labouring to make America Jewish."[18]

Ford's anti-Semitism was frightening not so much for its viciousness as for its combination of ignorance, unpredictable absurdity, utter conviction, and naïveté. Though not advocating violence in the European sense of pogroms, Ford had a hostility toward Jews that was perhaps equally disturbing in its open-endedness. One minute he would assume a dialect and laughingly relate how he had encountered a Jewish shopkeeper in Washington, D.C., who supposedly told him, "Well, I been readin' dis Dearborn *Independent* of yours. It's all right. It tells the truth about us." The next minute he would encourage Cameron to write about how Benedict Arnold had created a "Jewish front" in the American Revolution as an agent of Jewish bankers and warmongers. Or he would denounce Jay Gould as an avaricious "Shylock," even though the speculator was a lifelong Presbyterian. Or he would demand that engineers avoid using brass as a component in the Model T because it was a "Jew metal" (the engineers responded by using it when necessary and then covering it with black paint). Or he would propound such bizarre ideas, as he did in the early 1930s, that Hitler had been brought to power in Germany by wealthy, influential Jews in order to clean out the less prominent ones.[19]

However ignorant and malignant Ford's views were, they were exacerbated by another influence. By the early 1920s, his bigotry was being encouraged by someone ensconced at the very heart of his organization. Jealously guarding all outside access to Ford and looking after his personal financial affairs, this man viewed Jews as the bane of civilized society. At every opportunity, he encouraged his boss to do likewise.

In June 1920, Ernest G. Liebold, Henry Ford's business secretary and office manager, received a copy of *The Protocols of the Elders of Zion*. This text purported to be the proceedings of a conclave of Jewish leaders in the 1890s that ratified a plan for world domination. Translated by the Russian émigré and Bolshevik foe Boris Brasol, this version had come into the possession of a Madame Shishmareff, who was married to a lieutenant in the U.S. Army. In turn, she contacted Liebold, and arrangements were made to get him a copy. Within days, the *Protocols* were feeding the anti-Semitic attacks appearing in the Dearborn *Independent*. Liebold was thrilled, believing that this document provided concrete evidence of nefarious Jewish activity in the United States and around the world. "We took the *Protocols* at their face value," he explained later. "That's all we tried to do. In the various activities they [the Jews] performed, we could show a definite trend." The *Protocols* were an utter fabrication, but Liebold never indicated he knew that. It would not have mattered. For a man who loathed Jews and craved power at the Ford Company in equal proportion, such a distinction was beside the point.[20]

By the early 1920s, Liebold had gained considerable authority at the company through his personal relationship with Henry Ford. E. G. Pipp, who despised Liebold, believed he was poisoning the mind of his benefactor through flattery. "Mr. Liebold tilted back his chair, unbuttoned his coat, put his thumbs into the armholes of his vest, expanded his chest, and said: 'Mr. Ford, YOU don't have to think as other men think; YOUR thoughts come to you like a flash, from a sub-conscious mind, and you have your problems solved,' " Pipp described. He continued, "The door to the Ford mind was always open to anything Liebold wanted to shove in it, and during that time Mr. Ford developed a dislike for Jews, a dislike which [grew] stronger and more bitter as time went on." This partnership in bigotry had actually begun more than a decade before.[21]

Ernest Gustav Liebold had become Henry Ford's business secretary by a chain of circumstances. He had grown up in Detroit in a family of German Lutherans. After studying business, he took a job at the Peninsula Savings Bank in Highland Park in 1910 and slowly worked his way up from messenger to teller to bank officer. He eventually met James Couzens, who took an immediate liking to the hardworking young man. Couzens was involved in starting up a company bank in Highland Park to serve Ford employees, and he appointed Liebold first as head cashier, then to the board of directors, and then as its president. Liebold caught the attention of Henry Ford, who put him in charge of the D. P. Lapham Bank in Dearborn, an insolvent institution he had just purchased. Liebold, with his customary intelligence and efficiency, revived the Lapham Bank and impressed Ford greatly. By 1913, he was working directly for Ford and had received authorization to pay the industrialist's personal bills. He came gradually to handle Ford's business correspondence as well. Within a few years, he became Ford's office manager and gained power of attorney to sign Mr. and Mrs. Ford's personal correspondence and deal with their financial affairs. His salary was paid from Henry Ford's personal account rather than through the company.[22]

Liebold became a force to be reckoned with in the company. From his office in the engineering laboratory in Dearborn—right next to Henry Ford's office—he controlled access to the industrialist. He served as Ford's executive secretary, financial manager, accountant, and intermediary with the press, and stood at the center of every Ford project that did not involve the making of automobiles. Every day at midmorning, he would arrive at work, walk sedately from the garage to his office, and consult with his secretary, Hazel McConnell, and his assistant, Charlie Zahnow. Liebold's office suite was the picture of orderliness, and he sat for hours in his swivel chair behind a large desk managing Henry Ford's affairs and writing checks that often ran into the hundreds of thousands of dollars. His office also held a large safe, in which he kept over $1 million in cash.[23]

Liebold's power came not only from his abilities, but from taking advantage of Ford's notorious aversion to handling the details of his business. He realized that his boss had no patience for examining letters or documents or discussing the particulars of any financial or organizational issue. As Liebold commented, whenever he tried to discuss details with Ford "he'd get up and walk out. He just didn't want to be bothered about that. . . .

He'd say, 'I'll be back in a few minutes' or 'I'll be back later on.' That's the last I'd see of him." This habit created considerable opportunity for Liebold, who was delighted to work out various undertakings and submit them for his boss's approval. "All Mr. Ford had to say to Liebold was, 'Do this, do that,' and he'd carry out the most ambitious projects," reported one observer. Such an arrangement served the interests of both men.[24]

At the Chicago *Tribune* trial, Liebold established a news bureau to disseminate Ford's side of the story, and supervised a group of undercover operatives from a suite of rooms in the Medea Hotel in Mount Clemens. He supervised the building of the Henry Ford Hospital in Detroit and managed Ford's run for the Senate. A few years later, he organized the Ford for President boom, and became very interested in radio broadcasting because he thought it could be used to help Ford achieve high political office.[25]

Liebold performed even the most minor of tasks. When Ford became enthusiastic about a wood-burning train and wanted it restored and its cars decorated with paintings, Liebold called artist-in-residence Irving Bacon and gave him detailed instructions. When Ford hosted an elaborate banquet in honor of Thomas Edison, Liebold organized the affair. Ford's avid interest in antiques sent his office manager scouring the countryside in search of old steam engines or nineteenth-century furniture. When Ford complained that people were hounding him as he arrived and departed from work by automobile, Liebold procured a set of false whiskers that Ford actually wore in transit for a few days.[26]

In the words of Fred Black, Liebold "was riding high, wide, and handsome" in the Ford organization and was overheard to remark that soon "he expected to be General Manager." He supervised Henry Ford's interest in banks, real-estate projects, the DT&I Railroad, and mining and lumbering interests. "Liebold had tremendous power here in the twenties. . . . He had his finger in almost every pie," noted a secretary in Ford's office. Indeed, Liebold's responsibilities became so crushing that they drove him to a nervous breakdown in the early 1930s, when he disappeared from Dearborn for several days and holed up at a hotel in a remote area of Michigan to rest and recover his equilibrium.[27]

Though Liebold saw himself as an extension of Ford's will, an intricate relationship nonetheless developed between the two men. It was studiously formal. Throughout their many years of working together, no one ever heard them address each other except as "Mr. Ford" and "Mr. Liebold." Their respect was mutual, with Ford trusting many of the most important matters in his life to Liebold's discretion while the latter shouldered this responsibility with devotion. According to Harold Cordell, who worked in

Ford's office for many years, "Liebold was very devoted to him and, from what I could see, did his best to do what was right for Henry's interests."[28]

Occasionally, however, the Ford-Liebold relationship turned contentious. Though respectful, Liebold did not fear his boss; in the words of Irving Bacon, "He'd tell him right off the bat that he didn't agree with him, and why. He wasn't a bit afraid to tell Mr. Ford what he thought." Ford usually appreciated such candor, but occasionally tempers flared and resentments set in. "They'd get mad and refuse to speak to each other for months at a stretch, and Mr. Liebold would have to conduct his business in a more or less indirect fashion in order to get the things he wanted to put over," reported Cordell. "But they'd always get back together."[29]

Liebold's stern personality and efficiency were reflected in his physical presence. He always appeared a picture of neatness with his stocky frame, immaculate suits, starched shirts, wire-rim glasses, neatly groomed hair, and calm, stern demeanor. His personal life was cast in the same mold. He had married Clara Reich in 1910, and within thirteen years the couple had produced eight children. Apparently, he managed his family with the same efficiency he displayed at the Ford Motor Company. Henry Ford once told an associate, "When dinner time arrived at the Liebold household, Liebold marched his children around the table in military style, and when they had reached their places he commanded, 'Sitzen sie!' "[30]

Liebold's passion for order, however, alienated most people with whom he worked. He gained a reputation for being blunt, even brutal in his professional relationships, and appeared uninterested in personal friendships. "I make it a rule not to have any friends in the company—you must be in a position where you don't give a God-damn what happens to anybody," he once told Fred Black. Stories about Liebold's cold, tactless manner became widespread in the organization. J. L. McCloud, who headed the chemical-and-metallurgical laboratory for many years, encountered it unforgettably on Christmas Eve. "As I walked out I met Mr. Liebold and I said, 'Merry Christmas, Mr. Liebold!' He stopped and thought for a minute or two, and finally said, 'Well, all right.' "[31]

This tough demeanor and willingness to offend others became especially effective tools for Liebold to control access to Henry Ford. Reporters who wanted to interview the industrialist had to pass through his office manager first, and the route was not an easy one. "Liebold treated reporters badly," according to Fred Black, and "was very heavy-handed." By the 1920s, this screening had extended to many company executives, whom Liebold frequently insulted and then left cooling their heels. They deeply resented having their access to Ford blocked by a man who, in Harry Ben-

nett's words, "looked like a typical Prussian, and often acted like one." Many
of them, however, also feared Liebold, who had a small group of operatives
keeping tabs on Ford managers, the results of which went into elaborate
files.[32]

Liebold demonstrated his tactless manner in an incident involving
Ford's hobby of rescuing and restoring antique buildings. When a Virginia
state senator asked Ford to reconsider his removal of a building from the
Old Dominion, Liebold wrote a terse, insulting reply to the friendly letter
of inquiry. "It would appear that here in Dearborn where such other evi-
dences of our early history and civilization are being constructed, it would
be in its proper place, where maintenance and care could be given, instead
of permitted to disintegrate as its present condition shows," he said. Ford
clearly valued such toughness. When William Cameron once commented
that Liebold seemed to antagonize many people, Ford replied, "Well, when
you hire a watchdog, you don't hire him to like everyone who comes to the
gate."[33]

But Liebold, it was clear, used dogmatic, dictatorial methods not only
to protect his patron but to enhance his own position in the organization.
Many agreed with Fred Black that "Liebold had almost a Hitlerian desire
for power." One of Ford's workers in the 1918 senatorial campaign wrote a
bitter complaint about "Czar Liebold" to a newspaper editor. "E. G.
Liebold is the most disliked man I have ever come in contact with in all my
experience," he wrote. In turn, the editor, who had had his own run-ins with
Liebold, forwarded the letter to Edsel Ford and added his own complaint.
"Mr. Liebold has become a real menace to your father, yourself, and
your business," he warned. "His great greed for power and more power has
driven him to action akin to kaiserism."[34]

Perhaps Liebold's most notorious contribution to Ford came from his
central role in the Dearborn *Independent*. According to Liebold, Henry Ford
asked him to become involved in this journalistic venture in late 1918, when
delays had mounted. "You go out there and see what you can do to help out.
See if you can get the thing going," Ford said. Liebold found much disorga-
nization and inefficiency, so he deputized Fred Black and they fired about
half the employees and reformed the organization. Liebold claimed that
Ford also asked him to become editor of the paper when Pipp left, but he
demurred and recommended Cameron. Everyone knew who was really in
charge, however. As Cameron himself admitted, "I think the man who really
ran the thing was E. G. Liebold." With characteristic efficiency, Liebold
paid attention to the smallest detail, such as checking the paper for mis-
spellings and grammatical mistakes. When he found an error, a curt note to
the staff would explain, "I didn't want to be put in the position of being a

proofreader." Once, when Irving Bacon resisted doing illustrations for the newspaper, Liebold gave him "a browbeating look" and demanded, "Are you trying to tell me how to run this magazine?"[35]

In managing the *Independent*, Liebold focused on one particular goal. He hated everything Jewish, and he saw the publication as a vehicle for promoting this agenda. He did not mask his anti-Semitism. When clashing with another Ford operative at the Chicago *Tribune* trial, he explained the problem with a simple statement: "He was a Jew." When Liebold criticized Fred Rockelman for inflating his own importance in the company, he could not resist the observation, "His wife was half-Jewish." He related how Mrs. Rockelman had brought to the Dearborn Country Club several Jewish guests who talked so loudly and behaved so boorishly that Mrs. Ford took offense and complained to her husband. When denouncing government regulation of the American economy, Liebold observed that reputable sources had told him how "prominent Jewish financiers . . . conceived the idea of a Federal Reserve Bank" prior to 1912.[36]

Liebold's pro-German leanings, which he muted during World War I, supplemented his anti-Semitic fervor. Intensely proud of his heritage, he used his position to promote German achievements and activities. "Whenever any German delegation came to the office, the big red carpet was rolled out and royal honors were paid," Harold Cordell noted. "Whereas a United States Senator could just sit out in the anteroom for hours and wait for an audience." Historian Neil Baldwin, who has closely examined the evidence, argues convincingly that Liebold even served as an emissary to Ford from the rising Nazi movement in Germany during the early 1920s. In 1924, Liebold brought Kurt Ludecke, Adolf Hitler's primary fund-raiser in the United States, to meet with Ford in Dearborn and solicit money. Ford, though agreeing with Ludecke's slurs on the Jews, refused to offer financial assistance to the Nazi cause. Liebold always denied any connection between the Nazi movement and Ford. At the same time, however, without a shred of guilt, he admitted, "I always felt that the republication of the *International Jew* books in Germany had a large influence."[37]

According to Harry Bennett, Liebold constantly stirred up Ford's anti-Semitism. "I recall in particular one time when Liebold sat beside Mr. Ford at a big banquet," he wrote. "I saw Liebold lean over toward Mr. Ford and heard him whisper, 'See that man over there? He's a Jew.' And then I saw Mr. Ford look at the man Liebold had pointed out, and his expression changed." Another time, Liebold informed his patron, in a disapproving tone, that wastepaper from the newspaper was being collected and hauled away by a Jewish man. Ford, of course, subsequently decreed that "he didn't want any more wastepaper sold to the Jews. He didn't want them around the plant." Their shared pathology led Liebold and Ford to the crackpot theory that Jews had been behind the assassination of Abraham Lincoln. They became convinced that Lincoln's wartime authorization of greenback dollars had outraged a group of "international bankers," and these "Jewish internationalists" decided to kill the President. Liebold put several investigators on the case to gather evidence for an article in the Dearborn *Independent*. Not surprisingly, they found none.[38]

Liebold emerged as the prime mover in the "International Jew" articles. Those close to the scene described him as "the spark plug in the Jewish series." He insisted, "Our present campaign against the International Jew is based on facts which we have gathered for some time past and is not based on prejudice." He tried to position Ford's newspaper as a heroic defender of the truth, claiming, "We have been threatened and bombarded with Jewish letters. . . . However, we have set out to do our duty as we see it, and will die in the effort if we do not make a success of it." Liebold contended that the *Independent* faced subversion from "Jewish sources of distribution" and that in many city libraries "the Jews would go in there and borrow the paper and never return it."[39]

For all of Liebold's vigor in promoting the campaign against the Jews, he never usurped Henry Ford's authority. "Everything that was being done was because of Mr. Ford's wishes in carrying out the idea of revealing to the public the facts pertaining to certain Jewish activities," he wrote later. Throughout the 1920s, Ford made clear to Liebold his determination to pursue the Jewish bugaboo. When planning the newspaper attack, Liebold suggested that they use the heading "International Jew" to distinguish "good" members of the race from "bad" ones. Though Ford agreed, he insisted, "You can't single them out. You have to go after them all. They are all part of the same system." As he once proclaimed angrily, "We are going to print their names. We are going to show who they are."[40]

The anti-Semitism of Ernest Liebold and Henry Ford eventually created a full-blown crisis. Their partnership in bigotry had produced the "International Jew" series, but, not satisfied with that success, they initiated another attack on Jewish influence in America. This time they went too far. Their actions produced a lawsuit and a spectacular trial that, like the Selden and Chicago *Tribune* suits, brought Ford much publicity. The attention, however, revealed a side of Henry Ford that many had never seen.

On the morning of February 20, 1925, Aaron Sapiro filed a libel suit against Henry Ford and the Dearborn Publishing Company. A series of articles in the Dearborn *Independent* had characterized his attempts to organize farm cooperatives as a plot by Jewish international financiers to capture control of the American economy. Claiming defamation of character, Sapiro demanded restitution in the amount of $1 million "to vindicate myself and my race." Earlier in the decade, a series of skirmishes had been fought between Ford and various Jewish groups and individuals following the publication of "The International Jew." But now a major battle was joined as lawyers were hired and strategies were hatched.[41]

Ford's eagerness to participate in this trial reflected his warped judgment about the larger implications of his anti-Semitic crusade. He had never quite understood the impact of his attacks in the Jewish community. Blind to the prejudice and hatred spread by his newspaper, Ford genuinely believed that he was only attacking "bad" Jews, and that "good" Jews would support his crusade to reform the bad habits of the race. As publication of "The International Jew" unfolded, he had a falling out with Rabbi Leo Franklin of Detroit that seems to have mystified him. Franklin, leader of a prominent Reform temple in the city, had been a neighbor and longtime friend of Ford, and when the "International Jew" articles first appeared he believed that Ford had been swayed by evil advisers. Franklin thought the automaker would listen to reason and counseled patience, but he changed his mind as the articles continued. For several years, Ford had sent a new Model T to the rabbi every year, but in the summer of 1920, Franklin returned the gift. In an accompanying letter, he sorrowfully noted "an unfortunate idea that has taken possession of you . . . that must inevitably tend to poison the minds of the masses against the Jews." Ford telephoned a few days later, and his response spoke volumes about his naïveté: "What's wrong, Dr. Franklin? Has something come between us?"[42]

Angrier Jewish reactions to Ford's campaign arose in other quarters. The American Jewish Committee, under the leadership of attorney Louis Marshall, denounced "The International Jew" as "puerile and venomous drivel." Marshall also led a campaign to have Jewish newspapers refuse to accept advertising from the Ford Motor Company. Telegrams of protest from other Jewish groups and individuals streamed into the offices of the Dearborn *Independent;* sporadic boycotts of Ford automobiles cropped up in urban areas around the country. Herman Bernstein, editor of the *Jewish Tribune,* brought a libel suit against Ford when the latter claimed that Bernstein had told him the inside story of how Jews plotted war and planned to take over the world. To an extent, Ford responded to such pressure. "The Jewish articles must stop," he told Cameron and Liebold, and ordered an end to the "International Jew" series in January 1922.[43]

But the moratorium did not last long. Within a year, the *Independent* began a second wave of articles, which found evidence of undue Jewish influence in a host of places—the verdict in the case of Nathan Leopold and Richard Loeb, the Dawes Plan to reduce German reparations, the opposition to President Coolidge. The newspaper also launched a relentless attack against Captain Robert Rosenbluth of the U.S. Army, whom it accused of murdering his commanding officer, Major Alexander Cronkite, in 1918. Despite a ruling by an army board of inquiry that the shooting death had been a tragic accident, and oblivious to Rosenbluth's unblemished record as a veteran of World War I who had been gassed and wounded on the Western Front, the *Independent* began a years-long campaign against him. It suggested that Rosenbluth may have been a "dirty German Jew spy" or a Jewish Bolshevik agitator. After investigating the case at Ford's behest, the Department of Justice declined to press charges against Rosenbluth.[44]

In April 1924, the *Independent* initiated the series that embroiled it in national controversy. In "Jewish Exploitation of Farmers' Organizations," the newspaper attacked the efforts of Sapiro, claiming he was the leader of a Jewish conspiracy to unify American agriculture under a "Jewish holding company." For nearly a year, the articles detailed how "a band of Jews— bankers, lawyers, money-lenders, advertising agencies, fruit-packers, produce-buyers, experts—is on the backs of the American farmer." They fingered Sapiro as a particular villain.[45]

In certain ways, Sapiro made a logical target for muckraking journalism. In 1919, he had begun to organize farmers' organizations throughout the United States, and within a few years had formed the National Council of Farmers' Cooperative Marketing Associations as an umbrella group for some sixty regional associations. Representing almost a million farmers in the United States and Canada, Sapiro's organization used the classic tactic of cooperatives—withholding crops from the market temporarily, in order to force higher prices. But Sapiro's autocratic personality and managerial missteps created difficulties. He hired several incompetent subordinates, ridiculed other agricultural leaders, and made several bad decisions in marketing farmers' goods. Discontent with his leadership forced him to step down in 1924. There were also allegations of misappropriated funds and excessive legal fees.[46]

In the midst of these difficulties, Sapiro grew furious at the attacks on his character and agenda in Ford's "Jewish Exploitation" articles. After absorbing these assaults for several months, he finally struck back. In January 1925, he sent a thirty-one-page letter to Ford demanding a public retraction of the charges mounted in the Dearborn *Independent*. When none was forthcoming, he sued for libel. According to Liebold, when he cautioned that Cameron's zeal in attacking Sapiro might create legal problems,

Ford "told me to lay off Cameron, and that if Cameron could get us into a lawsuit, that would be just what he wanted."[47]

For a year after Sapiro filed his lawsuit, depositions were taken, and a trial date was set for March 1926. But Ford successfully sought a continuance until September, at which time his attorneys had the judge disqualified and gained another continuance. Finally, after two years of maneuvering, the case came to trial on March 15, 1927, in the U.S. District Court in Detroit. Judge Fred S. Raymond presided. The plaintiff was represented by William Henry Gallagher and Robert S. Marx; Ford was defended by U.S. Senator James A. Reed of Missouri, assisted by a team of seven attorneys.

During opening statements, the plaintiff's lawyers argued that the *Independent* was "Ford's mouthpiece" and that its attacks upon Sapiro were slanderous and had widened to include slanderous assaults on Jews as a whole. Ford's team countered with a complex defense. First, it contended that the newspaper was telling the truth by exposing Sapiro as "a grafter, faker, fraud, and cheat." Second, Ford's attorneys insisted that, under the law, you could not libel a race. "If Henry Ford authorized an attack on the Jewish *race*, that is something for which no *individual* can recover damages," Reed declared. Finally, Ford lawyers argued that the industrialist was the head of a corporation that printed the *Independent*, thus had no personal liability for the newspaper's contents unless it could be proved that he directed the articles to be written. According to Reed, Ford had not done so and "to this blessed day" had not even read the Sapiro series.[48]

Gallagher called William Cameron to the stand on March 18, and the editor spent the next six and a half days protecting Henry Ford. Gallagher pounded away at the witness, trying to gain an admission that Ford had directed his activities as editor and, more specifically, his writing of the "Jewish Exploitation" articles. Cameron claimed that Ford was only barely acquainted with the activities of his newspaper. He testified that Ford dropped by its offices "from time to time" and that his philosophy influenced the publication only sometimes, "in a general way." Cameron insisted that Ford not only never discussed the *Independent*'s editorial policy or content, but never read the newspaper. He would concede only one definite conversation with Ford about the Sapiro articles. Moreover, he claimed he could not recall talking with Ford "about any articles about any individual Jews." He doggedly stuck to this story as an incredulous Gallagher tried to break it down. But even Ford's people knew that Cameron was dissembling. "That was all done to take the heat off Mr. Ford," Liebold noted later. "As far as the activities on the Jewish question are concerned, they were prompted largely by Mr. Ford. He kept in touch with every phase of it."[49]

The next episode of high drama came when Aaron Sapiro was sworn in

as a witness. His attorneys highlighted Sapiro's rags-to-riches personal history and stressed his idealistic labors in the farm-cooperative movement.
Then Reed cross-examined him for two contentious weeks. Day after day,
the lawyer denigrated Sapiro's work, badgered the witness by mispronounc-
ing his name, and claimed that he had engaged in profiteering. The confrontation became a bitter exchange of sarcasm, anger, and invective. Reed
tried to establish that corruption rather than altruism had motivated Sapiro,
while the defendant insisted that a veneration of farmers and rural life had
inspired his career.[50]

As emotions intensified, Ford became increasingly nervous about his
own appearance as a witness. Originally, he had welcomed taking the stand,
but as the acrimony of the proceedings grew, he began to have second
thoughts. With memories of his performance during the Chicago *Tribune*
suit resurfacing, he sought to avoid being called. For several weeks, he
engaged in elaborate ploys to evade being subpoenaed. One time his attorneys claimed that a subpoena had been given to Ford's brother by mistake,
and in another instance that a subpoena dropped through Ford's car window
failed to touch him as it fell through his knees to the floorboard. In
Liebold's words, Ford sought "to do everything under the sun to get away
from the witness stand." Ford also became eager to keep Liebold from tes-
tifying. His office manager scrambled to avoid process servers for several
weeks, until they finally cornered him near his home and chased him for a
block to serve the subpoena.[51]

It was amid such machinations that Ford's mysterious "accident"
occurred on the road between his home and his office in Dearborn. Too bat-
tered to talk and in the care of his physicians, according to his attorneys,
Ford would be unable to appear in court for some time. Some newspapers
suggested that Ford had been the target of Jewish fanatics: "PLOT TO
ASSASSINATE FORD SEEN" and "FORD INJURED BY ASSASSINS:
HURLED OVER RIVER BANK IN CAR." Others were skeptical about
the injury. Attorneys for the plaintiff asked for an independent medical
examination to establish Ford's physical condition; Sapiro claimed that Ford
had "faked" the accident because his case was collapsing. The Ford organization reacted with a statement denying any assassination attempt and
assuring the public that the industrialist would recover steadily, if not
quickly.[52]

Then the Sapiro trial, just as it became a publicity circus, collapsed with
a final twist. Ford's attorneys, acting on information gleaned by one of their
operatives working the case, informed Judge Raymond that a juror had been
offered a bribe by a Jew to convict Ford. The juror, Mrs. Cora Hoffman,
angrily denied these charges in statements to the press. After this breach of

conduct, the judge had no choice but to grant a defense motion for a mistrial on April 21. A new trial was scheduled to begin in September.[53]

But Ford had seen enough. Under pressure, and increasingly unwilling to testify, he decided to throw in the towel. Summoning Fred Black to Fair Lane, he announced, "I want to stop the Dearborn *Independent!*" He ordered Black to come up with a plan for closure, and, indeed, on the last day of 1927, the newspaper quit publishing. Meanwhile, and even more important, however, Ford explored an out-of-court settlement with Sapiro. He enlisted journalist Arthur Brisbane; Joseph Palma, head of the New York office of the Secret Service; and Earl J. Davis, former assistant U.S. attorney general, as emissaries. They contacted Representative Nathan D. Perlman, a vice president of the American Jewish Congress, and Louis Marshall of the American Jewish Committee. Ford expressed regret about his role in the controversy and, after negotiation, agreed to release a formal apology and to make a cash settlement with Sapiro.[54]

Ford's apology was released to the major press agencies and published in newspapers on July 8. The retraction was complete—Marshall wrote most of it—as Ford confessed that he was "deeply mortified that this journal, which is intended to be constructive and not destructive, has been made the medium for resurrecting exploded fictions" such as *The Protocols of the Elders of Zion.* "I am fully aware of the virtues of the Jewish people as a whole," he continued. He pledged he would make amends to the Jews by "asking their forgiveness for the harm that I have unintentionally committed, by retracting so far as lies within my power the offensive charges laid at their door." But Ford also tried to save face. Asserting that he had not kept close watch on the *Independent* because of the "multitude of my activities," he claimed to be shocked upon examining its anti-Jewish articles. "To my regret I have learned that Jews generally, and particularly those of this country, not only resent these publications as promoting anti-Semitism, but regard me as their enemy," Ford wrote. He promised that "articles reflecting upon the Jews" would never again appear in his newspaper.[55]

The press generally welcomed Ford's statement, but opinion varied as to its sincerity. The Philadelphia *Record* described it as "A Gain for Tolerance"; the Indianapolis *Star* praised it as the means by which "Henry Ford Sets Himself Right." The Pittsburgh *Gazette Times* said, "There will be common satisfaction in Mr. Ford's confession of error and in his promise to sin no more against a great body of American citizens." Most Jewish publications accepted Ford's plea for forgiveness. The *American Hebrew* argued that his apology "breathes honesty and sincerity. . . . We forgive and will seek to forget." Prominent Jews also expressed approval. "It is never too late to make amends, and I congratulate Mr. Ford that he has at last seen the light," said Julius Rosenwald, the Chicago philanthropist. Louis B. Mayer, the Hollywood producer, wrote a personal letter to Ford offering his "sincere admiration and appreciation" for the apology.[56]

But many others questioned either the sincerity of the apology or the moral integrity of the person making it. *The Christian Century* did not know what to make of Ford's "baffling maneuver." Though approving of his rejection of anti-Semitism, the journal questioned his "passing the buck with a vengeance to Mr. Ford's employees." The Chicago *Tribune* found the apology and the explanation to be implausible, since Ford clearly served as the "authority and pay-roll" for the Dearborn *Independent*. *The Nation* acerbically suggested that Ford's claim to have just learned of Jewish resentment would be fantastic were it not for his "almost incredible simple-mindedness." The Richmond *Times-Dispatch*, though approving of his retraction of repugnant views, found his denial of knowledge about his newspaper's content to be ridiculous. It asserted that Ford's excuses "will be laughed at all over the United States."[57]

Indeed, much joking followed the release of Ford's apology. Will Rogers cracked, "He used to have it in for the Jewish people until he saw them in Chevrolets, and then he said, 'Boys, I am all wrong.' " The New York *Daily News* suggested that Ford could cement his new friendship with Jews by leaving the name "Ford" off his new car and calling it "the Solomon Six or the Abraham Straight-8." Songwriter and theatrical producer Billy Rose offered a satirical song entitled "Since Henry Ford Apologized to Me." Its lyrics included mocking stanzas such as these:

> *I was sad and I was blue,*
> *But now I'm just as good as you,*
> *Since Henry Ford apologized to me.*
> *I've thrown away my little Chevrolet,*
> *And bought myself a Ford Coupe,*
> *Since Henry Ford apologized to me.*[58]

But those who knew Ford understood the fundamental crassness of his "apology." Ernest Liebold claimed that Ford signed the statement just to be done with the matter: "He never even read that or knew what it contained. He simply told them to go ahead and fix it up." Cameron expressed amazement. "I know Ford too well not to be absolutely sure that his views set forth in [those] articles are still his views, and that he thinks today as he always did," he told an acquaintance. "I simply cannot understand his alleged statement." Soon after the apology, John McCloud was aghast to hear a Ford tirade against a Jewish lawyer in a meeting. McCloud concluded, "Mr. Ford, while he repudiated the articles, hadn't really changed his opinions one iota."[59]

In fact, Ford's anti-Semitism, called to account in the late 1920s, did not vanish. Instead, it retreated to the private realm. Understandably reluctant to discuss his views after the Sapiro trial, Ford occasionally let his real feelings slip. A couple of years after his apology, Liebold suggested that he sell the presses from the idle *Independent*, but Ford objected. "No, don't sell them," he said. "I made a deal with these Jews and they haven't lived up to their part of the agreement. I might have to go back after the Jews again." By the mid-1930s, Ford had resurrected the old charge that Jewish financial interests were maneuvering the world toward war. In public interviews he attributed rising tensions in Europe to the nefarious activities of "international financiers" and "money lenders." Once in a while he dropped the euphemisms and spoke frankly, as he did in 1940, when he leaned over and said to Dave Wilkie, the automobile editor of the Associated Press, while looking at a new army pursuit airplane, "I still think this is a phony war made by the international Jewish bankers."[60]

Most notoriously, in 1938 Ford accepted an honor from the German government of Adolf Hitler. According to Liebold, the German Embassy contacted him to inquire whether Ford would accept "The Order of the Grand Cross of the German Eagle." Liebold asked his boss, who replied, "You tell them that I'll accept anything the German people offer me." Thus, on July 30, he became the first American citizen to be decorated with this award, the highest bestowed upon a foreigner by the Reich, in a ceremony held in his Dearborn office. After two German consuls hung the beribboned cross and star around his neck, according to the Detroit *News*, they read "a congratulatory message from Reichsfuehrer Adolf Hitler felicitating Ford on his seventy-fifth birthday and citing him as a pioneer in making automobiles available to the masses." Present at the ceremony were Ernest Liebold and William Cameron.[61]

Henry Ford's anti-Semitic crusade of the 1920s started a long slide in his public career. To be sure, he had endured many earlier controversies, such as the Peace Ship, the sociological department, and the Chicago *Tribune* trial. But Ford's personal popularity had always sufficed to overcome difficulties. Now, however, his mindless bigotry against Jews indelibly stained his reputation and raised questions about his moral and ideological character that would linger for the rest of his life. When combined with the crisis in the Ford Motor Company regarding the decline of the Model T, the debacle of the Dearborn *Independent* revealed a man who had passed his peak.

Part Four

The Long Twilight

Twenty

Antiquarian

On October 21, 1929, Henry Ford presided at the largest, most lavish celebration in the history of his organization. He brought his old friend
Thomas Edison to Dearborn to commemorate the fiftieth anniversary of
one of the scientist's greatest inventions—the incandescent lamp. "Light's
Golden Jubilee," as Ford termed the event, saw many dignitaries descend
upon his headquarters for a special day of celebration. President Herbert
Hoover officiated at the ceremonial banquet, and Owen D. Young, chairman of General Electric, served as toastmaster. A high-profile assemblage
gathered for the event, including Will Rogers, Madame Curie, Orville
Wright, Jane Addams, Henry Morgenthau, John D. Rockefeller, Jr., and
Walter P. Chrysler.

A day earlier, the Edisons and the Fords, along with a few other dignitaries, toured a special landmark. At great cost and trouble, Ford had overseen the reconstruction of the laboratory, library, and machine shop from
Menlo Park, New Jersey, where Edison had worked during the late nineteenth century, when he developed the lightbulb. Edison was overwhelmed
by the faithfulness of the restoration, saying over and over, "I wouldn't have
believed it. It's amazing." He was especially astonished at the attention to
detail—the rebuilding of the nearby boardinghouse, the transfer of an old
elm-tree stump sitting outside the lab, the transport of seven railroad cars
full of "the damn New Jersey clay" that had surrounded his old facility. He
grew misty-eyed and once sat down for several minutes in one of his old lab
chairs, because "the memories of eighty-two years were flooding back." For
his part, Ford simply expressed great admiration for his hero and friend. As
he told reporters, "We are ahead of all other countries today, simply and
solely because we have Mr. Edison."[1]

The day of the event presented several memorable moments. Speaking
into a microphone in Berlin, Albert Einstein conveyed his congratulations

to Edison via the special transoceanic telephone circuit of the American Telegraph and Telephone Company. President Hoover praised Edison's invention and joked that the electric light relieved "the human race from the curse of always cleaning oil lamps, scrubbing up candle drips, and everlastingly carrying one or the other of them about." Edison attempted to speak but was overcome by emotion. Regaining his composure, he thanked the assembled guests, reserving special appreciation for one of them. "As to Henry Ford, words are inadequate to express my feelings," he said. "I can only say to you that, in the fullest and richest meaning of the term, he is my friend."[2]

The high point of the event came when Hoover and Ford, along with Francis Jehl, Edison's oldest living assistant, accompanied the inventor to the Menlo Park laboratory. Every household in the United States had been asked to turn off the lights on this special evening. Then Edison and Jehl re-enacted their first successful trial of the incandescent bulb. According to the breathless description of radio commentators: "You could hear a pin drop in his long room. Now the group is once more about the old vacuum pump. Mr. Edison has two wires in his hand. Now he is reaching up to the old lamp. Now he is making the connection. It lights!" At this point, electric lights were switched on all over the nation to illuminate the darkness and dramatize the impact of Edison's invention.[3]

Indeed, the live radio coverage of Light's Golden Jubilee played a central role in the proceedings. This event prompted tremendous publicity, and a chain of over one hundred radio stations carried the entire program coast to coast. Shortwave stations picked up the signals and broadcast them overseas. Hosted by Graham McNamee and Philip Carlin, who provided a moment-by-moment description of the proceedings, Light's Golden Jubilee was listened to by millions in the United States and abroad. The vast audience heard detailed accounts of the famous figures in attendance and the speeches of Hoover and Young, and turned on their own lights at the dramatic moment when Edison touched the two wires together.[4]

But this event did more than keep Henry Ford's name before the public. It also highlighted a passion in his life that had developed in old age. Light's Golden Jubilee dedicated the Thomas Edison Institute, a historical complex that aimed to recapture the American past. It included a large museum designed to hold the Americana that Ford had been collecting for the previous decade. The Menlo Park reconstruction was part of an American village being built to hold houses, farms, machine shops, and public buildings from the eighteenth and nineteenth centuries. Henry Ford had fallen in love with a certain vision of the American past, and he was determined to bring that vision to life in Dearborn.

This project sentimentalized the America of an earlier age. More fundamentally, however, Ford's great museum and reconstructed village reflected his conviction that history was the story of technological progress. Edison's lightbulb provided an inspiring example of the history that Ford wanted to memorialize. "I want to place here for all time the actual tools and housing used in what I consider one of the greatest achievements in the interest of human progress," he explained to the press a few days before the celebration. Engines, furniture, implements, and vehicles illustrated "the value to human progress of scientific research, unflinching persistence in the quest of the new and useful, and industry that is never discouraged by temporary failure. This is real history." And real history, not the fanciful accounts of the past that one encountered in textbooks, was what Ford wanted Americans to appreciate.[5]

The irony was striking. As this pioneering entrepreneur entered the twilight of his life, he seemed to turn away from the monuments of industrialism he had labored to create over the previous decades. Within shouting distance of the Rouge plant, with its tens of thousands of workers laboring at assembly lines, Great Lakes ships unloading at the docks, and coke ovens spewing out molten steel, lay a quiet rural town filled with horse-drawn wagons, corner drugstores, and blacksmith shops. Intellectually, Henry Ford was able to connect the two. But emotionally this task proved more difficult. He increasingly preferred Greenfield Village to the Rouge, and that was where he spent most of his time.

Henry Ford's interest in commemorating the American past arose almost imperceptibly from a series of events in his personal life. His pursuit of collecting *McGuffey Readers* starting in 1914 had been followed by the restoration of his boyhood home, beginning in 1919. Over the next seven years, Ford oversaw the restoration of the home, the barn and other outbuildings, and much of the farm equipment. He ransacked the area looking for original items and searched antique shops for duplicates. He set workmen to digging around the old house, and these amateur archaeologists discovered a number of artifacts, including a rusty pair of skates that he delightedly identified as having been his as a boy. The workmen also uncovered several dish fragments that were used to reproduce his mother's china pattern. Ford was a stickler for authenticity, determinedly hunting down an exact replica of the woodstove that had sat in the parlor and searching throughout the Midwest to find a red carpet runner identical to the one that had been on the stairway.[6]

His burgeoning interest in antiques led Ford to the Wayside Inn, a venerable colonial building near Sudbury, Massachusetts, that once had sheltered George Washington during the Revolution. It had fallen into disrepair by the early 1920s, and after a preservation trust contacted Ford, he decided to save the historic property. In 1923, he purchased the dilapidated building and ninety acres adjoined to it for $65,000 and started an extensive renovation of the old structure. Distressed by the presence of several seedy businesses nearby, he soon bought some twenty-five hundred acres of adjoining land and cleared them away, also restoring a gristmill, two sawmills, and an old country store. Eventually, Ford's agents purchased and rebuilt several other old New England houses on the Sudbury site and paid to reroute a busy highway. All told, Ford spent a bit over $2 million on the Wayside Inn project site during the six years of renovation, from 1923 to 1929. His success inspired him to complete a similar project with the Botsford Inn in Michigan.[7]

These endeavors fed what became a full-fledged mania for antique collecting. Ford began collecting household furnishings, machinery, clothing, and vehicles from the eighteenth and nineteenth centuries. In contrast to most antique-hunters, he sought not rare or valuable items but everyday objects. His staff of buyers fanned out nationwide as he authorized the purchase of innumerable items. In 1924, representatives of the old colonial capital of Williamsburg, Virginia, approached Ford and offered to sell him the entire town for $5 million in return for his sponsorship of a restoration campaign. He briefly considered the offer, but demurred, and John D. Rockefeller later took up the project.[8]

Ford put together a team of acquisition agents. William W. Taylor, an elderly New Englander, supervised the hunt for old treasures in the Northeastern section of the country; Frank Vivian, a Ford Motor Company executive, focused on the Western states. Israel Sack, an antique-dealer who specialized in furniture, sold many items to Ford throughout the 1920s. Charles Newton, a lawyer who handled many of the legal transactions entailed in Ford's historical projects, often accompanied him into the countryside to look for old pieces of farm machinery. Harold Cordell, a clerk in the Dearborn office, became the full-time bookkeeper and coordinator for the project.[9]

Ford's antique-buyers, fortified with their patron's unlimited funds, sent old items to Dearborn. But they were not always pleased with the result. When Israel Sack visited Dearborn, Ford greeted him, "Oh, Mr. Sack, I want to show you the wonderful job my cabinetmakers did repairing a desk. They put on sixteen coats of shellac." The antique-dealer saw workmen sanding the finish off an eighteenth-century desk and applying varnish until it gleamed like new. When a horrified Sack protested that the process was ruining the patina of the piece and destroying its value, Ford grew angry. But a few days later, after Sack explained in more detail, he understood and ordered a halt to such restorations.[10]

Ford himself often took a hand in the purchases. He would drop into antique stores and, according to an associate, "would walk around and say, 'I want this, I want that.' And before he got through, we'd have a carload out of that doggone place with no reference to price at all." When something caught his fancy, he would habitually say, "Pack it up and send it." Not surprisingly, Ford felt a particular sympathy for the small shopowner, who would often bring out his wife and line up his children to meet the famous visitor, who would buy out his whole stock. He liked to traverse the Michigan countryside looking for old engines and farm machinery. A. G. Wolfe, a family friend, occasionally went with Ford on these jaunts and witnessed his enthusiasm. Once, Ford spied a rusted old steam engine lying in the weeds in a rural area near Big Bay. He had operated one as a youth, and so decided to buy it. "I think he paid $500 for it. He should have got it for $50, but I think he wanted to help the fellow out a little bit," Wolfe reported. "It took us about three days to get the thing on the truck; it was heavy."[11]

Ford pursued an erratic course in his antique-purchasing. He would pay tens of thousands of dollars for a colonial highboy, and then refuse to spend a hundred dollars on a historically significant item. Harold Cordell found a rare wooden cane from colonial New England with a knob on one end and a small hole drilled in the other to hold a feather. When parishioners fell asleep during a long church service, a deacon would tickle women with the feather or whack men on the back of the head with the knob to awaken them. Cordell discovered one for $200, but Ford refused to pay. Cordell secretly purchased it, however, and eventually put it on display. Years later, when Ford saw the cane and read the placard describing it, he was fascinated. Thereafter, he always took visitors to see it, apparently not realizing it was an item he had rejected earlier. The Americana collection became a great source of pride for him. He liked to play tour guide for guests. "He had favorite spots and pieces all picked out, and would lead them from one to the other, and gave them a little dissertation on this one and that one, and they would go away perfectly happy," Edward Cutler reported.[12]

The hundreds of objects streaming into Dearborn began to pile up, first in Ford's office in the engineering laboratory, then in nearby nooks and crannies, and finally in various outbuildings. He secured a storehouse when a factory nearby fell vacant, and throughout the 1920s the three-acre site became the receptacle for this swelling collection of Americana. It also housed a workshop where craftsmen repaired and refurbished some of the thousands of items in the growing collection. Ford's hobby, however, developed into something much bigger, and he began to contemplate a permanent venue for displaying his artifacts.[13]

He first mentioned building a museum in 1919, on the way home from the Chicago *Tribune* trial. He had been embarrassed on the witness stand when his scanty knowledge of American history was exposed, but later grew angry about the unfairness of the examination. Ford believed that history, as taught in the schools, was a distorted, even irrelevant subject that dealt only with politics, wars, and wealthy elites. It failed to show how people had actually lived, which for Ford was the essence of history. "I'm going to start up a museum and give people a true picture of the development of the country. That's the only history that is worth observing," he told Ernest Liebold. "We'll show the people what actually existed in years gone by and we'll show the actual development of American industry from the earliest days."[14]

From this germ of an idea, Ford decided to build a museum in Dearborn to house his collection. In 1926, he and Edward Cutler chose a site on a tract of land sitting adjacent to the Ford Engineering Laboratory in Dearborn and only a couple of miles from the Fair Lane estate. Ford secured the services of a Detroit architect, Robert O. Derrick, who suggested a copy of Independence Hall in Philadelphia. Ford loved the idea and secured drawings and measurements of this historic structure from the city of Philadelphia. Derrick planned to correct mistakes in the building that threw things off center, but Ford wouldn't hear of it. "Oh, no!" he exclaimed. "Make it exactly the same, put in all the mistakes." Derrick drew up plans for a large exhibition hall that included balconies to display artifacts and a basement to contain storage areas, labs, and workshops. Ford balked. Unsettled by the prospect of employees remaining out of sight, he declared, "I could come in and they wouldn't be working. I wouldn't have it. I have to see everybody." He ordered his architect to revise the drawings to include no balconies and no basement.[15]

Derrick finally completed his plans to Ford's satisfaction. The replica of Independence Hall (complete with a copy of the Liberty Bell in its tower) was placed as the central entryway to a single-story facility with replicas of Philadelphia's Congress Hall and Old City Hall flanking it at each end of a long redbrick front façade. Behind this neocolonial façade sat a fourteen-acre exhibition hall under one roof, with the whole supported by dozens of pillars placed at strategic locations. In a small ceremony on September 27, 1928, Thomas Edison stuck a spade into a wet concrete cornerstone for the building, left his footprints, and then wrote his name. Over the next few months, the building was staked out, and construction began in earnest in April 1929. By the dedication of the Edison Institute at Light's Golden

Jubilee, the Independence Hall entryway had been completed, along with much of the front façade. Construction of the museum continued well into the following decade; portions of the teakwood floor were not completed until 1938.[16]

When the museum opened to the public, the huge building was filled with displays that often resembled the world's biggest rummage sale. Ford's staff packed every inch of available space with practical items from daily life in the past. The museum, in the words of one visiting journalist, presented a dream of history "as might have come out of 'Alice in Wonderland.' "

> Down these corridors are ranged in priceless vistas hundreds of old mahogany and maple and burled walnut chairs, highboys, desks, and tables that would make your common collector gnash his teeth in envy. . . . [There is] the vast array of kitchen utensils which ultimately will show series of every period from the wooden and pewter through the iron, tin, and Britannia ware to the aluminum and copper of today. Watches, mirrors, music boxes and band instruments, each probably the most complete collection in the world; all sorts of pianos and small organs—virginal, spinet, harpsichord, pianoforte, pienola, melodron, hurdygurdy—all are arranged in quaint juxtaposition. . . . Here are the high-wheeled bicycles and sewing machines, predecessors of the modern mimeograph, addressograph, and typewriter. . . . Here are hearses and barber chairs, hobby horses and cradles, early fire engines from New England, the first phonographs and movie cameras, all kinds of horse vehicles and the earliest automobiles in America.[17]

For Ford, this vast assemblage of material served to educate. In 1929, he announced that his museum would be a gift to the American people, the intent of which would be "commemorative and, above all, educative." "Improvements have been coming so quickly that the past is being lost to the rising generation, and I think it can be preserved only by putting it in a form where it may be seen and felt," he argued. "At least that is my idea of one side of education and the reason behind this collection." More specifically, Ford believed that seeing the actual material that had provided the stuff of American development, rather than just reading about it, would make a greater impact. "It helps a student to see with his eyes the practical story of progress," he explained.[18]

Even more, Ford was convinced that layers of rich meaning lay embedded in material objects waiting to be extracted. As William J. Cameron once noted, his boss read machines the way other people read books. They "were like a library to him. He could read in an old machine what the man had, what idea he had when he started it, what he had to work with," Cameron noted. Ford described how he could examine an object and discover "what the man who made them was thinking, what he was aiming at." Learning to see the charm and grace in utilitarian objects was part of education. "There's beauty in machinery, too," he asserted. "A machine that has been run fifteen years tells its own story."[19]

Amid his mountains of Americana, however, Ford reserved special affection for one category—fiddles. As a boy, he had learned to play a few tunes on an old fiddle, but he had given up the hobby when he departed for Detroit to study machinery and engineering. By the 1920s, the search for antiques had revived his interest in violins and he began to collect them. Ford's collection became one of the best in America, perhaps the world. Worth approximately $500,000, it included two Stradivarius violins, an Amati, a Guarnerius, a Bergonzi, and a Guadagnini. These instruments were supplemented by a dozen lesser models. All were kept in a steel vault and regularly taken out, treated with a special preservative mixture, and played by a symphony violinist. But Ford treated these priceless instruments with astonishing casualness. He regularly took one home to scratch out a few old melodies—"Turkey in the Straw" and "Home, Sweet Home" were among his favorites—for his own enjoyment. Even more shocking, he loaned out these rare and expensive instruments, on a whim, to anyone who caught his fancy. The recipients of his largesse ranged from skilled concert violinists to amateur musicians who, as guests in his home, might mention their admiration for one of his violins. "Want to take it home and try it? Go ahead," Ford would likely respond.[20]

His love of violins also inspired a burst of activity in the realm of country fiddling. In 1923, he crowned eighty-year-old Jep Bisbee, a champion fiddler from Michigan, as "King of the Country Fiddlers" at a contest held in Detroit and awarded him the Henry Ford Gold Cup. An elderly snow-shoe-maker from Maine, Mellie Dunham, next caught Ford's attention. Complete with his flowing white hair and beard, rustic manners, and colorful quotes—"I came to make some money and I make no bones about it, since me and Ma have had honor enough"—Dunham traveled to Dearborn amid much publicity to perform at a dance hosted by Ford. He played one of Ford's Stradivarius violins, with dozens of reporters and photographers covering the event. Using Ford's sponsorship, he went on to became a minor national celebrity as a fiddling craze swept the nation.[21]

But Ford's personal touch extended into many areas of the museum. Several artifacts from his own life found their way into the collections. Visitors could inspect a steam engine that had been used to run a threshing machine on William Ford's farm, which Henry had repaired in his youth. There was an old horse-drawn "bandwagon" that had transported Dearborn musicians, including Ford's fife-playing uncle, about the countryside in the late nineteenth century to perform at public celebrations. On the other hand, his pacifism disallowed the display of any weaponry or mementos associated with war.[22]

Ford's personal involvement extended into all areas of decision-making. Referring to the project as "my Smithsonian Institute," he wandered through his piles of antiques carrying a light, choosing what to keep and what to discard according to his own iconoclastic hunches and desires. After choosing, Ford would direct the specific placement of these objects on the museum floor. He also made many of the broader decisions about the museum, such as the choice of teakwood rather than oak for the flooring. He was particularly interested in the restoration of old cars. It became a dictum among the staff that Ford's personal opinions ruled the museum. "Mr. Ford had his own ideas of how he wanted things done, and you were liable to get into difficulty if you tried to use your own judgment," one of them explained.[23]

In fact, Ford seemed determined to reject altogether any notion of system. He maintained a staunch lack of interest in attempts to classify exhibits. The museum was a "plaything," and he happily mandated a haphazard arrangement of its antiques. In the formative stage of the project, Harold Cordell visited other museums to survey their organizational schemes and drafted a plan to govern the displays and the nature of future purchases according to thematic categories. Ford ignored it. He also buried a proposal from a curator of the University of Michigan museums—it was endorsed by Edsel—to set up a system of fellowships for graduate students in museum studies to work at his Dearborn institution. In Black's words, Ford "was afraid of bringing in experts whose opinions might run counter to his." The personal meaning of the relics for Ford was more important than upholding standards of the museum profession.[24]

Indeed, the museum assumed a central role in Ford's life. By the early 1930s, he seldom came to the Rouge plant and "actually put more hard work into the Museum than he did into the Ford Motor Company," according to Charles Sorensen. "The Museum was to be his monument." When Harold Hicks once urged Ford to complete the project, he replied, "Oh, no, I don't want to hurry up and get that done. If I get that done, I'll never have anything to do on this earth. When you don't have anything to do, then you're ready to die." A reporter from the New York *Times* saw firsthand the industrialist's affection for the museum's artifacts. "Henry Ford looked almost lovingly at the molds in which men made a half dozen candles at a time and when he turned to point out the good features of a covered wagon," he wrote.[25]

As Ford embraced the American past via his museum of everyday life, he contemplated an even more dramatic project. It would involve not just antiques to be savored, but an active re-creation of past life that would present visitors with a feast for all the senses and draw them into fuller participation. It also would provide a form of useful recreation that dovetailed happily with the new leisure culture of tourism in the early twentieth century.

In 1928, Samuel Crowther published an article in the *Ladies' Home Journal* that informed readers about his patron's newest project. "Henry Ford's Village of Yesterday," as the writer termed it, would be constructed in Dearborn but, unlike other real-estate developments springing up around the nation's cities, this one had no lots for sale. In Crowther's words, it would be a "village of the yesterdays showing every period of American history." It would be "an animated textbook" of the nation's experience, mixing a variety of productive activities from earlier periods, because, "while antiquarians may make period divisions, real life does not." It would display houses from various regions of the country, and men and women in period clothing who would use traditional modes of transportation, teach old methods of making daily products, and demonstrate various activities that defined daily life in the past. Ford, in Crowther's words, was creating "a living, working institution because he does not like 'dead' museums."[26]

Thus Ford planned a complement to his museum that would bring these items to life by re-creating for visitors the real, lived conditions of the American past. In many ways, Ford's historical village was a logical extension of his quest to present history in terms of the actual experience of ordinary men and women rather than the great-events approach of most textbooks. At the same time, it reflected Ford's keen sense of America's developing commercial culture of leisure and tourism. As Crowther noted, the village would support itself by charging an admission fee and selling articles that were made on the premises. With typical Fordian ambiguity, this idealized village would recapture the past and then market the result to vacationing consumers using the machinery of modern publicity.[27]

This idea probably stemmed from Ford's experience in rebuilding old structures such as his family homestead and the Wayside Inn. Having become addicted to bringing old buildings back to life, and inspired by the goal of educating the public about the real nature of the American past,

Ford sought to gather a group of houses and inns and sawmills and animate them. He chose Edward J. Cutler as manager for this historical reconstruction. A trained artist, Cutler had worked in the glass and drafting departments at Ford Motor Company since 1915, and Henry had tapped him to draft plans for a windmill replica to be placed on the family homestead. When Ford and Cutler picked out the Dearborn site for the museum in late 1926, they included enough land to house the village, approximately 245 acres in all. Over the next two years, Cutler drew up sketches of the project, laying out streets and placing buildings, and consulted regularly with his boss. He hit it off with Ford, in part because he understood the older man's aversion to long, written explanations. "Instead of writing things out, I would sit down with him on the ground and draw a sketch in the sand of what I was trying to do," Cutler noted. As with the museum, Ford pored over all plans and retained final authority for all decisions about the village.[28]

As it took shape, the general plan for Greenfield Village, which Ford named after the old township in which Clara had grown up, called for an idealized town rooted in no single region or culture. Two focal points defined its structure. First, the main street featured a string of shops and stores offering commercial services and commodities from the past. Second, a village green, anchored by a church at one end and a town hall at the other, provided a spacious civic space, emphasizing the communal aspect of traditional towns. Other residential, commercial, manufacturing, and agricultural buildings clustered around these central features. As did his antique-hunters, Ford's agents around the United States looked for historical structures that might fit into this master plan. By March 1928, a number of buildings had been purchased, dismantled, and sent to the Dearborn site to be reassembled. By the late 1930s, these historical structures numbered almost a hundred.[29]

The village's buildings fell into four categories.

First, Ford selected structures that illustrated aspects of daily life in the past. These were buildings used for residence, commerce, transportation, and a wide variety of productive endeavors. By the early 1930s, this group included the Clinton Inn, Waterford Country Store, Addison Ford Barn, Deluge Fire House, Loranger Grist Mill, Phoenixville Post Office, Smith's Creek Train Station, Village Blacksmith Shop, Sims Machine Shop, Tintype Studio, Hanks Silk Mill, Cooper Shop, Tripp Sawmill, Susquehanna Plantation House, Grimm Jewelry Store, Richart Carriage Shop, several slave cabins, and a nineteenth-century steamboat, the *Suwanee*. Greenfield Village also housed a number of windmills, covered bridges, and machine sheds.

Second, Ford gathered buildings associated with famous figures in America's past. These included Edison's Menlo Park laboratory; the Logan County Court House, where young Abraham Lincoln had argued several cases; the Stephen Foster House; McGuffey House; Noah Webster House; Luther Burbank Birthplace; and Wright Brothers Bicycle Shop. Significantly, this group of historical personalities included no politicians except Lincoln. Instead, Ford's choices reflected his admiration for practical achievements in industry, education, transportation, and science.

Third, since a town hall and church could not be found in original form, Ford ordered reproductions and had Cutler draw up plans. Working in the Greek Revival style from the early nineteenth century, the architect designed the town hall as a modest clapboard structure featuring tall shuttered windows and fronted by a quartet of fluted columns. He used the eighteenth-century Georgian style to design a chapel based on a Universalist church in Bradford, Massachusetts. Elegant and stately, this redbrick structure featured a tall, multilayered wooden steeple rising into the sky above a pillared entryway. The Chapel of Martha-Mary, named after the mothers of Clara and Henry, included bricks and doors from the old Bryant family home, in which the Fords had been married.

Fourth, the village contained a number of buildings associated with Ford's own life. There was a replica of the Bagley Avenue shop where he had built his first horseless carriage. The Owl Night Lunch Wagon, which he had frequented while working for the Edison Illuminating Company, offered hamburgers and other light fare to visitors. A quarter-scale reproduction of Ford's Mack Avenue plant sat along one village street; the Scotch Settlement School, which he had attended as a youth in Dearborn, sat on another. Eventually, in 1944, three years before Ford's death, his restored childhood home was also moved to the village. Mingling his own exploits with those of Lincoln, Burbank, Edison, and Foster reflected Ford's finely honed sense of promotion and publicity.[30]

As part of the Greenfield Village project, Ford launched an old-fashioned school designed to educate selected Dearborn youth. This experiment in education adopted a "learn by doing" philosophy that featured hands-on lessons, field trips, work-study programs, and arts and crafts. It was convened in 1929 in the one-room Scotch Settlement School with thirty-two students. As the school grew in size over the next few years, its classes met in other historic buildings; it moved into a new education-and-recreation structure in 1937. The Greenfield Village school taught children from kindergarten through high school, with some advanced technical training offered to high-school graduates. Emphasizing practical skills,

Ford's academy attempted to ease the transition from school to working in the real world.[31]

As with the museum, Ford viewed Greenfield Village in educational terms. "I deeply admire the men who founded this country, and I think we ought to know more about them and how they lived and the force and courage they had," he wrote in 1926. "The only way to show how our fore-fathers lived, and to bring to mind what kind of people they were, is to reconstruct, as nearly as possible, the exact conditions under which they lived." By faithfully reconstructing the real circumstances in which they had lived, Greenfield Village aimed to present "a history that is intimate and alive, instead of something in a book," Ford explained in 1929.[32]

Also like the museum, Greenfield Village displayed the personal imprint of Henry Ford on nearly every square foot within its boundaries. Although consulting with Cutler and others, he had the final say on the location of all buildings and exhibits in this outdoor site. The village fasci-nated him, and by the early 1930s, Ford was spending even more time there than at the museum. He loved its outdoor, real-life atmosphere and usually engaged in three favorite activities when there: tinkering with machinery and tools scattered about in various buildings, overseeing and inspecting construction projects, and visiting with schoolchildren.[33]

Ford found the village a haven from the burden of the Ford Motor Company. "I believe the pressures of Mr. Ford's work were relieved by the work in Greenfield Village," Cutler noted. "Several times he would make a crack, 'Well, I guess I'll have to leave you now, and go and make some more money for us to spend down there.' " For many years, Ford refused to let Cutler have a telephone in the village. When the manager protested that important communications from the Rouge would be needed, Ford replied, "Oh, forget that stuff. I came down here to get away from that gang." As Fred Black noticed, his boss headed to Greenfield Village "as an antidote for any worry or trouble that the business had caused him . . . and in five min-utes apparently forgot his business problems."[34]

Ford sought to involve Clara in, and gain her approval of, the village. He would drive her around the site, pointing out various buildings, dis-cussing plans for others, and asking her opinion. He often changed things if she disapproved. When the church was completed, for instance, the Detroit *News* published a story about the Mary-Martha Chapel, with the name of Henry's mother going first. But Clara sent word that *her* mother's name was to go first, and the title was changed officially. Another time, Henry, a noto-rious teetotaler, ordered antique liquor bottles removed from the barroom of the Clinton Inn. When Mrs. Ford came through, she noticed the change and ordered the bottles restored. Henry returned several days later and angrily asked why his instructions had not been followed. The supervisor explained that it was Mrs. Ford's doing, and "that's all there was to it. So they've been there ever since."[35]

Even though Ford genuinely loved Greenfield Village, he was not averse to making it economically self-sustaining or using it for publicity. As he once commented to Cutler, "It will never pay for itself. But you can't beat it as indirect advertising." Indeed, the attraction fit smoothly within the new culture of leisure and tourism that Ford's automobiles had promoted in modern America. From the very beginning, operation of the village was aimed at accommodating visitors. Workmen constructed an entrance "gate-house" for paying visitors, horse-drawn omnibuses were set to convey them about the streets, and student guides were hired to conduct tours. Employees dressed in period costumes demonstrated craft skills or impersonated historical figures to entice tourists. Sometimes these attempts at authenticity had unintended consequences. An actor who specialized in imitating Abraham Lincoln visited Ford and made an impression with his startling resemblance to the martyred President. Ford hired him to work in the Logan County Court House, where he would dispense "first-hand" information about Lincoln's life to delighted visitors. After a hard day's work, however, the actor fell asleep in the actual rocking chair in which Lincoln had been assassinated (Ford had purchased it during his antique-buying spree). The night watchman, unaware of Ford's hire, looked in on the building in the darkness, saw the tall, familiar figure slumped in the chair with his head lolling to one side, and fled in terror. Rushing into his supervisor's office, he choked out, "I've seen a ghost. Lincoln's up in the courthouse," and slapped his badge down, resigning on the spot. A quick investigation clarified the situation and calmed the watchman's nerves, but he suffered many jokes about the ghost episode over the next several weeks.[36]

The public responded to Ford's re-creation of the common man and his past. In 1929, even before the village opened, about four hundred people a day were requesting tours; by 1933, it had grown to a thousand a day. Some were admitted, but most were turned away politely. In June 1933, after completion of the gatehouse, the public finally gained admittance, with adult tickets costing twenty-five cents and children's ten cents. In 1934, the first year it was calculated, paid attendance at Greenfield Village totaled 243,000. By 1940, it had increased to about 633,000. In 1960, yearly attendance would surpass one million visitors for the first time.[37]

Not surprisingly, many intellectuals viewed Ford's history exhibits with disdain. They criticized Greenfield Village and the Ford Museum for their sprawling, diffuse nature, lack of intellectual coherence, and unsophisti-

cated clientele. In 1937, *The New Republic* described the nearly half-million
visitors to Dearborn as vacuous tourists who took in these attractions as a
matter of obligation. They were "silent Americans of the type of Mr. Ford
himself: those wind-burned, weather-beaten, middle-class and middle-aged
people whom one sees in the trailer camps outside Sarasota in the winter.
They descend upon the Ford exhibits . . . go in deep silence through the
museum and village. When it is all over they come out, saying nothing, pack
themselves into their cars again, and drive away." But average Americans
remained oblivious to the sneers of their intellectual betters. They flocked
to Dearborn to inspect the old steam engines, reverently survey Edison's
laboratory, imagine Lincoln arguing a case in the old courthouse, have their
likeness inscribed on a tintype photograph, romp on the village green, and
possibly learn a thing or two about their ancestors' lives.[38]

Henry Ford came to love Greenfield Village as perhaps his favorite spot
on earth. In 1935, a journalist who accompanied him on a tour of the facility noted, "As we drove slowly through the winding roads he pointed out
the various buildings which he had obtained in various parts of the country
and had erected in this town of his own making. There was a note of tender-
ness in his voice. . . . It was revealing to hear this man with a reputation for
hardness become almost sentimental over these relics of the past." But
Ford's growing sensitivity to the past also sought another outlet. Though
the Ford Museum and Greenfield Village may have reflected his ideas about
how to rediscover a useful history, these projects did not fully meet his personal needs. For that, Ford turned to an activity that engaged him physically
as well as emotionally.[39]

On August 15, 1924, New England dance instructor Benjamin Lovett
received a phone call from the hostess of the Wayside Inn. She informed
him that Henry Ford was visiting the area and wanted to meet him tomorrow to talk about dancing. Lovett, knowing Ford's disdain for modern ballroom techniques, immediately began brushing up on "the old-time
maneuvers." He consulted a number of dance manuals, refreshed his memory, and arrived the next morning confident he could handle any questions
that might be asked of him. After greeting Ford and his wife in the ballroom
of the Wayside Inn, however, Lovett was immediately stumped by the
automaker.

"Do you know the Ripple?" Ford inquired. "No, I don't," Lovett
replied. "I've heard of it somewhere, but I can't recall where. But I'll know it
the next time I see you." Ford appeared delighted. "Why, I caught him the

first time," he laughingly commented to Clara. Lovett was true to his word, however, and set out the next day to identify the elusive dance. Driving in his car, he contacted several professional acquaintances in Massachusetts, then motored into New Hampshire and Vermont, with no luck. Finally, Lovett found a crotchety old dance master near Burlington who solved the mystery. "Sure, I know," he said. "The Ripple is what we call the Newport Down East." Familiar with this latter dance, Lovett practiced the steps and went back to Ford in a few days to demonstrate his proficiency. The industrialist was very pleased. Subsequently, Lovett helped Ford organize several dance parties at the Wayside Inn, and then accepted an invitation to visit Dearborn for a week to do similar work. He would stay for the next twenty years, in a job that would bring him much fame and provide his patron with a great source of joy in his later life.[40]

Benjamin Basil Lovett was born in New Hampshire on February 2, 1876, and had been attracted to dancing as a teenager. His natural ability led him first to give lessons informally, and then to open up a small dancing school. Lovett studied with dancing masters in Boston and New York City, and his business prospered. In 1905, he married Charlotte L. Cooke, a graceful, pretty twenty-five-year-old secretary who shared his interest, and they opened several schools in Massachusetts that specialized in teaching the traditional dances of Anglo-America. A former student once described them as the "Fred Astaire and Ginger Rogers" of old-fashioned dancing. Their efforts brought notice, first in New England and then nationally, as Lovett was elected president of the International Association of the Masters of Dancing in 1913.[41]

In the meantime, as part of his larger embrace of the American past, Henry Ford had returned joyfully to the dances of his youth. It had begun innocently one evening when the Fords were entertaining a few old friends and the discussion turned to the dances they had enjoyed as young people. The group began listing them, and eventually the braver souls tried to replicate the various steps amid much merriment. Finally, Clara said to her husband, "Do you realize, Henry Ford, that we have danced very little since we were married?" This evening of reminiscing inspired the Fords to organize an old-fashioned dance at the Wayside Inn on their next visit, which in turn prompted them to contact Lovett. With the dance master's arrival in Dearborn in 1924, Ford's new interest took flight. He hosted a Halloween dance in the barn of the old Ford homestead, and followed by putting Lovett in charge of a wide-ranging program of instruction and recreation. "Mr. Ford's interest has been personal and continuous," Lovett wrote later. "As everyone knows, Mr. Ford is now the acknowledged patron of the Old American dances."[42]

With Ford's backing, Lovett launched a dance revival. Ford cleared out the whole southwestern corner of the large Ford Engineering Laboratory in Dearborn, enclosed it, and installed special wooden flooring. Lovett set up a schedule of dance classes in the evening and publicized them in the community. He organized a series of formal dances, to which Ford played host and invited friends and professional associates. Lovett also initiated a popular program to teach dance in the Dearborn public schools. In time, he expanded these endeavors to the national scene, where, with Ford's backing, he convened clinics throughout the country to teach traditional dance steps. By the 1930s, Ford had expanded Lovett's duties by appointing him head of the Greenfield Village schools.

Lovett cut a striking figure as the leader of Ford's dance revival. Stocky and elegant, he stood about five feet eight, but seemed taller because of his erect carriage. He always appeared in public neatly dressed in a suit, white shirt and tie, and shined shoes. With his dark hair slicked back against his head, and wire-rimmed spectacles, he struck everyone who saw him as perfectly groomed. As one of his former students observed, "He looked as though he had stepped out of a fashion magazine, even in his overcoat." Lovett's easy, confident walk—the product of his years of dance training— impressed many. He "gave the appearance of being very proper, prim, and precise," another student described. "I think he felt himself to be a model for posture, deportment, and dress."[43]

Lovett's reserved, occasionally stern personality matched his rather old-fashioned appearance. He seldom talked of his private life and insisted that his pupils adhere to traditional values of respect and punctuality. But his strong sense of propriety seldom degenerated into stuffiness. Good humor provided a tonic to his formal manner. When, in full view of a lunchtime crowd in the dining room of the engineering building, he spilled a chocolate sundae on his immaculate white suit, as the glass bowl crashed to the floor, he smiled ruefully at all the starers and said, "Well, I knew I should have worn my brown suit today." He was fond of teasing, often addressing a female teacher as the "Dean of Women," and greeting a small group of men at the Martha-Mary Chapel every morning with "Good morning, gentlemen. I think that includes most of you."[44]

Lovett brought considerable energy and confidence to his endeavors as a dance teacher for Ford. He loved his work, often arriving at the engineering laboratory, and later at Greenfield Village, cheerfully singing "I'm a Yankee Doodle Dandy." As an instructor, he insisted that students meet high standards but also provided much help and encouragement. "Mr. Lovett could really teach the dances. He was very particular and demanding in his instructions," recalled a former student. "For example, if you were to kick your foot out, you couldn't just kick your foot out. Your toe had to be pointed toward the floor. . . . It wasn't just any old way, but a certain way." Lovett would call out his dancing instructions in a pronounced Boston accent, directing students through various intricate steps as he walked around beating out the rhythm by striking together two short wooden batons. His considerable skills were crucial to his pedagogy. He and the equally skilled Mrs. Lovett awed and inspired students with their precise, graceful movements as they glided over the dance floor.[45]

Lovett's instructional talents met their greatest challenge in following one of his patron's directives to teach dancing to company executives. Managers dutifully attended the dance master's classes; as one observer noted ruefully, "For two solid weeks the top brass came to work wilted by nightly polkas and wondering if and when in all hell it would end." Ford supplemented these evening sessions with daytime interludes. He would drop by executive offices to offer pointers on dance steps that had been fumbled the night before, and on occasion after lunch even gave private instruction to associates in a large room near his private office at Fair Lane. J. L. McCloud clearly remembered the comical quality of these sessions, noting he "actually learned the Varsovienne by dancing with Mr. Ford and Charlie Sorensen." Harry Bennett once found himself caught in the middle of a good-natured disagreement between Ford and Lovett over the correct way to teach a certain dance. After Lovett complained that any dance expert watching Ford's version would say, "Why in the hell doesn't Mr. Ford hire a teacher who knows his business?," Ford surrendered, and watched a sweating Bennett spend the next half hour going through the steps with Lovett.[46]

The formal dances hosted by Ford at the ballroom became special events. They began promptly at nine o'clock on a Friday evening, lasted until midnight, and were studiously formal. Clara and Henry stood at the head of a receiving line to greet their guests, which consisted of a mix of Dearborn residents, company executives, and doctors from the Henry Ford Hospital. Guests were expected to follow the rules of decorum—polite requests for a dance, no cutting in, no crossing the middle of the ballroom—and to participate in the full range of traditional dances. As Ford explained, "Our complete repertoire is fourteen dances—the two-step, the circle two-step, the waltz, the schottische, the polka, the ripple, the minuet, the lanciers, the quadrille, the varsovienne, and so on through the infinite variety of combinations."[47]

Lovett served as caller for the dances, standing at the center of the stage in front of a microphone while behind him sat the dance orchestra, consisting of a violin, bass violin, cymbalum, accordion, and dulcimer. The Fords were a mainstay on the dance floor, and Lovett publicly praised his patron's skill: "He is a fine dancer, graceful, tireless, rhythmic, light on his feet, with a decided flair for the music of the dance, and, with Mrs. Ford, can give a notable exhibition on the floor of any old American dances." But in private, he offered another evaluation. According to Sorensen, Lovett complained that Ford "never quite caught the rhythm of dance music. The dance seemed a mechanical thing to him." Nonetheless, he appreciated Ford's enthusiasm. Indeed, Ford's passion for traditional dancing was so genuine that his wife often had to pull him off the floor at evening's end. The Fords frequently danced to phonograph music at home, and sometimes Henry even danced by himself to a record he liked.[48]

Lovett not only called many of the dances, but occasionally came down to the floor to participate directly. He had standing instructions to rescue Henry from "clodhoppers," their name for females who bungled the steps while dancing with their host. Upon noticing such a laborious scene, Lovett would approach Ford and his partner and ask if he could dance with their lovely guest. The relieved Ford would scurry off to find a more suitable partner. Lovett also found himself in the middle of a good-natured dispute between the Fords. The couple had a recurring disagreement about the best tempo for a waltz. Henry preferred a slower rhythm for full-swaying movement, whereas Clara liked it faster and more dramatic. They would stop in front of the bandstand, and she would request a quicker rhythm while he protested that it was fast enough. "Are you trying to get me into trouble?" Lovett would mutter to his patron, and then compromise by speeding up the tempo for thirty bars and slowing it down for the next thirty.[49]

Lovett admired Ford for the gracious, courteous manner he exhibited in hosting these events. Ford was helpful to everyone who attended, paying special attention to youthful participants and the elderly. He went out of his way to speak with strangers and gently urged everyone to dance. Ford, who always took up a position on the dance floor right in front of Lovett and the orchestra, established a special set of signals by which he helped the dance master manage the flow of the event. "If he is dancing with an elderly lady and she shows less agility than the other guests, he will signal me [to] slow the music a little. . . . He just winks at me," Lovett explained. "If at the end of a dance I see him fingering his hair, I know what music he wants for the next dance, and if I see him pulling his ear, I know what tune that indicates."[50]

For all of Ford's enthusiasm and Lovett's skill, however, not everyone enjoyed these dances. Some simply lacked a knack for dancing in the old manner. Mrs. Sorensen shared her husband's aversion to the activity, earning the secret name of "Dumb Dora" because of her inability to pick up the various steps. Some complained that, once there, you were forced to participate. Employees viewed the invitations as thinly disguised commands and resented being pressured to attend. "You felt that a lot of people just came because Mr. Ford wanted them to come, but they didn't have a very good time." Still others saw the events as rather stiff affairs and devoid of fun, which they attributed primarily to Mrs. Ford and her reserve. "She didn't mix as well as he did," noted one guest.[51]

Not just recreation but larger cultural issues lay at the heart of the dance revival mounted by Ford. Traditional dancing, he believed, also advanced a moral agenda. He saw the revival of the waltz and the two-step as an antidote to the degeneration of modern American culture represented by jazz and lurid dances such as the Black Bottom and the Charleston. In *Today and Tomorrow,* Ford complained that modern dancing had become commercialized (crowded onto cramped floors at supper clubs rather than spacious ballrooms) and privatized (two people using it as an excuse to engage in sensual groping). In contrast, he argued, "old American dancing was clean and healthful." It involved "rhythm and grace of motion, and people are thrown together and have to know one another. The old dances were social." Moreover, traditional dancing had rules of deportment that were still upheld at his balls. "There is no holding up two fingers for a dance and no 'cutting in.' The ladies do not enter the room unescorted and must slightly precede the gentlemen. . . . Everything is formal."[52]

Lovett shared his patron's view of the larger purposes of traditional dancing. He believed that it strengthened community ties by promoting "friendly relationships, neighborliness, and closer human understanding." He also felt that this activity taught self-discipline and self-respect. He became convinced that "social training" was the most important achievement of his classes. "We believe that physical, mental, and social benefit will come to every boy and girl in the public schools who is taught these old American dances and the social training that goes with them," he explained to his students and guests. "Among the benefits derived are consideration for others, courtesy under all circumstances, and an ease of manner which is far removed from the rudeness and selfishness which have crept into society these latter years." If he could start over again, Lovett wrote, "I would choose the same profession, for in my capacity of Dancing Master, I believe I am, in a practical sense, a builder of character."[53]

Lovett explained the Fordian moral agenda in a dance manual carrying the rather awkward title *Good Morning: After a Sleep of 25 Years, Old-Fashioned Dancing Is Being Revived by Mr. and Mrs. Ford* (1926). In addition to explaining traditional steps, it contained a moral primer on physical restraint and propriety that came straight out of Victorian culture. "There should not be bodily contact in the dance except through the arms. A gentleman should be able to guide his partner through a dance without embracing her as if he were her lover or her rescuer," Lovett said. The gentleman's right hand should have only its thumb and forefinger touching the lady's waist, as if it were holding a pencil. This was sufficient bodily contact to allow him to guide his partner through the dance.[54]

But *Good Morning* also took pains to place traditional dancing at the heart of a cultural retrenchment. In a conservative critique of modern values that smacked of nativism, the manual contended that dance reflected "the racial characteristics of the people who dance them." The degeneration of modern dance stemmed from the fact that there had been "imported into the United States of recent years dances that originated in the African Congo, dances from the gypsies of the South American pampas, and dances from the hot-blooded races of Southern Europe." As these waves of "foreign importations" swept over the United States, they encouraged the sensuality and moral laxity characteristic of modern dances and jazz culture. But, with Ford's backing, the revival of old-fashioned dances "is now shifting toward the style of dancing which best fits with the American temperament. There is a revival of the type of dancing which has survived longest among the Northern peoples."[55]

In 1937, Henry Ford commemorated his great regard for the dancing master from New England. Having built a beautiful ballroom on the second floor of a building appended to the Ford Museum, he named it Lovett Hall. Lovett would work for Ford until 1943, when the latter's physical and mental frailty finally forced him to give up one of his greatest passions. But for almost the previous two decades, Lovett and Ford had deployed swirling, waltzing couples and stamping square dancers as skirmish lines in a larger cultural campaign to reclaim and defend American values and practices from an earlier day. Ultimately, this crusade reflected Henry Ford's larger understanding of American history. Despite his penchant for crude comments that often captured headlines, those views were surprisingly complex and sophisticated.

To many observers, Ford's embrace of tradition as he entered old age appeared ironic to the point of farce. Indeed, the picture of the creator of the mighty Rouge factory growing misty-eyed over butter churns, blacksmith shops, and square dancing seemed ludicrous. After all, Ford had probably done more than any other individual to create the modern industrial mass-produced world that had overwhelmed America's agricultural past. "It is as if Stalin went in for collecting old ledgers and stock-tickers," said the

New York *Times*. How did Ford reconcile his industrial labors with his veneration for the horse-and-buggy world? Some observers offered a psychological diagnosis of split personality. "With his left hand he restores a
self-sufficient little eighteenth-century village; but with his right hand he
had already caused the land to be dotted red and yellow with filling stations," suggested *The Nation*. "With one side of his brain he has dismissed
all history as useless; with the other side he has indulged a passion which is
almost a mania for the kind of history he can understand." Others pointed
to guilt. *The New Republic* contended, "Mr. Ford might be less interested in
putting an extinct civilization into a museum if he had not done so much to
make it extinct."[56]

Ford's earlier rhetoric contributed to the problem. Since arriving on the
national scene in the early 1910s, he had missed few opportunities to
denounce history as the dead hand of the past restricting movement into the
future. In the 1919 Chicago *Tribune* trial, he gained much notoriety from
his reported statement that "history is bunk." Though newspaper headlines
oversimplified his testimony in this case—in fact, he stated only that history
"never served me very much purpose"—there is no question that Ford liberally applied the word "bunk" as he stridently denounced history throughout his career. He told the Chicago *Tribune* in 1916, "What do we care what
they did five hundred or one thousand years ago? It means nothing to me.
History is more or less bunk. It's tradition. We don't want tradition. We
want to live in the present and the only history that is worth a tinker's dam
is the history we make today." That same year, Ford told John Reed, "I don't
know anything about history, and I wouldn't give a nickel for all the history
in the world. . . . I don't want to live in the past. I want to live in the Now."[57]

Ford pushed the "bunk" concept well into the 1920s and 1930s. "History is bunk. What difference does it make how many times the ancient
Greeks flew their kites?" he said to the New York *Times* in 1921. Fifteen
years later, he was still attacking history textbooks as "just one man's misin-
formation or prejudices. Most history as written is bunk." By 1940, Ford
had worked himself into a kind of repetitive apoplexy. "I say history is
bunk—bunk—double bunk. Why, it isn't even true," he burst out in an
interview. "They wrote what they wanted us to believe, glorifying some
conqueror or leader or something like that."[58]

But Ford's "bunk" barrage masked a view of the past that was more
complicated and sophisticated than it appeared at first glance. First of all, he
saw history in surprisingly modern terms, not as the empirical recovery of
absolute truth but as *interpretations* of the past. As early as 1916, he reflected,
"History is being rewritten every year from a new point of view. So how can
anybody claim to know the truth about history?" When Ford denounced

history as bunk, therefore, he meant only traditional renderings of the past. His own notion of history turned on two central ideas—populism and progress—that lay at the heart of the American experience. These twin ideas inspired his historical collections and re-creations in Dearborn.[59]

Ford insisted that "real" history focused not on politicians, wars, and great events but on ordinary citizens and their daily labors. He constantly told associates that he was determined "to preserve what he appreciated as the contribution of plain men who never got into history." Fred Black often heard Ford claim that history was rooted in the everyday life and work of ordinary people. "He always said the history of America wasn't written in Washington, it was written out in the country," Black reported. Ford "was very enthusiastic about bringing to the attention of the present generation the development of the past, in mechanics, different little trades, how men made barrels, how men made horseshoes," as one employee put it. Ford's populist history focused on the struggle of ordinary people to survive and prosper.[60]

His public pronouncements elaborated on this theme. In the *Ladies' Home Journal*, he argued that in Greenfield Village, "by looking at the things that people used and the way they lived, a better and truer impression can be gained in an hour than could be had from a month of reading." In interviews, he said that his museum would "show in a material way the actual steps the people have made and therefore will constitute the true story of their minds." A reporter for the New York *Times* captured perfectly Ford's populist sense of history. In his museum, she wrote, "a pewter bowl from the humblest kitchen in the colonies would be of equal interest with one from that of George Washington."[61]

But Ford also believed that history must tell the story of progress, particularly in terms of technology and material life. While politicians bickered and orated, he concluded, "the real revolution was going on quietly in a laboratory." Over the past two centuries, the real changes in human life came not from parliamentary debates or presidential edicts but from such pioneering work as that of James Watt and the steam engine, Thomas Edison and electricity, and Alexander Graham Bell and the telephone. Ford was determined to promote this perspective at the Ford Museum and Greenfield Village. As he explained, the purpose of the facility was "to remind the public who visit it—and sometimes there are thousands a day—of how far and how fast we have come in technical progress in the last century or so. If we have come so far and so fast, is it likely we shall stop now?" Several years after the museum had opened to the public, he reflected on the "continuity of progress" that it tried to illustrate. "One of the eternal truths of this world is that there is nothing permanent in it except change, but the change is that of growth," he told a reporter. "To our students and to our visitors we are showing some of the changes which have taken place as generations have improved upon the past."[62]

This message of history as progress permeated information disseminated by the Ford organization. Jimmie Humberstone, a young man who led tours of Greenfield Village, habitually described it as "a complete exhibit of American historical progress." *Looking Forward Through the Past* (1935), the first handbook distributed to visitors to the village, also stressed this theme. "Behind us are limned the trails of progress we have traversed. No one can truly appreciate the present, or even dimly picture the future, who is insensitive to the past and to the advances men have made. . . . It is worthwhile to observe how our ancestors groped their way from the primitive to enlightenment."[63]

Ford's historical path of progress clearly led to a final destination: modern consumer society. In 1928, a journalist noted that his history showed a process whereby each generation added to the production of material goods, "forever relegating luxuries to the status of necessities and adding more luxuries." In an article entitled "The Idea Behind Greenfield Village," Ford stressed that modern Americans had grown accustomed to consumer comforts. But they needed to appreciate the work habits and skills of an earlier day, when their ancestors "were building toward today's standard of living which . . . is higher than has ever been attained elsewhere." In other words, while enjoying the fruits of consumer abundance, Americans should be careful not to lose sight of the work ethic that had produced them. Journalists took their cue from Ford and often described his museum and village as depicting progress toward modern consumer prosperity. In the words of one, these attractions represented "an engineer's vision of history . . . of the main advances of national life—the progress in general conditions of living, in invention and efficiency, in comfort and taste."[64]

There were also two other building blocks of Ford's view of "real" history: a sentimental attraction to the past, and a devotion to the practices and values of old-line American stock. These twin ideas of nostalgia and nativism reflected his growing cultural conservatism, which saw suspicious signs of decline everywhere in the modern world.

Ford disavowed any impulses of nostalgia in building the Dearborn museum and village. "I have not spent the twenty-five years making these collections simply to bring a homesick tear to sentimental eyes," he declared in 1932. "Its purpose is serious, not sentimental." Nonetheless, a nostalgic celebration of the past often influenced his public statements. In *Today and Tomorrow*, Ford claimed that our ancestors "knew how to order some parts of their lives better than we do. They had much better taste; they knew

more about beauty in the design of commonplace, everyday things." In
Looking Forward Through the Past, he expressed his hope that citizens would
realize that "something solid and vitally valuable in the past has escaped
us—and that we must strive back toward it at all costs."[65]

This sentimental regard for bygone days often appeared in "Mr. Ford's
Own Page," his ghostwritten column in the Dearborn *Independent.* In essays
entitled "The Small Town" and "The Old Ways Were Good," he condemned the crowded, noisy, nerve-wrenching nature of the modern city and
claimed that "in small communities the better qualities of our nature have a
chance." To those who mocked the backwardness of the past, he countered
with praise for "the old industry, the old thrift, the old preference of the
necessary rather than the unnecessary."[66]

Another *Independent* essay, however, let slip a disturbing aspect of Ford's
nostalgia. In a piece entitled "Change Is Not Always Progress," he contended that newness, in and of itself, did not always represent an advance.
Then Ford took an unsettling step. "The trouble with us today is that we
have been unfaithful to the White Man's traditions and privileges," he
stated. "We have permitted a corrupt orientalism to overspread us, sapping
our courage and demoralizing our ideals. There has always been a White
Man's Code, and we have failed to follow it." Here, of course, Ford linked
his sentimental regard for Greenfield Village to the anti-Semitism that
inspired his crusade against the Jews and to the prejudice against non-Anglo
cultures. Thus nativism as well as nostalgia shaped Ford's vision of the
"real" history of the common man in America.[67]

All in all, Ford's passion for Greenfield Village, the Henry Ford
Museum, and the dances of his youth suggested an underlying uneasiness
with the industrial world that he had created. Unquestionably, he was proud
of the modern society of consumerism and mass production his automobile
had helped launch. Like most Americans, he wanted to believe that technological change brought progress without destroying the simpler, enduring
values of the past. But Ford was haunted by a fear that, in many ways, such
had not been the case. History helped calm that anxiety. The village and the
museum, embodying Ford's populist, technological interpretation of the
past, helped assuage his personal sense of loss by locating the past and present in a single, upward trajectory in which ordinary people created extraordinary advances. This stabilizing vision connected dizzying change to older
traditions and values along a continuum. At the same time, Ford's history
projects offered another kind of emotional satisfaction by providing a *temporary* escape from the intensity of modern life. He could immerse himself
periodically in the warm feelings of Greenfield Village—he could play and
pretend—while always returning to the material comforts made possible by

the River Rouge. Ford strolled the streets of his little town and then rode home to Fair Lane in his chauffeured automobile.

Thus, as he entered the last period of his life, Henry Ford turned history to his own social and personal purposes. But in the end he was not able to escape modernity. Not long after Light's Golden Jubilee, the stock market crashed and the Great Depression slowly brought the consumer economy of the United States to its knees. Amid this disaster appeared a growing problem with industrial laborers who, desperate to defend their vulnerable positions, sought union protection. Confused and increasingly resentful, Ford struggled to deal with a situation never imagined by the simple, virtuous inhabitants of his mythical Greenfield Village.

Twenty-one

Individualist

In 1933, *Fortune* magazine offered the most in-depth analysis of Henry Ford and his company ever published by the press. Its reporters spent several weeks in Dearborn, interviewing the automaker and his managers, surveying the scene at the River Rouge plant and the Ford Engineering Laboratory, touring the Henry Ford Museum and Greenfield Village, and inspecting various agricultural projects. They also assembled an accurate, detailed reconstruction of company finances over the past decade.

In the resulting twenty-page article, *Fortune* reported that the Ford Motor Company's financial prospects looked bleak—a loss of $20 million in 1933, losses of $140 million from 1931 to 1933, and the likelihood of greater losses in the future. "Declining sales have changed Mr. Ford from one of the greatest U.S. money-makers to one of the greatest U.S. money losers," it observed. The company's domination of the automobile market was a thing of the past, for both General Motors and Chrysler, Ford's rivals among the "Big Three," had surged ahead and were showing a profit. The numbers were sobering. In 1933, according to Department of Commerce statistics, General Motors sold over 650,000 passenger cars and controlled 41 percent of the market. Chrysler sold 400,000 and had 25 percent of the market. Ford checked in with 325,000 and 21 percent. This situation, as *Fortune* reporters discovered, caused many observers of the industry to wonder if the Ford Motor Company was washed up.[1]

Fortune also noted a peculiarity that was reflected in the article's title: "Mr. Ford Doesn't Care." Henry Ford seemed unconcerned about his company's falling sales and declining revenues. "Through this din of whispering, Mr. Ford, at seventy, remains undisturbed, indifferent," the magazine observed. When pressed about the decline of his company and the advance of General Motors, he repeated his mantra that producing a good car would solve all problems. The "Chevrolet people," he admonished his own managers, were trying to "get you fellows' minds off your work. And they seem to have succeeded mighty well." Such incidents painted a clear, if unsettling, picture—while his company floundered, Henry Ford assumed a posture of benign neglect.

The *Fortune* article examined a final odd twist in the troubled company. On the one hand, its chief seemed to have lost much interest in the actual functioning of his enterprise and spent almost all his time with his historical hobbies and agricultural experiments. "Mr. Ford says that the Rouge is so big that it is no fun anymore," the magazine explained. On the other hand, he maintained an iron grip on his authority within the company. As the article concluded, "The first point to make again and again is that only one man runs it and he is Henry Ford." Refusing to share his decision-making power even as he stepped away from direct engagement in company affairs, Ford functioned by the mid-1930s as a kind of absentee landlord.[2]

None of this came as news to those inside his organization. During the first half of the 1930s, everyone could see Ford's declining interest in the company as he directed his energy to the Ford Museum and Greenfield Village, pursued special projects in education and rural development, and supervised the building of a new winter residence in coastal Georgia. Insiders also experienced manifestations of Ford's arbitrary power. Company managers were denied titles, and their responsibilities were not clearly designated. Personnel, and sometimes entire operations, appeared and disappeared magically. *Fortune* repeated the famous story of the salesman who met with a member of the Ford traffic department and then called back the next day to clarify an agreement. "Oh," said the telephone operator, "Mr. So-and-so isn't working here now." The startled salesman asked to speak to someone else in the traffic department. "Oh," the girl replied brightly, "we haven't got any traffic department any more." Ford would grow suspicious of someone "and all of a sudden he would find that he had an intense dislike and couldn't stand that certain guy around the plant. Then that man would just disappear and nobody knew what happened to him." As *Fortune* pointed out, "Like any other authority that is absolute, Mr. Ford's authority tends toward the extreme."[3]

Ford's intermittent engagement during the 1930s created a trio of major problems. First, the lines of authority in the company, which had been rather haphazard since its earliest days, now became tangled into a knot. Figures such as Edsel Ford, Charles Sorensen, and P. E. Martin occupied citadels of power, but none oversaw the complete institution or enjoyed the full confidence of its chief. Adding to this instability, Harry Bennett, an energetic, untutored, bullying ex-prizefighter, emerged as a dominant force in the company under Henry's patronage. Second, Ford's judgment on larger public issues proved to be as eccentric as his administrative decisions. Facing the grave social and economic issues of the Great Depression, he reacted with a series of platitudinous pronouncements that made him appear insulated from reality. He denounced the activist national government of President Franklin Roosevelt and engaged in a protracted battle with the New Deal. Third, Ford reacted badly to the rising discontent of industrial workers in the Depression-era economy. He helped create a series of spectacular, violent labor confrontations at the River Rouge plant that captured national headlines and sullied the reputation of his company.

This string of difficulties marked a decline in Henry Ford's career. After some three decades of groundbreaking innovations in American industry and influential interventions in national affairs, his eminent position began deteriorating rapidly. Though still respected as a leader in the making of the modern United States, he entered an inexorable spiral of decline into irrelevance. In the process, his image as a folk hero, reformer, and visionary, already tarnished by his misadventures with anti-Semitism, became even darker. In the 1930s, without ever quite realizing it, Henry Ford increasingly appeared as a problem.

In late 1929, only a few weeks after Light's Golden Jubilee, Henry Ford was invited to meet with President Hoover and other industrial leaders regarding the recent stock-market crash. The group, which included prominent businessmen such as Alfred P. Sloan, Pierre du Pont, and Owen D. Young, as well as Secretary of the Treasury Andrew W. Mellon, convened at the White House on November 21. They discussed the economic crisis that had beset the country and pondered various responses and policies. Reporters gathered to quiz the participants as they left the three-hour meeting. Since Hoover had announced his intention to issue a statement summarizing their collective conclusions, they politely muttered "no comment" or referred attention to the forthcoming declaration.

But Ford had his own idea. As the conference disbanded, according to newspaper accounts, "Mr. Ford broke through the throng in the Executive Offices" and strode through the clamoring journalists as his secretary distributed copies of a typed statement. Its contents created a sensation. First, true to his populist principles, Ford denounced the stock market as a forum for advancing "the promise of quick profits in speculation." Its recent difficulties, though unfortunate, reflected only a collapse of inflated value, and need not harm general business, which should return to its duty of producing good inexpensive products. Second, true to his belief in modern consumerism, Ford proclaimed the need for "increasing the purchasing power of our principal customers—the American people." That could be achieved, he argued, by lowering prices throughout the economy and by increasing the general wage level. "To make wages better and keep prices down requires that businessmen come back into business, as many are doing since stocks came down," he declared. After a quick lunch, Ford returned to the White House, consulted briefly with Hoover, and then released a second, dramatic statement. He announced a general wage increase for workers in the Ford Motor Company and promised that it would go into effect within ten days.

Other conferees were shocked by Ford's performance. He had not informed them of his ideas during their discussions. Indeed, the conference had agreed that the general wage scale should not be disturbed at present, and this principle had appeared in the President's summary, released after Ford's. With some understatement, newspapers noted, "Mr. Ford's colleagues, when informed of the contents of his statement, expressed surprise that such a personal utterance of policy should be made. They had expected enunciation of a policy representing the views of those at the conference only through President Hoover."

It was vintage Ford—the willingness to go it alone, the instinct to act decisively, the keen eye for publicity. He simply stole the show. Newspapers described how he had commandeered "the center of the stage" in Washington and hijacked Hoover's industrial conference "body, boots, and breeches." Ford's actions, garnering much favorable commentary, also demonstrated flaws that would become more pronounced as the Great Depression settled over the United States. His comments after the White House conference betrayed a superficial grasp of the complexities of the American economy. They revealed a naïve, almost obsessive belief that work and production would solve all problems in American business. Finally, Ford proved unable to keep his promise of higher wages. In little over a year, his company cut wages, as did nearly every other American business. Ford's brave façade at the White House, like much else about him during the 1930s, eroded under the onslaught of economic and social reality. He increasingly appeared as, at best, a slogan-spouting, irrelevant old man chained to the past, and, at worst, a dangerous reactionary.[4]

Ford's failure to grasp Depression-era problems became evident in a rash of public statements made throughout the first years of this economic disaster. Beginning in 1930, with a series of articles in *The Saturday Evening Post*, he offered a simplistic analysis of the massively complex issues of shrinking capital investment, endemic unemployment, and evaporating markets facing the American economy. This critique betrayed an equally limited appreciation of the problems facing ordinary Americans as jobs vanished, bankruptcies mounted, savings accounts disappeared, and mortgages were called in. Ford's bromides soon grew tiresome. But he would state them repeatedly in the following years.[5]

His analysis of the causes of the Depression showed his limitations. This economic disaster, he insisted, could be traced to one source: "speculation" in the stock market. A mania for making money by trading stocks had swept through American business in the 1920s, he argued, and diverted attention from the honest production of commodities. Sound business practice had given way to greed, producing "orgies" in the stock market and an epidemic of "extravagance, debt, and speculation." American prosperity, Ford contended, had encouraged bad habits, as businessmen "quit making goods and went to making money. . . . Their real business, for the time, was playing the stocks." This problem also infected ordinary citizens, Ford believed, who had been attracted by stories of "easy money and no work" in the stock market. They had accepted a delusion: that one "can get something for nothing—invest in stocks and get rich."[6]

Ford certainly put his finger on part of the explanation for the crash. Many observers, both at the time and in decades since, agree that excessive speculation encouraged the collapse of the stock market in 1929. But it was only one piece in a much larger mosaic of problems that included pyramid structures of corporations holding one another's stocks, growing poverty in the nation's agricultural sector, serious maldistribution of income, and a destabilization of the international debt structure by the late 1920s. Ford demonstrated little, if any, grasp of these larger, systemic problems in the American economy. In his view, business failure stemmed solely from an entrepreneur's or investor's own deficiencies. Ford believed that when his business dipped it was always "due to some defect in our own company, and whenever we located and repaired that defect our business became good again." When each entrepreneur put his own house in order, he preached, the Depression would lift.[7]

Ford's commentary moved from the simplistic to the trite in his reflections on the most pressing problem facing the United States—unemployment. He remained convinced that work was available if people would only take the initiative to look for it. "I found very early that being out of hire was not necessarily being out of work," he informed readers of *Business Week*. He blamed unemployment on slothful habits. "I have often thought that if the jobless . . . would set to work at work they see everywhere waiting to be done, they would quickly find that they had made good jobs for themselves," he declared in *The Saturday Evening Post*. For Ford, there was simply no excuse for poverty in modern America, since people only needed "to extract, convert, and distribute those things that nature has provided." This message, of course, offered scant comfort to the millions of people for whom jobs did not exist.[8]

Ford also blamed economic paralysis on a faulty understanding of money and its proper function in the economy. He relentlessly insisted that Americans confused money with wealth. Though money needed to circulate freely in order to facilitate the buying and selling of goods, he admitted, it had no intrinsic value. "Money . . . may represent wealth, but it is not wealth itself," Ford wrote. In the 1920s, however, businessmen had sought profits rather than producing solid products. The result had been disastrous, because "wealth consists of useful goods, and money which is made out of thin air does not add to the stock of goods and therefore does not add to wealth." This trend also increased the power of financiers and bankers, the old ideological bogeymen in Ford's populist worldview. For Ford, the economic crash had demonstrated that a "system of business in which the money lender too conspicuously thrives is not a truly prosperous system."[9]

His solution for the social and economic devastation of the Depression lay in a simplistic formula. He began with a one-word article of faith: production. Making tangible goods to meet the demand of consumers provided the bedrock of American prosperity. In Ford's words, "Plenty means production and still more production; production means wealth, and scarcity means poverty, and the entire social problem is poverty. . . . Production and the effects of production give the answer to practically all the things that trouble us."[10]

Ford followed the homily on production with praise for the necessity of work. Labor not only enriched society but bound it together, creating social respectability as well as banishing poverty. "Without it there is nothing," he wrote in 1930. "Work determines a man's place in the world; it indicates the caliber of his mind and character, and expresses the measure of his usefulness to his fellow men." In the best tradition of the American work ethic, Ford believed that the significance of labor lay in the moral realm as well as the economic. Any solution to the Great Depression must use this resource.[11]

He also contended that businessmen needed to refocus on the "fundamentals" of business, which consisted of three principles that he had promoted tirelessly since the 1910s: efficient mass manufacturing, low prices, and high wages. In 1934, Ford reiterated these fundamentals for *Elks Magazine*: "(1) Make or sell the best possible product at the lowest possible price. (2) The best possible product (or service) is one that best fills a real human need. (3) In the course of making or selling, pay the highest possible wages for the shortest possible number of hours." If sound business practices were revived, entrepreneurs would create "a system of normal, continuous and progressive supply and consumption, which will replace the periodically collapsing system under which we have been working."[12]

Finally, Ford lobbied throughout the 1930s for the decentralization of American manufacturing. His "village industries" were small factories built in rural areas or small towns where the workforce was drawn part-time from local farms. This attempt to "industrialize agriculture and agriculturalize industry," as Ford put it, employed people who owned small farms or truck gardens who worked shifts at the factory, which specialized in manufacturing a particular part. Workers would grow their own food and take time off during the warm months to plant, tend, and harvest their crops. The Ford Motor Company had opened seven such village industries by the mid-1930s in rural areas far outside Detroit, and their success seemed to point to a solution to larger economic problems. "Up through these country plants there has not been a person who needed help," Ford wrote. "They have raised so much of their own food that out of their wages they have always had a surplus." This project for integrating the country and the city, the farmer and the worker, not only appealed to his growing respect for American tradition but suggested a way for citizens to work and feed their families. That such a plan had little realistic application for urban industrial centers seems not to have disturbed Ford's utopian vision.[13]

But all of his prescriptions for recovery depended on a single, overarching dictum. The real need—and on this point he preached fervently—was for a resurgence of individual self-help and initiative. In pronouncements appearing regularly in venues such as *Business Week*, *The Saturday Evening Post*, and the New York *Times*, he urged Americans to help themselves in these trying times. Opportunities existed, Ford believed, and people "need not depend on employers to find work for them—they can find work for themselves." Self-reliance bolstered personal pride as well as economic well-being. "The great trouble today is that there are too many people looking for some one else to do something for them," he claimed in 1935. "The solution to most of our problems is to be found in every one doing something for himself." By marshaling their own talents to overcome adversity, people would "discover what is worth while and what is not worth while" and realize "there are no tricks which will take the place of work."[14]

In 1933, Henry Ford demonstrated his convictions about the Depression in confronting a local crisis. The Detroit banking structure was tottering, and many observers feared its total collapse. Early in the year, the Union Guardian Trust Company, a holding company that controlled the lion's share of the city's banking resources, lost its liquidity. The reckless speculation of Detroit banks, like many others around the country, had created this situation. The Reconstruction Finance Corporation (RFC) agreed to step in and provide a large loan to Union Guardian Trust to keep its banks operating if large investors, including Ford, would agree to guarantee an additional advancement of funds. After initially considering such support, Ford decided not to cooperate. The governor of Michigan declared an eight-day bank holiday to forestall collapse of most banking in Detroit. Ford then agreed to provide some $11 million in capital to create two new banks, whose managers he would select. Detroit's bankers refused this offer, and in March, General Motors, along with the RFC, established the National Bank of Detroit to stanch the financial bleeding. A few months later, Ford opened its own bank as well. Both of these new institutions did well. Throughout the controversy, Ford presented himself as a foe of reckless financiers and a friend of ordinary bank depositors, a position that he emphasized in a published pamphlet entitled *The Truth About Henry Ford and the Banking Situation.* The episode reinforced his view of banks as unproductive institutions that represented the interests of wealthy financiers. Rather than solutions, they appeared to him as part of the larger problem during the Great Depression.[15]

As the economic conditions deteriorated and banks began collapsing in smaller towns in Michigan, some of them also appealed to Ford for aid. Again, he refused. For example, a committee from L'Anse, a small town of four thousand where Ford operated two sawmills employing seven hundred people, requested a donation of $75,000 from Ford to reopen the Baraga County National Bank. He not only refused but issued a scathing public attack. Banks were part of "a system that has so lamentably failed in protecting the savings which working people have entrusted to it," he declared. "We have studied several communities in these matters and find that they do very well without banks as at present managed. A prosperous bank too often means a mortgaged community and such prosperity is the forerunner of depression."[16]

Ford pursued his formula for economic recovery—work and production, self-help, reconnection with the land—with several local projects. Observing growing privation among Detroit's working people, he urged them to plant gardens for sustenance and made some land available on Ford farms. "No unemployment insurance can be compared to an alliance between a man and a plot of land," he declared. Farmers, he assured readers, would be glad to lend small plots of land for such endeavors. As most city dwellers shook their heads in disbelief at this far-fetched plan, Will Rogers cracked that, since "most people got no room for a garden, what Mr. Ford will do is put out a car with a garden in it. Then you can hoe as you go."[17]

Ford also embarked on an extensive rehabilitation project in the community of Inkster. Incorporated in 1927, this African American town to the west of Dearborn had been devastated by the Great Depression as unemployment soared and its resources shriveled. Police protection, garbage collection, and utility service disappeared. Ford set up a community kitchen to provide meals and paid townspeople to clean up neighborhoods, drain stagnant water, and repair roads. He also opened a commissary to sell food and clothing at cheap prices or on credit, organized a medical clinic with doctors from the Rouge plant, and built a new high school. This initiative saved Inkster from some of the worst ravages of the Depression, and illustrated Ford's preference for private investment over public-welfare programs. But, like his garden plan, it repaired a few small tears in the social fabric of Detroit while doing little to stop its systematic unraveling.[18]

At the national level, Ford practiced his recovery preaching by releasing a new automobile. By 1931, the Depression had overtaken the company; sales of its Model A slumped significantly, and it had lost ground to General Motors and Chrysler. The founder responded by shutting down production of the Model A and offering a new model the following year, with an eight-cylinder, V-shaped engine. The Ford V-8, with its powerful engine and quick acceleration, gained legions of fans, including the outlaws John Dillinger and Clyde Barrow, who wrote Ford that his new car greatly aided their getaways. But it burned excessive amounts of oil, dampening enthusiasm among some consumers. The car sold only modestly, as did the Model B, an updated version of the Model A, and the company continued to lose money and position to its competitors. The failure of these moves revealed the threadbare quality of Ford's assertions about production and recovery. Making a good car revived neither the fortunes of the company nor the general state of the American economy.[19]

In late 1934, Ford demonstrated the bankruptcy of his position on the Great Depression. The United States lingered at a low point of economic activity, with unemployment hovering at around 22 percent, bankruptcies multiplying, investment standing some 88 percent below 1929 levels, soup lines in towns and cities all over the country, the gross national product and the consumer price index remaining about 25 percent below 1929 figures, and an atmosphere of despair settling over America. Ford's popular audience must have been amazed to read his assessment of the situation. In an essay entitled "Henry Ford Says This Is the Day of Opportunity," published in *Collier's*, Ford offered a view of the American scene so rosy it bordered on the hallucinatory.[20]

He assured readers that a single word pointed the way to economic salvation: "Work!" Owners of businesses and factories, Ford urged, "have to go back in and run them. They have to think about getting ahead. . . . They have to go on improving things and making them work." But he offered no specifics as to *how* bankrupt or capital-starved entrepreneurs should do this. To those out of work, Ford served up reassurances. "The way to stop unemployment," he asserted, "is to give these people something in place of relief. That will stop relief entirely. They'd get along." As to *how* they were to get along with no income, he simply said, "People know how to get along in a country like this. Nobody's going to starve in America." He dismissed the suggestion that desperate citizens might resist the abolition of relief, suggesting, "Oh, that's just revolution talk. Just give them a chance at making a living and see how quick they'll grab it."

Ford made the astonishing claim that present conditions offered great prospects for the small businessman. "You have to start your own business and look after it yourself," he instructed. "Where there was one opportunity when I was a young man, there are thousands now." He even seemed to think that failure offered opportunity. "Why, those homeless boys, those homeless boys riding around in box cars . . . Why, it's the best education in the world for those boys, that traveling around," he observed of the thousands of hobos tramping about the country. "They get more experience in a few months than they would in years of school." Ford's conclusion underlined the mindless quality of his optimism. "It's all right," he assured readers, "things are all right, but people have to start working again—and most of them will have to be self-starters." For millions of Americans unable to find jobs or driven from their homes in despair or struggling to find their next meal, such nostrums must have appeared surreal.[21]

Throughout the Great Depression, Ford continued pushing the same solution of production, self-help, work, and village industries. His muddled reading of this catastrophe reflected the old-fashioned aspects of his ideology. Obviously, his loyalty to traditional nineteenth-century values had remained strong even as he developed novel notions of mass production and consumerism. Ford's traditional mind-set also produced another important consequence. Observing the administration of President Franklin D. Roosevelt after 1933 and his innovative use of the national government for social and economic engineering, Ford bridled. The New Deal, he decided quickly, violated fundamental American values. With a typical combination of stubbornness and conviction, Ford dug in for a protracted battle with advocates of activist government.

In 1933, Henry Ford stood nose-to-nose with the new administration of Franklin D. Roosevelt. One of the chief executive's new agencies had tried to impose a code of competition on the automobile industry. Ford, unlike other automakers, refused to cooperate and vigorously defended his right to conduct business in a free, unencumbered market. The administration retaliated by threatening to withhold the symbol of national cooperation, the Blue Eagle, from display at Ford plants or on Ford automobiles. "Hell, that Roosevelt buzzard!" a fuming Ford responded. "I wouldn't put it on the car!" This reaction typified Ford's increasingly bitter opposition to the New Deal and his fervent defense of an older set of ideals glorifying individual initiative and enterprise.[22]

Ford's opposition to Roosevelt's administration and programs did not take long to develop. In the immediate aftermath of the President's inauguration in March 1933, he publicly wished the new government well and adopted a wait-and-see attitude regarding its policies. Privately, he was less sanguine. When Ford and a group of company executives listened to FDR's inaugural address on the radio in Edsel's office, some expressed tentative approval of the President's promises to take vigorous action against the Depression. But their leader looked skeptical. "The boss didn't say anything," William Cameron remembered. "He just shook his head." Within six months, expressions of goodwill vanished: the administration moved to regulate the production and sale of automobiles, and Ford resisted. As the New York *Times* noted of the Ford-Roosevelt standoff, "The world is about to witness the first and critical test between the old 'rugged individualism' which spread this nation across the map and the new 'robust collectivism' with which it is now proposed to keep it there."[23]

One of the New Deal's most significant creations, the National Recovery Administration (NRA), stood at the center of this confrontation. In June, only three months after Roosevelt took office, Congress passed and the President signed the National Industrial Recovery Act (NIRA), often described by historians as "the keystone of the New Deal." This measure promoted cooperation among business, government, and labor by authorizing the spending of $3.3 billion for public works, establishing a shorter workweek, and seeking to increase wages and payrolls. It also stipulated that codes of competition were to be established in all major industries, setting out wages, hours, and conditions for workers as well as prices for finished goods. Moreover, this legislation asserted the right of workers to organize and bargain collectively without retribution from their employer. The NRA was established to administer and enforce this landmark legislation. The National Automobile Chamber of Commerce drafted a code that was approved by the President and the NRA in the late summer of 1933. All automobile manufacturers agreed to sign the code but Ford.[24]

General Hugh S. Johnson, the flamboyant director of the NRA, stepped into the picture with typical bravado. Having forged a reputation as head of the Selective Service during World War I, this brigadier general had become a businessman in the 1920s, before joining the Roosevelt adminis- tration in 1933. A man of tremendous energy, Johnson had devised the Blue Eagle logo for the NRA, authored its slogan, "We Do Our Part," and cre- ated public enthusiasm through his efforts. Now he tackled the recalcitrant attitude of the nation's most prominent industrialist. Shortly after passage of the NIRA, he had secretly come to Dearborn to consult with Ford and gain his support and cooperation. Johnson talked at great length, and Ford "listened to him longer than any man I've ever known him to listen to," noted Cameron. "After he talked about two hours explaining his plan, the boss said, 'Well, General, you're making it awful hard for a young man to start in this country.' "25

Ford expressed his reservations throughout the summer, and when the automobile code finally went into effect, on September 5, he refused to sign an assent form. An angry Johnson began a campaign aimed at pressuring Ford to fall in line. When asked at a press conference if the administration intended to crack down on Ford, Johnson answered, "I think maybe the American people will crack down on him when the Blue Eagle is on other cars and he does not have one." A short time later, Johnson announced a boycott of Ford products by the federal government. In late October, he said that if he discovered evidence that the Ford Motor Company was violating wage and hour requirements of the NIRA, he would turn it over to the attorney general. The threat of government prosecution hung in the air.26

Ford struck back with even stronger words. The company released a statement attacking the head of the NRA for "assuming the airs of a dicta- tor." "The public has known the Ford Motor Company for thirty years and is not dependent on Mr. Johnson for information concerning it," the state- ment continued. "We suggest a code of fair publicity for Mr. Johnson's interviews." The company also issued a statement for *Time* magazine assert- ing "Signing a code is not in the law. Flying the Blue Eagle is not in the law. Johnson's daily expression of opinion is not in the law." The company sent a letter throughout the country soliciting support. It depicted Ford as an earnest supporter of recovery who endorsed certain parts of the NRA agenda. "Unfortunately, the Act includes some things which have nothing to do with recovery, and whose purpose seems to be to shift the American system of life and government over to some new and untried basis," the let- ter concluded.27

Ford pursued a subtle strategy in this dispute—meeting conditions on wages and hours as set by the automobile code, refusing to sign it because of government intrusion into business decisions, all the while conducting a public-relations campaign stressing his support for recovery. He presented himself as an advocate of workers and an opponent of government tyranny. Results were mixed with regard to public opinion: some applauded him for his principled stand, and others denounced him for impeding the fight against the Great Depression. Ford's battle with the NRA dragged on for two years, but he finally won the war. On May 25, 1935, the Supreme Court struck down the NIRA statute as unconstitutional, and the power of the NRA evaporated. Ford viewed this as a victory over malevolent forces that sought to destroy the American spirit of competition. "The NRA had that for its object, so has this share-the-wealth business," he told the New York *Times* a couple of months later. "Kill competition and the world will not progress."[28]

It was not just the struggle with the NRA that hardened Ford in his opposition to the growing power of the national government, but another, personal factor as well. He grew to hate the man who had created the New Deal. Though he never expressed it publicly, Ford's intense dislike of Roosevelt became an article of faith among his friends and co-workers.

The automaker and the President had clashed indirectly during the conflict over the NRA code, when FDR supported General Johnson in the government boycott of Ford products. Charles Edison, the son of Thomas Edison, worked for the NRA in New Jersey, and he tried to arrange a conciliatory meeting between the President and Ford. After Ford wrote a letter expressing his respect for the President, Edison read the passage to Roosevelt, who remarked with a smile, "If Henry will quit being a damn fool about this matter and call me on the telephone I would be glad to talk with him." But Ford would not make the first move, and neither would Roosevelt. Edison urged Ford to contact the White House, noting of Roosevelt, "He is, after all, the President of the United States," but Ford would not budge. Describing the situation as "like the famous case of the irresistible force meeting the unmovable body," Edison confessed that as a mediator "I guess I'm something of a flop." James Couzens, now a United States senator, stepped in to mediate and succeeded in getting Roosevelt to invite Ford to the White House. Ford, fearing that critics would interpret a visit as a ploy to renew government purchase of his vehicles, made his excuses. A meeting never happened.[29]

Publicly, Ford carefully avoided direct denunciation of FDR. He offered backhanded compliments, telling reporters, "The President was doing the best he could in an extraordinarily difficult situation." Or he used ambiguous rhetoric, observing that Roosevelt was "entitled to great credit for arousing the people to think. There is more public interest in national problems today than ever before." In letters whose content he knew would reach the President's ears, such as one he wrote to Charles Edison in 1933, he affirmed his respect for Roosevelt but added, "I have to make sharp distinction in my mind between the President and the NIRA. I cannot conceive of him as originating or crafting the act." Other times, however, Ford lifted the veil of diplomacy. In 1938, he told *Time* that Americans had "a leader who is putting something over on them, and they deserve it."[30]

Privately, Ford suffered no such restraints. Among colleagues, friends, and family, he criticized Roosevelt freely, often, and bitterly. He denounced the President and his minions for trying to destroy the private-enterprise system and the spirit of competition that fueled it. Joseph Zaroski, Ford's barber, once kidded his patron by asking if he was going to listen to one of FDR's Fireside Chats on the radio. Ford replied with "some language you don't hear in church," Zaroski recalled. Ford often commented to associates that "Roosevelt was too much of a sissy" ever to understand the hard-knocks, competitive world of business. He also liked to tell jokes about the President. One of his favorites had FDR fishing in a boat one day when he tipped it over and fell into the water. Two boys, fishing from the bank, threw down their poles, swam out, and pulled the victim to shore. A grateful Roosevelt informed them he was the President and promised to help them in any way he could. When one boy said his father was unemployed, FDR said he would find him a job. The other boy said his father was a businessman, and the President asked how he could help. "You can't do anything," the boy replied nervously. "If I tell my father who I pulled out of the water, he'll kill me!"[31]

Even after the two giants finally met at the White House in 1938, Ford's disapproval of Roosevelt persisted. Typically, FDR tried to charm his visitor. "Oh, Mr. Ford, I'm so glad to see you," he began. "My mother was so pleased to know that you were coming. She said, 'Franklin, I'm so glad that you're going to see Mr. Ford because Mr. Ford is not only a great man, he's a good man.' " Though polite, Ford resisted. During a lunch that was also attended by Edsel Ford and William J. Cameron, the President talked at length about his policies, including plans for the government to lend money to individuals to start business ventures with a repayment schedule of thirty-five years. After listening, Ford replied sourly, "You know, nobody pays a debt after thirty-five years." Upon leaving, he told FDR, "You know, Mr. President, before you leave this job, you're not going to have many friends, and then I'll be your friend." A few days later, Ford voiced his assessment of Roosevelt while walking through the Rouge with Walter G. Nelson, the company's manager of operations in northern Michigan. "Mrs. Roosevelt was a wonderful woman," Ford reported, "but that man was a rascal!"[32]

Ford's opposition to the New Deal reflected his deepest convictions about the mainsprings of American life. Put simply, he believed that private initiative, energy, and innovation had fueled the nation's material progress, and that government attempts to regulate the economic and social life of its citizens spelled doom. As early as 1931, even before FDR took office, Ford had begun railing against government intrusions into economic life. He noted that Washington was already paying soldiers and public employees, and some were now urging it to regulate the sale of industrial and agricultural products. Perhaps, he observed sarcastically, entrepreneurs should join the crowd "to make it unanimous and have us all live off the Government." Then all that was required "to be perfectly happy is a new kind of Santa Claus who will keep the Government well provided with money or anything else that it wants."[33]

Roosevelt's initiatives only exacerbated Ford's concerns. He believed that an activist federal government was inimical to the spirit of America. A close look at the NIRA, for example, clearly revealed that initiatives were being "put into law under cover of Recovery that were contrary to our whole American way of life and government." Promoting work, high wages, and reasonable working hours was a laudable goal, but forcing workers to join unions and regulating production and prices made for tyranny that "is impossible in America, which makes it all the more amazing that any American government should lend countenance to it." Under such regulation, "we can be told how much to pay for our materials whether they are worth it or not, how many cars to produce in a year, at what price to produce them, at what price to sell them, and every detail of our operation can be placed under control of a committee, one-third of whom are politicians and one-third of whom are labor leaders," Ford wrote. He especially abhorred two types who were filling the ranks of government: the "social theorist" who was determined to extract from businessmen support for the entire citizenry, and the representative of big finance who sought to use government power for "reestablishing money control of all our activities." This unholy alliance of antibusiness radicals and Wall Street financiers spelled "the destruction of the United States."[34]

Ford elaborated upon these themes in attacking the programs and provisions of the New Deal. He denounced plans for new taxes on business as destroying the very foundations of productivity and prosperity. "I have never objected to paying taxes, but I do object to government eating up the real wealth of this country on the pretext of giving it back to the people," Ford declared in 1935. "Industry can stand it, yes, but it would be like using the doors and woodwork of your house for fuel—pretty soon you have neither house nor fuel." A year later, he lit into Roosevelt's plans for government imposition of high wages. Ford said, "It is easy enough for a man who has never met a payroll or managed anything to sit on a commission and airily declare for higher wages, while at the same time imposing regulations which make the payment of these wages impossible." With the New Deal, Ford concluded, "the country has been given a postgraduate course in how not to do a number of different sorts of things. That experience should prove to be of great value to the country."[35]

As the Depression decade unfolded, the old populist in Ford increasingly moved to the fore. Like Huey Long, he denounced the federal government for allying itself with Wall Street to prey upon genuine "producers." He urged workers and businessmen to resist these "parasites" on behalf of American prosperity. He drew a parallel between government intrusion into the economy and speculation in the stock market. Government regulation of independent companies, Ford declared, dampened the creation of real wealth and promoted the interests of bankers, financiers, and other "money changers." "The politicians may not know it, but they are working right into the hands of that crowd," he said repeatedly. "Money lending is the only business that has prospered during the depression." After listening to one of his rants, a reporter wrote that Ford was determined to resist "the schemes of the money lenders to control America under the mask and pretensions of the New Deal." This critique, like much of the populist tradition, carried a whiff of anti-Semitism. Publicly, he denounced Wall Street bankers as secret partners in the New Deal coalition; privately, he identified Jewish financiers as culprits. "Mr. Ford seemed to feel quite strongly that there was a DuPont-Jewish-Roosevelt clique that was more or less tied together," reported one of his associates. "This was pretty deep in him."[36]

In 1936, Ford issued his definitive populist condemnation of the New Deal. Writing in *The Saturday Evening Post*, he described government and finance as "the two great businesses of today." These "parasites" had determined to "suck the lifeblood" out of the American economy in the interests of power and profit. "There is no difference, as far as the effect on the people is concerned, between overgrown finance and overgrown government," he argued passionately. "Both government and finance, whenever they get the chance, show the same avid desire to regulate and control the operations of producers."[37]

Ford's ideological confrontation with the Roosevelt administration revealed fully the individualist, producerist code of conduct that he believed had created American material prosperity. Within his company, that same rigid mind-set shaped his attitude toward a rapidly worsening problem—his company's relations with laborers. Workers' desperate search for economic security during the 1930s propelled them toward unionization, but this movement found a cold reception in Dearborn. Committed to an old-fashioned view of labor and its relationship to management that had been forged in the halcyon times of the Five-Dollar Day, Ford was unable to comprehend, let alone accept, the rationale for unionizing his company. This failure brought on spectacular episodes of labor strife, and also led him to promote to the top of his company one of the most controversial characters in its long history.

Twenty-two

Despot

On March 7, 1932, a crowd of some twenty-five hundred unemployed workers and radical agitators gathered on the outskirts of Detroit. After arriving on foot, by streetcar, and on buses, they organized themselves in the early afternoon and began moving toward Dearborn. Most of them had been present the night before at two mass meetings addressed by William Z. Foster, the Communist Party leader, whose fiery rhetoric escalated a sense of outrage. Describing their effort as a "hunger march," the marchers headed for the River Rouge plant, where they were determined to present grievances to the Ford Motor Company and demand jobs. Some seventy Detroit policemen monitored their progress as the protesters sang songs, chanted slogans, and waved placards saying "Come On Workers, Don't Be Afraid," "We Want Jobs!," and "Now Is the Time to Act!" When they arrived at Miller Road, which led to Gate 4, the main entrance to the Rouge, three dozen Dearborn police, supported by Ford security forces, blocked their way.

A confrontation erupted. The police demanded that the marchers refrain from violating private property, and when the crowd shouted its defiance and surged forward, the defenders fired several tear-gas canisters. The protesters responded with a hail of rocks and kept pushing forward. The police retreated in orderly fashion and gained support from the Dearborn Fire Department, which turned streams of water on the protesters from overhead passageways. More rocks greeted this tactic.

At this point, the escalating conflict halted for a peculiar interlude. The locked gate at the Rouge swung open, and a single automobile drove out. Next to the driver sat Harry Bennett, the Ford Company's head of security and chief labor negotiator, whose tough reputation had spread throughout Detroit. The car drove right up to the crowd. "Well, somebody yelled 'We want Bennett,' so like a fool I said, 'I'm Bennett,' and got out of the car," he described later. "Well, you should have seen those rocks. Honest, they came at me like a flock of pigeons." With typical bravado, Bennett went after one of the ringleaders when a rock struck him in the head and knocked him unconscious.[1]

When Bennett went down, the situation turned ghastly. The crowd pushed on, throwing bricks and stones, and this time defenders opened fire with shotguns and pistols. Witnesses reported that gunfire also came from ranks of the protesters. A full-scale, bloody riot erupted amid clouds of tear gas as the sound of guns, shouting, and shattering glass from plant windows punctuated hand-to-hand fighting between marchers and police and security men, all of whom were armed with wooden cudgels and lengths of metal pipe. As the battle raged, calls went out for support, and units from the Detroit police and the Michigan state police rushed toward the scene. When these reinforcements arrived, the marchers retreated in disarray. The smoke cleared on a horrifying site. Four men lay dead on the stone-littered ground, and thirty badly injured individuals were trying to drag themselves to safety or call out for help. Harry Bennett lay unconscious under the lifeless body of one of the march leaders, whose corpse, ironically, shielded the hated Ford operative.[2]

This violent confrontation caused a sensation around the country. *The New Republic* termed it the "Dearborn Massacre" and blamed the repressive policies of Henry Ford and his allies in the Dearborn Police Department for causing the tragedy. Ideological positions hardened and divided Detroit. Many of the marchers had been communists, and three days later they held a rally in a meeting hall where four caskets lay in state beneath a picture of Lenin while the band played a Russian funeral march. At the opposite end of the spectrum, the local American Legion passed a resolution promising to "tender to the Ford Motor Company and other Wayne County industries the assistance of our organization and pledge them the support of all members in any further emergency." One of the assistant prosecutors involved in the subsequent grand-jury investigation told journalists, "I don't care who knows it, but I wish they'd killed a few more of those damned rioters."[3]

The riot tragically highlighted the labor crisis that slowly enveloped the Ford Motor Company during the Great Depression. But it also illustrated another important development in the company's affairs during the 1930s: the central role played by Harry Bennett. After being knocked unconscious by the barrage of rocks, he was hailed for his courage by Ford supporters. But pro-union forces denounced Bennett's tactics, viewing him as "a cross between a spy and a gorilla," in the words of one magazine. Whatever was made of this controversial figure, one thing was clear. Henry Ford had placed Bennett in a position of authority during this period of labor agitation and backed him completely. The effects of this decision would resonate for many years.[4]

The tale of Harry Bennett's rise in the Ford Motor Company was remarkable. Through a combination of fortune and canniness, this disarmingly candid but ruthless roustabout climbed to the very apex of power in one of the nation's largest industrial enterprises. Trading on his close personal relationship with Henry Ford, Bennett became head of personnel and payroll and eventually took charge of labor relations. Given his connections to mobsters in the Detroit underworld, he surrounded himself with a small army of thugs and created an extensive spy system within the company. Bennett became Henry Ford's "pistol-packing errand boy," in the words of Charles Sorensen, and devoted himself utterly to his boss. By the early 1930s, he had become the second-most-powerful man in the Ford Motor Company.[5]

Bennett had been born in Ann Arbor, Michigan, in 1892 and grew up in Detroit. A rebellious, unruly child, he also demonstrated an artistic flair, studying painting and sculpture at the Detroit School of Fine Arts. He decided to join the navy in 1909, at age seventeen. As an enlisted sailor, Bennett had cruised to Central America, Europe, and Africa, and also drawn cartoons for a navy magazine and played clarinet in a service band. He became interested in boxing and fought a number of matches under the name Sailor Reese.[6]

In 1916, while on furlough in New York City and planning to re-enlist, Bennett accidentally made the most important acquaintance of his life. Along with a close friend, he had become embroiled in an argument with customs officials at Battery Park when things escalated into fisticuffs with the police. Arthur Brisbane, the noted journalist, wandered by during the fight and persuaded the authorities to release the young sailors. Bennett's friend promptly fled to the ship, but Brisbane asked the young Michigander to accompany him to Broadway to meet someone from his home state. A short time later, Brisbane introduced Bennett to Henry Ford, whom the journalist had known for a number of years. They chatted for a while, and Ford asked the sailor if he would like a job at his new plant under construction in Detroit. He promised a position as a security officer, explaining, "The men who are building the Rouge are a pretty tough lot, and I haven't got any policemen out there." Bennett accepted and returned to Detroit. Ford sent him to the Rouge "to be my eyes and ears." Upon arriving, Bennett promptly exchanged punches with a huge Polish foreman, and they knocked each other to the ground. Thus establishing his credentials, he began his career at the company, which he described in these simple words: "I am Mr. Ford's personal man."[7]

With Ford as his patron, Bennett rose steadily in the ranks over the next decade. After starting as the head of security at the Rouge, he played a key role in terminating the sociological department and prompting the resignation of the Reverend Samuel S. Marquis. By 1921, he was managing the Rouge employment office, and with the authority to hire and fire thousands of workers, his power grew substantially. As security chief at the Rouge, he also surrounded himself with a group of deputies who formed the core of the notorious Ford service department. This collection of street fighters, ex-convicts, underworld figures, and athletes numbered about three thousand by the early 1930s, and under Bennett's direction, they dominated daily life at the company. Spying on executives and assembly-line workers alike, intimidating employees, and keeping outsiders at bay, they carried out Bennett's orders as he sought to protect the interests of his employer. During this same period, he captured another source of power when Ford appointed him chief labor negotiator. The Great Depression saw Harry Bennett wielding authority on a par with Charles Sorensen and Edsel Ford. All the while, for those outside the company, he remained a shadowy figure about whom little was known. As late as 1938, *Forum* magazine noted that there was "a considerable body of myth built up around him, and in many minds he occupies the position that Rasputin did in Russia."[8]

Bennett's style contributed to his growing aura. Though small of stature, he displayed a larger-than-life personality. Habitually clad in a jaunty suit with a bow tie and fedora, he had a florid complexion and thinning brown hair carefully combed to cover a bald spot. His cocky, wisecracking air radiated streetwise experience. Physically, he was absolutely fearless, equally at home in the mayhem of a street brawl, the challenge of a personal fistfight, or a gun battle with gangsters. Bennett raised lions and tigers at his country home and occasionally brought a cub to his office to frighten visitors. He loved guns, practicing daily in his office with an air pistol that fired lead pellets, and often demonstrated his prowess. Irving Bacon recalled, "I dropped into his office one day, and sitting down in a chair, I noticed a pistol on his desk and asked, 'What kind of gun is that, Harry? Is it a German Luger?' He picked it up, and handing me a pencil, said, 'Hold it up, Bake.' He pulled up the gun and shot the pencil in half—close to my finger—William Tell fashion."[9]

His rugged charm and irreverent humor had a strange appeal. Fluent in the language of the street rather than the protocols of the boardroom, he eschewed corporate platitudes in favor of no-nonsense language. When a reporter accused Ford servicemen of being hoodlums, he responded, "They're a lot of tough bastards, but every goddam one of them's a gentleman." Bennett told the *American Mercury* how a gang of extortionists once fled from a meeting with him on a remote country road because they mistakenly thought he had brought the police. "They could have shot me dead, the dumb bastards," he said, laughing, "but they were sure that I had protection." He enjoyed his unsavory reputation. "The letters I get and the names they call me! Usually I can just read the first line and throw them away," he told *Fortune* in 1933. "But one fellow fooled me. He wrote me a nice, polite letter for a page and a half and right at the end it said, 'Bennett, you are a blank blank blank blank blank blank!' "[10]

Bennett's personal life came out of the same controversial mold as his career. He married three times and sired four daughters. All the while, he indulged in a continual round of parties, drinking, and carousing with cronies such as Harry Kipke, the former football coach at the University of Michigan. He loved to host rowdy events on his boat, where his favorite prank involved tripping a guest so that he fell overboard. The inebriated crowd would fish him out amid much merriment.[11]

Not surprisingly, Bennett lubricated his raucous lifestyle with generous applications of money. At the company, he sealed contracts by generously dispensing Ford cars, and sometimes dealerships, to influential individuals. Personally, though receiving only a modest salary, Bennett gained ample reward from a steady stream of valuable property. Ford gave him a twenty-eight-hundred-acre wilderness getaway in Clare County, Michigan, an eighty-four-hundred-square-foot cabin on Lost Lake, a valuable tract of land on the Detroit River near Grosse Ile, and a lodge on Harsen's Island on Lake St. Clair. He was especially fond of the *Estharr* (a combination of one wife's name and his), a seventy-five-foot yacht that he took on voyages with his cronies along the Huron River, onto Lake Michigan, and occasionally to the Caribbean. But Bennett's primary residence may have been the most outlandish result of Ford's largesse. Known as "The Castle," it sat on a large tract of land in the countryside near Ypsilanti. This little boy's fantasy was a sprawling stone structure featuring towers, an underground series of tunnels, false bookcases that became doors with the touch of a secret lever, and an underground cave room with specially manufactured stalactites and stalagmites, and tiger cages. It had a huge barroom decorated to look like the interior of a yacht with portholes, nautical clocks, and navigation instruments, all of which was surrounded by a large painted seascape where ships and lighthouses glowed with tiny electric lights when a switch was thrown.[12]

Bennett's easy way with substantial amounts of cash was evident to his friends. One evening in early December, Irving Bacon, Bennett, and Harry Kipke were relaxing at a lake near The Castle. After drinking much champagne, on a lark they crossed the lake in a canoe. A drunken Bennett fell into the frigid water and was pulled to shore by Kipke. To Bacon's astonishment, Kipke then went back out onto the lake. But, as soon became clear, he was paddling about and gathering up a large number of $20 and $50 bills that had been dislodged from Bennett's pockets and were now floating on the lake surface.[13]

But Bennett was not just a calculating roughneck who took advantage of a wealthy patron; he displayed talent in unexpected areas. A disciple of physical fitness, he exercised regularly and rode horses. He loved painting as much as fighting, and filled The Castle with his work, which ranged from nude studies to the seascape mural in his barroom. He also dabbled in sculpture and music. He was proficient on the saxophone and clarinet, playing the latter instrument to accompany his daughters on the piano and the former in the Shrine Band of Detroit, which performed occasionally at dances, concerts, and parties.[14]

For the most part, Bennett exercised power at the Ford Motor Company not through talent and personality but through fear. From his corner office in the basement of the administration building at the Rouge, he directed an army of henchmen in systematically creating an atmosphere of physical intimidation. The service department, filled with "hoodlums" and "punks," created a reign of terror at the Rouge. Anyone summoned to Bennett's office saw a number of these thugs lounging about waiting for orders, and ignored the obvious message at his peril. Some servicemen paraded along the assembly lines enforcing discipline and looking for slackers. Others fanned out among the workforce, temporarily taking real jobs so they could spy for Bennett and report any suspicious behavior or dissenting ideas. As the head of this repressive organization, Bennett gained a fearsome reputation among Ford workers. As one journalist noted, "They speak of him privately as if he were a combination of Dracula and J. Edgar Hoover."[15]

That same fear spread to Ford managers. Bennett's elaborate system of spies spread from the factory floor to executive offices, and he seemed to know everything that was said at the Rouge, who said it, and when he did so. He developed files on the personal transgressions—drinking, gambling, womanizing—of even the highest-placed executives. If Bennett couldn't get the goods on someone, he would try to lure the person into misbehavior. Lawrence Sheldrick reported how Bennett tried to talk him into going on a special railcar with representatives from the Budd Manufacturing Company on a trip to Chicago. But Sheldrick refused, sensing "one of his typical tricks, to get me off on this trip and then build up this story to the boss about me being wined and dined and getting drunk with our suppliers, and turn Mr. Ford against me." Indeed, Bennett encouraged disloyalty in the subordinates of the most powerful men in the company. He courted Russell Gnau, Charles Sorensen's executive assistant. "I know just about every time Mr. Sorensen went to lunch, Mr. Gnau would get up and go over to Bennett's office and the two of them would go some place for lunch," reported one observer.[16]

Bennett carefully cultivated an ethos of violence to enhance his mystique. Many in his organization were armed, and if a special alarm went off in his basement office, men with shotguns would appear almost immediately. Bennett bragged constantly about his underworld connections, and dark-suited characters with bulges under their coats were always loitering about his office. In fact, his mobster connections were so good that he was able to assist the police in solving several high-profile kidnapping and murder cases around Detroit. He enjoyed threatening violence to, or performing it on, anyone who blocked him. During a dispute, he once burst into Sorensen's office and threw off his coat to attack its occupant when Roscoe Smith, Sorensen's burly assistant, grabbed him from behind. "I learned a trick in the Navy of how to escape such a hold," Bennett described gleefully. "I relaxed. This caused Roscoe to relax. Suddenly I broke loose, turned, and pushing my left palm under Smith's chin, I slugged him with my right and broke his jaw." When this happened, Sorensen bolted for the door yelling, "Let me out of here! There's a madman loose!"[17]

Bennett reinforced his position in the company by cultivating powerful connections in the surrounding community, in Dearborn and elsewhere in the state of Michigan. He dispensed patronage by handing out jobs, favors, and automobiles. He built a political organization in Dearborn by donating money to public officials. "I don't think there is any doubt," noted a top Ford manager, "that Harry Bennett made and unmade the mayors and chiefs of police of Dearborn." Bennett's stooges formed a political organization called the Dearborn Knights that pressured voters and threatened opponents. He also acquired much influence among Wayne County judges. He successfully placed Harry Kipke on the Board of Regents for the University of Michigan, pushed a friend onto the City Council of Detroit, and struck up a friendship with the governor of Michigan. As the *American Mercury* reported, "Bennett is a power in Michigan politics. He is on intimate terms with practically every official in the state."[18]

For all his retainers in the service department and influential friends around Detroit, however, Harry Bennett's power at the company basically stemmed from one source—his close personal relationship with Henry

Ford. The two men had become nearly inseparable. According to Bennett, in the early 1920s Ford began meeting him at the Rouge late at night to inspect the premises and monitor the workforce. "They don't know when to look for us," Ford said, and "that keeps them on their toes and guessing all the time." Within a few years, he saw his security chief every day. "He usually called me the first thing in the morning, and often drove to my home to take me to work," Bennett recalled. Ford also telephoned Bennett every evening at nine-thirty. By 1930, this close friendship had bestowed enormous authority upon the head of security.[19]

The bond was unbreakable. When Ford heard reports about Bennett's antics or unsavory tactics, he would say with a smile, "That wasn't my Harry, was it?" When William J. Cameron criticized the security chief, Ford replied, "You know, you can say what you want about Bennett, but I think he's a pretty good Christian." By the 1930s, the two were seen together constantly, conversing about company affairs, discussing items in the newspaper, and laughing about the latest installment of "Iffy the Dopester," a cartoon strip in the *Free Press* they both enjoyed. Bennett summed up their relationship many years later: "I believe that Mr. Ford thought of me as a son. He was always extremely solicitous of my health, and, I think, felt as close to me as a father might."[20]

In addition to trust and camaraderie, respect flavored their relationship. Bennett admired Ford and fulfilled any request immediately and unquestioningly. But Ford also developed a very high opinion of his subordinate. He commented to friends about this ex-sailor's intelligence, and when a visiting reporter asked him to identify "the smartest guy he had ever worked with," Ford silently nodded at Bennett, who was driving the car. Sorensen once complained about something Bennett was doing in a meeting of company executives. Fred Black described the reaction: "Mr. Ford, with an icy-cold tone in his voice and a steely look, said, 'What is the matter, is he stepping on your toes?' Sorensen made no reply." When the company's production head had to steer clear of Bennett, others took notice.[21]

There were several reasons for Ford's embrace of Bennett. The colossal size of the company made it nearly impossible for its founder to keep tabs on its intricate operations. Harry Bennett could do it for him, and Ford came to believe that this task required a tough, ruthless personality. Once, when asked how he put up with Bennett, Ford said, "Well, what's the difference? If I put somebody else in his place, give them a few years, and they'll do the same thing."[22]

Bennett also offered Ford a substitute for his son. In the 1930s, as he grew older and his energy waned, Henry wanted someone to lean on in conducting the affairs of his company, and he remained convinced that Edsel was too soft for the job. Bennett appeared the picture of strength next to the younger Ford. Perhaps to toughen Edsel's character so he would assert himself, Henry set the security chief against his son. Bennett understood the game and maneuvered to isolate the Ford heir in the company by subtly berating him, bullying him, and freezing him out of the decision-making process. As he once noted, Edsel "was just a scared boy as long as I knew him. Mr. Ford blamed himself for this. He had always overprotected him." The son seemed determined to prove his father's point. Rather than fighting back, even though he was president of the company and sharply disapproved of Bennett, Edsel swallowed his objections and reluctantly endured his father's favorite.[23]

Finally, Ford proved susceptible to Bennett's shameless sycophancy. The latter skillfully manipulated the aging founder, convincing him at every turn of his utter devotion. When a friend once remarked to Bennett that he would tear down the Rouge's administration building if Ford told him to, the security chief replied, "You bet your God-damned life I would!" Bennett charmed Ford with his tough-guy demeanor and rough camaraderie, and went to great lengths to prove his eagerness. Harold Hicks once observed Bennett run from a room upon receiving an instruction from Ford, and then slow to a walk as soon as he was out of his sight. Such stratagems succeeded. As an old Ford family friend commented, it reached a point "where one couldn't tell what Mr. Ford wished and what Harry Bennett wished."[24]

Bennett's manipulation extended to subverting his rivals. Sometimes he gave Ford unfavorable information about them, garnered from his network of spies in the service department. More often, he used innuendo. He mastered the technique of dropping offhand remarks to Ford about other powerful men in the organization that called their judgment into question or disparaged their conduct. "Half of the injustices that took place around here were due to Bennett's whispering in the old man's ear," Lawrence Sheldrick contended. After planting suspicions, the subordinate would wait patiently for Ford to chime in with a negative comment about an individual, and then use this as an excuse to act. By the 1930s, Bennett had a stranglehold on the organization because of his control over hiring and firing, transfers, payroll, travel vouchers, and security. He had the power to hurt rivals, and he never hesitated to do so.[25]

As the Great Depression unfolded, Bennett's authority expanded further when he became the company's chief labor negotiator. In Bennett, Ford saw the perfect figure to lead his crusade against the union movement. As usual, the security chief said just what his boss wanted to hear. Organized labor, Bennett proclaimed, would never bully the company, because for every man in the Rouge who might want to strike "there are at least five who want their job and don't want a strike." He publicly denounced the primary autoworkers' union as "irresponsible, un-American, and no goddam good." When asked to explain the Ford position on unions, he did so with typical flair: "The Ford Motor Company will never make any agreement with any union, anytime, anywhere."[26]

Thus Harry Bennett occupied a strategic position regarding the company's growing labor problems. Enjoying the full confidence of his boss, and the loyalty of hundreds of thugs in his service department, he was confident of success. But events did not cooperate. Bennett's blustering, bragging persona and heavy-handed methods helped launch a bloody labor struggle that crippled the Ford operation throughout much of the Depression decade. It would not be resolved until matters teetered on the edge of disaster.

On May 26, 1937, Walter Reuther, president of a United Auto Workers local, and Richard T. Frankensteen, chief organizer for the UAW in Detroit, went to the River Rouge facility. Accompanied by a number of union organizers who sought to hand out leaflets entitled *Unionism, Not Fordism*, as well as some teachers, clergymen, reporters, and photographers, they mounted the overpass leading to the main gate of the factory. The contingent was about halfway across when a group of company toughs dressed in suits and hats appeared, and one of them barked, "Get the hell off here, this is Ford property." The organizers halted, uncertain what to do.

At this point, two of the Ford men grabbed Frankensteen, pulled his overcoat forward over his head to pin his arms, and began expertly to administer a severe beating. Some punched him in the face and head, while others kicked him in the groin, knocked him to the ground, and stomped on his stomach. Others were assaulted as well. "They would knock us down, stand us up, and knock us down again," Frankensteen said later. Reuther tried to get away, but he was seized, punched, and thrown down the concrete steps of the overpass, with Frankensteen bouncing right behind him. When photographers snapped pictures of the assault, the Ford deputies grabbed most of the cameras and stripped them of film. A few photographers escaped to their automobiles, however; one of them was chased at breakneck speed by Ford hoodlums until he took refuge in a police station. Back at the Rouge, a melee ensued, and dozens of union supporters were attacked and beaten. Within fifteen minutes, the Ford forces had swept the area of union sympathizers.

This vicious assault created a national furor. Newspapers and magazines ran photographs of the beating that vividly portrayed a bruised

Reuther and a profusely bleeding Frankensteen. Reporters gave firsthand accounts describing peaceful union organizers suffering violent attack. The UAW reported eighteen casualties from the confrontation, including one man who required attention from a brain specialist and four women who claimed that Ford goons had kicked them in the stomach. Homer Martin, president of the UAW, denounced the company's "paid thugs and mobsters" and claimed that "the principal Fordism of the Ford Motor Company is fascism." He characterized Harry Bennett as an "embryonic Hitler" and asserted that his "blackshirts" offered "a poor substitute for democracy and reason." In subsequent hearings held by the National Labor Relations Board (NLRB), a parade of witnesses competed to present the most chilling stories of Ford violence against union men.[27]

"The Battle of the Overpass," as it quickly became known, threw a spotlight on the labor controversy that had engulfed the company by the mid-1930s. Bennett tried to gloss over the situation, claiming that "there were no Ford service men involved" in the beating and that the incident had been staged by the UAW. A company news release claimed that the union needed "some dramatic occurrence to cover up its conspicuous failure to influence Ford employees" and that newspapers had been demanding a "Ford strike story." Cameron, Ford's spokesman, said that the union had sought the confrontation because it was confident of support from the NLRB, a "traveling court of inquisition." But such claims rang hollow in light of the bloody photographs and the eyewitness accounts of Ford aggression, and the UAW enjoyed a wave of national sympathy.[28]

Ford took a pounding in the press. Newspapers were so negative that Cameron complained about a "legal lynching" in the public print. *Time* magazine said that "the brutal beatings" at the overpass might end up hurting Ford more than their actual victims. Describing him as "narrow, intolerant, utterly prejudiced," *The Nation* accused him of flouting the law and called upon him "to do the right thing and end the shameful servitude of his workers to his own arbitrary will."[29]

The Battle of the Overpass tarnished the reputation of Henry Ford, a man previously known as a pioneer of humane industrial reform. Whereas the Highland Park plant had appeared an Eden of harmony and high wages in the 1910s, by the 1930s Ford's River Rouge factory resembled an armed camp. According to a company manager who drove to the Rouge on a summer evening in 1937, "The only thing I could see were a lot of Ford employees with baseball bats . . . and lead pipes. They were on picket duty." Henry Ford still regarded himself as an advocate of ordinary workers, but he now faced a volatile labor situation. It was fed by poverty (and fear of poverty) stemming from the Great Depression, and by oppressive working conditions at his factories that he refused to recognize. As discontented Ford workers considered unionization, the owner responded with angry, unstinting opposition. A man whose organization had been noted for progressive attitudes toward labor now appeared as a despot who abused his workers.[30]

This escalating labor controversy revolved around several issues. During the Depression, employment and production at Ford automobile plants declined steadily. For those who retained jobs, the general work atmosphere became polluted by new travails. The "speed-up" accelerated the assembly line to increase production and demanded a faster pace of work. The pace became so intense that men were forbidden to talk with one another, and had no opportunity to go to the toilet except when a substitute was available. The only break consisted of fifteen minutes for lunch, a situation that inspired considerable worker creativity. Consuming a couple of sandwiches, a bottle of coffee or milk, a piece of fruit, and perhaps a hunk of cake in fifteen minutes without choking required all the planning and ingenuity of Fordism itself. According to one worker, men would sneak their lunch boxes from the racks early and hide them near their posts, so they could use every available second to eat:

> At the first tick of the bell he reaches for his lunch with one hand, while the other is busy shutting off his machine. His legs seem to instantly lose their starch and he crumples into a sitting posture, usually upon the floor. The lid of the lunch box opens as if by magic, and quicker almost than the eye can follow he has a sandwich in hand and is chewing on the first bite. Fifteen minutes for the whole lunch means two and a half minutes for each of the articles mentioned. . . . Consequently he has to cut mastication to the limit and bolt his food if he was going to get it all down.[31]

The exhaustion and nervous tension created by the sped-up assembly line was exacerbated by Ford foremen, who drove workers relentlessly, constantly demanding greater and greater output. A worker described how the company, like many schools and colleges, had an official "yell" that could be heard above the noise of the machinery. Foremen kept a close eye on production numbers, constantly tallied output on an hourly basis, and "dashed back to the aisles—up one and down another—shouting 'Let's Go! Let's Go!' And the nearer it gets to the end of the hour the louder and more persistent becomes the yell." A "grinder" at the Rouge explained to a reporter that the machines he tended "take up the distance of a short city block." "By the time I'm at the last one the first machine has already stopped. The boss is shouting at me and I have to run back there, and then back down the line again to see that the last machine doesn't stand idle for a second. Now the boss tells me they're going to give me more machines." A maker of pinion gears reported that he had started on four machines several years earlier, then was assigned to six, and a few months earlier had become responsible for twelve. A worker on tire carriers reported that in 1925 daily shift production was 3,000 units produced by 160 men. By 1931, it was 6,970 units produced by 16.[32]

If such harsh working conditions were not enough, Harry Bennett's service department added more poison. Spying, harassment, and physical beating reached a crescendo of managerial tyranny by the mid-1930s. At an NLRB hearing in 1937, an ex-foreman from the Rouge plant testified that the service department maintained an elaborate espionage system whereby functionaries "snooped around," listened to employees both at work and after hours, and were authorized to fire them at any time. "Union talk," of course, was the worst crime, and smart workers "watched their step and kept their mouth shut" when servicemen, usually "identifiable by their cauliflower ears and broken noses," were skulking about. Walter Griffith, a longtime machinist at the Rouge, described workers' deep resentment of Bennett's henchmen, who drew generous salaries for intimidating workmen while doing little actual labor themselves. Griffith was particularly infuriated by the situation on payday, when long lines of workers waiting for their checks had to suffer the abuse of "a big Scotsman who was supposed to keep the men in line. He got very rough, struck several men, and pushed them around."[33]

Not surprisingly, this hostile atmosphere produced a deeply alienated workforce. Incidents of abuse and unwarranted firings piled one atop another. A boy sent on an office errand into the factory was fired by one of the service-department "spotters" for stopping to buy a chocolate bar at a lunch wagon. An older worker in the Ford employ for nearly twenty years was dismissed for using a piece of waste to wipe the oil from his arms a few minutes before the quitting bell rang. Not allowed to converse, workers developed the "Ford whisper"—talking in an undertone without moving one's lips while staring straight ahead at one's work—as a way to maintain human contact during work hours. But sometimes even this subtle resistance backfired. A worker named John Gallo was discharged after a "spotter" caught him "smiling" with co-workers after being warned earlier about "laughing with the other fellows." According to Walter Griffith, such incidents caused many Rouge workers to become "very bitter" toward Henry Ford.[34]

Corroboration of deplorable conditions at Ford factories came from an unlikely source. William J. Cameron publicly condemned unionization throughout the 1930s. In private, however, he offered a different view. "The Ford idea was no longer working. I know that Mr. Ford's idea and his philosophy didn't seem to be corresponded to by the practice in the shop in the later years," he confessed. "I knew it wasn't the boss's idea, the Ford idea, to drive men." The enterprise had grown so big that Ford could no longer control things, Cameron admitted, and the tactics of men like Harry Bennett were creating great ill will among even the most loyal workers. One longtime employee approached Cameron and recalled sorrowfully how men had been proud to bear the Ford name in the old days. "Now, Mr. Cameron, it's hell," he said. "It's a perfect hell."[35]

Against this backdrop of discontent, an inexorable process of polarization unfolded—Ford workers became receptive to unions as a way to redress their grievances, and their employer vowed to stop them. Throughout the 1930s, the UAW struggled to gain a toehold at the company, and the spectacle riveted national attention on Dearborn. The first stage of the contest began shortly after the inauguration of Franklin D. Roosevelt, when Ford workers at plants in Pennsylvania and New Jersey walked off the job, decrying wages and working conditions. They tried to associate with the American Federation of Labor, but Ford refused to recognize the union and crushed the insurgency. Later in 1933, the NRA Compliance Board recommended prosecuting the company for violations of Section 7A of the NIRA, which protected employees who sought to organize and bargain collectively. The Justice Department concluded that the case would be difficult, expensive, and controversial, however, and declined to prosecute.

In 1935, two developments shifted the terrain for this ongoing labor battle. First, congressional passage of the Wagner Act guaranteed workers the right to organize and bargain collectively and established the NLRB to administer and enforce this law. The same year saw the founding of the Committee for Industrial Organization (CIO) by John L. Lewis, head of the United Mine Workers, and other representatives of industrial unions. A short time later, the UAW affiliated itself with the CIO, thus setting the stage for a new unionization push at the Rouge. It began in the spring of 1937. A few months after the Battle of the Overpass came an NLRB ruling that found Ford guilty of violating the Wagner Act for interfering with unionization and firing workers who tried to organize. The struggle settled into a contest of wills over the next two years. As the company resisted, the UAW crusade bogged down. The union split into two contending factions—one associated with the CIO and the other with the AFL—each of whom tried to organize Ford workers.[36]

Throwing up breastworks to halt the union's drive for support, a determined Henry Ford marshaled all of his power and resources. He had always opposed unions, even in his earliest days as a reforming industrialist. Though declaring laborers needed better wages, he argued in 1916 that unions "mean [class] war, and I don't believe in war. Perhaps labor unions are necessary when the people haven't got any other defense against special privilege. But I think when we get the facts before the people, special privilege will die out." Ford believed that union labor was not needed at his factory because "we recognize human beings and their right to just wages." He continued to denounce unions in the 1920s. He often added an anti-Semitic slant to his earlier critique. Unions were organized not by laborers but by "these Jew financiers. The labor union is a great scheme to interrupt work. It speeds up the loafing," he told *Collier's* in 1923. "It's a great thing for the Jew to have on hand when he comes around to get his clutches on an industry."[37]

Thus Ford's hostility to unionization during the Great Depression was no sudden occurrence, but the end point of a long opposition. Yet an interesting question lingers—*why* did Ford reject unions, especially in light of his lifelong advocacy of high wages, shortened work hours, and other reforms for workers? In fact, his position was a complex one based on the same trio of convictions that fueled his criticism of the New Deal.

Ford's antiunionism sprang from a traditionalist ideology of rugged individualism. Even amid the severe dislocations of the Great Depression, he saw American society as a place where the individual stood on his own two feet, deployed his labor and talents to his best advantage, and competed. Unions defiled this vision. As an employer, he claimed that "a man could *ask* him to do anything, beg him, but he couldn't drive him." Unions also violated the individual integrity of the worker. "A man loses his independence when he joins a labor group of any kind, and he suffers as a result," Ford stated. Workers who joined unions lost a measure of their freedom because they paid dues to an organization and got little in return beyond political maneuvering and attempted coercion. Committed to the values of an earlier age, Ford remained convinced that the employer-employee relationship was an agreement between consenting individuals. "The main thing to consider, after all, is freedom," he stated in 1937. "That's the foundation of America. The men in our plants are free, and they are better off for it."[38]

Ford's individualist mind-set appeared even more clearly in his refusal to recognize such distinctions as "capital" and "labor." The notion of class differences involving power relations had no place in his worldview. He condemned "this habit we have of talking of 'labor' as if it was a class apart from others, as if 'labor' and 'business' were two antagonistic opponents," he declared. "Most of the business men of this country came out of labor.

Where else can they come from? I belong to 'labor.' It is all I have done all my life." Since Ford saw no distinction between workers who put forth a good effort and businessmen who sought to make a product efficiently, sell it at a low price, and pay high wages, bargaining between employers and employees made little sense. "We're all workers together, the men and I," he contended.[39]

Ford also believed that unions elevated class concerns above the primacy of the consumer. Modern mass production provided material goods efficiently and cheaply, he said, and they were entitled to the fruits of abundance. Consumers subsumed labor, since all workers purchased commodities. According to Charles Sorensen, who understood Ford's philosophy better than anyone, his boss opposed unions because, "when labor has the power to dictate wages and what it will give for the wage received, it claims for itself the first benefit of mass production. The consumer is forgotten."[40]

Ford's pronouncements throughout the 1930s continued to boost consumer interests. He repeatedly argued that interest groups of any kind, whether financiers or labor unions, hindered providing goods at reasonable prices. "There are thousands of things that could be produced cheaply today for the comfort and convenience of the common man except for control manifested by finance and organizations of one sort or another," he wrote in a 1937 antiunion article. In fact, he argued, the impetus for high wages came not from unions but from businessmen who realized that, "if we don't do our part to create a market by paying good wages, we can't sell our goods." In his view, the employer and the employee shared the same goal of spreading material prosperity and paying sufficient wages to promote consumption. "I have never bargained with my men, I have always bargained *for* them," Ford wrote in 1933. "It would be strange to set my men and me trying to get the better of each other. I think we have made better bargains for them than any could, or than they could make for themselves." By paying his men well, Ford had made them good consumers, and now unions threatened to interrupt the flow of abundance.[41]

Finally, Ford's populist streak led him to believe that unions had emerged in the 1930s as creatures of Wall Street forces who were determined to control the modern corporate state. He felt that labor organizations, much like Franklin Roosevelt's New Deal, were being manipulated by financiers to undermine independent, progressive businesses such as the Ford Motor Company. "Wall Street wants to stabilize things at some level," Ford stated. "They have industry pretty well controlled on the management side and if they can control labor, through the unions, they think they will have it stabilized. The unions were created by Wall Street—by capital—to bring about that control." Independent companies like his disrupted this process of corporate consolidation. If Wall Street could force them into union agreements, production could be regularized, competition stifled, and high profits guaranteed for even lackluster companies.[42]

In a 1937 interview with the Detroit *News*, Ford aired his views on the Wall Street manipulation of the union movement. "Financial interests in New York have always controlled a large part of American industrial management," Ford asserted. "But control of management is not enough for them. They must control labor also, else their whole scheme fails. They must have someone who can get the employees under command just as the managers are." This small group of financiers sought to control both employers and workers so they could set prices, dividends, and wages. "There is no mystery about the connection between corporation control and labor control," Ford concluded. "They are simply the two ends of the same rope." Thus Ford saw the great contest of the 1930s not as one between capital and labor, but between producers and nonproducers. On the one side stood independent, service-minded businessmen and workers; on the other, the allied forces of big finance, government bureaucracy, and labor organizations. At stake was the well-being of the American consumer.[43]

Ford's opposition to unions made for a vigorous ideological debate. But in light of the abuse of workers at his plants, it was indefensible. His high-minded depiction of enlightened businessmen and dedicated workers joined in a happy alliance of producers was a fantasy that did not reflect the reality of the Rouge under the domination of Harry Bennett's service department. Crucial questions remain unanswered. Did Henry Ford order the oppressive practices in his factories prevalent by the 1930s? Did he know about them and cynically look the other way? Or was he unaware of the ways in which Ford workers were driven, fired capriciously, intimidated, and physically assaulted?

The evidence is mixed, and the conclusions are often ironic. Charles Sorensen, one of Ford's greatest admirers, claimed that his boss knew about everything that went on at the Rouge. He argued that "one of the great myths about Henry Ford" was the notion that Bennett had duped the owner and created a tyrannical organization behind his back. Sorensen said flatly, "Bennett never had any real power other than that delegated to him by Henry Ford. He was a 'yes man' who did as he was told, and promptly." On the other hand, Keith Sward, one of Ford's sharpest critics, described as "credible" the assertion that he remained ignorant of the labor abuses at the Rouge. Although he refused to absolve Ford of blame, Sward offered the possibility that Bennett and others had done things in Ford's name that he would not have condoned.[44]

As for Ford, he never directly addressed the issue. Circumstantial evidence suggests a conclusion somewhere between the extremes: that Ford was partially aware of the abuse of labor, but failed to comprehend its scope because of his advanced age, his uncritical regard for Bennett, his blind hatred of unions, and the extra-company projects that were taking up most of his time. Whereas one can figure that Ford would fire employees for failure to work, it is harder to believe that he would approve goons' punching workers who were waiting in line for their paychecks.

Disputes with his own managers further twisted Ford's view of labor conditions in the company. A significant group of company executives, led by Edsel Ford, believed that unions were inevitable in the modern world and wanted to negotiate with the UAW. For Henry Ford, ever jealous of his own power and prerogatives, such opposition only strengthened his resolve to fight unionization. Regarding Edsel, of course, the personal reinforced the political. Long suspicious of his son's conciliatory personality, Henry found Edsel's views to be another confirmation of weakness. A furious Ford senior kept his son on the margins of the labor struggle. As his emissary, Bennett plunged ahead with an antiunion strategy based on harassment of organizers, intimidation of workers, and encouragement of factionalism within the union ranks between partisans of the CIO and those of the AFL. This strategy worked for a while.[45]

By 1940, however, the UAW-CIO began to gain the upper hand. Announcing a major campaign to unionize Ford, it lined up significant support among company workers as tensions again escalated. Moreover, General Motors and Chrysler had signed contracts with the union. Sitdown strikes at GM plants in Flint and Cleveland in 1936 had spread to other facilities, and when the governor of Michigan (with the backing of President Roosevelt) hesitated to enforce an injunction to evict the strikers, resistance collapsed. In February 1937, GM agreed to recognize the UAW as the collective-bargaining agency for its workers. At Chrysler, sitdown strikes had also crippled the company until Walter Chrysler had agreed to negotiate with John L. Lewis. In April, Chrysler declared that the UAW would be the principal bargaining agent for its workers and granted wages, hours, and working conditions similar to those at GM.[46]

The Ford Motor Company found itself increasingly isolated. It suffered a legal setback in early 1941, when the Supreme Court refused to review a decision by the U.S. Court of Appeals for the Sixth Circuit, which had supported the NLRB by holding that the company must reinstate some two dozen employees fired for union activity. A few weeks later, the UAW-CIO organized a massive strike at the Rouge, with thousands of picketers assaulting nonstriking workers who attempted to go to their jobs. Ford and Bennett continued their obstinate opposition. With the governor of Michigan and Edsel Ford serving as mediators, however, an agreement was finally reached to hold an election on unionization under the auspices of the NLRB. On May 21, 1941, workers received a ballot on which they could choose a union affiliate or no union at all. The result was clear—the UAW-CIO won about 70 percent of the total vote, the AFL about 27 percent. Less than 3 percent of the workers voted for no union at all. By mid-June, a formal contract had been drawn up between the company and the union, but Henry Ford refused to sign it. In a meeting with Sorensen and Edsel, he vowed to close down his plants rather than submit to unionization. When Sorensen suggested that the government might intervene if Ford would not sign, the old man replied angrily, "Well, if the government steps in, it will be in the motorcar business and it won't be me."[47]

The next day, however, Ford surrendered. In a sudden, spectacular turnabout, he agreed to everything the UAW wanted, and more—a union shop, wages equal to the highest paid by any competitor, and union dues to be withheld from paychecks by the company and turned over to the union. This settlement granted to the UAW the most favorable contract in the industry, and speculation about Ford's dramatic change of heart ran rampant. Some pointed to forthcoming NLRB hearings that would seriously damage the reputation of the company; others suggested that Ford's declining share of the automobile market or his desire to gain advantage over rivals motivated his action. But the truth of the matter, Sorensen claimed, lay elsewhere. Ford confided that he had gone home after the angry meeting with Sorensen and Edsel and informed his wife about his decision not to sign. Clara was horrified and told Henry that "there would be riots and bloodshed, and she had seen enough of that." She added that if he persisted in this course of action she would leave him. "She did not want to be around here and see me responsible for such trouble." "What could I do?" Ford told Sorensen. "The whole thing was not worth the trouble it would make. I felt her vision and judgment were better than mine." Clara Ford probably saved her husband from his own worst instincts.[48]

The agreement with the UAW marked not only Henry Ford's defeat in the labor wars but his eclipse on the national scene. His position as a powerful, respected public figure in modern industrial society over the past three decades had declined to the point of collapse. By the end of the Depression decade, Ford had become a tired old man. Weary of escalating problems at his great company, confronted with policy failures and managerial infighting, and increasingly beset by health problems, he entered the final stage of his life in disarray. Little did Ford know what lay ahead—a devastating personal tragedy that would cripple him emotionally, and a national crisis that would call the very survival of his company into question.

Twenty-three

Dabbler

In midsummer 1938, Henry Ford celebrated his seventy-fifth birthday in monumental fashion. On Friday, July 29, he attended, along with Clara, a pageant held at Ford Field in Dearborn. A crowd of forty thousand watched seven hundred performers re-enact scenes from Ford's life and the development of the city. After the event, the guest of honor dispensed "Fordisms" concerning the merits of production over Wall Street finance and stock-market speculation, the need to integrate farming and industry, and his belief in making wages high and prices low. "There will be no steps backward in this country. We are going to keep right on going forward, inventing things to make life better for our people," Ford assured reporters. "This country just cannot be stopped."[1]

The next day saw an acceleration of the celebration. In the morning, some thirty-five thousand people, including eight thousand schoolchildren, attended a gathering at the coliseum in the State Fairgrounds. Henry and Clara entered riding in a 1908 Model T. As they mounted the platform, the Department of Recreation Boys Band swung into "Happy Birthday," and the crowd joined in. A reporter noted that Ford, "visibly moved by the unselfish acclaim of the youngsters, was able only to bow and wave his reply." Then a giant cake appeared, surrounded by seventy-five girls dressed in different-colored skirts, followed by speeches, skits, dances, and a clown parade. Later that evening, Henry and Clara were guests of the city of Detroit for a dinner at the Masonic Temple attended by thirteen hundred. The tributes also came privately. A mountain of flowers arrived at Fair Lane from friends, associates, and admirers from around the world. Trucks brought the floral arrangements in such volume that they filled up the house and had to be stacked around the swimming pool.[2]

It is hard to imagine such a celebration for other business figures, such as John D. Rockefeller, Alfred P. Sloan, J. P. Morgan, or Pierre du Pont. It clearly demonstrated Ford's status as a national treasure, an oracle whose words of wisdom deserved attention. An odd twist in this birthday bash reinforced this image. Throughout the proceedings, Ford wore a necktie (and carried another in his pocket) fashioned from soybean fibers, which he held up periodically before launching into a commentary on the bright future for this industry. Despite his age, Ford appeared fascinated with new ideas and technologies. In fact, throughout the 1930s his interests had broadened. He spent much energy in a variety of activities far removed from the Rouge plant—not just the Ford Museum, Greenfield Village, and his beloved "village industries," but experimental soybean farms, practical educational projects, and innovative farm technologies. He not only had engaged in "a retreat to the land," as the New York *Times* termed it, but seemed to be distancing himself from the field in which he had succeeded so brilliantly: the making of automobiles.[3]

Indeed, during the Depression decade Ford gradually disengaged in many ways from his company. Though retaining ultimate authority to decide important matters such as labor policy and new models, he left much day-to-day decision-making to Harry Bennett, Edsel Ford, and Charles Sorensen. The company became a peculiar kind of autocracy, in which the autocrat was often absent. The public still encountered a Henry Ford who fired off salvos against the New Deal and fulminated against the UAW. It read newspaper and magazine accounts of his active role in steering the course of his enterprise. But in many ways this image of public engagement was an illusion.

The real Henry Ford, even if he periodically exhibited his old flair for the limelight, spent more time in private pursuits. On the day of his seventy-fifth birthday celebration, he seemed anything but a public hero. He dropped by one of his farm labs, where he often retreated to relax, about six different times. He appeared quite nervous and told the staff, "This is the worst day of my life!" Uncomfortable with all the fuss being made over him, and petrified of public speaking, he felt obligated to soldier on because so many people had worked hard to arrange matters.[4]

He occupied his days in Greenfield Village, discussing agricultural experiments with his chemists in their labs, exchanging ideas on education with teachers around the country, and enjoying a quiet pace of life at Fair Lane. Stepping away from the manufacturing world, he increasingly involved himself with projects that emphasized social improvement. His quiet private life was dominated by simple domestic pleasures, several hobbies, and regular rounds of travel. One of the wealthiest men in the world,

Ford could afford to dabble in the sunset of his life. He poked about in any nook and cranny that engaged his interest, enjoying every minute of it.

With the American economy in tatters and his company embroiled in labor wars, Henry Ford often retreated to the comfortable domestic cocoon that he and Clara had spun patiently over the previous two decades. Fair Lane, their estate on a picturesque stretch of the River Rouge in Dearborn, had been their home since the mid-1910s, and by the 1930s the couple had settled into familiar routines. Family affairs, personal interests, and social projects took up their time, and they followed a regular schedule. Henry and Clara ate breakfast together around eight-thirty, after which Henry would depart for his office at the engineering laboratory and his favorite haunts nearby, Greenfield Village and the Ford Museum. Clara would busy herself with domestic activities, charities, and social engagements on most days. They would eat a modest evening meal together in a small alcove off the dining room overlooking her "blue garden," and after a quiet evening the couple would retire at around 10:00 p.m.[5]

Clara supervised a considerable staff at Fair Lane in the 1930s—several maids, head butler, second butler, cook, houseman, and part-time laundress. Because of her extensive interest in flowers and landscaping, several men kept busy with horticultural duties, including the maintenance of several greenhouses. Henry oversaw the private powerhouse at the estate, with five men operating its steam engines to provide electricity, heat, and refrigeration for the estate. Charles Voorhess served as the chief electrical engineer at Fair Lane and supervised a number of Ford's personal projects. Several of the staff worked particularly closely with the couple—Rosa Buhler, the head maid; J. D. Thompson, the head butler; Alphonse de Caluwe, the head gardener; Robert Rankin, Clara's chauffeur; and Rufus Wilson, Henry's longtime driver. By all accounts, Clara was a demanding employer, polite and reserved.[6]

Henry's abundant energy flowed into many channels. He continued his fascination with birds, creating a sanctuary on the estate where wood ducks and herons populated the river running behind the house, and five hundred birdhouses, along with dozens of feeding stations, nourished some two hundred species on the grounds. Henry and Clara loved bird-watching, both from the sunporch at the rear of their house and on long walks through the estate's fields and forests. Once, the staff put white netting cloth over two cherry trees near the house to protect the fruit for use in cooking and preserving. As Ford went to work one morning, he saw a couple of robins entangled in the cloth webs. He ripped off the nets, and sternly instructed the groundskeeper, "Don't put that back no matter who wants it back on there. There's plenty of cherries for the birds and us, too." In fact, Ford loved many wild creatures. He ordered the staff to leave all hollow trees lying on the ground for the raccoons to live in. He often sat on the front porch of Fair Lane and fed the coons bread scraps from his table. "They were all that tame—they'd come right up and take it from his hand," reported a staff member.[7]

Ford also continued tinkering with watches. He had established a hide-away on the top floor of the Fair Lane powerhouse, to which he retreated frequently on weekends and evenings. He installed workbenches to hold all of his tools and collected friends' watches to repair or clean them. He still did this precision work well, although advancing age occasionally caused lapses. He once returned a repaired watch to one of the Fair Lane staff that the individual said was not his. "I wonder who the devil I got that watch from," a befuddled Ford replied. He also used the powerhouse room for various projects. Sacks of soybeans, oats, wheat, barley, and corn were sitting about for foodstuff experiments, and Ford, assisted by a couple of company engineers, also used the room for testing tractor engines.[8]

His domestic life had its quirky aspects. He continued his odd habit of soaking old razor blades in water and then mixing in olive oil to concoct a tonic for his hair. He seldom carried any money and would borrow small amounts from his driver and barber to purchase trifles. Like many older people, he occasionally had trouble sleeping. Staff members would see a light in his bedroom window in the early-morning hours, and if the insomnia was especially severe he would take a walk down to the powerhouse at 4 or 5 a.m.[9]

Friends and family tried to keep Ford from operating an automobile on weekends, when his driver was off, and they stayed clear of the vehicle if he managed to do so. Never a good driver, he had become a genuine menace behind the wheel. An agricultural chemist once sat white-knuckled in the passenger seat as Ford, after bouncing off a couple of curbs, sped through the entry gate to the automobile testing ground without stopping as the gateman, not recognizing the driver, came running after them yelling obscenities. Jerome Wilford, a young guide at Greenfield Village, had a har-rowing experience when he accompanied Ford on a wintry Saturday morning to inspect some building projects. The driver, after careening "across lawns, commons, and fields," bogged down in the snow. As Ford gunned the engine and spun the wheels at top speed to melt the ice, the car suddenly shot forward, splattering mud all over a newly painted building. That would "give the workmen something to do," he commented, before roaring off.[10]

During quiet evenings at Fair Lane, Clara loved to read books and magazines, and her husband browsed through articles and clippings that his staff had prepared for him. As they got older, Clara often read aloud to Henry. They had several radios scattered about the house and regularly listened to programs such as *Amos 'n' Andy*, *Jack Benny*, and *The Quiz Kids*. The Fords played phonograph records of old-time dance music, and took after-dinner walks through Clara's many rose gardens. Only occasionally did they attend a movie or a play. Though their serene domestic life seemed to suit the couple, Henry occasionally grew frustrated. When Edward Cutler mentioned that he and his family had gone to the movies the night before, his boss replied enviously, "We can't go and see those things. Every time we go outside of this place, we're on exhibition. We're like prisoners here. We just have to stay home."[11]

The Fords' weekend routine in the 1930s followed the same pattern. Henry would hike through the woods, chop wood, and putter in his experimental room while Clara worked in her gardens. In the afternoons, he would often drive her to Greenfield Village to inspect a new construction project. On Sunday mornings, after breakfast, Clara liked to read leisurely through the Sunday paper while Henry would visit the powerhouse. After a brief nap in the early afternoon, the couple strolled the grounds, taking in the orchard, the vegetable garden, and the greenhouses, all the while observing nature and looking for different species of birds. In the early evening, they walked along Clara's "trail garden," which meandered through the estate.[12]

The Fords entertained infrequently at Fair Lane. Once in a while Clara would host a luncheon, and old friends visited occasionally for dinner. Nor did the Fords attend many social functions. They loved hosting the old-time dances at Lovett Hall and enjoyed attending the weddings of their friends' children. By the 1930s, the deaths of old friends around Dearborn necessitated their presence at many funerals. Various members of the Bryant clan visited Fair Lane, but not the Fords, who were never a close-knit family. When Henry and Clara socialized, they did so quietly with the Bryants, or with local couples such as the Harry Snows, the Stanley Ruddimans, and the Clarence Davises. The Louis Iveses were their oldest and dearest friends. The Iveses and Fords went out for dinner, traveled on several trips together, and hosted wedding-anniversary celebrations for each other.[13]

The Fords maintained a close, comfortable relationship with clearly delineated roles into the late years of their marriage. Though never affectionate in the presence of others, they joked with each other and conversed easily. Clara dominated the domestic scene with determined efficiency. She campaigned so relentlessly for the installment of a watering system that her exasperated husband finally told Charles Voorhess, "Put in that damned lawn spray system. I don't want to hear any more about it." Another time, Henry wanted a telephone on the sunporch and instructed Voorhess to install one. When he had started the job, however, Clara appeared and nixed it, saying they already had enough phones in the house. Over a period of several days, Henry insisted and Clara refused, round and round. The phone did not go in.[14]

In certain ways, the couple offered contrasting personalities. Neither displayed emotions easily, and both were even-tempered, with Henry given to shyness and Clara exhibiting a cool reserve. She had acquired a sense of social position with her husband's stupendous success, and though always polite and often kind, she would put people in their place if crossed. Once, a loud, pushy man approached her at a reception at the Dearborn Country Club and addressed her in a breezy fashion. "With a little bow of the head, she just passed it off as if she didn't see him," according to Mrs. Ruddiman. More democratic and unself-conscious, Henry chatted with anyone who caught his interest. He often passed a friend and tapped him on the arm, something Clara would never dream of doing. Henry also dropped his genteel demeanor more easily, periodically indulging in a puckish sense of humor. At one of their rare dinner parties, Clara suggested that her guests have a glass of sherry after the meal. Henry, a notorious teetotaler, left the table in apparent disgust. He returned outlandishly a few minutes later, riding his bicycle into the dining room and carrying a bottle of champagne under his arm. Always the practical farm girl, Clara worried about the details and processes of daily life, whereas her more visionary husband was able to lay aside his worries and relax more easily.[15]

Their close relationship was based on respect and affection. Clara was fiercely proud of her husband and his accomplishments, and Henry treated his wife with a natural sweetness. He always left her with a kind word and touch. He knew she had an unreasonable fear of thunderstorms and lightning, and if absent from home when a storm hit, he always called to see if she was all right. He developed a particularly charming habit over the years that revealed his fondness for Clara as well as their shared interests. Upon returning to the house from work, he would whistle a special bird call as a signal to let his wife know he was about.[16]

With Henry tied less tightly to the daily operation of the company, the Fords enjoyed more recreational activities than they had in the past. In

1917, they had purchased a yacht, the *Sialia* (the ornithological name for the eastern bluebird), and taken several cruises, including one to Cuba. By the mid-1920s, they had bought two cargo ships and named them after their oldest grandchildren, the *Henry Ford II* and the *Benson Ford*. These freighters, outfitted with luxurious cabins, became their transportation of choice for regular trips on the Great Lakes. In 1935, Henry and Clara acquired a smaller, richly adorned yacht called the *Truant* for such jaunts. This craft transported them in leisurely fashion during the summer season to a special vacation spot. Each August, they visited the Huron Mountain Club, an exclusive resort some forty miles north of Marquette, Michigan. They owned a large cabin there, and spent several weeks deep in the woods, feeding the deer, relaxing in the wilderness, and taking an occasional excursion to Big Bay, a nearby village. Indeed, Henry so loved the little town that he bought it in the early 1940s and spent several million dollars restoring its lumber mill, fifty-two employee homes, and the local hotel.[17]

Travel throughout the Eastern United States became a hobby for the Fords in the late 1920s and the 1930s. They journeyed to New England, where they would visit the Wayside Inn, or Edsel's summer home on an island off the coast of Maine. Clara regularly traveled to New York City for shopping trips, occasionally accompanied by Henry but more often by small groups of her Dearborn friends. The Fords also headed southeast for winter vacations. Until 1931, they spent several weeks each winter in the "Mangoes," their home in Fort Myers, Florida, which was adjacent to Thomas Edison's winter residence. After Edison's death in that year, Henry and Clara shifted their attention to a several-hundred-acre plantation near Ways Station, Georgia, on the Atlantic coast, and wintered there over the following decade. On most of these trips the Fords traveled in their private railcar, the *Fair Lane*. Built for Ford in 1921, this eighty-two-foot car was constructed entirely of steel and featured a rear observation platform. Its interior, richly finished in walnut with elegant window draperies, had sleeping quarters, a drawing room, kitchen, and small dining room. The *Fair Lane* could accommodate eight passengers as well as a cook and a porter. It allowed the couple to travel comfortably in a homelike atmosphere, in which they could read, converse, and sleep according to their usual schedule.[18]

In their mature years, however, Henry and Clara derived the greatest joy from their role as grandparents. Edsel and Eleanor Ford's four children—Henry II had been born in 1917, Benson in 1919, Josephine (Dodie) in 1923, and William in 1925—often visited Fair Lane on weekends, when a chauffeur would bring them from Grosse Pointe to Dearborn. The two older boys spent more time with their grandparents in the 1920s, before departing for Eastern prep schools. The two younger children visited often in the 1930s and became particular favorites of their grandparents. Dodie was a bright, sweet girl; William, the very image of Edsel, allowed Henry and Clara to relive their son's childhood.[19]

The Fords provided their grandchildren with a wealth of activities. The youngsters swam in the pool, played raucous games in the bowling alley spiced by arguments over who would manually set up the pins, skated on the pond, and accompanied their grandfather to look for birds' nests in the fields and forest. Henry supervised the boys on overnight camping trips in the woods and joined them in riding bicycles all over the estate. Every spring he took them out to help drain maple sap and boil it down into syrup in a shack in the woods. He gave them impromptu driving lessons as they sat on his lap and helped steer the car. If the weather was bad, the children remained indoors and banged on the piano, played the wind-up Victrola, and explored the bays and towers of the big granite house. To the consternation of Edsel and Eleanor, Henry taught Billie how to shoot guns, and they would plunk away at tin cans with a .22 rifle. As part of the driving lessons, Henry took the boy out onto roads near Fair Lane, where they would drive "like a bat out of hell," according to the grandson's recollection. Once, a police officer stopped them, asking first the boy and then his grandfather for a driver's license. Neither had one, so the officer called Clara, who promised to take the matter in hand. When the two miscreants arrived home, she was waiting. "Bill, you go up to your bedroom," she said sternly. "And Henry, I want to talk to you."[20]

Henry was especially eager to have his grandchildren engage in practical, useful activities. He had drawing tables set up and made sure they were supplied with adequate paper, pencils, and crayons. He arranged for the building of a playhouse in the form of a two-room farmhouse, complete with miniature icebox, parlor stove, furniture, and sewing machine. A tiny barn sat behind, along with small-scale farm machinery, such as a miniature steam-powered threshing machine called the HEBENJOBILL after the names of the four grandchildren. Ford taught the children how to operate the machines. He also furnished a small wagon (and a small sleigh in winter) pulled by two black Shetland ponies so they could learn to drive an old-fashioned vehicle.[21]

The grandparents, especially Henry, spoiled Edsel's children. Young Henry and Benson regularly smashed up the many toy cars at Fair Lane; Dodie tore pages out of her grandmother's books and drew on them. According to Charles Voorhess, the grandchildren "had unlimited freedom" and could do whatever they liked. "There was no limit to it," he reported. Henry provided a screened-in sandbox and an elaborate tree house outfitted with Coleman lanterns, hardwood floors, stained walls, screened windows, and a stairway. On many Saturday mornings, he would take the boys to the engineering laboratory, where they engaged in much mischief. Driving a car around the interior, they would see how close they could come to the supporting columns without hitting them. Or they would take the time cards out of the rack, shuffle them up, and then replace them randomly. When anyone criticized such behavior, Henry replied, "Let them alone. They run wild when they're with me because the rest of the time they're cooped up like caged lions. They are so penned in at home by body-guards that when they are with me I want them to let loose." The grandfather may have had a point. Several kidnapping scares, along with threats from extremists during the labor wars, had deeply worried Edsel and Eleanor. Their estate in Grosse Pointe had become an armed camp, with eighteen bodyguards working twenty-four hours a day on several shifts, armed with tear-gas canisters and machine guns for an emergency. If family members ventured out for even a brief walk on the estate, guards monitored them with binoculars.[22]

The Fords' love of children, however, extended beyond their family. Both went out of their way to forge close relationships with a variety of youngsters. Henry took Dearborn boys who wanted cars to the Rouge, where they were scrapping old Model T's for the metal. Each boy would choose one of the more promising relics, and Ford would have his workmen rebuild the engines and refurbish the chassis until they looked like new. Clara was very fond of several children in the Bryant clan, especially her niece Grace Brubaker, who often accompanied her to social and community functions. Frances Bryant, another of Clara's nieces, married Irving ImOberstag, and their family became close to the Fords. Living across the Rouge River from Fair Lane, the children visited easily by crossing on stepping stones near the dam. Clara often had the oldest daughter spend the day with her, and they would have tea parties together.[23]

Children seemed to bring out Henry's playful, boyish side even in his seventies. He would gather up Dearborn kids and take them to the old Ford family homestead, where they would jump out of the barn hayloft into piles of hay, run races around the place (with Ford joining in, and often winning), and sit around crunching on apples. He took them on tours of the old house; they would gather in the parlor and sing songs around the pump organ while their host applauded. In the mid-1930s, Otto Stout, a local boy, floated down the River Rouge with a friend on a "raft" constructed of an old water heater and several other contraptions. As they came around the bend into sight of Fair Lane, an older man hailed them from the shore. At first, the boys thought they were in trouble, but, surprisingly, he only wanted a ride. When they worked their way to the shore, he asked permission to come aboard, and off they went. A short time later, the trio turned over the raft, however, and fell into the water. They made it safely to shore, soaking wet. But the elderly sailor, instead of "being angry, he just seemed excited to be a kid again," Stout recalled. Only then did the boys learn that he was Henry Ford. He took them up to the house, where Mrs. Ford helped them get some dry clothes and hot food.[24]

Henry also developed a grandfatherly relationship with Ann Hood. He first met her as a girl enrolled in the Scotch Settlement School in Greenfield Village, and she also took old-fashioned dancing lessons. Her father was Carl Hood, former principal of Dearborn High School, who now worked for Ford as head of the Edison Institute schools. The Hoods lived across the street from the Lovetts, and she became friendly with the dance instructors. Then, in the early 1930s, this vivacious and intelligent girl became a reporter and photographer for the school newspaper. As part of a story, she submitted a questionnaire to Ford about his early life, interviewed him at length, and wrote a brief biographical manuscript entitled "The Boy Henry Ford." He found her delightful. They struck up a friendship, talking and exchanging letters regularly even after she went off to college in the early 1940s. In 1934, Ford assisted Ann and her father on a trip to Europe, paying for cars, drivers, and lodging. This girl, like his own grandchildren and other youth in Dearborn, brought out many of Ford's most appealing characteristics—curiosity, high spirits, and generosity.[25]

Ford's relaxed domestic life was mirrored in his work routine. As *Fortune* observed in 1933, "He has no set program for his days, does whatever may come into his head." Not only advancing age but a significant change in his staff helped create this easing of professional burdens. Frank Campsall, Ford's private secretary, had gradually taken over many of Ernest Liebold's duties by the early 1930s, and he managed his boss's affairs quietly and efficiently. Campsall and Ford met briefly nearly every morning to discuss various activities and plans, and Ford came to rely upon his gracious, capable secretary, whom he eventually appointed to the board of directors for both the Ford Foundation and the Ford Motor Company.[26]

Though Ford had no set work schedule, he did follow a routine. After arriving at the engineering laboratory every morning, he would talk briefly with Campsall and then head next door to Greenfield Village to attend morning services in the Martha-Mary Chapel. He usually sat alone in a special place in the chapel gallery. He especially enjoyed hearing the children sing old hymns. Then he would wander about the village doing whatever he pleased—eyeing reconstruction projects, checking on the details of plans, dropping by Edward Cutler's office to look at sketches. According to Cutler, Ford always departed with a breezy "I'll see you later," and for all you knew "it might be two days or it might be ten minutes." For the rest of the day, he might check on exhibits at the Ford Museum or visit the Ford Farms to monitor ongoing agricultural experiments. Often he would drop by the chemistry labs he had established to test agricultural products, or go to a large farm near Macon, Michigan, where he had planted hundreds of acres of soybeans. He spoke with Harry Bennett on a daily basis; on rare occasions he would be driven to the Rouge to inspect the plant and consult with Charles Sorensen on production matters.[27]

Ford became renowned for avoiding his offices. He had one in the Rouge plant, but went weeks at a time without setting foot in it. Most often he used his office in the engineering laboratory, which was flanked by offices for Edsel, Liebold, Campsall, and Cameron; the entire complex served as a nerve center for the company. He dropped by daily, but seldom stayed for longer than a few minutes, to consult with Campsall or Cameron, and occasionally to chat with Edsel for a longer period of time. His office showed signs of neglect, often piled high with papers and artifacts such as old violins and children's games. But he did find one consistent use for the room. It contained a comfortable couch, and with advancing age sapping his energy, he would take a nap.[28]

Claiming that "everybody's office is my office," Ford visited his subordinates whenever he wanted to talk to them about some issue. The habit suited his nervous energy, but a larger purpose also lay behind it. Dropping by others' offices helped him manage his time more efficiently, because he could monitor matters and get more accurate information by "circulating," as he liked to call it. He trusted his own eyes and spontaneous interviews with his subordinates more than skillfully written official reports. Perhaps most important, by visiting others' offices he could avoid being trapped, either by an endless parade of supplicants winding past his door or by ambitious, talkative company executives who would tie him up for hours. By going to another's office, *he* could choose when the meeting was over. "I don't *want* an office with people coming in to see me," Ford once confessed to Charles Voorhess. "If I have a fellow come in to see me and I'm done with him, I can't kick him out. If I go to his place, and I want to get up, I can get up and get out, can't I?"[29]

The lunch roundtables at the engineering-laboratory building in Dearborn provided Ford his principal means of staying in touch with the activities of his company. Every day at 12:55 p.m., a group representing the engineering, production, and sales divisions would gather at a large round table in a private dining room. It included Edsel, Sorensen, P. E. Martin, Cameron, A. M. Wibel, Lawrence Sheldrick, W. C. Cowling, and three or four others (but not Harry Bennett). Occasionally special visitors would be invited. Ford would appear at one o'clock, shake hands with everyone, and invite them all to be seated. He usually consumed his "rabbit food" as the others, even if politely sharing Ford's fare on occasion, ate more heartily. He controlled the conversation, which often focused on company matters at some length, and he would absorb a great deal of information from the executives. He would listen and ask questions, often approving or disapproving various projects during these sessions. As a visiting journalist noted of Ford, at these daily lunches, "which may last anywhere from one to five hours, he is still 'the boss.' "[30]

Henry Ford maintained an impressive personal presence well into the Depression decade. Always well groomed and conservatively dressed, he went about in his trademark gray suits, wearing comfortable shoes that were handmade in the village and, in warm weather, a natty straw hat. He was soft-spoken and reserved in most circumstances, though giving glimpses of the nervous energy bubbling just beneath the surface. Speaking simply and directly, he treated others politely. Reporters who interviewed him in the 1930s were struck by his alert manner, youthful step, and raw energy. According to Anne O'Hare McCormick of the New York *Times*, Ford was "more nimble, physically and mentally, than most boys, and as constantly in motion as his conveyor system. . . . He is nervous, shifting from chair to chair as he talks. Sometimes he is fluent, often hesitant; he goes blank at some questions and springs to life at others, but always he seems a little fugitive, like quicksilver, and just on the point of escape." Ford seemed incapable of doing nothing. Even at his vacation homes, he had workshops with tools, nails, and lumber where he would steal away to build various projects. As Rufus Wilson summed up, "He had to be active. He just couldn't sit still."[31]

Exercise, of course, remained a critical part of Ford's daily regimen, and his physical stamina impressed everyone who came into contact with him. Even as an elderly man, he took his bicycle from the porch early each morning and rode to the back gate of the estate, then turned around and rode to the front gate, a total distance of about two miles. Cycling was better than walking, he once told a reporter, because "it keeps you one jump ahead of the mosquitoes." On many mornings, he would drop by the house of Clarence Davis, the son of old family friends who lived nearby, and the pair would go for a long walk. He also persisted in his lifelong habit of chopping wood; the Fair Lane staff would frequently glimpse him disappearing into the woods, dressed in overalls, with a large, newly sharpened ax carried over one shoulder. Even as an old man, Ford surprised more than one visitor by challenging him to a footrace. "I never in my life saw a man who could run as fast, and run fifty yards, as what Mr. Ford could do," a Fair Lane power-house engineer marveled. "He was in his seventies then."[32]

In certain aspects, Ford's personality mellowed in old age. Much of the time, and to most people, he appeared a courteous, somewhat shy older man who could be lovably eccentric. Never a big talker in private conversation, he tended to disguise his own feelings and opinions and draw other people out. "He was a good listener," acquaintances observed. He seldom used slang, or cursed beyond an occasional "damn." Nervous around women, he often seemed tongue-tied in their presence. Robert A. Smith, who worked in one of Ford's farm laboratories, was accompanied by his wife once when he met his boss. "He dropped his hat three different times while we were standing there talking," the younger man noted. Smith also commented on Ford's awkwardness when the lab hired a young woman with a college degree in chemistry. He always seemed startled by her presence, and embarrassed, but eventually came to like her and grew more comfortable.[33]

Ford's generosity grew in his old age. Employees at the Ford Farms and labs constantly received offers of help with their homes, such as putting up fencing, remodeling houses, and planting fruit trees. Irving Bacon had a serious heart attack in his fifties and spent nearly nine months in the Henry Ford Hospital. During this entire time, his boss took care to see that he was paid his usual salary. Ford gave an old house to Clarence Davis and his wife, who were expecting a child, and arranged to have it moved to a piece of land that Davis owned, where it was set on a new foundation and renovated.[34]

For all his attractive qualities, however, Ford nurtured a mean streak well into his seventies. He demanded that his wishes be followed in every province of his empire. He reacted angrily to any opposition and remained inordinately suspicious of unfamiliar people and ideas. Those who crossed him at the Ford Motor Company, or aroused mistrust in any way, found themselves dismissed by Harry Bennett. Staff members at Fair Lane discovered that if his instructions were not followed to the letter the courteous manner could evaporate and he would "chop off a head where necessary." They took great pains to keep Ford informed on even the tiniest matter, because actions taken without his knowledge aroused his "very quick temper." The powerhouse crew joked nervously that Ford "had at least a couple of personalities." At Greenfield Village, he shocked Edward Cutler by throwing a brick through a portrait of himself—he had never appreciated the likeness—that was painted on a glass panel above his door. Similarly, John McIntyre of the powerhouse crew once encountered Ford as he emerged from the woods around Fair Lane with a big ax on his shoulder.

"Hello there, Scottie, what do you think of my key?" Ford asked. When McIntyre asked what he meant, Ford replied testily, "Some of these people around here are locking up the doors on these outhouses. They think they're smart." Ford used his "key" to smash down the doors when he wanted to use the facilities.[35]

He gained a peculiar delight from keeping employees on edge. In the 1930s, he took a shine to a number of bright, capable young men at the Edison Institute, such as Wilbur Donaldson, Kenneth Petrack, and Jimmie Humberstone. Ford spent a lot of time ferrying them about among the many divisions of his enterprise, explaining and instructing. Having "built these boys up into such a state of ego that there was no living with them," according to one observer, Ford then set them loose among the company staff. His protégés strutted about attempting to give orders, and Ford feigned taking their advice, all the while laughing as experienced executives fumed. "He just did it to get the older men's goats," Lawrence Sheldrick concluded. On another occasion, two middle managers, one of whom worked at Greenfield Village and the other at the Henry Ford Museum, were bickering, and Ford chose to settle the matter in typical fashion. Secretly, he told each man to fire the other one, and then sat back laughing, along with a couple of confidants, as the two shouted and sputtered, neither agreeing to leave the premises.[36]

Ford's impish sense of humor remained constant, however, amid the benevolent gestures and mean-spirited outbursts. One day, Ford's barber, Joseph Zaroski, was at Fair Lane preparing to give his patron a haircut and shave, when Mrs. Ford stopped by. She commented that it seemed cold and brought her husband a sweater. Still unsatisfied, Clara then went in search of a blanket to cover his feet. Ford chuckled and said to Zaroski, "Well, I believe before you shave me I'm going to have a fur coat on." He continued to be fond of practical jokes and pranks in old age. Mrs. Stanley Ruddiman, whose gentility could shade into pomposity, was a favorite target for his teasing. She once wore to one of the old-fashioned dances a "very giddy spring hat," which she placed on a window ledge. When she retrieved it at the end of the evening, she was startled to see atop it a hand-lettered sign saying "For Sale." Ford had placed it there. Another time, she was having dinner with a friend when the waiter handed her a card that said, "The next dance is a waltz." She looked up as the orchestra started to play, and from across the room Ford, who had come in for dinner with Clara, winked at her. His joking also extended to his famous friends. When Will Rogers came visiting, Ford plotted with his driver to pull a scam. After bragging about his keen eyesight, he had the driver take out a penny, hold it out some distance away, and ask Rogers to identify the date on the coin. He could not do it. Then Ford, who had seen it beforehand, peered at the coin and said, "Yes, 1913 — is that right?" The driver nodded affirmatively as Rogers stared in amazement.[37]

Ford particularly liked to play tricks on his staff. One evening, he dropped by the powerhouse to talk to John McIntyre, and then left as the engineer started stoking the boilers in preparation for the night shift. With the fire roaring and the drafts opened, McIntyre became mystified when the steam pressure first failed to rise and then began dropping. After checking everything at the boilers, he inspected the pipes, only to discover that the big six-inch relief valve was wide open and all the steam pressure was flying out. "The old son-of-a-gun had opened the valve!" McIntyre exclaimed. When Ford came by a few days later, he told the powerhouse crew, "I gave Scottie a little bit of fun that night." Rufus Wilson also endured a prank when Ford visited the agricultural lab and went for a walk in the woods. A rainstorm sent Wilson to collect his boss, but Ford came back by a different route and decided to hide from his driver. The lab staff played along and said they had not seen Ford, all the while exclaiming, "He lost the boss!" About half an hour later, Ford appeared amid great merriment and relieved Wilson of his anxiety.[38]

Many who encountered Ford during the 1930s were struck by his delight in the company of ordinary people. When John McIntyre started working at Fair Lane, Ford sat down with him one day and remarked that he "liked to know the history of a man." In a couple of long conversations, he asked about McIntyre's upbringing and work history, and was especially interested to hear about his background in the coal mines around Pittsburgh. Ford's lack of pretension also surfaced in constant attempts to evade the staff at Fair Lane, who tried to keep track of him at all times after his 1927 car accident. He hated this attention and tried to escape. He had several maneuvers—crouching down on the passenger side of trucks leaving Fair Lane, hiding behind shrubs until the guards weren't looking, taking back ways off the estate and walking far around through the fields and woods. When he disappeared, the phones would start ringing with "Has anybody seen Mr. Ford?" As one of the staff observed, "You'd probably find him sitting along some old rail fence somewhere talking to some old farmer, just enjoying himself."[39]

Ford's unconventional notions about health and spirituality continued to play an important part in his life. He performed daily "eye exercises" to improve his vision, holding his eyes in cold water and moving them about, determinedly looking into the distance as far as he could for a period of time, moving his sight lines to the right and then the left, over and over. He was full of peculiar medical advice, telling friends that chronic colds could be cured by eating buckwheat pancakes, cold sores would disappear if the victim stopped eating eggs, and drinking too much coffee would cause deterioration in the strength of the fingernails. As for religion, Ford leavened his frequent attendance at the Martha-Mary Chapel with a continued belief in reincarnation. Robert A. Smith was surprised to hear his boss's views. During a casual conversation, Ford, who was relaxing with his feet up on a table, suddenly announced that he had been killed in the Civil War. "I guess I looked kind of startled," Smith remembered, so his boss "went on to explain that he had hunches that he was an engineer in the Union Army. And was killed in the Battle of Gettysburg." Ford later brought Smith a couple of books on reincarnation.[40]

For all his private preoccupations, Ford did not abandon his public career in the 1930s. He merely changed directions. His interests broadened, as he threw himself into numerous projects that engaged his public spiritedness. Ever restless and alert to new ideas, he initiated several educational endeavors that he hoped would improve the lot of average Americans in the same way that the Model T had done twenty years before.

Twenty-four

Educator

In 1930, Americans became aware of a new side of the nation's premier maker of automobiles. "Henry Ford will devote the remainder of his life to education, and in developing his ideas will spend perhaps $100,000,000," the New York *Times* announced. "Henry Ford has definitely begun the execution of a plan of education which has been forming in his mind for many years," added the *Ladies' Home Journal*. "It is his largest life work and he hopes it will be his most enduring contribution to the world."[1]

These stories explained how Ford planned to build throughout the country schools where one million youngsters could gain practical experience in a trade as well as book learning. Although the numbers proved to be hyperbolic, within a few years Ford had founded or funded educational projects that pursued his vision of practical education. His social idealism overflowed into other channels as well: crop experiments, tractor development, and community renovation. Stepping away from his earlier, wholehearted dedication to providing a sturdy automobile for the masses, Ford increasingly turned his attention to developing other kinds of vehicles for improving American life.

By 1930, Ford had become devoted to the reform of education. Convinced that it had been separated from real life, he agitated for change in numerous newspaper and magazine articles. "We have thought of getting an education and earning a living as two different kinds of activity, but they should not be very different from each other," he told *Good Housekeeping* in 1934. "While a child is acquiring an education he should be doing things that are close kin to the things he will have to do while he is earning a living. . . . Learn to do by doing—that's my favorite principle in education."[2]

In part, this emphasis on practical education stemmed from Ford's suspicions about book learning. In the 1920s, he had described reading as a "dope sickness" in modern life and insisted that real wisdom lay not in paper abstractions but in areas where people had to find real solutions to real problems. "I could never get much from books," he claimed in 1931. "When you have to solve a problem that nobody has yet thought about, how can you learn the solution from a book?"[3]

Ford pursued two goals in his pedagogy. First, he sought to tailor instruction to the needs of children rather than adults. "Children are our only real assets," Ford observed in *Nation's Schools*. "Nothing else is worth much, and all of our thinking, planning, and working are simply means for making our world a better place in which our children may live and work." He believed that instruction should augment children's natural eagerness to acquire knowledge about the world around them. "It isn't really necessary to teach children," he insisted in 1938. "All you need to do is let them learn. They're trying to learn all the time." This orientation led to Ford's second goal—the creation of productive, self-supporting citizens who could create and enjoy prosperity. A proper education would not just prepare brilliant students for college but train a body of well-informed citizens who could get good jobs and, in his words, "defeat poverty by providing plenty."[4]

As with so many other aspects of his worldview, Ford's notion of proper education was a curious combination of the modern and the old-fashioned. He embraced a model propounded by progressive educators, which held that learning was best achieved through hands-on activities, projects, and a child-centered curriculum. He also promoted the vocational training advocated by many educational efficiency experts. But in some ways, Ford supported a traditionalist, even reactionary model, whereby students met in one-room schoolhouses, recited from primers, and had older children tutoring younger ones. This potpourri of approaches betrayed his lack of pedagogical sophistication, but also revealed loyalties that were divided between tradition and innovation. He was willing to use new means (up-to-date curriculum and industrial training) to create traditional habits (the work ethic and character formation) to inspire modern success (efficiency and consumer prosperity). Ford's template for education reform was part John Dewey, part William H. McGuffey, and part Frederick Winslow Taylor.[5]

His ideas bore a variety of educational fruit. As early as 1916, he had started the Henry Ford Trade School at the Highland Park facility. Under the direction of Frederick E. Searle, it taught boys history, English, and chemistry while also training them in the mechanical arts, such as tool-and-die making. They were paid wages for the shop work; after graduation many of them joined Ford and some took jobs with other companies. By 1928, the school's enrollment stood at about two thousand. In 1931, it moved to the River Rouge plant, where it remained open until 1952.[6]

Henry Ford's interest in this practical-minded academy was genuine. When he found out that hundreds of students were waiting to get in, he boosted funding to raise enrollment. He believed that such trade schools provided a bracing dose of the real world to an ordinary curriculum sunk in theory and abstraction. As he described in a 1930 article, his school was one "in which academic training and industrial instruction go hand in hand." When a representative from Yale University approached Searle to ask if twenty theological students could come to the school for summer training, Searle took the gentleman to Ford, who asked the reason for the request. The Yale official said, "Well, when they get up in the pulpit and on the platform, after they've been in the shop they won't tell so many damned lies about industry!" Ford grinned and exclaimed, "Bring fifty of them!"[7]

He launched another educational project with the Edison Institute schools in Greenfield Village, seven of which he started between 1929 and 1943. Dedicated to instructing students from first grade through high school, they met in old buildings in the village, such as the Scotch Settlement School and the McGuffey House, and featured small classes, individual instruction, and a strong measure of practical projects and field trips. All students were expected to attend nonsectarian religious services every morning in the Martha-Mary Chapel. The Edison Institute High School (or Institute of Technology, as it was sometimes called) had its own building next to the Ford Museum with classrooms, laboratories, a library, and an auditorium.[8]

As with his trade school, Henry Ford took a personal interest in the Greenfield Village schools. Sitting in on classes and taking the children on excursions, he became known for his lax attitudes toward discipline. When children threw rocks through the windows of buildings, they were not punished. In fact, Ford delighted in one of their pranks. Creative students discovered that hard, smooth soybeans were the perfect ammunition for pea-shooters. As the children turned classrooms into pea-shooter battlefields, teachers cracked down and forbade the weapons. Ford, however, seemed as excited as the children, and mischievously brought bags of soybeans for the skirmishes.[9]

His success with the Edison schools prompted him to extend the project into the Michigan hinterland. In the 1930s, he began paying large subsidies to some fifteen school districts lying within a hundred-mile radius of Dearborn, in the rural, southeastern section of the state, where he owned great chunks of land. He also supported two schools in Michigan's Upper

Peninsula, as well as a trio of "Wayside Inn Schools" in Sudbury, Massachusetts. All of these institutions were modeled on the Edison Institute schools.[10]

The educational institution that earned Ford's greatest financial support, however, lay in the Georgia countryside, some fifty miles northwest of Atlanta. The Berry School, founded by Martha McChesney Berry in 1902, sought to bring college education to the people of the Southern backcountry. Its curriculum combined academic instruction with work programs in which poor students from rural areas filled jobs around the campus in farming, construction, cooking, and upkeep, both to learn skills and to support the institution. This "self-help college," with its emphasis on productive work and character formation, appealed greatly to Ford.

Berry and the Fords became acquainted in the early 1920s, and in 1923 Henry and Clara visited the campus. They were impressed by the young men's farming and carpentry and the young women's cooking and sewing. During a lunch that was cooked and served by female students in their log-cabin dining hall, Ford agreed with Berry that education must teach the hands as well as the mind, and expressed his admiration for the fact that the students of the school made everything on the campus, from buildings to roads to meals and clothing. At the end of the meal, the Fords volunteered to buy a new stove for the school and to rebuild its kitchen. These modest contributions presaged a flood of money over the next quarter-century. The Fords funded the construction of a dining hall and a dormitory; Henry purchased a dilapidated brick plant and modernized it to provide work for Berry students as well as steady income for the school. With the construction of the Ford Quadrangle, a beautiful campus of Gothic buildings, including classrooms, dormitories, a recreation hall, offices, and a chapel, the Fords contributed some $5 million to the Berry School.

From the mid-1920s to the mid-1940s, the Fords visited Berry once a year for a stay of several days. They would tour the grounds, inspect ongoing projects, meet with the students and staff, and enjoy the quiet rural atmosphere. Henry particularly loved the natural beauty of the surrounding countryside. While Clara observed the girls in their weaving, sewing, and dyeing of cloth, he would visit the students working in the fields and workshops, nose about the community, talk to old farmers, and hike in the local mountains. Ford felt so comfortable at the Berry School that he even overcame his aversion to public speaking. During one visit, Martha Berry asked him to come to the platform during a chapel meeting and say a few words to the students. Grimacing, he muttered, "Well, I suppose if she sent for me, I must go." Once at the podium, Ford began, "I've never made a speech in public, but it's very difficult to turn Miss Berry down. If I were going to speak, I think it would be easier to talk here than anywhere else." He then presented a short, heartfelt talk that affirmed his belief in training hands as well as minds. "As I look about the place, I know that all the money in the world wouldn't build a school like this," he concluded. "It takes a great deal more than money." Ford maintained a great admiration for Berry and her efforts. At her funeral in 1942, he looked at her grave and commented to several mourners, "Here rests the greatest teacher since the time of Christ, *the* Teacher."[11]

Ford's enthusiasm about educational reform was matched by his passion for research into new applications for that unfamiliar agricultural crop, the soybean. This plant had been known in China for thousands of years but, although introduced in the early twentieth century, had achieved little popularity in the United States. Around the beginning of the Depression decade, Ford began investing in research involving the soybean—planting and harvesting many varieties, and exploring its uses for food, oil, meal, fertilizer, and industrial applications. Like the village industries, this was part of his larger crusade to modernize the American farm and link it to industrial processes. Ford viewed soybeans as a commodity that could revive rural America and provide new products to enhance the lives of all consumers. As *Fortune* noted in late 1933, he "is as much interested in the soya bean as he is in the V-8."[12]

In 1929, Ford had established an agricultural laboratory in Greenfield Village to explore the new field of "chemurgy"—the uses of chemistry and other sciences to enhance agricultural production. He appointed Robert Boyer, a young, self-trained chemist, to manage the facility and its staff of a dozen young men from the Henry Ford Trade School. They experimented with a variety of vegetables and legumes to discover the possibilities of various plant material. Ford and Boyer would brainstorm about different possibilities, and the next morning a truckload of carrots or tomatoes would be dumped in front of the lab for processing. They examined nearly every vegetable imaginable. Ford even suggested that they try hemp, not realizing that this was another name for marijuana and one needed a special license to grow it. Once he had pulled some strings, a hundred pounds of the illegal seed arrived at Dearborn, along with a license. With seven acres of marijuana plants sprouting behind the Moir House in Greenfield Village, an hourly patrol made sure that people stayed out of the field. When Ford suggested looking at soybeans, Boyer's staff discovered that the bean had little water, high oil content, and made a high-protein meal after the oil was extracted.[13]

Ford ordered the planting of some three hundred varieties of soybeans on eight thousand acres on his farms. His chemists, after years of experimentation, made steady progress on two fronts: industrial and nutritional uses. Ford began informing the public about the soybean's potential. It had great market appeal because of its many uses—oil, food for humans and animals, fiber for cloth, and plastics. "Some day chairs, desks, doors, and other things now made of wood will be made from soy beans or similar materials," he predicted. This was only the beginning. Research would show that "many of the raw materials of industry which are today stripped from the forests and mines can be obtained from annual crops grown on farms."[14]

By the late 1930s, uses for the soybean in the Ford automobile had emerged. Soybean oil, when mixed with sand, made an effective coating in foundry molds for metal casting. The oil proved useful in producing a tough, easily applied enamel for finishing Ford automobiles. The meal residue provided the basic stuff for making plastic, which found its way into the manufacturing of gearshift knobs, dash controls, door handles, window trim, accelerator pedals, and horn buttons on Ford's line of cars. Most dramatically, however, Boyer's chemists discovered that it could be made into thick, hard sheets of plastic which could be molded into automobile bodies. Prototypes were made of parts such as trunk lids.[15]

Soybeans' potential as a food product also drew Ford's attention. He set up another lab to investigate this angle, under the direction of Dr. Edsel Ruddiman, his boyhood chum, who had been head of the school of pharmacy at Vanderbilt University. Ruddiman experimented with the food possibilities of this legume, as did Robert Smith, who worked at another small laboratory at the Ford Farms. These scientists discovered that soybean meal was 50 percent protein and 95 percent digestible, thus making it an ideal feed supplement for livestock. Things were more complicated for humans, however: soybean meal had an unpalatable taste, and soybean oil turned rancid quickly. Ruddiman developed a soybean biscuit that some managed to choke down, although one of Ford's associates described it as "the most vile thing ever put in human mouths." With varying degrees of success, experimenters flavored and shaped soybean meal to create cheese, croquettes, bread, butter, simulated meats, cookies, and ice cream. At Ford's insistence, Smith and Ruddiman even developed a form of milk. "We've gotten rid of the horse, now we've got to get rid of the cow," he liked to say. His researchers developed a "soy milk" that pleased Ford, though others found the taste unpleasant.[16]

As the Depression decade wore on, Ford mounted several public displays of advances in soybean utilization. At the Chicago World's Fair in 1934, he exhibited machinery for processing the legume into oil and meal. The following year, he funded and distributed a film entitled *Farm of the Future*, which explained the importance of connecting farm commodities to manufacturing in the modern world. In May 1935, Ford sponsored the first chemurgy conference ever held in the United States. Over three hundred prominent manufacturers, farmers, scientists, and businessmen met at the Dearborn Inn to discuss industrial uses of agricultural products. They founded the National Farm Chemurgic Council and, in the replica of Independence Hall at the Ford Museum, signed a document entitled "Declaration of Dependence upon the Soil and of the Rights of Self-Maintenance."[17]

Ford used his personal flair for publicity to promote this crusade. He wore ties made from soybean fibers and, in 1941, appeared in a suit fashioned completely from such material. Before the press, he jumped up and down on the sheets of soybean plastic developed by the Ford Motor Company, noting that "had that been sheet metal it would have been all bent out of shape." A bit later, when a plastic trunk lid had been installed on one of Ford's cars, he held a press conference. Grabbing an ax, he took a terrific swing at the plastic lid, and it bounced off, causing no dents or breaks in the surface (the ax's sharp edge had been blunted with a rubber boot). A beaming Ford told reporters that plastic-bodied cars would soon be quite common. "I wouldn't be surprised if our [soybean] laboratory comes to be the most important building in our entire plant," he declared. In August 1941, at a festival in Dearborn, Ford proudly unveiled a car with a body made completely of plastic.[18]

His deep interest in agricultural experiments led him into a cherished friendship with George Washington Carver. He first made the acquaintance of the African American plant scientist in 1937, at the annual chemurgical conference in Dearborn, where Carver had been invited to speak. Over the previous three decades, Carver had significantly enhanced Southern agriculture through his work at the Tuskegee Institute, where he developed hundreds of uses for crops such as the peanut and the sweet potato. Ford met with Carver in his suite at the Dearborn Inn, and the two struck up an instant friendship. Over the next six years, they exchanged many letters and visits; Ford toured Tuskegee to observe the agricultural experiments, and Carver went to both Dearborn and the Fords' winter home in coastal Georgia. Carver invited Ford to become a trustee of his foundation, and Ford built a replica of Carver's birthplace in Greenfield Village. The two men agreed that plants, for both nutritional and manufacturing possibilities, provided many solutions to human problems. Unlike just about everyone else, Ford enjoyed Carver's "weed sandwiches" and other vegetarian delights. Upon the scientist's death in 1943, Ford told *Fortune* magazine, "I have never known a man who knew so much about everything." In private conversation, he paid an even greater tribute. When an employee noted that Edison, in his view, was one of the greatest men who had ever lived, Ford replied, "I don't know. He was a great man, all right, but I think that Carver was really a greater man than Edison was."[19]

Tractor manufacturing provided a final Ford venture during the 1930s. Long interested in developing a sturdy, inexpensive tractor to lighten the workload of the American farmer, Ford had started a separate company, Henry Ford & Son, to manufacture the Fordson tractor in the 1910s. It enjoyed limited success with small, steady production quotas until manufacturing was transferred to Ireland, and then England, in the late 1920s. Around 1937, however, Ford's interest revived, and he declared publicly, "What the country needs right now is a good tractor that will sell for around two hundred and fifty dollars." Working with engineers such as Howard Simpson and Karl Schultz, Ford financed and then dropped two different models. Then Harry Ferguson, an Irish entrepreneur, approached him about a collaboration. Ferguson had developed two significant mechanisms—a linkage system by which implements could be directly attached to the tractor rather than pulled on wheels, and a hydraulic system by which the operator could raise and lower implements to control plowing and cultivation depth. After a demonstration at Dearborn in October 1938, Ford embraced this new technology. He put up money for development and tooling, and his engineers worked with Ferguson's team to create the Ford-Ferguson tractor. It went into production in the fall of 1939.[20]

Ford knew that farming had declined since the turn of the century, and the Depression had devastated the agricultural economy. He wanted to help farmers produce at a profit and improve the quality of their life. "In too many cases, farming has not only ceased to be profitable; it has also ceased to be interesting," he wrote in a publicity pamphlet for the new tractor. He and Ferguson believed that "farming can be made profitable, without increasing the cost of farm products to the consumer." Between 1939 and 1941, the Ford-Ferguson tractor captured 20 percent of the market and moved into second place, behind International Harvester. Even though the Ford Motor Company sold the tractors at a loss for many years, Henry Ford insisted on producing the machines for the benefit of farmers.[21]

Ford's educational and agricultural projects shared a common emphasis on practicality, useful achievement, and bettering the life of ordinary Americans. These same principles informed a significant development in his private life—the creation of a winter residence on Georgia's coast that involved not only a new private home but several endeavors to improve the life of local residents. As noted earlier, in the 1920s, Henry and Clara had first become acquainted with the area around Ways Station, Georgia, when traveling by train. Passing through Savannah on their trips to Florida, they were impressed by the natural beauty of the surrounding area. Ford began purchasing land in 1925 and eventually accumulated about seventy thousand acres, including several old plantations in Bryan County, about twenty miles south of Savannah.[22]

As the site for their new home, the Fords chose a lovely spot on the Ogeechee River that had been graced by an old plantation house in the antebellum era. They consulted with architects to draw up plans and bought The Hermitage, a dilapidated old mansion in Savannah that had been built of the famous "Savannah Gray Brick," which was no longer being manufactured. Workmen dismantled the old wreck of a building, cleaned each brick by hand, and transferred the lot to the new site. By 1936, a large, gracious structure had been completed. Built on a model of traditional plantation homes, it featured two-story pillars in the front along with a spacious veranda looking out on the river. Most of the furnishings came from the abundant holdings of the Henry Ford Museum. Henry outfitted an old rice mill with a restored steam engine, and this new powerhouse provided electricity, heat, and water to the residence. The Fords named their new home Richmond Hill.[23]

Starting in 1936, the Fords made a yearly pilgrimage to Richmond Hill sometime between January and March to spend several weeks. They enjoyed the warm weather and beautiful scenery far from the frozen fields and cold of Michigan winters. Clara would walk through the grounds, read, and entertain friends from Savannah; Henry toured the countryside, talking to farmers, inspecting old machinery, and monitoring a variety of projects. In this natural bird preserve, the couple frequently indulged in their hobby of bird-watching. They also entertained themselves and others in the community by hosting dancing parties. They usually imported Benjamin Lovett and the Dearborn orchestra for a series of dances held on the front lawn of Richmond Hill. Under the large trees facing the beautiful vista of the river, dozens of couples, including many pupils from the local school, danced waltzes and quadrilles.[24]

Ford saw his new Georgia residence as a base from which to launch several social projects to improve life in the area. Bryan County, like much of the rural area, was economically depressed, with a significant proportion of the population suffering from poverty and disease. Ford acted to help remedy the situation. After discovering that large bodies of standing water in the area bred mosquitoes and spread malaria throughout the community, he commenced an extensive drainage project. Earthmoving machines created a network of canals and drainage ditches through some seventy-five thousand acres. When the swampy ground had been drained sufficiently, roads were built into areas that had previously been inaccessible.[25]

At the same time, Ford moved to combat several diseases that were endemic among the poor citizenry. Malaria fever, which infected nearly 100 percent of the population, stood at the top of the list. He contacted the Georgia State Board of Health and the Winthrop Chemical Company, which manufactured atabrine, an antimalarial medication, to help plan a program. Twenty-one nurses were hired to visit each home in the community, examine residents, and dispense atabrine tablets to adults and quinine to children. Hookworms also were widespread, and victims of this malady received treatment. Through educational information and medication, rampant problems with syphilis, typhoid fever, and tuberculosis were also checked. John F. Gregory, Ford's superintendent at Richmond Hill, supervised much of this activity. Ford eventually funded a central facility in the county, the Ways Station Health Clinic, headed by Mrs. Constance Clark and Mrs. Sam Read, two local health workers. A pair of doctors from Savannah, C. F Holton and John Sharpley, visited the facility once a week to treat serious cases.[26]

On the educational front, Ford activated some of his pet pedagogical theories. Soon after arriving in Bryan County, he established the Ford Industrial Arts and Trade School to teach mechanics, drafting, wood- and metalworking, welding, printing, and furniture-making to local boys. In the spring of 1937, he assumed a major role in financing the local school district and embarked upon a program of construction and curricular development. He added science laboratories, dining rooms, and playgrounds to several schools, and provided bus transportation for students in outlying areas. He also encouraged the development of new classes and activities, such as a school newspaper, theater, gardening, home economics, photography, and music. To help solidify these advances, he provided a monthly salary supplement to each teacher, which made them among the best-paid in the state, and provided summer jobs to guarantee a respectable income. In addition, Ford constructed a small apartment complex for teachers only a block from the school, and a home for the principal adjacent to it.[27]

Ford supplemented these health and education endeavors with several community-service projects. In 1937, he built a Martha-Mary Chapel, which, like five other such structures in Michigan and Massachusetts, was modeled on the original in Greenfield Village. Standing near the school in Ways Station, it held a nondenominational service every morning for students as well as regular Sunday services and Sunday school. Ford funded construction of a large community house, which became the cultural and social center of the area. He also financed the building of an icehouse, a post office, a vehicle maintenance garage, a bakery, and a firehouse with a modern fire truck and ambulance.[28]

To revive depressed economic conditions in Bryan County, Ford undertook several agricultural projects. In 1937, he established a laboratory to investigate new uses for Southern crops, while starting a farming operation at Richmond Hill that eventually put some three thousand acres under cultivation. Ford's crews reclaimed hundreds of acres of old rice fields and engaged in the truck farming of vegetables, especially corn, sweet potatoes, and lettuce. Harry G. Ukkelberg, who had a degree in agriculture from the University of Minnesota, managed both the farming operation and the research laboratory. He oversaw the growing of crops such as the perilla plant, soybeans, castor beans, and tung trees. Ukkelberg and his assistants extracted starch from sweet potatoes and water chestnuts, and alcohol from several plants, which was blended with gasoline to fuel cars and tractors at Richmond Hill. The lab spent much time producing experimental plastics and rayon from natural products such as wood pulp, sawdust, and corncobs.[29]

Perhaps most important in economic terms, Ford rehabilitated a local sawmill and made it the most thriving industry in Bryan County. It provided jobs for area residents, many of whom were chronically unemployed. "We want to give them all work until this depression is over, and teach them how to work," Ford told a Richmond Hill supervisor. His acreage contained substantial growth of pine, hardwood, gum, and cypress trees that were harvested for lumber, railroad ties, and pulp. With the installation of large steam boilers and engines and the enlargement of the building, the mill began to produce lumber commercially. Ford took great personal interest in the facility and visited it every day when he was in residence. Typically, he was especially concerned with the efficiency and cleanliness of its operation. He determined how many board feet of lumber grew daily on his property, and set a quota for daily lumber production precisely at that amount. By 1940, approximately 670 workers were on the payroll at Richmond Hill, primarily working in the sawmill and farms. Ford eventually built some 235 houses for these employees and their families, to whom he charged no rent.[30]

Ford's many endeavors at Richmond Hill displayed a striking feature— the enlightened treatment of African Americans. Soon after arriving in Georgia, he made it known that anyone who was willing to work, regardless of race, would enjoy fair treatment and opportunity. He offered jobs to local black citizens at the sawmill and on the farms; by 1940, Richmond Hill employed 351 white workers and 320 African Americans. Although he never directly challenged educational segregation in the South, he made special efforts to improve the local schools for black children. He replaced seven small, ramshackle buildings throughout the county with a new school building and hired an African American principal, H. G. Cooper, to run it. Like Ford's other schools, it supplemented traditional academics with practical instruction in modern farming and the manual arts. On March 15, 1940, this modern institution was dedicated as the George Washington Carver School, and the scientist from Tuskegee participated in the ceremony. With tears running down his cheeks, he told listeners that it was one of the greatest days of his life. During Carver's stay, Ford also arranged to bring the former slave to a formal tea in Savannah, an occasion described by a contemporary magazine as "a landmark in the racial relations of the South."[31]

A genuine concern for African American progress lay behind Ford's actions. He frequently asked locals about the impact of the new black school and appeared excited at reports of improvement. "They seem to want better things, fix up their houses better, and so on. They've got more pride," Ford once commented to a Richmond Hill employee about African Americans. He stressed work as an endeavor to promote harmony and understanding between the races. Though blacks and whites remained separated in their churches and schools, it was a different story in the workplace at Richmond Hill. "Come to work, and the colored man works at one end of the log and the white man at the other," Ford said. "They work together just like brothers." Henry demonstrated a personal concern in many ways. Janie Lewis, an elderly black lady known locally as "Old Aunt Jane," had been born a slave and still lived in a decrepit shack near Richmond Hill. Henry and Clara built a modern home for her and provided food, clothing, and medical care for the rest of her life. One time, Ford visited a tough section of Savannah while Clara was inspecting a nursery school in which she was interested. He got out of the car and introduced himself to several young black men standing on the corner. The police arrived shortly thereafter to rescue the visitor, only to find him earnestly discussing the virtues of work with his new friends. When Clara finished her tour, according to the driver, Henry "shook hands with every colored person that was around there. There must have been fifteen or twenty of them. Those fellows were in their glory. The policemen were standing there laughing, much as to say, 'What a man!' "[32]

In fact, Ford's actions in Georgia reflected his longtime devotion to racial progress in Detroit. In the late 1880s, he had worked with William Perry, an African American acquaintance, manning a two-man crosscut saw to harvest lumber on his land in Dearborn. Ford later hired Perry to work at his company, where he stayed on the payroll until his death in 1940. In the

1910s, Ford expressed particular interest in getting African Americans into the Henry Ford Trade School. When he dropped by and saw young black men in the classes, Ford "stepped right up among them, shook hands with some of them, and said, 'I'm glad to see *these* fellows!' " By the late 1910s, black workers were being hired into a wide variety of jobs at the Ford Motor Company, including skilled machinist and white-collar positions. Ford contacted prominent black ministers to funnel dependable, hardworking members of their congregations into the company, and by 1929, its percentage of African American workers was greater than the percentage of blacks in the Detroit population. The Ford Motor Company became the largest employer of African Americans in the city, and they responded with fervent support. Black workers were the industrialist's staunchest allies during his struggle with striking CIO members throughout the 1930s.[33]

Ford's love for Richmond Hill gave it a special place in his heart. He loved his annual visits. "It seemed like when he came down here, he was like a boy out of school. They were holidays," noted one of the sawmill managers. "He'd come down here and relax and enjoy himself." While Clara enjoyed the beautiful flowers and foliage of the Southern climate or entertained friends, her husband prowled his vast acreage to check on the many projects under way. He would visit with the farmhands who were "chiseling out a post or putting up a fence. He'd take the mallet and chisel, and sit there and talk to the man, and he'd work there the whole afternoon. He could handle *any* tool." Or he would drop by to inspect the labors of carpenters "when they were building different houses. He'd take one man's saw out of his hand and stand there and talk to the man and saw that line. He could saw a line." Ford visited the sawmill daily, monitoring the lumber being cut, sharing stories with the workers, and listening to the engines to make sure the valves were in perfect adjustment.[34]

He displayed his democratic spirit at Richmond Hill, easily interacting with the laborers and sharing his interest in their work. Sometimes the consequences proved quite funny. One rainy day, John H. Tienken, a farmworker, was out in the field, unable to start a Fordson tractor to get it back to the barn. He was cussing enthusiastically when an older man wearing a straw hat and a pair of overalls came across the field and asked if he was having a problem. "Yeah, I sure as hell am," Tienken exploded. "I wish old Mr. Henry Ford had this damn Fordson shoved up his backside. I've been down here an hour in this rain." The stranger tinkered under the hood for a few minutes, and the tractor started. When Tienken came to work the next day, he saw the old gentleman standing around, and another worker identified him as Ford. Tienken muttered, "Oh my God," expecting to be fired. But

Ford spoke pleasantly, never mentioning the earlier incident, and Tienken remained in his employ for many years.[35]

On October 7, 1934, the *Ford Sunday Evening Hour* was broadcast for the first time on the full CBS radio network of eighty-six stations. As the show beamed out from Detroit's Orchestra Hall, which was filled to its capacity of two thousand seats, Edsel Ford performed the introductions on behalf of himself and his father. Edsel's wife, Eleanor, was in attendance, as were Henry and Clara, who sat in their special box, set above and to the left of the stage. The Detroit Symphony Orchestra followed with several short pieces by Wagner, Bach, Sibelius, and Mendelssohn, along with the traditional American songs "Uncle Remus" and "To a Wild Rose." Maria Jeritza, a soprano formerly with the Metropolitan Opera, performed selections composed by Tchaikovsky, Joyce, Grieg, and Romberg.

Perhaps the most unusual feature of the program, however, came during its six-minute intermission, when a portly, bespectacled gentleman with long gray hair and an earnest manner approached the microphone. In a rich, folksy voice "reminiscent of an earnest village parson," according to one description, he explained that each installment of the *Ford Sunday Evening Hour* would feature a brief talk on a public issue instead of advertising messages. In these commentaries, he noted, "we shall sometimes have to sound the personal note . . . about Mr. Ford and what he stands for." The speaker concluded with a promise "to make, if possible, a modest contribution to straight thinking and common sense," as Henry Ford nodded his approval from the box.[36]

For the next eight years, this promise would be kept, as the commentator, William J. Cameron, delivered hundreds of talks on history, morality and values, economics, government, and the lives of great Americans, distilling the philosophy of his boss and broadcasting it throughout the nation. This radio engagement constituted the final and most influential chapter in Cameron's lengthy career with Ford and his organization. Throughout the 1930s, it allowed this eloquent lay preacher to fulfill completely the role that he had played since the early 1920s: "Mr. Ford's representative to the outside world."[37]

Always intrigued by new technologies, Ford had toyed with radio throughout his career, but made a serious move into the field only in the 1930s. He sponsored a successful musical variety show featuring Fred Waring and the Pennsylvanians that ran from 1934 to 1937, as well as several high-profile sporting events such as the World Series. His most sustained and popular radio venture, however, was the *Ford Sunday Evening Hour.* With this show he sought to use radio's capabilities to share his love of music with a popular audience, advertise his company, and keep his views before the public. No one better served this latter purpose than the former newspaper editor who had worked closely with Ford for nearly twenty years.[38]

William J. Cameron had prepared long and well for his radio sojourn. Born in 1878 in Hamilton, Ontario, Cameron had grown up in Detroit and attended public schools there. After taking several college courses, he worked as a timekeeper for the Michigan Central Railroad and did some lay preaching in several small Michigan towns. In 1904, he found a position with the Detroit *News* as a reporter and staff writer, and took odd jobs as a public speaker. He rose steadily through the ranks of the newspaper to become one of its most valued journalists, eventually writing a column entitled "Reflections." In 1918, he followed the editor of the paper, Edwin G. Pipp, to the Dearborn *Independent.* Serving as a writer and reporter, he took over as editor following Pipp's resignation. Throughout the 1920s, Cameron penned hundreds of essays for "Mr. Ford's Own Page," in which he demonstrated a knack for conveying his boss's thoughts on a host of issues.[39]

Cameron emerged as a key figure in the anti-Semitic controversy that engulfed the *Independent* in 1927. Because he was editor of the newspaper, his testimony was crucial for determining the depth and nature of Ford's views on the Jews as well as his culpability in slandering Aaron Sapiro. Cameron absolved his boss of responsibility and took the rap. He insisted that Ford did not see advance copies of the newspaper articles and shouldered all blame for their content himself. Following the settlement of the lawsuit, Ford remained forever grateful for this act of loyalty.

Like Ford's, Cameron's ideological position had a strong populist streak. The rhetoric of "the people" suffused his writing, and he idealized American small-town life, maintaining the view that Protestants were socially and morally superior. Cameron denounced bankers, stockholders, and financial speculators for their greed and nonproductivity throughout his career. Once again like his patron, Cameron had a worldview infected by anti-Semitism, associating Jews with financial corruption and urban manipulation. In his case, however, the position was entangled with a curious set of religious ideas. Cameron was a disciple of the British-Israelite movement and headed an affiliate group in the United States called the Anglo-Saxon Federation. This sect believed that Anglo-Saxons were direct descendants of the lost tribes of Israel, and modern Jews were descended from other groups in Judea. Like other British Israelites, Cameron portrayed Anglo-

Saxon Christians and Jews as adversaries, the former being "true children of Israel" and the latter claiming a false birthright. This viewpoint influenced the anti-Semitic essays he wrote for Ford in the Dearborn *Independent* and led Cameron's Anglo-Saxon Federation to peddle pamphlet versions of *The Protocols of the Learned Elders of Zion*.[40]

After the debacle of the collapse of the *Independent*, Cameron took on a new role. He became the house intellectual and wordsmith for the Ford organization, where he kept busy composing greetings, remarks, and introductions for Henry and Edsel, writing press releases, and ghostwriting articles that appeared under Henry's name. In particular, Cameron became a personal public-relations officer for Henry Ford. "I never had an official function with the Ford Motor Company," Cameron confessed. "I would say that I acted as an interpreter for Mr. Ford." Gradually, his most important duty became handling the press. By the early 1930s, he was sitting at Ford's side during most interviews and interpreting his hazy pronouncements or convincing reporters to ignore his snap judgments about things of which he was ignorant. As Cameron noted of his protective role, "I felt I knew what he meant, and people who hadn't met him so often wouldn't know the background of what he was saying." Cameron's role as gatekeeper became the basis of his power. Even to see the industrialist one had to be cleared by his interpreter, and if he "did not think you were entitled to take up any of Ford's crowded time, you did not take it up."[41]

Then, in 1934, Ford launched the *Ford Sunday Evening Hour*, and the forum for Cameron's influence expanded. This program was aimed deliberately at a mass, middlebrow audience, none of its selections of classical pieces lasting more than ten minutes. Featuring a different conductor and soloist each week, the show opened and closed, at the special request of Henry Ford, with the "Children's Prayer" theme from *Hansel and Gretel*. In 1936, with its popularity swelling, it began broadcasting from the stage of the Masonic Temple in Detroit, which seated five thousand. By 1938, the *Ford Sunday Evening Hour* ranked as the fifth-most-popular program on radio, standing behind shows such as *Jack Benny* and *Charlie McCarthy* and ahead of others, such as the *Kraft Music Hall* and *Amos 'n' Andy*. By 1942, the show had some twenty-nine million listeners, who tuned in an average of 2.8 times a month.[42]

For many listeners, a highly anticipated feature of the show was the weekly talk during the intermission, which Cameron himself had suggested. When Henry and Edsel first conceived the idea for a radio show centered on the Detroit Symphony, they sought the writer's counsel about its content. He recommended that they avoid excessive commercials and have the announcer talk about something interesting during the intermission. The

Fords asked him to write an example of what he envisioned, so Cameron composed two or three brief talks. Several announcers auditioned unsuccessfully. Henry then asked Cameron to read his own work, and he performed so well that he was hired. Using his rich, soothing speaking voice fully, Cameron offered homilies that were heavy on old-fashioned common sense and village wisdom.[43]

Most listeners rightly considered Cameron to be Henry Ford's spokesman on the show. "That talking is a gift. I'm glad I never acquired it and I'll never try again," the audience-shy industrialist once told Charles Sorensen. "I can hire someone to talk for me that knows how." Having molded Ford's discourse for many years, Cameron proved perfect for this task. His six-minute talks, he explained later, were his own compositions but they reflected "Mr. Ford's attitude as I saw it." Cameron, benefiting from his years of experience, understood that Ford was an undisciplined, intuitive thinker who arrived at conclusions through flashes of perception rather than systematic analysis. "Mr. Ford had a twenty-five-track mind and there were trains going out and coming in on all tracks at all times," he once said of his boss's restless sense of inquiry. Moreover, Cameron grasped his boss's provincial mind-set. Ford, he once observed, inherited from his "rural, Populist background a terrible fear of monopolistic power holding everything down," a passion that fueled his attacks on financiers as well as his construction of steel mills and mines in order to control all aspects of his enterprise.[44]

Thus Cameron's radio talks turned time and again to themes dear to the heart of his patron—individual initiative, productivity, business as public service, the virtues of labor, uniting agriculture and manufacturing, and the foolishness of war. Titles from his first season include "American Individualism," "Thomas A. Edison," "The McGuffey Readers," and "A Day at Greenfield School." In later seasons they included "Peace Comes of Age," "Machines and Jobs," "Business and Recovery," and "The Method of Progress." Throughout these short addresses, Cameron explained the Ford perspective on issues such as industry's responsibility to the public, the evils of government regulation of business, the benefits of efficient production, and the necessity of high wages. Popularizing Ford's veneration of hard work, loyalty to family, experimentation and tradition, and the dignity and worth of ordinary Americans, Cameron distilled his benefactor's views into easily digestible morsels.[45]

Praise for Henry Ford the man was also a constant thread in the talks. The first address focused on "the personality behind the name" of his boss. Ford, he told the millions of listeners, was an unconventional magnate who seldom used his office, and spent most of his time talking directly to his managers and workers as he "circulated 'round." Though he lived his work and was devoted to manufacturing a useful car for ordinary people, Cameron continued, he also pursued educational and agricultural experiments. Ford foresaw a bright future of "undreamed progress, sound prosperity, and that social justice for which he has worked all his life." In such fashion, Cameron served as a conduit between Ford and his public. The following season, in a talk entitled simply "Henry Ford," he provided a brief biography that highlighted his employer's impressive list of accomplishments. "His greatest personal pleasure—creating more jobs," Cameron reported. "His constant goal—higher and yet higher wages . . . Says if he knew any better way of helping than by sticking to his job, he would do it. And so, at the age of 73, his face is in the light; he believes it is still early morning in America."[46]

Ford eagerly participated in this promotional project. He frequently dropped by Cameron's office to hear the next talk straight from the author and offer suggestions. He listened to the show regularly, either on the radio or by attending the live performance. For his part, Cameron embraced the notion of speaking for his innovative but verbally challenged patron. "William J. Cameron is Ford's voice, almost Ford's other self, for . . . he knows his employer's views and principles as well as Ford himself," a contemporary critic concluded. For millions of radio listeners, Cameron came to personify the great Detroit automobile company that had revolutionized modern life. Every Sunday evening for years, they heard a familiar statement—"You will hear from William J. Cameron of the Ford Motor Company"—that drove home the connection.[47]

Cameron worked very hard at shaping his weekly messages. Having settled in with his wife and four children in a comfortable Dearborn residence, he usually worked at his home library, often laboring into the early-morning hours. His output was prolific. He not only wrote and delivered several hundred radio talks, but composed countless speeches and newspaper and magazine articles over nearly twenty-seven years with the company. His written work ran into the many thousands of pages.[48]

Cameron brought several striking qualities of mind to his labors. He was well read, intelligent, and reflective, with spiritual interests that had produced a substantial library of religious tracts and, personally, "a ministerial manner and a very strict code of morals." Cameron's dignified demeanor and attitude of moral certitude occasionally drifted into pomposity. He felt qualified to comment on every area of human endeavor. "Like all too many preachers, W. J. Cameron . . . finds himself at home in many fields," a critic commented sharply. "Politics, economics, mechanics, finance, morals, psychology, history, life and death, right and wrong, taxation, sport, social problems—all are apparently within his competence." Yet Cameron retained an instinctive feel for the sensibilities of his middle-class audience. He also had a command of the English language that combined Victorian sentiment with a newspaperman's sense of brevity and human interest.[49]

One of the most fascinating aspects of Cameron's work for Ford, however, concerned not intelligence or productivity but a physical addiction. His alcoholism was an open secret in Ford Company circles. Something of a binge drinker, he underwent episodes of inebriation that caused great anxiety among the staff at the *Ford Sunday Evening Hour,* who worried that he would be unable to perform on the air. Cameron was assigned a special escort to watch over him on the afternoons of the broadcasts and convey him to the auditorium. In addition, Fred Black was always standing by to fill in if necessary. Cameron did deliver some of his addresses while drunk, but as a functioning alcoholic he always pulled off the performance without noticeable signs of trouble. Perhaps the most surprising dimension of this problem was his boss's tolerance of it. Ford's prohibitionist views were legendary, of course, but he put up with Cameron's weakness as he did no other individual's. A practical reason motivated Ford in part. "Cameron drunk is still a better writer and interpreter than anyone else I know," he once said. Cameron's shouldering of the blame in the Sapiro trial—according to a friend, the writer resumed drinking when "this Jewish thing blew up in his face"—probably prompted both guilt and tolerance in Ford. As well, Ford's reformist temperament inspired the progressive view that alcoholism was a disease, and he said to all concerned, "We're going to cure him."[50]

Thus, every week for eight years, Cameron overcame demon rum to deliver concise, stylized summations of his patron's view of the world. He perfected the role of small-town philosopher, reminding a modern society grown dizzy with bustle and sophistication of the virtues of traditional values. He approached the microphone with a dignified gait and exuded a solemn air. An audience member might "take him for the village preacher or perhaps the editor of the local paper" as he deployed a mellifluous speaking voice that exuded sincerity, wrote one journalist. His talks had an "almost sermon-like quality," in the words of another observer, and they were "pitched to a reverent yet homey plane." The overall effect was highly seductive. Indeed, one listener concluded that Cameron's weekly talks had "an accumulated effectiveness which only Roosevelt's Fireside Chats surpassed."[51]

Some contemporary analysts saw Cameron's inspirational performances as a kind of propaganda. A half hour of music created a receptive audience, orchestra and singers soothing listeners with light classics and American folk melodies. Cameron's "sermon-like" messages floated smoothly on this current of warm contentment. An academic expert in communications analyzed Cameron's rhetorical style, with its simplicity of theme, earnest delivery, positive images of progress, use of clichés and abstractions, occasional oratorical flourishes, down-home analogies, and patriotic allusions. He concluded that the speaker, with a superb grasp of his middle-class listeners, spoke to this group "in its own language" and fed back to it "its own ideals and symbols."[52]

In fact, Cameron became something of an institution during the Depression. "His Sunday night talks, repeated in the high and low places of America, are beginning to be recognized as shrewd commentaries on the American scene," a magazine noted. Some observers, in fact, found Cameron's popular appeal disconcerting. *The Christian Century* lumped Cameron with Huey Long and Father Coughlin as outspoken populist critics, but argued that he was the most dangerous of the three because of the "sweet reasonableness" of his attacks. *The Nation* attacked Cameron for "abysmal ignorance" and the promotion of "industrial dictatorship." A critic writing in the *Public Opinion Quarterly* denounced Cameron's talks as a form of manipulation that appealed to a hazy "American Way" in order to defend business against the encroachments of government regulation.[53]

But Ford was delighted with Cameron's efforts. Indeed, he was so pleased by the *Ford Sunday Evening Hour* talks that he paid to have them published, both as booklets and in several book-length collections. In his private box at the Masonic Temple along with Clara, he could be seen nodding in agreement as Cameron elaborated upon his dearest principles. Ford and "The Radio Pastor of Dearborn," as one magazine described Cameron, enjoyed a special relationship. Over the years, he came to appreciate the writer's ability to frame his own intuitive, often inchoate ideas into compelling, even eloquent forms. Cameron, perhaps more than any other individual, helped shape the positive aspects of Ford's image during the 1930s. Drawing upon comfortable populist aspects of his boss's worldview, he avoided extreme elements and did not directly attack Jews, FDR, or Wall Street. He prodded the process of evolution by which Ford became a national oracle whose thoughts, if not always endorsed, at least received respectful attention.

But Henry Ford was not destined to remain an elderly innovator dabbling in education, crop experiments, and radio entertainment. By the onset of a new decade, a looming crisis in the world forced him onto the public stage for a final performance. No one foresaw that it would be a tragedy. With his faculties failing, and betrayed by a long-standing family controversy, he stumbled deeper into a morass that threatened to engulf him. Eventually, the Ford family and key associates stepped in to avert disaster, but not before this King Lear of the automotive world had been brought low.

Twenty-five

Figurehead

In late August 1943, as the United States found itself engaged in global conflict during World War II, the Washington columnist Drew Pearson suggested in a radio broadcast that eighty-year-old Henry Ford's declining health might force the federal government to take over operation of his company. Ford reacted instantly and angrily. "I do not know how old or young this Pearson person is," he told reporters. "But tell him I'll meet him in any contest. I can lick him in anything he suggests. I never felt better physically in my life." He challenged the forty-six-year-old columnist to a footrace, a bicycle race, or a jumping contest to decide whose health was superior. The Detroit Retail Merchants Association sensed an opportunity and immediately offered to sponsor such a contest. It promised to clear a stretch of Woodward Avenue during its upcoming war-bond program and to provide judges and police protection for a physical competition.

Pearson good-naturedly accepted the challenge. Graciously noting that Ford would be a "formidable adversary," he promised to meet him "on foot, astride a bike, in a Model T, or in a contest of horseshoe pitching." With tongues slightly in cheeks, Michigan groups began lining up behind the Detroiter as a sentimental favorite. The Crack Pot Club of Grand Rapids, a businessmen's group, suggested that Pearson should start his training by "running a few preliminary heats with centenarians and gradually working up to the first team." The Detroit *Free Press* noted that, if a race did occur, "we would wager more than an apple on our home-town lad." Within a few days, Pearson realized the futility of either beating or losing to an eighty-year-old man in a physical contest. Ford, he asserted in another broadcast, had convinced even the most skeptical that "no one needs worry about the energetic way he is running his war plants." "My hat's off to him for his spunk," he noted, and backed away from the challenge.[1]

This commotion underlined the public perception of a vigorous Henry

Ford as he finished his eighth decade of life. Seemingly full of physical and mental energy, he delighted the press with his provocative statements and kept his hold on the public by dispensing nuggets of wisdom. On his eightieth birthday, he repeated many of his favorite maxims: industry would overcome poverty, money was good only for exchanging goods more easily, and industry and farming needed to be linked in common purpose. Ford reassured reporters about his excellent health and optimistic spirit. "If I felt any better," he remarked, "I'd have to run."[2]

But appearances deceived. Ironically, Pearson had been right in his original assertion. As his family and many colleagues knew all too well, Ford's physical and mental health were failing steadily. Since the late 1930s, he had been beset with various maladies, while his powers of perception and reason had slipped noticeably. He appeared increasingly unfit to meet the pressing challenges that bore down on his company in a tense, conflict-ridden world, and seemed equally unfit to resolve a personal struggle with his son. Those who cared about his welfare or depended upon his professional judgment were more and more worried about him.

By 1945, Ford's erratic behavior and troubling mental lapses had reached a crisis point. With his company foundering, Ford proved incapable of controlling the ebb and flow of power struggles that produced widening fissures in its structure. Unable to comprehend the impact of various policies and decisions, he oversaw a process of disintegration that raised the specter of chaos in one of the country's largest and most important corporations. Finally, with the assistance of his family, Ford would be removed from power in the company he had founded four decades before. The last two years of his life saw a drastic decline, as he drifted away and his wife struggled to shelter the man she loved from the public eye. It was a sad sight. Henry Ford, the vital, innovative man who had transformed modern society, spent his last days in an uncomprehending haze.

In the early 1940s, Ford still displayed many characteristics of a creative, productive individual. Engaged in an array of activities in industry, agriculture, education, and historical collecting, he kept a schedule that would have intimidated a much younger man. Walking the grounds of Greenfield Village, inspecting the exhibits at the Ford Museum, monitoring the experimental crops on his farms, auditing classes at the Henry Ford Trade School, visiting with reporters, dropping by his offices at the engineering building or the River Rouge plant, and consulting with Harry Bennett, Frank Campsall, Edward Cutler, Edsel Ruddiman, or Edsel Ford, he sometimes seemed in a blur of activity. He carried on a strenuous regimen of exercise, from bicycling every morning to taking long walks on his property, chopping wood, and making occasional outbursts of running that still surprised those who witnessed them. Rufus Wilson, Ford's driver, always carried an ax and a shovel in the trunk of the car, because his passenger frequently decided to "get out in the woods and whack at a log or chop down a dead tree" or dig up a piece of half-buried old farm machinery that he had spotted from the road.[3]

Ford continued to promote odd, and remarkably changeable, notions about diet, a tendency that polished his image as a lovable eccentric. He became convinced of the virtues of drinking warm rather than cold water, believing that the body wasted its precious energy to heat water into a usable form once it had been ingested. He had a special water heater rigged into his car so warm water would always be available and ordered a special "pollen water" from Maine for his personal use. He also grew enamored of wheat, describing it as a "divine and complete food" in its natural form. He would soak it for a day or two, until it was ready to sprout, and then eat the kernels for breakfast and throughout the day.[4]

Ford's lively image, however, masked deeper problems. By the 1930s, signs of failing health and a number of maladies were becoming evident. In 1932, near the age of seventy, he had surgery to repair a "strangulated femoral hernia" as well as an appendectomy. He suffered mounting tooth pain and degeneration, which demanded treatment, and he became irritable and impatient with the situation. He finally had dentures made by his dentist, James Melville Thompson, and most of those problems evaporated.[5]

More generally, Ford's physical activity waned along with his energy. By the early 1940s, the brisk walks had become strolls and the impulsive footraces disappeared almost entirely. Surviving letters from physicians, as well as a scattering of prescriptions and memoranda, show him inquiring about laxative products and the causes of impotence; doctors also informed him about treatments for blood pressure, excessive uric acid, and skin irritations, and about sedatives.[6]

Ford's odd views on health and his espousal of offbeat remedies exacerbated a worsening situation. Infatuated with the notion that diet and nutrition lay at the root of all illness, he remained suspicious of doctors and the practice of modern medicine. He had started the Henry Ford Hospital with the hope that its staff would find scientific proof for his theories, but their failure to do so caused him to lose interest. When the hospital's doctors were unable to find a cure for Clara Ford's arthritis with their scientific procedures, Henry chastised Frank M. Sladen, chief of medicine, and Roy D. McClure, chief of surgery, for failing to pursue dietary causes for the disorder. He put more and more faith in Lawson B. Coulter, a local chiropractor, who visited him twice a week for several years to manipulate his spine. Coulter also composed special diets for his patron—he was especially keen on avoiding fried foods and not mixing starches with meat or fruit—and urged Ford to avoid food cooked with aluminum pans and utensils. Many were suspicious of his expertise. As William Cameron once said of the chiropractor, "He was a very ignorant man."[7]

Ford's ideas on health, as they veered toward the crackpot, also posed a danger to others. One hot July evening in the late 1930s, an elderly friend fainted at one of the Fords' old-fashioned dances. F. Janney Smith, head of cardiology at Henry Ford Hospital, revived the man, took him out for some fresh air, and after a quick examination recommended that he go home until a fuller diagnosis could be made. Ford intervened and attributed the faint to the victim's drinking a glass of milk. To Smith's horror, he insisted that the old man go back into the ballroom and choose a partner for the next dance. Similarly, Ford frequently expressed skepticism when physicians diagnosed heart problems in friends. "Pay no attention to that doctor," he would snort. "All you have to do is get out of bed and lie on the floor for half an hour twice a day, and eat celery and carrots. Then you'll be alright."[8]

Ford's health theories posed a danger to himself as well. He refused to take medication unless the doctor could describe immediately the manufacturing process by which it had been made. When he felt ill, he had his chauffeur "take him for a fast ride with a little jouncing around," because he believed that jarring his body would restore its normal function. His dietary enthusiasms swung to wild extremes, likely bringing nutritional deficiencies in their wake. His excessive reliance on a wheat diet caused a medical specialist to warn him in the 1940s that he had been "starving to death." His suspicions about doctors took bizarre turns. In 1938, after suffering what turned out to be a stroke, Ford rejected the advice of his attending physician, Dr. McClure, and summoned his chiropractor for daily treatments.[9]

Ford's growing physical problems were accentuated by signs of mental deterioration. By the late 1930s, family members and colleagues had become concerned about his memory lapses, peculiar behavior, and declining analytical powers. Doctors diagnosed the onset of senility. In January 1936, Dr. Coulter was performing one of his osteopathic manipulations of Ford's spine and neck when things went awry. According to Dr. Sladen, the chiropractor put undue pressure on blood vessels in his aging patient's neck and caused "a cerebral vascular accident and consequent brain injury." Ford suffered a facial paralysis that lasted about three weeks, but the blow to his mental capacities seemed to linger. Then, in the spring of 1939, Clara summoned Sladen again to examine her husband, whose erratic thought processes were matched by general weakness and other physical complaints. Sladen diagnosed hardening of the arteries and "symptoms of developing senility" and said that Ford's behavior had not returned to normal after 1936. An incident in 1939 reinforced this evaluation. While attending a concert, the doctor saw the Fords in their special box and dropped by to say hello. To his astonishment, Henry angrily accused him of conspiring to keep Clara sick with arthritis. Sladen interpreted this as unreasonable irritability, a trait characterizing the early onslaught of senility. Typically, Ford refused to undergo an extensive examination, so a thorough analysis proved difficult. But Sladen noted that Clara began a subtle campaign to protect her husband and shelter him from the pressures of public life.[10]

Throughout this period, Ford suffered a series of strokes that contributed to his symptoms of mental failure. The 1936 episode, with its facial paralysis, exhibited certain signs of a mild stroke, and Dr. John G. Mateer, who became Ford's physician in the 1940s, concluded that it had been "a cerebral thrombosis or hemorrhage," an indication of arterial disease. In 1938, shortly after his seventy-fifth birthday, according to Charles Sorensen, Ford had another stroke that was carefully hushed up by the family. This was the incident after which he called in his chiropractor for treatments in defiance of his doctors from the Henry Ford Hospital. Finally, in August 1941, Ford suffered a more serious stroke that left him with an unclear mind for substantial periods. In Sorensen's evaluation, after this attack his boss's opinions hardened and "occasionally flared into hallucination." Ford became a "querulous, suspicious old man" who saw conspiracies everywhere and struggled with a fading memory.[11]

The combined impact of senility and strokes pushed Ford into an obvious spiral of decline. He had lost "his usual physical ability and mental alertness," noted Herman Moekle, the chief auditor for the company. Other longtime associates noted that on occasion Ford was unable to recall their names and had to ask them to identify themselves. "It seemed that he was rapidly becoming confused and dull," Irving Bacon observed. "His facial expression was changing. The keen-eyed, searching look was fading away."[12]

Even Ernest Liebold, never a paragon of human sympathy, was struck by the poignancy of Ford's mental decline around 1940. He witnessed his boss, increasingly stoop-shouldered and with a noticeably slower gait, struggling to communicate with his subordinates. "Sometimes situations arose when it was difficult to understand just what he was driving at or just what his reasons were," Liebold said. Ford would drop by the office in the morning to talk but could not remember the subject. He became confused about instructions he had given. Liebold was saddened by the spectacle. "It was just appalling to observe a man who had created something and had your greatest and highest respect, watching and seeing the thing going down in inches," he said. Like everyone else who encountered Ford's behavior, Liebold found his annoyance giving way to pity. "How can you hold a man responsible when his mind isn't functioning?" he decided. "He was no longer able to comprehend, he couldn't analyze things any more. Everybody here knew that."[13]

Yet, for all his growing mental and physical impediments, Ford still exhibited signs of liveliness and humor that delighted those close to him. On a trip to visit Richmond Hill in the early 1940s with Clara and several associates, Ford and his group traveled in two cars, one driven by Rufus Wilson, the other by Robert Rankin. Several hundred miles from their destination, Ford separated from his wife to ride in Wilson's car. Beset by an ornery urge, he persuaded Wilson to drive faster and faster as Rankin (and Clara) struggled to keep up. Hurtling down the highways at eighty-five miles an hour, the breathless group arrived at Richmond Hill several hours early and surprised the staff, who had nothing prepared yet. When Clara chastised her husband for driving so fast, he replied, "Callie, that Rankin was right on our tail. We were trying to get out of his way all the time!" Ford laughed about the incident for days afterward.[14]

But his declining mental and physical state became evident in his struggles to come to terms with a growing international crisis. By the late 1930s, the rise of fascism in Europe was raising the specter of war, and Ford, the old pacifist with a yen for publicity, could not stay on the sidelines. Following his heart rather than his head, he stumbled into controversy.

As tensions mounted and European nations edged toward war under the pressure of Nazi German expansionism, Ford resurrected his pacifist, populist principles. But his physical and mental deterioration complicated matters. "Ford was in bad health and worse morale. His memory was failing as rapidly as his obsessions and antipathies increased," Charles Sorensen reported. "Any mention of the war in Europe and the likelihood of this country's involvement upset him almost to incoherence." Ford tried to dampen enthusiasm for war at every turn. In a United States where many citizens still felt burnt by national involvement in World War I and were determined to avoid future foreign entanglements, Ford's commentary initially found an appreciative audience. Many approved his insistence that America stay free of any military involvement in the affairs of Europe.[15]

To those who recalled his comments during World War I, Ford's position was familiar. In conversation with friends, he insisted that war was the product of greedy financiers who sought profit in human destruction. He accused these conspiratorial elites of maneuvering European countries into armed conflict and trying to do the same with the United States. In 1939, he claimed that attacks on American merchant ships by German submarines were in fact acts of sabotage to fulfill "a scheme by financial war-makers to get this country into war." He remained obsessed with the Du Pont family, arguing that it was one of the leading "warmongers" who manipulated governments behind the scenes to make money. He praised English Prime Minister Neville Chamberlain for his peace efforts but claimed he was "running up against a bunch of war profiteers." He even became convinced that the declarations of war in September 1939 were a fraud to promote the selling of armaments. He refused to believe there was an actual shooting war in Europe until he was shown pictures of a Ford plant in England that had been bombed.[16]

In a 1940 article entitled "An American Foreign Policy" published in *Scribner's Commentator*, Ford despaired about the "work of destruction such as we see now in progress in Europe and threatening to spread to other parts of the world." The peoples of Europe had been "duped by the greedy financial groups seeking to extend their domination," he argued, and the United States "should NOT meddle in the affairs of other people." Several weeks later, he gave a long interview to the press at Richmond Hill, where he denounced both the Axis powers and England as oppressors of common people. The best result would see the combatants fight "until they both collapse. . . . There is no righteousness in either cause. Both are motivated by the same evil impulse, which is greed," Ford declared. "It is not the little people who are doing the fighting and the suffering who are the greedy ones. They are innocent of that." When both sides collapsed, Ford hoped, the United States could step in to broker a just peace and construct a world federation.[17]

Ford concocted fantasies of intervening to stop the European conflict. Forgetting the hard lessons of the Peace Ship debacle, he entertained the idea that he could somehow influence Hitler to halt the war. In January 1940, he summoned a young friend, James Newton, and another young man, and asked that they serve as his emissaries to Berlin. "I have an idea of how the hostilities might be stopped before they escalate. Of course, the key to it is Hitler. I think it's possible he might listen to my suggestions," Ford told them earnestly. "You know, he's following my example of producing a car for the millions. He got his engineers to come up with a cheap 'people's car'—Volkswagen. I think I just may have his respect, the door may be open." He offered his services as mediator and agreed to finance an expedition for the two men to feel out the German government. Wiser in the ways of the world than their patron, the two understood the futility of this naïve scheme and never followed up on the offer.[18]

In terms of public policy, Ford infuriated the American government when he reneged on an agreement to manufacture some six thousand Rolls-Royce engines for the British, saying he would do so only for the direct defense of the United States. "We are not doing business with the British Government or any other foreign government," he declared. "We have no agreement with anybody for the production of war materials and if and when we do have one it will be on that basis and with the United States Government only." He also publicly joined forces with prominent isolationists. In September 1940, he was named a member of the America First Committee, the leading organization of those opposing United States involvement in the conflict. "In joining the committee," reported the New York *Times*, "Mr. Ford said he believed immediate action must be taken to check the increasing trend toward war."[19]

Ford became close friends with Charles Lindbergh, whose transatlantic flight had made him a national hero before he emerged as the leading anti-war figure in the United States during the 1930s. The two had become acquainted in August 1927, when the pilot visited Dearborn as part of his cross-country tour promoting aviation. He consulted with Ford on his "flivver plane" project (later aborted) to manufacture small, inexpensive airplanes as a revolutionary transportation move. Lindbergh had taken the industrialist up in his *Spirit of St. Louis* and the Ford Tri-Motor for the only airplane rides of his life; Ford did not like flight and found the rides to be physically and mentally unnerving. Over the next ten years, the Lindberghs stayed with the Fords at Fair Lane on several occasions when the pilot visited Detroit to see his mother. In 1939, the two men renewed their friendship as they found common cause in opposing American entry into World War II.[20]

Lindbergh had become an outspoken advocate of American neutrality in the 1930s and a major force in the America First Committee, for which he solicited Ford's participation and financial support. Ford admired Lindbergh and thought him one of the greatest men in the world. He took the pilot to a meeting of the Moral Rearmament movement, another antiwar group, on one of his trips to Detroit, and responded eagerly to Lindbergh's overtures. "I want you to know how much encouragement you and Mrs. Ford have given to many of us by your acceptance of membership in the America First Committee," Lindbergh wrote to Ford in September 1940. "Your stand versus entry into the war has already had great influence, and, if we are able to keep out, I believe it will be largely due to the courage and support you have given us."[21]

Ford's isolationist views, in concert with his reputation for anti-Semitism and his longtime affection for Germany, raised suspicions and prompted an attack upon his motives in the fall of 1940. Two leftist publications, *Friday* and *PM*, accused him of being not only a fascist sympathizer but a financial supporter of the Nazi movement in both Germany and the United States. In an article entitled "American Merchants of Hate," *Friday* contended that Ford and William J. Cameron had arranged to give Fritz Kuhn, the leader of the German-American Bund, a job at the Ford Motor Company, along with an office. It published the facsimile of a letter to Kuhn from Cameron confirming the arrangement. *PM* charged Ford with a long list of transgressions: supporting publication of anti-Jewish tracts, maintaining "friendly relations with Hitlerism," employing American Nazis in his factories, generally disseminating "the Hitlerite type of anti-Jewish philosophy," and using "Nazi-Gestapo" methods in opposing the unionization of his workers.[22]

Ford's acceptance of the Grand Cross of the German Eagle from Hitler's government in 1938 struck many as a sign of his endorsement of Nazism. Later, others suspected that the company maintained its plants, and profits, in Germany not only during Hitler's ascendancy in the 1930s but after the declaration of war.[23]

Although Ford never answered these accusations personally, his spokesmen defended him. Cameron denounced "the defamation that is being so freely scattered" and pointed out that the letter printed by *Friday* was an obvious forgery—the letterhead stationery on which it appeared was that of a nonexistent organization ("The Anglo-Saxon Society of America"), the box it listed as a return address did not exist in the Dearborn Post Office, and the signature looked nothing like his. Cameron claimed that he and Ford had never even heard of Kuhn until reading about his Bund activities in New York. A perusal of company employment records revealed that Kuhn had worked for Ford for a few months, but had been dismissed in 1936 for failure to perform. He had been one of ninety thousand employees and never communicated at all with Ford or any other company manager. Neither Ford nor his company supported fascism around the world, Cameron insisted. Ernest Liebold also contended that "Mr. Ford had no contact with the anti-Semitic or Nazi movement in Germany." And there is scant evidence that Ford retained authority over its German branch, Ford-Werke, during World War II or profited from its wartime endeavors. By the late 1930s, Ford-Werke was controlled totally by German interests and had become, for all intents and purposes, a separate company. So, although Ford, like many Americans, may have been foolish in misreading Hitler and his movement, he was neither a Nazi nor a fascist. Nonetheless, the accusations provided much embarrassment.[24]

Despite his strenuous efforts to keep America out of World War II, Ford's support for neutrality wavered. On January 15, 1940, he made clear his determination to defend the United States at the dedication of a navy training school. "During this crisis our organization wants to do everything possible to help America and the President," he stated. "The Navy being our first line of defense, I feel that the training of these young men will vitally benefit our Nation." He also boasted that his factories could turn out a thousand planes a day if they ever needed to. "But remember, they are to be for defense only," he added. Privately, he expressed misgivings about the Germans and mused that the United States might be forced to help the British. According to Harry Bennett, Hitler's series of invasions in central Europe had caused Ford to declare, "He's just power drunk, like all the rest of them." The Luftwaffe bombing of the company's Dagenham plant, outside London, caused Ford's sympathy for England to rise further. By early 1941, he was overheard remarking at lunch, "You know what we have to do, Mr. Cameron? We have to get in 100% and help the British out," he declared. "They have to win."[25]

After the Japanese attack on Pearl Harbor and the subsequent German declaration of war on the United States, Ford abandoned all support for neutrality and lined up behind the war effort. He pledged his company to the manufacturing of armaments and published a statement repudiating anti-Semitism. In the name of "American community" and "national unity," Ford denounced "the hate-mongering prevalent for some time in this country against the Jew" and described it as a "distinct disservice to our country, and to the peace and welfare of humanity." He affirmed that, although war was a terrible business, "we are in it now, and the important thing is to finish it quickly, so that we can return to more useful, more serious matters." His shift of opinion seemed heartfelt. One morning, sitting in the Martha-Mary Chapel with James Newton, Ford listened to the schoolchildren singing a hymn. "Sometimes over there at the plant I look at those weapons rolling out and I think we've gone plumb crazy, killing each other off like this," he said. "Then I come here and watch these youngsters and I know it's worthwhile. We've got to win this war, so they can grow up in a free world."[26]

The Ford Motor Company threw itself into the war effort. Though it manufactured cargo trucks, tanks and tank destroyers, aircraft engines, and gliders at its factories around the country, its biggest contribution came with the mass production of B-24 Liberator bombers at a giant facility that arose in the Michigan countryside some twenty miles west of Dearborn. In January 1941, nearly a year before Pearl Harbor and following a request from Washington, the company had agreed to enter the field of military-airplane manufacturing. During a trip to California to inspect the factories of two aircraft companies, Consolidated and Douglas, Charles Sorensen and Edsel Ford had formulated a plan for a factory to build B-24s according to principles of assembly-line production. Henry Ford approved. By late spring, construction had begun on a plant near Ypsilanti, by a small stream called Willow Run. When it was finished, at a cost of nearly $50 million, Ford's L-shaped factory was nearly thirty-two hundred feet long, sat on eighty acres, with another hundred acres devoted to hangars, and was surrounded by seven concrete runways, each some sixty-two hundred feet long. Eventually, the factory would employ almost fifty thousand workers, studding the surrounding areas with houses, dormitories, and trailers to shelter them.[27]

Willow Run was really Sorensen's brainchild. On the California trip, he had sketched the first basic plan for the factory on a piece of stationery. In subsequent months, he managed the organization of the airplane's construction into nine subassemblies, oversaw the building of the facility with its mile-long assembly line, and coordinated affairs between the company and the federal government. The Willow Run project was, in Sorensen's own words, the "biggest challenge of my production career." Getting the factory up and running did not go flawlessly. Tormented by production glitches, labor shortages, and bureaucratic delays that created controversy (and some accusations of mismanagement), Willow Run spun its production wheels during the first year of the war. By August 1943, however, it was turning out 230 Liberators a month, and by August 1944 over 425 a month. "Bring the Germans and Japs to see it," Sorensen boasted. "Hell, they'll blow their brains out." By the war's end, the company had made over eighty-six hundred B-24s at the Ypsilanti facility. For millions of citizens, Willow Run became a symbol of America's tremendous productive capacity in wartime.[28]

Ford took great pride in his company's defense plant and visited it nearly every day during the first two years America was in the war. After a stop each morning for services at the Martha-Mary Chapel, he headed out in a car equipped with a two-way radio so company managers would know his arrival time. He had hired Lindbergh to work at Willow Run as an unpaid consultant—he flight-tested the bombers, developing modifications that improved their high-altitude performance, and served as a liaison between the production people and the flight crews—and the two visited frequently. Ford's arrival always generated interest. "Sometimes he would simply sit on a chair or desk and talk—about an engine he was developing, about the need for decentralizing factories so workmen could own a piece of land, about the effect of eating too much sugar, about his ideas for a parliament of man," Lindbergh described. "Sometimes he would take two or three company officers with him and inspect the factory lines. He was agile and untiring on these visits." Ford expressed great pride in Willow Run's scale of production, telling reporters, "The more we produce, the quicker it will be over and the sooner we can get back to the job of building up the country." "Two years ago he was an earnest pacifist," *Time* magazine stated in 1942. "Today, like the rest of the industry he is not only working for war but for war alone. . . . Henry Ford and his empire have converted themselves to war."[29]

Such pictures of Ford's involvement in war production at Willow Run, though bolstering the company's public relations and boosting the public's morale, had little to do with the truth. In fact, his participation in the real business of wartime production was far less than the public imagined. Beyond giving vague approval to plans and procedures already formulated by Sorensen and his managers at Willow Run, Ford did little of substance except lending encouragement as he roamed the plant. "Henry Ford had nothing to do with this program," Sorensen said of the company's conversion to war production. "With these matters in safe hands he went along as the glorified leader."[30]

If anything, Ford meddled and caused problems. With his mental state fluctuating wildly, he concocted conspiracies and hallucinated enemies. In late 1942, for example, he declared to Sorensen that he could no longer stomach William Knudsen, who must be dismissed from the organization. Knudsen, of course, had left Ford Motor Company twenty years earlier. Ford told associates he was being spied on, and expressed his distrust of army and air force officers who were stationed at the plant. He became convinced that an agent of the American government would kill him. "I was astonished to find an automatic pistol in a holster under the cowl of his car," Sorensen reported. "His chauffeur also packed a pistol." In more lucid moments, yet jealous of his own position and prerogatives, he encouraged managerial infighting at Willow Run. He tried to set Sorensen against Mead Bricker, who managed the bomber factory under Sorensen's supervision. Once he even told Bricker to attempt to fire his superior. "God, isn't that going to be funny when Bricker tells Charley to get out of the plant," Ford chortled to Harry Bennett. "Charley will fire him on the spot."[31]

Perhaps the best reflection of Ford's marginalization, however, came with the much-publicized visit of President Roosevelt to Willow Run on September 18, 1942. FDR's stopover at the bomber factory, part of a series of war-plant visits, agitated Ford greatly. Roosevelt, who had traveled by train, was two hours late, and Ford, annoyed by the delay, had left the welcoming party to roam the plant. When Roosevelt arrived, Ford was nowhere to be found; after a search by Harry Bennett's men, he was finally located talking with workers about a new machine tool. He then joined the President and First Lady, along with Donald M. Nelson, chairman of the War Production Board, Sorensen, and Edsel, for a tour of Willow Run. Riding in a car inside the facility, Ford was wedged in the back seat between the Roosevelts, with Edsel and Sorensen on jumpseats facing them and Nelson in the front seat beside the driver. As they moved along, Sorensen explained the various operations of the plant and the Roosevelts responded with enthusiastic questions and comments. FDR talked at length with his usual charm, but Ford pouted. Sorensen described the scene. "Sitting between the Roosevelts, who were good-sized people, he was almost hidden," Sorensen described. "He could not enter into the spirit of the event. When Edsel or I turned to look at him he would glare at us furiously." When Willow Run workers cheered the President, Ford only grew more infuriated. Sorensen's obvious expertise in explaining the plant's operation, as well as his reference to FDR as "the boss," did likewise. After a perfunctory goodbye in the President's private railcar, Ford sped off in his own automobile.[32]

Despite his minimal role, Henry Ford's wartime image as a patriotic producer reached great heights. In a cover story on March 23, 1942, *Time* magazine painted an admiring picture of the elderly industrialist as a "fighting pacifist." Noting that the American automobile industry had become a crucial part of the "miracle of war production," the article suggested that there was "no better sample than Henry Ford." This "America Firster," *Time* declared, had his reservations "bombed away at Pearl Harbor" and immediately devoted his industrial empire to winning the war. It portrayed him touring his factories and, at each stop, ordering, "Get a defense job going in there quick." As the article concluded admiringly, in his individualism, confidence, curiosity, and productivity, "Henry Ford is more like most Americans than most Americans realize." His wartime efforts demonstrated that "the whole U.S. nation was going to roll up its sleeves and fix Armageddon."[33]

The company's wartime ad series featuring its founder's life and achievements further burnished his personal image. Ford had banned advertisements describing the company's war work—he thought such efforts were in poor taste—but he happily assented to a plan based on his own life. John W. Thompson, who joined the public-relations staff in 1942, worked with Irving Bacon to develop ads focusing on key moments in

Ford's experience that revealed "the sources from which sprang the genius and success of the Ford Motor Company." Bacon's paintings depicted Henry as a boy building a waterwheel in the creek outside his school, repairing watches in his bedroom, having his first meeting with Thomas Edison, testing his first horseless carriage on the streets of Detroit, making a car that won the Transcontinental Race in 1909, and inaugurating the first assembly line in 1913. "Today, this philosophy and the skills developed through more than 40 years experience are being applied to America's vital needs," the ads said. "From this will arise new techniques to serve the nation even better when Ford resumes the production of sturdy, comfortable transportation, priced within the reach of the greatest number." According to Thompson, Ford took a great personal interest in these ads and suggested improvements.[34]

The military output of Willow Run and the outpouring of favorable publicity, however, only modified Ford's antiwar sentiments. He remained at heart a reluctant warrior. Throughout World War II, he spoke periodically on the need to end wasteful fighting as quickly as possible and get back to consumer production. At what turned out to be his last press conference—on his seventy-ninth birthday, on July 30, 1942—Ford told reporters that the present global conflict was "precipitated by greed, lust for power, and financial gain; it won't end until some sense of sanity has returned to those who believe in armed might for selfish gain." He hoped that the creation of a world federation and the renewal of peaceful production would make war obsolete. "The intensive production of the world's goods, new goods to serve human needs and legitimate desires—that is the broad highway to peace," Ford claimed.[35]

Indeed, at every opportunity Ford focused attention on his hopes for the postwar era. He suggested that factories such as Willow Run could be converted to the manufacture of prefab houses, complete with air-conditioning, central heating, and modern appliances, for millions of families now priced out of the housing market. Or they might be modified to produce large multiple-engine cargo and passenger planes. Ford also suggested conversion of war plants to agricultural uses, making not only tractors and other farm tools but new goods being developed in plastics, chemicals, and food. Whatever the specifics, Ford clearly entertained a happy postwar vision characterized by renewed consumer prosperity.[36]

The demands of World War II put great pressures on Henry Ford. Ideologically, this global conflict challenged his long-cherished commitment to peaceful solutions to international problems. Physically, it challenged a man whose health was declining as his mental processes grew steadily weaker and more erratic. His situation was complicated further by an ongoing, troubling personal relationship with his son. During World War II, it reached a tragic climax from which the father never fully recovered.

Edsel Ford could take it no longer. The onset of health problems, in concert with years of conflict with his father, had taken their toll. In 1943, in the middle of a war for which the Ford Motor Company was producing thousands of armaments, he determined to walk away from his work and his tormentors. Edsel decided that his situation had become intolerable following a particularly brutal confrontation with Henry. Fed up with his father's abuse and physically exhausted, after twenty-four years in the position, he decided to resign the presidency of the company that Henry had built.[37]

Throughout the 1930s, Edsel had walked the same tortuous path laid out for him in the previous decade—serving as the titular head of the great automobile company as his father maintained control over all important decisions and undermined his authority at every opportunity. The son, with his deep sense of loyalty and obligation, had attempted manfully to fill this position of prominence without power. The fact that he had established a fulfilling personal life helped him persevere. He, his wife, Eleanor, and their four children had settled into their beautiful Cotswold-style house and estate, Gaukler Pointe. Though they still socialized occasionally with Henry and Clara, the families had grown apart. Edsel's personal separation from his parents provided an emotional buffer.[38]

Professionally, he could not escape so easily. Tightly bound to his father and the company, the younger Ford labored dutifully. On the surface, he maintained a fairly normal work life. As president, Edsel kept an office in the administration building in Dearborn and, with characteristic calm, kindness, and dignity, ran an office that was a model of courteous efficiency. Sitting at his clean and orderly desk, he oversaw the business endeavors of the company as he wrote memoranda, responded to reports, and consulted with executives. Intelligent and hardworking, Edsel had a command of all aspects of the company's commercial operations and was perfectly at ease in discussions about production, sales, advertising, and labor. Even Henry had to admit grudgingly that Edsel "knows everything that's going on everywhere. I don't know how he does it, but he does." As an executive, his greatest strengths were an attention to detail and a belief in teamwork. Rather than issuing orders like his autocratic father, Edsel would listen carefully to managers' opinions, gather expert advice, and involve others in the decision-making process.[39]

Even as a young man, Edsel had appeared kindly, even-tempered, unfailingly polite, and reserved, and these characteristics stayed with him as a middle-aged executive. "In fact, he practically never turned any executives away who came to see him," reported A. J. Lepine, his administrative assistant. "He was there at the disposal of the executives of the company." Even when visitors talked at too great a length, Edsel remained patient rather than abruptly terminating the meeting.[40]

But Edsel's controlled exterior occasionally cracked to reveal an inner turmoil. "He is high-strung, nervous; when he is talking to you he tears sheets of paper into little bits, rolls up the bits, and pops them into a wastebasket," *Fortune* observed in 1933. "His voice and his manner are quiet." Indeed, Edsel's reserve seemed to provide a defense mechanism against an intrusive world. An associate who worked closely with him noticed that he "rarely exhibited enthusiasm. He rarely ever exhibited extreme distaste, and . . . I never saw him enthused or laugh about anything with anyone. He was always very solemn, serious. You never knew what was going on inside of his head." The younger Ford's emotional constraints seemed to mirror those imposed on him by his awkward professional situation.[41]

Art continued to be a passion in Edsel's life. An amateur painter, he dabbled at home for years before taking up photography as a hobby in the 1930s. His office displayed original paintings by the early-American painters Gilbert Stuart and John Trumbull. It was also decorated with several valuable antiques—Edsel had become an expert judge of colonial furniture—and the walls had been paneled in colonial style. Overall, the room exuded "a quiet dignity," in Lepine's words. Edsel and Eleanor had started collecting fine art in the early 1930s, and their home was adorned with works by van Gogh, Raphael, Degas, Matisse, and Frans Hals. They were longtime supporters of the Detroit Institute of Arts, and Edsel donated many works to its museum and hundreds of thousands of dollars to help boost its collections. He served as a commissioner of the institution from 1930 to 1943.

Edsel's most memorable artistic encounter came with the Mexican muralist Diego Rivera. An avowed communist and master of fresco, an artistic technique whereby paint was applied directly onto wet plaster, Rivera came to Detroit to put murals on the walls of the art institute's great garden court. Edsel paid for much of the project. The artist decided to depict the dynamic interaction of man and machine in this capital of automobile production and completed large portraits of assembly lines, machine shops, and chemical factories. The result was grandiose and controversial. Critics contended that the radical painter had created a grim picture of industrial Detroit and demanded that the murals be whitewashed or moved to a less conspicuous spot. Edsel, along with institute officials, held firm in support of Rivera's work. "I admire Mr. Rivera's spirit," Edsel told reporters. "I really believe he was trying to express his idea of the spirit of Detroit."[42]

Edsel's artistic sensibility spilled over into what became his professional passion in the 1930s—car styling, in partnership with E. T. Gregorie. He had been involved in automobile design since adolescence and had overseen development of the stylish Lincoln luxury line of cars in the 1920s, but he became serious about design during the 1930s. Gregorie's taste for clean, graceful lines drew Edsel's attention. They collaborated on designing Ford models early in the decade, Edsel providing broad aesthetic directives and retaining final approval while Gregorie did the actual designs. The collaboration was so successful that Edsel established a design department in the company in early 1935 with Gregorie as its head.[43]

Operating out of the engineering building in Dearborn, Gregorie and his assistants worked closely with Edsel in designing the new Lincoln Zephyr line introduced in 1935, the Mercury line introduced in 1939, and the Lincoln Continental. These models had been developed at the urging of the younger Ford, who sought to present consumers with a range of automobiles at various prices to compete with those of General Motors. Henry, of course, had resisted diversification because of his loyalty to the old Model T idea of a functional, inexpensive car for the masses. He acceded only grudgingly to Edsel's position. The new automobiles appeared slowly in the late 1930s, and, as Gregorie acknowledged, Edsel's fondness for sleek, simple lines, dignity, and elegance pervaded their designs.[44]

But behind this elaborate façade of work and fulfillment, an old problem eroded the foundation of Edsel Ford's life. As everyone knew, including himself, his position of authority was essentially a sham. His father stymied him and kept the reins of power firmly in his own hands, as he had since 1919. And he wielded that power with little tact. "There were times when Mr. Ford's attitude toward Edsel, in my judgment, reached pretty close to the point of persecution," Ernest Liebold said. Any action by the younger Ford was subject to the elder Ford's approval, noted another associate, and it was clear "that Henry Ford didn't trust Edsel's judgment too well." For the company president, the situation was equal parts frustration and humiliation.[45]

A profound difference in temperament explained much of this division. Fred Black noted that, whereas Edsel believed in organization, cooperation, and teamwork, his father "was not an organization man. He wanted to call all the signals and carry the ball." Edsel liked to gather facts, study them, and make deliberate judgments, but Henry made snap decisions based on intuition. Edsel listened carefully to reports on a situation as he considered the merits of various actions and often asked executives to present both sides of a problem. Henry, detesting complexity, was impatient with any kind of presentation and "on the basis of a hunch would come to a decision." Though Edsel was a model of courtesy and inclusion in his management practice, his father constantly pressured him to be tougher and more aggressive.[46]

This clash of sensibilities created many problems, such as Henry's contempt for Edsel's interest in automobile styling and design. Preoccupied with utilitarian issues of mechanical soundness and durability in Ford automobiles, he saw his son's aesthetic concerns as another sign that he was "too artistic for the automobile business." He did little to hide his disdain. In the 1930s, Ford dropped by Emil Zoerlein's engineering shop and noticed the acoustical work being done to lower noise levels in automobiles. Zoerlein showed him sound meters the company had purchased as part of a cooperative program with the University of Michigan and explained that Edsel was monitoring test results. Henry sneered, "Well, as far as I'm concerned, you can take these instruments and throw them out in the lake."[47]

Henry's suspicion of his son's artistic impulses translated into outright scorn for his friends and lifestyle. Since the 1920s, he had been convinced that Ernest Kanzler and "the Grosse Pointe crowd" were warping Edsel's character. He once uttered the supreme insult: "Kanzler and Edsel both ought to be bankers." Henry never tired of railing about Edsel's "high living" and the snobby "ear-piddlers" who were corrupting him and trying to get his money. According to a close associate, Henry carefully checked on all the parties Edsel gave or attended, bribed a servant to provide information on his son's private affairs, and once drove to Edsel's home to smash up his son's stock of liquor and wine. Clara Ford, to a certain extent, shared her husband's disapproval of their son's lifestyle. At an exhibit of modernist paintings in the Ford Museum sponsored by Edsel and Eleanor, she recoiled and asked that they be removed. "They get their idea of art and liking for certain things from the Rockefellers," she commented of her son and daughter-in-law. "She was *most* bitter!" noted an observer. "I could sense the feeling of bitterness, almost, toward her own son, because of his association with the Rockefellers."[48]

By the 1930s, Edsel's resigned attitude toward his father's criticism was giving way to resentment. He began to betray to close associates a cynical attitude of "Oh, what's the use?" The gap between the elder and younger Fords opened a little wider every year as their working relationship eroded. "Relations between Edsel and Henry Ford were now strained almost to the breaking point, and it became increasingly difficult for father and son to work together on anything," Charles Sorensen noted. Everyone who saw them together perceived the tension. "I wondered often how close Mr. Ford and Edsel really were," commented Emil Zoerlein. "Edsel always had a worried and a painful expression. Mr. Ford's expression was stern. . . . Mr. Ford and Edsel did not joke much with each other or tease each other."[49]

Public issues also entered the picture. Throughout the Depression era, Henry and Edsel quarreled over the company's labor policies, as Ford's struggle against unionization pushed father and son in different directions. Henry used every weapon at his disposal to fight against union inroads. Edsel disagreed, largely on practical grounds. He argued for an accommodation with the unions, contending that opposition was costing more than would acceptance of a union shop, and bringing bad publicity, too. Father and son had many long, heated arguments over labor policy, both becoming convinced that the other's approach would doom the company.[50]

Another divisive issue concerned Franklin D. Roosevelt. Henry's hatred of the President was legendary, yet Edsel had developed a friendship with FDR. He had met Roosevelt during World War I, and throughout the 1920s and 1930s had contributed generously to his therapeutic center for polio victims in Warm Springs, Georgia. Edsel visited him there in 1928 and shortly afterward gave the New York governor one of the new Ford Model A's, asking only for an autographed picture in return. The families exchanged birthday cards and holiday greetings for many years, and Edsel came to admire FDR for his courage, resiliency, and personal warmth. Thus it was little wonder that father and son wrangled sharply with regard to the President. On the two occasions they met FDR, Edsel behaved with his usual grace and Henry did little to hide his contempt.[51]

In the early 1940s, the company's involvement in war preparation further strained the relationship. The younger Ford, with his father's approval, had negotiated a deal for the company to manufacture Rolls-Royce engines for the British. Then, suddenly, Henry decided to squelch the deal and told the newspapers of his decision before apprising his son. "Well, I can't understand Father's statement of this. We've talked it over," a stunned Edsel told Fred Black. "He has never expressed any such attitude to me. It's very embarrassing to have this happen at this time, after a number of promises have been made." Humiliated once again, Edsel was left to pick up the pieces as he tried to explain the broken agreement.[52]

Harry Bennett, whom Edsel despised and Henry revered, became a constant source of friction. Henry had made the boisterous security chief a constant companion by the 1930s. Not surprisingly, this wounded Edsel, who viewed Bennett as a vulgar, violent, ignorant man who encouraged all of his father's worst instincts. In turn, Bennett regarded Edsel as a snob who, in his words, "hadn't the respect I thought he should have for men who came up through the ranks the hard way." He denigrated Edsel at every opportunity, and Henry would hear no criticism of Bennett from his son. This warped dynamic reached a climax when Henry appointed Bennett head of labor negotiations, a decision that infuriated Edsel. As his surrogate son and real son battled, the old man made clear his preference. "Over and over Henry Ford told me what a problem Edsel was to him," Sorensen reported. "Again and again I tried to impress upon him, without success, that his attempt to drive Edsel into line using Harry Bennett to annoy him and check his every move was breaking down Edsel's respect for him." But Henry remained determined to use Bennett to toughen up his son.[53]

Ironically, as hostility between Edsel and Bennett mounted, Edsel's relationship with Charles Sorensen improved markedly. For many years, the two had been rivals. "I do think that the old man set Sorensen against Edsel a great many times, deliberately," Lawrence Sheldrick said. "Edsel was aware of this, and I think it broke his heart." By the late 1930s, however, much of the hostility between the two had resolved into a workable arrange-ment. Sorensen's rough, even brutal management methods still upset Edsel, and the latter's quieter ways annoyed the hard-driving production chief. But several factors drew them together—Henry's growing instability, fear of Harry Bennett's rising influence, and genuine concern about the future of the company. In fact, as relations degenerated between the two Fords, Sorensen tried to serve as mediator, encouraging Edsel to persevere and urging Henry to curb his abusive behavior.[54]

By the 1940s, Henry's mental disintegration was producing outbursts that made the situation unbearable. His criticisms of Edsel became obses-sions, and increasingly bizarre directives reflected clouded judgments. In the spring of 1941, he decreed that Edsel's two eldest sons, Henry II and Benson, who had come to work for the company a few months earlier, should be banished as far away from Dearborn as possible. There appeared neither rhyme nor reason to the order. Sorensen and Edsel decided to visit Henry together, and the production chief threatened to quit if the Ford grandsons were sent away. Henry backed down, but Sorensen never forgot his countenance as Sorensen walked into his office with Edsel. "A look of hatred came over his face. I had never seen that expression before."[55]

In this highly charged atmosphere of family tension, an additional strain appeared. Edsel began to experience recurrent stomach pain and vomiting that proved resistant to treatment. "On one of our trips to Wash-ington, he was suddenly taken ill after a seafood dinner," Sorensen reported. "I got him back to our hotel rooms and called a doctor. Edsel was in such agony that I sat up with him all night." When the ailment was diagnosed as ulcers brought on by stress, the doctors advised him to cut back on work in order to ease his worries. Edsel attempted to do so, but with limited success. Henry, of course, was quick to blame his son's health problems on Grosse Pointe parties, alcohol consumption, and smoking. "If there is anything the matter with Edsel's health he can correct it himself," he told associates. "First, he will have to change his way of living. Then I'll get my chiropractor to work on him." Henry developed a standard prescription to remedy his son's health: "Edsel must mend his ways."[56]

Edsel's condition deteriorated. In January 1942, he underwent an operation for ulcers and surgeons removed part of his stomach. After the surgery, he improved slightly, but within months he began to lose weight and appeared increasingly wan and weak. To complicate matters, he also suffered undulant fever, an infectious, debilitating malady that is contracted from bacteria in unpasteurized dairy products. It is characterized by high fevers, chills, diarrhea, and weight loss, and at that time it was incurable. Ironically, it is likely that Edsel caught the fever by drinking milk from his father's farms. For years Henry had rejected the advice of medical and nutritional experts, insisting that pasteurizing milk was unnecessary. After Edsel was struck down, Henry stopped serving this milk in Greenfield Village and ordered Ray Dahlinger to get rid of all the cows on his farms. Nonetheless, he stubbornly insisted that his son's living habits were the source of his sickness. In November, Edsel returned to the hospital after a relapse and underwent another stomach surgery.[57]

It was becoming obvious to everyone but his father that Edsel was gravely ill. In the middle of this health crisis, Henry indulged in a shameful display that threatened to open a total breach with his only son. In a phone call on April 15, 1943, he ordered Sorensen to confront Edsel the next morning and demand a reform in his attitude and behavior. He reiterated his faith in Harry Bennett, declared he would support Bennett against every obstacle, and demanded that Edsel fully acquiesce in Bennett's authority over labor issues. To drive the point home, Henry ordered Sorensen to fire A. M. Wibel—the capable head of purchasing, who had worked at the company since 1912—because he had tangled recently with Bennett. Henry took an even harsher stand on personal issues. He insisted that Edsel end his long friendship with Ernest Kanzler and change his diet, drinking, and lifestyle. Sorensen was flabbergasted at this irrational tirade. "What a brutal thing to do to one's son!" he told himself. "To send me to tell him this!" The next morning, Sorensen visited Edsel and conveyed Henry's sentiments along with his own commiseration and support. The younger Ford, physically and emotionally exhausted, threw in the towel. "The best thing for me to do is to resign. My health won't let me go on," he said to Sorensen wearily. Henry backed away when Sorensen told the old man that he would follow Edsel out of the company, but this episode marked the breaking point for the son, who decided he could take his father's abuse no longer. Sadly, he would not have to.[58]

In late April, Edsel collapsed and was taken to his home at Gaukler Pointe. Eleanor then told the family, including Henry and Clara, what she had known since the operation in November: her husband had been diagnosed with incurable stomach cancer. When Henry heard that his son was dying, he refused to believe it. He frantically contacted the doctors at the Ford Hospital and demanded that they restore Edsel's health. He told associates, "You know, Edsel's not going to die." Henry's physician, Dr. Roy McClure, explained these irrational outbursts: "Henry Ford is a sick man, too. We must expect him to say and do unusual things." Throughout the month of May, Edsel remained bedridden at Gaukler Pointe as Eleanor and a team of doctors and nurses administered to his needs as best they could. But he steadily slipped away, occasionally mustering the energy to take a brief walk along the lakeshore. Finally, Edsel fell into a coma and at 1:00 a.m. on May 26, 1943, he died at age forty-nine.[59]

Henry Ford was shattered by his son's death. He went through Edsel's funeral "like a piece of stone," according to one observer, and was overheard muttering to himself, "Well, nothing to do, just work harder, work harder." Over the next few weeks, he went about in a daze. John McIntyre, the powerhouse engineer at Fair Lane, met the old man coming toward him on the path from the house and prepared to offer his condolences. But Ford "walked right past me and looked down at the cement. He didn't even see me," McIntyre said. "When the boy left, it just seemed to take something out of him." Ford tried to comfort himself with talk of reincarnation, telling Bennett, "Well, Harry, you know my belief—Edsel isn't dead." But Bennett knew better and described the death as "the greatest single catastrophe he ever suffered."[60]

In his pain, Henry lashed out at others and himself. He blamed the doctors for killing his son and denounced the medical profession. When it was suggested that he donate money to the cancer fund for medical research in his son's memory, he exploded in rage. He blamed everyone in the company who had clashed with his son (except Bennett), showing up at the River Rouge to announce, "I'm going to fire everybody around here who worried Edsel!" But he also wrestled with his own inner torment. "The Misses [sic] sits down and cries and gets over it, feels a little better. I just cannot do it," he told an associate. "I just have a lump here and there is nothing I can do about it." He compulsively revisited his own abusive treatment of his only child, which he knew in his heart to be the real problem. Alone with Bennett, he returned to the topic day after day as he tried to assuage his guilt.

"Harry, do you honestly think I was ever cruel to Edsel?" he would ask. "Well, cruel, no; but unfair, yes," Bennett answered. "If that had been me, I'd have got mad." Ford would reply, "That's what I wanted him to do—get mad."[61]

Though he could do nothing to bring back the son he had failed to remake in his own image, he made a pathetic attempt to enshrine Edsel's memory. In 1944, he dedicated the Edsel Ford Building at Greenfield Village. The small brick structure contained a replica of Edsel's boyhood workshop, which had sat over the garage at the Fords' old Edison Avenue home. It was filled with small machines and workbenches like the ones his son had tinkered with so many years before. "He wanted to preserve the things Edsel used when he was a boy on Edison Avenue. I thought he was quite sentimental about it," noted a friend.[62]

As Henry's agitation over Edsel's death subsided, a permanent cloud of gloom and guilt settled in its place. It became clear that he had suffered an emotional wound that could be bandaged but would never really heal. One day he came to get a haircut from Joe Zaroski and pulled out his wallet to show some family pictures. "Joe, look. This is Edsel when he was a little child, and I was very proud of him," Henry said. "My son had everything to live for, but he worked too hard and now he is gone." Zaroski glanced at Ford's face. "He had tears in his eyes. He was a lonely old gentleman." Bennett, who saw Ford every day, concluded that it was "impossible to describe how deeply the loss of his son hit him. After that he wasn't anti-Semitic or anti-Catholic or anything else. He was just a tired old man who wanted to live in peace."[63]

Edsel's death particularly accelerated Henry's mental decline. He seemed to lose both his zest for life and his tenuous grip on reality. "The sparkle went from his eyes," noted one associate. Ford began to live more in the past. As his memory failed with regard to immediate issues and personalities, he asked befuddled questions about basic matters that he knew already, or should have known. At times he seemed aware of his memory loss, but offered the sad explanation that he *wanted* to forget. "I put those things out of my mind so I won't have to worry about them," he told Rufus Wilson.[64]

Edsel's death also caused a brief rift between Henry and Clara. For years she had endured the tension between her husband and son, sharing some of Henry's misgivings about the boy's lifestyle yet sympathizing with Edsel's wish to lead his own life. Loyal to the two most important people in her life, she refused to choose between them. Edsel's passing, however, with its crushing load of grief, seems to have roused resentment over her husband's long persecution of their only child. For weeks after the funeral, they barely spoke; he walked the fields and woods of their estate, inconsolable, and she sat silently in the mansion, weeping and brooding. "After fifty-five years together their son was the one subject they could not discuss. The wound was too deep and painful," wrote an observer. Finally, one morning, Clara told Henry that the flowers were in bloom and they needed to gather some bouquets for the house. Handing him a basket and garden scissors, she led him into the gardens, where they spent the morning together. Although few words were spoken, they seemed to reconcile emotionally and move back into their familiar routines.[65]

In many ways, Edsel Ford's death claimed a second victim: it sent his father into an emotional nosedive from which he never really recovered. But Henry made one final, brash move that reflected some of his old fire. It created a crisis that damaged not only his personal well-being but that of the company he had headed for forty years.

The night before Edsel was buried, Henry Ford called Charles Sorensen. The production chief, who had grown used to his boss's occasionally bizarre communications in recent years, was nonetheless astonished. Ford announced his intent to take over again as president of the Ford Motor Company in order to allay any fears about its future. "My immediate reaction was 'impossible,' " noted a despairing Sorensen. "Mentally and physically he was unable to handle the job." Nonetheless, at a directors' meeting held on June 1, 1943, Henry Ford was elected president. Thus began what one historian of the company has called "the years of the Mad Hatter," as a mentally unstable Ford presided over the dissolution of his empire.[66]

Near chaos ensued. Almost immediately it became obvious that the founder was not up to the job. Henry fell into reveries for the past. He fantasized about the golden age of the company, telling Joe Galamb, "Joe, we have to go back to the old days, the Model T days. We've got to build only one car. There won't be any Mercury, no Lincoln, no other car—just the one Ford." Directors' meetings were a farce. Ford would enter the room with Bennett, walk around and shake hands with everyone, and then say, "Come on, Harry, let's get the hell out of here. We'll probably change everything they do, anyway." His mental lapses dismayed everyone who encountered them. Even Bennett had become concerned by the fall of 1943: "Mr. Ford was not himself at intervals. He was losing his memory, and on occasions his mind was confused." In such fashion, one of the world's largest industrial concerns began floundering and listing in the middle of a global war.[67]

Agitation and confusion reigned. Edsel Ford's family resented that the company directors, meeting only four days after his death, had reinstalled Henry in the presidency and surrounded him on the board with Bennett and several of his cronies. Eleanor, perturbed by the treatment her husband had endured for years from his father and Bennett, believed that her eldest son, Henry II, had been cast aside. She had several furious arguments with her father-in-law over the new company arrangement. Clara, in her quiet way, backed Eleanor by touting her grandson's qualities. But Henry remained obdurate. He distrusted his namesake because of the boy's conversion to Catholicism when he had married in 1940 and his bevy of wealthy friends from Grosse Pointe. He continued to back Bennett to the hilt.[68]

Other equally powerful divisions prevailed at the company. After Edsel's death, Sorensen assumed even greater responsibility for production at Willow Run and the Rouge, but he grew weary of Henry's feebleminded meddling and Bennett's hostility, and started to buckle under the strain. He contemplated retirement, and pleaded, at every opportunity, for Henry to bring his grandson into the company to take over. Meanwhile, Bennett stepped into the power vacuum and became de facto head of the company. He claimed to be the spokesman for Henry Ford, and whenever a decision needed to be made he would disappear for several hours, return insisting he had talked to his boss at Fair Lane, and issue a directive. No one felt secure enough to challenge him. Bennett moved ruthlessly to purge the company of all who had been allies of Edsel and Sorensen. By 1944, he had fired or pressured out A. M. Wibel, the purchasing manager; John Crawford, Edsel's most trusted assistant for many years; Fred Black, the public-relations man; Lawrence Sheldrick, the engineer who had played a key role in developing many Ford automobile models; E. T. Gregorie, the designer who had worked with Edsel; and several other executives.[69]

The wild card in this high-stakes poker game of corporate politics was Henry II. At the urging of his family, and with the help of Sorensen's connections, he had been released from the navy in August 1943 to return to Dearborn to participate in the management of the company. Immediately the twenty-five-year-old moved into his father's old office. Young Ford nosed about the company and studied its various operations, careful all the while to keep a low profile. Bennett distrusted him and did everything possible to isolate him, and most employees were afraid to be seen with the young man because of Bennett's hostility. Pleasant, tall, and handsome, if rather pudgy, and with no business experience and a poor student record including a withdrawal from Yale over a cheating scandal, Henry II did not seem to pose much of a threat. Only gradually did his toughness and determination emerge, as Sorensen glimpsed one day while sitting in young

Ford's office. Henry took a phone call from Bennett, who launched into a tirade over some company issue. Ford listened quietly and put the phone down after the explosion ended. "Young Henry was composed and resumed his talk with me as though nothing had happened," Sorensen reported. "The boy can take it, I said to myself happily; everything will work out all right."[70]

Henry II began to assemble a team of experienced, capable advisers. Mead Bricker and Logan Miller were key production managers at the Willow Run plant. John R. Davis was a sales manager whom Edsel had smuggled to California to protect him from Bennett's wrath in the prewar years, and who now returned to Dearborn. John Bugas, a former head of the Detroit office of the FBI, came to work after investigating wartime thefts at the River Rouge plant. Meeting secretly at the Detroit Club, where Bennett's men would have a hard time eavesdropping or planting bugs, this quartet showed young Ford the ropes. They plotted to oust Bennett and reform the company. Henry hated Bennett, later describing him as "the dirtiest, lousiest son-of-a-bitch I ever met in my life." But he moved cautiously, avoiding direct confrontation while making friends and allies in the Ford organization.[71]

Against this backdrop of uncertainty and intrigue, the situation with Sorensen reached a climax. Bennett's hostility to his old rival gained momentum when the elder Ford turned against his longtime deputy. Jealous of the favorable wartime publicity that was going Sorensen's way, Ford had become incensed about a 1942 article in *Fortune*, "Sorensen of the Rouge." It sang the praises of the plant manager and his endeavors to get Willow Run up and running, while barely mentioning Henry Ford. The piece struck a nerve with the old man, an associate noted, because it suggested he was "no longer being able to keep up with the activities" of his own company. Never one to share the limelight, Ford became suspicious that Sorensen was trying to push him to the sidelines. He exploded when he heard that Sorensen was sending out letters under the title "General Manager." "I'm the general manager here," he told Bennett, "and if I ever find out there's another general manager around here I'll fire him."[72]

Finally, Sorensen succumbed. Hemmed in by Bennett's maneuvers and deserted by Henry Ford, he departed for a vacation in Florida in early 1944 after telling Ford he was considering retirement. The old man, exhibiting signs of incomprehension, replied, "I guess there's something in life besides work." A few weeks later, on March 2, not quite a year after Edsel's death, Sorensen received a call from Frank Campsall, who conveyed the message that Henry Ford wanted him out. Although shocked, Sorensen immediately issued a statement of resignation. Though he had approved the firing, Ford never quite grasped either the gravity, or even the fact, of Sorensen's departure. According to Bennett, for months afterward his boss would get into the car and ask to go see Charlie.

> "Why, he's not here anymore," I'd answer.
> "He's not!" Mr. Ford would exclaim. "Where is he?"
> "He's gone," I'd say.
> And the next day Mr. Ford would say, "Let's go over and see Charley." After a while I just didn't answer.

Sorensen's departure, along with the enfeebled state of Henry Ford, made it clear that Harry Bennett had become the master of the Ford Motor Company.[73]

Over the next few months, Henry grew steadily more confused and exhibited irrational fears of persecution. According to Bennett, when Ford was at meetings or gatherings, "usually he didn't know where he was," and when the old man asked him to check the pills doctors had given him, Bennett discovered that they were "phenobarbital, a sedative." Then in early 1945, Ford suffered a debilitating stroke while on a trip to Richmond Hill. During the long car ride south in February, he began complaining of illness, and at a hotel stop in Nashville he was suffering from chills and disorientation. The next day, he seemed to recover, but then collapsed upon reaching his winter home. He lay down on a couch and refused to move. Clara believed he had "nerve exhaustion," and after a very short stay, during which her husband appeared completely listless, they returned to Dearborn. Back at Fair Lane, Ford remained mentally and physically languid and often failed to recognize old friends or associates. "He didn't want to go out or meet anyone," reported Mrs. Stanley Ruddiman. "During this period he depended very much on Mrs. Ford. . . . He didn't want her out of his sight." Ford, Bennett confirmed, was "in a constantly confused state, he was kept from going out in public, was carefully guarded, and was permitted to see no one outside the family."[74]

A few years later, in a deposition for a lawsuit, Dr. John G. Mateer, Ford's attending physician, described his patient's condition in the spring of 1945. Ford, he wrote,

> had no recollection. He had a memory of past events but not recent things, which is usual and typical in the development of senility. During rides with Henry Ford, he would ask the same question several times to which the doctor would make the same answer, and of this Mr. Ford had no recollection. . . .

Mr. Ford lost his initiative in starting conversations. . . . Mr. Ford became limited to "yes" and "no" answers.

During 1945, Mrs. Ford recognized her husband's mental impairment and protected him from any business talks. Henry Ford probably would not have been able to conduct business conversations intelligently. While Mr. Ford, even in his last year, would go to some social functions, Mrs. Ford was always there and protecting him. . . .

In May 1945, Mr. Ford did know and recognize his immediate family, but probably not many others beyond the family. . . . Mr. Ford was doing no reasoning.

The industrialist, Dr. Mateer concluded, could be characterized as "a pleasant vegetable."[75]

Henry Ford's collapse in early 1945 made the situation at the company intolerable. The family, particularly Eleanor and Clara, quietly planned to move the incapacitated president aside and elevate his eldest grandson into his place. The event that sparked the revolution, however, came accidentally. Around this same time, young Henry discovered a codicil to his grandfather's will that outraged the entire family. The document called for the company to be run by a board of trustees for ten years after the founder's death. The board would be headed by Bennett and consist largely of his friends and allies. No members of the Ford family were on it. Henry II immediately threatened to quit and write Ford dealers all over the country advising them to desert the company. After cooling the young heir down, John Bugas confronted Bennett about the codicil. Obviously perturbed at being smoked out, Bennett hauled out the original document and a carbon copy and burned them, pushed the ashes into an envelope, and told Bugas, "Take this back to Henry." Though the legitimacy of the document remained unclear—Bennett reported later that the elder Ford had carried the original codicil around in his pocket for a long time, scribbling things on it, including Bible verses, and that it was not even certain he had signed it— its very existence prodded the family into action. Clara joined Eleanor in pressuring Henry to step aside, and he stubbornly refused. Finally, when the Ford matrons threatened to sell their stock in the company if Henry II was not made president, the old man relented.[76]

Henry asked his namesake to come to Fair Lane. "My grandfather told me he was planning to step down and let me be president of the company," as young Henry later described the scene. "I told him I'd take it only if I had a completely free hand to make any changes I wanted to make. We argued about that—but he didn't withdraw his offer." Clara, sitting in on the meeting, voiced support for her grandson. "Henry, I think young Henry should take over," she told her husband. "Look, you're not well . . . and it's about time somebody got in there." Frank Campsall drew up a letter of resignation, and the founder signed it.[77]

A dramatic directors' meeting was held the next day, September 21, 1945. As Ford's letter of resignation was read, Bennett leaped to his feet, hurled a sarcastic congratulation to Henry II, and started to leave the room. Other directors prevailed upon him to stay, however, so he was present as the younger Ford was elected president of the company. The new chief officer wasted little time. As the meeting ended, he asked Bennett to come to his office. "I told him, then and there, that I had plans for reorganizing the company and that he didn't fit into them," Henry related. "I told him that John Bugas was taking over his job as industrial relations director the next day." "I was frightened to death that it wouldn't stick," Ford later confessed. Bennett blustered, angrily telling the young man, "You're taking over a billion-dollar organization here that you haven't contributed a thing to." But he seemed to accept his fate fairly calmly. Only later in the day did he explode. As Bugas sat in Bennett's office preparing to discuss the transition, Bennett whirled on him and exclaimed, "You dirty son of a bitch, you did this to me!" He pulled a .45 automatic from his desk. Bugas, the old FBI man, had anticipated the possibility of violence, and he calmly raised a .38 from the holster under his arm. "Don't make the mistake of pulling the trigger, because I'll kill you," he replied. "I won't miss. I'll put one right through your heart, Harry." Bennett set down his gun, and Bugas walked out, not at all sure he wouldn't be shot in the back. Bennett did not fire, however, and for the rest of the afternoon he burned papers in his office wastebasket, then left the plant for the last time. The next day, the new company president went to Fair Lane to tell his grandfather that Bennett had been fired. The old man took in the news, pondered it for a few moments, and responded quietly: "Well, now Harry is back where he started from."[78]

After handing over the reins of the company, old Henry fell ever deeper into a mental fog. Mrs. Ruddiman noticed that as his grandson took over the company he appeared curiously detached. "You would almost think he didn't know anything about it," she said. Over the next year and a half, she witnessed his transformation into a doddering old man childishly dependent upon his wife. "I don't think his mind wandered so much as that it didn't function. He would talk to you, but not as a person or individual he had known," Mrs. Ruddiman noted. "After he had gone, you had this feeling, 'I don't think he really knew me.' " Clara, shouldering the task of protecting her husband, who had become a mental invalid, performed brilliantly. She was "just beautiful in her love, attention, and steadfastness," Mrs. Ruddiman noted.[79]

From the autumn of 1945 to the spring of 1947, Henry Ford's life became a series of sad vignettes. Although enjoying periods of lucidity, much of the time he seemed unable to think rationally or speak coherently. He followed his wife about the house or sat staring into space. Every few days he went for a ride with Robert Rankin, and they explored the Dearborn area. When he felt perky, he would tell Rankin stories from his youth as, according to the driver, "he began to live in the past." Once in a while, Ford would be driven through Greenfield Village and try to give the "high sign" to people he recognized, although he never spoke. "The last time I saw him in the plant, he was standing in the middle of the laboratory floor, with a wan smile on his lips, like a lost child, and a faraway expression in his eyes— not noticing any person or thing in particular, and not knowing which way to turn," reported Irving Bacon. "The spirit of Henry Ford wasn't there any more." On his last vacation in the Upper Peninsula, he was observed trying to make a phone call. "He could hardly make it. His words were very weak, and Mrs. Ford took over the phone to finish the conversation," related an employee. "He sat there as if he were more or less in a daze, just looking at the floor. He didn't even look up." Although appearing emotionless most of the time, once in a while he said something suggesting that he was aware, at some level, of his unhappy state. When visiting the Moir House, where he had lived with Clara many decades before, he told Rankin, "I've got a lot of money and I'd give *every* penny of it right now just to be here with Mrs. Ford the same as I was in the old days."[80]

Henry Ford might have been better remembered, however, from an effort made a short time before. With perhaps his final flashes of awareness, he had tried to leave a valedictory in 1944 and early 1945, in the months before his last, devastating stroke. Sensing the gathering momentum of his own decline, he had struggled to compose a compendium of his basic principles for future generations to ponder. John W. Thompson became his assistant in this project. When he felt up to it, Ford would talk about issues he felt were important while Thompson took notes. Eventually, the two men began meeting in the engineering lab several mornings a week. Thompson used an Ediphone to record Ford's comments, and then had them typed up. Ford would review the text at the next session and indicate changes.[81]

The result was a thirty-two-page manuscript entitled "Thoughts for the Future." Loosely organized and written in short, simple sentences, the essay provided a final testimonial to Henry Ford's deepest beliefs. True to his old populist principles, he began by extolling "the people." He argued that Americans needed to express their individualism and remember that "government was not intended to dominate the people. It was designed merely to serve them." His pacifist convictions produced the assertion that "almost everything that is wrong in this world can be traced to war. It is the one blockade to moral and material progress." He urged all citizens to join in "the continuing fight for peace." Of crucial importance, of course, was identifying the "war makers" who stood to profit from mass killing. "You will find greed at the bottom of all wars," he wrote.[82]

Ford explained the ideals by which he had lived. He contended that the body must be nourished by "proper diet and exercise," the mind by "practical education," and the soul by "full acceptance of the individual's moral responsibility toward his fellow man." He reiterated his old belief in abundance. "The earth is a luxuriantly bountiful place. There is plenty of everything for everybody," he maintained. "We have not begun to find all that it holds for us nor how to make the best use of all it affords." He reaffirmed his loyalty to the land and argued that people must return to rural areas as new and productive ways to work the soil were discovered.[83]

In a particularly interesting passage, Ford acknowledged that pride in "the machine age" and "mass production" had produced a society of concentrated industrial production and impersonal cities. "We have fallen into a philosophy of bigness which is not good for the American way of life," Ford wrote. He acknowledged his own complicity. "In the race to see how fast and how cheaply we could produce these things we seem to have overlooked the human side of the picture—at least some of us have. We didn't do this knowingly," he wrote. "By increasing wages and making available more conveniences at lower and lower prices, we probably thought we were doing all we could for people." His solution, of course, lay in the plan he had been promoting for the last fifteen years: factories in the countryside or in small towns, where people could work both industrially and agriculturally.[84]

Ford concluded on an idealistic note. He said that "some form of religion exists in every man" as an impulse seeking "the principle of right and wrong, the power of good in the world." Moreover, religion and education must work as partners in the "teaching of moral law and the training of conscience." For Ford, the ultimate expression of morality and spirituality would be a "world organization" to ensure peace and prosperity. This "parliament of man," in Ford's view, would represent people from around the globe, mediate their differences, and guarantee order and abundance.[85]

According to Thompson, Ford tried to publish "Thoughts for the Future." Wartime restrictions on paper and political sensitivities, however, persuaded him to postpone publication, although he did have a few copies

run off at the print shop in Greenfield Village. Ford's final stroke aborted
the project, and it never found an audience, lying buried among his papers.
Nonetheless, this simple declaration of philosophy opened a window into
the mind of one the most influential figures in the making of modern America and illuminated his last thoughts. Within a short time, that window
would be closed forever.[86]

Epilogue

The Sage of Dearborn

The end came thick with irony. Almost eighty-four years earlier, in the summer of 1863, Henry Ford had been born by candlelight in a bedroom of his family's farmhouse. Now, during the first weekend of April 1947, torrential rains flooded the Dearborn area, knocking out electrical and telephone lines and forcing inhabitants once again to light candles for illumination. The clock also turned back in another way, as Ford showed some flashes of his old spirit on this Easter weekend. On Monday, April 7, he greeted family and friends, made several small jokes, and enthusiastically traveled about the area with his driver. As Robert Rankin noted with surprise, "He was just like his old self that day."[1]

Ford began his day in usual fashion with a good breakfast. Because of the electricity outage, Mrs. Rankin had prepared a meal of oatmeal, bacon, toast, prunes, and coffee and sent it with her husband for the Fords. After eating, Henry summoned Rankin to go for a ride to see the impact of the flooding. As they departed, he told his driver, "Your wife makes the best oatmeal that I've ever tasted in my life," and then joked that she should, because of her husband's Scottish ancestry. They briefly visited Greenfield Village, stopped by Ray Dahlinger's office, and then continued to the Rouge plant, where Rankin mistakenly turned into a one-way driveway. When he tried to turn around, Ford said mischievously, "Let's go anyway and see what will happen." He chuckled as people began yelling for them to go back—until they saw the passenger in the car. From there Rankin drove Ford to a small Congregational church, where Ford, who was wearing bedroom slippers and did not want to get out on the wet ground, talked briefly with the minister through the car window. Ford then visited the boat dock on the River Rouge, where he saw his two yachts, the *Benson Ford* and the *Henry Ford*.[2]

As they drove through Dearborn looking at the flood, Ford was fascinated by its impact. At one point he joked, "Yeah, the water must be going
down. You can see the tops of the cars now." The pair finished their tour by
driving through the town's Catholic cemetery, where Ford identified a
number of old friends and distant relatives, and then stopping for a longer
period at a small graveyard on Joy Road. Ford looked out at the headstones
for a while, and then said, "Rankin, this is where I'm going to be buried
when I die. In among the rest of my folks here." Upon returning to Fair
Lane, Ford walked to the powerhouse to consult with Charles Voorhess.
The generators had been knocked out by the flood, but while they were
there the lights flickered on briefly. "Well," Ford kidded Voorhess, "I'm
going up and tell Mrs. Ford that I've been down here and fixed it." The
engineer noted that his boss "looked to be in the best condition I'd seen in a
long time." Then the lights went out again; they would stay out for the next
two days. Voorhess and John McIntyre were unable to reach the coal bin but
managed to keep heat going for the house by stoking the furnace fire with
logs handed in through the window.[3]

Henry and Clara had a pleasant turkey supper by candles and kerosene
lamps as servants stoked a fireplace for additional heat. After the meal,
McIntyre went to the house to warn the Fords that continuing problems
with floodwater might keep the lights out all night. Ford had arisen from his
chair in the living room and came into the hall to shake hands. Now he put
his hand on McIntyre's shoulder and replied, "That's all right, Scottie. I
know you will stick by me; you've always done it for years. I never worry
about these things." Henry and Clara sat before the open fire in the living
room for a time, and she read to him. But the dim candlelight proved to be
a strain on her eyes, so they retired upstairs about 9 p.m.[4]

Ford undressed and drank a glass of warm milk to aid his sleep. Emerging from his bathroom to climb into bed, he suffered a coughing fit, but
recovered after a few minutes and went to sleep. Within a couple of hours,
however, he awoke, breathing heavily and complaining of a headache and
dry throat. As his condition worsened, Clara and the longtime maid, Rosa
Buhler, sent a messenger to get Rankin from his home. Rankin found a
working telephone at the Ford Engineering Laboratory and summoned Dr.
Mateer. The physician rushed to the scene from Grosse Pointe as Clara sat
quietly beside her husband on the bed, holding his head on her shoulder,
giving him sips of water, and comforting him in the candlelight. Mateer
arrived at the mansion just after midnight. Eve Dahlinger, alerted by Ford
servants, had also hurried to the residence, and was with Clara when Henry
Ford II and his wife arrived shortly before Mateer. They were all too late.
Henry Ford had died at approximately 11:40 p.m. on April 7, 1947, from a

massive cerebral hemorrhage. The doctor told Clara that Henry's stooping over to untie his shoelaces had probably caused a blood vessel to break, thus triggering the coughing and then the hemorrhage.[5]

Two days later, Ford lay in state at Greenfield Village as an enormous crowd gathered to pay their respects. Eventually, the mile-long line of some hundred thousand mourners filed by his open casket. The next day, Ford's funeral was conducted at St. Paul's Cathedral in Detroit before hundreds of invited guests, while a crowd of some thirty thousand gathered outside. After the service, his body was conveyed to the small cemetery on Joy Road and interred as police struggled to deal with another crowd, of around twenty thousand. Ford's headstone, a piece of white marble roughly three and a half feet by seven feet, displayed the engraving of a cross and the plain inscription:

HENRY FORD
July 30, 1863
April 7, 1947[6]

In the days following Ford's death, tributes appeared in newspapers and magazines, legislative resolutions and sermons, private telegrams and corporate news releases throughout the nation. The great majority of this commentary was favorable, noting the industrialist's huge impact on modern life. Much of it was even affectionate, recognizing his special status as a kind of American folk hero. Though some assessments, particularly in leftist and prolabor outlets, denounced Ford for his union-busting and anti-Semitic endeavors, they were buried in a landslide of praise. Most people seemed to venerate him, admire his accomplishments, and forgive his faults.[7]

Over the course of a long life, Henry Ford had become an American icon. By developing methods of mass production to bring cars to ordinary citizens, he had changed their lives irrevocably. The automobile had wrought a revolution, ending the isolation of rural life, boosting suburban development, creating a road-and-highway system along with accompanying service industries, making the car industry perhaps the keystone of America's modern economy, causing an expansion of the credit system through installment buying, and changing the nature of courtship and mating patterns. Henry Ford did more than any other single individual to wrench Americans out of the horse-and-buggy days of the nineteenth century and place them in the mobile world of the twentieth.

Moreover, Ford shaped not only how Americans led their lives in the modern era, but how they thought about those lives. His vision of a liberated, experience-seeking mass of citizens *defined* standards of modern contentment. Not just practical transportation but enriching new encounters, recreation, and enjoyment of a shiny, powerful machine itself paved the highway to happiness. Not just respectable prosperity but material abundance emerged as a sign of fulfillment. Ford's articulation of a consumer ethic helped recast popular ideas about "the pursuit of happiness" in a new mold for the modern era, and the automobile became its pre-eminent symbol. As one of political philosopher Isaiah Berlin's "hedgehogs"—unlike "foxes," who grasp many smaller things, hedgehogs understand one big thing—Ford grasped the central dynamic of modern life earlier than just about anyone else. Charles Sorensen once remarked that Ford was able to "demonstrate the superiority of an economy of abundance over one of scarcity, and to begin the elevation of a standard of living to a height never before dreamed of." The United States—indeed, the world—would never be quite the same.[8]

In leading this revolution, Ford developed a personal image that put an important modern twist on the American tradition of the self-made man. Like Theodore Roosevelt in politics, Will Rogers in entertainment, and Babe Ruth in sports, Ford attracted attention for who he was as well as what he did. With his instinctive sense of publicity, he skillfully manipulated the machinery of modern mass culture to keep his image and personality in the public eye. He used endless interviews, news releases, and a stream of ghost-written articles and books to make sure that people remained aware of his views and his projects. The idealism, eccentricity, or reactionary quality of his ideas only enhanced his aura, as did his penchant for folksy pronouncements. With his impressive achievements inflated even larger by publicity, Ford became America's first celebrity businessman.

His populist ideology and style completed the iconic image. Perhaps the wealthiest man in the world, Ford cherished his ties to common folk, and remained a loyal friend and defender of ordinary citizens throughout most of his life. He supported populism's producer ethic, its desire to remain close to the soil, and its suspicion of elite, urban financiers. Disdainful of Wall Street, he served proudly as the tribune of Main Street and sought to bring common people a comfortable, abundant life. At the same time, Ford's populism had changed over time. From its positive, idealistic form in his early life, it gradually mutated into a negative doctrine that searched for enemies and subversive agents, an impulse that created a mindless anti-Semitism and a hostility to labor unions. But most Americans preferred to remember the earlier Ford. Farmers and storekeepers, mechanics and janitors, machinists and office clerks, and all manner of people who worked for a living responded to Ford's lack of pretension and his interests and tastes. They sensed that, at heart, he was one of them.

For all his impact as an agent of historical change, however, Ford eventually proved the law of unintended consequences. He created the socioeconomic vehicle of consumer capitalism that carried Americans into the modern world and enthusiastically anticipated its promises of self-fulfillment. But then he perceived the growth of shallow materialism, licentious desires, and a declining work ethic, and became fearful of degeneration. Similarly, Ford pioneered the development of modern industrial capitalism with the assembly line, vertical integration of the production process, and high wages. Yet here, too, he blanched at the subsequent appearance of rationalized corporate bureaucracy, advertising, urban population growth, and yearly model changes. Like many Americans who experienced the relentless pace of historical change in the early twentieth century, he began to yearn for the past even while embracing the future.

Ford's response, in part, revealed his limitations as a historical actor. Reluctant to abandon older loyalties to work and productivity, thrift and prudence, he built only the foundation of modern corporate, consumer capitalism, leaving to others the task of constructing the entire edifice. In a more positive sense, however, Ford acknowledged his fears in a way that strengthened his bond with the people. He sought to counteract the unforeseen degradations of the assembly line and the Rouge factory by enshrining the past in the Ford Museum, old-fashioned dancing, and Greenfield Village. This ambivalence boosted his status as a folk hero, and he somehow managed to become a living symbol *both* of progress and of respect for older values. Ford was a halfhearted revolutionary whose misgivings, by mirroring those of his fellow citizens, created a bond of endearment.[9]

The law of unintended consequences also had an impact in his private life. To be sure, as Ford rose to prominence by the 1910s, his personal life overflowed with interesting experiences and fascinating people, and he enjoyed no small portion of happiness. But his wealth and fame also brought an overweening hubris full of pitfalls. Increasingly isolated from anyone who would tell him no, Ford stubbornly stayed with an outdated Model T and wasted his social capital on a misguided attack on Jews. Unchallenged and unwilling to analyze his convictions, he endorsed wrongheaded labor policies that plunged his company into chaos. Convinced that his success in making cars had demonstrated a gift for solving social problems, he addressed public issues about which he was ignorant. Reluctant to share the spotlight or delegate power, he mistreated the son who sought only to honor his legacy. Like Citizen Kane, Ford became a victim of his own powerful personality and great success.

In spite of all this, however, Ford's achievement was breathtaking. As one commentator has reminded us, his ideas "have been so generally adopted that people no longer realize how enormously original they were and how extraordinarily fruitful they have been." Committed to mass production, high wages, consumer values, and the judgment of the people, Ford imagined modern America and drew up the blueprint for its realization. As that dream came to life, he became a symbol of the sea change that remade the United States in the first half of the twentieth century. In *Middletown* (1929), Robert and Helen Lynd reported that for the average American the automobile had become crucial "for leisure-time as well as getting-a-living activities." In their words, "Ownership of an automobile has now reached the point of being an accepted essential of normal living." Frederick Lewis Allen, in his popular book *Only Yesterday* (1931), confirmed that the automobile had "changed the face of America." By the 1930s, streets and highways in every region of the country "bloomed with garages, filling stations, hot-dog stands, chicken-dinner restaurants, tearooms, tourists' rests, camping sites, and affluence." People understood that Henry Ford had brought about this transformation.[10]

Ultimately, he represented both the possibilities and the problems of America's democratic culture in the modern era. On the positive side, Ford embodied its devotion to opportunity, openness to new ideas, lack of pretension, reformist idealism, veneration of productive work, desire for material comfort, and concern for the dignity and welfare of ordinary citizens. On the negative side, he displayed its narrow-mindedness that edged into bigotry, anti-intellectualism that made a pride of ignorance, a paranoid view of social dynamics that tended to blame enemies rather than analyze causes, and faith in the redemptive power of material goods that too often overlooked questions of social cost and spiritual meaning. In all of these ways, Henry Ford *was* modern America. As the people's tycoon during the formative years of the American century, he embodied most of their greatest strengths and more than a few of their greatest weaknesses.

Acknowledgments

It is a pleasure to acknowledge the many individuals who contributed in some way to the completion of this book. At Alfred A. Knopf, my editor, Ashbel Green, used his legendary skills over the last several years to help shape the manuscript and give my prose whatever elegance it may have. His editorial assistant, Luba Ostashevsky, generously offered her own expertise to complete a host of tasks in the latter stages of the project.

At the Benson Ford Research Center in Dearborn, Michigan, the staff treated me with great kindness over the course of several years during my research stays. They helped me understand a "complicated" filing system, suggested new avenues of inquiry, and brought great mounds of material for my inspection with unfailing good cheer. Special thanks go to Linda Skolarus, who assisted with issues and requests far too numerous to list, and to Andrew Schornick, the Columbo of the archives, who often was able to find the most obscure materials hidden in the nooks and crannies of this large facility. The entire staff has my gratitude; this book could not have been completed without their help.

In the Department of History at the University of Missouri, many people played significant roles. The departmental staff—Patty Eggleston, Sandy Kietzman, Melinda Lockwood, Jenny Morton, Karen Pecora, Nancy Taube—helped relieve the burdens of a beleaguered chairman by taking care of business efficiently and well. Many colleagues offered sustenance (intellectual and otherwise) over the last few years in discussions, at lunches, or at Friday afternoon seminars: Carol Anderson, Richard Bienvenu, John Bullion, Win Burggraaff, Mark Carroll, Robert Collins, John Frymire, Lois Huneycutt, Abdullahi Ibrahim, Larry Okamura, Jeff Pasley, Mark Smith, Jonathan Sperber, John Wigger, Ian Worthington. Several research assistants—Mary Jane Edele, Mary Ann Fitzwilson, and, especially, Elizabeth Read—did wonderful work gathering and organizing research material. My pal of many years, Cindy Sheltmire, kindly proofread the manuscript when it first reached printed form. Catherine Damme deserves special credit. Her skillful assistance with research, editing, and word processing proved invaluable, while her comments on the text never failed to get me thinking about an important issue in a fresh way.

My agent, Ronald Goldfarb, has been a star. Whether negotiating contracts, offering shrewd career advice, or just being a friend, he continues to be indispensable to the successful completion of my books. I also owe special thanks to my good friend and fellow author, Steve Weinberg, whose encouragement and enthusiasm for the project never flagged, and to Sherrie Goettsch, whose photographic skills produced a picture where, contrary to tradition, I do not look as if a bill for overdue taxes had just arrived in the mail.

Much appreciation goes to my family, noted in the dedication, and to my in-laws and new neighbors, Tom and Vivian Sokolich. My boon companions at the farm—Oscar, Maxine, Elvis, Levon, Lucy, Loretta, Jesse, Roady, May, and George—provided hours of pleasant distraction. My greatest thanks, of course, go to Patti Sokolich Watts for her support, interest, assistance, and understanding over the last several years. The book goes to her with familiar words: "You're going to love it."

Notes

Many of the following notes refer to documents held in the Ford Archives at the Benson Ford Research Center, located at the Henry Ford Museum and Greenfield Village in Dearborn, Michigan. Most of the research for this book was conducted there. This facility is an enormous repository of materials on the life of Henry Ford and the history of the Ford Motor Company. It contains thousands of items—interview transcripts, news stories, publicity scrapbooks, letters and correspondence, company publications, memoranda, photographs, personal papers, and so on. All citations to this material will indicate the Ford Archives (FA).

Several matters in the notes require brief explanation. First, HF stands for Henry Ford. Second, the FA organizes its holdings according to a system of accessions, so citations to archival material will designate an accession number, followed by a box number. Third, the FA houses several hundred interviews with friends and associates of Henry Ford that were conducted and transcribed in the early 1950s. Citations note these "Reminiscences," as they are called, and page numbers refer to the transcriptions. All "Reminiscences" are in acc. 65 in the FA. Fourth, the FA has a large number of articles and manuscripts arranged topically in special files. Thus some of the notes will designate "Vertical File," followed by the name of the person, incident, or topic around which it is organized.

My analysis of Henry Ford and American culture has been bolstered by a huge scholarly literature on such topics as consumerism, populism, celebrity, and progressivism. Because of space limitations, the notes indicate only the most salient secondary sources I have consulted.

Prologue

1. HF, quoted in Charles Merz, "Our Second Billionaire," *World's Work*, April 1929, p. 110, and in Allan L. Benson, *The New Henry Ford* (New York, 1923), p. 330.
2. A fuller account of Ford and the Mount Clemens trial, complete with citations of sources, appears in chap. 13.
3. "Businessman of the Century," *Fortune*, Nov. 22, 1999, pp. 108–28; poll of fifty-eight academic business experts conducted by Blaine McCormick of the Baylor University School of Business on April 1, 2002, results forwarded to me by personal letter.

One • Farm Boy

1. HF, *My Life and Work* (Garden City, N.Y., 1922), pp. 24, 34.
2. William Ford's comment was reported by longtime Dearborn resident George F. Holmes, "Reminiscences," p. 94, in acc. 65, FA.

3. Ibid., p. 2.

4. For a standard history of Michigan, see Willis F. Dunbar and George S. May, *Michigan: A History of the Wolverine State* (Grand Rapids, 1965). On the rise of the Republican Party and its essential ideas, see Eric Foner's brilliant treatment in *Free Soil, Free Labor, Free Men: The Ideology of the Republican Party Before the Civil War* (New York, 1970).

5. HF, "Loose Notes," in acc. 1, box 14-2, FA.

6. Ann Hood, "The Boy Henry Ford," in acc. 653, box 1, FA. This manuscript, produced in the 1930s by a schoolgirl reporter, was based on a number of extensive interviews with HF.

7. On HF's early experiences in school, see Margaret Ford Ruddiman, "Memories of My Brother, Henry Ford," *Michigan History*, Sept. 1953, pp. 240–42, 251–52; William A. Simonds, *Henry Ford: His Life, His Work, His Genius* (Indianapolis, 1943), p. 34; Sidney Olson, *Young Henry Ford: A Pictorial History of the First Forty Years* (Detroit, 1997 [1963]), pp. 15–16; and the following in FA: HF, "Loose Notes"; Dr. Edsel Ruddiman, "Reminiscences," pp. 1–3; Hood, "Boy Henry Ford."

8. Ruddiman, "Memories of My Brother," p. 237; William Ford, Jr., quoted in Ford R. Bryan, *The Fords of Dearborn: An Illustrated History* (Detroit, 1997), p. 99; HF, "Loose Notes."

9. HF, quoted in Edgar A. Guest, "Henry Ford Talks About His Mother," *American Magazine*, July 1923, pp. 116, 11.

10. Among many works illuminating the dominance of Victorian values in nineteenth-century America, see Daniel Walker Howe, ed., *Victorian America* (Philadelphia, 1975); Karen Halttunen, *Confidence Men and Painted Women: A Study of Middle-Class Culture in America, 1830–1870* (New Haven, 1982); John F. Kasson, *Rudeness and Civility: Manners in Nineteenth-Century America* (New York, 1990).

11. Guest, "Ford Talks About His Mother," pp. 119, 14.

12. Ibid., pp. 119, 120.

13. Ibid., pp. 119, 13.

14. Ibid., p. 12; Ruddiman, "Memories of My Brother," p. 237.

15. Hood, "Boy Henry Ford"; Ruddiman, "Memories of My Brother," p. 237; HF, quoted in Allan L. Benson, *The New Henry Ford* (New York, 1923), p. 19.

16. Reynold M. Wik, *Henry Ford and Grass-Roots America* (Ann Arbor, 1973), p. 204.

17. HF, "Loose Notes"; Hood, "Boy Henry Ford"; Ruddiman, "Memories of My Brother," p. 242.

18. John G. Cawelti, *Apostles of the Self-Made Man* (Chicago, 1965), p. 208. For analyses of the *McGuffey Reader*, see Richard D. Mozier, *Making the American Mind: Social and Moral Ideas in the McGuffey's Readers* (New York, 1947); Dolores P. Sullivan, *William Holmes McGuffey: Schoolmaster to the Nation* (Rutherford, N.J., 1994).

19. HF, "The McGuffey Readers," *Colophon: A Quarterly for Bookmen*, Spring 1936, p. 587.

20. Harvey C. Minnich, ed., *Old Favorites from the McGuffey Readers* (New York, 1936); HF, "McGuffey Readers," pp. 587–603; HF, speech to Federation of McGuffey Societies, July 2–3, 1938, in acc. 1, box 113, FA; Harvey C. Minnich, *William Holmes McGuffey and His Readers* (New York, 1936), pp. v, vii. A useful overview of HF's adult attempts to memorialize McGuffey appears in Ford Bryan's paper, "The Fords and the McGuffey's," Oct. 10, 1998, in Vertical File—"Wm. McGuffey," FA.

21. Ford R. Bryan, *Henry's Lieutenants* (Detroit, 1993), p. 55; W. J. Cameron, "The McGuffey Readers: A Talk Given on the Ford Sunday Evening Hour, March 17, 1935," in Vertical File—"Wm. McGuffey," FA.

22. HF and James C. Derieux, "The Making of an American Citizen," *Good Housekeeping*, Oct. 1934, p. 121; HF, "McGuffey Readers," p. 587; Charles Voorhess, "Reminiscences," pp. 150–51.

23. Hamlin Garland, "The Homely Side of Henry Ford," in Vertical File—"Henry Ford–Biography," FA; William C. Richards, *The Last Billionaire* (New York, 1948), p. 165.

Two • *Machinist*

1. Margaret Ford Ruddiman, "Memories of My Brother, Henry Ford," *Michigan History*, Sept. 1953, p. 249; Edward J. Cutler, "Reminiscences," p. 185.

2. Ruddiman, "Memories of My Brother," pp. 244, 226; HF, *My Life and Work* (Garden City, N.Y., 1922), pp. 200, 22; Edgar A. Guest, "Henry Ford Talks About His Mother," *American Magazine*, July 1923, p. 12.

3. HF, *My Life and Work*, p. 22; Ruddiman, "Memories of My Brother," pp. 243–44.

4. Ann Hood, "The Boy Henry Ford," in acc. 653, box 1, FA; HF, "Personal Notebook," in acc. 1, box 12-5, FA; HF, *My Life and Work*, pp. 22–23; Ruddiman, "Memories of My Brother," pp. 242–43.

5. Ruddiman, "Memories of My Brother," pp. 249, 244.

6. Edison, quoted in Allan L. Benson, *The New Henry Ford* (New York, 1923), p. 38.

7. Guest, "Ford Talks About His Mother," p. 120; HF, quoted in William A. Simonds, *Henry Ford: His Life, His Work, His Genius* (Indianapolis, 1943), p. 34.

8. Hood, "Boy Henry Ford."

9. For details on the early history of the Ford family in Dearborn, and William Ford's early life in particular, see Sidney Olson, *Young Henry Ford: A Pictorial History of the First Forty Years* (Detroit, 1997 [1963]), pp. 5–15; Ford R. Bryan, *The Fords of Dearborn: An Illustrated History* (Detroit, 1997), pp. 93–98.

10. Margaret Ford Ruddiman, "Reminiscences," p. 41; Ruddiman, "Memories of My Brother," pp. 236–37, 245; Clyde Ford, "Reminiscences," p. 6.

11. Ruddiman, "Memories of My Brother," pp. 254, 226, 245, 41, 237.

12. Ibid., pp. 245–46, 227. Among a vast historiography on republican and free-labor ideology, see Steven Watts, *The Republic Reborn: War and the Making of Liberal America, 1790–1820* (Baltimore, 1987); Charles Sellers, *The Market Revolution: Jacksonian America, 1815–1846* (New York, 1991); Eric Foner, *Free Soil, Free Labor, Free Men* (New York, 1970).

13. Guest, "Ford Talks About His Mother," p. 119; Hood, "Boy Henry Ford"; Detroit *Free Press* article, quoted in Bryan, *Fords of Dearborn*, p. 102; HF, quoted in Olson, *Young Henry Ford*, p. 19.

14. HF, *My Life and Work*, pp. 22–23.

15. Ruddiman, "Memories of My Brother," p. 259.

16. Benson, *New Henry Ford*, pp. 33–34, 28–30, 25.

17. Gus Munchow, "Reminiscences," pp. 76–77; Benson, *New Henry Ford*, pp. 22–23.

18. Olson, *Young Henry Ford*, p. 88.

19. Ruddiman, "Memories of My Brother," pp. 249, 243–44.

20. Ibid., pp. 248–49, 246.

21. Ibid., pp. 246–47.

22. Ibid., pp. 268–69; Ruddiman, "Reminiscences," p. 94.

23. Ruddiman, "Memories of My Brother," p. 248; Dr. Edsel Ruddiman, "Reminiscences," p. 4.

24. Benson, *New Henry Ford*, p. 34; Horace L. Arnold and Fay L. Faurote, *Ford Methods and Ford Shops* (New York, 1915), p. 9; HF, *My Life and Work*, p. 24. This Arnold and Faurote book included a sketch of HF's life based on interviews with him.

25. Ruddiman, "Memories of My Brother," pp. 254–55; Frederick Strauss, "Reminiscences," p. 2.

26. Strauss, "Reminiscences," pp. 2–4.

27. "Fairlane Papers," unsigned 14-page HF interview, p. 11, in acc. 1, box 118, FA; Allan Nevins, *Ford: The Times, the Man, the Company* (New York, 1954), pp. 84–85.

28. HF, *My Life and Work*, p. 24; Olson, *Young Henry Ford*, p. 30; Nevins, *Ford: Times, Man, Company*, pp. 84–85.

29. Strauss, "Reminiscences," pp. 6–10.

30. HF, quoted in Simonds, *Ford: Life, Work, Genius*, pp. 35–38; HF, *My Life and Work*, p. 24.

31. HF, quoted in Olson, *Young Henry Ford*, p. 31; HF, *My Life and Work*, p. 27.

32. HF, quoted in Olson, *Young Henry Ford*, p. 33.

33. Ibid., pp. 34–38; HF, *My Life and Work*, pp. 25–28.

34. HF, *My Life and Work*, p. 29; Olson, *Young Henry Ford*, p. 45; Nevins, *Ford: Times, Man, Company*, pp. 108–11.

35. HF, *My Life and Work*, p. 29; Olson, *Young Henry Ford*, pp. 39–41, 46–48; Nevins, *Ford: Times, Man, Company*, pp. 104–10.

36. HF, *My Life and Work*, pp. 28–30; Ruddiman, "Memories of My Brother," pp. 264–65; Olson, *Young Henry Ford*, pp. 45–46.

37. HF, *My Life and Work*, p. 30, quoted in text. Ruddiman, "Memories of My Brother," p. 265; Olson, *Young Henry Ford*, p. 49.

38. "Mr. Ford Doesn't Care," *Fortune*, Dec. 1933, p. 134.

39. HF, "The McGuffey Readers," *Colophon: A Quarterly for Bookmen*, Spring 1936, p. 588; S. J. Woolf, "Mr. Ford Shows His Museum," New York *Times Magazine*, Jan. 12, 1936, p. 2.

Three • Inventor

1. Allan L. Benson, *The New Henry Ford* (New York, 1923), p. 108. Benson claimed that Edison made this statement to him.

2. A picture of this house—taken much later, in 1941—can be found in Sidney Olson, *Young Henry Ford: A Pictorial History of the First Forty Years* (Detroit, 1997 [1963]), p. 52.

3. The facts of Ford's career at Edison Illuminating Company are well known. For useful and accurate narratives of these years, see, for example, Olson, *Young Henry Ford*, pp. 53–56, 58–59, 68; Allan Nevins, *Ford: The Times, the Man, the Company* (New York, 1954), pp. 119–20, 135–36.

4. Dow, quoted in William A. Simonds, *Henry Ford: His Life, His Work, His Genius* (New York, 1943), p. 47. For another, similar interview, see Benson, *New Henry Ford*, pp. 57–58, 59–60.

5. Charles T. Bush and Claude Sintz, "Interview," March 3, 1952, in acc. 65, box 10–11, p. 24, FA; Ingram, quoted in Simonds, *Ford: Life, Work, Genius*, p. 48.

6. These stories were related by Jim Bishop, who was interviewed for Simonds, *Ford: Life, Work, Genius*, pp. 48–49.

7. HF, quoted in Olson, *Young Henry Ford*, p. 54; Frederick Strauss, "Reminiscences," pp. 37–38.

8. HF, *My Life and Work* (Garden City, N.Y., 1922), p. 29; Olson, *Young Henry Ford*, pp. 56–58.

9. HF confirmed this story in discussions with William Simonds for his *Ford: Life, Work, Genius*, quote from p. 47.

10. Olson, *Young Henry Ford*, p. 54.

11. HF, *My Life and Work*, 30; Olson, *Young Henry Ford*, p. 71.

12. See Nevins, *Ford: Times, Man, Company*, pp. 143–54; King is quoted on p. 145. See also Olson, *Young Henry Ford*, pp. 60–61.

13. Strauss, "Reminiscences," pp. 16–17.

14. Oliver Barthel, "Reminiscences," p. 48; Olson, *Young Henry Ford*, pp. 71–72.

15. HF's 1904 testimony in the Selden patent lawsuit is excerpted in Nevins, *Ford: Times, Man, Company*, p. 155; Margaret Ford Ruddiman's comments appear in her "Memories of My Brother, Henry Ford," *Michigan History*, Sept. 1953, p. 266.

16. HF, *My Life and Work*, pp. 30–31, describes the Quadricycle, and several photos of it have been reprinted in Olson, *Young Henry Ford*, pp. 76, 79.

17. Detroit *Free Press* and Detroit *Journal*, March 7, 1896; Olson, *Young Henry Ford*, pp. 72–73; Nevins, *Ford: Times, Man, Company*, pp. 148–49; Barthel, "Reminiscences," p. 26.

18. See Simonds, *Ford: Life, Work, Genius*, pp. 52–54, for HF's firsthand account of the first trial run of his Quadricycle and the subsequent encounter with William Wreford.

19. HF and Samuel Crowther, "The Greatest American," *Cosmopolitan*, July 1930, pp. 36–38. HF offered a similar account of this meeting in *My Life and Work*, pp. 234–35, and to Simonds, *Ford: Life, Work, Genius*, pp. 17–18.

20. For a shrewd analysis of Edison's achievements and image in this period, see Alan Trachtenberg, *The Incorporation of America: Culture and Society in the Gilded Age* (New York, 1982), pp. 65–68. See also Neil Baldwin, *Edison: Inventing the Century* (New York, 1995).

21. HF and Crowther, "Greatest American," pp. 187, 39. This was the first installment in a three-part series of articles on Edison authored by Ford with the assistance of Crowther. The other articles in *Cosmopolitan* were entitled "Edison's Life Story" (Aug. 1930) and "The Habits Which Make Edison the Greatest American" (Sept. 1930). These articles contain the fullest record of Ford's reflections on Edison's significance. Another useful piece in which Ford is quoted at length is F. D. McHugh, "Ford's Friend Edison," *Scientific American*, Nov. 1929, pp. 377–80.

22. HF and Crowther, "Greatest American," p. 193; HF and Crowther, "Habits," p. 54.

23. HF and Crowther, "Greatest American," p. 187.

24. Ibid., pp. 188, 189, 191.

25. Ibid., pp. 38–39.

26. Ibid., pp. 187–88.

27. HF and Crowther, "Habits," p. 208; HF and Crowther, "Greatest American," pp. 39, 187.

28. HF, *My Life and Work*, p. 33.

29. James J. Flink, *The Car Culture* (Cambridge, Mass., 1975), pp. 11–15.

30. HF, *My Life and Work*, p. 33.

31. Ibid.; Olson, *Young Henry Ford*, pp. 93–96; David Bell, "Reminiscences," pp. 8–10.

32. "Fairlane Papers," p. 11, in box 118, FA; Bush and Sintz, "Interview," p. 44.

33. Ford's "second car" now sits in the Henry Ford Museum in Dearborn; photographs of the car and its engine appear in Olson, *Young Henry Ford*, p. 97.

34. Ruddiman, "Memories of My Brother," pp. 267–68.

35. This letter is in FA, and it has been reproduced in Olson, *Young Henry Ford*, p. 98.

Four • Businessman

1. The story of this trip is related by Murphy's son-in-law, J. Bell Moran, in his book *The Moran Family: 200 Years in Detroit* (Detroit, 1949), p. 126. Moran apparently had in his possession Murphy's log of that trip. Allan Nevins, *Ford: The Times, the Man, the Company* (New York, 1954), p. 174, identified the July time frame for the Ford-Murphy expedition.

2. See Sidney Olson, *Young Henry Ford: A Pictorial History of the First Forty Years* (Detroit, 1997 [1963]), pp. 61, 90, 111–12, 114–15, for a discussion of Ford's relationship with Peck and Maybury in this period.

3. Ibid., p. 103; Nevins, *Ford: Times, Man, Company*, quote on p. 171.

4. "Ford's Automobile Has New Features and Is a Novel Machine," Detroit *Journal*, July 29, 1899.

5. Olson, *Young Henry Ford*, pp. 107–15, did a great deal of historical detective work in uncovering information about these prosperous Detroit backers of Ford's earliest manufacturing venture.

6. For information on William H. Murphy's life, see the biographical entry in Clarence M. Burton and M. Agnes Burton, eds., *History of Wayne County and the City of Detroit, Michigan* (Detroit, 1930), pp. 54–59; Moran, *Moran Family*, pp. 78–79; Olson, *Young Henry Ford*, pp. 116–17.

7. HF, *My Life and Work* (Garden City, N.Y., 1922), pp. 34–35.

8. William A. Simonds, *Henry Ford: His Life, His Work, His Genius* (New York. 1943), quote on p. 61; Allan L. Benson, *The New Henry Ford* (New York, 1923), pp. 61–62.

9. Detroit *Free Press*, Aug. 19, 1899; see also Nevins, *Ford: Times, Man, Company*, p. 177.

10. "First Automobile of the Detroit Co. Ready Tomorrow," Detroit *Journal*, Jan. 12, 1900; "Swifter Than a Race-Horse It Flew over the Icy Streets," Detroit *News-Tribune*, Feb. 4, 1900; Nevins, *Ford: Times, Man, Company*, pp. 178–79; Olson, *Young Henry Ford*, pp. 106–7.

11. Detroit *News-Tribune*, Feb. 4, 1900; Frederick Strauss, "Reminiscences," pp. 57–58; Olson, *Young Henry Ford*, pp. 107, 123; Nevins, *Ford: Times, Man, Company*, pp. 178–80.

12. William W. Pring, "Reminiscences," pp. 5, 9; Strauss, "Reminiscences," pp. 22–23; Oliver Barthel, "Reminiscences," p. 6.

13. Strauss, "Reminiscences," pp. 56–58.

14. Olson, *Young Henry Ford*, pp. 123–24; Nevins, *Ford: Times, Man, Company*, pp. 190–91; Strauss, "Reminiscences," pp. 57–58.

15. Detroit *Journal*, Nov. 30, 1901; Nevins, *Ford: Times, Man, Company*, p. 206.

16. Strauss, "Reminiscences," pp. 66, 7.

17. Barthel, "Reminiscences," pp. 7–11; Strauss, "Reminiscences," p. 66.

18. Pring, "Reminiscences," p. 16; Charles T. Bush, "Oral History," June 9, 1955, in acc. 65, box 10-10, pp. 9–11, FA.

19. Bush, "Oral History," pp. 9–11; Mrs. Wilfred C. Leland, *Master of Precision: Henry M. Leland* (Detroit, 1966), pp. 74, 96; Nevins, *Ford: Times, Man, Company*, pp. 211–12; Olson, *Young Henry Ford*, p. 154.

20. Moran, *Moran Family*, p. 127; Robert Lacey, *Ford: The Men and the Machine* (New York, 1986), pp. 289–95; Leland, *Master of Precision*, pp. 207–52.

21. "*Motor*'s Historical Table," *Motor*, March 1909.

22. Benson, *New Henry Ford*, pp. 69–70.

23. Bush, "Oral History," pp. 9–11. Italics added.

24. HF, *My Life and Work*, p. 36. Italics added. Oliver Barthel agreed with Ford's characterization of the company stockholders. Barthel described them as "speculative. I don't think any of them went into it with the idea of it being an investment. They were all speculators; that is, gamblers. They all went in on a gambling basis." (Barthel, "Reminiscences," pp. 7–11.)

25. See Alan Trachtenberg, *The Incorporation of America: Culture and Society in the Gilded Age* (New York, 1982), pp. 4–7; Olivier Zunz, *Making America Corporate, 1870–1920* (Chicago, 1990), pp. 4–10.

26. The literature on late-nineteenth-century social and cultural ferment in the United States is vast. For two particularly sweeping and stimulating analyses, see David Montgomery, *The Fall of the House of Labor: The Workplace, the State, and American Labor Activism, 1865–1925* (Cambridge, Mass., 1989); T. J. Jackson Lears, *No Place of Grace: Antimodernism and the Transformation of American Culture, 1880–1920* (New York, 1981).

27. Richard Hofstadter, *The Age of Reform: From Bryan to F.D.R.* (New York, 1959), pp. 4–5, 11–12.

28. HF and Samuel Crowther, "The Greatest American," *Cosmopolitan*, July 1930, p. 200.

Five • Celebrity

1. This description comes from the magazine *The Horseless Age*, as quoted in Sidney Olson, *Young Henry Ford: A Pictorial History of the First Forty Years* (Detroit, 1997 [1963]), 141.

2. Hrolf Wisby, "Style in Automobiles," *Scientific American*, Nov. 9, 1901.

3. For information on Winton's early career, see "The Winton Plant and Its Product," *Cycle and Automotive Trade Journal*, March 1, 1904, pp. 68–79; *Scientific American*, May 14, 1898, p. 309; Detroit *Free Press*, Oct. 6, 1901.

4. Detroit *Free Press*, Oct. 6, 1901; Olson, *Young Henry Ford*, p. 144; Allan Nevins, *Ford: The Times, the Man, the Company* (New York, 1954), quote on pp. 202–3.

5. Detroit *Free Press*, Oct. 11, 1901; Detroit *Journal*, Oct. 11, 1901.

6. Detroit *Tribune*, Oct. 11, 1901.

7. William A. Simonds, *Henry Ford: His Life, His Work, His Genius* (Indianapolis, 1943), p. 71; Detroit *News*, Detroit *Tribune*, and Detroit *Free Press*, all on Oct. 11, 1901.

8. Clara Ford to Milton D. Bryant, Dec. 3, 1901, in acc. 102, box 1, FA; Detroit *Tribune*, Oct. 11, 1901; Detroit *News*, Oct. 11, 1901.

9. Oliver Barthel, "Reminiscences," p. 8.

10. HF to Milton D. Bryant, Jan. 6, 1902, in acc. 102, box 1, FA.

11. HF, *My Life and Work* (Garden City, N.Y., 1922), p. 36.

12. John Kasson, *Amusing the Million: Coney Island at the Turn of the Century* (New York, 1978), pp. 106, 6–7. In addition to Kasson's splendid volume, a number of books have explored aspects of an emerging commercialized mass culture. See, for example, Lary May, *Screening Out the Past: The Birth of Mass Culture and the Motion Picture Industry* (New York, 1980); Lewis A. Erenberg, *Steppin' Out: New York Nightlife and the Transformation of American Culture, 1890–1930* (Chicago, 1981); David Nasaw, *Going Out: The Rise and Fall of Public Amusements* (New York, 1993).

13. Nasaw, *Going Out*, p. 4; see also pp. 2, 3, 9. See also Kasson, *Amusing the Million*, pp. 6, 106–7; May, *Screening Out the Past*, pp. viii, 235–36.

14. HF, *My Life and Work*, p. 37.

15. HF to Milton D. Bryant, Jan 6, 1902; Clara Ford to Milton D. Bryant, Dec. 3, 1901.

16. Detroit *Free Press*, Nov. 20, 1901; Barthel, "Reminiscences," p. 12.

17. Clara Ford to Milton D. Bryant, March 3, 1902, in acc. 102, box 1, FA.

18. *Automobile and Motor Review*, Sept. 27, 1902.

19. HF, *My Life and Work*, p. 50; Simonds, *Ford: Life, Work, Genius*, pp. 74–75.

20. Detroit *Journal*, Sept. 18, 1902.

21. Oldfield and Ford are quoted in William F. Nolan, *Barney Oldfield: The Life and Times of America's Legendary Speed King* (New York, 1961), p. 223. This is the only biography of the famous auto-racer, and it, along with Oldfield's *Saturday Evening Post* articles cited in note 23 below, supplies most of the information for my sketch of the famous racing driver.

22. Nolan, *Oldfield*, p. 54.

23. Barney Oldfield and William F. Sturm, "Wide Open All the Way," *Saturday Evening Post*, Sept. 19, 1925, p. 61. This was the first of a two-part article (the second part appeared in the subsequent, Sept. 26, number of the magazine) that supplies Oldfield's fullest reflections on his own career.

24. Oldfield and Sturm, "Wide Open All the Way," p. 21.

25. HF, *My Life and Work*, p. 51.

26. Oldfield and Sturm, "Wide Open All the Way," pp. 11, 50.

27. Ibid., pp. 11, 10; HF, *My Life and Work*, p. 51.

28. Detroit *Journal*, Sept. 13, 1902.

29. Oldfield and Sturm, "Wide Open All the Way," p. 11.

30. Clara Bryant Ford to Milton Bryant, Oct. 27, 1902, in acc. 102, box I, FA.

31. Oldfield and Sturm, "Wide Open All the Way," p. 52; HF, *My Life and Work*, p. 51; Lee Cuson, "Reminiscences," p. 5.

32. Oldfield and Sturm, "Wide Open All the Way," p. 54.

33. Oldfield's words appear in ibid. The best contemporary account of the Manufacturer's Challenge Cup can be found in "Detroit Race Thrills Thousands of Visitors," *Automobile and Motor Review*, Nov. 1, 1902, pp. 9–12. For general accounts of the race, see Olson, *Young Henry Ford*, p. 156; Nevins, *Ford: Times, Man, Company*, pp. 217–18; George DeAngelis, "Ford's '999' and Cooper's 'Arrow,'" *Antique Automobile*, Nov.–Dec. 1993, p. 310.

34. Oldfield and Sturm, "Wide Open All the Way," pp. 11, 52, 10.

35. HF, quoted in Detroit *Journal*, Oct. 27, 1902; HF, *My Life and Work*, p. 51.

36. HF, *My Life and Work*, p. 57. See DeAngelis, "Ford's '999,'" pp. 33–35, for details about this event.

37. DeAngelis, "Ford's '999,'" pp. 34–35.

38. HF, *My Life and Work*, p. 57.

39. Detroit *Tribune*, Jan. 13, 1904; Detroit *News*, Jan. 15, 1904; see also Detroit *Tribune*, Jan. 16, 1904; Detroit *Free Press*, Jan. 22, 1904.

40. This 1904 advertisement has been reproduced in David L. Lewis, *The Public Image of Henry Ford: An American Folk Hero and His Company* (Detroit, 1976), p. 30.

Six · Entrepreneur

1. "Auto Factory Built," Detroit *Journal*, June 19, 1903; "Ford Is King," *Horseless Age*, Jan. 13, 1904.

2. See the obituary "A. Y. Malcolmson, Auto Pioneer Passes Away," *Detroiter*, Aug. 6, 1923; newspaper stories covering his early career in the Detroit *Evening News*, April 1, 1903; Detroit *Free Press*, April 1, 1903 (quote), and Aug. 6, 1904. The "Hotter Than Sunshine" ad appeared, for instance, in the Detroit *Evening News*, Nov. 18, 1901, and the Detroit *Journal*, Sept. 18, 1901.

3. A. R. Malcolmson, in a 1942 interview quoted in Harry Barnard, *Independent Man: The Life of Senator James Couzens* (New York, 1958), pp. 29, 30. On Malcolmson's wives, see "Mrs. A. Y. Malcolmson Was a Talented Woman," Detroit *Free Press*, Dec. 7, 1901; "Sayings and Doings," Detroit *Free Press*, Jan. 2, 1903.

4. Allan L. Benson, *The New Henry Ford* (New York, 1923), p. 116, reports the results of an interview with James Couzens, Malcolmson's right-hand man, who explains HF and his boss's earliest contact. Allan Nevins, *Ford: The Times, the Man, the Company* (New York, 1954), p. 225, says that HF approached Malcolmson. Keith Sward, *The Legend of Henry Ford* (New York, 1948), pp. 15–16, suggests that Malcolmson approached HF. Sidney Olson, *Young Henry Ford: A Pictorial History of the First Forty Years* (Detroit, 1997 [1963]), pp. 160–62, argues for Livingstone's role in bringing the two together. But none of these scholars offers much evidence, and existing documents are not clear on the matter.

5. A copy of this agreement, witnessed by C. Harold Wills and Bella Roberts, is in FA. On John W. Anderson, and for the quotation, see his testimony, in "Additional Tax Case," transcript, 1927, pp. 1270–72, in acc. 940, box 14, FA.

6. John Wandersee, "Reminiscences," pp. 3–5.

7. HF to Malcolmson, Oct. 30, 1902, acc. 940, box 14, FA; Wandersee, "Reminiscences," pp. 7–8.

8. John W. Anderson to his father, W. A. Anderson, June 4, 1903, in FA; "New Auto Factory Built," Detroit *Journal*, June 19, 1903; "Ford Motor Company," Detroit *Evening News*, June 19, 1903.

9. Wandersee, "Reminiscences," pp. 7–9; John W. Anderson to W. A. Anderson, June 4, 1903.

10. Alexander Dow, quoted in William A. Simonds, *Henry Ford: His Life, His Work, His Genius* (New York, 1943), p. 79; John W. Anderson to W. A. Anderson, June 4, 1903.

11. The investors, their contributions, and their shares received are listed in "Minute Book," Ford Motor Company, vol. 2, entry for June 16, 1903, in acc. 85, FA. Olson, *Young Henry Ford*, pp. 170, 176–81, discusses the original stockholders at length. See also "New Auto Factory Built," Detroit *Journal*, June 19, 1903; "Ford Motor Company Has Been Organized," Detroit *Free Press*, June 20, 1903; "Ford Motor Company," Detroit *Evening News*, June 19, 1903.

12. John W. Anderson to W. A. Anderson, June 4, 1903; Wandersee, "Reminiscences," p. 9; Fred Rockelman, "Oral History," p. 10, FA.

13. HF, *My Life and Work* (Garden City, N.Y., 1922), pp. 53–54, 56.

14. Charles H. Bennett, "Reminiscences," p. 33; Wandersee, "Reminiscences," p. 36; Fred W. Seeman, "Reminiscences," p. 6; Rockelman, "Oral History," p. 13.

15. Bennett, "Reminiscences," pp. 48, 51; Wandersee, "Reminiscences," p. 13.

16. Frederick Strauss, "Reminiscences," p. 7; Wandersee, "Reminiscences," p. 37; Oliver Barthel, "Reminiscences," p. 27; and Seeman, "Reminiscences," p. 15.

17. See Myrle Clarkson's reminiscences in "We Old Timers," a column by George W. Stark, Detroit *News*, Sept. 16, 1941.

18. See "New Auto Factory," Detroit *Free Press*, May 13, 1904; "Ten Times Size of Present Plant," Detroit *Free Press*, May 29, 1904.

19. Bennett, "Reminiscences," p. 32.

20. Benson, *New Henry Ford*, pp. 117, 129–30. The author interviewed Couzens at length, and quotes him extensively throughout the book.

21. Much of the information on Couzens' early life and career comes from Barnard, *Independent Man*, chaps. 2–6. Barnard relies upon sources among Couzens' papers and a large number of oral interviews with Couzens' associates and family members.

22. Benson, *New Henry Ford*, p. 116.

23. Ibid., p. 103.

24. Ibid., pp. 104–5 for the quotation; Simonds, *Ford: Life, Work, Genius*, p. 79.

25. Barnard, *Independent Man*, p. 43; John W. Anderson to W. A. Anderson, June 4, 1903.

26. Benson, *New Henry Ford*, p. 119; *Ford Times*, July 1, 1908, p. 8; Wandersee, "Reminiscences," p. 34.

27. Henry L. Dominguez, *The Ford Agency: A Pictorial History* (Osceola, Wisc., 1981), pp. 9–10; Barnard, *Independent Man*, pp. 49–50, which includes his 1941 interview with Charles T. Bennett, quoted in the text.

28. Charles E. Sorensen, "Oral Reminiscences," pp. 44–45, 52, in acc. 65, box 66, FA; Rockelman, "Oral History," pp. 13, 27; Frank Bennett, "Reminiscences," pp. 35–36.

29. Simonds, *Ford: Life, Work, Genius*, p. 92; James Couzens, "What I Learned About Business from Ford," *System: The Magazine of Business*, Sept. 1921, p. 262.

30. Barnard, *Independent Man*, pp. 44–45, quoted in text; Benson, *New Henry Ford*, p. 130.

31. Barnard, *Independent Man*, p. 60. This close relationship also was attested to by Wandersee, "Reminiscences," p. 36, and Frank Bennett, "Reminiscences," p. 31.

32. Nevins, *Ford: Times, Man, Company*, pp. 250, 261, 272, 644, quoting from Treasurer's Records, Secretary's Reports, and other documents in FA; Detroit *Journal*, April 24, 1905.

33. HF, quoted in Milton A. McRae, *Forty Years in Newspaperdom* (New York, 1924), p. 393; Couzens, quoted in Benson, *New Henry Ford*, pp. 119–20. See corroborating testimony in Frank Bennett, "Reminiscences," p. 24.

34. Anderson's recollection of Ford's comments is quoted in Olsen, *Young Henry Ford*, pp. 168, 179.

35. Nevins, *Ford: Times, Man, Company*, pp. 260–61, discusses this situation in detail.

36. Ibid., pp. 275–78.

37. Frank Bennett, "Reminiscences," p. 49.

38. Vernon Fry quotes Gray in "Additional Tax Case," transcript, pp. 1314–15. For a discussion of this entire matter, see Nevins, *Ford: Times, Man, Company*, pp. 278–79.

39. Directors' minutes, Dec. 22, 1905, in acc. 85, FA.

40. "Detroit's Newest Auto Company," Detroit *Journal*, Dec. 4, 1905; "New Auto Plant," Detroit *Free Press*, Dec. 5, 1905.

41. Directors' minutes, Nov. 17, 1905, acc. 85, FA.

42. Rockelman, "Oral History," pp. 26–27; Charles H. Bennett, quoted in Nevins, *Ford: Times, Man, Company*, p. 331.

43. Chas. Bennett, "Reminiscences," pp. 93–96; Nevins, *Ford: Times, Man, Company*, pp. 330–31.

44. See Malcolmson obituary, Detroit *News*, Aug. 2, 1923; articles on the Aerocar Company bankruptcy and subsequent lawsuits in Detroit *Journal*, Sept. 24 and Oct. 17, 1907; Ernest Liebold's report on his 1919 meeting with Malcolmson in "Liebold Papers," in acc. 41, box 1, FA.

45. Rockelman, "Oral History," pp. 24–25.
46. Detroit *Journal*, Jan. 5, 1906.
47. Sorensen, "Oral Reminiscences," pp. 73, 79; Joseph Galamb, "Oral History," pp. 11, 17, in acc. 65, box 21-10, FA; Frank Bennett, "Reminiscences," p. 24.
48. Hugh Dolnar, "The Ford 4-Cylinder Runabout," *Cycle and Automobile Trade Journal*, 1906, pp. 108, 115–16.
49. Seeman, "Reminiscences," p. 25 (quote); Rockelman, "Oral History," pp. 23–24; advertisement, "The Successful Ford," *Cycle and Automobile Trade Journal*, vol. 10 (1905–6), p. 108, quoted in text. On sales figures, see Nevins, *Ford: Times, Man, Company*, p. 644, table compiled from records in FA.
50. "Successful Ford," p. 105; Wandersee, "Reminiscences," pp. 14, 19.
51. E. J. Finney, *Walter E. Flanders: His Role in the Mass Production of Automobiles* (privately printed, 1992), 2; Charles Sorensen, "The Early Years," ms., in acc. 65, box 66-9, pp. 113–14, FA; Flanders memo to James Couzens, July 19, 1906, quoted in Nevins, *Ford: Times, Man, Company*, p. 334.
52. Finney, *Flanders*, pp. 4–5; Max Wollering, "Reminiscences," pp. 4, 16–17, quoted in text.
53. Seeman, "Reminiscences," pp. 43–44. Wollering, "Reminiscences," p. 24, paints a similar picture of this system at Piquette Avenue.
54. George Brown, "Reminiscences," p. 19; "The Auto," Detroit *Journal*, Nov. 30, 1907.
55. Rockelman, "Oral History," pp. 30, 32; Brown, "Reminiscences," pp. 22–23, 175–76; Seeman, "Reminiscences," pp. 17–18.
56. Brown, "Reminiscences," pp. 24–25; Seeman, "Reminiscences," pp. 32–33.
57. Simonds, *Ford: Life, Work, Genius*, pp. 101–2.
58. HF, "Special Automobile Steels," *Harper's Weekly*, March 16, 1907, p. 386.
59. HF, *My Life and Work*, p. 59; Sorensen, "Oral Reminiscences," pp. 93–94.

Seven • Consumer

1. James J. Flink, *The Car Culture* (Cambridge, Mass., 1975), pp. 1–2, 154, 151; Robert and Helen Lynd, *Middletown: A Study in Modern American Culture* (New York, 1929), p. 253. See also Lendol Calder, *Financing the American Dream: A Cultural History of Consumer Credit* (Princeton, N.J., 1999).
2. HF, *My Life and Work* (Garden City, N.Y., 1922), pp. 65–66.
3. Ibid., pp. 67, 68.
4. Charles E. Sorensen, "Oral Reminiscences," pp. 107–9, in acc. 65, box 66-9, FA; Joseph Galamb, "Oral History," p. 15, in acc. 65, box 21-10, FA.
5. Galamb, "Oral History," pp. 15, 25.
6. Sorensen, "Oral Reminiscences," pp. 190, 112.
7. Charles J. Smith, "Reminiscences," pp. 3–4.
8. John Wandersee, "Reminiscences," pp. 19–20.
9. Sorensen, "Oral Reminiscences," pp. 104–5.
10. Charles Sorensen, "The Making of Men," ms., pp. 41–42, 109, in acc. 65, box 66-69, FA; Wandersee, "Reminiscences," pp. 22, 34.
11. Henry Ford, "Special Automobile Steels," *Harper's Weekly*, March 16, 1907, p. 386.
12. Smith, "Reminiscences," pp. 4–5; George Brown, "Reminiscences," pp. 45–46.
13. See Philip Van Doren Stern, *Tin Lizzie: The Story of the Fabulous Model T Ford* (New York, 1955), for much practical description and many photographs of this vehicle. Joseph Galamb, "Memorandum for the 1919 Additional Income Tax Case," in acc. 96, box 11, FA, provides a good summary of the Model T's features and their advantages. The description of the "nuzzling" Model T comes from Lee Strout White, *Farewell to the Model T* (New York, 1936), 14–15.

14. Sorensen, "Oral Reminiscences," pp. 125–26; see also Allan Nevins, *Ford: The Times, the Man, the Company* (New York, 1954), p. 396.

15. Brown, "Reminiscences," pp. 46–47.

16. The temporary halt on orders of the new Model T was announced in *Ford Times*, May 1909, p. 17.

17. Ford's Associated Press interview and the public reaction to it are discussed and quoted in "Henry Ford's Gospel of Spending," *Literary Digest*, Dec. 29, 1928, p. 10.

18. Headline and quotation originally in Tampa *Tribune*, Aug. 10, 1913. This statement is reprinted in HF, *My Life and Work*, p. 73. Although the first publication of the statement remains obscure, it regularly appeared in promotional copy for the Model T. See, for instance, its inclusion in *Ford Times*, June 1913, p. 366; "Eighth Wonder of the World Is 10 Years Old Today," Detroit *Free Press*, June 16, 1913.

19. HF, *My Life and Work*, pp. 67, 154; HF, *Today and Tomorrow* (New York, 1988 [1926]), p. 224.

20. William Leach, *Land of Desire: Merchants, Power, and the Rise of a New American Culture* (New York, 1993), pp. xiii–xiv. Among many works on the evolution of American consumer culture, see Warren Susman, *Culture as History: The Transformation of American Society in the Twentieth Century* (New York, 1984); Daniel Horowitz, *The Morality of Spending: Attitudes Toward the Consumer Society in America, 1875–1950* (Baltimore, 1985); Simon J. Bronner, ed., *Consuming Visions: Accumulation and Display of Goods in America, 1880–1920* (New York, 1989).

21. HF, in Bruce Barton, " 'It Would Be Fun to Start Over Again,' Said Henry Ford," *American Magazine*, April 1921, p. 7.

22. HF, *My Life and Work*, pp. 135–36, 148; HF, *Today and Tomorrow*, p. 253.

23. Henry Ford, "Why I Favor Five Days' Work with Six Days' Pay," *World's Work*, Oct. 1926, pp. 613–16. The bulk of this article was later reprinted in the *Congressional Digest*, Oct. 1932, pp. 242–44, as part of a symposium on American industry and the five-day workweek.

24. HF, *My Life and Work*, p. 154.

25. The literature on modern advertising is vast and growing. Particularly suggestive works include T. J. Jackson Lears, "From Salvation to Self-Realization: Advertising and the Therapeutic Roots of the Consumer Culture, 1880–1930," in Richard Wightman Fox and T. J. Jackson Lears, *The Culture of Consumption: Critical Essays in American History, 1880–1980* (New York, 1983); T. J. Jackson Lears, *Fables of Abundance: A Cultural History of Advertising in America* (New York, 1994); Roland Marchand, *Advertising the American Dream: Making Way for Modernity, 1920–1940* (New York, 1985); Pamela Walker Laird, *Advertising Progress: American Business and the Rise of Consumer Marketing* (Baltimore, 1998).

26. *Motor World*, Dec. 12, 1912, p. 20; Pelletier obituary, Detroit *Free Press*, Sept. 6, 1938; Sorensen, "Oral Reminiscences," pp. 97–98; Sorensen, "Making of Men," p. 25. See also David L. Lewis, *The Public Image of Henry Ford: An American Folk Hero and His Company* (Detroit, 1976), pp. 37–38, 48–49.

27. Articles in *Ford Times*: "Does Advertising Pay?," Dec. 1910, p. 109; "Living Advertising," April 1911, p. 222; "Suggestions for Advertising," Jan. 1912, pp. 130–31.

28. See the pamphlet *Ford Motor Cars*, 1912, p. 31; "Ford APL—1912," both in acc. 19, box 2, FA. For the promotion of the "winged pyramid" logo, see "Ford Trademark as a Window Sign," *Ford Times*, July 1912, p. 316. The 1912 Ford ad is in *Automobile Trade Journal*, in acc. 19, box 2, FA.

29. *Ford Times*, Nov. 1911, p. 64; July 1911, pp. 287–88.

30. For accounts of the race, see Stern, *Tin Lizzie*, pp. 63–75; "Ford No. 2 Winner of Great Auto Race," Seattle *Post-Intelligencer*, June 24, 1909; *Story of the Race*, FMC pamphlet, 1909 in acc. 717, box 5, FA (quote).

31. See ads in acc. 717, box 6, FA; Detroit *Journal*, July 12, 1909, p. 6; *Ford Times*, July 1, 1909, pp. 2, 6, 13; *Ford Times*, special "Trans-Continental Race Issue," July 15, 1909.

32. Ford ads, 1913–16, in acc. 19, box 2, FA; "Watch the Fords Go By," 1909, in acc. 175, box 1909–11, FA.

33. Ford ads, 1908, 1910, 1913, in acc. 19, box 2, FA.

34. "Ford Motor Cars," 1910, and "What the Motor Car Means to the Doctor," 1911, both in acc. 175, box 1909–1911, FA, and *Ford Times*, Nov. 1910, p. 91.

35. "Ford Motor Company," 1911, in acc. 175, box 1909–1911, FA; "Visiting Historic Places by Auto," *Ford Times*, April 1911, pp. 209–11; 1913 ad, *Horseless Age*, in acc. 19, box 2, FA.

36. *The Woman and the Ford*, 1912, in acc. 175, box 1912, FA.

37. F. L. Brittain, "Why Doesn't More Auto Copy Talk My Language?," *Ford Times*, Oct. 1910.

38. N. A. Hawkins, "The Man Who Does Things," *Ford Times*, 1908, p. 4.

39. Brown, "Reminiscences," p. 19; "The Auto," Detroit *Journal*, Nov. 30, 1907; Peter E. Revelt, "Errant Bookkeeper Becomes Ford's First Sales Genius," *Ward's Quarterly*, Fall 1967, p. 59; "Hawkins Pardoned," Detroit *Free Press*, Dec. 25, 1896.

40. Brown, "Reminiscences," p. 20.

41. Hawkins explained his early career at Ford in great detail in "Additional Tax Case," transcript, 1927, in acc. 940, box 14, FA. His testimony was reported nearly verbatim in the Detroit *News*, Feb. 2, 1927, pp. 1–2.

42. Arthur J. Lacey's testimony, in "Additional Tax Case," transcript, 1927, in acc. 84, FA; Hawkins, quoted in Detroit *News*, Feb. 2, 1927, pp. 1–2.

43. Hawkins, Detroit *News*, Feb. 2, 1927, pp. 1–2.

44. These essays by Norval A. Hawkins appeared in *Ford Times* on April 1, 1909, p. 5; Sept. 29, 1908, pp. 8–9; Jan. 15, 1909, p. 4; March 1, 1912, pp. 194–95; April 15, 1909, p. 5.

45. Miriam Trichner, "Detroiters at Play: Norval Hawkins, a Modern Midas," Detroit *Times*, Dec. 1, 1913; "Ford Motor Company Minutes, 1908–1910," in acc. 940, box 14, FA.

46. Detroit *News*, Feb. 2, 1927, pp. 1–2.

47. Ibid.; *Ford Times*, June 1912, p. 283.

48. Norval A. Hawkins, *The Selling Process: A Handbook of Salesmanship Principles* (Detroit, 1920), pp. 1–218.

49. Ibid., pp. 68, 219–21.

50. Ibid., pp. 229–45.

51. Revelt, "Ford's First Sales Genius," pp. 59–60; Sorensen, "Making of Men," pp. 10–11, 26–27; Charles E. Sorensen, *My Forty Years with Ford* (New York, 1956), p. 39 (quoted).

52. Brown, "Reminiscences," pp. 110–11. Allan Nevins noted that this story was corroborated by C. H. Wills, Jr. (See Nevins, *Ford: Times, Man, Company*, p. 581.)

53. This incident was first noted in *Pipp's Weekly*, Aug. 25, 1923, p. 7, quoted in text. HF later offered a version of the story in Ralph Waldo Trine, *The Power That Wins: Henry Ford and Ralph Waldo Trine in an Intimate Talk on Life* (Indianapolis, 1929), p. 163.

Eight • Producer

1. These figures come from tables in David A. Hounshell, *From the American System to Mass Production, 1800–1932* (Baltimore, 1984), p. 224; and Allan Nevins and Frank Ernest Hill, *Ford: Expansion and Challenge, 1915–1933* (New York, 1957), p. 685.

2. Henry Ford, "Machinery, the New Messiah," *Forum*, March 1928, pp. 359–64.

3. "To Make It All Ford," *Motor Age*, vol. 10 (Sept. 1906), p. 9; "Ford Company in Highland Park," Detroit *Journal*, March 9, 1907; "Ford Co. Plans Fine Building," Detroit *Journal*, June 10, 1908.

4. David L. Lewis, "Ford and Kahn," *Michigan History*, Sept.–Oct. 1980, pp. 17–28.

5. See Clarence Hooker, *Life in the Shadows of the Crystal Palace, 1910–1927: Ford Workers in the Model T Era* (Bowling Green, Ohio, 1997), pp. 26–27; Hounshell, *From American System to Mass Production*, pp. 226–27.

6. This description relies heavily upon Nevins and Hill, *Ford: Expansion and Challenge*, pp. 454–56.

7. Much of this is detailed in *Ford Factory Facts* (Detroit, 1912), in FA, a Ford publication that

took the reader on a step-by-step guided tour through the Highland Park plant. See also Hounshell, *From American System to Mass Production*, pp. 228–33.

8. Detroit *Journal*, quoted in Nevins and Hill, *Ford: Expansion and Challenge*, p. 461. See also Hounshell, *From American System to Mass Production*, pp. 234–37.

9. The production statistics come from Hounshell, *From American System to Mass Production*, p. 224. Colvin's sixteen articles appeared in *American Machinist*, May 8–Nov. 27, 1913; the quotations come from his "Building an Automobile Every 40 Seconds," *American Machinist*, 1913, p. 759; and "Special Machines for Auto Small Parts," *American Machinist*, 1913, p. 442.

10. The statistic on American car production comes from Colvin, "Building Automobile Every 40 Seconds," p. 757. See also "Ford Factory Is a Wonderful Place," New Orleans *Picayune*, Nov. 12, 1912; "Figures on Ford Production Amaze," Jackson, Michigan *Press*, Oct. 18, 1913; "New Idea in the Big Ford Factory," San Francisco *Chronicle*, Nov. 17, 1912; "Ford's Gigantic Output Marvel in Auto Industry," Toledo *Blade*, Jan. 18, 1913. Clipbook No. 1, in FA, is filled with such news articles.

11. "Single Model Is Ford Secret," Providence *Tribune*, July 6, 1913; "Save Thousands by Elimination of Waste Motion," *Christian Science Monitor*, Nov. 9, 1912; "Make Ford Auto and Start in 2½ Minutes—This Remarkable Record Caught in Moving Pictures at the Factory," Los Angeles *Times*, June 22, 1913; "Rise of Ford Is like a Fairy Tale," Indianapolis *Star*, March 9, 1913.

12. *Ford Factory Facts*, pp. 44, 10.

13. HF, *My Life and Work* (Garden City, N.Y., 1922), p. 80.

14. Ibid., p. 81. Ernest G. Liebold, in his "Reminiscences," vol. 3, p. 167, claimed that HF told him the watch factory story. See also W. C. Klann, "Reminiscences," pp. 20–22; Charles Sorensen, "The Early Years," ms., pp. 123–24, acc. 65, box 66-9, FA.

15. Hounshell, *American System to Mass Production*, pp. 218–49, has offered a persuasive account of the development of the Ford assembly line based on an exhaustive examination of the evidence.

16. Klann, "Reminiscences," pp. 27–31.

17. Ibid., pp. 46–51; Horace L. Arnold and Fay L. Faurote, *Ford Methods and the Ford Shops* (New York, 1915), p. 116; Hounshell, *From American System to Mass Production*, pp. 248–49.

18. Klann, "Reminiscences," p. 55.

19. Ibid., pp. 47, 55, 60, 63, 68–71; Harold Wibel, "Reminiscences," p. 21.

20. Clarence W. Avery, "How Mass Production Came into Being," *Iron Age*, June 13, 1929, p. 1638.

21. Klann, "Reminiscences," pp. 79, 80; Clarence Avery, "Speech at Dinner for 35-Year Employees, Dec. 19, 1944," p. 3, in acc. 23, box 8, FA; Hounshell, *From American System to Mass Production*, p. 255.

22. See Arnold and Faurote, *Ford Methods and the Ford Shops*.

23. Ibid., pp. 32, 307.

24. Ibid., pp. 95, 102–3, 104.

25. Ibid., p. 135.

26. "Ford Factory Is an Ideal," *Interstate Motorist*, June 20, 1914; S. S. Thompson, "Through the Ford Factory," Boise, Idaho, *News*, June 7, 1914; "New Ford System," Houston *Chronicle*, May 30, 1914.

27. "Ford Production Industrial Marvel," Washington, D.C., *Times*, Sept. 27, 1913; "Assemble Complete Car in Two and One-Half Minutes," Grand Rapids *Herald*, June 8, 1913; "Auto Is Built in Two Hours," Detroit *Journal*, June 2, 1913; "Record Broken at Ford Factory," Louisville *Herald*, May 10, 1914; "Ford Motor Car Reduced to $500," Chicago *Tribune*, Aug. 3, 1913.

28. "Ford Motor Co. Employees, the Most Expensive Picture That Was Ever Taken," Grand Rapids *Herald*, Aug. 29, 1913, "Ford Army Gets Paid on a Daily Schedule," Chicago *Evening Post*, June 2, 1913; "Half Million Fords in Use—Every Third Car a Ford," Boston *Post*, April 26, 1914, also in Indianapolis *Star*, April 26, 1914.

29. Frank Vivian, "Reminiscences," pp. 6–9; *Ford Times,* July 1915, p. 455.

30. For biographical information on Wills, see Ford R. Bryan, *Henry's Lieutenants* (Detroit, 1993), pp. 289–94; Jack Woodward, "Childe Harold Wills," *Special-Interest Autos,* Aug.–Oct. 1977, pp. 30–33, 60–61; M. D. Henry, "Childe Harold Wills: A Career in Cars," *Automobile Quarterly,* Fall 1966, pp. 136–45.

31. Alfred P. Sloan, *Adventures of a White-Collar Man* (New York, 1941), p. 72; Edward J. Cutler, "Reminiscences," p. 185; Henry, "Childe Harold Wills," p. 136.

32. Allan Nevins, *Ford: The Times, the Man, the Company* (New York, 1954), p. 227; Oliver Barthel, "Reminiscences," p. 46.

33. Charles H. Bennett, "Reminiscences," p. 97; Fred W. Seeman, "Reminiscences," p. 25.

34. Charles E. Sorensen, "Oral Reminiscences," acc. 65, box 66-9, pp. 77–79, FA; Seeman, "Reminiscences," p. 8; Fred Rockelman, "Oral History," p. 11; and Nevins, *Ford: Times, Man, Company,* p. 227, where the author relates the story of Wills and the Ford trademark that he heard from Wills' son, Harold Wills, Jr.

35. John Wandersee, "Reminiscences," p. 12; Rockelman, "Oral History," p. 13; Sorensen, "Oral Reminiscences," p. 44.

36. Charles Sorensen, "The Making of Men," p. 42, in acc. 65, box 67-8, FA; Irving Bacon, "Reminiscences," 14–16.

37. Woodward, "Childe Harold Wills," p. 60, based on an interview with Wills' daughter, Virginia Wills Chauvin; Sorensen, "Making of Men," pp. 50, 52, 42.

38. Sorensen, "Oral Reminiscences," pp. 43–44, in acc. 65, box 66-9, and pp. 41, 49–52, box 67-8, FA.

39. On Wills' pioneering role in developing vanadium, see Rockelman, "Oral History," pp. 50–51; Wandersee, "Reminiscences," p. 20; Nevins, *Ford: Times, Man, Company,* pp. 348 ff., which relates Wills' own account as told to his son, Harold Wills, Jr. See also Henry, "Childe Harold Wills," p. 138.

40. John F. Dodge, testimony, in Dodge case, in acc. 572, box 20, "Wills" folder, FA; Sorensen, "Making of Men," pp. 53, 59.

41. HF, *My Life and Work,* pp. 80–81.

42. On Taylor and scientific management, see Samuel Haber, *Efficiency and Uplift: Scientific Management in the Progressive Era* (Chicago, 1964); Daniel Nelson, *Frederick W. Taylor and the Rise of Scientific Management* (Madison, Wisc., 1980); Daniel T. Rodgers, *The Work Ethic in Industrial America, 1850–1920* (Chicago, 1978), pp. 53–57. Historians such as Alfred Chandler, *The Visible Hand: The Managerial Revolution in American Business* (Cambridge, Mass., 1977), and Olivier Zunz, *Making America Corporate, 1870–1920* (Chicago, 1990), have stressed that Taylorism was the foundation for a much broader rationalization of modern corporate capitalism under the auspices of a new managerial class.

43. Arnold and Faurote, *Ford Methods and the Ford Shops,* p. 20; Hounshell, *From American System to Mass Production,* p. 251 quoted in text.

44. Wibel, "Reminiscences," pp. 22–24; O. J. Abell, "Making the Ford Motor Car," *Iron Age,* June 6, 1912, pp. 1457–58; Charles Madison, "My Seven Years of Automotive Servitude," in David L. Lewis and Laurence Goldstein, eds., *The Automobile and American Culture* (Ann Arbor, 1983), pp. 17–18. In fact, Max Wollering claimed in his "Reminiscences" that he had used a stopwatch as early as 1907 to systematize work functions.

45. Abell, "Making the Ford Motor Car," pp. 1457–58; Fred H. Colvin, "Making Rear Axles for the Ford Auto," *American Machinist,* July 24, 1913, p. 148; Klann, "Reminiscences," pp. 37, 54.

46. Arnold and Faurote, *Ford Methods and Ford Shops,* p. 119. See Stephen Meyer, *The Five Dollar Day: Labor Management and Social Control in the Ford Motor Company, 1908–1921* (Albany, N.Y., 1981), pp. 60–64, for a revealing discussion of the assembly line's impact at Ford.

47. Daniel T. Rodgers, *The Work Ethic in Industrial America, 1850–1920* (Chicago, 1978), remains a splendid analysis of the work ethic and its role in American industrialization.

48. HF, *My Life and Work,* pp. 3, 9, 92.

49. Ibid., p. 120; Judson C. Welliver, "Henry Ford, Dreamer and Worker," *American Review of Reviews*, Nov. 1921, p. 482.
50. HF, *My Life and Work*, pp. 83, 279, 77, 80; HF, "Mass Production," *Encyclopaedia Britannica* (New York and London, 1929), vol. 15, p. 40.
51. HF, *My Life and Work*, pp. 103, 77–79; HF, "Mass Production," p. 40.
52. HF, *My Life and Work*, pp. 110–11.
53. HF, "Mass Production," pp. 40–41; HF, *My Life and Work*, pp. 105–6.
54. HF, *My Life and Work*, pp. 103, 278–79.
55. HF, "Mass Production," p. 41.
56. Ibid., pp. 38, 39.
57. Sorensen, "The Early Years," pp. 61–62.

Nine • Folk Hero

1. Julian Street, "Detroit the Dynamic," *Collier's*, July 4, 1914, pp. 24–27.
2. For an exhaustive account of the Selden court battle, see William Greenleaf, *Monopoly on Wheels: Henry Ford and the Selden Automobile Patent* (Detroit, 1961). See also Allan Nevins, *Ford: The Times, the Man, the Company* (New York, 1954), pp. 284–294; David L. Lewis, *The Public Image of Henry Ford: An American Folk Hero and His Company* (Detroit, 1976), pp. 20–21.
3. "Ford on the Selden Association," *Cycle and Automobile Trade Journal*, Oct. 1, 1903, pp. 17, 48; Ford ads, *Horseless Age*, Jan. 27, 1904, and March 30, 1904; Ford ad in *Cycle and Automobile Trade Journal*, April 1, 1904.
4. Among the most insightful works on progressivism are Richard Hofstadter, *The Age of Reform: From Bryan to F.D.R.* (New York, 1959); Robert Wiebe, *The Search for Order, 1877–1920* (New York, 1967); James T. Kloppenberg, *Uncertain Victory: Social Democracy and Progressivism in European and American Thought, 1870–1920* (New York, 1986); Daniel Rodgers, *Atlantic Crossings: Social Politics in a Progressive Age* (Cambridge, Mass., 1998).
5. Ford ads, *Horseless Age*, Jan. 27, 1904, and March 30, 1904; Ford ad, New York *Herald*, Jan. 14, 1906.
6. "What Henry Ford Has to Say in Reply," *Automobile*, May 2, 1907, pp. 735–36.
7. Henry Ford, "Ford Against the Selden Patent," Detroit *News Tribune*, Feb. 17, 1907.
8. See Nevins, *Ford: Times, Man, Company*, pp. 415–37; Lewis, *Public Image of Ford*, pp. 23–24.
9. "A Significant Event," *Ford Times*, Feb. 1911, pp. 172–74, 183, quoted in text; "Ford Victory Pleases Many," Detroit *Journal*, Jan. 11, 1911; "Motor Car News," Detroit *Journal*, Jan. 18, 1911; Nevins, *Ford: Times, Man, Company*, pp. 437–38.
10. *Horseless Age*, Jan. 11, 1911, pp. 120–26, and Jan. 18, 1911, p. 145; *Motor World*, Jan. 12, 1911, pp. 1–3; "Ford the Fighter," Detroit *Free Press*, March 1, 1910; "Changes in Automobiledom," Detroit *Free Press*, Jan. 12, 1911; "Henry Ford's Victory," Detroit *Journal*, Jan. 11, 1911; "One Man's Example," Fort Wayne *Independent*, Aug 12, 1913.
11. HF, *My Life and Work* (Garden City, N.Y., 1922), p. 63; "Liberating an Industry," in *A Series of Talks Given on the Ford Sunday Evening Hour by W. J. Cameron, 1934–1935* (Dearborn, Mich., 1935), pp. 50–52.
12. "Henry Ford in Fifteen Years Rises to Be, in Point of Income, One of the Richest Men in the World," St. Paul *Pioneer*, Aug. 24, 1913; Harry M. Nimmo, "A Talk with Henry Ford," *Harper's Weekly*, May 29, 1915, p. 519.
13. See, for instance, stories dated July 9, 1914, in Cincinnati *Times-Star*, Indianapolis *News*, and Louisville *Post*. See "Henry Ford; or How to Be Happy on a Million a Month," *Current Opinion*, Aug. 1914, p. 95.
14. "Henry Ford, Looking into the Future, Sees 500-Lb. Cars Going 200 Miles an Hour," Detroit *Journal*, July 16, 1913.
15. "Ford's Folly Brings Millions: Modest Beginnings and Great Accomplishments of Automobile Manufacturer Told—His Life Is Simple," Pasadena *News*, Sept. 17, 1913; "How Ford's

Folly Grew," Omaha *Bee*, Sept. 28, 1913; "Henry Ford; or How to Be Happy on a Million a Month," p. 95; Harry M. Nimmo, "A Talk with Henry Ford," *Harper's Weekly*, May 29, 1915, p. 520; Chicago *Herald*, quoted in Frank Bonville, *What Henry Ford Is Doing* (Seattle, 1920), p. 13.

16. "Henry Ford; or How to Be Happy on a Million a Month," p. 95; Nimmo, "Talk with Henry Ford," p. 520.

17. "Henry Ford; or How to Be Happy on a Million a Month," p. 95; Nimmo, "Talk with Henry Ford," pp. 518, 520.

18. Flint *Journal*, Sept. 24, 1913; "How Ford's Folly Grew"; "Henry Ford; or How to Be Happy on a Million a Month," p. 96.

19. Nimmo, "Talk with Henry Ford," pp. 519–20.

20. Ibid., p. 518.

21. Gerald Stanley Lee, "Is Ford an Inspired Millionaire?," *Harper's Weekly*, March 14, 1914, pp. 9, 10.

22. "Ford ads from 1908," Acc. 19, box 2, FA.

23. *The Carriage Dealer's Opportunity* (1909), p. 5, in FA; *Ford Motor Cars* (1909), p. 4, in FA.

24. Ford ads, Detroit *Free Press*, March 20, 1910; *Horseless Age*, March 30, 1904; Detroit *Free Press*, March 27, 1910; see also *The Woman and the Ford* (1912), in FA.

25. *Ford Motor Cars* (1912).

26. On Hubbard's life and magazines, see David A. Balch, *Elbert Hubbard* (New York, 1940), esp. pp. 261–64; Frank Luther Mott, *A History of American Magazines, 1885–1905* (Cambridge, Mass., 1957), pp. 639–48; Jackson Lears, *No Place of Grace: Antimodernism and the Transformation of American Culture, 1880–1920* (New York, 1981), pp. 68, 86, 89.

27. Elbert Hubbard, "A Little Journey to the Workshop of Henry Ford," *Ford Times*, June 1912, pp. 243, 244.

28. Ibid., pp. 244, 245.

29. Elbert Hubbard, "Henry Ford," *Fra*, Nov. 1913, pp. 33–38.

30. Elbert Hubbard, *One of the World Makers* (East Aurora, N.Y., 1912).

31. See "Ford's Chat with President Wilson Big Boost for Car: Popular Manufacturer Continually in Public," Birmingham *Herald*, July 12, 1914; James Flink, *The Car Culture* (Cambridge, Mass., 1975), p. 68; "Ignorance of Ford Told by Roosevelt," Wisconsin *News*, March 2, 1921.

32. Gerald Stanley Lee, "The Clue to Mr. Ford," *Everybody's Magazine*, Jan. 1916, p. 92; "Why They Love Henry," *New Republic*, June 27, 1923, p. 111; "Have You a Case of Ford-osis?," *Detroit Saturday Night*, Jan. 28, 1928, p. 2.

33. Fred L. Black, "Reminiscences," p. 174; *Motor Age*, Jan. 15, 1914, p. 16; Chicago *American*, July 2, 1934.

34. HF, "How I Made a Success of My Business," *System: The Magazine of Business*, Nov. 1916, pp. 448–49.

35. HF, "Ford Asks Readers to Name His Hospital—What's Your Idea?," Cincinnati *Post*, July 4, 1914.

36. Charles E. Sorensen, *My Forty Years with Ford* (New York, 1956), pp. 27–28; E. G. Pipp, *The Real Henry Ford* (Detroit, 1922), pp. 39, 41; Black, "Reminiscences," p. 158.

37. Samuel S. Marquis, *Henry Ford: An Interpretation* (Boston, 1923), pp. 36–37.

38. Ibid., pp. 15–18, 23–24, 9.

Ten • Reformer

1. "Henry Ford Gives $10,000,000 in 1914 Profits to Workers," Detroit *Journal*, Jan. 5, 1914.

2. Headlines, in Detroit *Journal*, Jan. 5, 1914; Detroit *Free Press*, Jan. 6, 1914; *Motor World*, Jan. 8, 1914; Keokuk, Iowa, *Gate City*, Jan. 6, 1914; New York *Sun*, Jan. 11, 1914; St. Louis *Post-Dispatch*, Jan. 11, 1914. Statistics on newspaper coverage appear in David L. Lewis, *The Pub-*

lic Image of Henry Ford: An American Folk Hero and His Company (Detroit, 1976), p. 71. The farm-boy cartoon appeared in the Cincinnati *Times-Star,* Jan 9, 1914.

3. On letters to Ford, see *Ford Times,* March 1914, p. 253; Lewis, *Public Image,* p. 73. On the unruly crowd at Highland Park see, for instance, "10,000 in Line at Ford Motor Works," Minneapolis *Journal,* Jan. 6, 1914, quoted in text; "Ford Is Pleased as Gigantic Mob After Positions Storms Factory," Joliet *Herald,* Jan. 7, 1914; "Idle Men Riot at Ford Plant," Chicago *Tribune,* Jan. 13, 1914.

4. See Stephen Meyer, *The Five Dollar Day: Labor Management and Social Control in the Ford Motor Company, 1908–1921* (Albany, N.Y., 1981), pp. 71–72. My account of the labor problem at Ford relies heavily upon Meyer's skillful, painstaking analysis.

5. Ibid., p. 100.

6. Ibid., pp. 79–88.

7. Ibid., pp. 75–78.

8. Ibid., pp. 99–108.

9. See the front-page stories, "New Industrial Era Is Marked by Ford's Shares to Laborers," Detroit *Free Press,* Jan. 6, 1914; and "Henry Ford Gives $10,000,000 in 1914 Profits to His Employees."

10. For a good account of this meeting, see Allan Nevins, *Ford: The Times, the Man, the Company* (New York, 1954), pp. 532–33.

11. HF, *Today and Tomorrow* (Portland, Ore., 1988 [1926]), pp. 9, 158.

12. There is a large interpretive literature on populism. See, for example, Lawrence Goodwyn, *The Populist Moment: A Short History of the Agrarian Revolt in America* (New York, 1978); Robert C. McGrath, Jr., *American Populism: A Social History, 1877–1898* (New York, 1993); James Turner, "Understanding the Populists," *Journal of American History,* vol. 67 (1980), pp. 354–73.

13. Richard Hofstadter, *The Age of Reform: From Bryan to F.D.R.* (New York, 1959), pp. 4–5, 11–12. HF, quoted in John Reed, "Industry's Miracle Maker," *Metropolitan Magazine,* Oct. 1916, p. 67.

14. HF, quoted in "Ford Says Square Deal Is His Aim," Cleveland *Leader,* April 29, 1914; and in "Ford Says Plan Is Common Sense," Middletown *Journal,* Jan. 9, 1914.

15. HF, quoted in Samuel S. Marquis, *Henry Ford: An Interpretation* (Boston, 1923), p. 39; and in "Ford Tells Why He Gave $10,000,000 to Workers," Chicago *Examiner,* Jan. 12, 1914.

16. HF, quoted in "Henry Ford, Who Made 26,000 Employees Happy," New York *Sun,* Jan. 11, 1914; in "Ford Tells Why He Gave $10,000,000 to Workers"; and in "Ford Says Square Deal Is His Aim."

17. "Ford Tells Why He Gave $10,000,000 to Workers"; "Aid Man Who Sweats, Says Ford," Detroit *Journal,* Jan. 7, 1914; "Ford Likes Birds, but Not Wall St.," New York *Tribune,* Jan. 12, 1914.

18. Harry M. Nimmo, "A Talk with Henry Ford," *Harper's Weekly,* May 29, 1915, p. 520; Garet Garrett, "Henry Ford's Experiment in Good Will," *Everybody's Magazine,* April 1914, p. 470.

19. Garrett, "Ford's Experiment," p. 468.

20. Ibid., p. 473; Nimmo, "Talk with Ford," p. 518.

21. Nimmo, "Talk with Ford," p. 520; Gerald Stanley Lee, "Is Ford an Inspired Millionaire?," *Harper's Weekly,* March 14, 1914, p. 10; Garrett, "Ford's Experiment," p. 465.

22. "Millionaire Ford's Tastes Are Worker's," San Francisco *Bulletin,* Jan. 17, 1914. See Clipbook No. 1, in FA, for many other articles publicizing Ford's populist characteristics.

23. "Henry Ford Gives $10,000,000 in 1914 Profits to His Employees."

24. Couzens to William Robinson, Nov. 15, 1915, and Feb. 23, 1916, quoted in Harry Barnard, *Independent Man: The Life of Senator James Couzens* (New York, 1958), p. 94. Differing accounts of the origin of the Five-Dollar Day idea can be found in Charles E. Sorensen, *My Forty Years with Ford* (New York, 1956), p. 139, who credits Ford, and E. G. Pipp, *Henry Ford: Both Sides of Him* (Detroit, 1926), p. 48, who credits Couzens.

25. Couzens, quoted in "Henry Ford Gives $10,000,000 in 1914 Profits to His Employees"; in "It Pays to Pay Good Wages to Ford Workers, Says James Couzens," Detroit *Journal*, April 24, 1916; and in "Unity Is Urged to Aid Business," Denver *Post*, April 29, 1914.

26. James Couzens, "Why I Believe in High Wages," Detroit *Saturday Night*, April 29, 1916.

27. Couzens, quoted in " 'Crazy Ford' They Called Him, Now He's to Give Away Millions," St. Louis *Post-Dispatch*, Jan. 11, 1914; and in "It Pays to Pay Good Wages to Ford Workers, Says James Couzens."

28. Couzens, quoted in "Henry Ford, Who Made 26,000 Employees Happy."

29. Barnard, *Independent Man*, pp. 70–71, 77.

30. Ibid., pp. 77–78.

31. Ibid., pp. 70, 81–83. See also B. C. Forbes, "Multi-Millionaire Couzens Tells Why He Quit Business," *Forbes*, Dec. 22, 1922, p. 307.

32. Barnard, *Independent Man*, pp. 85–90.

33. "It Pays to Pay Good Wages to Ford Workers, says James Couzens."

34. "James Couzens' Life Story: A Remarkable Man's Fight," Detroit *News*, Oct. 18, 1915; Barnard, *Independent Man*, pp. 96–97, quoted in text; Ford R. Bryan, *Henry's Lieutenants* (Detroit, 1993), pp. 70–73; Forbes, "Couzens Tells Why He Quit Business," p. 310, quoted in text.

35. Lewis, *Public Image*, pp. 73–75, quoted in text.

36. "World's Economic History Has Nothing Equal to Ford Plan," Detroit *Journal*, Jan. 5, 1914; "Social Justice Animates Ford, He Is Not for Multi-Millionaires," Toledo *Blade*, Jan. 6, 1914; "Puts Capital and Labor on Equal Basis," Grand Rapids *Press*, Jan. 5, 1914; "Ford Factory Has a Heart," Keokuk *Gate City*, Jan. 6, 1914; "Industrial Readjustment Seen in Ford's Act, Henry Ford's Act Is That of a Far-Sighted Businessman," Chicago *American*, Jan. 6, 1914; "Aid Man Who Sweats, Says Ford," Detroit *Journal*, Jan. 7, 1914. For other stories on Ford's populist background, see "Henry Ford, Poor Farmer Boy, Who Earns $100 a Minute and Is Going to Share Profits with His Workmen," Wilkes-Barre-*Times Leader*, Jan. 7, 1914; "Henry Ford, Who Boosts Men's Pay, Lowers Work Hours, Was Poor Boy," Kalamazoo *Press*, Jan. 7, 1914.

37. "Prosperity Sharing," Cleveland *Plain Dealer*, Jan. 6, 1914; New York *Globe*, quoted in "Press Opinions of the Ford Plan," Detroit *Free Press*, Jan. 9, 1914; "The Ford Profit Sharing," Omaha *News*, Jan. 7, 1914.

38. "The Ford Example," New York *Times*, Jan. 11, 1914; "An Experiment," Philadelphia *Telegraph*, Jan. 8, 1914; Cleveland *Leader*, quoted in "Press Opinions of the Ford Plan"; "The Labor World Has Been Startled," Des Moines *Capital*, Jan. 8, 1914; "The Henry Ford Idea," Peoria, Illinois, *Transcript*, Jan. 8, 1914.

39. "Attitude Fair, Says Gompers," St. Louis *Post-Dispatch*, Jan. 11, 1914; "Illinois Labor Unions Rejoice at Precedent of Ford People," Joliet *Herald*, Jan. 8, 1914; "Ford Is Sincere, Is Labor Man's View," Toledo *News*, Jan. 8, 1914; "Union Leader Lauds Ford's Wage Increase," Chicago *Examiner*, Jan. 6, 1914.

40. *Wall Street Journal*, quoted in "Press Opinions of the Ford Plan"; Syracuse *Journal*, Jan. 13, 1914; "Tilton Lauds Ford, but Doubts Plan's Success," Detroit *Free Press*, Jan. 6, 1914.

41. Sorensen, *My Forty Years with Ford*, p. 141; automakers quoted in "Economic Mistake," Keokuk *Gate City*, Jan. 9, 1914; "Ford's Plan Economic Mistake," Piqua, Okla., *Call*, Jan. 9, 1914. For impact on auto industry, see Alfred D. Chandler, *Giant Enterprise: Ford, General Motors, and the Automobile Industry* (New York, 1964), p. 18; Ed Cray, *Chrome Colossus: General Motors and Its Times* (New York, 1980), p. 109.

42. "The Ford Plan of Distribution," Pontiac, Michigan, *Press*, Jan. 8, 1914; "Ford Profit-Sharing Plan," Manchester *Union*, Jan. 8, 1914; Grand Rapids *Press*, Jan. 8, 1914.

43. John Reed, "Why They Hate Henry Ford," *Masses*, Oct. 1916, p. 11; Reed, "Miracle Maker," p. 11.

44. "Jo Labadie Praises Ford for Gift to Men, Socialist Leader Also Commends Auto King,"

Detroit *Times*, Jan. 8, 1914; "Ford's Plan Defended by Minister," Detroit *Free Press*, Jan. 12, 1914.

45. Untermyer and Darrow, both quoted in "Industrial Readjustment Seen in Ford's Act," Chicago *American*, Jan 6, 1914.

46. Eugene V. Debs, "Editor's Note" to "Some More Ford," *National Rip-Saw*, Feb. 1916, p. 6; Kate Richards O'Hare, "A Conversation with Henry Ford," *National Rip-Saw*, March 1916. On O'Hare's career, see Sally M. Miller, *From Prairie to Prison: The Life of Social Activist Kate Richards O'Hare* (Columbia, Mo., 1993).

47. Upton Sinclair, "Henry Ford Tells," *Reconstruction*, May 1919, pp. 129–32.

48. John R. Commons, "Henry Ford, Miracle Maker," *Independent*, May 1920, pp. 160–61, 189–91.

49. Ida Tarbell, *All in the Day's Work: An Autobiography* (Boston, 1939), p. 289.

50. "Jo Labadie Praises Ford for Gift to Men"; Lee, "Is Ford an Inspired Millionaire?," p. 9.

51. Reed, "Miracle Maker," pp. 12, 64–65.

Eleven • Victorian

1. "New Industrial Era Is Marked by Ford's Shares to Laborers," Detroit *Free Press*, Jan. 6, 1914.

2. For a good overview of the Ford wage plan and its sociological dimension, see Samuel L. Levin, "Ford Profit Sharing, 1914–1920," *Personnel Journal*, Aug. 1927, pp. 75–86.

3. "Henry Ford Gives $10,000,000 in 1914 Profits to His Employees," Detroit *Journal*, Jan. 5, 1914; Couzens, quoted in "Ford Again Staggers the World," *Motor Age*, Jan. 8, 1914, p. 64; and in Levin, "Ford Profit Sharing," pp. 78–79.

4. Allan Nevins, *Ford: The Times, the Man, the Company* (New York, 1954), pp. 458, 526–29; Samuel S. Marquis, *Henry Ford: An Interpretation* (Boston, 1923), pp. 136, 148, quoted in text.

5. "Mr. Lee's Talk to First Group of Investigators, April 15, 1914," in acc. 940, box 17, FA; John R. Lee, "The So-Called Profit Sharing System in the Ford Plant," *Annals of Personnel and Employment Problems in Industrial Management*, May 1916, pp. 299, 301–2, 304.

6. *Helpful Hints and Advice to Employees: To Help Them Grasp the Opportunities Which Are Presented to Them by the Ford Profit-Sharing Plan* (1915), p. 3, in FA.

7. Ibid., p. 13.

8. Ibid., p. 15.

9. Ibid., pp. 21–30, 28.

10. Ibid., pp. 12, 14, 16, 18, 21, 29, 35, 37, 6, 12, 23, 38, 39.

11. See O. J. Abell, "The Ford Plan for Employees' Betterment," *Iron Age*, Jan. 29, 1914, p. 307; Stephen Meyer, *The Five Dollar Day: Labor Management and Social Control in the Ford Motor Company, 1908–1921* (Albany, N.Y., 1981), pp. 127–28.

12. John A. Fitch, "Ford of Detroit and His Ten Million Dollar Profit Sharing Plan," *Survey*, Feb. 7, 1914, p. 547.

13. *Factory Facts from Ford* (1915), p. 43, in FA.

14. Nevins, *Ford: Times, Man, Company*, p. 531; "Profit Sharing Bearing Fruit," Grand Rapids *News*, April 8, 1914.

15. *Helpful Hints and Advice*, pp. 32–34, 17–21; *A Brief Account of the Educational Work of the Ford Motor Company* (1916), p. 11, in FA; Levin, "Ford Profit Sharing," p. 85.

16. Ernest G. Liebold, "Reminiscences," vol. 3, pp. 214, 231.

17. "Final Report and Testimony Submitted to Congress by the Commission on Industrial Relations," *Senate Documents*, vol. 26, 64th Congress, 1st Session, p. 7627.

18. Marquis, *Ford: An Interpretation*, p. 152.

19. Sarah Terrill Bushnell, "Henry Ford's Industrial Policy: 'Give Men a Chance, Not Charity,' " *National Magazine*, July 1920, pp. 155, 156.

20. HF, quoted in Fitch, "Ford of Detroit and His Ten Million Dollar Profit Sharing Plan," p. 550; and in Marquis, *Ford, An Interpretation*, p. 153.

21. HF, quoted in Otto McFarley, "Detroit Has Strangest School in the World," Toledo *News*, June 27, 1914; and in Garet Garrett, "Henry's Ford's Experiment in Good Will," *Everybody's Magazine*, April 1914, p. 469.

22. HF, quoted in Garrett, "Ford's Experiment," p. 270. See also HF, *My Life and Work* (Garden City, N.Y., 1922), p. 128; Willis J. Abbott, "Ford Tells Why He Gave $10,000,000 to Workers," Chicago *Examiner*, Jan. 12, 1914; "Squalid Homes Banned by Ford," New York *Times*, April 19, 1914; Marquis, *Ford: An Interpretation*, pp. 153–54.

23. Ford R. Bryan, *Henry's Lieutenants* (Detroit, 1993), p. 206.

24. Ibid., pp. 205–6; Allan Nevins and Frank Ernest Hill, *Ford: Expansion and Challenge, 1915–1933* (Detroit, 1957), p. 332.

25. "Common Cause," Detroit *Free Press*, April 17, 1904; "Equal Morals for Each Sex," Detroit *Journal*, March 2, 1910.

26. "Detroit Men of Affairs" (feature story on Marquis), Detroit *Journal*, July 7, 1906.

27. Marquis, *Ford: An Interpretation*, p. 147.

28. Samuel S. Marquis, "The Ford Idea in Education," *National Educational Association of the U.S. Addresses and Proceedings*, 1916, pp. 910–12.

29. Marquis, *Ford: An Interpretation*, pp. 109–10.

30. Ibid., pp. 98–101.

31. Marquis quoted in John Reed, "Industry's Miracle Man," *Metropolitan Magazine*, Oct. 1916, p. 64; Marquis, "Ford Idea in Education," pp. 913, 917.

32. "Lecture by Dr. Marquis, Delivered Before the Advisors of the Educational Department at Detroit, January 11, 1917," pp. 1–4, in acc. 293, box 1, FA.

33. Samuel Gompers to Marquis, Feb. 5, 1918; Marquis to Gompers, Feb. 11, 1918; Ida Tarbell to Marquis, Jan. 20, 1916, and May 12, 1916, all in acc. 293, box 1, FA.

34. Reed, "Miracle Man," pp. 12, 64.

35. "Dean Marquis Labors in the Ford Vineyard," New York *Tribune*, Nov. 28, 1915; Marquis, *Ford: An Interpretation*, pp. 140–42.

36. Samuel S. Marquis, "The Man—a Three-Cylinder Engine," *Ford Times*, Feb. 1912, pp. 135–37. The reprinted pamphlet was entitled *The Man: On the Scientific Self-Management of a One Man-Power Three Cylinder Engine* (Detroit, 1912). The citations below refer to the *Ford Times* version.

37. Marquis, "Three-Cylinder Engine," p. 135.

38. Ibid., pp. 135–36.

39. Ibid., p. 137.

40. Charles E. Sorensen, *My Forty Years with Ford* (New York, 1956), p. 155; Marquis, *Ford: An Interpretation*, pp. 140–42, 155.

41. Otto McFarley, "How Ford Taught United States to Many Workers," Toledo *News*, June 29, 1914; Lee, "So-Called Profit Sharing System," pp. 305, 306.

42. HF, quoted in New York *Times*, April 19, 1914.

43. See Peter Roberts, *English for Coming Americans* (New York, 1909); Lee, "So-Called Profit Sharing System," p. 306.

44. Samuel S. Marquis, untitled document on history of Ford profit-sharing and sociological activities, p. 9, in acc. 293, box 1, FA; Bushnell, "Ford's Industrial Policy," p. 157; "Assimilation Through Education," *Ford Times*, June 1916, p. 407.

45. "Assimilation Through Education," p. 410; Editorial, *Ford Times*, Dec. 1916, p. 195; "A Motto Wrought into Education," *Ford Times*, April 1916, p. 407; Marquis, "Ford Idea in Education," pp. 911–12; "Better Workmen and Citizens," *Ford Times*, Feb. 1917, pp. 315–17.

46. "Assimilation Through Education," p. 410; McFarley, "How Ford Taught United States."

47. "Better Workmen and Citizens," *Ford Times*, Feb. 1917, pp. 315, 318; Marquis, "Ford Idea in Education," p. 912.

48. Marquis, "Ford Idea in Education," p. 915; McFarley, "How Ford Taught United States."
49. Meyer, *Five Dollar Day*, pp. 157–58; *Helpful Hints and Advice*, p. 32; Marquis, "Ford Idea in Education," p. 913; *A Brief Account of the Educational Work of the Ford Motor Company* (1916), p. 12, in FA.
50. "From Codfish to Motor Cars," *Ford Times*, Aug. 1915, p. 31.
51. "The Making of New Americans," *Ford Times*, Nov. 1916, p. 151; "Codfish to Motor Cars," pp. 29–30; "Motto Wrought into Education," p. 408.
52. Reed, "Miracle Maker," p. 12.
53. Ibid., p. 64.
54. "Final Report and Testimony," p. 7629.
55. "The Ford Uplift," New Haven, Conn., *Journal-Courier*, May 13, 1914; "Ford's Feudal System," St. Albans, Vt., *Messenger*, May 13, 1914.
56. "Paternalism at the Ford Works," Portsmouth, N.H., *Herald*, April 24, 1914.
57. John A. Fitch, "Ford of Detroit, and His Ten Million Dollar Profit Sharing Plan," *Survey*, Feb. 7, 1914, p. 548; Reed, "Miracle Maker," p. 64.
58. William Pioch, "Reminiscences," p. 62; John R. Lee, "Mr. Lee's Talk to Investigators on July 7, 1914"; and W. M. Purves, "The Investigators' Standing with Employees and Others, June 21, 1915," both in acc. 940, box 17, FA; Levin, "Ford Profit Sharing," p. 85.
59. B. C. Forbes, "Men Who Are Making America: The Story of Henry Ford, Most Paradoxical Among Americans," *Leslie's*, April 26, 1917, pp. 483, 497; C. J. Shower, "Guiding the Workman's Personal Expenditures," *Automobile*, March 14, 1918, p. 547; "A Benefactor," Cedar Rapids *Gazette*, May 5, 1914; "Henry Ford, Who Made 26,000 Employees Happy," New York *Sun*, Jan. 11, 1914.
60. The literature on progressivism is vast. For a recent compelling discussion of this current in American political culture, see Steven J. Diner, *A Very Different Age: Americans of the Progressive Era* (New York, 1998), esp. chap. 8. My summary of progressive assumptions is drawn from pp. 200–202.
61. Marquis, "Ford Idea in Education," p. 914.
62. Ida Tarbell, *All in the Day's Work: An Autobiography* (New York, 1939), pp. 289–90.
63. Ida Tarbell, *New Ideals in Business: An Account of Their Practice and Their Effects upon Men and Profits* (New York, 1917), pp. 127–29.
64. John R. Commons, "Henry Ford, Miracle Maker," *Independent*, May 20, 1920, pp. 189–90.
65. Ibid., p. 191.
66. Samuel M. Levin, "The End of Ford Profit Sharing," *Personnel Journal*, Oct. 1927, pp. 161–70; HF, *My Life and Work*, p. 130.

Twelve • Politician

1. B. C. Forbes, "Men Who Are Making America: The Story of Henry Ford, Most Paradoxical Among Americans," *Leslie's*, April 26, 1917, p. 483; Samuel S. Marquis, *Henry Ford: An Interpretation* (Boston, 1923), p. 55.
2. This description is drawn from Harry Barnard, *Independent Man: The Life of Senator James Couzens* (New York, 1958), pp. 5–6, 99, which in turn is based upon the transcript of a 1926 interview with Couzens deposited in the Couzens papers.
3. *Ford Times*, Feb. 1915, p. 192; "Henry Ford to Push World-Wide Campaign for Universal Peace," Detroit *Free Press*, Aug. 22, 1915.
4. Edward Marshall, "Commercialism Made War, Says Henry Ford," Indianapolis *Star Magazine*, April 11, 1915; Kate Richards O'Hare, "A Conversation with Henry Ford," *National Rip-Saw*, March 1916, p. 8; HF, "Concerning Preparedness," *Farm Life*, March 1916, p. 17.
5. HF, "Concerning Preparedness," p. 17; HF, "Humanity—and Sanity," advertisement template, in acc. 1, box 193, FA.

6. Dozens of newspapers carried stories on Ford's announcement. For a particularly full one, see "Ford Hires Liner in Peace Crusade," New York *Times*, Nov. 25, 1915.

7. See, for instance, "Ford to Captain Peace Crusade in Chartered Liner," Philadelphia *Evening Telegraph*, Nov. 24, 1915; "Peace Ship Will Sail in December," New York *Evening Post*, Nov. 24, 1915; "Prominent People to Go with Ford," Wheeling *Intelligencer*, Nov. 26, 1915; "To End War by Wireless," Boston *Post*, Nov. 28, 1915. On Ford's brief speech, see Louis P. Lochner, *Henry Ford: America's Don Quixote* (New York, 1925), pp. 41–44.

8. "Henry Ford, Peacemaker," New York *Evening World*, Dec. 2, 1915; "Henry Ford's Crime," Seattle *Times*, Dec. 6, 1915; "The Ford Expedition," New York *Herald*, Dec. 6, 1915.

9. "Ford Meets Difficulties in Filling His Peace Ship," New York *Sun*, Nov. 26, 1915; Louisville *Herald*, Dec. 2, 1915.

10. These editorials are excerpted in "Editorial Opinions on Henry Ford's Peace Mission," Detroit *Free Press*, Nov. 27, 1915.

11. Ibid.

12. "Depew Puts Ford in Barnum Class; Calls Trip Absurd," New York *Press*, Nov. 29, 1915; "Beats Barnum, Says B. Sunday," Houston *Chronicle*, Dec. 5, 1915; "Ford 'a Clown Strutting on Stage,' Says Mr. Parker," New York *Telegram*, Dec. 1, 1915.

13. "Joy Riders of Peace," Philadelphia *Ledger*, Nov. 27, 1915; "The Clown," New York *Evening World*, Dec. 2, 1915; New York *Sun*, Nov. 27, 1915; New York *World*, Nov. 25, 1915; "Not to Be Ridiculed," Paterson, N.J., *Press-Guardian*, Nov. 26, 1915.

14. See accounts in the Philadelphia *North American*, Dec. 5, 1915; New York *Telegraph*, Dec. 6, 1915; New York *American*, Dec. 6, 1915. A full-page collection of cartoons appeared in the Los Angeles *Times*, Dec. 18, 1915. A brief account of the *Oscar II*'s departure can be found in J. Timberlake Gibson, "Henry Ford's Peace Ship: Not a Better Idea," *Smithsonian*, Dec. 1974, pp. 94–96.

15. "Ford Ship Is Scene of War," Springfield *News*, Dec. 13, 1915; "Peace Angels War on Ford Ship over Wilson Message," New York *World*, Dec. 13, 1915; "Threat to Quit Peace Ship," New York *Mail*, Dec. 13, 1915.

16. New York *World*, Dec. 21, 1915; Florence Lattimore, "Aboard the Oscar II," *Survey*, Jan. 15, 1916, pp. 458–59; Allan Nevins and Frank Ernest Hill, *Ford: Expansion and Challenge, 1915–1933* (New York, 1957), p. 42; New York *American*, Dec. 19, 1915; Troy *Record*, Dec. 28, 1915.

17. Gibson, "Ford's Peace Ship," p. 95.

18. Lattimore, "Aboard the Oscar II," p. 458; David L. Lewis, *The Public Image of Henry Ford: An American Folk Hero and His Company* (Detroit, 1976), p. 90; New York *Times*, Dec. 15, 1915.

19. Gibson, "Ford's Peace Ship," p. 95; Nevins and Hill, *Ford: Expansion and Challenge*, p. 45. For a sympathetic if unconvincing account of the *Oscar II*'s voyage by one of the participants, see J. E. Jones, "The Truth About the Henry Ford Peace Expedition," *National Magazine*, March 1916, pp. 961–68.

20. Nevins and Hill, *Ford: Expansion and Challenge*, p. 45.

21. Lochner, *Ford: America's Don Quixote*, p. 122.

22. "Ford Back, Plans a New Peace Drive," New York *Tribune*, Jan. 3, 1916; "Henry Ford Back, Admits an Error, Denies Deserting," New York *Times*, Jan. 3, 1916; Lewis, *Public Image*, p. 91.

23. "Henry Ford Back, Admits an Error, Denies Deserting"; HF, "Humanity—and Sanity" appearing, for example, in the New York *Evening Post*, April 28, 1916; HF, "Concerning Preparedness," *Farm Life*, March 1916; Lewis, *Public Image*, p. 91.

24. HF, *My Life and Work* (Garden City, N.Y., 1922), p. 245.

25. "Ford's Farewell Message to U.S.," Houston *Chronicle*, Dec. 5, 1915; Marshall, "Commercialism Made War, Says Henry Ford."

26. "Ford Makes His Will; Says He's for Allies," New York *Evening Sun*, Dec. 3, 1915; HF,

"Concerning Preparedness," p. 17; Marshall, "Commercialism Made War, Says Henry Ford."

27. HF, "Humanity—and Sanity."

28. Marshall, "Commercialism Made War, Says Henry Ford."

29. Ibid.; HF, "Concerning Preparedness," p. 17; HF, "Humanity—and Sanity."

30. Marshall, "Commercialism Made War, Says Henry Ford"; Lochner, *Ford: America's Don Quixote*, p. 18.

31. Hedley G. Stacey, "Reminiscences," p. 29. For an analysis of the antiwar tradition in populism, see Richard Hofstadter, *The Age of Reform: From Bryan to F.D.R.* (New York, 1959), pp. 85–86, 271–72, although Hofstadter believes that populists objected more to "institutional militarism" than to war itself, and distinguishes between wars of conquest and wars for humanity.

32. Stacey, "Reminiscences," pp. 29–30; "Henry Ford to Push World-Wide Campaign for Universal Peace"; HF, "Concerning Preparedness," p. 17; Marshall, "Commercialism Made War, Says Henry Ford."

33. Lochner, *Ford: America's Don Quixote*, p. 44; "Mr. Ford's Own Page," Dearborn *Independent*, Nov. 22, 1919, p. 3. See also HF's statements, quoted in Detroit *News*, Feb. 22 and May 7, 1916, and in New York *Times*, April 23, 1916.

34. HF, in Detroit *Free Press*, Aug. 15, 1915; "Henry Ford to Push World-Wide Campaign for Universal Peace"; HF, "Concerning Preparedness"; Kate Richards O'Hare, "A Conversation with Henry Ford," *National Rip-Saw*, March 1916, pp. 6, 8.

35. Marshall, "Commercialism Made War, Says Henry Ford"; O'Hare, "Conversation with Henry Ford," pp. 6, 8.

36. "Ford Makes His Will, Says He's for Allies," New York *Evening Sun*, Dec. 3, 1915; Lochner, *Ford: America's Don Quixote*, pp. 17, 42.

37. New York *American*, Jan. 3, 1916; and Saginaw, Mich., *Herald*, Jan. 6, 1916.

38. New York *Times*, March 2, April 7, April 23, and April 26, 1916; Nevins and Hill, *Ford: Expansion and Challenge*, pp. 114–15.

39. New York *Times*, April 8 and April 23, 1916.

40. See the cache of letters in acc. 63, box 4, FA; Reynold M. Wik, *Henry Ford and Grass-Roots America* (Ann Arbor, 1972), pp. 167–68.

41. Wik, *Ford and Grass-Roots America*, p. 168; Ernest G. Liebold, "Reminiscences," pp. 283–89; acc. 62, FA, containing several documents that reveal Ford's advertising support for the Wilson campaign; "Henry Ford Out in Support of Wilson," New York *World*, Sept. 15, 1916.

42. "'Out of the Shops in Eight Hours' Is Ford's Wilson Cry," New York *World*, Oct. 7, 1916.

43. HF, "Humanity and Your Vote," Detroit *Evening News*, Nov. 4, 1916.

44. "Henry Ford Offers His Factory Free," New York *Herald*, Feb. 6, 1917, quoted in text; HF, *My Life and Work*, p. 246, quoted in text; Nevins and Hill, *Ford: Expansion and Challenge*, p. 56.

45. For good summaries of Ford Motor Company's wartime endeavors, see Nevins and Hill, *Ford: Expansion and Challenge*, pp. 63–76; and Lewis, *Public Image*, pp. 93–96.

46. HF testimony, July 15, 1919, in "Henry Ford vs. The Tribune Company et al., Circuit Court for the Country of Macomb, State of Michigan, Transcript of Court Record, May 13–August 14, 1919," in FA; *Pipp's Weekly*, March 25, 1922, p. 7; Ray Stannard Baker, *Woodrow Wilson: Life and Letters* (New York, 1927–39), vol. 8, p. 209.

47. HF to John Magnum, July 1918, in acc. 62, box 60, FA.

48. "Ford Now in Open as Senate Candidate," New York *Tribune*, Sept. 8, 1918; "Proverbs of Henry Ford," *Detroit Saturday Night*, Aug. 7, 1918; "Ford Declares for Suffrage," New York *Tribune*, July 24, 1918.

49. HF, "Why Henry Ford Wants to Be a Senator," *World's Work*, Sept. 1918, pp. 522–27.

50. See "Fear of Attack on Ford," New York *Herald Tribune*, Nov. 1, 1918; excerpts from newspaper editorials, in "What Michigan Thinks of Henry Ford and His Candidacy," *Detroit*

Saturday Night, July 13, 1918, p. 2, and Aug. 3, 1918, p. 16; Newberry ads, in *Detroit Saturday Night*, July 6, 1918, p. 5, and July 13, 1918, p. 4.

51. McAdoo to HF, June 15, 1918; Baruch to HF, June 20, 1918; Commons to HF, June 8, 1918, all in acc. 62, box 60, FA.

52. "Ford, the Apostle of Efficiency," *Union*, Aug. 16, 1918; "Henry Ford Is Progressive, Therefore He Suffers Abuse," New York *American*, Sept. 9, 1918.

53. Frank Parker Stockbridge, "Henry Ford, Amateur," *World's Work*, Sept. 1918, pp. 504–15.

54. South Haven, Mich., *Daily Tribune* and Flint *Journal* editorials, both excerpted in "Michigan's View of Ford," New York *Tribune*, July 10, 1918.

55. "Two Presidents of the United States Write Commander Newberry," advertisement, *Detroit Saturday Night*, Oct. 26, 1918, p. 12. The ad also contained a briefer, less caustic letter against Ford from William Howard Taft.

56. "Mr. Ford and the Senatorship," *Outlook*, June 26, 1918, p. 332; Port Huron *Times-Herald*, Oswosso *Times*, Sanilac County *Times*, and Grand Rapids *News*, all excerpted in "Michigan's View of Ford."

57. Liebold, "Reminiscences," p. 296; Nevins and Hill, *Ford: Expansion and Challenge*, pp. 121–24.

58. New York *Tribune*, April 30, 1916.

Thirteen • Legend

1. Reinhold Niebuhr, "How Philanthropic Is Henry Ford?," *Christian Century*, Dec. 9, 1926, pp. 1516–17.

2. Arthur Pound, "The Ford Myth," *Atlantic Monthly*, Jan. 1924, pp. 41–49.

3. "Why They Love Henry," *New Republic*, June 27, 1923, pp. 111–12.

4. "John F. Dodge and Horace E. Dodge vs. Ford Motor Company, Henry Ford et al., Michigan Records and Briefs, January 1919," pp. 9–14, 331–32, in FA. Hereafter cited as Dodge Suit Record.

5. Allan Nevins and Frank Ernest Hill, *Ford: Expansion and Challenge, 1915–1933* (New York, 1957), pp. 90–91, 96; Dodge Suit Record, pp. 1–3.

6. Ernest G. Liebold, "Reminiscences," p. 177.

7. *Pipp's Weekly*, March 12, 1921, p. 5, and Jan. 19, 1924, p. 5; "Dodges Threaten Him, Ford Testifies," New York *World*, Nov. 16, 1916.

8. Liebold, "Reminiscences," p. 177; Dearborn *Independent*, Oct. 8, 1915; Dodge Suit Record, pp. 351–52.

9. HF, quoting his own testimony, in *My Life and Work* (Garden City, N.Y., 1922), p. 162; "Ford Makes Reply to Suit Brought by Dodge Brothers," Detroit *Evening News*, Nov. 4, 1916.

10. HF, *My Life and Work*, pp. 161–62; "Ford Says He Will Fight to the Highest Court," Detroit *Free Press*, Nov. 14, 1916.

11. Nevins and Hill, *Ford: Expansion and Challenge*, pp. 101–4.

12. "The Ford Imagination," Streator, Ill., *Times*, Nov. 15, 1916.

13. "Sees Dodge Fight on Ford Smelter Backed by Trust," Detroit *Journal*, Jan. 10, 1917.

14. "Ford, the Pioneer of Our $100,000,000 Market," New York *Evening Mail*, Nov. 18, 1916.

15. Samuel S. Marquis, *Henry Ford: An Interpretation* (Boston, 1923), pp. 65–66.

16. See Vertical File—"Henry Ford's Camping Trips and Other Vacations," FA, for a complete listing of these trips.

17. Dorothy Boyle Huyck, "Over Hill and Dale with Henry Ford and Famous Friends," *Smithsonian*, June 1978, pp. 88–94; Paula Wilens Metzler, "In Nature's Laboratory," *Conservationist*, July–Aug. 1977, p. 30.

18. Harvey Firestone, *Men and Rubber* (Garden City, N.Y., 1926), pp. 198, 215.

19. Metzler, "In Nature's Laboratory," pp. 30–33, 47; David L. Lewis, "The Illustrious Vagabonds," *Antique Automobiles*, Nov.–Dec. 1972, p. 7; "John Burroughs' Reputation All That Saved Edison Party," Poughkeepsie *Star*, Aug. 21, 1918.

20. Firestone, *Men and Rubber*, p. 226; Charles J. Smith, "Reminiscences," p. 42; Lewis, "Illustrious Vagabonds," pp. 7–8; F. W. Loskowske, "Reminiscences," p. 25.

21. Lewis, "Illustrious Vagabonds," p. 8; "Ford, Edison and Burroughs Show 'Pep' By 'High Kicking,' " Fort Dodge *Messenger*, Aug. 26, 1918; Huyck, "Over Hill and Dale," p. 90; Smith, "Reminiscences," p. 43; Loskowske, "Reminiscences," p. 16.

22. Loskowske, "Reminiscences," pp. 16, 19; Smith, "Reminiscences," pp. 41–42.

23. Burroughs, quoted in Firestone, *Men and Rubber*, pp. 214, 216.

24. Ibid., pp. 235, 233.

25. "Mr. Ford Demonstrates He's Not Afraid of Work; Repairs His Damaged Car," Connellsville, Pa., *Courier*, Aug. 21, 1918.

26. Firestone, *Men and Rubber*, pp. 213, 227; "Henry Ford Chops Wood," Philadelphia *Record*, Aug. 22, 1918.

27. Firestone, *Men and Rubber*, pp. 191, 192; Huyck, "Over Hill and Dale," pp. 91–94.

28. Firestone, *Men and Rubber*, p. 188; Ford, *My Life and Work*, p. 240; Lewis, "Illustrious Vagabonds," p. 9; Loskowske, "Reminiscences," pp. 9, 33, 13–14.

29. Charles E. Sorensen, *My Forty Years with Ford* (New York, 1956), p. 18; Lewis, "Illustrious Vagabonds," pp. 8–9.

30. Huyck, "Over Hill and Dale," pp. 91–92; Loskowske, "Reminiscences," pp. 29, 31; Firestone, *Men and Rubber*, p. 230.

31. For a pioneering example of the abundant historiography on the early-twentieth-century recreation boom, see John Kasson, *Amusing the Million: Coney Island at the Turn of the Century* (New York, 1978). Warren James Belasco, *Americans on the Road: From Autocamp to Motel, 1910–1945* (Baltimore, 1997), provides an insightful analysis of automobile touring and camping as part of this larger trend.

32. Metzler, "In Nature's Laboratory," p. 30; "Ford's Nerves Reason for Trip, Says Edison," Pittsburgh *Dispatch*, Aug. 18, 1918; Loskowske, "Reminiscences," p. 36.

33. Lewis, "Illustrious Vagabonds," p. 6; Metzler, "In Nature's Laboratory," pp. 30–33, 47.

34. Loskowske, "Reminiscences," pp. 12, 16–17; Huyck, "Over Hill and Dale," pp. 88–94.

35. "The Edison-Ford Motor Jaunt to North Carolina," New York *Commercial*, Sept. 21, 1918.

36. Detroit *News*, May 14, 1919; Detroit *Times*, May 28, 1919; Detroit *Free Press*, May 13, 1919; Chicago *Tribune*, May 10, 1919; New York *Tribune*, May 25, 1919.

37. Detroit *Times*, May 22, 1919; Detroit *Free Press*, May 13, 1919; New York *Tribune*, May 25, 1919; Detroit *Times*, May 24, 1919.

38. Liebold, "Reminiscences," p. 295; "Ford Sues for a Million," New York *World*, Sept. 8, 1916.

39. "Henry Ford at Bay," *Forum*, Aug. 1919, p. 136; Liebold, "Reminiscences," pp. 298–301.

40. "Professor Lauds Opinions of Ford," New York *World*, Aug. 2, 1919; "Ford's Teachings Upheld by Bishop," New York *World*, July 26, 1919; "Doctrines of Ford Not Those of Reds," New York *World*, July 30, 1919.

41. "Asks Son of Ford About Huge Profit," New York *World*, July 11, 1919; "Clergyman Made Ford Flag Design," New York *World*, Aug. 2, 1919. See also, for instance, the description of the trial in Nevins and Hill, *Ford: Expansion and Opportunity*, pp. 129–42; David L. Lewis, *The Public Image of Henry Ford: An American Folk Hero and His Company* (Detroit, 1976), pp. 103–8; Jonathan N. Leonard, *The Tragedy of Henry Ford* (New York, 1932), pp. 158–61.

42. "About Ford and Benedict Arnold," *Pipp's Weekly*, Oct. 15, 1921, p. 1.

43. See, for instance, the reports of Ford's testimony in "The Grilling of Henry Ford," *Literary Digest*, Aug. 9, 1919, pp. 44–46; "Henry Ford at Bay," *Forum*, Aug. 1919, pp. 129–44.

44. "Trying to Drill History into Henry Ford," *Pipp's Weekly*, Oct. 22, 1921, p. 5.

45. "Grilling of Henry Ford," pp. 44–46; "Henry Ford at Bay," pp. 131–32.

46. Boston *Post,* July 16, 1919; Philadelphia *North American,* July 20, 1919; negative editorials, Chicago *Tribune,* Aug. 21, 1919.

47. See acc. 62, box 4, FA, for numerous examples of the signed "Brisbane letters" received by the Ford Motor Company.

48. Acc. 62, box 5, FA, contains hundreds of such letters, including the ones quoted from in this paragraph.

49. "The 'Ignorant' Mr. Ford," Fairbury, Neb., *Journal,* July 22, 1919; "Henry Ford Proves His Ignorance in Court, Bless His Old Heart!," San Jose *News,* July 20, 1919.

50. Sorensen, *My Forty Years with Ford,* p. 30.

51. Marquis, *Henry Ford: An Interpretation,* p. 9; Sorensen, *My Forty Years with Ford,* pp. 146, 27; E. G. Pipp, *The Real Henry Ford* (Detroit, 1922), p. 24; John Kenneth Galbraith, "The Mystery of Henry Ford," *Atlantic Monthly,* March 1958, p. 47.

52. Lewis, *Public Image,* pp. 130, 129, 213; Fred L. Black, Ben Donaldson, and Walter Blanchard, "Reminiscences," p. 42; Liebold, "Reminiscences," quoted in Nevins and Hill, *Ford: Expansion and Challenge,* p. 607.

53. Judson C. Welliver, "Henry Ford, Dreamer and Worker," *American Review of Reviews,* Nov. 1921, pp. 481–95, esp. pp. 481, 493.

54. Charles Merz, "The Canonization of Henry Ford," Dearborn *Independent,* Nov. 27, 1926, pp. 617–18, 628.

55. For a good description and analysis of this newspaper's founding, see chap. 11, "The Dearborn Independent," in Ford R. Bryan, *Beyond the Model T: The Other Ventures of Henry Ford* (Detroit, 1997), pp. 101–6.

56. HF, quoted in Detroit *News,* Nov. 22, 1918; *History of the Dearborn Independent,* n.d., in acc. 44, box 14, FA; Black, Donaldson, and Blanchard, "Reminiscences," p. 3.

57. "Ford in Action," *Pipp's Weekly,* Sept. 1927; Black, Donaldson, and Blanchard, "Reminiscences," pp. 2, 8–9, 15.

58. Lewis, *Public Image,* p. 135; Black, Donaldson, and Blanchard, "Reminiscences," pp. 17–19, 65; Liebold, "Reminiscences," p. 442.

59. "Mr. Ford's Own Page," Dearborn *Independent,* Jan. 11, 1919.

60. Black, Donaldson, and Blanchard, "Reminiscences," p. 20.

61. HF, *My Life and Work,* p. 20.

62. Reviews of *My Life and Work,* in Greensboro *Daily News,* Jan. 21, 1923; *International Book Review,* Jan. 1923; "Finding the Winning Card in Business," New York *Times,* Oct. 15, 1922; "Ford: Pioneer, Not Superman," *Nation,* Jan. 3, 1923, pp. 17–18; Lewis, *Public Image,* pp. 215–16.

63. Fred L. Black, "Reminiscences," p. 158.

Fourteen • *Visionary*

1. Allan Nevins and Frank Ernest Hill, *Ford: Expansion and Challenge, 1915–1933* (New York, 1957), pp. 8–9, 92; David L. Lewis, *The Public Image of Henry Ford: An American Folk Hero and His Company* (Detroit, 1976), p. 109.

2. Nevins and Hill, *Ford: Expansion and Challenge,* pp. 8–9; Ed Cray, *Chrome Colossus: General Motors and Its Times* (New York, 1980), p. 137.

3. Otheman Stevens, "Henry Ford Organizing Huge New Company to Build Better, Cheaper Car," Los Angeles *Examiner,* March 5, 1919.

4. "Henry Ford Defies Fellow Stockholders and Says He Will Proceed to Build Cheap Car," Los Angeles *Sunday Times,* March 16, 1919.

5. "Ford Company Officials in Dark on New Scheme," New York *Herald,* March 7, 1919; "Ford Would Build New Car Himself," *Automobile Topics,* March 8, 1919, p. 539.

6. *Automotive Industries,* April 3, 1919, p. 773; "Ford Automobile Holdings of Many Millions

Reported Sold to General Motors," New York *Herald,* April 18, 1919; "Argument Centers About the Fordlet," *Automobile Topics,* March 15, 1919, p. 655; *Automotive Industries,* July 3, 1919, p. 39.

7. "What Shall We Call the Baby," New York *Herald,* March 16, 1919; "Ford Motor Company—New Car Development," in acc. 62, box 89, FA.

8. Ernest G. Liebold to Gaston Plantiff, March 19, 1919, Gaston Plantiff folder, acc. 62, box 107, FA; "Argument Centers About the Fordlet," *Automobile Topics,* March 15, 1919, p. 655.

9. R. T. Walker, "Reminiscences," pp. 40–45; Dana Mayo, "Memo," in acc. 940, box 19, FA; William N. Mayo, "Reminiscences," pp. 21–25, 15, 32; John W. Anderson, testimony Jan. 27, 1927, in "Minority Stockholders' Tax Cases," in acc. 940, box 19, pp. 1325–41, FA.

10. "Ford Would Build New Car Himself," *Automobile Topics,* March 8, 1919, p. 539; *Motor Age,* April 3, 1919, 15.

11. Anderson testimony, in "Minority Stockholders' Tax Cases," pp. 1325–41; Stuart Webb, quoted in New York *Times,* Feb. 5, 1927; Mayo, "Memo."

12. "Ford Auto Company Gets $75,000,000 Loan," New York *World,* July 12, 1919; *Automobile Topics,* July 17, 1919, pp. 134, 146. For a fuller explanation of the financial intricacies of the minority stock purchase, see Nevins and Hill, *Ford: Expansion and Challenge,* pp. 109–13.

13. "Purchase Paves Way for New Ford Era," *Motor Age,* July 17, 1919, pp. 10–11.

14. Mary Louise Gregory Brand, "Reminiscences," p. 4.

15. See Detroit *Journal,* June 16, 1915; "Ford Buys Thousand-Acre Site for Blast Furnaces and Plant," *Automobile Topics,* June 19, 1915, p. 435; Edsel Ford to dealers, March 21, 1919, acc. 78, box 1.

16. Frank C. Riecks, "Reminiscences," p. 9; Walker, "Reminiscences," p. 48; HF, quoted in "New Ford Blast Furnaces in Detroit to Cost $8,000,000," New York *Herald,* June 25, 1916.

17. William F. Verner, "Reminiscences," pp. 16–17; "Ford Motor Company Minutes from Director's Meeting," Nov. 28, 1916, in acc. 940, box 24, FA; Mayo, "Reminiscences," p. 14.

18. George Brown, "Reminiscences," p. 121; "An Outside Vision," *Ford Times,* Oct. 1916, p. 106.

19. "Ford to Build Blast Furnaces at Rouge to Cost $8,000,000," Detroit *Free Press,* June 24, 1916; "Progress Being Made on Ford Plant," *Iron Age,* Dec. 19, 1918, p. 1520; *Detroit Saturday Night,* March 3, 1917; Verner, "Reminiscences," p. 12; Nevins and Hill, *Ford: Expansion and Challenge,* pp. 204–5.

20. Ford R. Bryan, *Henry's Lieutenants* (Detroit, 1993), pp. 219–24; Mayo, "Reminiscences," p. 24; Verner, "Reminiscences," p. 21; Riecks, "Reminiscences," pp. 9, 67, 24.

21. Detroit *News,* May 18, 1920; see also Nevins and Hill, *Ford: Expansion and Challenge,* pp. 208–10.

22. Charles E. Sorensen, *My Forty Years with Ford* (New York, 1956), p. 159; HF quoted in William Pioch, "Reminiscences," p. 35. For discussions of "vertical integration" in early-twentieth-century American industry, see Glenn Porter, *The Rise of Big Business, 1860–1910* (Arlington Heights, Ill., 1973), pp. 43–54; Alfred D. Chandler, Jr., *Strategy and Structure: Chapters in the History of the American Industrial Enterprise* (Cambridge, Mass., 1962), pp. 116–20, 122–24, 144, 170–71; Alfred D. Chandler, Jr., *The Visible Hand: The Managerial Revolution in American Business* (Cambridge, Mass., 1977), pp. 363–65, 472–73; Olivier Zunz, *Making America Corporate, 1870–1920* (Chicago, 1990), pp. 12, 14.

23. HF, *My Life and Work* (Garden City, N.Y., 1922), pp. 146, 147, 149–50, 151–52, 155.

24. Sorensen, *My Forty Years with Ford,* p. 157; Verner, "Reminiscences," pp. 13–14; Riecks, "Reminiscences," p. 22.

25. "An Outside Vision," *Ford Times,* Oct. 1916, p. 106.

26. John H. Van Deventer, "Ford Principles and Practice at River Rouge," *Industrial Management,* Aug. 1922, pp. 65–66, and Sept. 1922, p. 132.

27. Evans Clark, "The Super-Trust Arrives in America," New York *Times,* Dec. 13, 1925.

28. Riecks, "Reminiscences," p. 39.

29. For a brief sketch of Sorensen's life and career, see Bryan, *Henry's Lieutenants*, pp. 267–73; a much longer, autobiographical account can be found in Sorensen, *My Forty Years with Ford.*

30. See Bryan, *Henry's Lieutenants*, pp. 267–73; Ibid.

31. Christy Borth, *Masters of Mass Production* (Indianapolis, 1945), p. 261; Sorensen, *My Forty Years with Ford*, pp. 125–27, 130, quoted in text from 137–38, 169–70; Norman J. Ahrens, "Reminiscences," quoted in Nevins and Hill, *Ford: Expansion and Challenge*, pp. 650–51.

32. Charles Voorhess, "Reminiscences," as noted in special collection, acc. 940, box 24, FA; Ernest G. Liebold, "Reminiscences," p. 198; Sorensen, *My Forty Years with Ford*, pp. 7–8.

33. Voorhess, "Reminiscences"; Mead Bricker, "Reminiscences," pp. 55–56.

34. Sorensen, *My Forty Years with Ford*, pp. 156–58, 171–72, 173.

35. Ibid., pp. 180–91.

36. "The Ford Riddle," *Detroit Saturday Night*, Feb. 5, 1921, p. 1; P. E. Haglund, "Reminiscences," p. 66.

37. Walker, "Reminiscences," pp. 113–15; Sorensen, *My Forty Years with Ford*, pp. 74–75.

38. Voorhess, "Reminiscences"; Sorensen, *My Forty Years with Ford*, pp. 144–46; Walker, "Reminiscences," pp. 113–15, quoted in text; Bryan, *Henry's Lieutenants*, pp. 155, 224.

39. Bryan, *Henry's Lieutenants*, pp. 213–14, 268.

40. Philip Haglund, "Reminiscences," quoted in Nevins and Hill, *Ford: Expansion and Challenge*, p. 280; Verner, "Reminiscences," pp. 41–42; Bricker, "Reminiscences," pp. 53–55, 58; Frank Hadas, "Reminiscences," quoted in Nevins and Hill, *Ford: Expansion and Challenge*, p. 280; Herman L. Moekle, "Reminiscences," as noted in special collection, acc. 940, box 24, FA.

41. L. E. Briggs, "Reminiscences," p. 9; W. C. Klann, "Reminiscences," pp. 253–57; Edwin G. Pipp, quoted in Nevins and Hill, *Ford: Expansion and Challenge*, p. 275.

42. Haglund, "Reminiscences," and Theodore Mallon, "Reminiscences," both quoted in Nevins and Hill, *Ford: Expansion and Challenge*, pp. 280–81.

43. E. G. Pipp, "Ford's Secret Service," *Pipp's Weekly*, June 11, 1921, pp. 1–4.

44. Harry B. Hanson, "Reminiscences," pp. 289, 291, 305–7.

45. H. C. Doss, "Reminiscences," p. 51.

46. Sorensen, *My Forty Years with Ford*, pp. 15, 154–55.

47. Ibid., pp. 25–26, 4–6.

48. Ibid., pp. 6, 27; Frank Hadas, "Reminiscences," quoted in Nevins and Hill, *Ford: Expansion and Challenge;* p. 280; Verner, "Reminiscences," pp. 41–42.

49. Sorensen, *My Forty Years with Ford*, pp. 27–28.

50. Ibid., pp. 5–6, 33–34; E. G. Pipp, *Pipp's Weekly*, Jan. 29, 1924, pp. 4–5; Hanson, "Reminiscences," p. 291; Joseph Galamb, "Reminiscences," p. 32.

51. Sorensen, *My Forty Years with Ford*, pp. 100, 159–60; see also Bryan, *Henry's Lieutenants*, p. 268; Hanson, "Reminiscences," p. 290; Christy Borth, *Masters of Mass Production* (Indianapolis, 1945), p. 261.

52. Barbara Carritte [Marquis' daughter], "Reminiscences," quoted in Nevins and Hill, *Ford: Expansion and Challenge*, pp. 349–50; HF, *My Life and Work*, pp. 197–99.

53. "European Trip, 1921," folder, in acc. 38, box 45, FA; Galamb, "Reminiscences," quoted in Nevins and Hill, *Ford: Expansion and Challenge*, p. 282; Bricker, "Reminiscences," p. 55; Fred L. Black, "Reminiscences," p. 128.

54. Sorensen, *My Forty Years with Ford*, pp. 143, 35, 149.

55. Hanson, "Reminiscences," pp. 303, 305.

Fifteen • Moralist

1. Sarah T. Bushnell, *The Truth About Henry Ford* (Chicago, 1922), p. 39.

2. Samuel S. Marquis, *Henry Ford: An Interpretation* (Boston, 1923), pp. 36, 165; Edwin G. Pipp, *The Real Henry Ford* (Detroit, 1922), p. 43; Charles E. Sorensen, *My Forty Years with Ford* (New York, 1956), pp. 11, 34.

3. Elizabeth Breur, "Henry Ford and the Believer," *Ladies' Home Journal*, Sept. 1923, pp. 8, 122; Norman Beasley, "Ford Answers: 'You Should Go into Business for Yourself,' " *Forbes*, Nov. 15, 1928, p. 12.

4. Breur, "Henry Ford and the Believer," pp. 8, 122, 124, 127.

5. Ford R. Bryan, *Clara: Mrs. Henry Ford* (Dearborn, 2001), pp. 15–16, 23–24.

6. Bryan, *Clara*, pp. 25–27; see also Margaret Ford Ruddiman, "Memories of My Brother Henry Ford," *Michigan History*, Sept. 1953, pp. 261–62.

7. Bryan, *Clara*, p. 28.

8. Ibid., pp. 29–30; Ruddiman, "Memories of My Brother," pp. 264–65.

9. Bryan, *Clara*, pp. 31–58; Sorensen, *My Forty Years with Ford*, pp. 15–16; Clara quoted in Ruddiman, "Memories of My Brother," p. 266.

10. Clara quoted in Bryan, *Clara*, pp. 35–37; Sidney Olson, *Young Henry Ford: A Pictorial History of the First Forty Years* (Detroit, 1997 [1963]), pp. 60, 65.

11. Bryan, *Clara*, pp. 67–68. The photos are reproduced on pp. 45, 47, 72, 78 in ibid., and on p. 67 in Olson, *Young Henry Ford.*

12. Bryan, *Clara*, pp. 102–8; Sorensen is quoted on p. 104.

13. Clara quoted in William A. Simonds, *Henry Ford: His Life, His Work, His Genius* (Indianapolis, 1943), pp. 142–43. See also Charles Voorhess, "Reminiscences," p. 39; Clara Snow, "Reminiscences," p. 42.

14. Frederick L. Collins, "Mrs. Henry Ford," *Delineator*, April 1927, p. 8; Clara Ford and Sorensen, quoted in Bryan, *Clara*, pp. 66, 103–4.

15. Louise Clancy and Florence Davies, *The Believer: The Life Story of Mrs. Henry Ford* (New York, 1960), pp. 158–60; Sorensen, *My Forty Years with Ford*, pp. 268–71.

16. Harry Bennett, *We Never Called Him Henry* (New York, 1951), p. 102.

17. Bryan, *Clara*, pp. 56, 111–12; Collins, "Mrs. Henry Ford," p. 73.

18. Bryan, *Clara*, pp. 108–10, 262–63; Sorensen, *My Forty Years with Ford*, p. 16.

19. Olson, *Young Henry Ford*, p. 65; Bryan, *Clara*, pp. 109, 158; Collins, "Mrs. Henry Ford," p. 73.

20. Bryan, *Clara*, pp. 108, 116–17, 152, 199–200; Collins, "Mrs. Henry Ford," p. 73; Alphonse de Caluwe, "Reminiscences," p. 29.

21. E. Genevieve Gillette, "More Beauty, More Profit: Mrs. Henry Ford Reviews Possibilities of Roadside Markets," *American Motorist*, Oct. 1928, pp. 9, 28.

22. "Ford Peace Gift to Follow Wife's," New York *Tribune*, Nov 24, 1915; "A Convert to the Cause of Suffrage," *Woman Citizen*, Nov. 30, 1918, p. 549.

23. "Establish Home for Girls," *Michigan Churchman*, Nov. 1921, p. 15; Ford Office Correspondence, acc. 62-2, box 7, FA; New York *Times*, July 8, 1926.

24. Harold Hicks, "Reminiscences," pp. 162–63.

25. Breur, "Henry Ford and the Believer," p. 127; Collins, "Mrs. Henry Ford," p. 73.

26. Breur, "Henry Ford and the Believer," p. 127.

27. *Pipp's Weekly*, May 6, 1922, p. 2; Sorensen, *My Forty Years with Ford*, p. 14; Rosa Buhler and J. D. Thompson, "Reminiscences," p. 65; Edward J. Cutler, "Reminiscences," p. 63.

28. Breur, "Henry Ford and the Believer," p. 8; "Spirit of 76! Henry Ford Talks to Bernarr Macfadden," *Liberty*, Oct. 28, 1939, p. 8.

29. For background on Ford and this booklet, see David L. Lewis, "Introduction," *The Case Against the Little White Slaver* (Detroit, 1992 [1916]). All following citations to this work are from this edition.

30. Lewis, "Introduction," *Little White Slaver*, n.p.

31. Anon., *Little White Slaver*, pp. 4, 5–6.

32. Ibid., pp. 11–14, 15–17; HF, statement at end of vol. 4 of ibid., n.p.

33. Ibid., pp. 13, 17–18, 19, 64, 65.

34. Ibid., p. 5.

35. Ibid., pp. 14–15, 48, 21, 49–50.

36. Ibid., pp. 50, 37–39, 46, 22.

37. Ibid., pp. 29–36, 51; Lewis, "Introduction."
38. Cameron Wilkie, "If You Could Spend an Hour with Henry Ford," *Christian Herald*, July 20, 1929, p. 5; P. L. Atkinson, "Smooth-Running Henry Ford," *Physical Culture*, June 1923, p. 126.
39. HF, *Three Interviews on Prohibition* (Detroit, 1930), pp. 3–4, 5, 16.
40. Ibid., p. 12.
41. Ibid., pp. 10, 11, 15, 16.
42. Ibid., pp. 6, 20, 13.
43. Ibid., pp. 1–2, 5.
44. Norman Beasley, "The Commonest Thing We Do We Know Least About: An Interview with Henry Ford," *Redbook*, May 1935, p. 59.
45. Frank Parker Stockbridge, "Henry Ford, Amateur," *World's Work*, Sept. 1918, p. 515; "Mr. Ford Doesn't Care," *Forbes*, Dec. 1933, p. 134.
46. Elbert Hubbard, "A Little Journey to the Workshop of Henry Ford," *Ford Times*, June 1912, p. 243.
47. John Reed, "Industry's Miracle Maker," *Metropolitan Magazine*, Oct. 1916, pp. 10, 68.
48. Ida M. Tarbell, "Every Man a Trade and a Farm," *McCall's*, July 1927, p. 79. Tarbell quotes at length from her discussions with HF in May 1915.
49. "Ford Thoughts," as set down by James Martin Miller, *Success*, May 1923, p. 35. See also Reynolds M. Wik, *Henry Ford and Grass-Roots America* (Ann Arbor, 1973), p. 43.
50. HF, quoted in Wik, *Henry Ford and Grass-Roots America*, p. 12; "Ford Thoughts," p. 35; HF, telegram to Branch Manager, Poughkeepsie, N.Y., Feb. 22, 1922, in acc. 1, box 3, FA.
51. Andrew S. Wing, "The Sort of a Man Henry Ford Is When You Meet and Talk with Him," *Farm and Fireside*, Feb. 1926, pp. 4, 5; Andrew S. Wing, "A Farmer Visits Henry Ford," *Farm and Fireside*, Sept. 1925, pp. 3, 49.
52. Ford R. Bryan, "Revival of Old-Fashioned Harvesting," pp. 1–4, in Vertical File—"Farming," FA.
53. N.a., "The Dearborn Flour Mill," pp. 1–3, in Vertical File—"Ford Farms," FA.
54. Reed, "Miracle Maker," pp. 11, 67; Detroit *News*, May 11, 1930; Tarbell, "Every Man a Trade and a Farm," p. 80.
55. Wing, "Farmer Visits Henry Ford," p. 3.
56. Judson C. Welliver, "Henry Ford, Dreamer and Worker," *American Review of Reviews*, Nov. 1921, pp. 494, 485.
57. HF, *My Life and Work* (Garden City, N.Y., 1922), pp. 15, 204.
58. Sorensen, *My Forty Years with Ford*, p. 232; HF quoted in Welliver, "Henry Ford, Dreamer and Worker," pp. 482–83.
59. Sorensen, *My Forty Years with Ford*, pp. 233–36; Wik, *Henry Ford and Grass-Roots America*, pp. 84–87.
60. Wik, *Henry Ford and Grass-Roots America*, pp. 87–96.
61. "Henry Ford at Bay: The Extraordinary Trial at Mt. Clemens," *Forum*, Aug. 1919, pp. 142–43; HF, *My Life and Work*, p. 200. See also Wik, *Henry Ford and Grass-Roots America*, p. 88.
62. HF, "We Don't Know Enough," *Country Home*, Aug. 1931, p. 5; Welliver, "Henry Ford, Dreamer and Worker," pp. 482–83; Ford interview, Washington *Evening Star*, May 28, 1930; Wing, "Farmer Visits Henry Ford," p. 46; "Experimenting with the Soy Bean," *Ford News*, March 1933, pp. 49–51; Reynolds M. Wik, "Henry Ford's Science and Technology for Rural America," *Technology and Culture*, Summer 1962, pp. 247–58.
63. Welliver, "Henry Ford, Dreamer and Worker," p. 485. See Clipbooks 1919–1923, in FA, for a sampling of news stories on Ford's initiatives in this area.
64. "Henry Ford at Bay," p. 142.
65. HF, "Why Henry Ford Wants to Be Senator," *World's Work*, Sept. 1918, pp. 525–26; "Henry Ford Wants Cowless Milk and Crowdless Cities," *Literary Digest*, Feb. 26, 1921,

p. 42; "Henry Ford at Bay," p. 143. See also "Ford Thoughts," p. 36; Wing, "Sort of a Man Ford Is," p. 52.

66. HF, *My Life and Work*, pp. 190, 189, 192.
67. "Spirit of 76," p. 8.

Sixteen • Positive Thinker

1. Oliver Barthel, "Reminiscences," pp. 70–73; "Henry Ford, Discussing His Religion, Says I Believe in a Master Mind," London *Express*, Nov. 4, 1928; William C. Richards, *The Last Billionaire* (New York, 1948), p. 411.
2. See HF, "Looking Under the Human Hood," *Rotarian*, Jan. 1947, p. 10, and HF, "Rock of Ages," *Woman's Home Companion*, July 1943, where he recalled his early religious training; Dr. Edsel Ruddiman, "Reminiscences," p. 3; Margaret Ford Ruddiman, "Reminiscences," pp. 38–39.
3. HF, quoted in Sidney Olson, *Young Henry Ford: A Pictorial History of the First Forty Years* (Detroit, 1997 [1963]), p. 31; Samuel S. Marquis, *Henry Ford: An Interpretation* (Boston, 1923), p. 92.
4. "Henry Ford Says I Believe in a Master Mind"; Ralph Waldo Trine, *The Power That Wins: Henry Ford and Ralph Waldo Trine in an Intimate Talk on Life* (Indianapolis, 1928), pp. 76–77, 80.
5. "Ford and Trine: A Christmas Conversation About Life, Work, Vision, Religion, and Immortality," *Psychology*, Feb. 1929, p. 55; Irving Bacon, "Reminiscences," p. 155; Artemus Litogot, "Reminiscences," quoted in Peter Collier and David Horowitz, *The Fords: An American Epic* (New York, 1987), p. 132.
6. Charles H. Wood, "Ford Makes Some Amazing Revelations," *Forbes*, Jan. 1928, p. 10; "Henry Ford Says I Believe in a Master Mind."
7. "Henry Ford Says I Believe in a Master Mind." On Ford's familiarity with Emerson, see Allan L. Benson, *The New Henry Ford* (New York, 1923), pp. 331–32. See also Trine, *Power That Wins*, pp. 14, 15.
8. "Henry Ford Says I Believe in a Master Mind"; Ralph Waldo Trine, "The Religion of a Practical Man," *New McClure's*, Feb. 1929, p. 67.
9. "The Amazing Things Henry Ford Told Frazier Hunt About Himself," *Cosmopolitan*, Feb. 1926, p. 25; "Henry Ford Talks of Mind-Reading in Dialogue with Ralph Waldo Trine," Boston *Post*, n.d., in Vertical File—"Misc.," FA.
10. "Henry Ford Says I Believe in a Master Mind."
11. "Ford Says He Reads Bible Every Day," New York *Times*, July 25, 1929; HF, "Looking Under the Human Hood," p. 11.
12. "Henry Ford Says I Believe in a Master Mind"; "Ford and Trine: A Christmas Conversation," p. 54.
13. HF, "Rock of Ages," *Woman's Home Companion*, July 1943; HF, "Looking Under the Human Hood," p. 10; William A. Stidger, "At the Height of 80 Years," *Christian Herald*, July 1943, pp. 15–16; HF, "Faith," *American Magazine*, Feb. 1941, p. 9; S. J. Woolf, "Ford, at 80, Expounds His Faith," New York *Times Magazine*, July 25, 1943, pp. 6, 23.
14. On Trine, see Donald Meyer, *The Positive Thinkers: A Study of the American Quest for Health, Wealth, and Personal Power from Mary Baker Eddy to Norman Vincent Peale* (New York, 1965), pp. 25, 60, 61, 88, 92–95.
15. Trine, *Power That Wins*, pp. 11–12.
16. Charles S. Braden, *Spirits in Rebellion: The Rise and Development of New Thought* (Dallas, 1963), pp. 13–20, 28, 35, 49; Jackson Lears, *No Place of Grace: Antimodernism and the Transformation of American Culture, 1880–1920* (New York, 1981), pp. 38, 53–54; Meyer, *Positive Thinkers*.

17. Nathan G. Hale, Jr., *Freud and the Americans: The Beginnings of Psychoanalysis in the United States, 1876–1917* (New York, 1971), pp. 231–32, 229, 244; Braden, *Spirits in Rebellion*, pp. 14–18; Meyer, *Positive Thinkers*; Lears, *No Place of Grace.*

18. Norman Beasley, "Ford Answers: 'Should You Go into Business for Yourself,' " *Forbes*, Nov. 15, 1928, p. 11; P. L. Atkinson, "Ford's Message to Young Men of Today," *National Brain Power*, June 1923, p. 72; M. K. Wisehart, "Henry Ford Talks to Young Men," *American Magazine*, Aug. 1929, p. 160, quoted in text.

19. Atkinson, "Ford's Message to Young Men," p. 14; Albert Sidney Gregg, "Henry Ford's Half Dozen," *Leslie's Illustrated Weekly*, Dec. 31, 1921, p. 908; Benson, *New Henry Ford*, pp. 67–68, 210, 270, 273–74; Bacon, "Reminiscences," p. 155.

20. Wisehart, "Henry Ford Talks to Young Men," pp. 160, 45; HF, "As I See It: A Common Sense Editorial," *National Brain Power*, June 1923, p. 11.

21. Trine, *Power That Wins*, pp. 37–38, 47, 61–63, 16–17, 35. See also "Henry Ford Talks of Mind-Reading."

22. Trine, *Power That Wins*, pp. 15–16, 21, 22.

23. Ibid., pp. 161–62, 165–66.

24. Detroit *Times*, March 29, 1926; William C. Richards, *The Last Billionaire: Henry Ford* (New York, 1948), pp. 292–93, quoted in text; David L. Lewis, *The Public Image of Henry Ford: An American Folk Hero and His Company* (Detroit, 1976), p. 229.

25. For insightful treatments of nineteenth-century food and health reformers, see Stephen Nissenbaum, *Sex, Diet, and Debility in Jacksonian America: Sylvester Graham and Health Reform* (Westport, Conn., 1980); James C. Whorton, *Crusaders for Fitness: The History of American Health Reformers* (Princeton, N.J., 1982).

26. Trine, *Power That Wins*, pp. 107, 108, 111; Keith Sward, *The Legend of Henry Ford* (New York, 1948), pp. 108–9.

27. Trine, *Power That Wins*, p. 119; "Spirit of 76! Henry Ford Talks to Bernarr Macfadden," *Liberty*, Oct. 28, 1939, pp. 7–8.

28. Norman Beasley, "The Commonest Thing We Do, We Know Least About," *Redbook*, May 1935, pp. 59, 164. See also Trine, *Power That Wins*, p. 107.

29. Detroit *News*, August 9, 1919; Sward, *Legend of Henry Ford*, p. 108; Lewis, *Public Image*, p. 229; Robert Lacey, *Ford: The Men and the Machine* (New York, 1986), p. 240.

30. Barthel, "Reminiscences," pp. 77–78; Sward, *Legend of Henry Ford*, pp. 108–9; Trine, *Power That Wins*, pp. 114, 127–28; Baltimore *Sun*, Feb. 10, 1921.

31. For revealing discussions of this trend, see Lears, *No Place of Grace*, pp. 26–32; Gail Bederman, *Manliness & Civilization: A Cultural History of Gender and Race in the United States, 1880–1917* (Chicago, 1995), pp. 170–215.

32. Ann Fabian, "Making a Commodity of Truth: Speculations on the Career of Bernarr Macfadden," *American Literary History*, 1991, pp. 51–76; Lisa Grunberger, "Bernarr Macfadden's *Physical Culture*: Muscles, Morals, and the Millennium," Ph.D. dissertation, University of Chicago, 1997, esp. pp. 1–20.

33. P. L. Atkinson, "Smooth-Running Henry Ford," *Physical Culture*, June 1923, pp. 24–25, 126–27; P. L. Atkinson, "Introducing Henry Ford Himself," "Ford's Message to Young Men Today," and "Making the Ancient God Vulcan Look like Thirty Cents," all in *National Brain Power*, June 1923, pp. 12–13, 64–65, 14–16, 72, 26–28, 60–61; "Spirit of 76," pp. 7–8; Bernarr Macfadden, "Henry Ford's Secret for Success and Happiness," *Physical Culture*, Jan. 1940, pp. 12–13, 77–78. The advertisement appeared in *National Brain Power*, June 1923, p. 65.

34. Atkinson, "Smooth-Running Ford," pp. 24–25, 126.

35. Ibid., pp. 126, 127; Macfadden, "Ford's Secret for Success and Happiness," p. 78.

36. Norman Beasley, "Keep Interested and Stay Fit: An Intimate Interview with Henry Ford," *Psychology*, Nov. 1923, pp. 7–9.

37. Trine, *Power That Wins*, pp. 128, 69.

38. Charles E. Sorenson, *My Forty Years with Ford* (New York, 1956), p. 18; Allan L. Benson, *The New Henry Ford* (New York, 1923), p. 201.

39. John Côté Dahlinger, *The Secret Life of Henry Ford* (Indianapolis, 1978), pp. 80, 215. John Dahlinger was the son of Evangeline Dahlinger and, most likely, Henry Ford.

40. Ibid., p. 15.

41. Ibid., pp. 15, 16, 27.

42. Ibid., pp. 8–9, 26, 87.

43. Ibid., pp. 32, 80.

44. Ibid., pp. 23, 70.

45. Ibid., pp. 101, 14.

46. Ibid., pp. 16, 90, 91; "Boss of 7,000-Acre Farm Got Start as Floorwalker in Detroit 12 Years Ago," Detroit *Times*, Sept. 27, 1918; Ford News Bureau, news release, n.t., n.d., in Vertical File—"Ray Dahlinger," FA.

47. Dahlinger, *Secret Life*, pp. 16, 91.

48. Ibid., pp. 18, 16, 22.

49. Ibid., pp. 22–24.

50. Ibid., pp. 24, 89–91, quoted in text; Al Esper, "Reminiscences," p. 25; "Boss of 7,000-Acre Farm Got Start as Floorwalker," quoted in text.

51. "Boss of 7,000-Acre Farm Got Start as Floorwalker"; Ray Newman, "Reminiscences," p. 9; F. W. Loskowske, "Reminiscences," pp. 44, 121–22; Bacon, "Reminiscences," p. 72; Harold Hicks, "Reminiscences," pp. 137, 175–76; Edward J. Cutler, "Reminiscences," pp. 164–66, 171; Roy Schumann, "Reminiscences," pp. 142–44; Esper, "Reminiscences," p. 74.

52. Hicks, "Reminiscences," pp. 137, 175–76; Esper, "Reminiscences," pp. 25, 71; Eugene Farkas, "Reminiscences," p. 296.

53. Cutler, "Reminiscences," pp. 142, 165–66; Esper, "Reminiscences," p. 80; Emil Zoerlein, "Reminiscences," p. 235; Schumann, "Reminiscences," pp. 140–42; Loskowske, "Reminiscences," pp. 121–22.

54. Hicks, "Reminiscences," p. 45; Schumann, "Reminiscences," p. 144; Bacon, "Reminiscences," pp. 66, 152–53; Farkas, "Reminiscences," p. 350.

55. Dahlinger, *Secret Life*, pp. 4, 17.

56. Ibid., pp. 35, 5. Irving Bacon observed John Dahlinger's plethora of expensive toys when he visited the Dahlinger estate to do some painting ("Reminiscences," p. 65).

57. Dahlinger, *Secret Life*, pp. 11, 43, 56.

58. Ibid., pp. 41, 35–36, 50.

59. Ibid., pp. 34, 35, 43–44.

60. Bacon, "Reminiscences," pp. 65, 120–122; Dahlinger, *Secret Life*, p. 198.

61. Hicks, "Reminiscences," p. 122. See also Dahlinger, *Secret Life*, p. 32.

62. Dahlinger, *Secret Life*, pp. 29–30, 154; Harry Bennett, *We Never Called Him Henry* (New York, 1951), pp. 102–3; Hicks, "Reminiscences," p. 179.

63. Elizabeth Breur, "Henry Ford and the Believer," *Ladies' Home Journal*, Sept. 1923, p. 8.

64. Bacon, "Reminiscences," pp. 142–43; Bennett, *We Never Called Him Henry*, p. 105.

65. Rosa Buhler and J. D. Thompson, "Reminiscences," pp. 68–69; Ford R. Bryan, *Clara: Mrs. Henry Ford* (Dearborn, 2001), pp. 100–102.

66. Fred L. Black, "Reminiscences," p. 30.

67. Dahlinger, *Secret Life*, pp. 72, 77, 161; Constance Clark, "Reminiscences," p. 19.

68. Dahlinger, *Secret Life*, pp. 213–14, tells the story of Eve's being summoned to Ford's deathbed. Henry Ford II confirmed it in an interview with Robert Lacey on April 17, 1986, which is quoted in Lacey, *Ford: Men and Machine*, pp. 468–69, p. 733.

Seventeen • Emperor

1. Will Rogers, *Wit and Philosophy from Radio Talks of Will Rogers* (New York, 1930), p. 33; Donald Day, *Autobiography of Will Rogers* (New York, 1962), p. 206; San Francisco *Chronicle*, Feb. 15, 1930.

2. Will Rogers, "The Grand Champion," *American Magazine*, Dec. 1929, pp. 34–37.

3. Charles Merz, "The Canonization of Henry Ford," *Independent*, Nov. 27, 1926, pp. 617–18, 628.

4. See Alfred D. Chandler, Jr., *Giant Enterprise: Ford, General Motors, and the Automobile Industry* (New York, 1964), pp. 111–13, 145–47; David Farber, *Sloan Rules: Alfred P. Sloan and the Triumph of General Motors* (Chicago, 2002), pp. 48–50; Allan Nevins and Frank Ernest Hill, *Ford: Expansion and Challenge, 1915–1933* (New York, 1957), pp. 470–75.

5. Nevins and Hill, *Ford: Expansion and Challenge*, pp. 405, 415, 685.

6. International sales figures can be found in ibid., pp. 685–86. On Germany, see Mary Nolan, *Visions of Modernity: American Business and the Modernization of Germany* (New York, 1994), esp. chap. 3, "The Infatuation with Fordism," pp. 30–57. On the broader European scene, see Charles S. Maier, "Between Taylorism and Technocracy: European Ideologies and the Vision of Industrial Productivity in the 1920s," *Journal of Contemporary History* 5 (1970): 27–51.

7. Nevins and Hill, *Ford: Expansion and Challenge*, pp. 673–83.

8. Ibid.; Maurice Hinds, "Henry Ford Conquers Russia," *Outlook*, June 29, 1927, pp. 280–83.

9. Merz, "Canonization of Ford," p. 618. Two examples of the massive publicity attending Ford can be found in Jerome Davis, "Henry Ford, Educator," *Atlantic Monthly*, June 1927, pp. 803–10; and "Ford's Plan to Double Jack's Pay," *Literary Digest*, July 18, 1925, p. 14.

10. Sales figures appear in Nevins and Hill, *Ford: Expansion and Challenge*, pp. 415, 685.

11. Theodore F. McManus and Norman Beasley, *Men, Money, and Motors* (New York, 1929), p. 228; B. C. Forbes, "How Ford Dealers Are Treated," *Forbes*, May 15, 1927, p. 19.

12. The fullest treatment of Ford's Muscle Shoals project appears in Reynold M. Wik, *Henry Ford and Grass-Roots America* (Ann Arbor, 1973), pp. 106–25; the quote comes from "Ford Fights Banks on Muscle Shoals," New York *Times*, March 18, 1922.

13. Wik, *Ford and Grass-Roots America*, pp. 116–23; "Ford's Muscle Shoals Case Under Fire," New York *Times*, April 20, 1924.

14. Reinhold Niebuhr, "How Philanthropic Is Henry Ford?," *Christian Century*, Dec. 9, 1926, pp. 1516–17.

15. Rexford Guy Tugwell, "Henry Ford in This World," *Saturday Review of Literature*, Aug. 7, 1926, pp. 17–19.

16. Waldemar Kaempffert, "The Mussolini of Highland Park," New York *Times Magazine*, Jan. 8, 1928, pp. 1–2, 22.

17. Robert Littell, "Henry Ford," *New Republic*, Nov. 14, 1923, p. 304.

18. Edmund Wilson, "The Despot of Dearborn," *Scribner's*, July 1931, pp. 24–35.

19. B. C. Forbes, "The New Henry Ford: The Democrat Turned Autocrat," *Forbes*, May 15, 1927, pp. 16–20.

20. Allan L. Benson, *The New Henry Ford* (New York, 1923), p. 42; HF, *Today and Tomorrow* (Garden City, N.Y., 1988 [1926]), pp. 224, 253; Charles E. Sorensen, *My Forty Years with Ford* (New York, 1956), p. 35.

21. HF, "Machinery, the New Messiah," *Forum*, March 1928, p. 363; HF, "My Philosophy of Industry," *Forum*, April 1928, pp. 488–89.

22. HF, quoted in James C. Young, "Ford to Fight It Out with His Old Car," New York *Times*, Dec. 26, 1926.

23. Allen L. Benson, "Ford, After His Hardest Year," *Cosmopolitan*, Dec. 1927, p. 172.

24. Judson C. Welliver, "Henry Ford, Dreamer and Worker," *American Review of Reviews*, Nov. 1921, p. 494; Mary Lee, "Henry Ford Tells Us We Should Work," New York *Times*, May 16, 1926; G. A. Nichols, "What Will Take the Place of Advertising in Ford's Marketing Scheme?," *Printer's Ink*, June 17, 1926, p. 17.

25. David L. Lewis, *The Public Image of Henry Ford: An American Folk Hero and His Company* (Detroit, 1976), p. 127.

26. "$7,000,000 for Ford Ads," New York *Times*, Aug. 17, 1923; *Automotive Industries*, Aug. 16,

1923; Franklin Russell, "So Ford Is Advertising," *Printers' Ink*, July 17, 1924, pp. 41–44; Lewis, *Public Image*, pp. 189–91. The new advertising policy was announced within the company in "General Letters 1421 and 1425," in acc. 572, box 10, FA.

27. "Ford's $7,000,000 Fund for Advertising," *Pipp's Weekly*, Aug. 25, 1923, pp. 6–7.

28. The Ford Motor Company advertisements discussed above, and many others, can be found in acc. 19, box 3, FA.

29. G. A. Nichols, "What Will Take the Place of Advertising in Ford's Marketing Scheme?," *Printer's Ink*, June 17, 1926, pp. 17–20; Lewis, *Public Image*, pp. 189–91.

30. Ernest Liebold to Midwest Reserve Trust Co., Aug 21, 1921, in acc. 285, box 36, FA; *The Ford Plan*, company brochure (1924), in acc. 951, box 18, FA; Henry L. Dominguez, *The Ford Agency: A Pictorial History* (Osceola, Wisc., 1981), p. 32.

31. HF, "When Is a Business Worth While?," *Magazine of Business*, Aug. 1928, pp. 133–36.

Eighteen • Father

1. Charles E. Sorensen, *My Forty Years with Ford* (New York, 1956), p. 301.

2. "Clara Ford" folder, in acc. 1, box 18, FA; Faye Beebe, "Reminiscences," p. 3; 1901 Christmas letter, in Vertical File—"Ford, Edsel," FA.

3. Beebe, "Reminiscences," p. 5; Mrs. Stanley Ruddiman, "Reminiscences," pp. 89, 92, 94; Charles Voorhess, "Reminiscences," p. 46.

4. Samuel Crowther, "An Interview with Edsel B. Ford," *Youth's Companion*, 1929, p. 10, draft, in acc. 572, box 3, FA; HF to Edsel Ford in acc. 1, box 1, FA; Beebe, "Reminiscences," p. 5; John Wandersee, "Reminiscences," pp. 52–53; Charles J. Smith, "Reminiscences," pp. 23–24; Ruddiman, "Reminiscences," p. 97.

5. Beebe, "Reminiscences," p. 11; Edsel's drawings, in acc. 1, box 27, FA; Henry Dominguez, *Edsel Ford and E. T. Gregorie* (Warrendale, Pa., 1999), pp. 28–30; Irving Bacon, "Reminiscences," pp. 7, 108; Ruddiman, "Reminiscences," p. 94.

6. Ford R. Bryan and Henry Dominguez, "Remembering Edsel Ford on the Centennial of His Birth," *Dearborn Historian*, Autumn 1993, pp. 101–4; Crowther, "Interview with Edsel Ford," p. 12 quoted in text.

7. "The Boy Finds New Use for His Runabout," *Motor World*, Jan. 24, 1907, p. 274; Crowther, "Interview with Edsel Ford," pp. 10–11; Dominguez, *Ford and Gregorie*, pp. 31–35.

8. Edsel Ford's testimony, in "Henry Ford vs. The Tribune Company et al., Circuit Court for the County of Macomb, State of Michigan, Transcript of Court Record, May 13–Aug. 14, 1919," pp. 5397–98, in FA (hereafter cited as Tribune Suit Record); George Brown, "Reminiscences," p. 99.

9. Brown, "Reminiscences," pp. 99–100; W. C. Klann, "Reminiscences," pp. 23–24.

10. For accurate, concise summaries of Edsel Ford's life, see Ford R. Bryan, "Edsel Bryant Ford," in *Henry's Lieutenants* (Detroit, 1993), pp. 113–21; Richard Bak, "The Edsel Enigma," *Hour*, Dec. 1997–Jan. 1998, pp. 57–75; Dominguez, *Ford and Gregorie*, pp. 21–54.

11. Detroit *Free Press*, Nov. 2, 1916; Bak, "Edsel Enigma," p. 60; Clara Ford to Mrs. Meade, Oct. 24, 1919, in acc. 940, box 7, FA.

12. Bryan, "Edsel Ford"; Bak, "Edsel Enigma"; Bryan and Dominguez, "Remembering Edsel Ford."

13. Edsel Ford to R. J. Pearce, Oct. 20, 1917, in Vertical File—"Ford, Edsel," FA; Edsel Ford, quoted in Bak, "Edsel Enigma," p. 60.

14. Bryan and Dominguez, "Remembering Edsel Ford," pp. 101–2; Edsel Ford's testimony, July 10, 11, 14, 1919, Tribune Suit Record, pp. 5360–5600.

15. Fred L. Black, "Reminiscences," p. 53; Smith, "Reminiscences," p. 27; Eugene Farkas, "Reminiscences," p. 353.

16. These two stories of Henry humiliating Edsel are recounted in Dominguez, *Ford and Gregorie*, pp. 26–27.

17. Voorhess, "Reminiscences," p. 14; Joseph Galamb, "Reminiscences," p. 131; Dahlinger, quoted in Harold Hicks, "Reminiscences," p. 174; Black, "Reminiscences," p. 53.

18. Howard Simpson, "Reminiscences," p. 115; Sorensen, *My Forty Years with Ford*, pp. 304–5, 302.

19. Simpson, "Reminiscences," pp. 121–22.

20. Hicks, "Reminiscences," pp. 173–74; William J. Cameron, "Reminiscences," pp. 98–100; Farkas, "Reminiscences," p. 353, describing Campsall.

21. Sorensen, *My Forty Years with Ford*, pp. 304–305; Hicks, "Reminiscences," p. 173; Cameron, "Reminiscences," pp. 98–100.

22. Cameron, "Reminiscences," pp. 98–100; Sorensen, *My Forty Years with Ford*, p. 301; Ruddiman, "Reminiscences," p. 97.

23. Crowther, "Interview with Edsel Ford," pp. 3–4.

24. Hicks, "Reminiscences," p. 174; Simpson, "Reminiscences," p. 115; Klann, "Reminiscences," pp. 119–20.

25. Black, "Reminiscences," p. 58; Voorhess, "Reminiscences," pp. 86–87.

26. Galamb, "Reminiscences," pp. 140–41; Sorensen, *My Forty Years with Ford*, p. 302; Simpson, "Reminiscences," pp. 31–32.

27. Sorensen, *My Forty Years with Ford*, p. 302; Voorhess, "Reminiscences," p. 14; Hicks, "Reminiscences," p. 48; Galamb, "Reminiscences," pp. 131, 140–41.

28. Black, "Reminiscences," p. 54; William F. Verner, "Reminiscences," p. 44; Voorhess, "Reminiscences," p. 47.

29. Kanzler memo, Jan. 26, 1926, in acc. 1, box 116, FA.

30. Allan Nevins and Frank Ernest Hill, *Ford: Expansion and Challenge, 1915–1933* (New York, 1957), pp. 61–62, 271; Sorensen, *My Forty Years with Ford*, pp. 307–8.

31. Sorensen, *My Forty Years with Ford*, pp. 307, 310; W. G. Nelson, "Reminiscences," pp. 103–4.

32. Lawrence Sheldrick, "Reminiscences," pp. 47–48, quoted in text; Hicks, "Reminiscences," p. 175; Farkas, "Reminiscences," pp. 218–19; Galamb, "Reminiscences," p. 133; Nevins and Hill, *Ford: Expansion and Challenge*, p. 411; Sorensen, *My Forty Years with Ford*, p. 310.

33. James Dalton, "What Will Ford Do Next?," *Motor*, May 1926, pp. 30–31, 84, 102.

34. James C. Young, "Ford to Fight It Out with His Old Car," New York *Times*, Dec. 26, 1926.

35. William F. Sturm, "The Fords and the Future," *Liberty*, Sept. 25, 1926, pp. 42, 47–48; B. C. Forbes, "Ford Loses Motor Leadership," *Forbes*, April 15, 1927, pp. 9–10, 32.

36. Simpson, "Reminiscences," pp. 110–11; Sorensen, *My Forty Years with Ford*, p. 219, quoted in text; Young, "Ford to Fight It Out," quoted in text.

37. Sorensen, *My Forty Years with Ford*, pp. 219, 221.

38. Sheldrick, "Reminiscences," p. 46; Sorensen, *My Forty Years with Ford*, pp. 309–10, 222.

39. Sheldrick, "Reminiscences," pp. 37, 41; Peter Winnewisser, *The Legendary Model A Ford* (Iola, Wisc., 1999), pp. 7–11.

40. Sorensen, *My Forty Years with Ford*, pp. 223–24; Al Esper, "Reminiscences," p. 70; Galamb, "Reminiscences," pp. 108, 138; Nevins and Hill, *Ford: Expansion and Challenge*, p. 447.

41. Sheldrick, "Reminiscences," pp. 83–84; Farkas, "Reminiscences," p. 355.

42. Sheldrick, "Reminiscences," pp. 30–31; Ernest G. Liebold, "Reminiscences," p. 846; Nevins and Hill, *Ford: Expansion and Challenge*, p. 450.

43. Winnewisser, *The Legendary Model A*, pp. 7–8, 15.

44. New York *Times*, May 26, 1927; Sheldrick, "Reminiscences," pp. 40–41.

45. Sorensen, *My Forty Years with Ford*, pp. 219–20; New York *Times*, July 25, 1927; Winnewisser, *Legendary Model A*, p. 15; David A. Hounshell, *From the American System to Mass Production, 1800–1932* (Baltimore, 1984), p. 288; David L. Lewis, *The Public Image of Henry Ford* (Detroit, 1976), p. 200; Nevins and Hill, *Ford: Expansion and Challenge*, p. 458.

46. "New Ford," *Time*, Aug. 22, 1927, pp. 35–36; New York *World*, quoted in "A Country Editor's Scoop on the New Ford Car," *Literary Digest*, Dec. 3, 1927, p. 54; Lewis, *Public Image*, p. 199; Washington *Post*, July 27, 1927.

47. "Strut, Miss Lizzie!," *Nation*, Dec. 14, 1927, p. 672; newspaper stories extracted in "Henry Ford as Super-Showman and Salesman," *Literary Digest*, Dec. 17, 1927, p. 10.

48. Fay Leone Faurote, "Henry Ford Still on the Job with Renewed Vigor," *Industrial Management*, Oct. 1927, pp. 194, 195; Allan L. Benson, "Ford After His Hardest Year," *Cosmopolitan*, Dec. 1927, pp. 30–31; Charles H. Wood, "Ford Makes Some Amazing Revelations," *Forbes*, Jan. 1, 1928, pp. 10–11; "The Dramatic Story Behind Ford's New Car," New York *Times*, Dec. 18, 1927; HF, quoted in ad released nationwide, Dec. 2, 1927, reproduced in Winnewisser, *Legendary Model A Ford*, p. 19; HF and Samuel Crowther, "Progress," *Magazine of Business*, June 1928, p. 707.

49. Lewis, *Public Image*, pp. 201–3.

50. See Winnewisser, *Legendary Model A Ford*, pp. 16–21, 33–39, for a variety of photos of the new model.

Nineteen • Bigot

1. Ford R. Bryan, *Clara: Mrs. Henry Ford* (Dearborn, 2001), pp. 200–201; Detroit *Times*, April 1, 1927.

2. Harry Bennett, *We Never Called Him Henry* (New York, 1951), p. 53.

3. Fred L. Black, Ben Donaldson, and Walter Blanchard, "Reminiscences," pp. 3, 15; "Henry Ford at Bay," *Forum*, Aug. 1919, p. 129, quoted in text; E. G. Liebold to W. S. Pendelton, Nov. 26, 1918, in acc. 62, box 62, FA.

4. Black, Donaldson, and Blanchard, "Reminiscences," pp. 17–19; Ernest G. Liebold, "Reminiscences," p. 1261; Black, "Reminiscences," pp. 21, 148–49.

5. "Why," pp. 1–4.

6. "The International Jew: The World's Problem," Dearborn *Independent*, May 22, 1920.

7. *The International Jew* (Dearborn, 1920–22), 4 vols.

8. Ibid., vol. 4, pp. 231, 233.

9. Ibid., pp. 239–45.

10. Leo P. Ribuffo, "Ford and the International Jew," in his *Right, Center, Left: Essays in American History* (New Brunswick, N.J., 1992), pp. 71, 73. Ribuffo's thorough article has provided a foundation for my interpretation in this chapter.

11. Ibid., p. 89; "We Have Given Up the Ford Agency," Sioux City *Daily Tribune*, Sept. 28, 1921; "Brickbats Coming Our Way," *Pipp's Weekly*, Dec. 8, 1923, p. 2.

12. Norman Hapgood, "The Inside Story of Henry Ford's Jew-Mania," *Hearst's International*, June 1922, pp. 14–15, 17; Ribuffo, "Ford and the International Jew," pp. 77–78.

13. Irving Bacon, "Reminiscences," p. 231; Liebold, "Reminiscences," p. 492; James Martin Miller to Samuel Untermeyer, July 9, 1925, reprinted in *Henry Ford Must Choose*, pamphlet, in Vertical File—"Henry Ford—Anti-Semitism," FA; and Allan L. Benson, *The New Henry Ford* (New York, 1923), pp. 354–56.

14. Robert Littell, "Henry Ford," *New Republic*, Nov. 14, 1923, p. 303; "Peace Object, Says Ford, in an Attempt to Justify His Anti-Semitic Attitude," New York *World*, Feb. 17, 1921; HF, *My Life and Work* (Garden City, N.Y., 1922), pp. 250–51.

15. Judson C. Welliver, "Henry Ford, Dreamer and Worker," *American Review of Reviews*, Nov. 1921, p. 492; Emil Zoerlein, "Reminiscences," p. 64; Detroit *Free Press*, Aug. 7, 1922; Liebold, "Reminiscences," pp. 409–10, 1434–35; Andrew S. Wing, "The Sort of a Man Henry Ford Is When You Meet and Talk with Him," *Farm and Fireside*, Feb. 1926, p. 52.

16. Allan L. Benson, quoted in "The Jewish Bloc in Mr. Ford's Presidential Path," *Literary Digest*, Aug. 25, 1923, p. 48; Black, Donaldson, and Blanchard, "Reminiscences," p. 29; Rosika Schwimmer, "The Poisoned Henry Ford," *Jewish Tribune*, Dec. 5, 1924, quoted in Neil Baldwin, *Henry Ford and the Jews: The Mass Production of Hate* (New York, 2001), p. 59. I have relied extensively on Baldwin's exhaustive book on Ford and the Jewish controversy for materials and insight in this chapter.

17. Wing, "Sort of a Man Henry Ford Is," p. 51.

18. Ribuffo, "Ford and the International Jew," p. 80; Black, Donaldson, and Blanchard, "Reminiscences," pp. 30–32; Baldwin, *Henry Ford and the Jews*, p. 171; HF, *My Life and Work*, p. 251.

19. Bacon, "Reminiscences," p. 63; *International Jew*, vol. IV, pp. 67–69; HF conversation with John Burroughs, quoted in Baldwin, *Ford and the Jews*, p. 89; Harold Hicks, "Reminiscences," pp. 178–79; Zoerlein, "Reminiscences," p. 65.

20. Liebold, "Reminiscences," pp. 467–68; Robert Singerman, "The American Career of the Protocols of the Elders of Zion," *American Jewish History*, Sept. 1981, pp. 48–78.

21. "What Started Mr. Ford Against the Jews," *Pipp's Weekly*, March 5, 1921.

22. Liebold, "Reminiscences," pp. 2–19; Ford R. Bryan, *Henry's Lieutenants* (Detroit, 1993), pp. 169–70; Baldwin, *Ford and the Jews*, pp. 24–25; Bacon, "Reminiscences," pp. 11–12.

23. Bacon, "Reminiscences," pp. 66, 198–99.

24. Ibid., p. 234; Liebold, "Reminiscences," pp. 23, 41, 365.

25. Bacon, "Reminiscences," pp. 41–42; Liebold, "Reminiscences," pp. 297, 299; Bryan, *Henry's Lieutenants*, p. 171; Liebold to Gaston Plantiff, July 11, 1918 in acc. 62, box 20, FA; William J. Cameron, "Reminiscences," p. 36; Charles Voorhess, "Reminiscences," pp. 78–80.

26. Bacon, "Reminiscences," pp. 83, 131, 251; Liebold, "Reminiscences," pp. 21–22.

27. Black, "Reminiscences," p. 130; Bacon, "Reminiscences," pp. 58, 97–98; Harold Cordell, "Reminiscences," p. 10; Liebold, "Reminiscences," p. 1142.

28. Cameron, "Reminiscences," p. 53; Black, "Reminiscences," p. 131; Cordell, "Reminiscences," pp. 14, 8–9.

29. Bacon, "Reminiscences," p. 236; Cordell, "Reminiscences," p. 9.

30. Bryan, *Henry's Lieutenants*, pp. 169, 173; Bennett, *We Never Called Him Henry*, p. 48, quoted in text.

31. Black, "Reminiscences," p. 131; J. L. McCloud, "Reminiscences," pp. 112–13.

32. Black, "Reminiscences," p. 132; Liebold, "Reminiscences," p. 259; Cordell, "Reminiscences," p. 15; Mrs. Stanley Ruddiman, "Reminiscences," p. 129; Bennett, *We Never Called Him Henry*, p. 48.

33. E. G. Liebold to Senator Lloyd Warren, in acc. 572, box 4, FA; Cameron, "Reminiscences," p. 38.

34. Black, "Reminiscences," p. 134; William Cody to Richard English, and Richard English to Edsel Ford, both in acc. 6, box 31, FA.

35. Liebold, "Reminiscences," pp. 425–26, 436, 444; Cameron, "Reminiscences," p. 8; Bacon, "Reminiscences," pp. 231, 68.

36. Liebold, "Reminiscences," pp. 297, 1161, 484.

37. Cordell, "Reminiscences," p. 10, Baldwin, *Ford and the Jews*, pp. 186–89; Liebold, "Reminiscences," pp. 1533, 1544.

38. Bennett, *We Never Called Him Henry*, p. 49; Black, "Reminiscences," p. 132; Liebold, "Reminiscences," pp. 499, 451–52.

39. Black, Donaldson, and Blanchard, "Reminiscences," p. 36; Liebold to Dr. Michael Shander, June 30, 1920; and to George F. Oberge, Oct. 22, 1920, both in acc. 940, box 12, "FMC—Anti-Semitism" folder, FA; Liebold, "Reminiscences," p. 446.

40. Liebold, "Reminiscences," pp. 456–58.

41. Ribuffo, "Ford and the International Jew," p. 94; Baldwin, *Ford and the Jews*, pp. 210–11.

42. Baldwin, *Ford and the Jews*, pp. 121–33; Leo Franklin to HF, June 14, 1920, in acc. 572, box 2, FA.

43. Baldwin, *Ford and the Jews*, pp. 147–48, 236; Ribuffo, "Ford and the International Jew," pp. 89–91.

44. Ribuffo, "Ford and the International Jew," pp. 91–92; Gene Smith, "The American Dreyfus," *American Heritage*, Nov. 1994, pp. 93–94.

45. Ribuffo, "Ford and the International Jew," pp. 92–93; Baldwin, *Ford and the Jews*, pp. 209–10.

46. Baldwin, *Ford and the Jews*, pp. 204–8; Ribuffo, "Ford and the International Jew," pp. 92–93; Grace H. Larsen and Henry E. Erdman, "Aaron Sapiro: Genius of Farm Cooperative Promotion," *Mississippi Valley Historical Review*, Sept. 1962, pp. 242–65.

47. Ribuffo, "Ford and the International Jew," p. 94; Liebold, "Reminiscences," p. 492.

48. Baldwin, *Ford and the Jews*, pp. 218–19; Ribuffo, "Ford and the International Jew," pp. 94–95.

49. "Cameron Kept on Libel Stand," Detroit *News*, March 25, 1927; Baldwin, *Ford and the Jews*, pp. 220–22; Liebold, "Reminiscences," p. 492.

50. Ribuffo, "Ford and the International Jew," p. 96; Baldwin, *Ford and the Jews*, pp. 222–23.

51. Ribuffo, "Ford and the International Jew," p. 96; Liebold, "Reminiscences," pp. 492–95; Keith Sward, *The Legend of Henry Ford* (New York, 1948), pp. 153–54.

52. Ribuffo, "Ford and the International Jew," p. 96; Baldwin, *Ford and the Jews*, pp. 222–23; David L. Lewis, *The Public Image of Henry Ford: An American Folk Hero and His Company* (Detroit, 1976), p. 144.

53. Ribuffo, "Ford and the International Jew," pp. 96–97; Baldwin, *Ford and the Jews*, pp. 223–24.

54. Black, "Reminiscences," p. 50; Baldwin, *Ford and the Jews*, pp. 224, 233–38, 255.

55. For the complete text of Ford's apology, see Baldwin, *Ford and the Jews*, pp. 238–40.

56. "The Ford 'Retractor,' " *Literary Digest*, July 23, 1927, pp. 8–9; Louis B. Mayer to HF, July 23, 1927, in Vertical File—"HF—Anti-Semitism," FA.

57. Editorial, *Christian Century*, July 21, 1927, p. 867; "Henry Ford," *Nation*, July 20, 1927, p. 47; "Ford 'Retractor,' " p. 9.

58. "Will Rogers at the Annual Dinner," *S.A.E. Journal*, Feb. 1929, p. 114; New York *Daily News*, quoted in "Apology to Jews," *Time*, July 20, 1927, p. 14; Rose's song, reprinted in Lewis, *Public Image of Ford*, p. 147.

59. Liebold, "Reminiscences," p. 1384; Cameron, quoted in Baldwin, *Ford and the Jews*, p. 243; John L. McCloud, "Reminiscences," p. 348.

60. Liebold, "Reminiscences," p. 504; untitled report of Ford's statements on Jews, 1927–42, prepared by American Jewish Committee, Jan. 31, 1942, p. 18, in acc. 940, box 12, "FMC—Anti-Semitism" folder, FA.

61. Liebold, "Reminiscences," p. 1528; "Reich Honor Is Bestowed," Detroit *News*, July 31, 1938.

Twenty • Antiquarian

1. "Edison Young Again as He Relives the Past," New York *Times*, Oct. 21, 1929, quoted in text; William A. Simonds, *Henry Ford and Greenfield Village* (New York, 1938), pp. 134–35; William Greenleaf, *From These Beginnings: The Early Philanthropies of Henry and Edsel Ford, 1911–1936*, pp. 104–5; HF, quoted in Paul D. Paddock, "Edison to Remake First Light," *Popular Mechanics*, April 1929, p. 941.

2. "World Will Hear Edison Celebration," New York *Times*, Oct. 21, 1929; "Edison's Golden Day," *Literary Digest*, Nov. 2, 1929, pp. 10–11.

3. "Edison's Golden Day," p. 11; and "Stenographic Report of the Proceedings of Light's Golden Jubilee," p. 16, both in Vertical File—"Lights Golden Jubilee," FA.

4. "World Will Hear Edison Celebration"; "Stenographic Report of Light's Golden Jubilee," pp. 1–16.

5. A. M. Smith, "Edison Memorial Built by Ford's Persistence," Detroit *News*, Oct. 13, 1929.

6. Fred L. Black, "Reminiscences," p. 34; A. G. Wolfe, "Reminiscences," pp. 49–51.

7. Samuel Crowther, "Henry Ford: Why I Bought the Wayside Inn," *Country Life*, April 1925, pp. 43–45; New York *Times*, Feb. 17, 1924; "A Mid-West Victorian Inn," *Mentor*, June 1929, pp. 11–13; Greenleaf, *From These Beginnings*, pp. 85–90.

8. Charles Messer Stow, "Henry Ford, Historian," *Antiquarian*, April 1929, pp. 47, 100;

Greenleaf, *From These Beginnings*, pp. 77–83; "Henry Ford Asked to Buy Ancient Virginia Town," Detroit *Free Press*, Aug. 31, 1924.

9. Black, "Reminiscences," p. 36; Frank Vivian, "Reminiscences," pp. 49–59; Israel Sack, "Reminiscences," pp. 23–30; Harold Cordell, "Reminiscences," pp. 57–58, 61; Wolfe, "Reminiscences," p. 51.

10. Sack, "Reminiscences," pp. 37–38.

11. Edward J. Cutler, "Reminiscences," p. 131; Cordell, "Reminiscences," p. 69; Sack, "Reminiscences," p. 34; William J. Cameron, "Reminiscences," p. 84; Wolfe, "Reminiscences," pp. 163–64.

12. Cordell, "Reminiscences," pp. 58–59; Cutler, "Reminiscences," p. 68.

13. Charles A. Selden, "Ford Renews the Past for a Machine Age," New York *Times Magazine*, Sept. 16, 1928, p. 8; Ruth Kedzie Wood, "Henry Ford's Greatest Gift," *Mentor*, June 1929, p. 5; Henry A. Haigh, "The Ford Collections at Dearborn," *Michigan History Magazine*, Jan. 1925, pp. 34–35.

14. Ernest G. Liebold, "Reminiscences," p. 890.

15. Geoffrey C. Upward, *A Home for Our Heritage: The Building and Growth of Greenfield Village and Henry Ford Museum, 1929–1979* (Dearborn, 1979), p. 26; Robert O. Derrick, "Reminiscences," pp. 1–2, 5, 8–9.

16. Upward, *Home for Our Heritage*, pp. 22–23, 52–57.

17. Eunice Fuller Barnard, "Ford Builds a Unique Museum," New York *Times Magazine*, April 5, 1931, p. 3.

18. Wood, "Ford's Greatest Gift," p. 2; Samuel Crowther, "Henry Ford's Village of Yesterday," *Ladies' Home Journal*, Sept. 1928, p. 10; "The Making of an American Citizen," *Good Housekeeping*, Oct. 1934, p. 121.

19. Cameron, "Reminiscences," pp. 80–81; S. J. Woolf, "Mr. Ford Shows His Museum," New York *Times Magazine*, Jan. 12, 1936, p. 20; Mary Lee, "Henry Ford Tells Us We Should Work," New York *Times*, May 16, 1926.

20. William C. Richards, *The Last Billionaire* (New York, 1948), pp. 116–23.

21. "Fiddling to Henry Ford," *Literary Digest*, Jan. 2, 1926, pp. 33–38; David L. Lewis, "The Square Dancing Master," pp. 4–6, in Vertical File—"Henry Ford—Dancing," FA.

22. Barnard, "Ford Builds a Unique Museum," pp. 2–3; Selden, "Ford Renews the Past," p. 8.

23. Upward, *Home for Our Heritage*, pp. 11–12; Charles Voorhess, "Reminiscences," pp. 170–71, 174; Liebold, "Reminiscences," pp. 895, 901–2.

24. Cutler, "Reminiscences," p. 132; Cordell, "Reminiscences," pp. 63–65; Black, "Reminiscences," pp. 44–45.

25. Charles E. Sorensen, *My Forty Years with Ford* (New York, 1956), p. 19; Harold Hicks, "Reminiscences," quoted in Upward, *Home for Our Heritage*, p. 75; Cameron, "Reminiscences," p. 95; Woolf, "Mr. Ford Shows His Museum," p. 1.

26. Crowther, "Ford's Village of Yesterday," pp. 10–11, 116–18.

27. Ibid., p. 118.

28. Henry A. Haigh, "Henry Ford's Typical Early American Village at Dearborn," *Michigan History Magazine*, July 1929, p. 508; F. D. McHugh, "Ford's Friend Edison," *Scientific American*, Nov. 1929, p. 379; Cameron, "Reminiscences," p. 69; "Greenfield Village's E. J. Cutler Dies, 78," Detroit *News*, March 9, 1961; Upward, *Home for Our Heritage*, pp. 26, 177. For an insightful sketch of Cutler's career, see Ford R. Bryan, *Henry's Lieutenants* (Detroit, 1993), pp. 81–87.

29. Upward, *Home for Our Heritage*, pp. 21–22.

30. For a detailed description of the many buildings in Greenfield Village, see ibid., pp. 26–47, 80–110.

31. Ibid., pp. 77–78, 97–101.

32. HF, *Today and Tomorrow* (Garden City, N.Y., 1988 [1926]), p. 229; HF, "Foreword" to Wood, "Ford's Greatest Gift," p. 2.

33. Voorhess, "Reminiscences," pp. 157, 158; Barnard, "Ford Builds a Unique Museum," pp. 2–3; Cutler, "Reminiscences," p. 135; Upward, *Home for Our Heritage*, p. 77.

34. Cutler, "Reminiscences," p. 138; Black, "Reminiscences," p. 35.

35. Voorhess, "Reminiscences," pp. 157–58; Upward, *Home for Our Heritage*, pp. 45, 29, with William Simonds quoted on the latter page.

36. Cutler, "Reminiscences," p. 121; Upward, *Home for Our Heritage*, pp. 89–93; Richards, *Last Billionaire*, pp. 189–90, quoted in text.

37. Upward, *Home for Our Heritage*, p. 76; David L. Lewis, *The Public Image of Henry Ford: An American Folk Hero and His Company* (Detroit, 1976), p. 280; Barnard, "Ford Builds a Unique Museum," p. 4.

38. "Mr. Ford Collects," *New Republic*, April 28, 1937, p. 352.

39. S. J. Woolf, "Ford Answers Wealth-Sharers," New York *Times Magazine*, July 7, 1935, p. 16.

40. "Henry Ford Shakes a Wicked Hoof," *Literary Digest*, Aug. 15, 1925, p. 38, quoted in text; "Reminiscences of Benj. B. Lovett," p. 6, in acc. 572, box 7, FA, quoted in text; Eva O. Twork, *Henry Ford and Benjamin Lovett: The Dancing Billionaire and the Dancing Master* (Detroit, 1982), pp. 53–54.

41. "Reminiscences of Lovett," pp. 1–5; Bryan, *Henry's Lieutenants*, p. 183; former student quoted in Twork, *Ford and Lovett*, pp. 24–28.

42. Richards, *Last Billionaire*, pp. 103–4, quoted in text; Twork, *Ford and Lovett*, pp. 53–55; "Reminiscences of Lovett," p. 17.

43. Interviews with Paul Major, Lucile Webster, and Mark Stroebel, quoted in Twork, *Ford and Lovett*, pp. 27–28, 138, 143–44.

44. Interviews with Mark Stroebel, Lucile Webster, Gino Caporali, and Helen Holmes, quoted in Twork, *Ford and Lovett*, pp. 110–11, 143–44, 138–40, 144, 183.

45. Interviews with Frank Caddy, Mark Stroebel, Patricia Damon, and Margaret Hair, quoted in Twork, *Ford and Lovett*, pp. 190, 143, 195–96.

46. Richards, *Last Billionaire*, pp. 106, 109–11; Sorensen, *My Forty Years with Ford*, pp. 20, 21; J. L. McCloud, "Reminiscences," p. 338, quoted in text; Twork, *Ford and Lovett*, pp. 59–60, quoted in text.

47. Richards, *Last Billionaire*, pp. 108, 114; Keith Sward, *The Legend of Henry Ford* (New York, 1948), pp. 260–61; McCloud, "Reminiscences," p. 353; Benjamin Lovett to International Press Photo Service, Oct. 6, 1926, in acc. 572, box 7, FA; HF, *Today and Tomorrow*, pp. 227–28.

48. "Reminiscences of Lovett," pp. 17, 19; Sorensen, *My Forty Years with Ford*, p. 21; Twork, *Ford and Lovett*, p. 81.

49. Richards, *Last Billionaire*, pp. 109, 111–12.

50. "Reminiscences of Lovett," p. 18.

51. McCloud, "Reminiscences," p. 353; Derrick, "Reminiscences," p. 23; "Mr. Ford Doesn't Care," *Fortune*, Dec. 1933, p. 64; Howard Simpson, "Reminiscences," p. 124.

52. "Reminiscences of Lovett," pp. 6–7; HF, *Today and Tomorrow*, pp. 226–27.

53. Lovett to International Press Photo Service; "Reminiscences of Lovett," pp. 9–10, 14, 20; Lovett, quoted in Detroit *News*, March 25, 1928.

54. Benjamin B. Lovett, *Good Morning: After a Sleep of 25 Years, Old-Fashioned Dancing Is Being Revived by Mr. and Mrs. Ford* (Dearborn, 1926), pp. 13–14.

55. Ibid., 14–15.

56. New York *Times*, Nov. 13, 1935; "Henry Ford, Antiquarian," *Nation*, June 30, 1926, p. 714; "Mr. Ford Collects," pp. 353–54.

57. Ford's 1919 testimony, reproduced in John B. Rae, ed., *Henry Ford* (Englewood, N.J., 1969), p. 54; Chicago *Tribune*, May 23 and May 25, 1916; HF, quoted in John Reed, "Industry's Miracle Maker," *Metropolitan Magazine*, Oct. 1916, p. 66.

58. "History Is Bunk, Says Henry Ford," New York *Times*, Oct. 29, 1921; Fred C. Kelly, "Ford Urges Nation to Shun War and Stock Gambling," New York *Times*, Oct. 27, 1935; HF, quoted in Reynolds M. Wik, *Henry Ford and Grass-Roots America* (Ann Arbor, 1973), p. 206.

59. HF, quoted in Reed, "Miracle Maker," p. 66.

60. Cameron, "Reminiscences," pp. 84, 126–27; Black, "Reminiscences," p. 9; an associate on the Greenfield Village project, quoted in Roger Burlingame, *Henry Ford* (New York, 1955), p. 16.

61. Crowther, "Ford's Village of Yesterday," p. 10; F. D. McHugh, "Ford's Friend Edison," *Scientific American*, Nov. 1929, p. 379; Glen F. Jenkins, "Mr. Ford of Greenfield Village," *Christian Science Monitor*, May 22, 1935, p. 3; Barnard, "Ford Builds a Unique Museum."

62. Anne O'Hare McCormick, "Ford Scans the Current Tides," New York *Times Magazine*, Oct. 21, 1934, p. 1; Henry Ford, "Thinking Out Loud," *American Magazine*, Oct. 1934, p. 19; Black, "Reminiscences," p. 43; McHugh, "Ford's Friend Edison," p. 379; Woolf, "Ford Shows His Museum," p. 2.

63. Selden, "Ford Renews the Past," p. 8; Paul Paddock, "Edison to Remake First Light," *Popular Mechanics*, April 1929, p. 940; Haigh, "Ford's Typical Village," p. 508; *Looking Forward Through the Past*, 1935, n.p., in FA.

64. Selden, "Ford Renews the Past," p. 8; HF and Arthur Van Vlissinger, Jr., "The Idea Behind Greenfield Village," *American Legion Monthly*, Oct. 1932, p. 8; Barnard, "Ford Builds a Unique Museum," pp. 2–3.

65. HF and Van Vlissinger, Jr., "Idea Behind Greenfield Village," p. 8; HF, *Today and Tomorrow*, pp. 226, 228–29; *Looking Forward Through the Past*.

66. See "The Small Town" and "The Old Ways Were Good," in *Ford Ideals*, collection of "Mr. Ford's Own Page" editorials (Dearborn, 1926), pp. 296–99, 341–44, in FA.

67. "Change Is Not Always Progress," in *Ford Ideals*, pp. 361–64.

Twenty-one • Individualist

1. "Mr. Ford Doesn't Care," *Fortune*, Dec. 1933, pp. 63–69; U.S. Department of Commerce statistics, compiled in tables in Alfred D. Chandler, Jr., *Giant Enterprise: Ford, General Motors, and the Automobile Industry* (New York, 1964), pp. 3–7.

2. "Mr. Ford Doesn't Care," pp. 121–28, 131–34.

3. Ibid., p. 126; Charles Voorhess, "Reminiscences," p. 21; Howard Simpson, "Reminiscences," pp. 107–9.

4. On HF and the 1929 White House conference, see "Ford's Wage Rise Comes as a Surprise," New York *Times*, Nov. 22, 1929; "Ford Announces Immediate Wage Increase," Detroit *Free Press*, Nov. 22, 1929; articles in Detroit *News* and Detroit *Times*, Nov. 22, 1929.

5. These articles were condensed from the third volume of Ford's writings, published in 1930. See HF and Samuel Crowther, *Moving Forward* (New York, 1930).

6. HF and Samuel Crowther, "The Fear of Overproduction," *Saturday Evening Post*, July 12, 1930, p. 4; HF and Samuel Crowther, "Toward Abolishing Poverty," *Saturday Evening Post*, Aug. 16, 1930, p. 18; HF and Samuel Crowther, "Management and Size," *Saturday Evening Post*, Sept. 20, 1930, p. 25; HF and Samuel Crowther, "The Way to Wealth," *Saturday Evening Post*, May 17, 1930, p. 4.

7. S. J. Woolf, "Ford Answers Wealth-Sharers," New York *Times Magazine*, July 7, 1935, p. 16; "Ford Urges Nation to Shun War and Stock Gambling," New York *Times*, Oct. 27, 1935; HF and Crowther, "Way to Wealth," p. 3. On deeper problems contributing to the Great Depression, see Robert L. Heilbroner, *The Economic Transformation of America* (New York, 1977), pp. 173–77; David M. Kennedy, *Freedom from Fear: The American People in Depression and War, 1929–1945* (New York, 1999), pp. 40–43, 70–79.

8. "Henry Ford on Unemployment," *Business Week*, June 8, 1932, p. 19; HF and Samuel Crowther, "Unemployment or Leisure," *Saturday Evening Post*, Aug. 2, 1930, pp. 102, 105.

9. Woolf, "Ford Answers Wealth-Sharers," p. 2; HF, "A Rich Man Should Not Have Any Money," *Cosmopolitan*, March 1932, pp. 52–53, 164–65; "Ford Urges Nation to Shun War and Stock Gambling"; HF and Crowther, "Way to Wealth," p. 4; HF and Samuel Crowther,

"Toward Abolishing Poverty," *Saturday Evening Post*, Aug. 16, 1930, pp. 18, 19; Samuel Crowther, "Should the Profit System Be Destroyed? An Interview with Henry Ford," *Elks Magazine*, Dec. 1934, p. 8.

10. HF and Crowther, "Way to Wealth," pp. 4–5; Crowther, "Should Profit System Be Destroyed?," p. 10; Samuel Crowther, "Our Job: An Interview with Henry Ford," *Saturday Evening Post*, Oct. 31, 1936, p. 5.

11. HF and Crowther, "Management and Size," p. 154; HF and Crowther, "Toward Abolishing Poverty," p. 120.

12. HF and Crowther, "Way to Wealth," p. 3; "Ford, Wages, and Depression," *Business Week*, Feb. 22, 1933, pp. 10–11; "Should the Profit System Be Destroyed?," p. 10; HF and Crowther, "Toward Abolishing Poverty," p. 18.

13. HF and Samuel Crowther, "There Is No Santa Claus," *Saturday Evening Post*, May 16, 1931, p. 97; "Ford, Wages, and Depression," p. 11; "Mr. Ford on Farm and Factory," Detroit *News*, June 1, 1932; Crowther, "Our Job: An Interview with Henry Ford," p. 7.

14. "Henry Ford on Self-Help," *Business Week*, June 15, 1932, p. 1; "Ford Urges Nation to Shun War and Stock Gambling"; Woolf, "Ford Answers Wealth-Sharers," p. 16; HF and Crowther, "There Is No Santa Claus," p. 96.

15. See Howard R. Neville, *The Detroit Banking Collapse of 1933* (East Lansing, Mich., 1960); David L. Lewis, *The Public Image of Henry Ford: An American Folk Hero and His Company* (Detroit, 1976), pp. 238–41; Ford Motor Company, *The Truth About Henry Ford and the Banking Situation* (Detroit, 1933), in FA.

16. "Ford Refuses to Aid Bank in Michigan," Detroit *Times*, May 28, 1932.

17. "Henry Ford on Self-Help," *Business Week*, June 15, 1932, p. 1; "Ford Urges Nation to Shun War and Stock Gambling"; Rogers, quoted in Lewis, *Public Image*, p. 234.

18. William Greenleaf, *From These Beginnings: The Early Philanthropies of Henry and Edsel Ford, 1911–1936* (Detroit, 1964), pp. 121–27.

19. Lewis, *Public Image*, pp. 206–8; Allan Nevins and Frank Ernest Hill, *Ford: Expansion and Challenge, 1915–1933* (New York, 1957), pp. 593–96; Allan Nevins and Frank Hill, *Ford: Decline and Rebirth, 1933–1962* (New York, 1962), pp. 63–64.

20. The statistics come from Heilbroner, *Economic Transformation of America*, pp. 179, 185; and Richard N. Current et al., *American History: A Survey* (New York, 1987), p. 707.

21. "Henry Ford Says This Is the Day of Opportunity," *Collier's*, Nov. 10, 1934, pp. 7–8, 26.

22. Ernest G. Liebold, "Reminiscences," p. 1406.

23. William J. Cameron, "Reminiscences," p. 147; New York *Times*, Sept. 3, 1933.

24. Alan Brinkley, *Voices of Protest: Huey Long, Father Coughlin, and the Great Depression* (New York, 1983), p. 60; Sidney Fine, "The Ford Motor Company and the N.R.A.," *Business History Review*, Winter 1958, pp. 353–55, 358–59.

25. Brinkley, *Voices of Protest*, p. 4; Fine, "Ford Motor Company and the N.R.A.," pp. 358–60; Cameron, "Reminiscences," p. 22. Acc. 52, box 8, FA, contains transcripts of phone conversations between HF and Johnson as they set up their June meeting, and a letter from Johnson to HF, June 27, 1933, thanking him for his hospitality on the recent visit to Dearborn.

26. Detroit *News*, Aug. 30, 1933; Fine, "Ford Motor Company and the N.R.A.," pp. 360–63.

27. Company statement, in acc. 52, box 8, "NRA Misc." folder, FA; "Ford Is Out," *Time*, Nov. 6, 1933, pp. 20–21; W. J. Cameron to Arthur Brisbane, Sept 12, 1933, in acc. 52, box 8, FA.

28. Fine, "Ford Motor Company and the N.R.A.," pp. 365–69, 385; Woolf, "Ford Answers Wealth-Sharers," p. 16.

29. Charles Edison to HF, Oct. 8 and 9, 1933; transcript of phone call from Edison to HF, Oct. 7, 1933; and HF to Edison, Oct. 6, 1933, all in acc. 52, box 8, FA. See also Fine, "Ford and the N.R.A.," pp. 364, 369–70.

30. Harold N. Denny, "Ford Calls NRA a Step Toward an Era of Justice," New York *Times*, Jan. 11, 1934; HF to Charles Edison, Oct. 6, 1933, in acc. 52, box 8, FA; "Like a Dream," *Time*, May 9, 1938, p. 10.

31. Voorhess, "Reminiscences," pp. 49, 50; Emil Zoerlein, "Reminiscences," p. 66; Joseph Zaroski, "Reminiscences," pp. 12–13; Tom Phillips, "Reminiscences," pp. 20–21.

32. Cameron, "Reminiscences," pp. 151–52; W. G. Nelson, "Reminiscences," pp. 56–57.

33. HF and Crowther, "There Is No Santa Claus," p. 25.

34. HF to Charles Edison, Oct. 6, 1933.

35. Philip Kinsley, "An Interview with Henry Ford," Chicago *Tribune*, July 12, 1935; Crowther, "Our Job: An Interview with Henry Ford," p. 5.

36. Crowther, "Our Job: An Interview with Henry Ford," p. 7; HF and Crowther, "There Is No Santa Claus," p. 96; Kinsley, "Interview with Henry Ford"; Zoerlein, "Reminiscences," p. 233. On Huey Long and his similar populist critique of FDR and the Wall Street establishment, see Kennedy, *Freedom from Fear*, p. 237.

37. Samuel Crowther, "The Only Real Security: An Interview with Henry Ford," *Saturday Evening Post*, Feb. 1, 1936, p. 58.

Twenty-two • Despot

1. "Mr. Ford Doesn't Care," *Fortune*, Dec. 1933, p. 131. Bennett offers a similar but longer account in his memoir, Harry Bennett, *We Never Called Him Henry* (New York, 1951), pp. 92–94.

2. For the fullest contemporary account, see "4 Die in Riot at Ford Plant," Detroit *Free Press*, March 8, 1932.

3. Oakley Johnson, "After the Dearborn Massacre," *New Republic*, March 30, 1932, pp. 172–74.

4. "Mr. Ford Doesn't Care," p. 131.

5. Charles E. Sorensen, *My Forty Years with Ford* (New York, 1956), p. 8. For a good short synopsis of Bennett's life and career, see Ford R. Bryan, *Henry's Lieutenants* (Detroit, 1993), pp. 29–34; Bennett relates his own version of events in *We Never Called Him Henry*.

6. Bennett, *We Never Called Him Henry*, pp. 14–15; John H. O'Brien, "Henry Ford's Commander in Chief: Harry Bennett and His Private Army," *Forum*, Feb. 1938, p. 68; John McCarten, "The Little Man in Henry Ford's Basement," *American Mercury*, May 1940, pp. 13–14; Bryan, *Henry's Lieutenants*, p. 29.

7. Bennett, *We Never Called Him Henry*, pp. 5–13; "Little Man in Ford's Basement," p. 7.

8. Bennett, *We Never Called Him Henry*, pp. 33–34; Bryan, *Henry's Lieutenants*, pp. 30–31; O'Brien, "Ford's Commander in Chief," p. 68.

9. O'Brien, "Henry Ford's Commander in Chief," p. 68; "Little Man in Ford's Basement," pp. 9, 203; Fred L. Black, "Reminiscences," p. 140: Irving Bacon, "Reminiscences," pp. 204, 250.

10. "Little Man in Ford's Basement," pp. 10, 202; "Mr. Ford Doesn't Care," p. 131.

11. Bryan, *Henry's Lieutenants*, p. 30; Bacon, "Reminiscences," pp. 206–7; Black, "Reminiscences," p. 140.

12. O'Brien, "Ford's Commander and Chief," pp. 68, 71; "Little Man in Ford's Basement," pp. 205–7; Bryan, *Henry's Lieutenants*, p. 31.

13. Bacon, "Reminiscences," pp. 258–60.

14. O'Brien, "Ford's Commander and Chief," p. 68; "Little Man in Ford's Basement," pp. 205–7; Bryan, *Henry's Lieutenants*, p. 32.

15. Al Esper, "Reminiscences," p. 89; Charles Voorhess, "Reminiscences," pp. 20, 25–26; Anthony Harff, "Reminiscences," pp. 58–60; "Little Man in Ford's Basement," pp. 8–9; O'Brien, "Ford's Commander and Chief," p. 69.

16. Lawrence Sheldrick, "Reminiscences," pp. 86–88; Hayward S. Ablewhite, "Reminiscences," pp. 60–62; Harff, "Reminiscences," pp. 61–62.

17. George Brown, "Reminiscences," pp. 128–29; O'Brien, "Ford's Commander and Chief," p. 70; Bacon, "Reminiscences," pp. 248, 202.

18. Voorhess, "Reminiscences," pp. 21, 25–26; Ablewhite, "Reminiscences," pp. 65, 62; Black, "Reminiscences," pp. 140–41; Esper, "Reminiscences," pp. 88–90; Brown, "Reminiscences," pp. 146–49; "Little Man in Ford's Basement," p. 10.

19. Bennett, *We Never Called Him Henry*, pp. 37–38.

20. Esper, "Reminiscences," p. 27; Voorhess, "Reminiscences," pp. 27–28; Cameron, "Reminiscences," p. 176; Harff, "Reminiscences," pp. 75–76; Bennett, *We Never Called Him Henry*, p. 63.

21. Mrs. Stanley Ruddiman, "Reminiscences," p. 79; Peter Collier and David Horowitz, *The Fords: An American Epic* (New York, 1987), p. 166; Voorhess, "Reminiscences," p. 25; Black, "Reminiscences," p. 138.

22. Ablewhite, "Reminiscences," p. 89; Emil Zoerlein, "Reminiscences," pp. 235–36.

23. Black, "Reminiscences," pp. 136, 139, 140–41; Herman L. Moekle, "Reminiscences," pp. 160–61; Bennett, *We Never Called Him Henry*, p. 23.

24. Black, "Reminiscences," p. 135; Harold Hicks, "Reminiscences," p. 177; Ruddiman, "Reminiscences," p. 79.

25. Black, "Reminiscences," p. 135; Sheldrick, "Reminiscences," pp. 86–87.

26. Esper, "Reminiscences," pp. 88–90; "Ford Men Counted Non-Union by 5 to 1," New York *Times*, March 25, 1937; "Little Man in Ford's Basement," p. 207; O'Brien, "Ford's Commander and Chief," p. 67.

27. "Ford: Frankensteen Gets a Beating, U.A.W. Gets Tremendous Impetus," *Newsweek*, June 5, 1937, p. 7; "Ford Men Beat and Rout Lewis Union Organizers," New York *Times*, May 27, 1937; "Threatens Arrest of Ford Men in Riot," New York *Times*, May 28, 1937; "Ford Men Called Typical Hoodlums," New York *Times*, July 9, 1937.

28. "Ford Company Lays Riot to Newspapers and Union," New York *Times*, May 28, 1937; "Ford's Spokesman Assails the NLRB," New York *Times*, July 22, 1937; "Frankensteen Gets a Beating," p. 8; "NLRB Finds Ford Guilty of Violating Labor Law," New York *Times*, Dec. 24, 1937.

29. Cameron quoted in "Ford's Spokesman Assails NLRB"; "On the Overpass," *Time*, June 7, 1937, p. 69; Oswald Garrison Villard, "Issues and Men," *Nation*, April 24, 1937, p. 467.

30. Esper, "Reminiscences," pp. 88–89.

31. Robert L. Cruden, "The Great Ford Myth," *New Republic*, March 16, 1932, pp. 117–18; W. J. Cunningham, *"J8": A Chronicle of the Neglected Truth About Henry Ford and the Ford Motor Company* (Detroit, 1931), pp. 38–40, in FA.

32. Cunningham, *"J8,"* pp. 23–25; Cruden, "Great Ford Myth," pp. 117–18.

33. "Ex-Foreman Stirs Row in Ford Case," New York *Times*, July 15, 1937; Walter Griffith, "Reminiscences," p. 31.

34. Cunningham, *"J8,"* pp. 61–62; Keith Sward, *The Legend of Henry Ford* (New York, 1948), pp. 312–13; Griffith, "Reminiscences," p. 31.

35. Cameron, "Reminiscences," pp. 219–20, 275–76, 278–79.

36. Blow-by-blow accounts of this struggle can be found in Allan Nevins and Frank Hill, *Ford: Decline and Rebirth, 1933–1962* (New York, 1962), pp. 28–54, 133–67; Sward, *Legend of Ford*, pp. 342–421.

37. Charles N. Wheeler, "Close-Up View of Henry Ford and His Ideas," Chicago *Tribune*, May 23, 1916; John Reed, "Industry's Miracle Maker," *Metropolitan Magazine*, Oct. 1916, p. 67; Charles W. Wood, "If I Were President: Henry Ford Tells Where He Stands on All of the Great Issues of the Day," *Collier's*, Aug. 4, 1923, p. 6.

38. Tom Phillips, "Reminiscences," p. 21; " 'Shun Unions,' Ford Advises Workers," New York *Times*, Feb. 20, 1937; "Will Never Recognize Any Union," New York *Times*, April 6, 1937; "Ford Hints Pay Raise in Fight with CIO," New York *Times*, April 11, 1937.

39. F. Raymond Daniell, "Ford Confidently Faces a Labor Duel," New York *Times*, Oct. 17, 1937; "Ford Hints Pay Raise"; Ablewhite, "Reminiscences," p. 29.

40. Sorensen, *My Forty Years with Ford*, p. 254.

41. "Ford Hints Pay Raise"; "Will Never Recognize Any Union"; HF to Charles Edison, Oct. 6, 1933, in acc. 52, box 8, FA.

42. "Ford Says His Men May Join Anything," New York *Times*, April 14, 1937. See also " 'Shun Unions,' Ford Advises Workers"; and Daniell, "Ford Confidently Faces Labor Duel," for similar statements from HF about Wall Street direction of unionization.

43. A. M. Smith, "Ford Gives Viewpoint on Labor," Detroit *News*, April 29, 1937.

44. Sorensen, *My Forty Years with Ford*, pp. 256–57; Sward, *Legend of Henry Ford*, pp. 333–35.

45. Moekle, "Reminiscences," p. 159; Sorensen, *My Forty Years with Ford*, pp. 259–62. The escalating feud between Henry and Edsel Ford will be examined in more detail in chap. 24.

46. Alfred D. Chandler, Jr., *Giant Enterprise: Ford, General Motors, and the Automobile Industry* (New York, 1964), pp. 196–97; Nevins and Hill, *Ford: Decline and Rebirth*, p. 135. See also Sidney Fine, *Sit Down: The General Motors Strike of 1936–37* (Ann Arbor, 1969).

47. David L. Lewis, *The Public Image of Henry Ford: An American Folk Hero and His Company* (Detroit, 1976), pp. 253, 261–66; Sward, *Legend of Henry Ford*, p. 417; Sorensen, *My Forty Years with Ford*, pp. 268–69.

48. Lewis, *Public Image*, pp. 266–68; Sorensen, *My Forty Years with Ford*, pp. 268–71.

Twenty-three • Dabbler

1. "Henry Ford Has a New Tie, and He's Still Looking Ahead," and "Ford Watches Town Pageant," Detroit *Free Press*, July 30, 1938.

2. "9,000 Party Experts Throw a Real One for Henry Ford," Detroit *Free Press*, July 31, 1938; "Happy Children Lift Voices in Jubilee Tribute to Ford," Detroit *News*, July 31, 1938; "Detroit Honors Genius of Ford, Its No. 1 Citizen," Detroit *Free Press*, July 31, 1938; "1,500 Diners Toast Ford on Birthday," Detroit *News*, July 31, 1938; W. R. Brewer, "Reminiscences," pp. 14–15.

3. "Henry Ford, 75," *Newsweek*, Aug. 8, 1938, p. 10; Anne O'Hare McCormick, "The Future of the Ford Idea," New York *Times Magazine*, May 22, 1932, pp. 1–2.

4. Robert A. Smith, "Reminiscences," pp. 21–22.

5. Mrs. Stanley Ruddiman, "Reminiscences," p. 65.

6. John McIntyre, "Reminiscences," pp. 3–4. Voorhess, Buhler, de Caluwe, Rankin, and Wilson have contributed reminiscences to the FA, and they offer rich material on the Fords' domestic life during this period.

7. Voorhess, "Reminiscences," pp. 35–36; Brewer, "Reminiscences," pp. 16–17, 8–9.

8. McIntyre, "Reminiscences," pp. 6–8; Donn P. Werling, *Henry Ford: A Hearthside Perspective* (Warrendale, Pa., 2000), pp. 16, 37–38.

9. William Clay Ford, quoted in David L. Lewis, *Ford Country: The Family, the Company, the Cars* (Sydney, Ohio, 1999), p. 16; Joseph Zaroski, "Reminiscences," p. 6; McIntyre, "Reminiscences," p. 20.

10. Smith, "Reminiscences," p. 22; Jerome S. Wilford, quoted in Lewis, *Ford Country*, pp. 63–64.

11. Ruddiman, "Reminiscences," pp. 48–49; Ford R. Bryan, *Clara: Mrs. Henry Ford* (Dearborn, 2001), pp. 262–64; Voorhess, "Reminiscences," pp. 36–39; McIntyre, "Reminiscences," p. 24; Edward J. Cutler, "Reminiscences," p. 97.

12. McIntyre, "Reminiscences," p. 22; de Caluwe, "Reminiscences," pp. 26–28; Ruddiman, "Reminiscences," p. 46.

13. Ruddiman, "Reminiscences," pp. 115–17, 118, 125, 131; Voorhess, "Reminiscences," p. 48.

14. Ruddiman, "Reminiscences," pp. 69–70; Voorhess, "Reminiscences," pp. 40–41, 45.

15. Ruddiman, "Reminiscences," pp. 68–69, 73, 76, 84, 86; Bryan, *Clara*, pp. 250–51.

16. Cutler, "Reminiscences," p. 99; Ruddiman, "Reminiscences," p. 77; Bryan, *Clara*, p. 248.

17. Ford R. Bryan, *Friends, Families, and Forays: Scenes from the Life and Times of Henry Ford* (Dearborn, 2002), pp. 363–69, 414–19; Ruddiman, "Reminiscences," pp. 47–48.

18. Voorhess, "Reminiscences," pp. 39–40; Ruddiman, "Reminiscences," p. 60; Bryan, *Friends, Families, and Forays*, pp. 353–62, 370–75.

19. Voorhess, "Reminiscences," pp. 46–47; Ruddiman, "Reminiscences," pp. 66–67; W. R. Brewer, "Reminiscences," and Lawrence Sheldrick, "Reminiscences," quoted in Carol Gelderman, *Henry Ford: The Wayward Capitalist* (New York, 1981), pp. 214–15.

20. Brewer, "Reminiscences," and Sheldrick, "Reminiscences," quoted in Gelderman, *Ford: Wayward Capitalist*, pp. 214–15; John Côté Dahlinger, *The Secret Life of Henry Ford* (Indianapolis, 1978), pp. 71, 74; McIntyre, "Reminiscences," p. 24; William Clay Ford, interview in Detroit *News*, 1993, quoted in Lewis, *Ford Country*, pp. 15–16; Werling, *Ford: Hearthside Perspective*, p. 138; "Fords Relish Memories of Auto Giant's Heart, Legacy," Detroit *News*, June 18, 1995.

21. Ernest G. Liebold, "Reminiscences," p. 1486; Werling, *Ford: Hearthside Perspective*, p. 98.

22. Voorhess, "Reminiscences," pp. 188–89; Dahlinger, *Secret Life*, pp. 35–38; Werling, *Ford: Hearthside Perspective*, p. 98; Brewer, "Reminiscences," and Sheldrick, "Reminiscences," quoted in Gelderman, *Ford: Wayward Capitalist*, pp. 214–15; Henry Dominguez, *Edsel: The Story of Henry Ford's Forgotten Son* (Warrendale, Pa., 2002), pp. 272–73.

23. Rufus Wilson, "Reminiscences," pp. 25–26; Ruddiman, "Reminiscences," pp. 108–10.

24. Brewer, "Reminiscences," p. 11; Andrew Hild, "He Was a Nice Man," Detroit *Sunday News Magazine*, April 3, 1977, pp. 60–63; Stout, quoted in Werling, *Ford: Hearthside Perspective*, p. 99.

25. Eva O'Neal Twork, *Henry Ford and Benjamin B. Lovett: The Dancing Billionaire and the Dancing Master* (Detroit, 1982), pp. 196–97; Sidney Olson, *Young Henry Ford: A Pictorial History of the First Forty Years* (Detroit, 1997 [1963]), p. 39; Ford R. Bryan, *Henry's Lieutenants* (Detroit, 1993), p. 296; William A. Simonds, *Henry Ford: His Life, His Work, His Genius* (Indianapolis, 1943), p. 238; Allan Nevins and Frank Hill, *Ford: Decline and Rebirth, 1933–1962* (New York, 1962), p. 407; series of letters from Ann Hood to HF, 1934 to 1943, in acc. 1, box 138, FA.

26. "Mr. Ford Doesn't Care," *Fortune*, Dec. 1933, p. 63; Bryan, *Henry's Lieutenants*, pp. 59–65.

27. Cutler, "Reminiscences," p. 135; S. J. Woolf, "Ford Answers Wealth-Sharers," New York *Times Magazine*, July 7, 1935, pp. 1–2.

28. Irving Bacon, "Reminiscences," pp. 66–67; Woolf, "Ford Answers Wealth-Sharers," p. 1; Voorhess, "Reminiscences," p. 36.

29. A. G. Wolfe, "Reminiscences," pp. 210–11, quoted in text; Samuel Crowther, "Our Job: An Interview with Henry Ford," *Saturday Evening Post*, Oct. 31, 1936, p. 5; Woolf, "Ford Answers Wealth-Sharers," p. 1; Fred C. Kelly, "Ford Urges Nation to Shun War and Stock Gambling," New York *Times*, Oct. 27, 1935; Voorhess, "Reminiscences," pp. 67, 36.

30. Nevins and Hill, *Ford: Decline and Rebirth*, pp. 56–57; Charles E. Sorensen, *My Forty Years with Ford* (New York, 1956), p. 176; Woolf, "Ford Answers Wealth-Sharers," p. 2.

31. Ruddiman, "Reminiscences," pp. 38–40, 44, 67–68; Kelly, "Ford Urges Nation to Shun War"; McCormick, "Future of Ford Idea," p. 2; Wilson, "Reminiscences," p. 20.

32. McIntyre, "Reminiscences," pp. 9–11; Ruddiman, "Reminiscences," pp. 44, 103–4; F. Raymond Daniell, "Ford Confidently Faces a Labor Duel," New York *Times*, Oct. 17, 1937.

33. Voorhess, "Reminiscences," pp. 47, 42–44; Roy Schumann, "Reminiscences," p. 145; Smith, "Reminiscences," pp. 25–26.

34. Schumann, "Reminiscences," p. 146; Bacon, "Reminiscences," p. 67; Ruddiman, "Reminiscences," pp. 104–5.

35. Voorhess, "Reminiscences," p. 76; McIntyre, "Reminiscences," pp. 20, 16; Cutler, "Reminiscences," p. 135.

36. Sheldrick, "Reminiscences," pp. 187–89; Werling, *Ford: Hearthside Perspective*, p. 141; Voorhess, "Reminiscences," pp. 61–62, 65.

37. Zaroski, "Reminiscences," p. 3; Ruddiman, "Reminiscences," pp. 54, 69–70; Werling, *Ford: Hearthside Perspective*, p. 141.

38. McIntyre, "Reminiscences," pp. 18–19; Smith, "Reminiscences," pp. 19–20.

39. McIntyre, "Reminiscences," pp. 17–18; Brewer, "Reminiscences," pp. 10–11.
40. Ruddiman, "Reminiscences," pp. 44, 63; Smith, "Reminiscences," p. 21.

Twenty-four • Educator

1. New York *Times*, Feb. 14, 1930; Samuel Crowther, "Educating for Leadership: Henry Ford Explains His New Schools for a Million Children," *Ladies' Home Journal*, Aug. 1930, p. 12.
2. HF and James C. Derieux, "The Making of an American Citizen: A Manufacturer and a Social Psychologist Think Our Schools Should Do a Better Job," *Good Housekeeping*, Oct. 1934, p. 20.
3. *Ford Ideals: Being a Selection from Mr. Ford's Page in the Dearborn Independent* (Dearborn, 1922), p. 412; William Greenleaf, *From These Beginnings: The Early Philanthropies of Henry and Edsel Ford, 1911–1936* (Detroit, 1963), pp. 137–39; Fred C. Kelly, "Mr. Ford Talks of Many Things," *Barron's*, Jan. 26, 1931, p. 5.
4. Arthur B. Moehlman, "Don't Neglect the Children," *Nation's Schools*, April 1942, p. 18; "Not Teaching—Learning," *Forum*, Sept. 1938, p. 122; HF, quoted in Samuel Crowther, "The Only Real Security," *Saturday Evening Post*, Feb. 1, 1936, p. 7, and in Crowther, "Educating for Leadership," p. 69; HF and Derieux, "Making of an American Citizen," p. 117.
5. My discussion of HF's educational ideology has been influenced by David B. Tyack, *The One Best System: A History of American Urban Education* (Cambridge, Mass., 1974); Lawrence A. Cremin, *The Transformation of the School: Progressivism in American Education, 1876–1957* (New York, 1961); Stephen S. Mucher, "Making Sense of Henry Ford's Educational Progressivism(s): A Tale of Two Schools," unpublished paper, in Vertical File—"HF, Schools," FA.
6. H. E. Gronseth, "Ford's Vocational Schools," *Automotive Industries*, Aug. 29, 1936, pp. 276–78, 292; n.a., "Henry Ford Trade School," and Keith Glassley, "History of Henry Ford Trade School," both in Vertical File—"Henry Ford Trade School," FA; Ford R. Bryan, *Henry's Lieutenants* (Detroit, 1993), pp. 236–40; Ford R. Bryan, *Beyond the Model T: The Other Ventures of Henry Ford* (Detroit, 1990), pp. 179–80.
7. Crowther, "Educating for Leadership," p. 69; Frederick Searle, "Reminiscences," pp. 4, 36.
8. Madeline J. Straight, "Henry Ford: Schoolmaster," *Nation's Schools*, May 1942, pp. 14–17; "Edison Institute Schools," in Vertical File—"Edison Institute Schools," FA; Greenleaf, *From These Beginnings*, pp. 147–50.
9. Greenleaf, *From These Beginnings*, p. 149; J. L. McCloud, "Reminiscences," p. 385.
10. Bryan, *Beyond the Model T*, p. 176; Greenleaf, *From These Beginnings*, pp. 143–46; "Edison Institute Schools."
11. On the Fords and the Berry School, see Mrs. Inez Henry, "Reminiscences," pp. 15–45; Harnett T. Kane, *Miracle in the Mountains* (Garden City, N.Y., 1956), pp. 201–15; Greenleaf, *From These Beginnings*, pp. 141–43; David G. Roberts, "The Berry School Plant," unpublished paper, 1986, in Vertical File—"Berry School," FA. All of these sources are quoted in text.
12. "Mr. Ford Doesn't Care," *Fortune*, Dec. 1933, p. 134. For a good survey of Ford's soybean project, see Reynold M. Wik, *Henry Ford and Grass-Roots America* (Ann Arbor, Mich., 1972), pp. 148–55.
13. Robert Boyer, "Reminiscences," pp. 15–19; Bryan, *Henry's Lieutenants*, pp. 45–50; Robert A. Smith, "Reminiscences," pp. 27–28.
14. HF, quoted in "Economic Liberation for the Farmer," *Ford News*, June 1934, pp. 108–9; and in "Automobiles and Soy Beans: An Interview by Arthur Van Vlissingen, Jr., with Henry Ford," *Rotarian*, Sept. 1933, n.p., in Vertical File—"Soybeans," FA.
15. "Automobiles and Soybeans"; "Economic Liberation for the Farmer," p. 109.
16. David L. Lewis, "Henry Ford and the Magic Beanstalk," p. 5, unpublished paper, 1991, in

Vertical File—"Soybeans," FA; "Economic Liberation for the Farmer," p. 109; Smith, "Reminiscences," pp. 7–8, 13; Joseph Galamb, "Reminiscences," pp. 115–16.

17. "Economic Liberation for the Farmer," p. 108; Lewis, "Ford and the Magic Beanstalk," p. 6; Wik, *Ford and Grass-Roots America*, p. 154; Bryan, *Beyond the Model T*, pp. 112–13.

18. Rusty Davis, "Henry's Plastic Car: An Interview with Lowell E. Overly," *V-8 Times*, n.d., pp. 46–51, in Vertical File—"Soybeans," FA; David L. Lewis, *The Public Image of Henry Ford: An American Folk Hero and His Company* (Detroit, 1976), pp. 283–87.

19. HF, quoted in "The '43 Ford," *Fortune*, Feb. 1943, p. 112; see also Albert DeLorge, "Reminiscences," p. 21; Ford R. Bryan, "A Prized Friendship: Henry Ford and George Washington Carver," *Ford Museum and Greenfield Village Herald*, 1983, pp. 90–95.

20. Allan Nevins and Frank Hill, *Ford: Decline and Rebirth, 1933–1962* (New York, 1962), pp. 124–25, quoted in text; Lewis, *Public Image*, pp. 287–88.

21. HF, preface, company pamphlet on new Ford-Ferguson tractor, n.t., 1941, in Vertical File—"Tractors—Ford Ferguson," FA; "Henry Ford and Harry Ferguson Revolutionize Farming," *Ford Field Magazine*, July 1939, pp. 10–15; Nevins and Hill, *Ford: Decline and Rebirth*, pp. 124–25; Lewis, *Public Image*, pp. 287–88.

22. On the Fords at Richmond Hill, see Stuart Kinzie, "Mr. Ford Lends a Hand," *Scribner's Commentator*, April 1941, pp. 21–26; Franklin L. Long and Lucy B. Long, *The Henry Ford Era at Richmond Hill, Georgia* (Richmond Hill, Ga., 1998), pp. 1–12; Ford R. Bryan, *Friends, Families, and Forays: Scenes from the Life and Times of Henry Ford* (Dearborn, 2002), pp. 403–13.

23. Long and Long, *Ford Era at Richmond Hill*, p. 3; Bryan, *Friends, Families, and Forays*, pp. 405–7.

24. Mrs. Harry Gill, "Reminiscences," pp. 7–8; Bryan, *Beyond the Model T*, p. 189; Bryan, *Friends, Families, and Forays*, p. 411; Long and Long, *Ford Era at Richmond Hill*, p. 5.

25. Long and Long, *Ford Era at Richmond Hill*, p. 2.

26. Constance Clark, "Reminiscences," pp. 16–19; Gill, "Reminiscences," pp. 2–3; Long and Long, *Ford Era at Richmond Hill*, pp. 2–3; Kinzie, "Ford Lends a Hand," pp. 23–24; Bryan, *Beyond the Model T*, pp. 190–91.

27. Typed brochure, March 1940, in acc. 587, box 70, FA, detailing various educational activities at Richmond Hill; Kinzie, "Ford Lends a Hand," p. 24; Long and Long, *Ford Era at Richmond Hill*, p. 6.

28. Gill, "Reminiscences," pp. 4–7; Long and Long, *Ford Era at Richmond Hill*, pp. 4–5; Bryan, *Beyond the Model T*, p. 188.

29. Bryan, *Beyond the Model T*, pp. 192–94.

30. W. B. Eidson, "Reminiscences," pp. 7, 30; Tom Phillips, "Reminiscences," pp. 2–9; Long and Long, *Ford Era at Richmond Hill*, pp. 9, 11.

31. Bryan, *Beyond the Model T*, pp. 194, 189, 193; Robert Rankin, "Reminiscences," pp. 45–46; Kinzie, "Ford Lends a Hand," p. 24.

32. DeLorge, "Reminiscences," pp. 27–28; Phillips, "Reminiscences," p. 13; Bryan, *Beyond the Model T*, pp. 194–95; Rankin, "Reminiscences," pp. 43–45.

33. Searle, "Reminiscences," p. 37; David L. Lewis, "Working Side by Side," *Michigan History Magazine*, Jan.–Feb. 1993, pp. 25–30.

34. Mrs. Stanley Ruddiman, "Reminiscences," p. 47; Phillips, "Reminiscences," p. 24; Eidson, "Reminiscences," pp. 29–30.

35. John H. Tienken, "The Ford Farms," memoir, in Vertical File—"Richmond Hill," FA.

36. *A Series of Talks Given on the Ford Sunday Evening Hour by W. J. Cameron, 1934–1935* (Dearborn, 1935), pp. 7–11.

37. "Mr. Ford Doesn't Care," p. 126. See Bryan, *Henry's Lieutenants*, pp. 53–57, for a biographical sketch of Cameron.

38. On Ford's radio projects, see Bryan, *Beyond the Model T*, pp. 91–96; Lewis, *Public Image*, pp. 311–15.

39. Bryan, *Henry's Lieutenants*, pp. 53–57.

40. See "Cameron Renamed as President of the Anglo-Saxon Federation," July 2, 1935, news-paper clipping, in Vertical File—"Cameron, W. J.," FA; see also Neil Baldwin, *Henry Ford and the Jews* (New York, 2001), pp. 261–67, for Cameron's association with the British-Israelite movement. On this sect, see also Michael Barkun, *Religion and the Racist Right: The Origins of the Christian Identity Movement* (Chapel Hill, N.C., 1994), pp. 3–31.

41. William J. Cameron, "Reminiscences," p. 155, quoted in text; "Mr. Ford Doesn't Care," p. 134; William C. Richards, *The Last Billionaire* (New York, 1948), pp. 150, 260; Fred L. Black, "Reminiscences," p. 148, quoted in text.

42. "Radio Favorites," *Fortune*, Jan. 1938, pp. 88, 91; "Four Hundred Fords," *Newsweek*, Dec. 31, 1945, p. 85.

43. Cameron, "Reminiscences," pp. 221–22; Harvey Pinney, "The Radio Pastor of Dearborn," *Nation*, Oct. 9, 1937, pp. 374–76.

44. Charles E. Sorensen, *My Forty Years with Ford* (New York, 1956), p. 29; Cameron, "Reminiscences," pp. 228, 95, 24.

45. See "Contents," in *Series of Talks 1934–1935*; "Contents," in *A Series of Talks Given on the Ford Sunday Evening Hour by W. J. Cameron, 1935–1936* (Dearborn, 1936).

46. *Series of Talks, 1934–1935*, pp. 12–15; *Series of Talks, 1935–1936*, pp. 90–93.

47. Fred Black, quoted in John W. Spalding, "The Radio Speaking of William John Cameron," *Speech Monographs*, March 1959, p. 49; Ben Donaldson, transcript of interview with him, Fred L. Black, and Walter Blanchard, p. 67, in acc. 65, box 7, FA; Ken McCormick, "Spokesman for Henry Ford," *Radio Guide*, Dec. 1939, p. 4.

48. Cameron, "Reminiscences," p. 227. Cameron's surviving radio talks alone fill boxes 5, 6, 7, 8 in acc. 44, FA.

49. Black, "Reminiscences," pp. 160, 141–42; Pinney, "Radio Pastor of Dearborn," p. 374.

50. Black, "Reminiscences," pp. 142–45; Lewis, *Public Image*, p. 326; David L. Lewis, "The Ten Most Important People in Henry Ford's Life," *Car Collector*, June 1978, p. 28.

51. McCormick, "Spokesman for Henry Ford," p. 4; Spalding, "Radio Speaking of Cameron," p. 48; Lewis, *Public Image*, p. 326.

52. Pinney, "Radio Pastor of Dearborn," p. 376; Spalding, "Radio Speaking of Cameron," pp. 51, 55.

53. McCormick, "Spokesman for Henry Ford," p. 4; Paul Hutchinson, "Heretics of the Air: Mr. Ford's Mr. Cameron," *Christian Century*, April 17, 1935, pp. 508–10; Pinney, "Radio Pastor of Dearborn," p. 376; Thomas S. Green, "Mr. Cameron and the Ford Hour," *Public Opinion Quarterly*, Oct. 1939, pp. 669–75.

Twenty-five • Figurehead

1. The Ford/Pearson incident was covered in the Detroit *Free Press*: "Ford Hands Challenge to Commentator," Aug. 25, 1943; "Drew Pearson Accepts Ford Battle Bid," Aug. 25, 1943; "Ford's Challenge," Aug. 27, 1943; "Crack Pots Send Pearson 'Pot of the Month,' " Aug. 30, 1943; "Pearson Backs Up on Ford Challenge," Aug. 30, 1943. These articles are quoted in the text.

2. "Henry Ford, 80," and "If I Felt Better I'd Have to Run, Ford Says at 80," both in Detroit *News*, July 30, 1943.

3. Rufus Wilson, "Reminiscences," pp. 8–9.

4. Ibid., pp. 8, 15; Raymond J. Jeffreys, *God Is My Landlord* (Tecumseh, Mich., 1967 [1947]), p. 36.

5. Documents on HF's hernia operation, in acc. 572, box 7, FA; Mrs. Stanley Ruddiman, "Reminiscences," p. 40; Robert Rankin, "Reminiscences," p. 74; Ernest G. Liebold, "Reminiscences," pp. 1305–6.

6. Al Esper, "Reminiscences," p. 105; letters, reports, and prescriptions from Drs. B. R. Shurly, Lawson B. Coulter, and I. R. Peters, in acc. 1, box 113, FA.

7. Dr. F. Janney Smith, "Reminiscences," pp. 24–25; Ford R. Bryan, *Beyond the Model T: The Other Ventures of Henry Ford* (Detroit, 1990), pp. 201–3, on the Ford Hospital; Dr. Lawson B. Coulter, letters and memos to HF, in acc. 572, box 7, FA; Liebold, "Reminiscences," pp. 1313–18; William J. Cameron, "Reminiscences," p. 184.

8. Smith, "Reminiscences," pp. 22–23.

9. Ibid.; Jeffreys, *God Is My Landlord*, pp. 81, 93; Charles E. Sorensen, *My Forty Years with Ford* (New York, 1956), p. 266.

10. Statement of Dr. Frank Sladen, July 26, 1951, in *Edgar Leroy Bryant v. Clara Ford Estate*, in acc. 513, box 12, FA.

11. Statement of Dr. John G. Mateer, July 17, 1951, in *Edgar Leroy Bryant v. Clara Ford Estate*, in acc. 513, box 12, FA; Sorensen, *My Forty Years with Ford*, pp. 266, 271–72, 313; Allan Nevins and Frank Hill, *Ford: Decline and Rebirth, 1933–1962* (New York, 1962), p. 242; David L. Lewis, *The Public Image of Henry Ford: An American Folk Hero and His Company* (Detroit, 1976), p. 291.

12. Herman L. Moekle, "Reminiscences," pp. 185–86; E. F. Wait and Logan Miller, "Reminiscences," cited in Nevins and Hill, *Ford: Decline and Rebirth*, p. 242; Irving Bacon, "Reminiscences," pp. 210–11.

13. Liebold, "Reminiscences," pp. 1323–24, 1220–21, 1191, 1176–77.

14. Rankin, "Reminiscences," pp. 52–54.

15. Sorensen, *My Forty Years with Ford*, pp. 273–74.

16. "Ford Blames 'Sabotage' in Submarine Disasters," New York *Times*, June 20, 1939; "Ford Believes War Threat Is Just a 'Big Bluff,' " Detroit *Free Press*, Aug. 29, 1939; Wilson, "Reminiscences," p. 36.

17. HF, "An American Foreign Policy," *Scribner's Commentator*, Dec. 1940, pp. 3–6; "Ford Urges All Aid to British and the Axis; He Sincerely Hopes They Both Collapse," New York *Times*, Feb. 16, 1941.

18. James Newton, *Uncommon Friends: Life with Thomas Edison, Henry Ford, Harvey Firestone, Alexis Carrel, and Charles Lindbergh* (New York, 1987), p. 107.

19. "Government Cancels Plans to Have Henry Ford Produce Airplane Engines," *Commercial and Financial Chronicle*, June 29, 1940; "Ford in America First," New York *Times*, Sept. 25, 1940.

20. Esper, "Reminiscences," pp. 48–49; Lindbergh to Frank Hill, Nov. 13, 1959, in acc. 940, box 27, FA.

21. Wilson, "Reminiscences," p. 32; Lindbergh, interview with Frank Hill, Oct. 27, 1959, in acc. 940, box 27, FA; Lindbergh to HF, Sept. 22, 1940, in acc. 1, box 141, FA.

22. Michele Sayers and A. E. Kahn, "American Merchants of Hate," *Friday*, Sept 27, 1940, p. 4; Henry Paynter, "Henry Ford: Richest Anti-Semitic Propagandist in U.S.," *PM*, Aug. 14, 1940, p. 8. Harold Lavine, "Fifth Column Literature," *Saturday Review of Literature*, Sept. 14, 1940, p. 16, made a similar attack on Cameron and Ford for "fascist" leanings.

23. Ken Silverstein, "Ford and the Fuhrer," *Nation*, Jan. 24, 2000, pp. 11–16.

24. William J. Cameron, form letter, n.d., in "PM and Friday—Attack on Mr. Ford and Mr. Cameron" folder in acc. 44, box 15, FA; Cameron, "Reminiscences," p. 213; Liebold, "Reminiscences," p. 1533. Silverstein, "Ford and the Fuhrer," argues that Ford Motor Company profited directly from wartime production of Ford-Werke; Neil Baldwin, *Ford and the Jews: The Mass Production of Hate* (New York, 2001), assigns moral responsibility to the company. I find Silverstein's evidence unpersuasive, and Baldwin's accusation reasonable but overdrawn. Ford Motor Company's rebuttal, *Research Findings About Ford-Werke Under the Nazi Regime* (Dearborn, 2001), and the conclusions of Simon Riech, "The Ford Motor Company and the Third Reich," *Dimensions: A Journal of Holocaust Studies*, Winter 1999, strike me as more convincing in their assertion of Ford-Werke's separation from the parent company by the U.S. entry into the war in 1941.

25. "Ford Pledges His Help in the World Crisis," New York *Times*, Jan. 16, 1941; "1,000 Planes a Day—Easy Task, Henry Ford Says," Washington *Post*, June 11, 1940; Harry Bennett, *We*

Never Called Him Henry (New York, 1951), p. 122; Wilson, "Reminiscences," pp. 36–37; Russell Gnau to Charles Sorensen, March 19, 1941, in acc. 38, box 93, FA.

26. "Ford Repudiates Bias Against Jews," New York *Times*, Jan. 12, 1942; "The '43 Ford," *Fortune*, Feb. 1943, p. 113; James Newton, *Uncommon Friends*, p. 112.

27. "The '43 Ford," pp. 112–13, 208, 210; "Sorensen of the Rouge," *Fortune*, April 1942, pp. 79, 114, 116, 120; Nevins and Hill, *Ford: Decline and Rebirth*, pp. 188–208.

28. Sorensen, *My Forty Years with Ford*, pp. 282, 281, 286–92; "Sorensen of the Rouge," pp. 79–80, 114, 116; Lewis, *Public Image*, pp. 348–62, esp. pp. 351–52 for Sorensen's wartime comments.

29. "The '43 Ford," pp. 113, 208, 210; Charles Lindbergh to Frank E. Hill, Dec. 6, 1959, pp. 4–5, in acc. 940, box 27, FA; HF, quoted in n.t., *Rotarian*, Sept. 1944, n.p., in Vertical File— "World War II," FA; "The Battle of Detroit," *Time*, March 23, 1942, pp. 10, 14.

30. Sorensen, *My Forty Years with Ford*, pp. 313, 317.

31. Ibid., pp. 313, 317; Bennett, *We Never Called Him Henry*, pp. 155–59.

32. Sorensen, *My Forty Years with Ford*, pp. 292–97, 315; Lewis, *Public Image*, pp. 356–57.

33. "Battle of Detroit," pp. 10–14.

34. Acc. 19, boxes 168, 169, 170, FA; John W. Thompson, "Reminiscences," pp. 42–43.

35. "Ford at 79 Expects War to End in a Few Months," Detroit *News*, July 30, 1942; "Ford at 79 Is Optimistic About Post War Prosperity," Columbus *Dispatch*, July 30, 1942; "Ford, 79 Today, Hopes His Plants Can Help Shorten War," *Daily Mining Journal*, July 30, 1942.

36. "From Bombers to Houses," *Motor*, Oct. 1942, p. 206; "Ford Plans to Build Big Post-War Planes," New York *Times*, Nov. 13, 1943; "Ford to Abandon Aviation in Peace," New York *Times*, March 30, 1945.

37. Sorensen, *My Forty Years with Ford*, p. 321; Liebold, "Reminiscences," p. 1176.

38. Liebold, "Reminiscences," p. 1486.

39. A. J. Lepine, "Reminiscences," pp. 26–29, 31–32, 35.

40. Ibid., pp. 24–26, 66–67, 61–64.

41. "Mr. Ford Doesn't Care," *Fortune*, Dec. 1933, p. 132; E. T. Gregorie, "Oral History," pp. 64–65, FA.

42. Lepine, "Reminiscences," pp. 7, 25, 70; Henry Dominguez, *Edsel: Henry Ford's Forgotten Son* (Warrendale, Pa., 2002), pp. 135–54.

43. For a complete survey of Edsel's design projects, see Henry Dominguez, *Edsel Ford and E. T. Gregorie: The Remarkable Design Team and Their Classic Fords of the 1930s and 1940s* (Warrendale, Pa., 1999).

44. Ibid., pp. 38, 86–87, 201–3, 51.

45. Liebold, "Reminiscences," p. 1493; Esper, "Reminiscences," pp. 95–96.

46. Fred L. Black, "Reminiscences," pp. 49, 53.

47. Gregorie, "Oral History," p. 23; Emil Zoerlein, "Reminiscences," pp. 71–72.

48. Bennett, *We Never Called Him Henry*, pp. 147, 164, 26; Hayward S. Ablewhite, "Reminiscences," pp. 73–74.

49. Zoerlein, "Reminiscences," pp. 72–73; Sorensen, *My Forty Years with Ford*, pp. 311–12.

50. Black, "Reminiscences," p. 59; Sorensen, *My Forty Years with Ford*, pp. 311, 259–60.

51. Dominguez, *Edsel*, pp. 117, 261; Douglas Brinkley, *Wheels for the World: Henry Ford, His Company, and a Century of Progress* (New York, 2003), p. 471.

52. Black, "Reminiscences," pp. 55–56. See also Sorensen, *My Forty Years with Ford*, pp. 274–76.

53. Bennett, *We Never Called Him Henry*, p. 149; Sorensen, *My Forty Years with Ford*, pp. 27, 261–63, 314; Black, "Reminiscences," pp. 54–55; Ablewhite, "Reminiscences," p. 72.

54. Lawrence Sheldrick, "Reminiscences," pp. 83, 311–12; Sorensen, *My Forty Years with Ford*, pp. 301–2, 304–5, 313.

55. Sorensen, *My Forty Years with Ford*, pp. 314–15.

56. Ibid., pp. 317–18, 323.

57. Sorensen, *My Forty Years with Ford*, pp. 317–19; Bennett, *We Never Called Him Henry*, p. 164; Dominguez, *Edsel*, pp. 306–7.

58. Sorensen, *My Forty Years with Ford*, pp. 320–22.

59. Dominguez, *Edsel*, pp. 311–13; Cameron, "Reminiscences," p. 110, quoted in text; Sorensen, *My Forty Years with Ford*, pp. 323–24, quoted in text.

60. Cameron, "Reminiscences," p. 110; John McIntyre, "Reminiscences," p. 27; Bennett, *We Never Called Him Henry*, p. 165.

61. Liebold, "Reminiscences," pp. 1175–76; Gus Munchow, "Reminiscences," p. 60; Bennett, *We Never Called Him Henry*, pp. 166, 168.

62. Charles Voorhess, "Reminiscences," pp. 165–66; Geoffrey Upward, *A Home for Our Heritage: The Building and Growth of Greenfield Village and Henry Ford Museum, 1929–1979* (Dearborn, 1979), p. 119.

63. Joseph Zaroski, "Reminiscences," p. 23; Bennett, *We Never Called Him Henry*, p. 168.

64. Robert A. Smith, "Reminiscences," p. 19; Voorhess, "Reminiscences," p. 34; Tom Phillips, "Reminiscences," p. 22; Wilson, "Reminiscences," pp. 34–36.

65. Louise Clancy and Florence Davies, *The Believer: The Life Story of Mrs. Henry Ford* (New York, 1960), pp. 199–201.

66. Sorensen, *My Forty Years with Ford*, p. 324; Bennett, *We Never Called Him Henry*, p. 167; Nevins and Hill, *Ford: Decline and Rebirth*, pp. 243, 250.

67. Joseph Galamb, "Reminiscences," p. 30; Bennett, *We Never Called Him Henry*, pp. 167, 170.

68. Sorensen, *My Forty Years with Ford*, pp. 324–25, 327.

69. Joe McCarthy, "The Ford Family," *Holiday*, Aug. 1957, p. 78; Nevins and Hill, *Ford: Decline and Rebirth*, pp. 257–59.

70. Sorensen, *My Forty Years with Ford*, pp. 328–29; see also Nevins and Hill, *Ford: Decline and Rebirth*, pp. 254–56.

71. McCarthy, "Ford Family," p. 78; Nevins and Hill, *Ford: Decline and Rebirth*, pp. 264–65; Henry Ford II, interview with David Lewis, early 1980s, p. 27, in FA.

72. Liebold, "Reminiscences," p. 1186; Bennett, *We Never Called Him Henry*, pp. 136, 165.

73. Sorensen, *My Forty Years with Ford*, pp. 329–30; Mrs. Frank Campsall, "Reminiscences," pp. 12–13; Bennett, *We Never Called Him Henry*, pp. 172, 176.

74. Bennett, *We Never Called Him Henry*, pp. 176, 178; Roy Bryant, "Reminiscences," pp. 45–47; Ruddiman, "Reminiscences," pp. 98–99; John McIntyre, "Reminiscences," pp. 29–30.

75. Statement of Dr. John G. Mateer, July 17, 1951, in *Edgar Leroy Bryant v. Clara Ford Estate*, in acc. 513, box 12, FA.

76. McCarthy, "Ford Family," p. 78; Nevins and Hill, *Ford: Decline and Rebirth*, pp. 248–50, 265–66, 268; Bennett, *We Never Called Him Henry*, p. 174.

77. McCarthy, "Ford Family," p. 78; HF II, interview with Lewis, p. 26; Nevins and Hill, *Ford: Decline and Rebirth*, pp. 260–61.

78. HF II, interview with Lewis, p. 29; Nevins and Hill, *Ford: Decline and Rebirth*, pp. 268–69; Bennett, *We Never Called Him Henry*, p. 178; Irving Bacon, "Reminiscences," p. 211; McCarthy, "Ford Family," p. 79.

79. Ruddiman, "Reminiscences," pp. 98–101.

80. Voorhess, "Reminiscences," p. 189; Rankin, "Reminiscences," pp. 32–36; Edward J. Cutler, "Reminiscences," p. 163; Bacon, "Reminiscences," pp. 210–11; Wallace G. Beesley, "Reminiscences," p. 27.

81. Thompson, "Reminiscences," pp. 43–45.

82. HF, "Thoughts for the Future," pp. 2–3, 5–8, 11–14, in Vertical File—"Ford, Henry, Thinking About," FA.

83. Ibid., pp. 9, 15, 16–19.

84. Ibid., pp. 19–23.

85. Ibid., pp. 24–27, 28–32.

86. Thompson, "Reminiscences," p. 46.

Epilogue • *The Sage of Dearborn*

1. Robert Rankin, "Reminiscences," p. 67.
2. Ibid., pp. 66–69.
3. Ibid., pp. 66, 69–70; Charles Voorhess, "Reminiscences," pp. 191–92.
4. John McIntyre, "Reminiscences," pp. 31–32; Mrs. Stanley Ruddiman, "Reminiscences," p. 102.
5. Rankin, "Reminiscences," pp. 71–73; Ruddiman, "Reminiscences," pp. 102–3; "Henry Ford Dies in Cold, Oil Light," Detroit *Times*, April 8, 1947; Henry Ford II, interview with David Lewis, 1986, p. 37, in FA; Ford R. Bryan, *Clara: Mrs. Henry Ford* (Dearborn, 2001), p. 297.
6. "Detroit Dynasty," *Time*, April 21, 1947, pp. 28–29; David L. Lewis, *The Public Image of Henry Ford: An American Folk Hero and His Company* (Detroit, 1976), pp. 476–77.
7. Sigmund Diamond, *The Reputation of the American Businessman* (Cambridge, Mass., 1955), pp. 141–44, 156–65, and Lewis, *Public Image*, pp. 474–76, provide convenient excerpts from the vast commentary after Ford's death.
8. Charles E. Sorensen, *My Forty Years with Ford* (New York, 1956), p. 35.
9. See David Farber, *Sloan Rules: Alfred P. Sloan and the Triumph of General Motors* (Chicago, 2002), for an insightful analysis of an industrialist who offers an interesting contrast to Ford in his creation of a full-fledged corporate structure that was completely attuned to values of rationalized decision-making, market research, credit, and advertising.
10. R. L. Bruckberger, *Image of America* (New York, 1959), p. 181; Robert S. Lynd and Helen M. Lynd, *Middletown: A Study in Modern American Culture* (New York, 1929), p. 253; Frederick Lewis Allen, *Only Yesterday: An Informal History of the 1920s* (New York, 1931), p. 136.

Index

A Note About the Author

Steven Watts is professor of history at the University
of Missouri. He is the award-winning author of four
books, including *The Magic Kingdom*, a biography of
Walt Disney. His many articles and essays have
appeared in the *Journal of American History*, the
American Quarterly, and *American Studies.*
He lives in Columbia, Missouri.

A Note on the Type

This book was set in Janson, a typeface long thought to have been made by the Dutchman Anton Janson, who was a practicing typefounder in Leipzig during the years 1668–1687. However, it has been conclusively demonstrated that these types are actually the work of Nicholas Kis (1650–1702), a Hungarian, who most probably learned his trade from the master Dutch typefounder Dirk Voskens. The type is an excellent example of the influential and sturdy Dutch types that prevailed in England up to the time William Caslon (1692–1766) developed his own incomparable designs from them.

Composed by North Market Street Graphics, Lancaster, Pennsylvania

Printed and bound by Berryville Graphics, Berryville, Virginia

Designed by Iris Weinstein